Prophets of the Bible

and their prophecies... understanding God's ways

Second Edition

By

John R. Barber

"I am conscious that this book is going out before it is ready, but at some point a halt has to be called, or, to revert to the sea metaphor, one has to burn one's boats and face what comes. If Christians are encouraged to work at the book of Daniel afresh, so altogether we come nearer to feeling its heartbeat, then any effort of mine will have been worthwhile." **Joyce Baldwin, 1977, Preface to "Daniel"**

"God has told us enough about the future to enable us to stand firm, to do exploits, to bring understanding, to endure suffering, to be refined, to resist evil, and to find rest." **David Pawson, Unlocking the Bible**

"We are not diplomats but prophets, and our message is not a compromise but an ultimatum." **Aiden Wilson Tozer**

"We are all at times unconscious prophets." **Charles Haddon Spurgeon**

ISBN 978-0-9537306-4-3

First Edition: September 2020

Second Edition: January 2022

Published by: John Barber, Southend, England

Website: www.jrbpublications.com

Please note: a very late addition to this second edition of this book is a new chapter put at the end, titled: "Chapter 22: A New Ending".

Copyright © John Barber 2020, 2021, 2022 - all rights reserved

Contents

Bible Quotations 10
Dedication 11
About the Book 12
    Outside the Camp 13
    About the Book (contents)... 13
    About the Book (cover).. 13
About Bible versions and referencing 14
About the Author 16
Glossary 17
Acknowledgements 19
Preface to the First Edition...24
Preface to the Second Edition 31
Chapter 1: Introducing the prophets..33
    Our approach.. 35
    The test for a true prophet 37
    The trials and tribulations of the prophets....................................... 38
    How God spoke to the prophets.. 39
    How prophets communicated their message 40
    What was the message of the prophets? 41
    How the prophets show us God is for real.. 42
Chapter 2: The prophets in context 43
    Why context is important 43
    Introducing the figures 46
    Figure 1 – Bible Timeline.. 48
    Figure 2 – The Christian Bible and the Hebrew Bible........................ 49
    Figure 3 – Bible chronology (1) 50
    Figure 4 – Bible chronology (2) 51
    Figure 5 – Kings of the Bible 52
    Figure 6 – Prophets of the Bible 53
    Figure 7 –Wilderness Journey.. 54
    Figure 8 – Tabernacle and Temple 55
    Figure 9 – 7 Feasts of and 5 Offerings to YHWH 56
    Figure 10 – Twelve Tribes of Israel (after entering Canaan)............... 57

Figure 11 – Israel, Judah (divided kingdom) & surrounding kingdoms map .. 58
Figure 12 – Assyrian Empire (650 BC) 59
Figure 13 – Babylonian Empire (540 BC) 60
Figure 14 – Persian Empire (400 BC) 61
Figure 15 – Greek Empire (320 BC) 62
Figure 16 – Roman Empire around the time of Christ 63
Figure 17 – The Ten Commandments 64
Figure 18 – The Gospel 65
Figure 19 – Seven churches of Revelation 66
Figure 20 – Israel and its surrounding neighbours today 67

Chapter 3: Prophets, priests and kings 68
The Bible – chronology, division, order 68
Introducing prophets, priests and kings 69
The Bible – an overview 69
Looking at the priests 72
Looking at the kings 74
Jesus – Prophet, Priest and King 75
Pre-, actually in it, and post-Exile 77

Chapter 4: The Genesis account and prophets 81
Introducing Genesis 81
Adam (and Abel and Seth) 84
Enoch 85
Noah 86
Abraham 87
Isaac 88
Jacob 89
Joseph 91

Chapter 5: Moses and wandering in the wilderness 93
The books of Moses 93
About Moses 93
Exodus, Leviticus, Numbers, Deuteronomy 94
Moses and the Law 98
Religious worship 99
Blessings and curses 101
Law and grace 102
Moses the prophet 103
Other prophets 105
Christ in the Pentateuch 106
Moses and Jesus 109

Chapter 6: Balaam and assorted false prophets **110**
   Introducing the false prophets 110
   Surveying the Bible for false prophets 111
   Balaam 113
   Verses revealing attributes of and approaches to false prophets 116
   True and false prophets compared 121

Chapter 7: Deborah and other women prophets **122**
   Miriam 122
   Deborah 123
   Huldah 125
   Sarah 126
   Abigail 126
   Hannah 127
   Esther 128
   Other Old Testament women prophets 129
   New Testament women prophets 129
   Jesus and women 130
   Women false prophets 132

Chapter 8: From Joshua, through Judges to Samuel **133**
   Joshua 133
   Judges 135
   Ruth 137
   Samuel 138

Chapter 9: David, Nathan and Gad **141**
   David 141
   Nathan 145
   Gad 146
   More on prophets in David's day 147

Chapter 10: Elijah and Elisha **149**
   Elijah 149
   Elisha 154
   Applying lessons 158

Chapter 11: Unnamed, unknown and less known prophets **160**
   Unnamed prophet (1) 161
   Unnamed prophet (2) 161
   Ahijah 162
   Shemaiah 163

Unnamed prophet (3) 163
Hanani 164
Jehu 164
Unnamed prophet (4) 165
Micaiah 166
Unnamed prophet (5) 166
Sons of Asaph 167
Iddo 167
Azariah 167
Eliezer 168
Unnamed prophet (6) 168
Oded 168
Mordecai 169
Urijah 169
Baruch 170
Prophets who are not recognised as prophets 170
Job 171
Solomon 171
Nehemiah 172
Nebuchadnezzar 172
Cyrus 173

Chapter 12: The major prophets (Isaiah to Daniel) 174
Overview 174
Isaiah 176
Jeremiah 184
Ezekiel 193
Daniel 203

Chapter 13: The minor prophets (Hosea to Malachi) 213
Overview 213
Hosea 215
Joel 219
Amos 222
Obadiah 228
Jonah 231
Micah 234
Nahum 239
Habakkuk 242
Zephaniah 246

Haggai 249
Zechariah 253
Malachi 262

Chapter 14: Prophets of the New Testament 268
Transitioning from the Old to the New 268
John the Baptist 272
John the Divine (Apostle) 275
As for today 279

Chapter 15: Digging deeper into prophecy 281
Making the case 281
Bruising the Serpent's head (Genesis 3:14,15) 287
Enoch and the Lord's coming with His saints (Jude verses 14,15) 289
The Lord, my Lord and Melchizedek the Priest (Psalm 110) 290
The Suffering Servant (Isaiah 52:13-53:12) 291
The time of Jacob's trouble (Jeremiah 30:7 etc.) 293
The New Covenant (Jeremiah 31:31-34 etc.) 294
The battle of Gog and Magog (Ezekiel 38, 39) 295
The new (third) Temple (Ezekiel 40-48) 296
Daniel and the Antichrist (Daniel 7) 297
Daniel's seventy weeks (Daniel 9:24-27) 298
The restoration of Israel (and the Gentile inclusion) (Amos 9:10-15) 300
The destruction of the Temple and signs of the End Times (Matthew 24) .. 301
The Abomination of Desolation (2 Thessalonians 2:3-4) 302
The Two Witnesses (Revelation 11:1-14) 304
The woman and the dragon (Revelation 12:1-3) 305
The Mark of the Beast (Revelation 13:15-18) 307
The Mystery of Babylon (Revelation 17:1-9) 308
The Battle of Armageddon and the Lord's return (Revelation 19 etc.) 309
The Millennium (the thousand-year reign of Christ) (Revelation 20:1-6) 310
The new heaven and the new earth (Revelation 21,22) 311

Chapter 16: Learning from the prophets 313
Personal reflections 313
More afterthoughts 322
Prayer of praise and thanksgiving 325
Prayer of intercession and supplication 326

Chapter 17: Tying up loose ends 327
Why a new ending when the lesson is endeth? 327
Bible 328
Truth 330
Church 332
Israel 335
Rapture 338
Community 340
Spirit 342
Apologetics 345
Blood 347
Gospel 349

Chapter 18: More loose ends 353
Covenant 353
Fear 356
Holiness 360
Idolatry 365
Trinity 368
Suffering 371
Eternity 373
Prayer 377
Faith 381
Grace 384

Chapter 19: My twelve favourite Bible characters 389
Introduction 389
Jephthah 389
Job 390
Abraham 390
Jacob 391
Elijah 392
Obadiah 392
Jeremiah 393
Daniel 393
Stephen 394
Barnabas 395
Ruth 395
Mary Magdalene 396
Conclusion 396

Chapter 20: Twelve more favourite Bible characters 397
- Moses 397
- Caleb 398
- Boaz 399
- Hannah 399
- David 400
- Isaiah 401
- Hosea 402
- Hezekiah 403
- Nehemiah 404
- John the Baptist 406
- Paul 407
- Priscilla 408

Chapter 21: 2020, 2021 and the prophetic 410
- An extraordinary undertaking 410
- 2020 410
- 2021 419

Prophets' Poem 426

Questions 429

"Lord, how long?" – a phoenix from the ashes – a Covid prayer 433

Psalm 69 – a meditation for times of trouble 442

The Brethren 445
- Why the Brethren 445
- About the Brethren 446
- The Pilgrim Church 448

The Unprofitable Servant 449
- J.N.Darby and E.B.Pusey 449
- The Parable applied 450

Another twelve favourite Bible characters 452

Of making many books 455
- Past writings 455
- Blog e-books 456
- Future plans 457

Join all the glorious names 459

The Prophets and the Gospel 461

Chapter 22: A New Ending 463

Bible Quotations

"Would God that all the Lord's people were prophets, and that the Lord would put his spirit upon them!" **Numbers 11:29**

"Do not call conspiracy all that this people calls conspiracy, and do not fear what they fear, nor be in dread. But the Lord of hosts, him you shall honor as holy. Let him be your fear, and let him be your dread." **Isaiah 8:12,13 (ESV)**

"Go, set a watchman; let him announce what he sees." **Isaiah 21:6 (ESV)**

"Surely the Lord God will do nothing, but he revealeth his secret unto his servants the prophets." **Amos 3:7**

"And it shall come to pass afterward, that I will pour out my spirit upon all flesh; and your sons and your daughters shall prophesy, your old men shall dream dreams, your young men shall see visions: And also upon the servants and upon the handmaids in those days will I pour out my spirit." **Joel 2:28,29**

"And from the days of John the Baptist until now the kingdom of heaven suffereth violence, and the violent take it by force. For all the prophets and the law prophesied until John." **Matthew 11:12,13**

"Pursue love, and earnestly desire the spiritual gifts, especially that you may prophesy." **1 Corinthians 14:1(ESV)**

"All scripture is given by inspiration of God, and is profitable for doctrine, for reproof, for correction, for instruction in righteousness: That the man of God may be perfect, thoroughly furnished unto all good works." **2 Timothy 3:16,17**

"No prophecy of the scripture is of any private interpretation. For the prophecy came not in old time by the will of man: but holy men of God spake as they were moved by the Holy Ghost." **2 Peter 1:20,21**

"God, who at sundry times and in divers manners spake in time past unto the fathers by the prophets, Hath in these last days spoken unto us by his Son, whom he hath appointed heir of all things, by whom also he made the worlds; Who being the brightness of his glory, and the express image of his person, and upholding all things by the word of his power, when he had by himself purged our sins, sat down on the right hand of the Majesty on high." **Hebrews 1:1-3**

Dedication

This book is dedicated to those who have laid and will lay down their lives for Christ and His cause; and to the Remnant seeking to know and to do God's will:

"*After this I beheld, and, lo, a great multitude, which no man could number, of all nations, and kindreds, and people, and tongues, stood before the throne, and before the Lamb, clothed with white robes, and palms in their hands; And cried with a loud voice, saying, Salvation to our God which sitteth upon the throne, and unto the Lamb. And all the angels stood round about the throne, and about the elders and the four beasts, and fell before the throne on their faces, and worshipped God, Saying, Amen: Blessing, and glory, and wisdom, and thanksgiving, and honour, and power, and might, be unto our God for ever and ever. Amen. And one of the elders answered, saying unto me, What are these which are arrayed in white robes? and whence came they? And I said unto him, Sir, thou knowest. And he said to me, These are they which came out of great tribulation, and have washed their robes, and made them white in the blood of the Lamb. Therefore are they before the throne of God, and serve him day and night in his temple: and he that sitteth on the throne shall dwell among them. They shall hunger no more, neither thirst any more; neither shall the sun light on them, nor any heat. For the Lamb which is in the midst of the throne shall feed them, and shall lead them unto living fountains of waters: and God shall wipe away all tears from their eyes.*" **Revelation 7:9-17**

About the Book

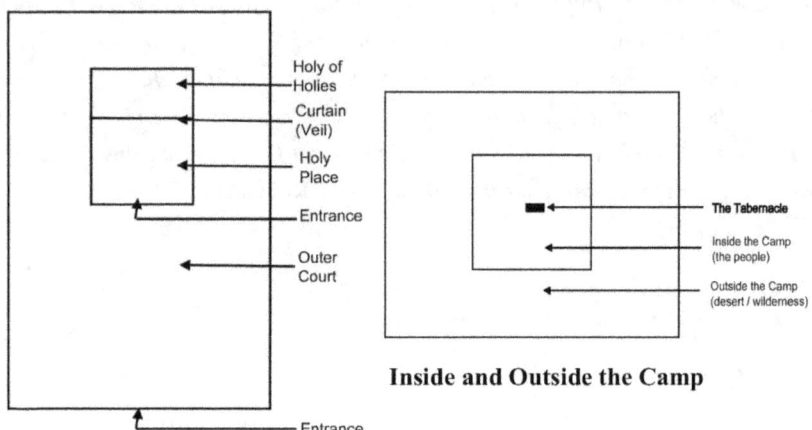

Inside and Outside the Camp

The Tabernacle (Tent)

"*Let us, then, go to him **outside the camp**, bearing the disgrace he bore*".

"*... we have confidence to enter the Most Holy Place by the blood of Jesus, by a new and living way opened for us through the curtain, that is, his body ... And so Jesus also suffered outside the city gate to make the people holy through his own blood. Let us, then, go to him **outside the camp**, bearing the disgrace he bore. For here we do not have an enduring city, but we are looking for the city that is to come.*" **Hebrews 10:19-20, 13:12-14**

Outside the Camp

Prophets of the Bible is the third published book under the umbrella of ***JRB Publications***. The texts quoted earlier from the Book of Hebrews stress the significance of going inside "the veil" and then outside "the camp" and is represented diagrammatically on the previous page concerning the Tabernacle that was set up under Moses during the Israelites journey in the Wilderness. These texts also form the background for the author, who believes it is necessary to go first "inside the veil" and then "outside the camp", in his writings in this series.

About the Book (contents)

Prophets of the Bible tries to identify *every* prophet in the Bible, named and unnamed, recognised as a prophet at the time, or they said or did something which the author identifies as being prophetic that made him or her a prophet for at least that period; and then to relate a succinct, contextual account of their lives and ministries, together with God's eternal purposes and its relevance for today. **It is a book intended for ALL, irrespective of church or any other affiliation!**

About the Book (cover)

Front Row 1:
1. Moses encounters God in the burning bush (Exodus 3).
2. Elijah appoints Elisha to become his successor (2 Kings 2).

Front Row 2:
1. John baptising in the river Jordan (Matthew 3:1-12).
2. Jesus is transfigured and talks to Moses and Elijah (Matthew 17:1-13).

Back Row 1:
1. Deborah and Barak go into battle (Judges 4,5).
2. Hosea and Gomer, his faithless wife (Hosea 3).

Back Row 2:
1. Jeremiah in the cistern – Ebed-Melech about to help (Jeremiah 38:7-13).
2. Jonah spewed up onto shore by the big fish (Jonah 2:10).

Back Row 3:
1. Ezekiel in the valley of dry bones (Ezekiel 37:1-14).
2. Daniel in the lion's den (Daniel 6:16-23).

About Bible versions and referencing

Up to quite late on in this project, I took the view having a statement right at the start, as "*All Bible quotations are from the King James (Authorized) version*", would cover what I needed in order to explain what version of the Bible I was using when I quoted from it. Other than the few occasions when I quoted from a different version, often for pragmatic reasons, including when the alternative's wording seemed better if trying to make certain points, I kept to the KJV, or so I had thought. I was fairly confident given I tended, as a matter of course, to cut and paste relevant texts from my **Biblegateway** application when in KJV mode.

But then I was to have one of those "*child caught with his hand in the cookie jar*" moments and my reviewers spotted not all was KJV; best practice requires me to own up to the fact. While at the time it seemed a finicky and almost irrelevant point, I decided it was a fair cop and tried to make amends. However, there could still be a tiny few non-KJV quotes in what follows. I now realise what happened – rather than quoting direct from my online application, I sometimes included and adapted text from other sources and often these included non-KJV Bible quotes.

As for why I favour the KJV over other Bible versions, I give reasons in *Acknowledgements*, but then this book is not about the relative merits of different versions, and discussion is for another time and place. I also quote heavily from the Bible, believing it makes some points better than me. So, there you have it – an explanation of my use of Bible versions. It brings me to another related point, to do with referencing. I have tried to ensure what I wrote was well researched, accurate and non-abrasive. At the same time, I was not aiming at an academic leaning audience but rather ordinary folk keen to know more about the Prophets of the Bible, who are up for serious study. Other than acknowledging my main sources up front and, if I do directly quote, give the source, I go little further than that. I do not, for example, include a bibliography, list of references or footnotes.

I was of the view that not only would I lose readers in the wood, I would find myself lost trying to separate the wood from the trees. Even so, I have read widely and, thanks to the Internet, besides reading much material online, have watched numerous videos, especially on the more challenging aspects of Bible prophecy. While I have included a glossary, it is not extensive and I admit to sometimes using long words and technical terms more likely to be seen in academia. In trying to get straight to the subject, I may sometimes assume knowledge that is not there.

Please bear with me. I am mindful that for some English is not their first language or unfamiliar with aspects of British culture and humour. Then there is my seemingly irreverent disdain for the those who might dictate choice of words or style, especially when I write in the language of the ordinary man. Finally, I can only pass on the advice: go to the Internet (assuming you have access) for explanation and, if you have access, check out good concordances or dictionaries.

About the Author

John Barber was born in Rochford Hospital, just outside Southend, UK (forty miles east of London) in 1951. He grew up and has lived in Southend for most of his life, having in earlier life travelled widely. He lives with Jolly (his wife), Matthew (his son) and three cats, at their home in Southend (they also have a home in Trivandrum, India, where some of their family live, and visits there when they can). He holds three degrees: BA (Hons.), B.Sc. (Hons.) and PGCE. He has had three careers: secondary school science teacher, software engineer and computer consultant (including twelve years running his own business), and then as community worker; and has been involved in serving the community in a wide variety of ways, taking on both paid and unpaid roles. He enjoys wide reading, assorted sports and nature walking, although he is a lot more restricted these days. He is an ordinary guy, who likes ordinary things and mixes with ordinary folk.

He is now "retired" but remains a gospel-preaching, community activist and a watchman on the wall. His main "community" activity is hanging out with homeless folk and their helpers. He has some health issues but is grateful to God for being able to make a difference. He reflects on his past wide-ranging activities and observations, notably as a Christian involved in the wider community, in his book ***Outside the Camp***. He has written several other books, relating to his interests in education, community and church history, as well as e-books based on his observations of the world as he sees it and just being interested in what is going on around him. His most recently book (prior to this) is a devotional based on the Song of Solomon. Many of which can be found in electronic form, and are freely available as downloads from his website **jrbpublications.com**. He blogs, often forthrightly, regularly on an assortment of issues and, besides "watch and pray", he seeks to "test and weigh" what goes on in the world and the perplexing events happening, and shares - sometimes controversially - thoughts on many subjects.

He is committed to serving God's mystery, the church, irrespective of the denominational label. While a member of Providence (Strict) Baptist Church for much of his Christian life, he has been a member of the Plymouth Brethren, including as an elder of his local assembly (which closed six years ago) and, as intimated earlier, his PB association has had a significant impact on his thinking. He serves the whole church as and when he is able, including as a Bible teacher and community activist. His wish is to point people to Christ and pass the baton onto the next generation of God's servants. While "About the author" is written by way of introducing people to this little-known author, he would much rather point people to Christ: "*How is your beloved better than others ... My beloved is radiant and ruddy, outstanding among ten thousand*" (Song of Solomon 5:9,10).

Glossary

The intention of the author is to define terms and acronyms before they are used, although sometimes that is not possible without making the book unwieldy. The following are some used in the book, where an explanation may help.

Apocalyptic is about forecasting the ultimate destiny of the world.

Apologetics goes beyond merely 'apologising' for one's faith. It derives its meaning from the Greek "*apologia*", meaning a 'reasoned defence'.

Cessationism versus continuationism involves a theological dispute as to whether spiritual gifts remain available to the church (continuationist), or whether their operation ceased with the Apostolic Age of the church (cessationist).

Charismatic relates to exercising a compelling charm which inspires devotion in others. Often used when referring to charismatic movement, which places special emphasis on the use of spiritual gifts, including prophecy, in the church.

Church: strictly "*ekklesia*" – a called-out assembly or congregation (typically of Christians), sometimes universal, but often used to depict an organisation etc.

Covenant: a strong, solemn agreement between two parties

Day of the Lord: identifies events that take place at the end of history, when God deals with humankind, specifically in judgment.

Dispensation: the method or scheme according to which God carries out his purposes towards men.

DV: (Latin: *Deo volente*) God willing

Ecclesiology: theology as applied to the nature and structure of the church.

Eschatology: theology concerned with the final events of history, or the ultimate destiny of humanity.

Gnosticism: a collection of religious ideas originating in the first century AD, emphasising personal spiritual knowledge over the orthodox teachings, traditions.

"**good and bad**": in the context, for example when describing a king, is a relative term and often relates to whether that king honoured God and did right or not.

imo, imho: in my opinion; in my humble opinion

Israel: in the course of the book it has sometimes been a choice between using Israel, Judah or Jews in the text, especially following the divided kingdoms of Israel and Judah. When Israel is used, it usually describes God's Covenant people, although sometimes it refers to the land they were promised or have occupied.

KJV: King James Version (the main version of the Bible used in the book) – other versions occasionally used include the English Standard Version (ESV), the New International Version (NIV) and the Message (MSG).

Last days: used in Bible prophecy to refer to the time when historical events would reach a final climax.

Messiah: promised deliverer of the Jewish nation prophesied in the Hebrew Bible.

Millennium: a period of a thousand years – as far as the prophets were concerned, this is a period that will be inaugurated with the coming of the Messiah.

NT: New Testament.

OT: Old Testament.

PB: Plymouth Brethren (comprising "Open" and "Closed" sections).

Social justice: a concept of fair and just relations between the individual and society, as measured by the distribution of wealth, opportunities for personal activity, and social privileges.

Watchmen in the Bible were guards responsible for protecting towns and military installations from surprise enemy attacks and other potential dangers. Their job was to keep watch and warn the townspeople of impending threats.

YHWH: (short for Yahweh or Jehovah) is the name often ascribed, especially in the Old Testament, to God, and is often translated as "The Lord".

Acknowledgements

I became a Christian aged fifteen, and became part of a set-up associated with the Plymouth Brethren. Not long after, I went along to the church Bible study, which as I recall was a somewhat stuffy occasion and one where the men came in suits and the ladies wore hats. The untypical speaker for that first visit was one Winston Chilcraft, who reminded me of a mildly unkempt, absent-minded professor. His subject that evening was Elijah and Naboth's vineyard, and it was presented alongside a backdrop – a map of the Middle East. The story was set in the Northern kingdom (Israel) and found in 1 Kings 21. As was pointed out, it needed to be understood in the context of what was happening in surrounding countries.

The synopsis was, wicked King Ahab wanted to buy a vineyard. Its owner, Naboth, did not want to sell. Ahab's wife, Queen Jezebel (even more wicked), hatched a plan to falsely accuse and then kill Naboth and thus acquire the vineyard. All this was revealed to the prophet Elijah, who exposed Ahab. I got to know brother Winston in the years following and I attribute my fascination with the prophets a lot to him. A few years ago, I attended his funeral. I recall someone making the apt remark that when Winston got to heaven one of his first ports of call would have been to seek out and quiz one of the minor prophets!

The Plymouth Brethren were keen to *"rightly divide the word of truth"* (2 Timothy 2:15), and since they regarded *"all scripture is given by inspiration of God, and is profitable…"* it should not be surprising that this included the less well-known parts of the Bible. In my mid-to-late teens, I recall lessons on aspects of the Law of Moses, Wilderness Wanderings and Tabernacle worship, to fine detail, and all sorts of Bible-related subjects being taught at the Young People's Bible class I attended - some quite obscure and I doubt would be covered in most other places. I became fascinated, for example, with the Song of Solomon (my last book-writing project), as one or other brother shared a Christ-related thought in the morning meeting. This at least is one aspect of PB-ism that I am grateful for.

In later years, I have found myself associating with the Strict Baptists, specifically Providence Grace Baptist Church. While they have a deep love of scriptures, their heritage was not so much about studying those nooks and crannies that so fascinated the Brethren. I found myself leading a number of their Bible studies in the last few years, which is ongoing. We agreed for the last several studies it should be on the prophets of the Bible, which has provided a springboard for this book as well as opportunities to preach, especially on my India visits.

While I have access to all sorts of books and commentaries on the prophets, the one that stands out is what was introduced to me when I was a university student – the Tyndale commentaries covering each book of the Bible. I like the fact it focuses on explanation rather than application, although there is a place for both. As with all resources I have referred to, it was not so much in order to get a verse-by-verse analysis of the text but more in order to get a steer on what is pertinent and to ensure what I write is sound. One recent resource that has come to hand is *A Pathway into the Bible* by my friend Stuart Kimber. This has proved a great help, especially concerning the writing prophets. I have sometimes been tempted to write "Go and read Stuart's book to find out more." As it is, he has kindly allowed me to plagiarise some of his material and encouraged me on the way.

I am not a big NIV fan but I do like the study Bible I have, which I use when on the road in England and India. I especially like its introductions to each Bible book and often find its notes and cross-references helpful as a source for what I write, especially when doing a synopsis of a Bible book, and is available online from **biblestudytools.com**. There is much else on the ubiquitous Internet, where so much "good stuff" can be found, as well as the thoughts of those who give a fascinating range of views on the subject, along with that found in dusty old books. I appreciate the resource **biblegateway.com**, where I can read the Bible in many different versions and, if need be, I can go to a specialist resource for the original language. I make no apology that I have favoured the King James Version (KJV), which is testimony to the fact that dinosaurs are not yet extinct. A complementary resource is the King James Version Audio Bible which can also be accessed from **biblestudytools.com**. On many occasions I have listened to the Bible being read while reading the text at the same time it was spoken.

While I do not like **YouTube** banning contrary voices, what I mention here can all be accessed from it. Lots of online sermons and studies have helped, but one resource I have consistently gone to, especially when covering major and minor prophets, that I have found invaluable, is the *Unlocking the Bible*" series by David Pawson. I learned of his death while writing this book. This does what it says on the cover – unlock the Bible. It has proved an incredible resource. One unlikely, recently discovered resource that neatly summarises each Bible book, is named *The Bible Project*. One even more recent helpful discovery is the *One Hour, One Book* series by Dr. Randall D. Smith. There is a lot of helpful material, when you know where to look, including from less salubrious sources, and all of it needs to be weighed. I also listen to and reflect on the deliberations of those with prophetic insights, people like Jacob Prasch, and other prickly types the Christian establishment shy away from. And always books to read, like ***God's Ultimatum*** by David Gardner and ***The Prophetic Guide to the End Times*** by Derek Prince that are two pertinent recent examples. While I like to think what I present are my own God-given thoughts, credit must go to where credit is due.

Looking back on my life, starting from when I attended Sunday School as a child under a strict yet kind, prim and proper, near retired headmistress (Miss Rafan) who loved the Lord and His Word; and then as a teen under my ever so patient Covenanter leader (Bryn Jones), and latterly my faithful father-in-law, Evangelist Varghese Matthai, who had confidence in me when others did not, as well as my early mentors, many have helped to inform and shape my thoughts for this book. I thank members of Providence Baptist, my church, for keeping me on my toes. I have appreciated exchanges with and thoughts of brothers and sisters in Christ, often unbeknown to them, who have helpfully shared their insights. One I should mention, not so much because of her deep insights on the prophets but more due to giving me the time and space to write, and care, is my wife Jolly. I do need to give glory to God, not just for helping me to understand but seeing me through often puzzling and painful experiences, without which I doubt I could empathise with the prophets, and whose amazing grace hardly begins to cover it.

Then, practically speaking, there are those who have assisted me in getting the words typed into the computer to a form people can read. I am grateful that in my friend Paul Barnes I had a very thorough proof reader. No doubt the final version will contain errors but that is most likely me doing further, customary tinkering and trying to make the book look pretty. While I have yet to see the final product, I should mention Ian Hutchins (www.hutchinscreative.co.uk) for doing the typesetting and final cover design and the folk at 4edge for printing the book (www.4edge.co.uk). Given they did a great job last time, I have no doubt they will do so again. I thank Paul Slennett, owner of Southend Christian Bookshop, who is not only a good example of a "golden oldie" community activist who understands the prophetic but who has provided sound advice due to his knowledge of the book trade. One discovery rather late on was an online resource that makes freely available images from the Bible (www.freebibleimages.org), some I have used, with permission, in this book - notably the cover. Then there have been those who on the way have encouraged me at times when the going was getting tough, for example: Paul Saunders, Keith Williams and John Hymus.

As for opinions expressed, biases implied, these are the author's. About selection of material, some of what might have been covered has not been, and I can only apologise in advance if I miss something important, yet even great expositors do so. As for intended audiences, it is intended for anyone with an interest in Bible prophets, who wants to know more. I welcome those who do not share my take on eschatology. I have no delusions of grandeur about readership, and if more than a few read it, that is a bonus. This project concerns some of the legacy I want to leave for them who come after me, and if it be good, then glory goes to God.

I did think about who to dedicate the book to, starting with the memory of my early Plymouth Brethren (a much misunderstood and maligned group) mentors, especially Winston Chilcraft who I recently discovered (like me) had Jeremiah down as his favourite prophet (I know the feeling, brother). While writing this, I learned of the death of his son, Steve, who like his dad lived to promote the cause of Christ, and while there is no guarantee that faith is transmitted from one generation to the next, it was good to witness both father and son serving the Lord.

Leaving a legacy, matters. This was brought home when considering the life and death of Bible characters. When it comes to my son, Matthew, I pray without wanting to sound pretentious that he will be like Elisha, who had a double portion of Elijah's spirit. I sadly see a new generation, brainwashed by a godless culture and let down by the shepherds (of the church). What we now desperately need (among other things – but then this book is about prophets) is a prophetic voice.

The recent news of the partings of Ravi Zacharias, David Pawson and Jim Packer – each in their own way have blessed me – makes me realise their shoes need to be filled. As well as martyrs, I dedicate this book to those of the next generation (who I suspect will comprise those least likely in human eyes; it is Him that must have the glory) who will pick up the prophet's mantle and regardless of title, status or whether or not they do predict the future, will convey God's heart and mind to this and future generations (if the Lord tarries), who desperately need to know.

My final acknowledgement concerns those who take time to read this book. As I am often at pains to point out, I do not have delusions of grandeur this will be read by many. All I can say, is I have given it my best shot and, whether few or many read this, it is all in the Lord's hands. Since I began the project at the start of 2020, there have been momentous events happening around us that few would have foreseen and my more than mere gut feel is there is more to come, and possibly even more earth shattering and unpredicted, and is why I am keen not to delay getting this book out. Being part of a faithful remnant is never easy, as the prophets of the Bible can testify, even though our goal is glory, but encouraging one another helps.

Writing as I do is my way of doing this, for the message of the prophets is one that gives hope and inspiration for times like these. The aim here is not to speculate on what might be the future but to face it, without fear, knowing the one who holds all the keys will always do right. I anticipate many of those who do read this will be part of that faithful remnant; I want to acknowledge you!

Following the first edition of this book, and prior to this second edition – this time directly via Ingram and deciding to focus on the buying online route, given a lack of interest by more traditional outlets to partner with this project – there have been more folk to acknowledge for their help, including some who have read parts and given valuable feedback, including suggestions for a better approach to get the "punters" interested. I am grateful to Jim Holmes (www.greatwriting.org.uk) for his professional advice, including getting signed up with Ingram so that people, potentially, anywhere in the world, including booksellers, who now have the opportunity to order online (the logical way for folk like me to go). I thank Chandi Chirwa for his help in producing videos, that are available on YouTube, in order to promote the book. Then I must mention Richard Barker (www.richards-watch.org) for encouraging me to think through the part modern day prophets have to play, along with friends like Chris Moyler for encouraging me to relate Bible prophecy to prophecy today and world events. I must also thank Peter Hall for stepping into the breach and doing some helpful last-minute proof reading. We live in a time when it easy to be discouraged. When I began work on this second edition, I discovered Dutch Sheets and his "*Give Him 15*" daily broadcasts (www.dutchsheets.org), an example of such encouragement that has affected this writing. Finally, I acknowledge "the Remnant", to whom I dedicate this second edition. More than anyone else, I write for today's often despised true believers.

Footnote (February 2021): When I wrote this section for the first edition, I included an acknowledgement of Ravi Zacharias, David Pawson and Jim Packer, three high profile Christians, whose quite different ministries had impacted me significantly, and who died while I was preparing the book. Since that time, what appears irrefutable revelations of acts of sexual impropriety have come to light concerning Ravi Zacharias. There is a temptation to follow the lead of some, and withdraw mention of him here. That in my view would be dishonest. I am appalled by and cannot excuse what he did and, like us all, he must give an account before his maker. But the fact remains, as an apologist of the faith, his contribution was monumental, including for this book. The acknowledgement therefore remains.

Preface to the First Edition

When I did my customary Google search on a subject I wanted information on - in this case it was to the question, *"**Why do books have a preface?**"* – I got what I felt was a decent answer on my first hit: *"The preface is a place for the book's author to tell the reader how this book came into being, and why. It should build credibility for the author and the book ... Here the author should explain why they wrote the book, and how they came to writing it. The author should be showing the reader why they are worth reading."* I had been thinking of going straight into the main content but it only seemed right and proper I produce this "I-hope-folks-will-read" preface beforehand. I also have to confess, even though I have often been guilty in the past, my aversion to giving too many personal anecdotes and reflections in a book that is meant to be mainly objective. While I use the first person in this preface, I will avoid doing so in the chapters that follow, at least until I get to the beyond Chapter 16, where I will offer a personal view.

Sometimes personal perspective is inevitable, and by having a preface we can get the personal bits out of the way, clear the decks by stating the axioms on which we base our writing, and partly to cover ourselves from accusations of being an omniscient, narcissist, know it all. My approach to understanding scripture is non pre-tribulation (rapture), pre-millennial, advocating engaging with the culture, Israel has not been replaced, prophecy can be and often is fulfilled on more than one level, OT types matter and unless it is clearly not the case should be taken literally; and this will affect my writing. I do so mindful of better and more learned people than me who see things differently. It is helpful before delving into the important, objective exegesis to try and ensure it is not about me, but rather the Prophets of the Bible and what they said. As a gospel preaching, community activist, I want to be true to my calling when I write, mindful of my limitations, as well as to be beholden to the truth and the need to respect sound scholarship.

According to Wikipedia: *"In religion, a prophet is an individual who is regarded as being in contact with a divine being and is said to speak on that entity's behalf, serving as an intermediary with humanity by delivering messages or teachings from the supernatural source to other people. The message that the prophet conveys is called a prophecy. Claims of prophethood have existed in many cultures throughout history, including Judaism, Christianity, Islam, in ancient Greek religion, Zoroastrianism, Manichaeism, and many others"*. When I did another Google search looking for something more "Christian", one response to the question: *"**What is a prophet in the Bible?**"* was *"In a general sense, a prophet is a person *who speaks God's truth to others. The English word prophet comes from the Greek word 'prophetes', which can mean 'one who speaks forth' or 'advocate.' Prophets are also called 'seers," because of their spiritual insight or their ability to see' the future. In the Bible, prophets often had both a teaching and revelatory role, declaring God's truth on contemporary issues while also revealing details about the future."* In this book, I go with this broader definition.

I am sure readers will agree with me that defining key terms is important to save misunderstanding down the line and, while I go with this definition, it will be with a couple of caveats. Clearly there are many characters in the Bible who meet this criteria, and the principal ministry of many was simply to hear God and speak His truth, applicable to the situation prevailing at the time, regardless of any future predictions they might make; and there are many who did just that who traditionally are not regarded as prophets, yet what they said or did was significant. Some, not usually regarded as prophets, relayed God's message and sometimes that included predicting future events, and that too was significant. Besides being seers, prophets were watchmen, whose solemn job was to stand watch over the land and warn them of impending danger.

As well as true prophets, the Bible tells us of false prophets whose message was NOT of God, just as is the case today and, as for us, we need the spirit of discernment, to *"Quench not the Spirit. Despise not prophesyings. Prove all things; hold fast that which is good."* (1Thessalonians 5:19-21.) Putting aside the question, "Are there prophets today?", we need people around who will simply step up to the plate and take on the role of watchmen.

"Significant" is important because, in God's dealing with His people, Israel, especially, and also with the nations generally, there were invariably prophets around saying what needed to be said. At least it was the case in Old Testament times. But it is not just for that time and the setting in which the prophets spoke, but also for our own time, including prophecies to take place, although over-dwelling on what could be a controversial subject can be unhelpful. Trying to maintain that balance on what the prophets taught, how it was received and understood at the time, what was actually meant and lessons we can take away, including on unfulfilled prophecy, is why I am keen to write this book.

I hope to cover all well-known prophets as well as those less well known, with the focus on what made them tick and why their message was relevant then and now. I recognise, to do full justice to what is a significant section of the Bible (well over a quarter) would require a library of books, and what I am producing is one book of not many pages. I hope to cover or at least introduce the more significant lessons and apologise in advance for what I anticipate as many important things I might miss. I will attempt to open up my subject, say something about the prophets themselves, reflect on their message, state pertinent facts and suggest possible present-day applications. I hope this book will encourage earnest readers to do deeper study on prophetic scriptures and the context in which these are placed. When it comes to scripture, the following could be borne in mind:

1. "[The Bereans] *received the word with all readiness of mind, and searched the scriptures daily, whether those things were so."* (Acts 17:11.)

2. *"All scripture is given by inspiration of God, and is profitable for doctrine, for reproof, for correction, for instruction in righteousness: That the man of God may be perfect, thoroughly furnished unto all good works."* (2 Timothy 3:16-17.)

3. *"No prophecy of the scripture is of any private interpretation. For the prophecy came not in old time by the will of man: but holy men of God spake as they were moved by the Holy Ghost."* (2 Peter 1:20-21.)

It is worth explaining how I came to tackle a subject which could well have taken me way out of my depths. Whether or not I am listened to or read, I know I am in good company with the prophets, who were often dismissed in their day and treated abysmally, even when doing something as important as speaking on God's behalf things they needed to know. I regard writing this book is an important undertaking, possibly my most important project to date, mindful as I rapidly approach my three score and ten years, and with failing health, my time will soon run out and there are many other things I could be doing, like putting my feet up. It may be my way of passing the baton to future generations to help them treasure the Bible and live it! I write, I hope with due humility, because I believe what I say needs saying, and I may be one such to do so and thus make a difference.

It is true *"of making many books there is no end"*, and, while most of what I am about to write may have already been written, we do well to reinforce these points. While I have seen much, there may be much I don't get or miss, and gaps in my understanding on subjects, such as New Testament prophecy, prophecy today and unfulfilled prophecy. I explained earlier, why I have a fixation on the prophets of the Bible. While I do not know the Bible as well as I ought, I know it better than most, especially this part of it, which from what I can make out is not anywhere nearly as well covered in standard church teaching contexts as it ought to be.

There is something else though: Around the turn of the millennium, I embarked on my third career, which might be best described as a community worker. I wrote about this in my book ***Outside the Camp***, which along with many of my writings is freely available online in my website. The title that has some bearing on my PB background is based on the text: *"Wherefore Jesus also, that he might sanctify the people with his own blood, suffered without the gate. Let us go forth therefore unto him without the camp, bearing his reproach."* (Hebrews 13:12,13). In the past six years I have regularly maintained a blog. It covers all manner of subjects; many, controversially, trying to figure out the world about me. I think reflecting on the prophets, their message etc., will help. I add a caveat though; the need for humility – good, well-read people, including on the prophets, may reach different conclusions when applying this to current events, often to do with their beliefs and understanding (or lack of) but also it is often the case no-one knows for sure.

It seemed to me that a common theme of the prophets, especially when it came to Israel, the main intended audience of many prophecies, was the need to be faithful to YHWH, but also to do justice when it comes to the people around them, especially the poor and oppressed. I am exercised that having gone inside the veil (which separates the Holy of holies from the Holy Place), Hebrews 6:19, in order to commune with the Almighty, we need to then go out into the wider world, with all its contradictions and counters to godly living. What takes place there matters a lot, including our own involvement, even if we cannot fully understand many of the reasons for and implications of. This can be a contentious area, yet one that if we are to follow in the footsteps of the prophets we cannot avoid.

Even as I write, I am noticing well known Christian leaders speaking in God's name, offering a view of the world and an understanding of scripture I believe to be in error. While it is important to do good, we must also be obedient to scripture. Not only are there true prophets and teachers today, there are also false ones who lead people astray. This can have a huge untoward impact. While we can disagree on things of lesser importance with professing believers, it is important we are beholden to the truth and we *"earnestly contend for the faith."* (Jude verse 3.)

When we think of what was prophesied, some of it related to things that were to happen in the prophet's lifetime, but much that happened centuries after, e.g. concerning the first coming of the Messiah (Jesus – the helpless Babe of Bethlehem), and some that is yet to happen, e.g. concerning the future of Israel and the second coming of the Messiah (Jesus – the all-conquering King of kings). This may be a controversial subject with views among Christians polarised. As a young man, I found such subjects occupied older, Bible-savvy men – and now I am one! I do not believe Israel (people and land) has been replaced; I believe there is a body of yet to be fulfilled prophecy that helps us understand world events, although I recognise some scholars will think differently. Some prophecy, e.g. the latter chapters of Daniel, have considerably occupied some and, while I do not intend to duck the exegetical challenges, I realise I may disappoint some.

While I intend to focus on what prophets said at the time and how it applied to the situation in which they were placed or reflecting on, one would be doing a disservice to ignore the fact that there is good deal that has yet to come to pass. Besides, considering prophecy from a viewpoint of what was understood at the time, we cannot ignore future fulfilments or the Jewish mindset that allowed for an initial fulfilment and a final one. While focusing on Old Testament prophets and prophecies, one significant New Testament prophecy is the Book of Revelation, where a blessing is promised to those who read it, and many intended recipients underwent persecution. While this book will not consider Revelation (or any other book come to that) in great depth, it will help to prepare the ground for a study of events prophesied that are yet to be fulfilled and which complement and incorporate many of the prophesies of the Old Testament prophets.

When I began writing this book, at the start of 2020, I could hardly have reckoned on the rapid unravelling of tumultuous events taking place in the world, along with culture and other wars and conflicts, changes in the church, such as persecution of believers globally, revival in difficult places and moves toward apostasy and false ecumenism where Christianity had become better established; all of which is consistent with what the prophets did predict for these last days (and that was before Covid-19 lockdown and civil unrest due to Black Lives Matter and other "anti" movements, and who knows what the next calamity is to befall – subjects which in the past would have interested the Hebrew prophets).

While diversity, equality, and tolerance can be good things, these preoccupations have often been distractions replacing the emphases on the three things the Holy Spirit is in the world to convict people of – *"And when he is come, he will reprove the world of sin, and of righteousness, and of judgment."* (John 16:8.) There is a widespread tendency to cherry-pick the Bible to suit people's views. For many it includes ignoring the Old Testament, including the prophetic. Because I believe studying the prophets can be a necessary corrective, I write as I do. While it is true, we are under the New Covenant, not the Old, God has not changed and we need to study both Old and New Testaments to get a balanced, complete view of what God thinks. As for studying the prophets, it will enlighten and encourage us living in a world that is a long way from what God intended. Even when we feel powerless, we can prepare, knowing whatever happens, His will does prevail!

My final point, before introducing the prophets, is that while I see my role as a watchman on the wall, I do not see myself as a prophet in any traditional sense. I am God's unprofitable servant at best and have often rebelled against the one I claim to serve. In the process, I have experienced brokenness and as a result I have been able to value more my covenant relationship with a patient, holy, gracious God, and this along with my prophecy insights enables me to inform and encourage others and not be over bothered what other people think. While the focus of this book is on the Old Testament rather than the New, it is chiefly because there are many more OT prophets than NT; and present-day prophetic gifts, given my church background, is not an area I felt qualified to speak on, even though I believe in the gift of prophecy and that prophets exist today. For the sake of balance, I will consider the place of prophecy today, including the gift of prophecy, and will add my own personal perspective. Some I reckoned have had a genuine prophetic gift, whose ministries I personally benefited from, as well as false prophets who do the opposite, just as the Bible warned us would happen.

I have found lack of knowledge of the Bible to be sadly rife among Christians, especially the Old Testament. But as one of my teenager mentors told me, *"The New is in the Old concealed and the Old is in the New revealed."* Nowhere better is this seen than in prophetic utterances. Besides encouraging those wanting to better understand the prophets and to make some sort of sense of this crazy world in which we live in the light of what the prophets said, I want this book to honour the Lord. I intend in the chapters that follow to expand on these considerations.

But like the Apostle Paul, you can never reckon on the final "finally" and, as the project extends, more "must share" thoughts come my way. Here it is to do with a question some may ask: why continue reading this book when there is *The Book* – the Bible? If that is what you are thinking then go for it, and God bless you, for the vast majority, including among Christians, do not seriously read the Bible and that is one main reason why the world and the church is in the mess it is. The other thought is peoples' fixation with what the future holds. It has ever been thus and as I look at a world more runaway than when Michael Green wrote his **Runaway**

World in 1968, that got me in the path of serious thinking theologically; people will understandably be asking such questions and often turning to one of the many false prophets for answer. My response is, it is likely God has told you enough of what you need to know. While reading my book will mean you will know more, there is a lot God has not said as well as a lot of rabbit holes I have not gone down. What I am saying is, do what my PB mentors urged this once keen-to-change-the-world youngster to do – be faithful regarding what God is telling you now. All I can add is it will all turn out good in the end - at least for those who follow the Lord - and while it is possible you may join the band of martyrs referred to in the book of Revelation, our job is to serve Him, even as mere unprofitable servants.

Preface to the Second Edition

When I produced the first edition, as far as I was concerned that was it – no second bite of the cherry, so to speak. But events have transpired and it seemed opportune now to go to a second edition, allowing me to add bits that occurred after the book went for publishing. One reason is, it was pointed out to me there may have been some infringements of copyright (now rectified). Another is there were inevitable typos, brought about mainly by me tinkering with the text right up to the last moment. Those which I have spotted, I have corrected. I am grateful to those who have suggested how I can improve the presentation, including the cover, and have taken on-board some of their suggestions. Then, as I surveyed the content of the first edition, there were things I felt I should change, mainly by way of incorporating extra thoughts, and this I have done.

The urge to tinker will continue, given this is a huge subject where more can be said, although I have no plan for a third edition or delusions of grandeur that a world awaits my every thought. I have added four new chapters (18 - 21) where I address ten further topics that relate to the subject of this book and two chapters devoted to consideration of my favourite Bible characters. The last chapter I title ***2020, 2021 and the prophetic***, and is my most controversial and possibly my most important. I have added new, for want of a better word, appendices, covering stuff that seem to me to be relevant and appropriate that I would like to get off my chest, especially given my writing days may well be numbered. Thinking about it, there may be several books included in this, and if readers were to dip in here and there, given there is only so much time in the day, that is totally acceptable.

I write Chapter 21 by way of a journal, reflecting and updating on world events and the deliberations of certain prophets over a period of three months (December 2020 to February 2021). I hope readers bear with me, although I anticipate criticism, but what I have to say regarding events that have occurred, especially in 2020, and might occur in 2021, relates to my motivation for and content in writing my book in the first place and they strangely relate; it seems to me that the prophets of old were always enquiring God concerning what was going on around them at the time and as this affected God's people. It relates to the thought prophecy is not something airy fairy but is to do with real world happenings. Sometimes He chooses to speak into these through the prophetic; often He does not. Moreover, the prophetic touches on all sections of the Bible, and is partly my justification for seeming sometimes to go off-topic in my second edition.

Questions relating to modern day prophecy, just as with what to make of unfulfilled prophecy, are huge and, while opening up these subjects, I realise I have only just begun and more can and no doubt will be said in the future. I still see myself as a bit of an outsider that is not going to be welcomed with open arms among certain elites in Christian circles, but then that is ok since it isn't about me and, whoever we are, we are each accountable to the Lord, who has the last word and we are each obliged to use whatever gift we have and opportunity that comes our way. I am not writing to ingratiate myself with anyone but rather to honour the Lord and encourage His people to do exploits, and to delve into His Word deeper, and to discover more of the treasure that is contained therein.

My burden is for God's people to know His Word. If this helps then great; like William Tyndale, I would want to say the equivalent concerning them that think they have a monopoly on interpreting scripture: *"If God spares me… I will cause the boy that driveth the plough to know more of the Bible than thou doest"*. As for me, I will continue to marvel at His grace. Moreover, by not being in the running to win popularity contests, I feel I am in good company with the prophets of old.

Finally, I confess to have rather gone on. And even now, right up to the very last moment, I have been unable to resist tinkering with the text. What was initially meant to be minor additions to and changes from the first edition have become much more than that, and as a result the book has grown in size by a third. I can think of at least two reasons for this. Firstly, my publish date extended by three months, during which time new and pertinent profound (imo) came to me and, while mindful of the need to avoid delusions of grandeur and tendencies of narcissism, I wanted to share these. Secondly, the extended Corona Lockdown, with this old codger being told to stay at home, meant I had the time to make these additions. Many of these were to do with relating what was written 2000+ years ago with our often-troubling times. But I do so remembering the words of Jesus:

"Let not your heart be troubled: ye believe in God, believe also in me. In my Father's house are many mansions: if it were not so, I would have told you. I go to prepare a place for you. And if I go and prepare a place for you, I will come again, and receive you unto myself; that where I am, there ye may be also. And whither I go ye know, and the way ye know. Thomas saith unto him, Lord, we know not whither thou goest; and how can we know the way? Jesus saith unto him, I am the way, the truth, and the life: no man cometh unto the Father, but by me … But the Comforter, which is the Holy Ghost, whom the Father will send in my name, he shall teach you all things, and bring all things to your remembrance, whatsoever I have said unto you. Peace I leave with you, my peace I give unto you: not as the world giveth, give I unto you. Let not your heart be troubled, neither let it be afraid." (John 14:1-6; 26-27.)

Chapter 1: Introducing the prophets

In order to help us cover our subject to an acceptable level, we have divided the book into twenty-one chapters, often containing discrete sections covering specific prophets or particular aspects of the vast subject of prophets and prophecy. These are not equal in size and represents a progression in our journey. As noted in the Preface, the coverage is not fully comprehensive; justice is hardly done concerning many, maybe most, of the prophecies in the Bible. But this book is for Joe Bloggs and Jane Doe, to encourage ordinary folk to dig deeper into the Bible and learn more about Bible prophets. It is also written by a little known, ordinary bloke that claims no outstanding ministerial or theological pedigree. His main claims are he loves the Lord, has seriously studied the subject, and has being doing so for most of his life, has benefited from "sound" teaching, has tried to cast aside factional hang-ups and popular talking points and is himself on a journey.

Chapter 1: Introducing the prophets – this chapter.

Chapter 2: The prophets in context – before embarking on studying specific prophets, we need to establish a context in order to understand their ministries.

Chapter 3: Prophets, priests and kings – while this book is about prophets, they operated alongside priests and kings. Here we explore that relationship.

Chapter 4: The Genesis account and prophets – Genesis is not known for its prophets but they existed. Understanding Genesis is vital to our further studies.

Chapter 5: Moses and wandering in the wilderness – Moses is a giant among prophets, and what took place, before entering the Promised Land, is significant.

Chapter 6: Balaam and assorted false prophets – the Bible is full of false prophets as well as true ones. We will look at these but will focus on Balaam.

Chapter 7: Deborah and other women prophets – while most prophets were male, there were prophetesses of which Deborah is one of the best known.

Chapter 8: From Joshua, through Judges to Samuel – Samuel was a giant in Israel's national development, but firstly we must fill the gap following Moses.

Chapter 9: David, Nathan and Gad – most prophets of the Bible operated under the kings of Israel and Judah. Nathan and Gad did so under David.

Chapter 10: Elijah and Elisha – Elijah and Elisha were two quintessential prophets who were prolific in their ministries, of which much is recorded.

Chapter 11: Unnamed, unknown and less known prophets – there are other prophets, often not well known or named, which we cover for completeness.

Chapter 12: The major prophets (Isaiah – Daniel) – given how much they wrote and did, there is potentially a great deal of material that needs covering.

Chapter 13: The minor prophets (Hosea – Malachi) – while they wrote less than the "majors", what they wrote and did was nevertheless hugely significant.

Chapter 14: Prophets of the New Testament – while concentrating on the Old Testament, prophets and prophecy still played a vital part in the New.

Chapter 15: Digging deeper into prophecy – while we cannot delve into every End Time prophecy, we can begin to have a go; here we look at twenty examples.

Chapter 16: Learning from the prophets – having gone through the prophets of the Bible, we take a last look, deriving lessons from their lives and ministries.

Chapter 17: Tying up loose ends – not planned but it seemed to the author there are many relevant topics impacting this book. Here he considers ten of them.

Chapter 18: More loose ends – the first of four Second Edition additions. It covers a further ten relevant topics that are related to this book.

Chapter 19: Twelve favourite Bible characters – considers the author's twelve favourite Bible characters, including some surprises, and why they are favourites.

Chapter 20: Twelve more favourite Bible characters – considers twelve more of the author's twelve favourite Bible characters, and why they are favourites.

Chapter 21: 2020, 2021 and the prophetic – considers current world events and what modern day prophets have to say about what is going on, as a journal.

Prophets' poem – is part of the author's personal response to the above.

Questions – on chapters 1 - 21, which readers may care to attempt to answer.

Covid prayer – is a prayer the author wrote earlier on during Covid-19 lockdown.

Psalm 69 – a meditation for times of trouble – a meditation on Psalm 69.

The Brethren – considers the Plymouth Brethren movement and its relevance.

Of making many books – provides an overview of the author's other writings.

Our approach

Regarding this book, the intention is to cover all the prophets of the Bible found by using a Bible search on the term "*proph*" and anything else relevant, and that includes groups of prophets, of which there were a number, unnamed prophets and those we do not normally regard as prophets but yet still prophesied, plus false prophets. While we cannot guarantee great depth, we will endeavour to discuss the lives of the prophets themselves (when this is known), the context in which, and events taking place, when they operated, and their all-important message. If all we manage is to provide the setting in which prophets did their stuff and give an outline of the work undertaken and events happening, then we have done our job to encourage folk to search the Scriptures, including the prophetic ones.

Putting aside the New Testament, which we will get to: if – as some suggest – prophets *proper* began with Elijah and ended with Malachi and, except for the later ones that lived during and after the Exile, these all operated alongside the kings of Israel and Judah, and it was God's gracious provision to raise up prophets to speak to kings and people, for "*surely the Lord God will do nothing, but he revealeth his secret unto his servants the prophets.*" (Amos 3:7) – if that was all we have prophecy wise, then there would still be much to ponder on today as to what they said and did, and yet the God of Israel continues to speak.

The prophets – bearing in mind the loose working definition in the Preface – were a rather eclectic lot, and while there may be common characteristics among the many we come across when reading the Bible, there were huge variations too. They come from all walks of life and comprised a wide range of characters and temperaments. While there were wide variations in their message, a common theme was God's holiness and justice as well as His love and mercy. While they prophesied primarily to Judah and Israel, there were important messages for the surrounding nations too. While not quite going along with the list provided in the Talmud (48 male and 7 female), the central text of Rabbinic Judaism and the primary source of Jewish religious law and Jewish theology, as to who the prophets of the Old Testament were, it is a useful check in identifying the prophets we need to discuss. A few from their list have been rejected in this book as not meeting the criteria set out in the Preface, and a few not on their list have been added. When it comes to the New Testament, there were few named prophets, although given the extent of the gift usage, there were many more unnamed or unknown. The role of the NT prophet changed from prophesying to nations to more building up the church. One important observation is that as far as the Bible goes, the message of the prophets is generally a lot more important than their lives, and it is hardly surprising that in most cases we know so little about them.

A good deal of what the Hebrew prophets prophesied only came to pass after their deaths, sometimes long after, and one is reminded of the words of the poet Longfellow: "*Though the mills of God grind slowly, yet they grind exceeding small; Though with patience He stands waiting, with exactness grinds He all.*" What was said came to pass and, from what we can make out from the historical record, did so exactly as the prophets predicted, which if this were a book on Bible apologetics would furnish good evidence the Bible is true and YHWH is the true and living God. Some prophecies related to the first coming of Israel's promised Messiah, which, while it may be a view non-believing Jewish folk would likely reject, was something that the early Christians repeatedly referred to. This is evidenced by the number of Old Testament references cited in the New when it applies these to the birth and death and other events concerning Jesus' life.

The same application is true concerning the second (yet to happen) coming of the Messiah, which is spoken about many times in the Old Testament and referred to in several places in the New, especially the book of Revelation. This is for some the main interest when it comes to the prophets of the Bible. Yet for others such texts, of which there are many, are rather dismissed. Often this is to do with how those who interpret and expound the Scriptures view them. The author has little doubt that Israel has *not* been replaced by the church, that Jesus will personally return to the earth, there will be a literal millennium yet to take place, and unless it is clear that this is not the case, prophecies are to be interpreted literally, yet recognising that many Christians do not hold those positions. But this is what will determine our approach in this book. And as with all things, balance is needed and, in the first fourteen chapters especially, when the subject of unfulfilled prophecy does inevitably arise, it will be discussed more from the perspective of how it was understood at the time, and will be light when trying to apply this to current events, mindful that good and learned men have got it very wrong in the past when attempting to do so. In Chapter 15, we explore what to expect in the Last Days as relating to some of these prophecies. In Chapter 16 we reflect on some of the lessons learned. In Chapter 17, which was an afterthought, we consider related subjects to our prophecy studies, where the Bible provides a view. Chapters 18, 19, 20 and 21 are additions by virtue of going to a second edition.

While it is not the intention to dismiss altogether those whose understanding of Bible prophecy differs from that of the author, one is mindful there are those who do not take what the prophets said as true, divinely inspired or to be taken literally, often not believing the events they wrote about have taken place or would take place; and when it comes to actual prophecies, these were not made at the time when the prophets lived (for how could they have known?), and were added later. Several of the prophets, especially those dealing with miracles or prophecies fulfilled a lot later, fall into that category. This is *not* the approach taken in this book, but rather that what was prophesied in the Bible either took place at the time or, as would become evident, there is a future fulfilment, to be taken literally. Many books have been written on interpreting the prophets and apologetics. Readers interested in the rationale should refer to these. As far as this book is concerned, while not beyond explaining why the author believes as he does, it is written based on the belief that what took place was how the Bible described it.

Before moving on to consider further background (Chapters 2 and 3), and then onto each individual prophet that is deemed to be such (in the author's opinion), there is more general stuff that applies, and given its importance, this needs to be reflected on, which we will return to when we wind up in the final chapters.

The test for a true prophet

If we search the Scriptures, we find a lot that is said or implied concerning who are the true prophets and who are the false prophets: e.g., *"But the prophet who presumes to speak a word in my name that I have not commanded him to speak, or who speaks in the name of other gods, that same prophet shall die.' And if you say in your heart, 'How may we know the word that the Lord has not spoken?'— when a prophet speaks in the name of the Lord, if the word does not come to pass or come true, that is a word that the Lord has not spoken; the prophet has spoken it presumptuously. You need not be afraid of him."* (Deuteronomy 18:20-22.)

At least two common points should be inferred here: firstly, in the case of true prophets, what they prophesy will come to pass; and, secondly, they speak truth concerning the one true God. The penalty for those who fail to meet that criteria is a severe one – death. Yet, as will be discussed in Chapter 6, there were many false prophets to be found throughout the Bible. The warning Jesus gave, *"And many false prophets will arise and lead many astray"* (Matthew 24:11), is poignant, particularly given that false prophets are often not seen to be such by many, often due to their charismatic personality and even miraculous powers and what they spoke was all too often what the people wanted to hear.

It also has a bearing on the controversial question (at least among many Christians the author has associated with in the past) of whether there are prophets today. Just as there are false prophets, there are true ones too; and sometimes it is hard to tell which is which, yet we are required to test prophecy, if truly from God. Just as with Christian leaders (e.g. pastors, priests) today, the matter of what constitutes a call can be a contentious one, especially if the said person does not speak the word of the Lord, which in the author's experience is often the case. Moreover, there were some who prophesised without any record of them having been called by God to be prophets, whose "prophesies" were and are accepted as coming from the Lord. The matter of how God spoke to the prophets generally is an interesting one, which we will get to – and perhaps begs the question as to how God speaks to those of us who are not prophets and how we are guided by Him.

Yet even though we have scant information about the lives of many of the prophets, there are several accounts of God having called individuals to be prophets, ranging from the likes of Isaiah who saw the Lord high and lifted up, to Amos who was spoken to while carrying out the humble tasks of looking after sheep and fig trees. Some prophets, such as Elijah, simply appeared on the scene without any introduction. What is striking is that the prophets were from all sorts of backgrounds, operated under quite different circumstances and varied widely in temperament. While they operated in the supernatural, they were quite ordinary and had the same range of human flaws and foibles as do the rest of us. Two of the arguably greatest of the prophets failed big time. Moses failed to give God the glory when he struck the Rock, and as a result was not allowed to enter the Promised Land. Elijah, soon after his amazing mountain-top experience, fled Jezebel in a fit of depression, wanting only to die. Yet they were, at least at the time they prophesied, devoted to serving the Lord, and were honoured as such.

We are reminded that *"God hath chosen the foolish things of the world to confound the wise; and God hath chosen the weak things of the world to confound the things which are mighty"* (1Corinthians 1:27), and ours is not to reason why it is that God called some to be prophets, and how He did so, but we should be glad He did because of the important role they had, from which we all benefit.

The trials and tribulations of the prophets

The words of Jesus to the religious leaders of His day are poignant: *"Woe to you! For you build the tombs of the prophets, and your fathers killed them."* (Luke 11:47.) While the Bible account does not record much by the way of prophets being killed because of their prophesying (although other historical sources tell us some, e.g. Isaiah, were) there is plenteous evidence of prophets being persecuted and attempts on their lives (as with Jeremiah and Daniel). As for tombs, we know some died natural deaths as the tombs of some (Ezekiel, Nahum, Haggai, Zechariah and Malachi) survive to this day and are places of pilgrimage.

The lives of the prophets were not easy and most suffered deprivations. Often their message of rebuke and warning did not go down well, because they did not say what the people wanted to hear, especially the powers that be. They were often reviled and misunderstood, and much worse, and their existence could be a lonely one. Sometimes, suffering hardship was because God instructed them to do odd things when it came to communicating the message He gave them. In Isaiah's case, this included walking around the city naked; Jeremiah was told not to marry; Ezekiel had to lie on his side for days on end, surviving on starvation rations - all in order to make important points. Without self-pitying, prophets like Elijah and Jeremiah often remonstrated with God – why me? The lot of a prophet was not enviable. Their consolation was being in and knowing the will of God and that God was with them; and while they had direct knowledge of God's thoughts and intentions, although often without the full big picture, it came at a hefty price.

How God spoke to the prophets

The Lord declared "*If there is a prophet among you, I the Lord make myself known to him in a vision; I speak with him in a dream.*" (Numbers 12:6.) Dreams and visions were certainly important ways God spoke to His prophets and there are several examples of Him having done so. Indeed, we were reminded, when the Holy Spirit came on the Day of Pentecost, that "*it shall come to pass in the last days, saith God, I will pour out of my Spirit upon all flesh: and your sons and your daughters shall prophesy, and your young men shall see visions, and your old men shall dream dreams.*" (Acts 2:17.) Expect more to come!

Yet it seemed too that when God spoke, it was in a variety of ways. It may have been a voice from heaven or through an intermediary, typically an angel. It could be through events taking place or might simply be a message that was impressed, as it were, upon the prophet's heart by the Lord. But whatever the method that was employed, the prophets heard from God and recognised their solemn duty was to pass on that message by whatever means to those for whom the message was intended. "*For the prophecy came not in old time by the will of man: but holy men of God spake as they were moved by the Holy Ghost.*" (2 Peter 1:21.)

While we may not be prophets, God promises: "*I will instruct thee and teach thee in the way which thou shalt go: I will guide thee with mine eye.*" (Psalm 32:8.)

How prophets communicated their message

As we saw earlier, some of the prophets were actors, and rather good at it. The important thing was to get the message out, which they sought to do in the most effective way possible, as instructed by the Lord, even though often their words were rejected. Two obvious ways of communicating were speaking and writing.

It can be misleading, though, when referring to the later prophets (four majors and twelve minors) as the writing prophets, given they have books written with their names as titles, since the writing prophets both spoke and wrote, as did some of the prophets before them. It would have been a tremendous experience to see the prophets speaking their message while in full flow with something important to say, whether to an individual such as a king or to crowds small and large. All we have to go by now is what they wrote or what was written about them.

While the translators have often done a good job in translating their words into the vernacular, inevitably things get lost in the translation, such as the depth and precision of word meaning, use of illustrations, use of acrostics and different types of figurative language, and the beauty and emotion behind the words used, often with the intention at the time to make the message more memorable. One notable feature is the use of poetry as well as prose, with the former aimed at the heart and the latter the head. It was written so that God's people knew what He thought and felt. These writings often detailed what was to happen, whether it was to do with confronting Israel's enemies, future events or getting Israel to repent (***teshuvah*** - literally "return"); saying what would happen if they did not.

While the Old Testament particularly addressed Israel, with the New addressing additionally those who were not Israel, even in the Old, God was interested in the other nations; and while they could not be expected to follow the law of Moses *per se*, the prophets made it clear that they were expected to act rightly and were to be judged if they did not do so. But in Israel's case, He wanted especially to appeal to their hearts, given that God was married to Israel (e.g. as referred to in Hosea and Jeremiah), with Israel the faithless bride, yet still loved by her heavenly husband, longing that she returned to Him, and thus the use of poetry.

What was the message of the prophets?

While the message of the prophets varied from prophet to prophet, there was a lot of repetition, both with individual prophets repeating the same message and other prophets bringing the same message, often to a different group of listeners.

A lot of prophecy was generic in nature – *e.g.* Israel (and other nations) needing to repent of their sins or else face God's anger and judgement; or God's love and compassion was such that He wanted to bless His people. Yet a lot was more specific and related to the needs of the hour as the prophets saw these, or rather as God saw things, instructing them in what to say. A lot of prophecy related to the coming of the Messiah and the Last Days.

Especially in the times of the kings, and after that the Exile and return from Exile, God wanted to guide His people as to how they should act or how He would act on their behalf when they did. Many prophecies were remarkably specific in nature and we can now look back at the fulfilment of many as being precisely as the prophets had predicted. Some seemed unlikely at the time, e.g. Ezekiel predicting the destruction of Tyre, Jeremiah that of Babylon, Obadiah that of Edom, and Nahum Nineveh – all seemingly impregnable places, yet it did happen.

Often the prophet was unaware of timescale – sometimes prophecies were fulfilled immediately, and some, nearing three thousand years later, are yet to be fulfilled. When walking in his beloved Lake District, the author might view the mountains from some strategic spot, seeing one distant mountain seeming right up close behind another one, but the reality was there was significant unseen space between the two. It could be said, this is how the prophets saw the coming of the Messiah. What seemed like one coming, culminating in the Day of the Lord, was two, separated by a long period (two thousand years at least), in which attention was being drawn to the church rather than Israel, with so much about the church the prophets would not have reckoned with. God only told prophets what they needed to know and it is for later generations to work out their actual fulfilment.

An example of a prophecy that has more than one fulfilment (of which there are many) is found in Daniel 11, which was fulfilled exactly as prophesied four hundred years later under Antiochus Epiphanes, and yet even has a final fulfilment under the coming Antichrist. Another is when Matthew speaks of the boy Jesus returning from Egypt (Matthew 2:15), he claims it fulfilled what Hosea had prophesied: "*out of Egypt I called My son*", (Hosea 11:1) which, when understood at the time, would have been taken to mean Israel coming out of Egypt.

How the prophets show us God is for real

While it is the intention of this author to speak to the mind by saying it as it is, so to speak, concerning the prophets of the Bible, encouraging readers to think through what they read here and to go and find out for themselves what it is the Bible teaches, it is also intended to speak to the heart. There is a tendency in all of us to accept something as true and important with our minds and it goes no further than that. But in the case of the prophets in particular, and the Bible in general, if we accept it to be true, consistency at the very least demands we do something about it. The prophets found, time after time, God to be real, who said what he meant and did what he said, and He was not to be messed with.

The remarkable thing about these prophecies is that, except for those yet to be fulfilled, several hundred prophecies have been fulfilled down to the tiniest detail, even when the timing appeared delayed and it happened in ways not always expected. While this is not a book on apologetics, the many examples we find in the Bible of fulfilled prophecy, which we will get to, shows the Bible to be true. God is to be obeyed and, whether one does so out of fear or love, it matters and is the difference between going on to experience God's blessings or God's curses; as Israel, the main intended audience of the Hebrew prophets, should have known very well if they had taken seriously Deuteronomy 28-30.

While those of us living today might fret over what is happening all around us and God's apparent silence, the God we are called to love with all our hearts and minds is the same One proclaimed by the prophets, who has our best interests at heart, whose promises are *yea and amen* and, like the prophets, we are called to obey Him fully. For it is, above all, all about Him, mindful that same God still does wondrous things. There is a tendency for all of us *not* to take God seriously. As an example from two prophets we will get to, when Elisha had been picked up the "mantle" from his mentor, Elijah, following Elijah being suddenly whisked away in a chariot of fire, and confronted with his first of many challenges to come, he asked the question *"where is the Lord God of Elijah?"* (2 Kings 2:11) and found out then and thereafter the God of Elijah was for real. Different time and different context but the word of the Lord through the last of our OT prophets is ever pertinent: *"prove me now herewith, saith the Lord of hosts"* (Malachi 3:10).

Chapter 2: The prophets in context

Why context is important

There is a tendency for all of us to succumb to our prejudices and the viewpoints of those who get to us first. We are more inclined to believe things that fit in with how we see the world, regardless of facts that suggest differently and without knowing the bigger picture or getting the right balance. No doubt this could happen with our studies of the prophets, and this chapter is written to help remedy this and provide useful references for when we come to the chapters that follow.

Granted, it is better that readers know but a little if it comes down to choosing that or loving God a lot, and it is far better to concentrate on studying the Bible, even without reliance on extra help. After all, we do not have to go to the experts before we begin to study; true wisdom and understanding often resides with those who love and fear God as opposed to those with deep intellect and knowledge. If all this book does is to get folk digging deep into the Bible, then that is great! Yet context is all important, else our understanding of the Bible will be limited. This chapter opens up this whole context business, providing maps and charts that the author has found helpful, along with tools, resources and learned commentaries.

What we have done is to take several images, the majority of which can be found on the Internet, including charts and maps that in one way or another relate to some aspect of our study, and we include these in this chapter, along with a comment to help explain the relevance of their inclusion. But before we do, there are a number of principles that anyone serious about understanding the Bible, specifically the prophets, ought to take into consideration. These have continually been taken into account by the author in the course of researching for this book.

1. **Study all that the Bible says about the prophets and their words.**

    There is a temptation to pick the easy or nice bits and ignore the more difficult bits pertaining to each prophet. It is important to study all that is written. Often it cannot be done in a single sitting, but we gain much if we study the whole.

2. **Get to know well all sixty-six books that make up your Bible.**

    The prophets and their message can only be properly understood with reference to the rest of the Bible, from Genesis to Revelation. It is good to get into the habit of regular Bible study that involves systematically going through the whole Bible. This is a lifetime business; there are always new things to see.

3. **Even if you use a particular translation, also use other translations.**

   While the author has opted for the King James Version, as much because that is the translation he is most familiar with and its memorable language, readers may well have other preferences. We are in fact spoilt for choice. It is good to read a passage in more than one translation in order to get a fresh perspective.

4. **Find out what is written in the original languages.**

   Few who read their Bibles do so in the original languages, but words and the way these are arranged matter. Sometimes it helps to refer to the original text using excellent on- and offline commentaries and dictionaries on the subject.

5. **Understand the history of the period in which the prophets wrote.**

   It will come as no surprise to discover much went on while the prophets wrote affecting their ministries. We can find out much by reading all of the Bible, but also non-Bible writings explaining pertinent historical events.

6. **Understand the geography of the period in which the prophets wrote.**

   The map of the region, especially relating to the countries surrounding Israel (often opposing it), and the rise and fall of different empires, was continually changing. As with the history, this too had a bearing on what was written.

7. **Have some archaeological awareness relating to events recorded.**

   While not seeing the artefacts of the period the prophets operated in, thanks to many amazing archaeological finds we now know a lot, and among other things it often confirms what the prophets said, adding further insight.

8. **Understand the culture – especially Jewish culture.**

   For most readers, the culture and mindset that typically influences us is *not* Jewish. It can put us at a disadvantage when attaching significance to the prophetic writings. There is also something we can loosely refer to as *Midrash*, which among other things gives insights as to how the Jews viewed prophecy.

9. Learn from those who know their stuff.

Watch, listen and read! While readers are encouraged to go direct to the Bible to gain understanding, rather than read the musings of those deemed "expert", there are some wonderful resources out there, some of which are mentioned in the *Acknowledgements* section of this book. We are often spoilt for choice.

10. Pray to the Lord to open your eyes and help you to understand.

The Bible is no ordinary book – it is God's Word. We should approach our studies prayerfully, seeking the guidance of the Holy Spirit to reveal the truth.

Before we get to the remainder, the baulk of this chapter, it is worth reminding ourselves that while the message of the prophets was often for a specific time and place, often it was and is more widely applicable. Just as God does not change, his message through the prophets, or whoever, is timeless. But in our quest to understand the context, and our desire to relate this message to the times we live in, we need to exercise due caution. The author has endeavoured to concentrate on sound Bible exegesis, at least up to Chapter 20, and does so mindful of his own background, axioms and interests, his advice to readers is to bear this in mind and, more than any other consideration, try to understand what the Bible teaches us.

Introducing the figures

Here, then, are the figures and accompanying explanations that help further to provide the context as well as further background in studying the prophets. It is suggested that when reading the chapters that follow, these can be referred to:

Figure 1. *Timeline of the Bible* – the Bible recounts the story of God's dealing with humankind, starting from "in the beginning", going on until the end of time.

Figure 2. *Bible (Hebrew and Christian)* – the way Jews and Christians lay out the Old Testament are different, even though the content is the same. The two ways used for categorising and ordering the books are laid out side by side.

Figure 3. *Chronology (1)* – from the beginning to the death of Jesus. There are many key dates relating to Bible events given and several are approximations. While we do not refer to all of them, many that relate to this book are included.

Figure 4. *Chronology (2)* – from the divided kingdom to the end of the Old Testament, and is further elaboration of some of the events shown in Figure 3.

Figure 5. *Kings of the Bible* – basic details of every king of Israel and Judah.

Figure 6. *Prophets of the Bible* – details of Elijah, Elisha, Writing Prophets.

Figure 7. *Wilderness journey* – suggested route of the children of Israel following escape from Egypt; forty years in the wilderness and entering the promised land.

Figure 8. *Tabernacle (in the wilderness) layout and the Temple in Jesus' time.*

Figure 9. *Feast and offerings* – these played an important part of Israel's religious life. The seven prescribed feasts and five prescribed offerings are laid out here.

Figure 10. *Map of Israel* - showing the land allocated to the twelve tribes, after the Israelites had entered Canaan, the Promised Land.

Figure 11. *Map of the divided kingdom and the surrounding nations* – this would have been around the time of Amos and shows nations he prophesied against.

Figure 12. *Map of the Assyrian empire, 650 BC.*

Figure 13. *Map of the Babylonian empire, 540 BC.*

Figure 14. *Map of the Persian empire, 490 BC.*

Figure 15. *Map of the Greek empire, 320 BC.*

Figure 16. *Map of the Roman empire around the time of Christ.*

Figure 17. *The Ten Commandments* – central to the Law and the Covenant.

Figure 18. *A simple Gospel presentation* – central to the New Covenant.

Figure 19. *Seven churches in Revelation.*

Figure 20. *Israel and its neighbours today.*

Note: all the figures included are because the author has found them to be helpful to support the narrative that follows in Chapter 3 onwards, and thinks the reader may do so too. A few were produced from scratch but most were taken as *freebies* from the Internet and cannot be edited (in case of error or ambiguity) and may lack in resolution. Most were originally produced in colour.

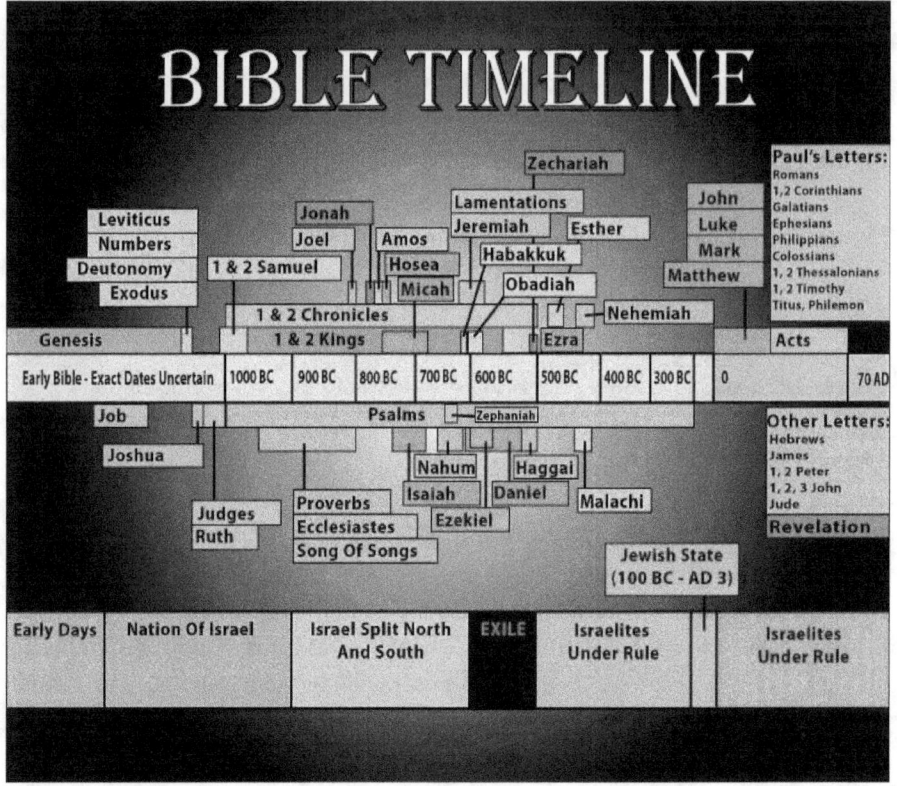

Figure 1 – Bible Timeline

This figure shows each book of the Bible according to when they appear in the timeline, relating to events described in those books or when they were written.

Figure 2 – The Christian Bible and the Hebrew Bible

The books of the Bible are often categorised according to type. When it comes to the Old Testament, while the content is the same, the Hebrew and Christian Bible orders, categorises and sometimes names the books differently. In the Hebrew Bible, Judges, Samuel and Kings are deemed prophecy and Daniel is not.

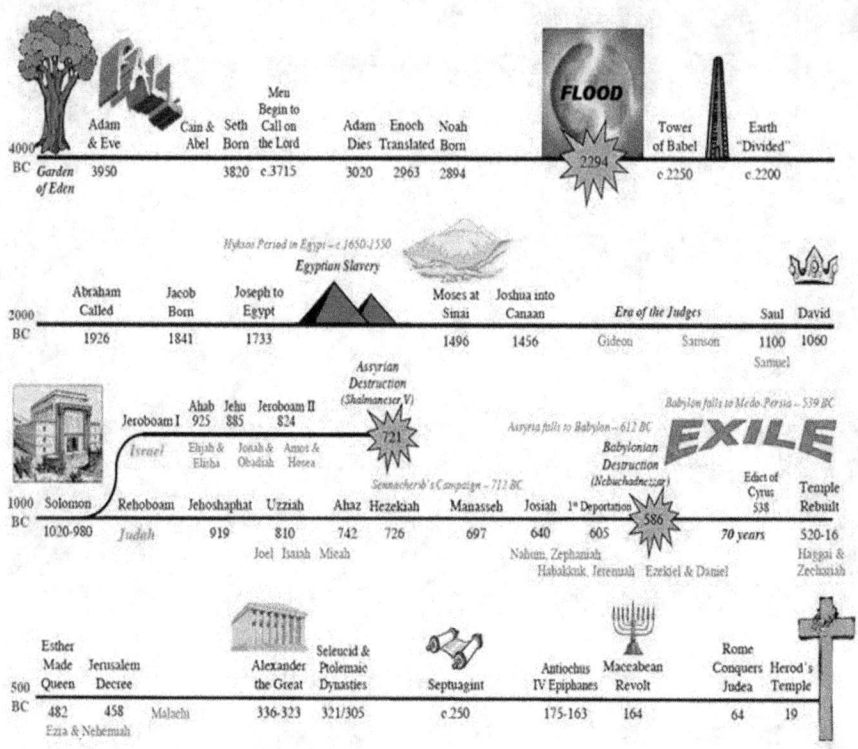

Figure 3 – Bible chronology (1)

Helpful in understanding the subject matter of this book is finding where various happenings fit into the historical timeline. This figure highlights broadly many of the main events that feature in the Bible story, with a particular focus on Israel.

800 Death of Elisha 2Kings 13:18-21

782 Jeroboam II becomes king of Israel and reigns 41 years

Jonah sent to prophesy against Nineveh – Jonah 1:1-3

Amos & Hosea prophesy to Israel; Isaiah & Micah to Judah

722 Fall of Israel / Assyrian Captivity – 2Kings 17:3-6

716 Hezekiah becomes king of Judah and reigns 29 years

650 Nahum sent to prophesy against Nineveh – Nahum 1:1-3

640 Josiah becomes king of Judah and reigns 31 years

Zephaniah and Habakkuk prophesy to Judah

612 Fall of Nineveh – Nahum 3:18-19

608 Josiah killed at Megiddo – 2Kings 23:29

Jeremiah prophesies to Judah, mainly regarding its demise

Four bad kings: Jehoahaz, Jehoiakim, Jehoiachin, Zedekiah

Babylon dominant world power – defeats Assyria, then Egypt

605 Daniel taken to Babylon and begins his ministry

598 Ezekiel taken to Babylon, begins his ministry five years later

586 Fall of Jerusalem

539 Persians overthrow the Babylonian empire

Cyrus edict for Jews to return to their land

537 Jews begin to return to Israel under Zerubbabel

Haggai and Zechariah prophesy

458 Jews return to Israel under Ezra

444 Jews return to Israel under Nehemiah

Malachi prophesies

Figure 4 – Bible chronology (2)

The study of the prophets, particularly the later prophets, is helped by knowing when the prophets operated and what was going on at the time. The above chart attempts to do so for writing prophets, excluding Joel and Obadiah, whose dates are disputed; unlike with, for example, Zechariah, whose exact dates we know.

Kings of Judah and Israel

Saul	1050-1010 BC
David	1010-970
Solomon	970-930

Judah (and Benjamin)					Israel (Ten Northern Tribes)				
King	Reign		Character	Prophets	King	Reign		Character	Prophets
1. Rehoboam	931-913	17 years	Bad	Shemaiah	1. Jeroboam I	931-910	22 years	Bad	Ahijah
2. Abijah	913-911	3 years	Bad		2. Nadab	910-909	2 years	Bad	
3. Asa	911-870	41 years	Good		3. Baasha	909-886	24 years	Bad	
					4. Elah	886-885	2 years	Bad	
					5. Zimri	885	7 days	Bad	
					6. Omri	885-874*	12 years	Bad	Elijah
4. Jehoshaphat	870-848*	25 years	Good		7. Ahab	874-853	22 years	Bad	Micaiah
5. Jehoram	848-841*	8 years	Bad		8. Ahaziah	853-852	2 years	Bad	
6. Ahaziah	841	1 years	Bad		9. Joram	852-841	12 years	Bad	Elisha
7. Athaliah	841-835	6 years	Bad		10. Jehu	841-814	28 years	Bad	
8. Joash	835-796	40 years	Good	Joel	11. Jehoahaz	814-798	17 years	Bad	Jonah
9. Amaziah	796-767	29 years	Good		12. Jehoash	798-782	16 years	Bad	Amos
10. Uzziah (Azariah)	767-740*	52 years	Good		13. Jeroboam II	782-753*	41 years	Bad	Hosea
11. Jotham	740-732*	16 years	Good	Isaiah	14. Zechariah	753-752	6 mo	Bad	
12. Ahaz	732-716	16 years	Bad	Micah	15. Shallum	752	1 mo	Bad	
13. Hezekiah	716-687	29 years	Good		16. Menahem	752-742	10 years	Bad	
14. Manasseh	687-642*	55 years	Bad-repent		17. Pekahiah	742-740	2 years	Bad	
15. Amon	642-640	2 years	Bad	Nahum	18. Pekah	740-732*	20 years	Bad	
16. Josiah	640-608	31 years	Good	Habakkuk Zephaniah	19. Hoshea	732-712	9 years	Bad	
17. Jehoahaz	608	3 mo	Bad						
18. Jehoiakim	608-597	11 years	Bad	Daniel	722 BC Fall of Isreal / Assyrian Captivity				
19. Jehoiachin	597	3 mos	Bad	Ezekiel					
20. Zedekiah	597-586	11 years	Bad	Jeremiah					
Destruction of Jerusalem, 9th Av, 586 BC, Babylonian Captivity									

Figure 5 – Kings of the Bible

This is one of the author's favourites and is a figure frequently referred to when he was trying to work out (at least, when there were kings of Israel and Judah around) who were the kings reigning in the Northern and Southern Kingdoms (whose doings we can then check out) at the time the prophesies were made, along with what was going on during their reigns, and their dates (and a reminder of their character – good or bad), and when the different prophets were prophesying.

PROPHETS OF THE BIBLE

PROPHETS	PROPHESIED TO/ABOUT	KINGS WHO RULED DURING PROPHET'S TIME	APPROX DATES (B.C.)
Jonah	Nineveh (Assyria)	Jeroboam II	Before Northern Kingdom of Israel Captivity (780-740)
Nahum	Nineveh (Assyria)	Manasseh, Amon, Josiah	Before Southern Kingdom of Judah Captivity (658-615)
Obadiah	Edom	Zedekiah	Before Southern Kingdom of Judah Captivity (590-586)
Hosea	Israel	Jeroboam II, Zechariah, Shallum, Menahem, Pekahiah, Pekah, Hoshea	Before Northern Kingdom of Israel Captivity (780-731)
Amos	Israel	Jeroboam II	Before Northern Kingdom of Israel Captivity (790-779)
Isaiah	Judah	Uzziah, Jotham, Ahaz, Hezekiah, Manasseh	Before Southern Kingdom of Judah Captivity (760-681)
Jeremiah/ Lamentations	Judah	Josiah, Jehoahaz, Jehoiakim, Jehoiachin, Zedekiah	Before Southern Kingdom of Judah Captivity (626-585)
Joel	Judah	Joash	Before Southern Kingdom of Judah Captivity (830-798)
Micah	Judah	Jotham, Ahaz, Hezekiah, Manasseh	Before Southern Kingdom of Judah Captivity (740-695)
Habakkuk	Judah	Jehoiakim, Jehoiachin	Before Southern Kingdom of Judah Captivity (609-597)
Zephaniah	Judah	Amon, Josiah	Before Southern Kingdom of Judah Captivity (640-626)
Ezekiel	Exiled Judah in Babylon	Jehoiachin, Zedekiah (Babylonian Captivity)	During Southern Kingdom of Judah Captivity (593-571)
Daniel	Exiled Judah in Babylon	Jehoiakim, Jehoiachin, Zedekiah (Babylonian Captivity)	During Southern Kingdom of Judah Captivity (605-536)
Haggai	Returned Remnant of Judah	Governor Zerubbabel	After Southern Kingdom of Judah Captivity (520)
Zachariah	Returned Remnant of Judah	Governor Zerubbabel	After Southern Kingdom of Judah Captivity (520-518)
Malachi	Returned Remnant of Judah	Governor Nehemiah	After Southern Kingdom of Judah Captivity (420-415)
Elijah	Israel	Ahab, Ahaziah, Joram	During Northern Kingdom (870-845)
Elisha	Israel	Joram, Jehu, Jehoahaz	During Northern Kingdom (845-800)

Figure 6 – Prophets of the Bible

This figure refers to Elijah, Elisha and the "writing" prophets, giving dates when they operated, the places they prophesied to and who were in charge at the time.

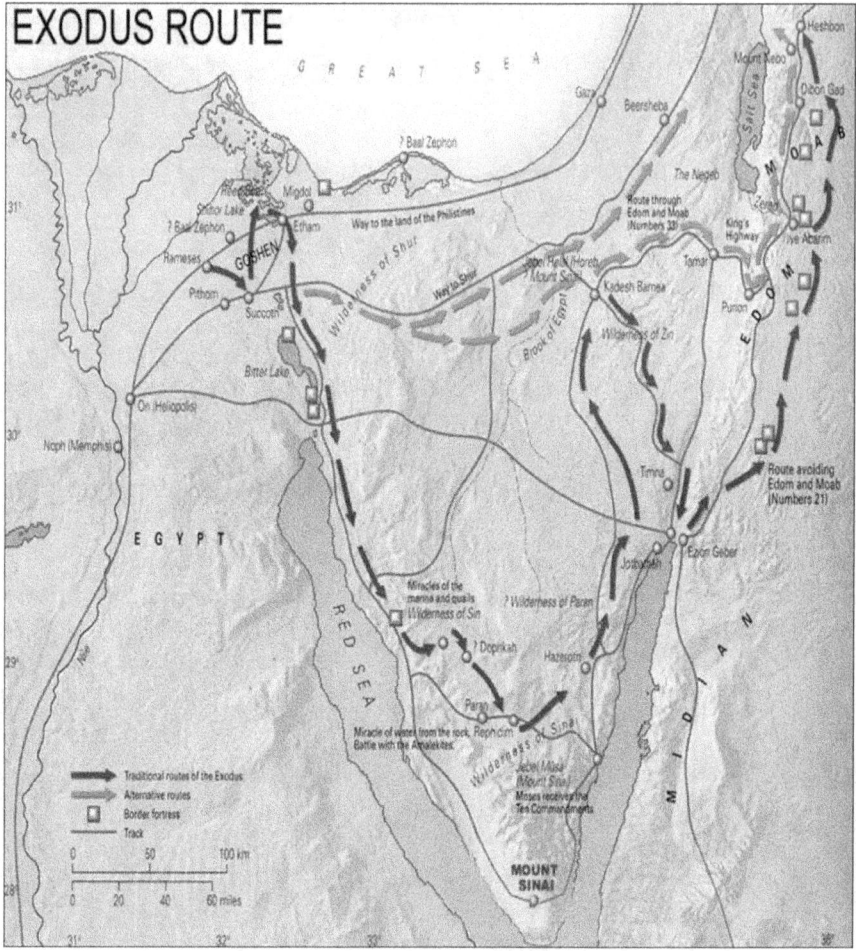

A particular interest of this book is the journey of the Children of Israel between leaving Egypt and entering the Promised Land; the many and varied happenings along the way, when there was the giving of the Law and establishment of civic and religious life. During this time, they spent forty years "wandering" in the wilderness, encountering obstacles and being tested. We cannot be sure of the exact route they took and this is a frequently disputed subject, *e.g.* the mountain on which Moses was given the Law, but many think it is as shown on this map.

Figure 7 – Wilderness Journey

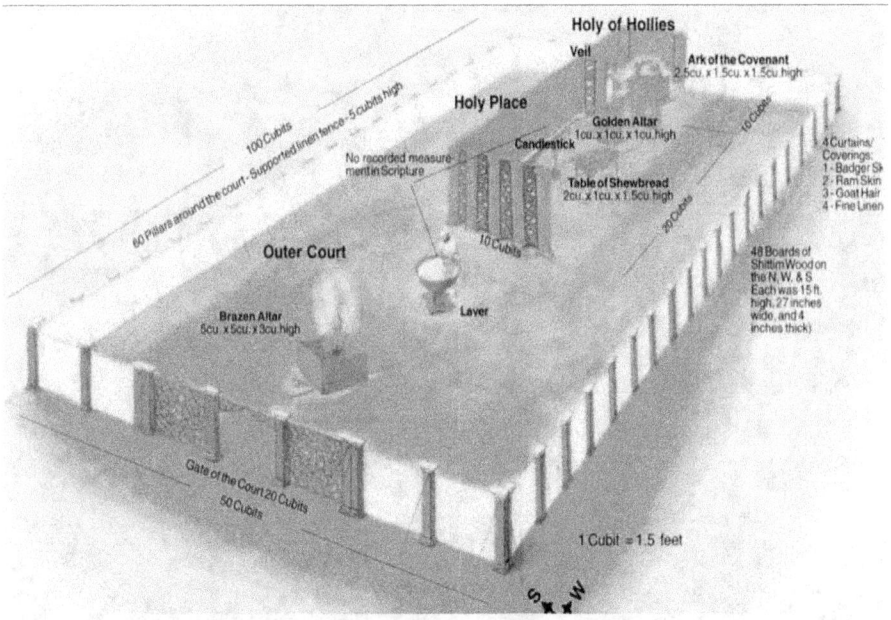

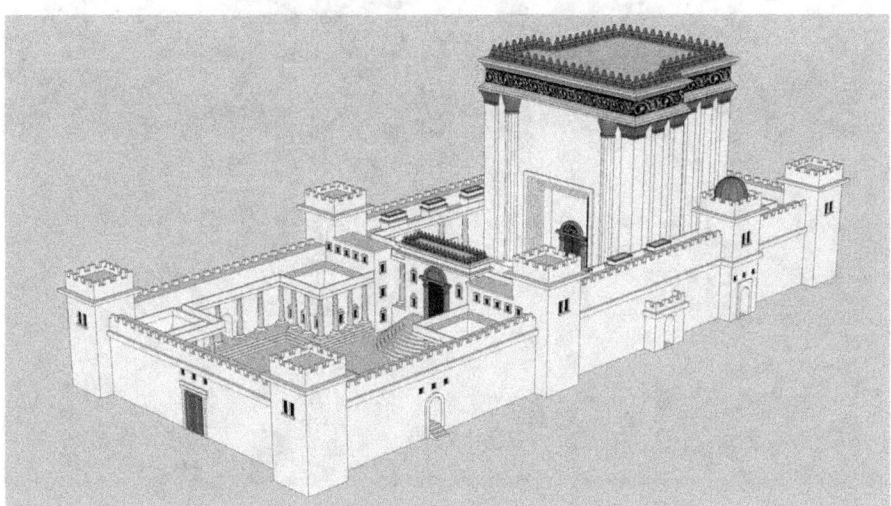

Figure 8 – Tabernacle and Temple

Another interest of this book is the Tabernacle in the Wilderness that was replaced by the (first) Temple built by Solomon, to be destroyed by the Babylonians, with the (second) Temple built on return from Exile and rebuilt by Herod (shown here), and destroyed in AD 70. There is a popular belief there will be a third Temple.

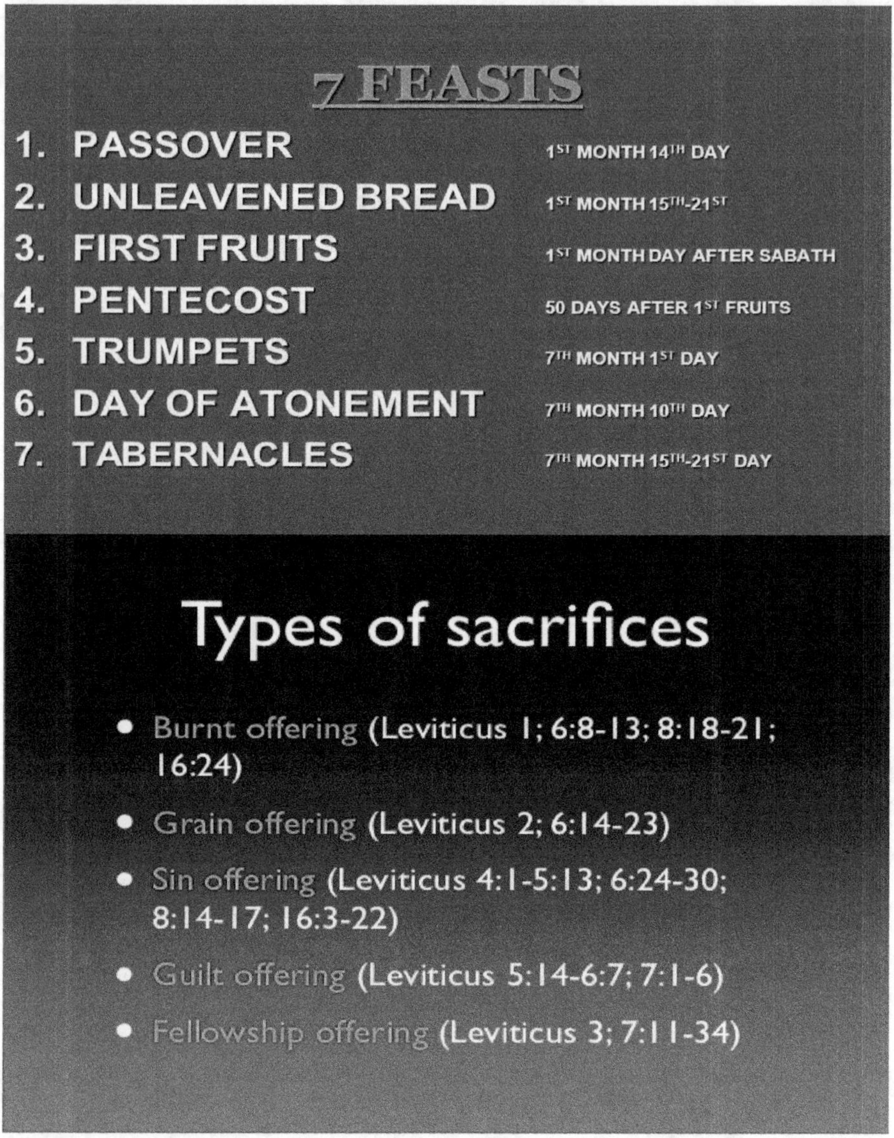

7 FEASTS

1. **PASSOVER** — 1ST MONTH 14TH DAY
2. **UNLEAVENED BREAD** — 1ST MONTH 15TH-21ST
3. **FIRST FRUITS** — 1ST MONTH DAY AFTER SABATH
4. **PENTECOST** — 50 DAYS AFTER 1ST FRUITS
5. **TRUMPETS** — 7TH MONTH 1ST DAY
6. **DAY OF ATONEMENT** — 7TH MONTH 10TH DAY
7. **TABERNACLES** — 7TH MONTH 15TH-21ST DAY

Types of sacrifices

- Burnt offering (Leviticus 1; 6:8-13; 8:18-21; 16:24)
- Grain offering (Leviticus 2; 6:14-23)
- Sin offering (Leviticus 4:1-5:13; 6:24-30; 8:14-17; 16:3-22)
- Guilt offering (Leviticus 5:14-6:7; 7:1-6)
- Fellowship offering (Leviticus 3; 7:11-34)

Figure 9 – 7 Feasts of and 5 Offerings to YHWH

Feasts and offerings were an important and central part of Jewish life and worship. Ever since the destruction of the Temple in AD 70, sacrifices have not been offered but Jews today still observe the feasts, as do some Israel-sympathising Christians. The figures shown above are a reminder of what these were.

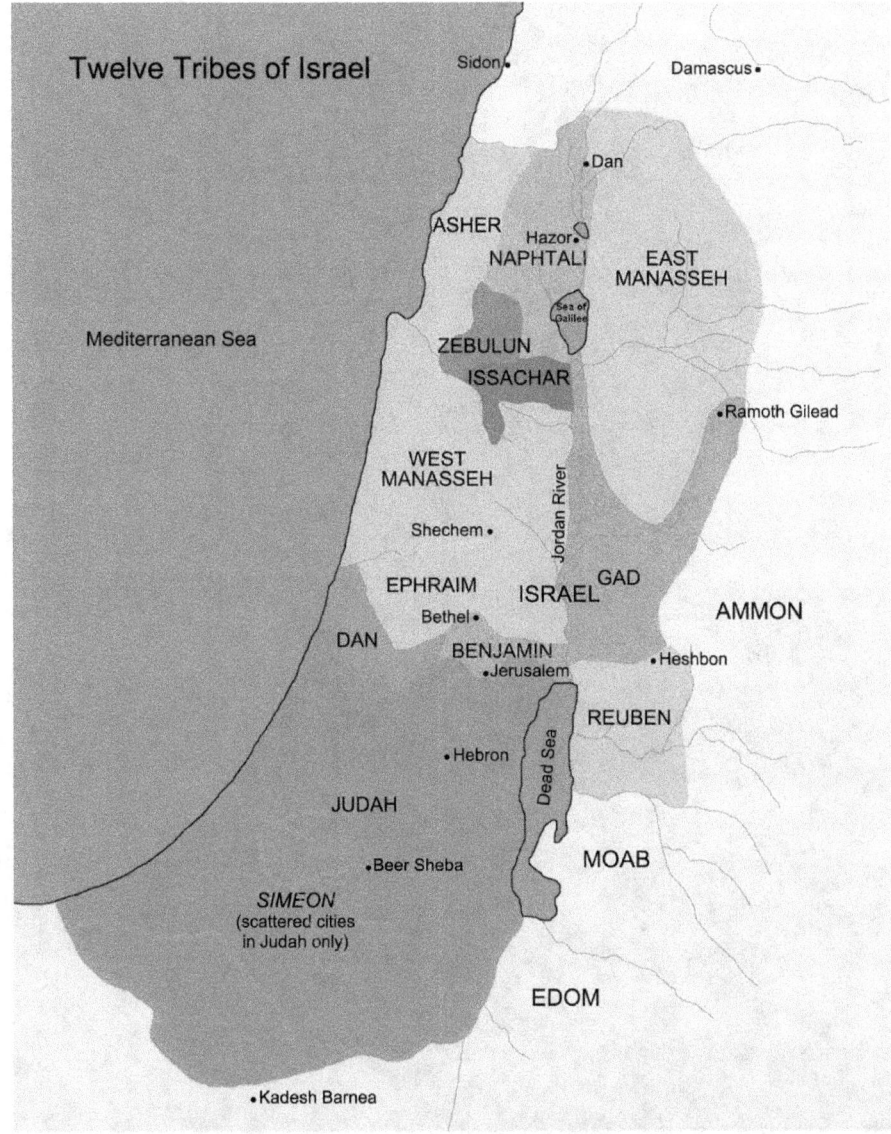

Figure 10 – Twelve Tribes of Israel (after entering Canaan)

Following entering the Promised Land, the land was allocated according to tribe. These allocations remained until Israel and Judah were taken into exile.

Figure 11 – Israel, Judah (divided kingdom) & surrounding kingdoms map

This is how the region looked, geographically speaking, around the time when Amos prophesied. Notably, all the countries surrounding Israel and Judah (that had by then divided) feature (unfavourably) in his prophesies.

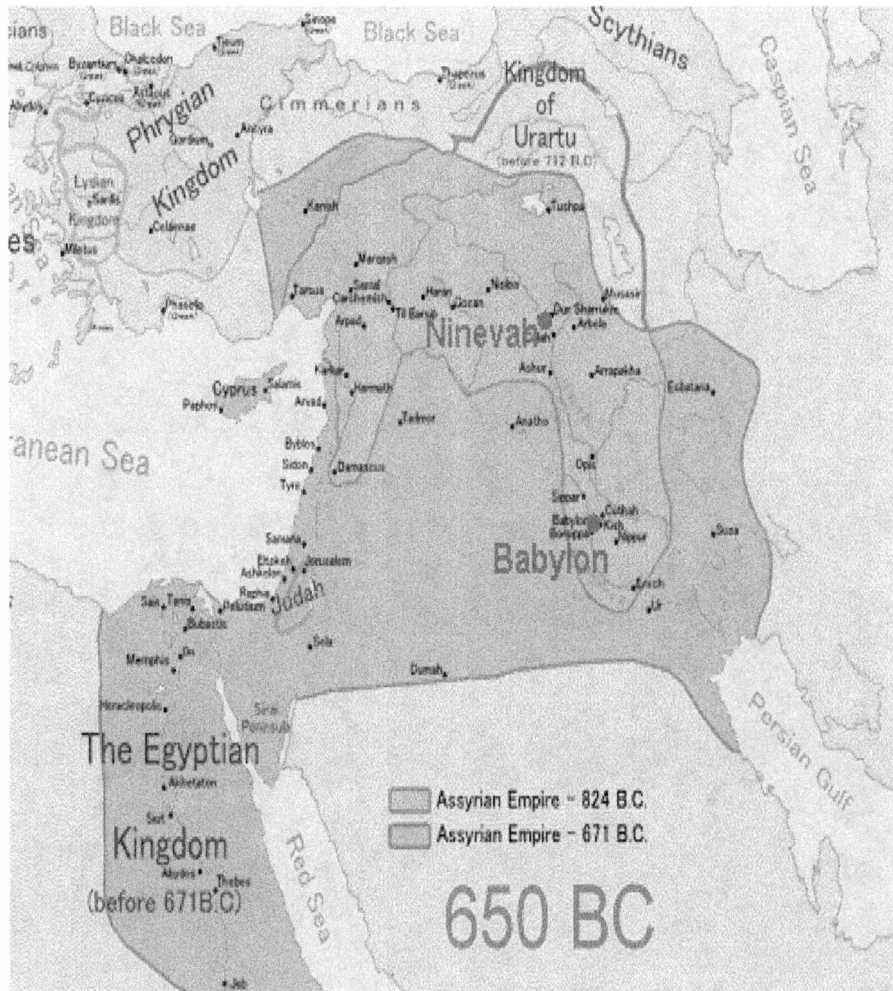

Figure 12 – Assyrian Empire (650 BC)

Assyria is the first of the great empires to feature in the Bible narrative, other than perhaps that of Nimrod. They were a constant thorn in Israel's side, and conquered and took the Northern Kingdom of Israel into captivity in 722 BC, and tried, unsuccessfully, to do the same with the Southern Kingdom of Judah, under king Hezekiah, and only failed because of God's intervention. Around the time represented in this map, 650 BC, Nahum prophesied of its demise as Jonah had done earlier, and this occurred at the hands of the Babylonians in 612 BC.

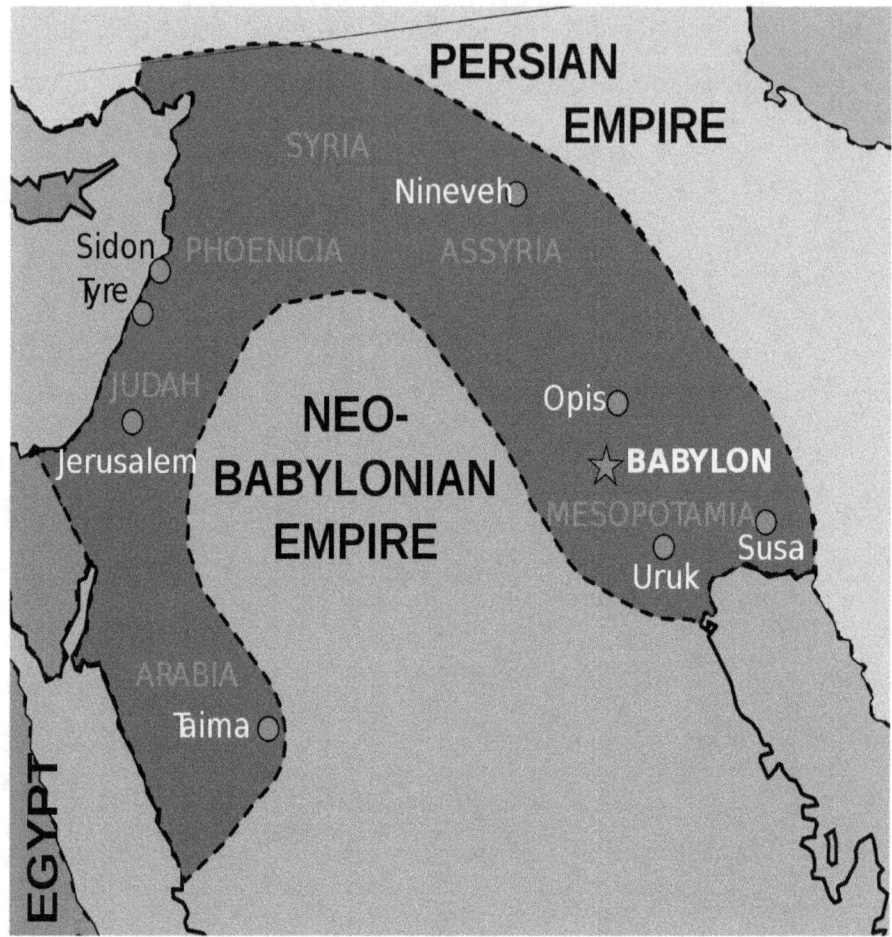

Figure 13 – Babylonian Empire (540 BC)

When King Hezekiah received a delegation from Babylon, with their "get-well card", and proudly showed off his treasures, few would have thought that Babylon would be at the unlikely centre of the next great empire after Assyria. It was they who took Judah into exile in Babylon, which lasted seventy years, as prophesied by the prophet Jeremiah. A year after the date to which the map relates, the Babylonians were conquered by the next great empire, the Medo-Persians.

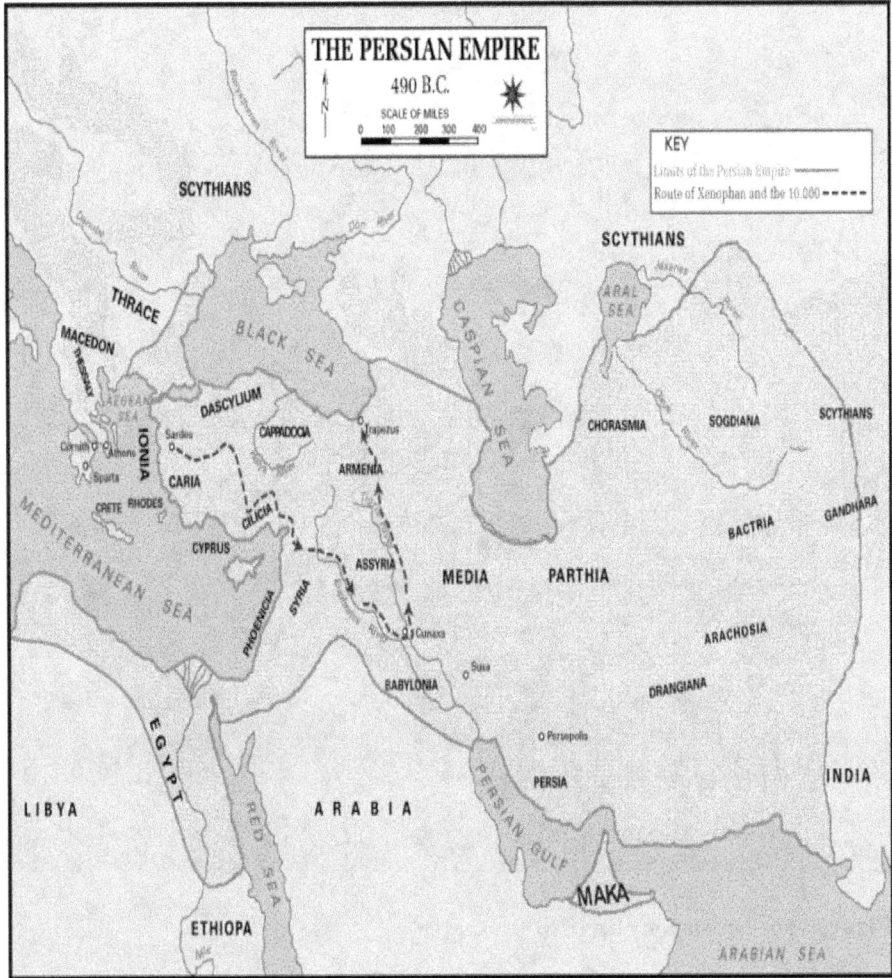

Figure 14 – Persian Empire (490 BC)

After the Babylonians, came the Persians, who conquered them. As far as Israel was concerned, they were generally benevolent, giving them a fairly free reign, and this was particularly so with their rulers, some mentioned by name in the Bible. They allowed the Jews to get on with their lives and practice their religion, unhindered. It was the decree of Cyrus that allowed them to return to their land.

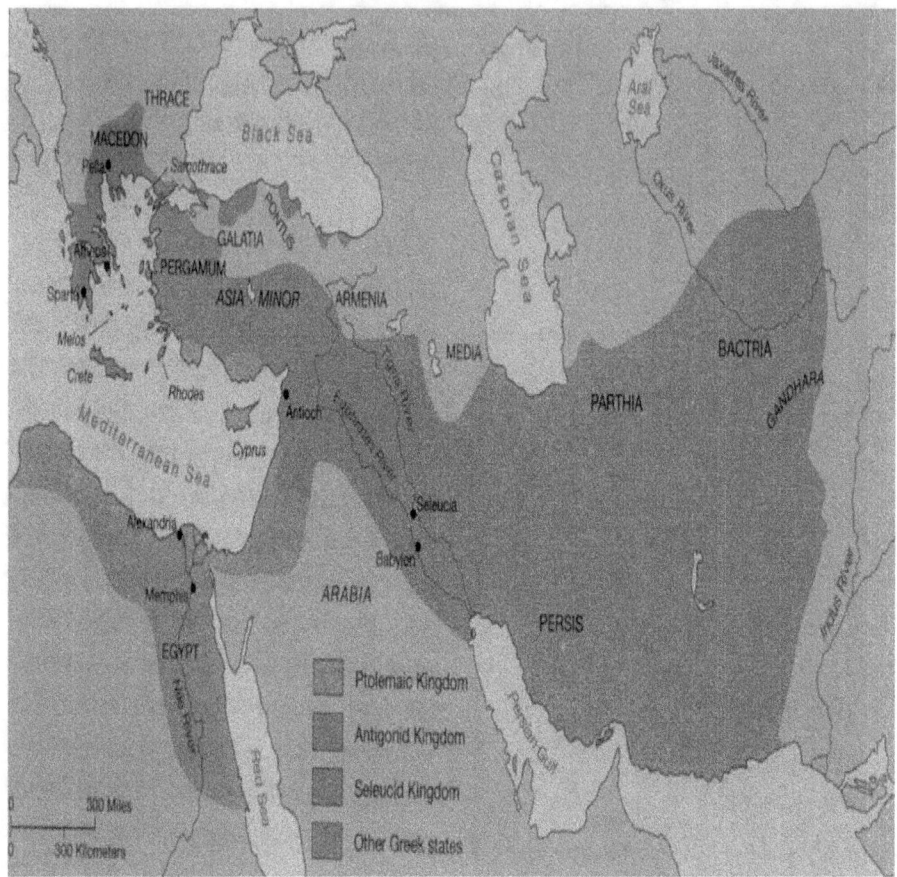

Figure 15 – Greek Empire (320 BC)

Before the Greek Empire took over from the Persians, there were a number of conflicts and battles fought between the two, with the Greeks, under Alexander the Great, eventually coming out on top. The Greek Empire came and went during the Inter-Testament period (replaced by the Romans) and some of that history was exactly foretold by the prophet, Daniel. Notably, Greek culture and thought has significantly influenced the Christian church, even up to the present time.

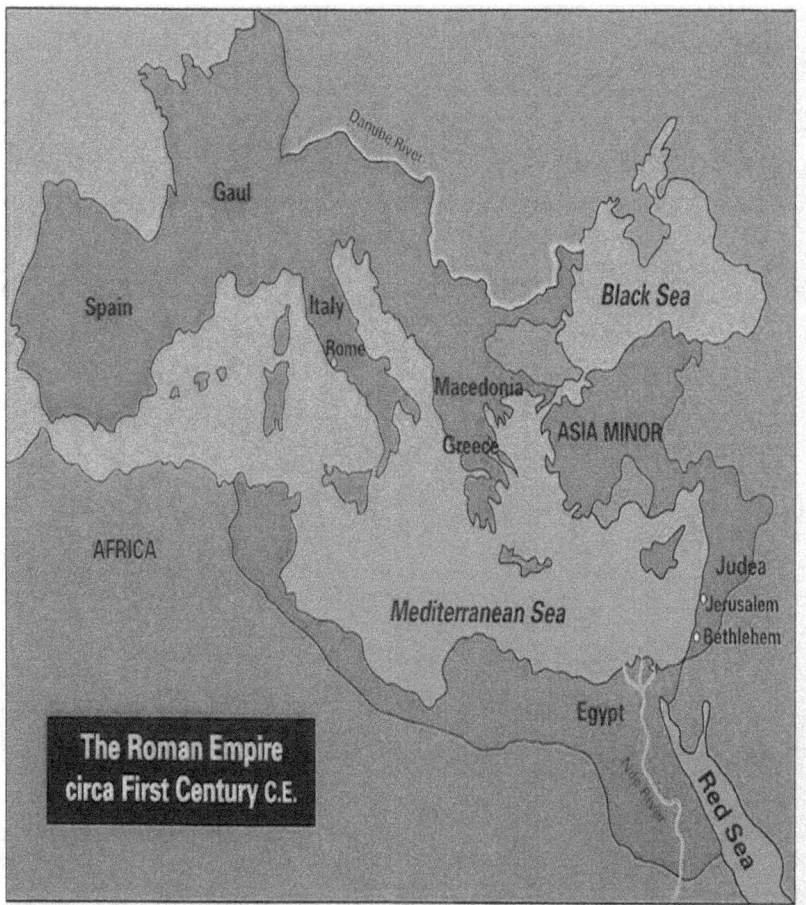

Figure 16 – Roman Empire around the time of Christ

The Roman Empire came into its own in the first century BC. The first two centuries of the Empire saw a period of unprecedented stability and prosperity known as the Pax Romana ("Roman Peace") and it was during the time of Roman ascendancy that included the New Testament period. While not over-sympathetic to "The Way", part of the reason for the success of the gospel in its early years, which spread throughout the Roman empire, might be attributed to Roman rule.

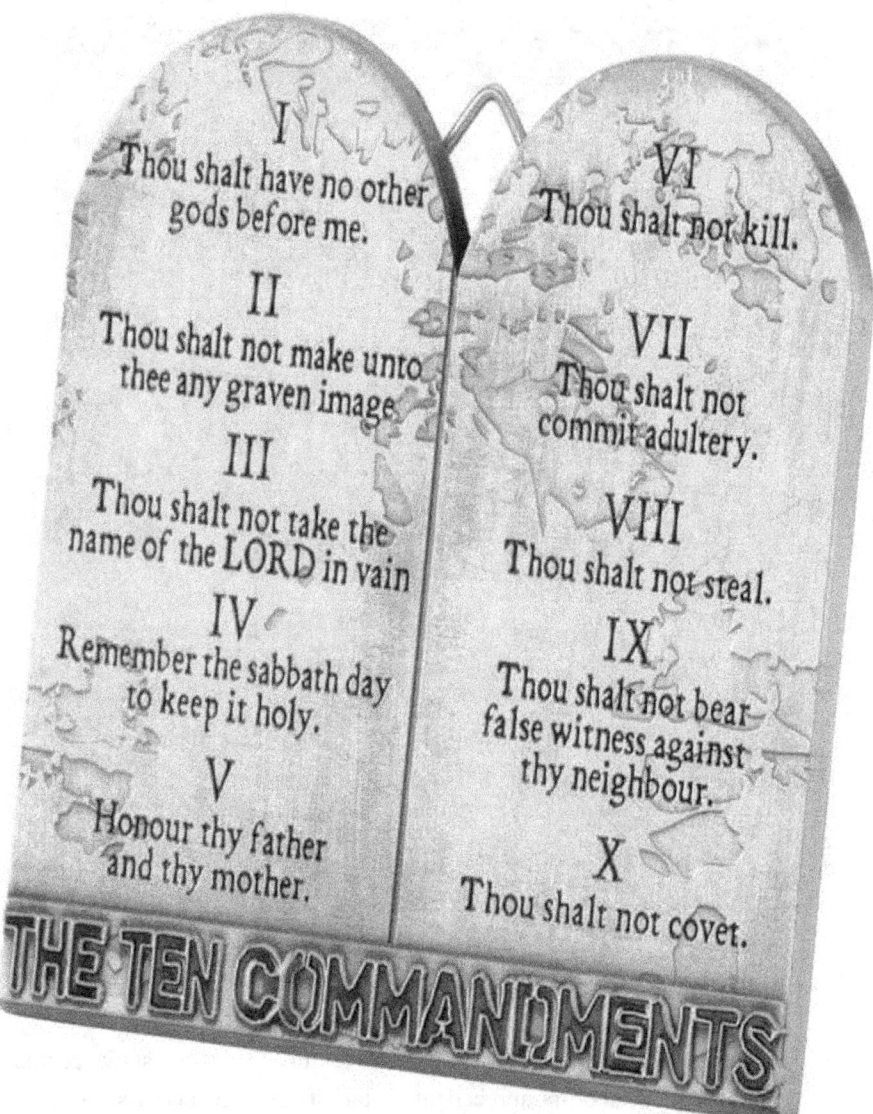

Figure 17 – The Ten Commandments

The Ten Commandments, here portrayed written on tablets of stone, which was how they were given to Moses (and took place twice), was at the very heart of the Jewish Law, including being placed in the Holy of holies, and has come to influence legal codes of many nations thereafter, even until the present day.

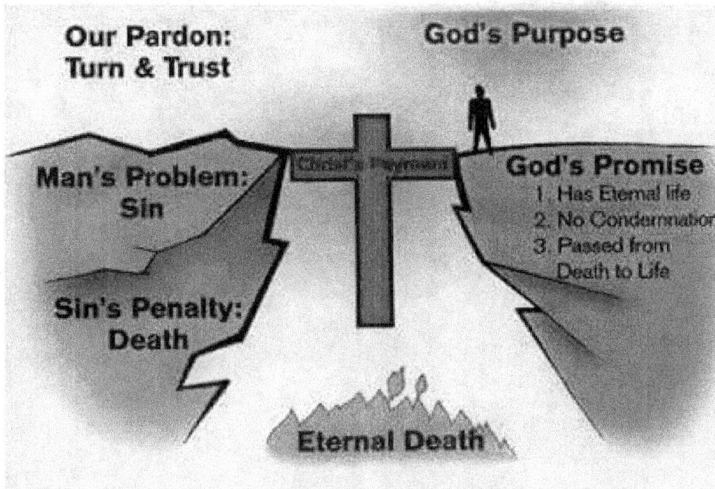

Figure 18 – The Gospel

The Gospel is so simple that the least educated and worst sinner can understand it, and yet so profound that many so-called wise and noble cannot. While there are all sorts of implications and ramifications for those who admit to being Christian need to recognise, the story of how sinners can be saved by God's grace and not by their own human endeavours, as depicted in this figure, is a truly wonderful and important one the prophets of the Bible had at best glimpses into.

Figure 19 – Seven churches of Revelation

The final, and, in terms of not yet having been fulfilled, as well as perhaps the most profound, prophecy of the Bible is that contained in Revelation. But it was addressed initially to the seven churches in Asia Minor, as depicted above, by way of both warning and encouragement in the light of trials and testing that had and were to come and were to be faced. These churches have long ago ceased to exist.

Figure 20 – Israel and its surrounding neighbours today

This figure shows Israel now back and living in a fraction of the land that was promised to Abraham, including what is referred to as "the Occupied Territories". It is surrounded by hostile nations (little has changed), as well as those with which it has some form of peace accord. The future, humanly speaking, is uncertain and yet is one of the important themes that is considered in **Prophets of the Bible**.

Chapter 3: Prophets, priests and kings

A lot of the Old Testament makes reference to three groups of people: prophets, kings and priests, as they feature in the nation of Israel. They were, in their own ways, leaders of the nation, although there were elders and officials too, but it was always God's intention that He would lead them. One esteemed Bible commentator has made the observation, when we consider the two-thousand-year Bible history of Israel leading up to the coming of Jesus, that if we were to divide this into four roughly equal periods, when considering its leadership, this was dominated by patriarchs, prophets, kings and priests respectively. It was never quite that simple though. Prophets and priests featured in the three last periods and there was considerable overlap and interaction between prophets, kings and priests (the place of these in the Old Testament, especially the last two, we will consider in more depth in this chapter). That same commentator observed that in those two thousand years, no styles of leadership worked entirely satisfactorily, which is why they needed someone who could combine all three offices. They got that in Jesus, their Messiah, who we will consider, but whom they rejected. Before we do so, we will consider the history of Israel through the lens of the Bible.

The Bible – chronology, division, order

When we consider the Old Testament chronologically (see Figures 1 and 2 in Chapter 2), we can do so with reference to the Christian Bible, which can be viewed in three sections: History, Genesis through to Esther (seventeen books); Poetry, Job through to Song of Solomon (five books) and Prophecy, Isaiah through to Malachi (seventeen books) - total thirty-nine books. Regarding Prophecy, this can be divided into two sections: the four major prophets and Lamentations; the twelve minor prophets. But there is also the Hebrew Bible.

Books are arranged differently in the Hebrew Bible, which can also be viewed in three sections: the Law, Genesis through to Deuteronomy (five books); the Prophets, Joshua through to the twelve minor prophets, treated as one book (eight books); the Writings, Psalms through to Chronicles (eleven books) - total twenty-four books). Prophecy too can be treated in two parts: Former Prophets, Joshua, Judges, Samuel, Kings; the last two, both one book; and the Latter Prophets, Isaiah through to the minor prophets, with Daniel included in the Writings, along with Lamentations and Ruth, with Samuel, Kings and Chronicles each one book.

In many ways, the Hebrew Bible approach suits that taken by this book. The prophets, unsurprisingly, are mostly in the part of the Hebrew Bible called "the Prophets", although they appear in the Law and the Writings. The kings appear mainly in the Prophets, but some appear in the Writings too, notably Chronicles.

There is an important distinction that could be made with reference to Kings and Chronicles appearing in different sections of the Hebrew Bible, rather than next to each other as in the Christian Bible. Kings (and Samuel) were written from a prophet's perspective, with a focus on the kings of both Israel and Judah; Chronicles was written from a priestly perspective with a focus on the kings of Judah and the line of David, from which the Messiah would come.

For the sake of balance, while we see repetition between Kings and Chronicles, there are important differences too, and for a fuller understanding of the prophets of the Bible, Kings and Chronicles needs to be studied. As for priests, they appear in all three sections of the Hebrew Bible. While not a focus of this book, they played an important part in our story and interacted with both kings and prophets.

Introducing prophets, priests and kings

While the focus of attention in this chapter is on the prophets, priests and kings of the Old Testament, something should be said about the New. The first and most important thing to mention is that the Jesus we read about in the New Testament is prophet, priest *and* king. We will return to this point later in the chapter, after we have set out our store. As for the offices, while prophets do exist under the New Covenant, which is what the New Testament is primarily about, there are aspects not seen in the Old, like no priests, even though many churches today are led by priests. While there are "leaders" in the church, which we will also get to, priests do not apply in the same way as the Old. Jesus is our Great High Priest and the teaching of the "priesthood of all believers" takes on added importance. As for kings, the King the church follows is Jesus. However, as citizens on earth, we are obliged to obey earthly rulers (kings) unless it stops us obeying King Jesus.

The Bible – an overview

We will now embark on a rapid journey through the Old Testament, identifying prophets, priests and kings on the way, before picking up again specifically on priests and kings, while prophets are comprehensively covered in the remaining chapters of this book - for they appear in one way or another in almost every book of the Old Testament, along with their prophetic utterances.

The Bible begins with the creation story, with God creating human beings in His own image, seeking to have a relationship with them. We see at the outset the origins of sin (with other origins to follow), and also the beginning of the way to redemption, one of the major themes of the Bible. We learn how humankind multiplied, but also of their rebellion toward God, whence God sent a flood to destroy the earth. Even following the flood, the human propensity to do wrong continued; for example, in building the Tower of Babel, and God destroying it.

This brings us to a central theme of the Bible and the focus of the Old Testament, Israel. We start with God calling Abraham: *"Now the Lord had said unto Abram, Get thee out of thy country, and from thy kindred, and from thy father's house, unto a land that I will shew thee: And I will make of thee a great nation, and I will bless thee, and make thy name great; and thou shalt be a blessing"*, Genesis 12:1-2. It was with that great nation God wanted to establish His covenant, which might be likened to that of marriage. We follow the story through Isaac and Jacob, then the Patriarchs and then a four-hundred-year stay in Egypt when they became slaves and Israel's population increased to over a million.

This brings us to Moses, God's prophet and more, to lead Israel out of Egypt into the Promised Land. The forty years spent in the wilderness was a testing period and one when the Law was given (covered in Chapter 5). Following possessing the land under Joshua, there was a further period, mainly to do with Israel and God's dealing with it under the Judges (covered in chapter 8). This was followed by a period of Israel following the kings and, following the death of Solomon, the division of the kingdom into the ten northern tribes (Israel) and two southern tribes (Judah). Both were eventually to go into Exile; Israel under the Assyrians and Judah under the Babylonians.

The rest of the Old Testament relates to considering the Babylonian Exile and the return of a remnant of those who were exiled, under Zerubbabel, Ezra and Nehemiah respectively. The four hundred years before the coming of Jesus are part covered in the Apocrypha, which most Protestant do not regard as the inspired Word of God. Full autonomy for Israel never happened and there was always some foreign power controlling their fate, which was a mixture of some good and a lot that was not good. Dates and timelines are shown in Figures 3 and 4 in Chapter 2. The sad story of the Old Testament is that it was a lot to do with the ups and often downs of Israel, as they broke their covenant with the Lord and were disobedient to Him, to be later restored because of God's mercy.

This brings us to the New Testament; but before we do, let us bridge the gap by considering the last, and often neglected, book of the Hebrew Bible, Chronicles. Given it was written centuries after Samuel and Kings, the content of which would have been well known to the readership and referred to by the author - possibly the priest, Ezra - one might ask what the intention was behind this writing.

To understand this better, we should put ourselves in the shoes of the Jewish readership. They had returned from exile to the Promised Land, but things were far from what they desired and hoped. One salutary thought is that only a small proportion of the descendants of the Exiles actually returned. They were looking for the awaited descendant of David to come as their Messiah, and to restore the land to its former glories and better, as had been foretold by the prophets.

The Temple, whose story David is so much part of, even though he was not allowed to build it, represented the Messianic hope that God would dwell among His people and all the promises made, going back to Abraham, would be fulfilled. The lineage of David, and the importance of Temple worship were two themes emphasized in Chronicles but not in Kings. The very last verse of Chronicles is: *"Thus saith Cyrus king of Persia, All the kingdoms of the earth hath the Lord God of heaven given me; and he hath charged me to build him an house in Jerusalem, which is in Judah. Who is there among you of all his people? The Lord his God be with him, and let him go up"* 2 Chronicles 36:23, leaving open the door of hope.

What was being looked forward to was the coming of the Son of David, Jesus the Messiah. While the prophets saw this at best as a shadow as they looked forward to the Kingdom being restored and the Day of the Lord, the Gentiles were to play an important part, even though never discounted in the Old Testament. We turn to the Church (Jew and Gentile) age, covered in the New Testament and whose story can be found in the annals of history, until such time Jesus comes again.

The issue of the Temple following the return from exile is an interesting one that is covered in future chapters, including the one described in Ezekiel 40-48, suggesting that following the rebuilding of the Temple when the exiles returned and the destruction of Herod's rebuilt Temple in AD 70 there will be a "Third" Temple. It is one of many items of discussion among students of Bible prophecy. It is argued by some Christians, especially who see that temple irrelevant as far as the New Covenant goes, that Jesus is the Temple: *"And the Word was made flesh, and dwelt among us, (and we beheld his glory, the glory as of the only begotten of the Father,) full of grace and truth"* John 1:14; and in Jesus' own words: *"Tear down this Temple, and in three days I will build it again"*, John 2:19.

Looking at the priests

Note: This book is about the *Prophets of the Bible*, and as a future project another two books could be written: *Priests of the Bible* and *Kings of the Bible*. To do the subjects justice, this would require the same forensic trawl through the Bible as was the case for this book. The best we can do for now is to provide overviews on priests and kings, with an emphasis on how they related to the prophets.

The priesthood of ancient Israel was the class of male individuals who were patrilineal descendants from Aaron (the elder brother of Moses), who served in the tabernacle, Solomon's temple and the second temple until the destruction of Jerusalem in AD 70. The High Priest was the chief religious functionary in the temple of Jerusalem, and before the temple was built, the tabernacle; whose unique privilege was to enter the Holy of Holies once a year on Yom Kippur, the Day of Atonement, to burn incense and sprinkle sacrificial animal blood to expiate his own sins and those of the people of Israel. A priest is required to act as a mediator. He is one who represents YHWH to His subjects and in return them to Him. He acts as an ambassador, a chosen vehicle through whom YHWH has chosen to serve the people, to represent Him, on His behalf.

Besides priests featuring in other religious worship, e.g. of Baal, they featured long before the office was established under Moses, and as recorded in the books of Exodus and Leviticus.

The first mention of priest is Melchizedek, King of Salem (Genesis 14:18), which we will return to when we consider Jesus as Priest. Moses' father-in-law, Jethro, was the priest of Midian (Exodus 3:1). There were priests among the Israelites when they came out of Egypt (Exodus 19:22, 24).

As for the false priests who served false gods, there were priests of On (Genesis 41:45), priests of Dagon (1 Samuel 5:5), priests of the high places (1 Kings 12:32), and priests "*of them that are no gods*" (2 Chronicles 13:9).

At Mount Sinai, God designated Aaron and his descendants to serve as priests (Exodus 28:1, 29:44; 30:30; 40:13-15; Numbers 3:3). One of the twelve tribes of Israel, Levi, was assigned priestly duties, although not all Levites were priests. Only those designated could perform priestly duties, not other Levites (Numbers 16:1-3; 17:1-10; 18:1-3), not Moses or his descendants (1 Chronicles 23:13). The Levitical priests had to be between 30 and 50 years old (Numbers 4:3), unblemished

- e.g. not lame (Leviticus 21:16-23), have a proper marriage (Leviticus 21:9, 14) - i.e. not married to a harlot or a divorced woman or a widow other than a priest's widow (Ezekiel 44:22).

While the other tribes of Israel were given an inheritance, when it came to dividing up the land, this was not so for the tribe of Levi, for the Lord was their inheritance (Deuteronomy 10:9). The standards of ritual holiness and actual holiness among priests were high, and when two of Aaron's sons offered *unauthorized fire* before the Lord (Leviticus 10:1), without further ado, God struck them down dead.

Among the duties of the priests was to teach the people (Leviticus 10:8-11), serve as judges to resolve controversy (Deuteronomy 21:5), offer sacrifices (Exodus 29:38-42), assess impurity (Leviticus 13-15), burn incense (Exodus 30:7-8), bless the people (Numbers 6:22-27), bless God (Deuteronomy 10:8), keep the tabernacle (Numbers 3:38; 4;16), take care of the altar (Leviticus 6:8-13), the lamps, and the showbread (Leviticus 24:1-9), prepare the holy things for each day's journey (Numbers 4:5-15), continue the sacred fire (Leviticus 6:12-13), and blow the trumpets (Numbers 10:1-10).

As for the high priest, he was God's leader over the priests. Aaron served as the first high priest (Exodus 40:12-13). Aaron's son, Eleazer, replaced him as high priest when he died (Numbers 20:26-28).

The position of high priests continued through the time of Christ (Matthew 26:3) until the destruction of the temple by the Romans in 70 AD. Their duties included: direct the work of the priests and Levites (Numbers 3:4), inquire of the Lord (Judges 20:28), consecrate other priests (Exodus 29:1-37), maintain the golden candlestand with its fire (Leviticus 24:1-4), burn incense daily (Exodus 30:7-8), and offer sacrifices on the Day of Atonement (Hebrews 5:1, Leviticus 16, 23) the one day he could enter the Holy of Holies.

Regarding the priesthood, as far as Israel is concerned, this was maintained until at least the second temple was destroyed. For a period, when there was no temple following the destruction of the first temple, i.e. during the Exile, priests appeared not to function, although the line was maintained. Between the Law being given to Moses at Mount Sinai to Solomon building the temple, priests operated out of a tabernacle (tent).

As far as Christians are concerned, this was replaced by a better-than-that-of-Aaron priesthood, a priesthood of the order of Melchizedek. He was the man who blessed Abraham after returning from battle: "*And Melchizedek king of Salem brought forth bread and wine: and he was the priest of the most high God. And he blessed him, and said, blessed be Abram of the most high God, possessor of heaven and earth: And blessed be the most high God, which hath delivered thine enemies into thy hand. And he gave him tithes of all.*" (Genesis 14:18-20.)

Looking forward to the King that was to come, the psalmist declared: "*The Lord said unto my Lord, sit thou at my right hand, until I make thine enemies thy footstool... The Lord hath sworn, and will not repent, Thou art a priest for ever after the order of Melchizedek.*" (Psalm 110: 1,4.)

A final "priest thought" concerns the different roles of priests and prophets, sometimes bringing the two into conflict (nothing new considering church life today) but one story when the two worked together involved Nathan the prophet and Zadok the priest. It concerned Adonijah, one of David's son, who resolved to take David's throne as he neared death. But the two got wind of the plan, let the king know what was being hatched and stopped him: "*And let Zadok the priest and Nathan the prophet anoint him there king over Israel: and blow ye with the trumpet, and say, God save king Solomon.*" (1Kings 1:34.) And they did!

Looking at the kings

Kings feature throughout the Bible, starting with Nimrod, who was "*a mighty hunter before the Lord*" (Genesis 10:9), and long before Israel had a king. We use the term "king" loosely. It could be them who ruled over a city, like the five kings who fought against the four kings, referred to in Genesis 14; them who ruled over nations, including Israel from the time of Saul, of which there are many examples; and them who ruled over empires, like Cyrus (Persian) and Nebuchadnezzar (Babylonian). While our kingly focus, as far as this book is concerned, is on Israel (and Judah), it was not God's intention for Israel to have a king, and rather He, YHWH, should be their King, but the people insisted they have a king and be like other nations, and God acceded to their request. While Israel's kings, and later Israel and Judah when the kingdom was divided, were meant to follow the Law and rule wisely, justly etc., they managed to do so with varying success.

Following the Exile, Israel had varying degrees of autonomy although, except for a short period (167 BC to 37 BC) under the Maccabees, they were always ruled over by someone else, with varying degrees of benevolence, at least until 1948, when

Israel became a sovereign, albeit secular, state. Kings in Bible times were usually autocratic, ranging from very bad to quite good. While in the two thousand years following Christ, attempts were made, when Christians were in the ascendency, to have a theocracy, but rarely succeeded and will not do so before Christ returns to reign, yet engaging with government is a contemporary issue.

Figure 5 in Chapter 2 shows a timeline for the kings of Israel and Judah. The first three kings, Saul, David and Solomon, ruled over a united kingdom. When the kingdom divided, Israel and Judah followed different routes. While our chart indicates kings were either good or bad, it was rarely that simple. More often than not, the fortunes enjoyed or otherwise by people in the land had a lot to do with how well the king behaved. The kings of Judah were a mixture of good and bad, while those of Israel were all bad. Yet sometimes bad kings had good points, e.g. Jehu; and good kings had bad points such as not removing the high places. Sometimes a king started off good and turned bad later, e.g. Solomon; and, on rare occasions, a king started off bad and turned good, e.g. Manasseh.

All too often, a bad king followed a good one, and vice versa. The tragedy was that both the kingdoms of Israel and Judah came to ignominious endings, and that was a lot down to their turning their backs on God. Throughout – and especially during – the time of the kings, there were prophets around to guide them in God's ways and, more often than not, they engaged with the kings who were reigning. Sometimes, happily, they were listened to and their words were heeded, but all too often they were ignored and rejected, with often disastrous results. As far as this book is concerned, examples of that interaction are given in Chapters 9-13.

Jesus – Prophet, Priest and King

In exceptional cases, individuals in the Old Testament combined more than one office. For example, while Ezekiel and Zechariah are both known to us as prophets, they were also priests. It might be argued that Moses was king and priest as well as prophet. After all, he led the children of Israel and when God was angry with them over worshipping the golden calf, he interceded on their behalf, as a priest. The same might be said of King David. As we will see, he wrote half the Psalms, some of which are prophetic. As for being a priest, he did make a sacrifice and lead the worship when the Ark of the Covenant came to the city (2 Samuel 6 12-15). But the one who fully and wonderfully combined all three offices was Jesus and it is He whom we will consider now, as we conclude this chapter.

But Jesus is a lot more than Prophet, Priest and King – He is God. According to the Nicene Creed: *"We believe in one Lord, Jesus Christ, the only Son of God, eternally begotten of the Father, God from God, Light from Light, true God from true God, begotten, not made, of one Being with the Father."* According to John: *"In the beginning was the Word, and the Word was with God, and the Word was God. The same was in the beginning with God. All things were made by him..."* (John 1:1-3.) According to the writer of the Hebrews: *"God, who at sundry times and in divers manners spake in time past unto the fathers by the prophets, Hath in these last days spoken unto us by his Son, whom he hath appointed heir of all things, by whom also he made the worlds; Who being the brightness of his glory, and the express image of his person, and upholding all things by the word of his power, when he had by himself purged our sins, sat down on the right hand of the Majesty on high."* (Hebrews 1:1-3.)

As a Prophet, Jesus called the world to turn from sin and return to the Father, and was put to death for doing so. Crowds identified Him as *"Jesus the prophet"* (Matthew 21:11). He spoke of Himself as a Prophet: *"No prophet is accepted in his own native place"* (Luke 4:24). Among His many prophecies, a few days before His death, He foretold His death and resurrection (Matthew 16:21–28).

Peter cited Moses when he preached Christ: *"For Moses truly said unto the fathers, A prophet shall the Lord your God raise up unto you of your brethren, like unto me; him shall ye hear in all things whatsoever he shall say unto you. And it shall come to pass, that every soul, which will not hear that prophet, shall be destroyed from among the people. Yea, and all the prophets from Samuel and those that follow after, as many as have spoken, have likewise foretold of these days."* (Acts 3:22-24.)

Given that a priest is a mediator between God and human beings who offers a sacrifice to God on behalf of all, notably on the Day of Atonement, the Jewish high priest went into the Holy of Holies, for his sins and the sins of the people; that was what Jesus did, although not for His sins, since He was sinless. The writer of the letter to the Hebrews compared Jesus to Melchizedek, a greater high priest. Because He is both divine and human, Jesus is the perfect mediator. He is not only the perfect Priest, holy and sinless, but the perfect sacrifice. The sacrifice of Jesus need never be made again. Jesus *"entered once for all into the sanctuary, not with the blood of goats and calves but with his own blood, thus obtaining eternal redemption"* (Hebrews 9:12). Jesus continues His role as Priest. *"He is always able to save those who approach God through him, since he lives forever to make intercession for them"* (Hebrews 7:25).

Jesus is spoken of as a King in the Gospels. Gabriel announced to Mary that the Lord God would give her son the throne of David His father, and He would rule over the house of Jacob for ever. Magi looked for a newborn King of the Jews. When Jesus last entered Jerusalem, crowds hailed Him as a King. He was arrested for making Himself King, and the soldiers mocked Him as one. When Pilate asked if He were King of the Jews, Jesus replied, *"You say so"*; and He clarified, *"My kingdom does not belong to this world"* (John 18:36). The charge written against Jesus was *"Jesus the Nazarene, the King of the Jews"*. Jesus announced the kingdom of God. His mission was to have God reign in the hearts of all and to have peace and justice in the world. Jesus exercised His royal office by serving.

He is foretold as King: "I*n thy majesty ride prosperously because of truth and meekness and righteousness"* (Psalm 45:4). His return is keenly anticipated: *"King of kings, and Lord of lords"* (Revelation 19:16).

Pre-, actually in it, and post-Exile

And on a lightish note: A challenge facing those of us authors who undertake serious research with a view of presenting it in a way that is comprehensive and palatable to ordinary folk, who are averse to dry, academic treatises, is, how do we divide the necessary content so that everything worth covering is covered and keep those who want to know God interested and just those whose interests are mainly academic? Maybe it is OCD or autism, but having felt some satisfaction that the sixteen chapters, plus a bonus five at the end, cuts the mustard, this author realised he had not given due justice to presenting the bigger picture of the Exile.

The Exile (of Judah into Babylon), along with the Exodus (of Israel from Egypt into the Promised Land), are the two big standout, dominating events of the Old Testament, occupying the thoughts of successive prophets; and, considering the modern situation, are remarkably relevant. We will cover Exodus when we do Moses, but given we have prophets before the Exile (concerned with the Exile to come), e.g. Isaiah and Jeremiah as well as Habakkuk and Zephaniah, prophets who lived through the Exile, i.e. Ezekiel and Daniel, and prophets who came with the return from exile, i.e. Haggai, Zechariah and Malachi, we face the challenge of where to present the big picture (at least an overview). This is the response:

There were two Exiles: the first involved the ten Northern tribes of Israel by the Assyrians, around 722 BC; the second involved the two Southern tribes of Judah by the Babylonians around 586 BC. It is this Exile we are concerned with here, although in both cases the reason for the Exiles was God's final judgment concerning their sin despite being given and ignoring many warnings. The main justification for including it here, besides being convenient to do so, is that it represents the transition from kings and prophets to prophets and priests (with prophets fading out altogether following the end of the Old Testament and until the New begins), and prepares us for the One who is Prophet, Priest and King, i.e. Jesus, the One that prophets in all of these periods were looking forward to.

It is helpful to view both the sending into exile and the returning from exile following the decree of Cyrus in 536 BC, having conquered Babylon in 539 BC.

Sending into exile (deportations):

1. 606 BC, and included the Royal Court, including Daniel.

2. 597 BC, and included craftsmen, including Ezekiel.

3. 586 BC, and included the rest (but not all, especially if poor).

Returning from exile:

1. 537 BC, comprising fifty thousand from the tribes of Judah and Benjamin, led by Zerubbabel, under King Xerxes / Cyrus (rebuilding the social life).

2. 458 BC, comprising eighteen hundred, mainly priests and Levites, led by Ezra, under King Artaxerxes (concerned with rebuilding the religious life).

3. 444 BC, comprising a few craftsmen, led by Nehemiah, under King Artaxerxes (concerned with rebuilding the physical life).

Some of the scattered ten tribes, and some of the two tribes that had been exiled to Babylon, drifted back later.

This second Exodus was a bits-and-pieces, stop-start approach, compared to the first Exodus under Moses, with only a few of the exiled Jews actually choosing to return. While the Exile was anticipated with foreboding, notably by Habakkuk, and the Babylonians, like the Assyrians, could be and were cruel – and the Bible says little of life in exile – it appears those exiled were generally treated well and could get on with their lives and even prosper (why one reason many later stayed).

When it came to the Persians, who conquered Babylon, their rulers, beginning with Cyrus the Great, were very sympathetic and encouraged the return from exile. While work to rebuild the temple began soon after their return, work halted in 520 BC, partly through apathy and partly through being discouraged by the Samaritan inhabitants, to resume, with prophets Haggai and Zechariah encouraging them, with work completed in 516 BC. The third post-Exile prophet, Malachi, prophesied after the third return, around 440 BC.

Much of what we know about life after return from exile can be found in the Books of Ezra (meaning "help") and Nehemiah (meaning "comfort"); although it is just one book in the Hebrew Bible, with perhaps Ezra as author. One commentator, noting remarkable similarities in approach between the two books, divides Ezra chapters as 1-2 return (1), 3-6 rebuild, 7-8 return (2) and 9-10 reform; and Nehemiah chapters as 1-2 return (3), 3-7 rebuild, 8-10 renew and 11-13 reform; with chapter 9 in both confessing of national sins. (The numbers 1,2 and 3 in brackets refer to the first, second and third returns from exile.)

If there was a sadness, it was that while there was a semblance of returning to God and some high points, it was often half-hearted and mixed with wrong attitudes. One particular event of interest was Esther becoming queen in 479 BC, with the book named after her describing how the Jewish people were delivered from nigh certain annihilation thanks to what she and her uncle Mordecai did.

Mention should be made of the books of Kings and Chronicles. They say little of the time of exile and nothing after, yet both end on positive notes concerning King Jehoiachin and the Cyrus decree respectively. Both Jehoiachin and his grandson, Zerubbabel, who led the first return, were part of the Davidic line that led to Jesus.

As we bow out of the Old Testament, four hundred years before the awaited Messiah, whom Israel was to reject, OT readers nevertheless can look forward to the promise of David's descendant on the Throne. Those of us who accept the Messiah has come can look forward to His glorious coming again. The beautifully haunting words of the author's favourite Christmas (Advent) carol seem apt:

1 O come, O come, Immanuel,
and ransom captive Israel
that mourns in lonely exile here
until the Son of God appear.
Refrain:
Rejoice! Rejoice! Immanuel
shall come to you, O Israel.
2 O come, O Wisdom from on high,
who ordered all things mightily;
to us the path of knowledge show
and teach us in its ways to go. Refrain
3 O come, O come, great Lord of might,
who to your tribes on Sinai's height
in ancient times did give the law
in cloud and majesty and awe. Refrain
4 O come, O Branch of Jesse's stem,
unto your own and rescue them!
From depths of hell your people save,
and give them victory o'er the grave. Refrain
5 O come, O Key of David, come
and open wide our heavenly home.
Make safe for us the heavenward road
and bar the way to death's abode. Refrain
6 O come, O Bright and Morning Star,
and bring us comfort from afar!
Dispel the shadows of the night
and turn our darkness into light. Refrain
7 O come, O King of nations, bind
in one the hearts of all mankind.
Bid all our sad divisions cease
and be yourself our King of Peace. Refrain

Chapter 4: The Genesis account and prophets

Introducing Genesis

Where better to start our study of Bible prophets than at the beginning, in the Book of Genesis. Genesis is not known for providing us with an abundance of prophets, even though it covers a period of over two thousand years; significant, as it is longer than the entire period covered by the rest of the Old Testament. Yet it is vital to our study of the prophets; missing it out would be tantamount to reading a book from halfway through. "Genesis" means *origin* or *beginning*, for it tells us how much that is significant in the world as we know it now, came into being.

Like the proverbial football match, sometimes seen as a game of two halves, Genesis can be divided, unequally it is true, into two halves:

Part 2 is nearly four times as long as Part 1, and it only covers four generations of mainly one family (that of Abraham), and a period of not much more than two hundred years; one-tenth the period covered by Part 1. If we are to work on the basis that the Bible, including Genesis, is the Word of God, it reflects what God deems important; and, tantalizingly, sometimes omits certain details. Part 1 tells us for the first time about much God deemed important: the creation of the world, how He established two genders, the creation mandate, the institution of marriage, the origin of sin, the pathway to redemption, angels and demons, sacrifices and offerings, how nations began, culture and industry, and a lot more besides.

The significant origin not covered is that of God Himself, and all we know is He was there right at the start, *"In the beginning God"* (1:1); and it is a mind-blowing thought that God always was, is, and ever shall be. Part 1 tells us of how He wanted to have a relationship with those He created and how they fell out of His favour through disobedience (despite being given free rein, they did the one thing that was forbidden), even though God still wanted to (and did) extend His favour to humankind. We read, prior to the Flood, *"And it repented the Lord that he had made man on the earth, and it grieved him at his heart"* (6:6); and yet, despite man's rebellion, God continued to graciously reach out to man.

It is not our intention to get embroiled in arguments as to whether or not planet earth was created in six days and is less than ten thousand years old; that there was a great flood covering at least the then known world; and other "unlikely" happenings, like two highly significant trees, a talking snake, the "mysterious" mark of Cain, a race of giants – a hybrid between angels and humanity - and a tower (Babel) from which we can trace how the nations of the world began. Rather, this book is written on the assumption it all happened, as Genesis 1-11 states, and all these origins are highly significant, even if the majority opinion among those who pontificate over its veracity is that Genesis Part 1 is myth.

Before moving onto Part 2, it is worth dwelling on two points about God's creation, which helps further inform us why He dealt with humankind in the way He did, through the prophets that were to come: "*God created man in his own image, in the image of God created he him; male and female created he them. And God blessed them, and God said unto them, be fruitful, and multiply, and replenish the earth, and subdue it*" (1:27-28); "*And God saw everything that he had made, and, behold, it was very good*" (1:31).

Part 2 talks about one important origin not covered in Part 1, – that of the nation of Israel. Much of what is written is concerning the people who comprised that nation, and that focus remains throughout the Old Testament. Even in the New Testament, where the emphasis is on the Gentiles, Israel was never far from God's thoughts, who have still to play a significant part in prophecy yet to be fulfilled.

One of the big questions, to which we do not have a perfect answer, is, "Why did God choose the Jews – and for what purpose?" One poet put it, "*How odd of God to choose the Jews*"; although, for the sake of balance, one response was, "*But not so odd as those who choose a Jewish God yet spurn the Jews.*" The conundrum of mistreatment and dismissal of Jews, to this day, including by "Christians", and at the same time their resilience and survival, is a major one that remains.

While it may not be entirely clear why God should choose Abraham and His descendants to be His special people, despite constantly falling away thereafter, we do get some insights into the reasons why: "*For thou art an holy people unto the Lord thy God: the Lord thy God hath chosen thee to be a special people unto himself, above all people that are upon the face of the earth. The Lord did not set his love upon you, nor choose you, because ye were more in number than any people; for ye were the fewest of all people: But because the Lord loved you, and because he would keep the oath which he had sworn unto your fathers, hath the Lord brought you out with a mighty hand, and redeemed you out of the house of bondmen, from the hand of Pharaoh king of Egypt.*" (Deuteronomy 7:6-8.)

And to this day, Jewish people have been vilified by many; but we can only point to what God thinks, and challenge those who consign Jewish folk to being now irrelevant, which as we will see will not let them off the hook when they disobey God and are made even more accountable because they are God's chosen people; and those who do oppose them will find they are opposing God and will reap the consequences. We will not be able to understand the Hebrew prophets if we ignore God's special relationship with Israel that is unique among the nations, and the Genesis account of how Israel came to be.

Part 2 begins: *"Now the Lord had said unto Abram, Get thee out of thy country, and from thy kindred, and from thy father's house, unto a land that I will shew thee: And I will make of thee a great nation, and I will bless thee, and make thy name great; and thou shalt be a blessing: And I will bless them that bless thee, and curse him that curseth thee: and in thee shall all families of the earth be blessed."* (12:1-3.) Chapters 12 to 24 record events in Abraham's life, and, after briefly turning our attention to his son, Isaac, the remaining chapters (25 to 50) are mainly about Jacob and, to a lesser extent, his younger son Joseph, and other sundry events. Genesis ends with Jacob and his family (by this time numbering seventy) living in Egypt, where they remained for four hundred years, with the story being picked up again in Exodus, and Moses being the main character.

As far as Genesis goes, the only one we can find in the book, identified as a prophet, was Abraham. It was when God told Abimelech, king of Gerar, who had designs on Abraham's wife, Sarah, *"Now therefore restore the man his wife; for he is a prophet, and he shall pray for thee, and thou shalt live: and if thou restore her not, know thou that thou shalt surely die, thou, and all that are thine"* (20:7). There is no mention anywhere else in the Old Testament that anyone else mentioned in Genesis was a prophet, although the Talmud cites the three Patriarchs, Abraham, Isaac and Jacob, as all being prophets.

Unexpectedly maybe, in the New Testament, another Genesis figure is spoken of as a prophet: *"And Enoch also, the seventh from Adam, prophesied of these, saying, Behold, the Lord cometh with ten thousands of his saints, To execute judgment upon all, and to convince all that are ungodly among them of all their ungodly deeds which they have ungodly committed, and of all their hard speeches which ungodly sinners have spoken against him"* (Jude, verses 14-15).

For our study, we will look at five persons from Part 1 as being possible prophets: Adam, Abel, Seth, Enoch and Noah; and four persons from Part 2: Abraham, Isaac, Jacob and Joseph. We do not know enough about Abel, Seth and Enoch to comment, but the Bible recalls all the others doing acts of foolishness or plain wrong, and yet God was able to use them all. They all played vitally significant roles in what is after all His Story.

Adam (and Abel and Seth)

It is strange that the first "prophet" we cite is not regarded as such by most Christians and Jews (although Muslims believe Adam to be a prophet). The intention is not to be controversial but rather to work within the loose definition of a prophet as someone who has heard directly from God and has passed on what he has heard. While the first part is definitely true of Adam, who daily communed with God in the Garden of Eden, we can only surmise that Adam passed on to those who came after him what he had heard; for how else would we know about what God did at the beginning – including, notably, concerning one of his descendants (Jesus): "*it shall bruise thy (*the serpent – Satan*) head, and thou shalt bruise his heel*" (3:15)?

After Adam and Eve were driven from Eden, upon eating the forbidden fruit, God gave them animal skins to wear as a covering, an early indication of the principle of redemption by blood, which was to become a recurring theme of the Bible.

We also see a contrast with Adam and the second Adam (Jesus) in the New Testament: "*For as in Adam all die, even so in Christ shall all be made alive*", 1 Corinthians 15:22.

Regarding Abel, we know little other than what we are told – "*And Abel, he also brought of the firstlings of his flock and of the fat thereof. And the Lord had respect unto Abel and to his offering: But unto Cain and to his offering he had not respect. And Cain was very wroth, and his countenance fell*" (4:4-5) – and being subsequently murdered by his jealously outraged older brother. We are told in the New Testament, "*By faith Abel offered unto God a more excellent sacrifice than Cain, by which he obtained witness that he was righteous, God testifying of his gifts: and by it he being dead yet speaketh*" (Hebrews 11:4). What is clear is, unlike his brother, Abel believed God and showed future generations how offerings were to be made, including the importance of blood sacrifices.

We know even less about Seth than we do Abel. But we are told: "*And Adam knew his wife again; and she bare a son, and called his name Seth: For God, said she, hath appointed me another seed instead of Abel, whom Cain slew. And to Seth, to him also there was born a son; and he called his name Enos: then began men to call upon the name of the Lord"* (4:25-26). Checking out the descendants of Seth and Cain, only in Seth's line do we find those who feared God, and just maybe that was the legacy Seth passed on that Cain did not. Just as with Adam, so with Abel and Seth, whether these could be regarded as prophets depends on how one regards prophets, yet all three acted prophetically.

Enoch

All we know about Enoch from the Old Testament is: *"And Enoch lived sixty and five years, and begat Methuselah: And Enoch walked with God after he begat Methuselah three hundred years, and begat sons and daughters: And all the days of Enoch were three hundred sixty and five years: And Enoch walked with God: and he was not; for God took him."* (5:21-24.) In the New Testament, there are two references to Enoch. Firstly: *"By faith Enoch was translated that he should not see death; and was not found, because God had translated him: for before his translation he had this testimony, that he pleased God."* (Hebrews 11:5.) Secondly: *"And Enoch also, the seventh from Adam, prophesied of these, saying, Behold, the Lord cometh with ten thousands of his saints, To execute judgment upon all, and to convince all that are ungodly among them of all their ungodly deeds which they have ungodly committed, and of all their hard speeches which ungodly sinners have spoken against him."* (Jude vv14,15.) The NT throws further light thereby on this intriguing first OT reference of one who walked with God.

About Methuselah, one possible meaning of his name is "his death sends". It is interesting to note that the year Methuselah died, something very big was sent – the Flood. Methuselah's name may well include a prophecy that on the day of his death the Flood (which his death sends) came.

The intriguing prophecy, though, is what Jude quoted from the Book of Enoch. This contains unique material on the origins of demons and giants, why some angels fell from heaven, a partial explanation of why the Great Flood was morally necessary, and exposition of the thousand-year reign of the Messiah. While the book of Enoch is generally not considered part of the Canon, the fact that Enoch prophesied concerning the End Times cannot be denied and neither can that strange mix of angels interacting with humankind: *"That the sons of God saw the daughters of men that they were fair; and they took them wives of all which they chose. And the Lord said, My spirit shall not always strive with man, for that he also is flesh: yet his days shall be an hundred and twenty years. There were giants in the earth in those days; and also after that, when the sons of God came in unto the daughters of men, and they bare children to them, the same became mighty men which were of old, men of renown."* (6:2-4.) While this amazing prophecy qualifies Enoch as a prophet, just as remarkable was that he walked with God throughout his life and was taken by God without dying.

Noah

Most people know about Noah's Ark, the building of which (a long way from any water) did enable eight people to escape the Great Flood and also preserved the animal species. They may not be surprised at statements like *"Noah was a just man and perfect in his generations"* (6:9), or finding him being referred to as *"a preacher of righteousness"* 2 Peter 2:5, and, along with Daniel and Job, put up as an example of righteous living (Ezekiel 14:20). *"But Noah found grace in the eyes of the Lord"* (6:8) gives telling insights into Noah, the man of righteousness, and how God ever acts toward those who follow His righteous ways.

The context was straightforward: God was grieved the world had turned from Him and decided to destroy its inhabitants by sending a flood: *"And the Lord said, I will destroy man whom I have created from the face of the earth; both man, and beast, and the creeping thing, and the fowls of the air; for it repenteth me that I have made them"* (6:7). Jesus Himself declared: *"They did eat, they drank, they married wives, they were given in marriage, until the day that Noah entered into the ark, and the flood came, and destroyed them all"* (Luke 17:27). As for Noah's faith, we are told: *"By faith Noah, being warned of God of things not seen as yet, moved with fear, prepared an ark to the saving of his house"* (Hebrews 11:7).

One can only but imagine, having been told to build the Ark and doing what he was told, with no water for miles around, what this preacher of righteousness said during the decades it took to build the Ark. As far as his prophetic credentials were concerned, these were impeccable, preaching the same message: the actuality of sin that needed to be repented of and judgment if they did not, year after year, but with no response other than ridicule and rejection.

After the Flood we learn: *"And Noah built an altar unto the Lord; and took of every clean beast, and of every clean fowl, and offered burnt offerings on the altar. And the Lord smelled a sweet savour; and the Lord said in his heart, I will not again curse the ground any more for man's sake; for the imagination of man's heart is evil from his youth; neither will I again smite any more every thing living, as I have done. While the earth remaineth, seedtime and harvest, and cold and heat, and summer and winter, and day and night shall not cease.*" (8:20-22.) Then he was told to "B*e fruitful, and multiply, and replenish the earth*" (9:1), which is what he set out to do. Besides relaying this message and doing what God said, we read of him correctly prophesying regarding his sons, Ham, Shem and Japheth.

Abraham

We noted earlier how Part 2 of Genesis began with God calling out Abraham to a land God will show him and give to his descendants, along with the promise of being a great nation and a blessing.

Abraham is regarded as the founder of the nation of Israel and father of the faithful. His lineage continued through his son Isaac, even though prior to that he had another son, Ishmael; and that continued through Jacob, even though he had an older twin, Esau. Abraham, Isaac and Jacob are known as the three patriarchs (heads of the Jewish line) and God (YHWH) was often referred to as the God of Abraham, Isaac and Jacob. While the chapters relating to Abraham concerned how he settled and prospered, under God, in the land God was to give to him, important recurring themes were around having a son, especially given Sarah, his wife, was beyond child-bearing age, and how his faith was exercised and tested.

What makes him particularly interesting is: "*Abraham believed God, and it was imputed unto him for righteousness: and he was called the Friend of God*" (James 2:23). His faith was outstanding, not just because he believed things that humanly speaking were impossible, but in demonstrating that we are imputed righteousness though faith and, despite a few hiccups, remain true to the divine calling. He underwent much trial and tribulation, and yet carried on and God prospered him. His faith was tested, notably regarding his heir, whom he had to wait an inordinate long time for, which he was later called upon to offer as a sacrifice. He made mistakes such as lying to King Abimelech and sleeping with Sarah's maid, Hagar. Yet his was a special relationship with God, who often confided in him regarding His intentions, such as the destruction of Sodom and Gomorrah in judgment, even allowing Abraham to successfully intercede on their behalf.

Upon his death, the fulfilment of God's promise seemed a very long way off: the only part of the Promised Land he possessed was a small plot to build the family tomb. An example of his prophetic calling was God telling Abraham precisely what was to happen and insights into the ways of God, who is never in a hurry but always on time – His time: "*And he said unto Abram, Know of a surety that thy seed shall be a stranger in a land that is not theirs, and shall serve them; and they shall afflict them four hundred years; And also that nation, whom they shall serve, will I judge: and afterward shall they come out with great substance. And thou shalt go to thy fathers in peace; thou shalt be buried in a good old age. But in the fourth generation they shall come hither again: for the iniquity of the Amorites is not yet full*" (15:13-16).

Despite all this, the promise that caused Abraham to venture out in faith remains one of the most important in Bible history and, arguably, still has not received its final fulfilment, and it happens because Abraham obeyed. Without knowing it, Abraham was looking far into the future, including to the promised Messiah. Jesus was to say to the unbelieving Jews of His day: "*Your father Abraham rejoiced to see my day: and he saw it, and was glad*" (John 8:56). Abraham is significant because just like his grandson, Jacob, God says he is significant and goes as far as referring to him as His friend: "*But thou, Israel, art my servant, Jacob whom I have chosen, the seed of Abraham my friend.*" (Isaiah 41:8.)

Isaac

Given Part 2 of Genesis is dominated by the narratives concerning Abraham and Jacob (with the story of Joseph thrown in), it might be tempting to overlook Isaac. But he was a patriarch too, an essential link in the lineage began with Abraham and ending with Jesus, and would be celebrated as such throughout Jewish history. He communicated directly with God on more than one occasion, something his grandson, Joseph, had not managed in spite of his pivotal role. An intriguing aspect concerning Isaac is of typology. When he enquired of his father before he was about to be sacrificed, "B*ehold the fire and the wood: but where is the lamb for a burnt offering?*" (22:7), he was told: "*my son, God will provide himself a lamb for a burnt offering*" (22:8).

Two thousand years later, God did provide His Son as a sacrifice for our sins. While a lamb was found as a substitute for Isaac, Jesus was obedient and He became that substitutionary sacrifice. It is notable that Isaac was at least willing. Another type, covered in chapter 24, was when Abraham instructed his servant to find a bride for Isaac, reminding us of the Holy Spirit searching for a bride for God's Son, Jesus. As for things Isaac accomplished, the one that sticks out is him unstopping wells that had been stopped, and another spiritual application beckons. Isaac's prophetic credentials are seen in that he held firm to the promise that was given to his father, Abraham, being reassured by God of its fulfilment.

When he was effectively duped, when it seemed that he was close to death, into passing the birthright onto Jacob over his son Esau, whom he wrongly favoured despite God's will on the matter, it was not expected that Isaac had so many years left in him, yet he was still around when Jacob, who had fled as a result, returned twenty years later. We are told: *"And the days of Isaac were an hundred and fourscore years. And Isaac gave up the ghost, and died, and was gathered unto his people, being old and full of days: and his sons Esau and Jacob buried him"* (35:28,29). If nothing else, this final phase of Isaac's life reminds us of the vagaries and unpredictability of life and, in Isaac's case, one whose life we can look back upon and honour.

Jacob

One thing that strikes some about Jacob was his unlikeability. Unlike Esau, who might be seen as a man's man (although caring little of the things of God but, rather, living for the moment), Jacob was a mummy's boy, and sneaky with it. His very name means "supplanter", and this he did with respect to trying to steal the birthright, thus incurring the anger of older brother Esau, even though Esau was not the right person to pass on the promise God gave to their grandfather, Abraham; and, importantly, was not God's choice. After doing the dirty on Esau, with the complicity of mother, Rebecca, he spent the next twenty years, having had to flee, outconned by his uncle Laban. All through that period he was being refined and chastened by God to become the very person God wanted him to be.

Two key events were to define Jacob's life. Firstly, when he came to Bethel (*"House of God"*), and secondly, when he came to Peniel (*"Face of God"*).

And so Jacob came to a place he was to name Bethel, with nothing other than what he carried, running from a brother that had vowed to kill him: *"And he dreamed, and behold a ladder set up on the earth, and the top of it reached to heaven: and behold the angels of God ascending and descending on it. And, behold, the Lord stood above it, and said, I am the Lord God of Abraham thy father, and the God of Isaac: the land whereon thou liest, to thee will I give it, and to thy seed; And thy seed shall be as the dust of the earth, and thou shalt spread abroad to the west, and to the east, and to the north, and to the south: and in thee and in thy seed shall all the families of the earth be blessed. And, behold, I am with thee, and will keep thee in all places whither thou goest, and will bring thee again into this land; for I will not leave thee, until I have done that which I have spoken to thee of. And Jacob awaked out of his sleep, and he said, Surely the Lord is in this place; and I knew it not."* (28:12-16.)

After finding his uncle Laban, Jacob falls in love with his daughter, Rachel, but ends up, as a result of Laban's duplicity, having to marry Leah, her older sister, before marrying Rachel, and having to work for Laban for fourteen years as a price and then a further six years for the livestock. He then returns home, but not before having to meet his brother, Esau. Understandably, Jacob is apprehensive of what might happen. But before the meeting, which happened to turn out well, he had two divine encounters. As the result of his second encounter, an all night wrestling match with a mysterious being that is cause of speculation who this might be, his thigh was put out of joint and would thereafter be a reminder of what took place. More significantly, this man who twisted and deceived to get his way, was finally out manoeuvred and became, in essence, a broken man, and showed how it might be with any of us who want to get close to the Lord.

"*And Jacob went on his way, and the angels of God met him. And when Jacob saw them, he said, This is God's host: and he called the name of that place Mahanaim.*" (32:1,2.) And later: "*And Jacob was left alone; and there wrestled a man with him until the breaking of the day. And when he saw that he prevailed not against him, he touched the hollow of his thigh; and the hollow of Jacob's thigh was out of joint, as he wrestled with him. And he said, Let me go, for the day breaketh. And he said, I will not let thee go, except thou bless me. And he said unto him, What is thy name? And he said, Jacob. And he said, Thy name shall be called no more Jacob, but Israel: for as a prince hast thou power with God and with men, and hast prevailed.*" (32:24-28.)

There Jacob settles back into the land of promise, bringing up his family, with his story later intertwining with that of Joseph, who was to become the family deliverer. Jacob continues to seek God, and God continues to bless and reaffirm His promises: "*And God appeared unto Jacob again, when he came out of Padanaram, and blessed him. And God said unto him, Thy name is Jacob: thy name shall not be called any more Jacob, but Israel shall be thy name: and he called his name Israel. And God said unto him, I am God Almighty: be fruitful and multiply; a nation and a company of nations shall be of thee, and kings shall come out of thy loins; And the land which I gave Abraham and Isaac, to thee I will give it, and to thy seed after thee will I give the land.*" (35:9-12.)

As he approached his end, Jacob makes two (at least) profound prophetic statements: firstly, in blessing Joseph's younger son, Ephraim, ahead of his older brother, Manasseh (48:8-14); secondly, in prophesying over his own sons, including Judah: "T*he sceptre shall not depart from Judah, nor a lawgiver from between his feet,* until Shiloh come; and unto him shall the gathering of the people be"* (49:10) – the significance of which is seen years later. *"And when Jacob had made an end of commanding his sons, he gathered up his feet into the bed, and yielded up the ghost, and was gathered unto his people"* (49:33).

Joseph

Toward the end of the Joseph story, which begins in chapter 37 and dominates the remaining chapters of Genesis, we read: *"And Joseph said unto them, Fear not: for am I in the place of God? But as for you, ye thought evil against me; but God meant it unto good, to bring to pass, as it is this day, to save much people alive. Now therefore fear ye not: I will nourish you, and your little ones. And he comforted them, and spake kindly unto them."* (50:19-21.) God turning something meant for evil, for good, pretty much summarizes the main thrust of the story of Joseph and was a welcome response to his still guilt-ridden brothers, who out of jealousy had sold him into slavery, thinking now father Jacob was dead and buried, Joseph, now with the power to do so, would exact his revenge.

It is an unusual and unexpected story with many twists and turns, yet, as Genesis Part 2 to the end of the Old Testament is very much to do with God's dealing with His specially chosen people, we can reflect that Joseph played an important part in ensuring the continuance of the line and the establishing of a nation.

It was Joseph as a dreamer of his own dreams and as an interpreter of the dreams of others, having heard from God, that leads us to identify him as a prophet. Those dreams that were recounted were all highly significant insofar that they all predicted future events in which Joseph was to play a major and positive role. The first concerned him being given prominence over the rest of the family, the unwise telling of which, along with him flaunting his *"amazing technicolor dreamcoat"*, given to him as a sign of his father's special favour over that of his brothers, had roused their anger and led to him being sold by them as a slave, and ending up living in Egypt. But God, in accordance with His grand design, had great plans for Joseph, who in turn sought to honour Him.

After having been put in charge of the household of an Egyptian official, Joseph found himself in prison after being falsely accused by his master's wife of trying to rape her. There he managed to correctly interpret the dreams of two fellow inmates, the butler and the baker, and thus gained a reputation as an interpreter of dreams; and was later able to interpret that of Pharaoh regarding seven years of plenty followed by seven years of famine. He was elevated to a high position to manage the situation, during which he met his brothers who had come to Egypt for food because of the famine. This led to reconciliation and bringing his father Jacob, and his children and grandchildren, to live in Egypt.

Having brought his family to Egypt and under royal protection, he lived out his years in relative peace, ending with one final prediction: *"And Joseph took an oath of the children of Israel, saying, God will surely visit you, and ye shall carry up my bones from hence. So Joseph died, being an hundred and ten years old: and they embalmed him, and he was put in a coffin in Egypt."* (50:25,26.)

What follows is Jacob's family living in relative peace under a sympathetic Pharaoh, and the family of seventy growing to over a million in the next four hundred years, of which period very little is recorded. If there is an observation to make, it is this: while God always keeps His promises, it is in His time frame, and various things had to be put in their place. Things changed during that time, including a Pharaoh who was anything but sympathetic. We next pick up the story of how God dealt with His chosen people under Moses and the Exodus.

Concerning the bones of Joseph, the Children of Israel brought these out of Egypt, when they did leave Egypt; and these were buried in Shechem, in a parcel of land that Jacob had bought from the sons of Hamor, for a hundred pieces of silver, and this is recorded in Joshua 24:32. Keeping and later burying Joseph's bones, over four hundred years after his death, seems rather strange – and yet it happened; and not only were Joseph's wishes recorded in the Bible, so were them being carried out, suggesting significance. The promise God gave to Abraham and passed down through Isaac and Jacob, in particular involving that to do with taking possession of the Promised Land, is one of the highlights of the Bible narrative and is one that is not lost on Joseph, nor his descendants. Joseph was looking far into the future and the outworking of God's purposes, and in so doing it could be said that he too was acting prophetically.

The matter of the bones that would have been carefully secured over that time is representative of the hope that was never lost, even if for a lot of that time it looked unlikely to happen. It would later come to represent Israel's hope in their Messiah coming to reign, a hope that 3500 years later has been kept alive as Christians await His Second Coming, which many Jews see as His first.

Chapter 5: Moses and wandering in the wilderness

The books of Moses

At the very end of the Pentateuch (the first five books of the Bible, which comprise Genesis, Exodus, Leviticus, Numbers and Deuteronomy), we read: *"And there arose not a prophet since in Israel like unto Moses, whom the Lord knew face to face, In all the signs and the wonders, which the Lord sent him to do in the land of Egypt to Pharaoh, and to all his servants, and to all his land, And in all that mighty hand, and in all the great terror which Moses shewed in the sight of all Israel"*, Deuteronomy 34: 10-12.

In Chapter 4, we argued why an understanding of the Book of Genesis is essential to our overall understanding of the prophets of the Bible. The same is true about the remaining four books of the Pentateuch, with its focus on the Covenant God made with His special, chosen people Israel, and in setting out the Law which Israel was expected to obey; as well as what perhaps was the most momentous event of the Old Testament, the Exodus of Israel from Egypt into the Promised Land and the remarkable happenings in their wilderness journey. God promised to bless; Israel promised to obey: that, in essence, was the Covenant.

The main character in these four books is Moses. Before we get to the Covenant and Law, and how God dealt with Israel, and how Israel responded, we need to go back to when Moses was born and the situation that was prevailing at the time.

We ended Genesis with Jacob taking his family of seventy to Egypt to live, under the patronage of a sympathetic Pharaoh. Four hundred years later, that family had grown to over a million, and the then Pharaoh was anything but sympathetic. Not only did he force the Hebrews into slave labour but, in order to reduce their size and remove any threat, he ordered the new born baby boys to be killed.

About Moses

Enter Moses, born at the time the baby boys were being killed. So that she could save him, his mother hid the baby in the bulrushes, to be later discovered by Pharaoh's daughter who adopted and brought him up as her own son where he lived a privileged life with a well-rounded education, up to the age of forty. It was then that he stood by a Hebrew slave who was being beaten by his Egyptian taskmaster, whom he killed; soon realising his action had been seen and retribution would be exacted. He fled as a result and spent the next forty years living in the wilderness, taking care of sheep, etc. It was there he had an encounter with God ("I AM WHO I AM"), and he then spent the next forty years leading the Jewish people out of Egypt, to just before they entered the Promised Land.

One commentator has summarised Moses' life as forty years spent thinking he was a somebody, the next forty years learning he was a nobody and the final forty years discovering how God can use a nobody (all experiences prior to that God was able to use). There is much in Moses' life that is instructive concerning how He dealt with and could use His prophets, despite their faults. When Moses met God at the site of the burning bush, he used many excuses to try to escape the task God had given him to do, to liberate and lead his people; but, as invariably happens, God won the argument. Thereafter, Moses was to be mightily used by God to lead His people from captivity to the verge of entering the Promised Land.

The fact he could not enter himself was due to God's judgment, because he did not give God the glory when it came to him striking as opposed to speaking to the rock as God had instructed him. Yet we read of times his authority was being questioned and undermined, although he was repeatedly affirmed by the Lord; and this included by the two people closest to him, Aaron and Miriam, whom God after judged for their rebellion against the man He had appointed:

"Now the man Moses was very meek, above all the men which were upon the face of the earth. And the Lord spake suddenly unto Moses, and unto Aaron, and unto Miriam, Come out ye three unto the tabernacle of the congregation. And they three came out. And the Lord came down in the pillar of the cloud, and stood in the door of the tabernacle, and called Aaron and Miriam: and they both came forth. And he said, Hear now my words: If there be a prophet among you, I the Lord will make myself known unto him in a vision, and will speak unto him in a dream. My servant Moses is not so, who is faithful in all mine house. With him will I speak mouth to mouth, even apparently, and not in dark speeches; and the similitude of the Lord shall he behold: wherefore then were ye not afraid to speak against my servant Moses?" Numbers 12:3-8.

Exodus, Leviticus, Numbers, Deuteronomy

"Exodus" means "*a going out; a departure or emigration, usually of a large number of people*"; and the thrilling story of how the Jewish people escaped from Egypt to camping by Mount Sinai, where the Law was given to Moses, is recounted in

Chapters 1-18. The story of the plagues, the celebration of the Passover, the crossing of the Red Sea and the early experiences of wandering in the wilderness, including instances of grumbling contained in that account, is enormously significant and an important part of Israel's shared history that provides a backdrop for the work of the later prophets.

Throughout that forty-year period, Moses heard from God, often on a daily basis. Some of this was prophecy, including far into the future; a lot of it was the receiving of the Law (613 commandments in total, including the Ten Commandments), covering all aspects of life; and some was instructions as to how to deal with the people and their enemies, which was made more difficult because of their propensity to break the Law. Interwoven between these things was a narrative of various happenings, which serve to instruct us.

From Exodus 19, through the Book of Leviticus and the first ten chapters of the Book of Numbers, the Bible narrative is about the people that remained camped at Mount Sinai for over a year and the giving of the Law, including precise details of what God intended and expected. For the remainder of the Pentateuch (Numbers 11 to 36 and the Book of Deuteronomy), our attention is drawn firstly to the Children of Israel wandering in the wilderness for the next thirty-eight-and-a-bit years, and then as they were about to enter the Promised Land – not under Moses' leadership but that of Joshua, who Moses had been mentoring.

Ironically, from Sinai to the Promised Land, the journey could have taken two weeks, and it nearly did. When ten of the twelve men that Moses sent out to spy out the land came back with unfavourable reports as to why this could not be done, the people accepted that report and rebellion followed, born out of unbelief, and was one of a number in the years following. It was part of God's judgment that only Joshua and Caleb, the two spies that gave favourable reports, who believed God, would be able to enter the land. All the rest died before then.

The Book of Leviticus is to do with God graciously providing a way for people to live in His presence.

The Book of Numbers maps Israel's journey from Mount Sinai, through the Wilderness of Paran, and onto the Plains of Moab, overlooking the Promised Land, combining both Law and narrative.

The Book of Deuteronomy is to do with Moses recounting and reinforcing the Law, and new laws, to what was now a new generation who were not there to hear Moses recount the Law at Sinai. In a series of speeches, Moses counsels them as to how they should act and their need to be faithful to God. He also hands over the baton to his successor, Joshua, and goes off to die.

But, before we consider the main subject of this chapter, the life of the prophet (i.e. Moses) and what it was that he prophesied, as well as other examples of prophets and prophecies that can be found in the Pentateuch, we need to reflect on Israel's wilderness experience, given it is essential to our understanding of the rest of the Bible, and tied in with what future prophets had to say:

1. God's holy Covenant with Israel.

2. The Law.

3. Religious worship.

4. Blessings and curses.

God's holy Covenant with Israel

There is enough about the character of God worth discussing to fill the rest of this book, but for this section we will consider one attribute: holiness. Holiness is to do with perfection and being set apart, which for God is a given but for humankind something to aspire to. God commands His people to be like Him: *"And ye shall be holy unto me: for I the Lord am holy,"* (Leviticus 20:26); and He reminds them, *"For thou art an holy people unto the Lord thy God: the Lord thy God hath chosen thee to be a special people unto himself, above all people that are upon the face of the earth,"* (Deuteronomy 7:6). It is also something His New Covenant people need: *"But as he which hath called you is holy, so be ye holy in all manner of conversation; because it is written, Be ye holy; for I am holy."* (1 Peter 1:15,16.) Moreover, just as Israel was called to be a kingdom of priests to God and a holy nation, so has the Church. Without recognising and respecting God's holiness, we will not be able to understand the message of the prophets.

There is much in the Bible, and especially the Pentateuch, that humanly speaking is difficult to comprehend concerning modern sensibilities. The Law includes instructions, to execute those who break parts of it, that might be deemed vastly disproportionate by today's standards, e.g. stoning the man gathering sticks on the

Sabbath: "*And while the children of Israel were in the wilderness, they found a man that gathered sticks upon the sabbath day. And they that found him gathering sticks brought him unto Moses and Aaron, and unto all the congregation. And they put him in ward, because it was not declared what should be done to him. And the Lord said unto Moses, the man shall be surely put to death: all the congregation shall stone him with stones without the camp.*" (Numbers 15:32-35.)

Or wiping out whole nations: men, women and children, *e.g.*: "*When the Lord thy God shall bring thee into the land whither thou goest to possess it, and hath cast out many nations before thee, the Hittites, and the Girgashites, and the Amorites, and the Canaanites, and the Perizzites, and the Hivites, and the Jebusites, seven nations greater and mightier than thou; And when the Lord thy God shall deliver them before thee; thou shalt smite them, and utterly destroy them; thou shalt make no covenant with them, nor shew mercy unto them:*" (Deuteronomy 7:1-2.)

We raise these examples, not so we can defend God (He does not need it), or explain God's justice (He is answerable to no-one), but rather to make the point that God is holy, and we will not begin to understand God if we do not get this. If we do get this, while we may still confess our own ignorance, we might also see marvels beyond belief. Repeatedly, Moses and Israel would find out what God's holiness meant in real terms, and that in their dealings with God, and their dealings with everyone else, holiness was a principal consideration. One aspect of this is God's mercy, without which the Israelites could never have survived.

This brings us to the real point of what took place at Mount Sinai, of which the giving of the Law, while being an important part of what took place, was not the most important. It is here God made His Covenant with His people, much as in a similar vein a man and a woman makes a covenant with each other when they marry. As far as the Mosaic Covenant goes, it is about God and Israel coming together to make a contract, agreeing on promises, stipulations, privileges, and responsibilities. For His part, God promises to protect and bless Israel, and in return Israel promises to obey God's Law. While there is the sense of fear and reverence, there is also the mutual love between the two parties.

While God remained ever faithful to the Covenant He made with Israel on Mount Sinai, the same cannot be said for Israel, who continually broke it. As well as Moses, during forty years wandering in the wilderness, later prophets confronted Israel with the fact they had broken the Covenant, along with the consequences.

Moses and the Law

The matter of keeping the Law was one of the big issues the Jewish-dominated Church had to come to terms with in its early days, as what started off as predominantly Jewish became increasingly Gentile, and we read about some of its conclusions in Acts 15. The Law was far more than the Ten Commandments, which has become the basis of the legal code adopted by countries like the UK and USA. Most would see many of the other laws given by God to Moses as the Israelites camped around Mount Sinai, as not applicable to Christians today.

Rather than argue concerning specifics, we might consider the following:

1. The rule and norm for God's holiness was God's Law.

2. Underpinning the Law was the need for moral purity, actual and ritual.

3. Everyone, high and low, were considered as equal under the Law and judges were required to be impartial.

4. While the Law provided the harshest of penalties for certain offences, it was always fair and just; e.g. distinguishing intentional and unintentional, as well as proportionate in its provisions and in seeking restoration.

5. The Law governed all aspects of life for Israel.

6. The Law provided for ways to settle disputes.

7. The Law addressed issues like hygiene, social justice, sexual morality, family life, dealing with the poor and foreigners, there are many principles that are mind-bogglingly amazing and applicable.

8. How to treat employees who are fellow Hebrews.

9. How to deal with people (and animals) who inflict various kinds of personal injury, deliberately or by accident.

10. How to deal with thefts and negligence concerning other people's property.

11. How to act responsibly towards women, widows, orphans and aliens.

12. How to ensure justice, especially for the poor and for foreigners.

13. How to celebrate God's involvement in community life by leaving the land uncultivated every seventh year so that the poor could benefit, by observing every seventh day as a day of rest for everyone, and by observing three annual religious festivals in God's honour.

14. Gentile Christians can still say "Amen!" to many of the sentiments of the Psalmist, e.g. "*O how love I thy law! it is my meditation all the day*", Psalm 119:97; and "*More to be desired are they than gold, Yea, than much fine gold; Sweeter also than honey and the honeycomb*" Psalm 19:10.

15. An important section of the Law might be described as "religious" and to do with worship, which we will consider in the next section.

16. There is the question of how Christians, especially Gentiles, come to terms with the Law, and how they apply the principles, if not the "letter".

Religious worship

A good deal of the Law was to do with religious worship – how Israel was to approach God (YHWH), along with God's expectations regarding worship. Worship of God was a central part of the life of the nation of Israel, and at its centre (literally) was the Tabernacle (Tent), which was later replaced with a temple. When it came to interceding to God on behalf of the people, this was given to priests, drawn from the tribe of Levi. This prescribed worship told us much about God and how that covenant relationship was to play out, and would feature significantly when we consider the later prophets. In a real sense, God dwelt in the Holy of holies, right from the time the Tabernacle was constructed and commissioned until the glory of God left the Temple in Ezekiel 10.

Worship centred around the Tabernacle, situated in the centre of the Israelite camp, comprising three sections: the Outer Court, the Holy Place and the Holy of Holies, including five offerings to do with thanking God and saying sorry, six Tabernacle furniture items, highly symbolic, along with seven annual feasts. Much could be said of these, which would feature significantly in our later Old and New Testament studies. It could be said that every part foreshadowed something deeper and more spiritual, but given the focus of our book, these are mentioned mainly in passing, with the subjects meriting further profitable study.

Offerings

1. The Burnt Offering.
2. The Meat Offering.
3. The Peace Offering.
4. The Sin Offering.
5. The Trespass Offering.

Tabernacle

1. The Altar of Burnt Offering.
2. The Laver.
3. The Table of Showbread.
4. The Lampstand.
5. The Altar of Incense.
6. The Ark of the Covenant and Mercy Seat.

Feasts

1. Pesach or Passover.
2. Unleavened Bread.
3. Firstfruits.
4. Shavuot, the Festival of Weeks.
5. Rosh Hashanah, or The Feast of Trumpets.
6. Yom Kippur, or The Day of Atonement.
7. Sukkot, or The Feast of Booths.

Blessings and curses

In the final section of Deuteronomy, that deals with Moses' last words and death, he sets out the choice the Israelites needed to make, and provided warnings and ultimatums should they make the wrong choice. If they were to listen and obey, there would be blessings. If they were to rebel, there would be devastation and exile from the land; i.e. curses. It could be summarised:

"See, I have set before thee this day life and good, and death and evil; In that I command thee this day to love the Lord thy God, to walk in his ways, and to keep his commandments and his statutes and his judgments, that thou mayest live and multiply: and the Lord thy God shall bless thee in the land whither thou goest to possess it. But if thine heart turn away, so that thou wilt not hear, but shalt be drawn away, and worship other gods, and serve them; I denounce unto you this day, that ye shall surely perish, and that ye shall not prolong your days upon the land, whither thou passest over Jordan to go to possess it. I call heaven and earth to record this day against you, that I have set before you life and death, blessing and cursing: therefore choose life, that both thou and thy seed may live: That thou mayest love the Lord thy God, and that thou mayest obey his voice, and that thou mayest cleave unto him: for he is thy life, and the length of thy days: that thou mayest dwell in the land which the Lord sware unto thy fathers, to Abraham, to Isaac, and to Jacob, to give them." (Deuteronomy 30:15-20.)

The reason we bring up the matter of blessings and curses here is that this is a recurring theme throughout Israel's history, which over and over again reveal blessings when Israel obeys and curses when they do not. When prophets warned them of the consequences of straying from the Mosaic Covenant, which later came to pass, they could have just as easily been referring to the blessings and curses that are so graphically listed and described in these later chapters of Deuteronomy.

As we will see, Israel (ten northern tribes) were taken into exile by the Assyrians in 722 BC, and Judah (two southern tribes) were taken into exile by the Babylonians in 586 BC. While a remnant from the Judah exile returned from 539 BC, that did not happen for the ten tribes. Until Israel became a sovereign state in 1948, without national repentance, those that lived in the Promised Land always did so under the patronage of a foreign power exercising its control over them.

Before completing this chapter, we will consider five further topics, although as with all our studies in the books of the Bible, there is so much more that is worth pondering, but the focus for this book has to return to prophets and prophecy:

1. Law and grace.

2. Moses the prophet.

3. Other prophets.

4. Christ in the Pentateuch.

5. Moses and Jesus.

Law and grace

It is written: "*For the law was given by Moses, but grace and truth came by Jesus Christ*", John 1:17. It would be wrong, though, to conclude that Israel and the Old Testament is exclusively about law, and the Church and the New Testament is only about grace. God has always been gracious, and His dealings with His people as recorded in the Old Testament provide plenteous evidence. While Christians are not bound to follow all the letter of the Law, they do need to uphold its principles. The following is universally applicable, as much now as it was then: "*Thou shalt love the Lord thy God with all thy heart, and with all thy soul, and with all thy mind. This is the first and great commandment. And the second is like unto it, thou shalt love thy neighbour as thyself. On these two commandments hang all the law and the prophets.*" (Matthew 22:37-40.)

The relationship between the Law and the Gospel is one that is explored to some depth in the New Testament. One thing is clear: people cannot be saved by keeping the Law, which at best reveals God's expectations of His people, even though they fail to keep it due to having a sinful nature. It is one reason why a system of sacrifices was introduced under the Law of Moses, with Jesus being the ultimate and perfect sacrifice.

If there is a significant difference between the Old and New Covenants, it is in the latter we find the Law being written on people's hearts, as was prophesied by Jeremiah: "*But this is the covenant which I will make with the house of Israel after those days' declares the Lord, 'I will put My law within them and on their heart I will write it; and I will be their God, and they shall be My people*'", Jeremiah 31:33; and also by Ezekiel: "*And I will give them one heart, and put a new spirit within* them. *And I will take the heart of stone out of their flesh and give them a heart of flesh"* Ezekiel 11:19.

While recognising positive aspects, a lot is made of the shortcomings of the Law in the New Testament - not that the Law was anything but perfect but those who followed it were imperfect - as well as the importance of faith; for example, referring back to Deuteronomy:

"Even as Abraham believed God, and it was accounted to him for righteousness. Know ye therefore that they which are of faith, the same are the children of Abraham. And the scripture, foreseeing that God would justify the heathen through faith, preached before the gospel unto Abraham, saying, in thee shall all nations be blessed. So then they which be of faith are blessed with faithful Abraham. For as many as are of the works of the law are under the curse: for it is written, cursed is every one that continueth not in all things which are written in the book of the law to do them. But that no man is justified by the law in the sight of God, it is evident: for, the just shall live by faith. And the law is not of faith: but, the man that doeth them shall live in them. Christ hath redeemed us from the curse of the law, being made a curse for us: for it is written, Cursed is every one that hangeth on a tree: That the blessing of Abraham might come on the Gentiles through Jesus Christ; that we might receive the promise of the Spirit through faith." (Galatians 3:6-14.)

Moses the prophet

While on the subject of keeping the Law, in his final speeches Moses prophesied that Israel would turn away from obeying the Law and would be sent into exile; but, because God is faithful when it came to keeping His Covenant, there is invariably a way for His people to return to Him and for the blessings to be restored, which still remains a hope. He also foresaw what Jeremiah and Ezekiel were to later prophesy: *"And the Lord thy God will circumcise thine heart, and the heart of thy seed, to love the Lord thy God with all thine heart, and with all thy soul, that thou mayest live."* (Deuteronomy 30:6.)

As discussed in Chapter 3, while he would be regarded as primarily a prophet, Moses was probably unique in the Old Testament in combining the offices of prophet, and to a lesser extent priest and king, and part of his prophesying was to look forward to the one, Jesus, who was to perfectly combine all three roles: *"The Lord thy God will raise up unto thee a Prophet from the midst of thee, of thy brethren, like unto me; unto him ye shall hearken"*, Deuteronomy 18:15, even though, like all the prophets, what he saw was a shadow of what was to come. If we were to cite only examples of pure prophesying, i.e. predicting future events, over and above Moses hearing what God was saying on a regular basis and sharing this with the people, we would still be spoiled for choice.

Besides suggesting doing so could be a useful exercise, let us leave one example of how Moses not just predicted what was about to happen, e.g. regarding the plagues of Egypt, or far into the future, as discussed in the last paragraph, but in the not-so-distant future, e.g. following Israel's first battle after crossing the Red Sea, against the Amalekites, which they won: *"And the Lord said unto Moses, write this for a memorial in a book, and rehearse it in the ears of Joshua: for I will utterly put out the remembrance of Amalek from under heaven. And Moses built an altar, and called the name of it Jehovah nissi: For he said, Because the Lord hath sworn that the Lord will have war with Amalek from generation to generation."* (Exodus 17:14-16.) History records that it was as Moses predicted.

Before moving on, and since the focus of this book is on the prophets themselves, and since one person who commented on an earlier draft felt not enough was said about Moses the man, for example his meekness (i.e. humility). Another striking aspect of Moses' life was his communion with God, which was a daily occurrence in that the Lord spoke to him face to face (Exodus 33:11; Deuteronomy 34:10). This could be when alone on the holy mountain or in a tent that was set up for the purpose. This intimate communion meant like Abraham before him and later with Amos, he was able to change God's mind - in this case it was about washing His hands of them because of the golden calf incident and Moses pleading for them.

Another example was when he asked to be shown God's glory and God responded, albeit a glimpse: *"And it came to pass, as Moses entered into the tabernacle, the cloudy pillar descended, and stood at the door of the tabernacle, and the Lord talked with Moses."* (Exodus 33:9.) *"And the Lord spake unto Moses face to face, as a man speaketh unto his friend."* (33:11.) *"Now therefore, I pray thee, if I have found grace in thy sight, shew me now thy way, that I may know thee, that I may find grace in thy sight: and consider that this nation is thy people. And he said, My presence shall go with thee, and I will give thee rest. And he said unto him, If thy presence go not with me, carry us not up hence. For wherein shall it be known here that I and thy people have found grace in thy sight? is it not in that thou goest with us? so shall we be separated, I and thy people, from all the people that are upon the face of the earth. And the Lord said unto Moses, I will do this thing also that thou hast spoken: for thou hast found grace in my sight, and I know thee by name. And he said, I beseech thee, shew me thy glory. And he said, I will make all my goodness pass before thee, and I will proclaim the name of the Lord before thee; and will be gracious to whom I will be gracious, and will shew mercy on whom I will shew mercy. And he said, Thou canst not see my face: for there shall no man see me, and live. And the Lord said, Behold, there is a place by me, and thou shalt stand upon a rock: And it shall come to pass, while my glory passeth by, that I will put thee in a clift of the rock, and will cover thee with my hand while I pass by: And I will take away mine hand, and thou shalt see my back parts: but my face shall not be seen."* (33:13-23.)

In going up the mountain the second time to receive the law, his forty days of fasting was not only exceptional, it was miraculous for he drank no water (34:28), and there is also a parallel with the greater Prophet Jesus. When he came down from the mountain, he did not know that the skin of his face shone (an example perhaps of his humility): "*And when Aaron and all the children of Israel saw Moses, behold, the skin of his face shone; and they were afraid to come nigh him ... And till Moses had done speaking with them, he put a vail on his face*" (34:30,33). This story is picked up in 2 Corinthians 3:7-18. As for greatness, the writer to the Hebrews in making the comment how much greater Jesus is than any who have lived, cites Moses as arguably the best example of human greatness: "*And Moses verily was faithful in all his house, as a servant.*" (Hebrews 3:5.)

There are other NT references. For example, there was the mysterious manner of his death, that the Lord buried Moses (Deuteronomy: 34:6), and Satan had a dispute concerning his body (Jude verse 9). We consider later that it was Moses (along with Elijah) who Jesus meets with when he is transfigured: (Matthew 17:1–8, Mark 9:2–8, Luke 9:28–36 and 2 Peter 1:16–18). Some argue he is one of the two witnesses that will appear to boldly defy the Antichrist (Revelation 11:1-12). The last mention of Moses is "*And they sing the song of Moses the servant of God, and the song of the Lamb, saying, Great and marvellous are thy works, Lord God Almighty; just and true are thy ways, thou King of saints.*" (Revelation 15:3.)

Other prophets

As far as the books of Exodus through Deuteronomy goes, the standout prophet was Moses whom God repeatedly affirmed in that role, often when his authority was being undermined. But there were other prophets too, including Miriam, discussed in Chapter 7, as well as false prophets, like Baalam, discussed in Chapter 6. Aaron, besides being a priest, was also a prophet, but only insofar as he was Moses' spokesman.

One unexpected account of a group of people being bestowed the gift of prophecy, albeit temporarily, reads: "*And Moses went out, and told the people the words of the Lord, and gathered the seventy men of the elders of the people, and set them round about the tabernacle. And the Lord came down in a cloud, and spake unto him, and took of the spirit that was upon him, and gave it unto the seventy elders: and it came to pass, that, when the spirit rested upon them, they prophesied, and did not cease. But there remained two of the men in the camp, the name of the one was Eldad, and the name of the other Medad: and the spirit rested upon them; and they were of them that were written, but went not out unto the tabernacle: and they prophesied in the camp.*" (Numbers 11:24-26.)

While some, including Joshua, objected to others taking on the prophetic role, Moses' reply was surprisingly modern and maybe sets a precedent for our attitude today: "*…would God that all the Lord's people were prophets, and that the Lord would put his spirit upon them!*" (Numbers 11:29.)

One unlikely "prophet", whom we would probably overlook when searching out prophets is Phinehas, brought to our attention because the Talmud names him as a prophet. He was a priest, a grandson of Aaron and son of Eleazar. Displeased with the immorality with which the Moabites and Midianites had successfully tempted the Israelites to intermarry and to worship Baal (Numbers 25:1–9), Phinehas personally executed an Israelite man and a Midianite woman while they were together in the man's tent, running a javelin or spear through the man and the belly of the woman, bringing to an end the plague sent by God to punish the Israelites for sexually intermingling with the Midianites.

He is commended by God (Numbers 25:10-13), as well as in Psalm 106:28-31, for having stopped Israel's fall into idolatrous practices brought in by Midianite women, as well as for stopping the desecration of God's sanctuary. After the entry to the land of Israel and the death of his father, he was appointed the third High Priest of Israel, and served at the sanctuary of Bethel (Judges 20:28). While he spoke prophetically, his actions and its results may be seen as prophetic.

Christ in the Pentateuch

One aspect of prophecy that can be overlooked is how particular events may be seen as types and shadows of things to come, which some Christian traditions emphasise more than others. We know this is a valid way of looking at things, given the number of references given in the New Testament linking an event, happening or saying in the Old with some profound truth. This is particularly noticeable concerning the person of Jesus. We have already seen in Chapter 4 how Isaac was willing to be sacrificed by his father Abraham but was saved in a nick of time by the provision of a lamb to be sacrificed instead, prefigured how Jesus was a willing sacrificial Lamb, dying for the sins of humankind. We conclude with four further examples of types, one each from Exodus, Leviticus, Numbers and Deuteronomy, which might be considered prophetic.

One of the most significant celebrations in the Jewish calendar, still, is the Feast of the Passover. Passover was first celebrated just prior to the Israelites leaving Egypt in haste for their Promised Land. There had already been plagues as God sought for Pharaoh to let His people go, but Pharaoh's heart was hardened; and then the final plague when the Angel of Death flew over the land and slew the firstborn son of each house. The Hebrews were spared by staying indoors, but before that a lamb had to be slaughtered and its blood had to be put over the door. God declared: *"And the blood shall be to you for a token upon the houses where ye are: and when I see the blood, I will pass over you, and the plague shall not be upon you to destroy you, when I smite the land of Egypt"*, Exodus 12:13.

As far as Christians are concerned, Christ is the Passover Lamb, and because He shed His blood when He was crucified, its application is good enough to save us. We read, when Jesus celebrated the Passover, just prior to his crucifixion: *"And as they were eating, Jesus took bread, and blessed it, and brake it, and gave it to the disciples, and said, Take, eat; this is my body. And he took the cup, and gave thanks, and gave it to them, saying, Drink ye all of it; For this is my blood of the new testament, which is shed for many for the remission of sins. But I say unto you, I will not drink henceforth of this fruit of the vine, until that day when I drink it new with you in my Father's kingdom. And when they had sung an hymn, they went out into the mount of Olives."* (Matthew 26:26-30.)

When we come to Leviticus, one of the most important (maybe *the* most important) aspects of religious life is what took place on the Day of Atonement each year, which was described in detail in Leviticus 16. During this time, the High Priest enters the Holy of Holies on behalf of himself and his family, sprinkling the blood of slain animals over the Mercy Seat for a sin atonement. The New Testament reflects on this event, directly or otherwise, as being highly important, given sin atonement was essential if we are to have fellowship with a holy God. In particular, the writer of the Hebrews argues that Christ is both a High Priest and an atoning sacrifice, and is better than that provided under the Law because His priesthood, and the efficacy of His shed blood, is Eternal.

One aspect taking place at the end of this Feast was the High Priest laid his hands on a goat's head, referred to as the Scapegoat, symbolically transferring the sins of the people to the animal, which was then released into the wilderness. *"And Aaron shall lay both his hands upon the head of the live goat, and confess over him all the iniquities of the children of Israel, and all their transgressions in all their sins, putting them upon the head of the goat, and shall send him away by the hand of a fit man into the wilderness: And the goat shall bear upon him all their iniquities unto a land not inhabited: and he shall let go the goat in the wilderness."* (Leviticus 16:21,22.) Jesus is our Scapegoat, and we are told: *"Let us go forth therefore unto him without the camp, bearing his reproach."* (Hebrews 13:13.)

One of the most memorable Bible verses is, *"For God so loved the world, that he gave his only begotten Son, that whosoever believeth in him should not perish, but have everlasting life"*, John 3:16. But we need to consider the verses preceding: *"And as Moses lifted up the serpent in the wilderness, even so must the Son of man be lifted up: That whosoever believeth in him should not perish, but have eternal life"*, John 3:14,15. This refers to yet another incident in Israel's wilderness sojourn, when the people grumbled against God. Here God sent fiery serpents to punish, that bit the people and many died. The people cried to God, confessing their sin. *"And the Lord said unto Moses, Make thee a fiery serpent, and set it upon a pole: and it shall come to pass, that every one that is bitten, when he looketh upon it, shall live"*, Numbers 21:8 – which is what happened – and in a sense is what will happen when we look to Jesus the Saviour of mankind.

We read in Deuteronomy 21:23, referring to what the Israelites did with the Canaanite kings that they had conquered: *"His body shall not remain overnight on the tree, but you shall surely bury him that day, so that you do not defile the land which the Lord your God is giving you as an inheritance; for he who is hanged is accursed of God"*; which, as we saw earlier, was picked up in the NT: *"For as many as are of the works of the law are under the curse: for it is written, Cursed is every one that continueth not in all things which are written in the book of the law to do them. But that no man is justified by the law in the sight of God, it is evident: for, The just shall live by faith. And the law is not of faith: but, The man that doeth them shall live in them. Christ hath redeemed us from the curse of the law, being made a curse for us: for it is written, Cursed is every one that hangeth on a tree."* (Galatians 3:10-13.)

Where the Canaanite kings conspired against the Lord and was punished accordingly, Jesus, being the Lord's anointed, did the unthinkable: He gave up His life as a ransom for many. He became a curse for us so that the blessing of Abraham might come to the Gentiles. We have salvation because He was cursed. One goal of Jesus' death and resurrection was to bring the blessing of Abraham to all nations. Jesus being cursed means that others will be blessed.

Moses and Jesus

According to Wikipedia: *"The transfiguration of Jesus is a story told in the New Testament when Jesus is transfigured and becomes radiant in glory upon a mountain. The Synoptic Gospels (Matthew 17:1–8, Mark 9:2–8, Luke 9:28–36) describe it, and the Second Epistle of Peter also refers to it (2 Peter 1:16–18). It has also been hypothesized that the first chapter of the Gospel of John alludes to it (John 1:14). In these accounts, Jesus and three of his apostles, Peter, James, and John, go to a mountain (the Mount of Transfiguration) to pray. On the mountain, Jesus begins to shine with bright rays of light. Then the prophets Moses and Elijah appear next to him and he speaks with them. Jesus is then called 'Son' by a voice in the sky, assumed to be God the Father...."*.

Christian preachers down the centuries have made much of this important event, including the significance of Jesus meeting with Moses, representing the Law, and Elijah, representing the prophets, and how both the Law and the Prophets were fulfilled in the life, death and ministry of Jesus. As we turn from Moses to Joshua, who leads the Children of Israel into the Promised Land, and then up to the coming of Jesus some thirteen hundred years later, we might reflect that while the focus of the Old Testament is on Israel, and that of the New on the Church, the overriding focus has to be on God whose grand design was to call a people for Himself, whether it be Israel or the Church, and prophecy should be seen in that light. How Israel and the Church, as God's Covenant people, are to become reconciled as one, is unravelled in the Bible story, and is still to happen.

Chapter 6: Balaam and assorted false prophets

Introducing the false prophets

This book is about *true* prophets in the Bible. But when we read through the Bible, we come across many *false* prophets. We are warned that in the days we are living there will be false prophets, for what they speak is not the truth and likely lead people astray who follow them. This chapter discusses false prophets, a subject we will return to when we consider lessons learned, and in our final chapter.

We have broadly defined a true prophet as one who hears directly from the Lord and passes on what he or she has heard, even if not generally recognised as a prophet. A false prophet also passes on a message, but it is not one from the Lord. In this chapter we will identify some of the false prophets of the Bible, especially those who purport to speak in the name of YHWH, as well as false gods; and at the end will consider Balaam, of which the Bible has much to say, for he encapsulates many of the characteristics and attributes of false prophets.

Much has been written in the Bible concerning false prophets (often coupled with false teachers and prophecy) and why they needed to be called out as such. We finish by quoting verses the author considers particularly significant, but firstly some general points we can cite to help us distinguish true from false prophets. When testing the prophets as we must, these are tests we can apply:

	True prophet	**False prophet**
1	Leads hearers from error to truth	Leads hearers from truth to error
2	Often suffers at the hands of men	Often praised by men
3	Honours YHWH, opposes sin	Dishonours YHWH, endorses sin
4	Hears from YHWH	Does not hear from YHWH
5	Prophecies come to pass	Prophecies do not come to pass
6	Lives a godly life that bears fruit	Lives an ungodly, fruitless life
7	Appeals to the godly	Appeals to the ungodly
8	Appeals to seekers after truth	Appeals to those who accept error
9	Life marked by humility	Life marked by pride
10	Says what people don't want to hear	Says what people do want to hear

11	Not adept at blending in, lonely	Adept at blending in, popular
12	Not always credible and impressive	Often credible and impressive
13	YHWH honours them	YHWH judges them
14	Sheep in sheep's clothing	Wolves in sheep's clothing
15	Beholden to the Word of God	Negligent of the Word of God
16	Feeds the sheep	Fleeces the sheep
17	Not interested in money	Interested in money
18	May perform miracles, without show	May perform miracles, with show
19	Has a servant heart	Seeks prestige and honour
20	Many have existed / exist	Many more have existed / exist

Surveying the Bible for false prophets

As we survey the Bible, looking for examples of false prophets, it should be borne in mind that warnings against false prophets and prophecy were numerous. Texts concerning some of the more significant examples are given below. It should also be realised that opposition to God's word or His prophets came from various sources, not just false prophets. When we consider Moses, while God gave him many warnings about false prophets, except for Balaam, whom we will get to, he did not have to confront false prophets (and even with Balaam, it was only after the event that Balaam's involvement was realised). The only prophets that challenged him were Aaron and Miriam, and both of these were true prophets.

The first recorded head-on clash between true and false prophets came when Elijah confronted *"the prophets of Baal four hundred and fifty, and the prophets of the groves four hundred, which eat at Jezebel's table"* (1 Kings 18:19) at Mount Carmel in a fire-sent-from-heaven-contest to decide who was the true God. A similar outnumbering occurred when: *"the king of Israel gathered the prophets together, about four hundred men, and said unto them, Shall I go against Ramoth-Gilead to battle, or shall I forbear? And they said, go up; for the Lord shall deliver it into the hand of the king"* (1 Kings 22:6) – only to be opposed by Micaiah, the one true prophet of the Lord, who told the king the opposite was the case.

Nehemiah is best known for his leadership when it came to building the walls of Jerusalem, when a remnant of the Jewish people returned following the Exile.

While, as far as Nehemiah was concerned, and most commentators on what took place, recognised he was doing the right thing, it was not without opposition, and one of those opposing him was a prophetess: *"My God, think thou upon Tobiah and Sanballat according to these their works, and on the prophetess Noadiah, and the rest of the prophets, that would have put me in fear"* (Nehemiah 6:14).

Isaiah, Jeremiah and Ezekiel were all aware of the false prophets that were opposing their message and their person by leading the people astray. Isaiah saw in them propagators of a great deception, with an eagerness to speak smooth words that were at odds with the word he had given, yet gained wide acceptance.

It was the same under Jeremiah. The threat of exile by the Babylonians was imminent and yet the people dismissed Jeremiah's warnings and refused to return to the Lord. As far as the false prophets were concerned, everything was going to turn out alright and calls for repentance were not needed. How wrong they were shown to be. One of his opposers, named Hananiah, was mentioned several times. Jeremiah predicted he would soon die because of his lies, and die he did. Another lying prophet that incurred similar judgment was Shemaiah the Nehelamite.

While Jeremiah was prophesying in Jerusalem, Ezekiel was doing the same in Babylon. He too prophesied against the false prophets and that God was opposed to and will judge them. They prophesied their own thoughts and not God's; they prophesied peace when there was no peace. All these true prophets of God not only had to confront false prophets but had to suffer as a result, for the people and their rulers more often than not sided with the false rather than true.

When we consider the minor prophets, opposition to their prophesying was commonplace, but notably it was Micah who faced false prophets. Micah several times had to oppose false prophets who wanted nothing to do with negativity and doom. They covered their ears at the voice of God's mouthpiece. The people of Samaria and Jerusalem took the god of their imagination to be the one true God of the Covenant. But that Covenant threated punishment for disobedience as well as blessing for obedience (Deuteronomy 8:20). With their cities under judgment, their lives hanging by a thread, and their children about to be cursed beyond cure, they preferred prophecies about plenty. They, in effect, did what false prophets often did and provided false comfort, but Micah declared God will judge them.

As far as the New Testament goes, false prophets (often coupled with false teachers) were a threat to the Church (see quotes given below) and did cause much damage.

Simon Magus (Acts 8:9-24), Bar-Jesus (Acts 13:6), the girl who foretold the future (Acts 16: 16-18), Jezebel (Revelation 2:20), and the False Prophet (Revelation 13:11-18) are all examples of false prophets identified in the New Testament. That false teaching and prophecy is prevalent, is the case to this day. An obvious example are perpetrators of the prosperity gospel. Proving what is true, and calling out what is false, was a necessary challenge then, as it is now. One of the bones of contentions concern prophets whose prophecies relate to some of the big events of our day and whether or not (and how) there will be revival. There are some that believe true prophets ceased to exist once the New Testament was completed. We will return to these thoughts in later chapters.

One further sobering thought, as we move from examples of Bible false prophets to the one false prophet the Bible has much to say about, is to recall the words of Jesus as He responded to this important question: *"Tell us, when shall these things be? and what shall be the sign of thy coming, and of the end of the world? And Jesus answered and said unto them, take heed that no man deceive you. For many shall come in my name, saying, I am Christ; and shall deceive many ... And many false prophets shall rise, and shall deceive many."* (Matthew 24:3-5,11.) It has ever been thus that whenever we come across the genuine article pertaining to spiritual matters in the Bible, there is also the counterfeit. This is nowhere more so than when we come to prophets who purport to speak in God's name.

Balaam

As suggested earlier, Balaam is not only a significant figure when dealing with the subject of false prophets, but is an important one in the overall Bible story, with three whole chapters devoted to his story, as part of Israel's wilderness wanderings, right near the end. The Promised Land was in sight and soon the Israelites would be entering it. Balaam is referred to several times elsewhere in the Bible, in Deuteronomy, Joshua, Nehemiah and Micah, as well as three times in the New Testament, and can be seen as an example not to follow. While Balaam is one of the bad guys, a false prophet, and his counsel and stirring-ups were so destructive (including twenty-four thousand Israeli deaths), as was his greed, yet his prophecies were beautiful and amazing, and even looked forward to the Messiah to come. His story is also very instructive for our deliberations.

Balaam is introduced as a diviner in the Old Testament, whose story is found in the Book of Numbers (22 to 24). Balaam, the son of Beor, is introduced as a prophet for hire, although we know little about him other than that he delved into the occult and earned his living by doing so. While he did not follow YHWH, he knew a lot about Him. Balaam earned his living by plying his dark art trade and was evidently motivated by greed. His encounter with the angel of the Lord, who at first he did not see, along with his talking donkey who did see the angel, is the one story that many, who know little more than this, might know. Though the positive blessings he delivers upon the Israelites are well described, he is looked back on as a "wicked man" (2 Peter 2:15, Jude 1:11, Revelation 2:14).

Balaam refused to speak what God did not speak and would not curse the Israelites, even though King Balak of Moab offered him a lot of money to do so. Balak was fearful of what the Israelites might do to Moab, based on what they had done already to other nations in their wilderness sojourn, even though God had commanded Moses to leave Moab alone. Balaam's error and the source of his wickedness can be seen when sabotaging the Israelites as they entered the Promised Land. According to Revelation 2:14, Balaam told King Balak how to get the Israelites to commit sin by enticing them with sexual immorality and food sacrificed to idols. The Israelites fell into transgression due to these traps and God sent a deadly plague to them as a result (Numbers 31:16).

As for going back with the emissaries of King Balak, it was the wrong thing to do because what Balak wanted was for Balaam to curse Israel, realising force of arms could not prevent Israel from doing to Moab what a short time earlier it had done to the Amorites, when conquering them, even though if he had known the God of Israel he would have realised that was not the plan. Something about the powers of darkness and the power of the curse led Balak to believe Balaam was his man to curse Israel, something he was prepared to richly reward him for doing.

So Balaam returned with Balak's people and God allowed him to go. The strange encounter with the angel of the Lord only confirmed to Balaam he could only speak the words the Lord was to give him. For that he could thank his donkey, who saw the angel when Balaam had not, refused to continue to his certain death, and was beaten for her troubles. *"What have I done unto thee, that thou hast smitten me these three times?"* Numbers 22:28 and following are among the most profound utterances of the Bible and it took a donkey to make them.

What then follows, after Balaam meets Balak, are three oracles which he gets to utter from three different positions where the Israelites could be viewed. What Balak wanted was a curse, and instead Balaam gave a blessing: *"He hath said, which heard the words of God, which saw the vision of the Almighty, falling into a trance, but having his eyes open: How goodly are thy tents, O Jacob, and thy tabernacles, O Israel! As the valleys are they spread forth, as gardens by the river's side, as the trees of lign aloes which the Lord hath planted, and as cedar trees beside the waters. He shall pour the water out of his buckets, and his seed shall be in many waters, and his king shall be higher than Agag, and his kingdom shall be exalted. God brought him forth out of Egypt; he hath as it were the strength of an unicorn: he shall eat up the nations his enemies, and shall break their bones, and pierce them through with his arrows. He couched, he lay down as a lion, and as a great lion: who shall stir him up? Blessed is he that blesseth thee, and cursed is he that curseth thee."* (Numbers 24: 4-9.)

After that third oracle, angry Balak sent Balaam on his way, but not before Balaam delivered his fourth and most profound oracle as it looked forward to Israel's coming Messiah: *"I shall see him, but not now: I shall behold him, but not nigh: there shall come a Star out of Jacob, and a Sceptre shall rise out of Israel, and shall smite the corners of Moab, and destroy all the children of Sheth"* (Numbers 24: 17). But the story does not end there. What Balaam could not do through cursing, he nearly succeeded in doing by enticing Israel into idolatry and sexual immorality (Numbers 25, 31). While the plan failed, it was not before twenty-four thousand Israelites were killed in a plague, part of God's judgement. In the bloody war of vengeance that ensued against the Midianites, who had been the instruments of enticing Israel to sin, Balaam was killed (Numbers 31:8).

Balaam's life was one of conundrums and enigmas. He had, for example, earlier declared: *"Who can count the dust of Jacob, and the number of the fourth part of Israel? Let me die the death of the righteous, and let my last end be like his!!"* (Numbers 23:10). Sadly, he would not commit to living the life of the righteous. While he was one who delved into the forbidden, dark arts, he also gave some of the most profound prophecies in the Bible. For one whose life was motivated by greed, he recognised he could not withstand God; even though, as a result, his love of money would not be realised until later. While Balaam is an example of a false prophet we should shun, he had insights into divine truth not to be ignored.

Balaam was a tragic figure who made the wrong choice, despite knowing the right one. It is a choice all of us are called to make – to either side with YHWH, or not. As for blessings and curses, this great theme of the Bible the prophets would often return to. As far as God was concerned, Israel was a nation He was committed to blessing, despite apostasy (even though cursing was the result of sin and was why Jesus became a curse to save us). While the Church is not Israel, granting a blessing is God's intention for both. Sometimes He brings judgment to get their attention. Blessing the world is what the people of God are about. God's intention is that the world, firstly through Israel and then the Church, be blessed.

Verses revealing attributes of and approaches to false prophets

(Quotations are from the ESV and KJV in the order the verses appear in the Christian Bible. This is a far from complete list but is illustrative of the seriousness in which God views and deals with the false prophets of the Bible and now.)

Numbers 12:6

Hear now my words: If there be a prophet among you, I the Lord will make myself known unto him in a vision, and will speak unto him in a dream.

Deuteronomy 13:1-3

If a prophet or a dreamer of dreams arises among you and gives you a sign or a wonder, and the sign or wonder that he tells you comes to pass, and if he says, 'Let us go after other gods,' which you have not known, 'and let us serve them,' you shall not listen to the words of that prophet or that dreamer of dreams. For the Lord your God is testing you, to know whether you love the Lord your God with all your heart and with all your soul.

Deuteronomy 18:20-22

But the prophet who presumes to speak a word in my name that I have not commanded him to speak, or who speaks in the name of other gods, that same prophet shall die.' And if you say in your heart, 'How may we know the word that the Lord has not spoken?'— when a prophet speaks in the name of the Lord, if the word does not come to pass or come true, that is a word that the Lord has not spoken; the prophet has spoken it presumptuously.

Isaiah 8:20

To the law and to the testimony: if they speak not according to this word, it is because there is no light in them.

Isaiah 9:15

The ancient and honourable, he is the head; and the prophet that teacheth lies, he is the tail.

Isaiah 29:10

For the Lord hath poured out upon you the spirit of deep sleep, and hath closed your eyes: the prophets and your rulers, the seers hath he covered.

Isaiah 30:10

Which say to the seers, see not; and to the prophets, Prophesy not unto us right things, speak unto us smooth things, prophesy deceits:

Isaiah 56:10-11

His watchmen are blind; they are all without knowledge; they are all silent dogs; they cannot bark, dreaming, lying down, loving to slumber. The dogs have a mighty appetite; they never have enough. But they are shepherds who have no understanding; they have all turned to their own way, each to his own gain.

Jeremiah 5:30-31

An appalling and horrible thing has happened in the land: the prophets prophesy falsely, and the priests rule at their direction; my people love to have it so, but what will you do when the end comes?

Jeremiah 6:14

They have healed the wound of my people lightly, saying, 'Peace, peace,' when there is no peace.

Jeremiah 14:14

And the Lord said to me: "The prophets are prophesying lies in my name. I did not send them, nor did I command them or speak to them. They are prophesying to you a lying vision, worthless divination, and the deceit of their own minds.

Jeremiah 23:16

Thus says the Lord of hosts: "Do not listen to the words of the prophets who prophesy to you, filling you with vain hopes. They speak visions of their own minds, not from the mouth of the Lord.

Jeremiah 23:21

I did not send the prophets, yet they ran; I did not speak to them, yet they prophesied.

Jeremiah 28:8-9

The prophets who preceded you and me from ancient times prophesied war, famine, and pestilence against many countries and great kingdoms. As for the prophet who prophesies peace, when the word of that prophet comes to pass, then it will be known that the Lord has truly sent the prophet.

Lamentations 2:14

Your prophets have seen for you false and deceptive visions; they have not exposed your iniquity to restore your fortunes, but have seen for you oracles that are false and misleading.

Ezekiel 13:9

My hand will be against the prophets who see false visions and who give lying divinations. They shall not be in the council of my people, nor be enrolled in the register of the house of Israel, nor shall they enter the land of Israel. And you shall know that I am the Lord God.

Ezekiel 13:16, 17

To wit, the prophets of Israel which prophesy concerning Jerusalem, and which see visions of peace for her, and there is no peace, saith the Lord God. Likewise, thou son of man, set thy face against the daughters of thy people, which prophesy out of their own heart; and prophesy thou against them.

Ezekiel 14:9, 10

And if the prophet be deceived when he hath spoken a thing, I the Lord have deceived that prophet, and I will stretch out my hand upon him, and will destroy him from the midst of my people Israel. And they shall bear the punishment of their iniquity: the punishment of the prophet shall be even as the punishment of him that seeketh unto him;

Ezekiel 22:28

Her prophets have smeared whitewash for them, seeing false visions divining lies for them, saying, 'Thus says the Lord God,' when the Lord has not spoken.

Micah 2:6

Prophesy ye not, say they to them that prophesy: they shall not prophesy to them, that they shall not take shame.

Micah 3:5

Thus says the Lord concerning the prophets who lead my people astray, who cry "Peace" when they have something to eat, but declare war against him who puts nothing into their mouths.

Micah 3:11

Its heads give judgment for a bribe; its priests teach for a price; its prophets practice divination for money; yet they lean on the Lord and say, "Is not the Lord in the midst of us? No disaster shall come upon us."

Matthew 7:15-16

Beware of false prophets, who come to you in sheep's clothing but inwardly are ravenous wolves. You will recognize them by their fruits. Are grapes gathered from thornbushes, or figs from thistles?

Matthew 24:11

And many false prophets shall rise, and shall deceive many.

Matthew 24:24

For false christs and false prophets will arise and perform great signs and wonders, so as to lead astray, if possible, even the elect.

Acts 20:28-31

Take heed therefore unto yourselves, and to all the flock, over the which the Holy Ghost hath made you overseers, to feed the church of God, which he hath purchased with his own blood. For I know this, that after my departing shall grievous wolves enter in among you, not sparing the flock. Also of your own selves shall men arise, speaking perverse things, to draw away disciples after them. Therefore watch, and remember, that by the space of three years I ceased not to warn every one night and day

2 Peter 2:1-3

But false prophets also arose among the people, just as there will be false teachers among you, who will secretly bring in destructive heresies, even denying the Master who bought them, bringing upon themselves swift destruction. And many will follow their sensuality, and because of them the way of truth will be blasphemed. And in their greed they will exploit you with false words. Their condemnation from long ago is not idle, and their destruction is not asleep.

1 John 4:1

Beloved, do not believe every spirit, but test the spirits to see whether they are from God, for many false prophets have gone out into the world.

Jude 1:3,4

Beloved, when I gave all diligence to write unto you of the common salvation, it was needful for me to write unto you, and exhort you that ye should earnestly contend for the faith which was once delivered unto the saints. For certain people have crept in unnoticed who long ago were designated for this condemnation, ungodly people, who pervert the grace of our God into sensuality and deny our only Master and Lord, Jesus Christ.

Revelation 2:20

Notwithstanding I have a few things against thee, because thou sufferest that woman Jezebel, which calleth herself a prophetess, to teach and to seduce my servants to commit fornication, and to eat things sacrificed unto idols.

Revelation 19:20

And the beast was taken, and with him the false prophet that wrought miracles before him, with which he deceived them that had received the mark of the beast, and them that worshipped his image. These both were cast alive into a lake of fire burning with brimstone.

True and false prophets compared

We can see from the above verses (and there are more we could quote) that false prophets were prevalent in Bible times. It often seemed that they were listened to more than the true prophets. But what about today? This is a sticky subject and a controversial one, where opinion among Christians is markedly divided. Most will agree there have been and are false prophets, and, depending on whether one believes there are prophets today, who the true ones are. We continue to address this controversial matter in later chapters of this book. What we can say is that the Bible is clear as to what criteria makes both true and false prophets, and it is beholden upon the people of God to test and weigh words from the lips of those purporting to be prophets, whether or not these are truly from God.

While we need to take heed of the true and turn from the false and, right now, this has resulted in painfully controversial rows among respected Christian leaders as to what is true. We need to be patient, recognising God moves in mysterious ways and rarely acts exactly as we think He should. He may and often does delay the fulfilment of prophecy. Sometimes prophecy depends on how people respond and He may change His mind (examples of which we will see in chapters that follow), but always He honours His true prophets, noting in some quarters "prophets" are put on a pedestal and in others the opposite is true.

Chapter 7: Deborah and other women prophets

A general survey of the secular historical record would suggest that in almost every sphere of life – literature, culture, science, governance etc. – men featured a great deal more than women, despite there being many exceptions. In today's culture, including in church circles, there has in recent years been an effort to redress the balance, and things like creating gender equality in all aspects of life has become important. While the role of women, particularly when it comes to church leadership and the like, may be a contentious one, it is not a subject for this book other than the observation that this "imbalance" applies to the Bible too.

When it came to Old Testament prophets, if the Talmud is to be believed, there were forty-eight prophets and only seven prophetesses. While, unsurprisingly, there were many more times men than women who fulfilled the office of prophet, the women who did were formidable characters who discharged their duties with credit. Of the seven prophetesses mentioned (Miriam, Deborah, Huldah, Sarah, Abigail, Hannah and Esther), the first three were given that title in the Bible account, but as for the other four, cases can be made that these were indeed prophets, even though there is nothing in the respective narratives to say they were. As far as this chapter is concerned, we will consider all seven, starting with those definitely identified as prophets, followed by those other women in the Old Testament we can make a case for as being prophets, followed by New Testament women prophets, followed by women false prophets in the Bible.

Miriam

While not mentioned by name in Exodus 2, Miriam is believed to be the older sister of Moses, the very one who had the brave, quick wit to go to and advise Pharaoh's daughter, who adopted baby Moses as her own, and which was the alternative to death. It was almost eighty years later that she features again, and that was when the children of Israel were able to escape Egypt by crossing the Red Sea. We read: "*And Miriam the prophetess, the sister of Aaron, took a timbrel in her hand; and all the women went out after her with timbrels and with dances. And Miriam answered them, Sing ye to the Lord, for he hath triumphed gloriously; the horse and his rider hath he thrown into the sea*" (Exodus 15:20-21).

Miriam was clearly looked upon as a leader, especially among the women, and we find the first of a number of associations between music (and dance) and prophecy. We do not know much about Miriam, besides her being the brother of Aaron and married to Hur (who held Moses' arms up when he fought the Amalekites), and her grandson played an important part in the construction of the Tabernacle. It appears, along with brother Aaron, she was part of Moses' "inner circle". Centuries later, another prophet could look back when speaking to Israel: *"For I brought thee up out of the land of Egypt, and redeemed thee out of the house of servants; and I sent before thee Moses, Aaron, and Miriam"* (Micah 6:4).

There was one story where Miriam played a major part but it did not redound to her credit. *"And Miriam and Aaron spake against Moses because of the Ethiopian woman whom he had married: for he had married an Ethiopian woman... And the Lord spake suddenly unto Moses, and unto Aaron, and unto Miriam, Come out ye three unto the tabernacle of the congregation. And they three came out... And the Lord came down in the pillar of the cloud, and stood in the door of the tabernacle, and called Aaron and Miriam: and they both came forth ... And the cloud departed from off the tabernacle; and, behold, Miriam became leprous, white as snow: and Aaron looked upon Miriam, and, behold, she was leprous... And Miriam was shut out from the camp seven days: and the people journeyed not till Miriam was brought in again."* (Numbers 12:1, 4, 5, 10, 15.) If anything, it shows her pride and jealousy, but also God's severity and His mercy, for He heard Moses' prayer, and Miriam's leprosy went away.

As for her end: *"Then came the children of Israel, even the whole congregation, into the desert of Zin in the first month: and the people abode in Kadesh; and Miriam died there, and was buried there"* (Numbers 20:1). It was in the final (fortieth) year of Israel's wilderness wanderings, when later Aaron, followed by Moses, also died, thus handing over the leadership of the people to a new generation. While we may look with consternation at how Miriam, who had been such a support to Moses and inspired leader among the people, might have refrained from her criticism, there was little doubt her role was an important one; and other Jewish records talk of people mourning her death. From the young girl who saved her brother, to the older woman who led the people in worship, to the very old woman who helped lead the people, Miriam will always be looked upon as the prophetess who played an important part in Israel's story.

Deborah

We read in Chapter 8 of the period of the Judges (Deborah was one of them). It recounted the ups and downs of Israel when in the Promised land, after they had entered in under Joshua, and before the kings (beginning with Saul) began to reign.

What happened was Israel sinned; they were oppressed by one or other of their neighbours; they cried to God; God sent them a deliverer (judge) who helped rescue them, and then there was a period of peace. This happened time and time again. The story of Deborah, found in Judges 4 and 5, occurred in one such cycle. One remarkable thing about Deborah was that she was a prophet and a judge, and the only obvious woman prophet between Miriam and Huldah (under Josiah).

The story begins: "*And the children of Israel again did evil in the sight of the Lord, when Ehud was dead. And the Lord sold them into the hand of Jabin king of Canaan, that reigned in Hazor; the captain of whose host was Sisera, which dwelt in Harosheth of the Gentiles. And the children of Israel cried unto the Lord: for he had nine hundred chariots of iron; and twenty years he mightily oppressed the children of Israel. And Deborah, a prophetess, the wife of Lapidoth, she judged Israel at that time. And she dwelt under the palm tree of Deborah between Ramah and Bethel in mount Ephraim: and the children of Israel came up to her for judgment.*" (4:1-5.)

Even from this beginning, we learn a number of things. One is that Israel lived under an oppressor that possessed much military might. Another is that Israel was in another of its "*cried unto the Lord*" periods. Yet another is, while we know little of Deborah's background other than being married to Lapidoth (no other reference is found of him), she judged Israel, had a certain presence and was respected by people coming to her for counsel.

What this remarkable woman did was bring together different tribes of Israel to go to war under the generalship of a reluctant Barak, and then she told them the strategy they needed to adopt, as from the Lord: "*And Deborah said unto Barak, Up; for this is the day in which the Lord hath delivered Sisera into thine hand: is not the Lord gone out before thee? So Barak went down from mount Tabor, and ten thousand men after him. And the Lord discomfited Sisera, and all his chariots, and all his host, with the edge of the sword before Barak; so that Sisera lighted down off his chariot, and fled away on his feet.*" (Judges 4:14-15.) The result was a mighty victory with a twist (Jael (a woman) killed Sisera using a tent peg), followed by a period of peace and prosperity, at least until the next cycle.

Judges 5 is devoted to Deborah's song: "*Then sang Deborah and Barak the son of Abinoam on that day, saying, Praise ye the Lord for the avenging of Israel, when the people willingly offered themselves. Hear, O ye kings; give ear, O ye princes; I, even I, will sing unto the Lord; I will sing praise to the Lord God of Israel... The inhabitants of the villages ceased, they ceased in Israel, until that I Deborah arose, that I arose a mother in Israel. ... So let all thine enemies perish, O Lord: but let them that love him be as the sun when he goeth forth in his might. And the land had rest forty years."* (5:1-3,7,31.)

The details of the battle were recorded, including Sisera's inglorious end (by a woman and not a male warrior) and Israel's predicament that under Deborah, a "mother in Israel", achieved a mighty victory with God's help. This prophet and judge was also prepared to lay her life on the line for the sake of the people, whom God was well able to use even though (*she was only*) a woman.

Huldah

Huldah comes to our attention during the reign of good King Josiah, when she provided timely reassurance and stern counsel from the Lord. The context was the discovery of scrolls of the Law that hitherto had been overlooked, when having a clear out / clean-up of the Temple, that had long been neglected. Josiah realised that things were not right in the relationship between God and Israel, and sought counsel from, of all people, a woman, albeit a knowledgeable one.

"*So Hilkiah the priest, and Ahikam, and Achbor, and Shaphan, and Asahiah, went unto Huldah the prophetess, the wife of Shallum the son of Tikvah, the son of Harhas, keeper of the wardrobe; (now she dwelt in Jerusalem in the college;) and they communed with her*" (2 Kings 22:14). We know little more about Huldah the person than what we read here. We know more about her husband, who appeared to have had an important position in the royal household.

Her response was clear and unambiguous: "*And she said unto them, Thus saith the Lord God of Israel, Tell the man that sent you to me, Thus saith the Lord, Behold, I will bring evil upon this place, and upon the inhabitants thereof, even all the words of the book which the king of Judah hath read: Because they have forsaken me, and have burned incense unto other gods, that they might provoke me to anger with all the works of their hands; therefore my wrath shall be kindled against this place, and shall not be quenched. But to the king of Judah which sent you to enquire of the Lord, thus shall ye say to him, Thus saith the Lord God of Israel, As touching the words which thou hast heard; Because thine heart was tender, and thou hast humbled thyself before the Lord, when thou heardest what I spake against this place, and against the inhabitants thereof, that they should become a desolation and a curse, and hast rent thy clothes, and wept before me; I also have heard thee, saith the Lord. Behold therefore, I will gather thee unto thy fathers, and thou shalt be gathered into thy grave in peace; and thine eyes shall not see all the evil which I will bring upon this place. And they brought the king word again."* (1 Kings 22:15-20.)

Huldah fully grasped the significance of the discovery, mindful of God's nature and purposes, promises and warnings. Because she was a prophet, she was able to counsel what needed to happen next. Unlike what was often the case, the king heeded the word of the prophet and did what Huldah said and for a period the land enjoyed peace and a measure of prosperity. Sadly, it was only a temporary respite from the Lord's anger, which Huldah had revealed; and for Israel, following the death of Josiah in an ill-advised military operation, it was tragically downhill after that. We are ever grateful for Huldah, for her timely counsel, saying what needed to be said, without mincing her words, which in Josiah's case were well received.

Sarah

We read concerning Sarah: *"Through faith also Sara herself received strength to conceive seed, and was delivered of a child when she was past age, because she judged him faithful who had promised. Therefore sprang there even of one, and him as good as dead, so many as the stars of the sky in multitude, and as the sand which is by the sea shore innumerable."* (Hebrews 11:11-12.)

While our focus in those chapters of the Bible, where Sarah is given an occasional mention, is understandably on her husband, Abraham, it is clear Sarah's role was a significant one. While she may never have uttered any word of prophecy, her actions might be deemed to be prophetic, as her whole life was a testimony to the hope of a promise fulfilled hundreds of years on, and to this day sets an example: *"Look unto Abraham your father, and unto Sarah that bare you: for I called him alone, and blessed him, and increased him"* (Isaiah 51:2); and *"Even as Sara obeyed Abraham, calling him lord: whose daughters ye are, as long as ye do well, and are not afraid with any amazement"* (1 Peter 3:6).

Abigail

The story of Abigail in the Bible is an unusual one, with an interesting, unexpected twist, and is told, almost in its entirety, in 1 Samuel 25. We learn, *"Now the name of the man was Nabal; and the name of his wife Abigail: and she was a woman of good understanding, and of a beautiful countenance: but the man was churlish and evil in his doings; and he was of the house of Caleb"* (1 Samuel 25:3). Nabal was a man of churlish character that David, then an outlaw, came to for help, whose emissaries were rudely sent away. This made David angry, especially given the presence of him and his band had provided security for Nabal, who resolved then to kill him and may have done so if Abigail had not intervened as she did.

"But one of the young men told Abigail, Nabal's wife, saying, Behold, David sent messengers out of the wilderness to salute our master; and he railed on them ... Then Abigail made haste, and took two hundred loaves, and two bottles of wine, and five sheep ready dressed, and five measures of parched corn, and an hundred clusters of raisins, and two hundred cakes of figs, and laid them on asses." (1 Samuel 25:14, 18.) With tact and wisdom, Abigail managed to win David over and he changed his mind when it came to seeking revenge:

"And when Abigail saw David, she hasted, and lighted off the ass, and fell before David on her face, and bowed herself to the ground ... And David said to Abigail, Blessed be the Lord God of Israel, which sent thee this day to meet me...." (1 Samuel 25:23,32.) Not long after that, Nabal died and David married Abigail. Her wise, God-inspired, God-fearing actions saved the day and averted a disaster.

Hannah

Hannah is an integral part of the Samuel story. She was barren, prayed to God for a son and promised to dedicate him to the Lord's service: *"And she was in bitterness of soul, and prayed unto the Lord, and wept sore. And she vowed a vow, and said, O Lord of hosts, if thou wilt indeed look on the affliction of thine handmaid, and remember me, and not forget thine handmaid, but wilt give unto thine handmaid a man child, then I will give him unto the Lord all the days of his life, and there shall no razor come upon his head."* (1 Samuel 1:10,11.)

She had a son and she carried out her promise, with Samuel later becoming a great prophet. *"For this child I prayed; and the Lord hath given me my petition which I asked of him: Therefore also I have lent him to the Lord; as long as he liveth he shall be lent to the Lord. And he worshipped the Lord there."* (1 Samuel 1:27,28.) Her amazing prayer, reminiscent in part to Mary's Magnificat, could be seen as prophetic, on top of her earlier prayer and her dedication, concerning Samuel:

"And Hannah prayed, and said, My heart rejoiceth in the Lord, mine horn is exalted in the Lord: my mouth is enlarged over mine enemies; because I rejoice in thy salvation. There is none holy as the Lord: for there is none beside thee: neither is

there any rock like our God... The Lord maketh poor, and maketh rich: he bringeth low, and lifteth up. He raiseth up the poor out of the dust, and lifteth up the beggar from the dunghill, to set them among princes, and to make them inherit the throne of glory: for the pillars of the earth are the Lord's, and he hath set the world upon them. He will keep the feet of his saints, and the wicked shall be silent in darkness; for by strength shall no man prevail. The adversaries of the Lord shall be broken to pieces; out of heaven shall he thunder upon them: the Lord shall judge the ends of the earth; and he shall give strength unto his king, and exalt the horn of his anointed."* (1 Samuel 2:1-2, 7-10.)

Esther

The story of Esther, recounted in the Book of Esther, is a remarkable one. While God is never mentioned, when reading between the lines it would seem clear God was active in carrying out His purposes, in particular preserving His special people, Israel, and using as His instrument, Esther, to do so.

Esther had found herself, it would seem by quirk of fate, to be queen to the ruler of the Persian Empire, King Ahasuerus. In doing so, she hid her Jewish identity, but when it became clear that all the Jews in the Empire were going to be killed because of the wicked designs of the king's prime minister, Haman, action needed to be taken; and as encouraged by her mentor, her uncle, Mordecai, she responded: *"For if thou altogether holdest thy peace at this time, then shall there enlargement and deliverance arise to the Jews from another place; but thou and thy father's house shall be destroyed: and who knoweth whether thou art come to the kingdom for such a time as this? Then Esther bade them return Mordecai this answer, Go, gather together all the Jews that are present in Shushan, and fast ye for me, and neither eat nor drink three days, night or day: I also and my maidens will fast likewise; and so will I go in unto the king, which is not according to the law: and if I perish, I perish.."* (Esther 4:14-16.)

The story is a fascinating one, full of action and because God is in the equation, even though not mentioned. It was not chance happenings, and Esther by her brave and appropriate responses, managed to save the Jewish people from annihilation. One could only imagine what might have been if she had not acted as she had. Jewish people to this day remember this event when each year they celebrate the Feast of Purim. There is no greater honour than to have been raised up by God *for such a time as this*, and that honour fell upon a woman, Queen Esther. The need today for people to be raised up for "such a time as this" is all too evident.

Other Old Testament women prophets

It is not the intention here to prolong the citing of further examples of women prophets, other than refer to one woman, discussed in Chapter 8, Ruth the Moabites, and another woman whom we will simply refer to as Mrs Isaiah, since we do not know her name. Ruth was arguably every bit a prophet as Sarah, Abigail, Hannah and Esther, but is not referred to as such in the Talmud, likely because she was not a Hebrew. Moreover, the Law had hard things to say when barring those from Moab from their community. No doubt Ruth knew this but it did not deter her returning to Bethlehem with her mother-in-law, Naomi: *"...for whither thou goest, I will go; and where thou lodgest, I will lodge: thy people shall be my people, and thy God my God"* (Ruth 1:16).

Her meeting and marrying Boaz (a definitely good guy) is one of the lovely stories of the Bible, as was her being an ancestor of Jesus. While like these other four ladies she did not prophesy, her life was every bit as prophetic. While the Old Testament focuses on Israel and the New on the Church, that are now mainly Gentiles along with Jews who believe in Jesus their Messiah, the way God dealt with Ruth was a sign for future generations that there is a place in His purposes and blessings for those who are not the physical descendants of Abraham.

As for Mrs Isaiah, other than being mother of Isaiah's children, all we can find out about her from the Bible is: *"I went to the prophetess; and she conceived, and bore a son. Then said the Lord to me, Call his name Mahershalal hashbaz"* Isaiah 8:3. Whether she was a prophetess in her own right or her relationship with her husband was such he would run over his prophecies with her, or merely because she was married to a prophet is a matter for discussion (but not here). It is not one the author has strong views on either way, but is mentioned here for completeness.

New Testament women prophets

When the baby Jesus was brought to the Temple, there is a lovely story of the first prophetess mentioned in the New Testament: *"And there was one Anna, a prophetess, the daughter of Phanuel, of the tribe of Aser: she was of a great age, and had lived with an husband seven years from her virginity; And she was a widow of about fourscore and four years, which departed not from the temple, but served God with fastings and prayers night and day. And she coming in that instant gave thanks likewise unto the Lord, and spake of him to all them that looked for redemption in Jerusalem."* (Luke 2:36-38.)

In his sermon on the Day of Pentecost, after the Holy Spirit had fallen upon the believers there gathered, Peter quotes from the Book of Joel: *"And it shall come to pass in the last days, saith God, I will pour out of my Spirit upon all flesh: and your sons and your daughters shall prophesy, and your young men shall see visions, and your old men shall dream dreams"* (Acts 2:17). We can infer that the gift of prophesy, along with other gifts of the Holy Spirit, was available men and women, although, as discussed in Chapter 14, there are widespread differences between the Old and New Testaments in the use of the gift of prophesy.

As for an example of women prophets after Pentecost, we find: *"And the same man had four daughters, virgins, which did prophesy"* (Acts 21:9). It is perhaps a mind boggling thought that Philip had not one but four daughters who prophesied.

While the gift of prophesy was encouraged among women in the early Church, we should note Paul's teaching: *"But every woman that prayeth or prophesieth with her head uncovered dishonoureth her head: for that is even all one as if she were shaven"* (1 Corinthians 11:5); and, *"But I suffer not a woman to teach, nor to usurp authority over the man, but to be in silence"* (1 Timothy 2:12).

Finally, there is one (at least) lovely story of women being prophetic without saying a word. We refer to the story told in Matthew 26 and Mark 14, when a little before Jesus was arrested we learn of a remarkable an act of devotion: *"There came unto him a woman having an alabaster box of very precious ointment, and poured it on his head, as he sat at meat"* (Matthew 26:7). This led to much consternation from among His disciples, who felt the oil should have been sold and the money then given to the poor. Jesus' response was: *"Verily I say unto you, wheresoever this gospel shall be preached in the whole world, there shall also this, that this woman hath done, be told for a memorial of her"* (Matthew 26:13). The author recalls having heard moving sermons in the past of *a woman having an alabaster box of very precious ointment* and can confirm this to be the case.

Jesus and women

One of the many remarkable aspects of Jesus' short ministry was concerning the way he interacted with women, and especially those of ill repute, which stands out by the way he honoured and treated them, regardless. One was Mary Magdalene who became part of His inner circle. We know something of the dark side of her early life because we are told that Jesus expelled seven demons from her (Luke 8:2). Some have suggested she was the unnamed woman (likely a prostitute) who washed Jesus' feet with her tears and dried them with her hair (Luke 7:36-38), as discussed earlier. There is a remarkable passage recorded in John 20:1-18 when she visited the tomb in which Jesus was laid, following His crucifixion, to anoint His body, but instead was greeted, to her astonishment, by the living Christ (she being the first person to see Jesus after He had risen) who told her to go to His disciples and tell them that He was alive!

Another story concerned the women at the well at Samaria, recorded in John 4:1-30. In the extraordinary dialogue that ensued, which began with Jesus asking her for water and ended with Him telling her He could give living water such that those receiving would never thirst again, Jesus discerned something of her dark past – she had been married five times and was now living with a man who was not her husband. She realised this was the Christ and went back to her people to recount what had happened. Likely, these two women would not be regarded as prophets, yet gained unique insights concerning Jesus and used the opportunity that was afforded to them to tell others, just as a prophet might do.

One of the lovely stories of the Bible was Elisabeth who was carrying John the Baptist meeting Mary, carrying Jesus, with John leaping in his mother's womb. Both spoke prophetically. In Elisabeth's case: *"And it came to pass, that, when Elisabeth heard the salutation of Mary, the babe leaped in her womb; and Elisabeth was filled with the Holy Ghost: And she spake out with a loud voice, and said, Blessed art thou among women, and blessed is the fruit of thy womb. And whence is this to me, that the mother of my Lord should come to me? For, lo, as soon as the voice of thy salutation sounded in mine ears, the babe leaped in my womb for joy. And blessed is she that believed: for there shall be a performance of those things which were told her from the Lord"* Luke 1:42-45.

In Mary's case: *"My soul doth magnify the Lord, And my spirit hath rejoiced in God my Saviour. For he hath regarded the low estate of his handmaiden: for, behold, from henceforth all generations shall call me blessed. For he that is mighty hath done to me great things; and holy is his name. And his mercy is on them that fear him from generation to generation. He hath shewed strength with his arm; he hath scattered the proud in the imagination of their hearts. He hath put down the mighty from their seats, and exalted them of low degree. He hath filled the hungry with good things; and the rich he hath sent empty away. He hath helped his servant Israel, in remembrance of his mercy; As he spake to our fathers, to Abraham, and to his seed for ever"* Luke 1:46-55.

Women false prophets

Just as there were men false prophets, there were also women false prophets, both in the Old Testament, e.g. Noadiah (Nehemiah 6:14), who went out of her way to discourage Nehemiah from building the wall (although the Bible record does not have her down as false *per se*), and the "*daughters of your people who prophesy out of their own imagination*" (Ezekiel 13:17); and the New Testament, e.g. "*a certain damsel possessed with a spirit of divination*" (Acts 16:16), and Jezebel of Thyatira (Revelation 2:20) who brought false teaching. The church had been taken in and Jesus took them to task: "*Notwithstanding I have a few things against thee, because thou sufferest that woman Jezebel, which calleth herself a prophetess, to teach and to seduce my servants to commit fornication, and to eat things sacrificed unto idols*" (Revelation 2:20).

The ability to deceive and lead people astray was evident among women, just as it was among men. The fact that in the Bible women false prophets held a certain sway is further evidence women prophets were taken seriously in Bible times, in what were, after all, male-dominated societies.

Chapter 8: From Joshua, through Judges to Samuel

Joshua

We have begun to set the scene for the emergence of the prophets *en masse* by considering the origins of everything in Chapter 4, the giving of the Law and the establishing of the Covenant between God and His chosen people, Israel, in Chapter 5, and, by way of diversions, albeit important ones, reflecting on false prophets in Chapter 6, and women prophets in Chapter 7. During all that period, the one prophet to emerge that is usually seen as especially significant is Moses. If prophets really came into their own and were there throughout the duration, it was during the period of the Kings, which we will soon get to. Before that, we need to consider the period preceding, following on from the death of Moses.

The transition between Moses dying, and handing over the baton for leading the people to Joshua, was relatively smooth. We read at the end of the Pentateuch: *"And the Lord said unto him, This is the land which I sware unto Abraham, unto Isaac, and unto Jacob, saying, I will give it unto thy seed: I have caused thee to see it with thine eyes, but thou shalt not go over thither. So Moses the servant of the Lord died there in the land of Moab, according to the word of the Lord. And he buried him in a valley in the land of Moab, over against Bethpeor: but no man knoweth of his sepulchre unto this day. And Moses was an hundred and twenty years old when he died: his eye was not dim, nor his natural force abated. And the children of Israel wept for Moses in the plains of Moab thirty days: so the days of weeping and mourning for Moses were ended. And Joshua the son of Nun was full of the spirit of wisdom; for Moses had laid his hands upon him: and the children of Israel hearkened unto him, and did as the Lord commanded Moses. And there arose not a prophet since in Israel like unto Moses, whom the Lord knew face to face, In all the signs and the wonders, which the Lord sent him to do in the land of Egypt to Pharaoh, and to all his servants, and to all his land, And in all that mighty hand, and in all the great terror which Moses shewed in the sight of all Israel."* (Deuteronomy 34:4-12.)

And then onto the Book of Joshua, which is about possessing the Promised Land, and it was evident that Moses was a hard act to follow and yet as invariably happens God raises up and equips those who take their place: *"Now after the death of Moses the servant of the Lord it came to pass, that the Lord spake unto Joshua the son of Nun, Moses' minister, saying, Moses my servant is dead; now therefore arise, go over this Jordan, thou, and all this people, unto the land which I do give to them, even to the children of Israel. Every place that the sole of your foot shall tread upon, that have I given unto you, as I said unto Moses."* (Joshua 1:1-3.)

We had already come across Joshua when the Israelites fought their first major battle under his generalship (Exodus 17), as Moses' servant during the giving of the Law at Mount Sinai (Exodus 24), and after during the Wilderness wanderings when he was likely mentored by and learned much from Moses, coming to further prominence when as one of the twelve appointed to spy out the Promised Land (Numbers 14), it was he, who along with Caleb were alone in bringing back promising reports and urging the people that notwithstanding the obstacles they could go and possess the land with the Lord's help.

God had His hand on Joshua from the outset: *"Be strong and of a good courage: for unto this people shalt thou divide for an inheritance the land, which I sware unto their fathers to give them. Only be thou strong and very courageous, that thou mayest observe to do according to all the law, which Moses my servant commanded thee: turn not from it to the right hand or to the left, that thou mayest prosper withersoever thou goest. This book of the law shall not depart out of thy mouth; but thou shalt meditate therein day and night, that thou mayest observe to do according to all that is written therein: for then thou shalt make thy way prosperous, and then thou shalt have good success. Have not I commanded thee? Be strong and of a good courage; be not afraid, neither be thou dismayed: for the Lord thy God is with thee whithersoever thou goest."* (Joshua 1:6-9.) From what we read, Joshua obeyed and God blessed him.

While Joshua strikes us as more a leader and general than a prophet in the sense of foretelling the future, we note throughout the time Joshua led the people, God was telling Joshua what he needed to do and what would happen as a result of obedience (e.g. conquering Jericho) and of disobedience (e.g. routed at Ai due to there being sin in the camp – revealing, as if the Israelites needed to be reminded, that God is a Holy God and cannot be disregarded or treated with contempt).

What takes up much of the rest of the Book of Joshua is accounts of the various conquests and the dividing up of the land among the tribes of Israel. And to reinforce the message of the Blessings and Curses, discussed in Chapter 5, these were recited once again in Joshua 8, in fulfilment of what Moses said should happen: *"And it shall come to pass, when the Lord thy God hath brought thee in unto the land whither thou goest to possess it, that thou shalt put the blessing upon mount Gerizim, and the curse upon mount Ebal"* (Deuteronomy 11:29).

After a period of relative peace, and given what had happened prior to Joshua becoming leader and after a period when the people were mostly obedient, Joshua gives his farewell speech, just as Moses did, before he died (Joshua 23 & 24). The theme of blessing when the people obeyed and cursing when the people disobeyed was his central message. The section begins: *"And it came to pass a long time after that the Lord had given rest unto Israel from all their enemies round about, that Joshua waxed old and stricken in age. And Joshua called for all Israel, and for their elders, and for their heads, and for their judges, and for their officers, and said unto them, I am old and stricken in age: And ye have seen all that the Lord your God hath done unto all these nations because of you; for the Lord your God is he that hath fought for you."* (23:1-3.)

It is notable that there is no succession in leadership given, other than a sort of leadership we will get to when we come to the Book of Judges, apart from offices, elders, judges and officers, given here. Significantly, it was always God's intention that He would be Israel's King, and what mattered was keeping the Covenant (discussed in Chapter 5). The choice before the people was a simple one: either obey or disobey. The people agreed to obey and the Covenant was re-established with this new generation. And soon after Joshua died.

Much of the rest of the Old Testament is about how each succeeding generation obeyed the Covenant (or not), and the message of future prophets was often to do with dealing with the consequences of disobedience.

Judges

Which brings us to the Book of Judges. The term "judge" is a misnomer. These might be best seen as trouble-shooters, raised up when Israel was oppressed by an enemy within the land they occupied, invariably as a result of disobeying the Covenant they had agreed to at the end of the Book of Joshua. They were a rather diverse bunch but, from what we can make out, all were raised up for a purpose.

This title is assigned to twelve persons in the Book of Judges: Othniel, Ehud, Shamgar, Deborah, Gideon, Tola, Jair, Jephthah, Ibzan, Elon, Abdon and Samson; plus at least one more, Samuel, discussed in the Book of Samuel – and, as far as authentic prophets go, is the only one considered at length in this chapter; although one of the judges, Deborah, was a prophet too (discussed in Chapter 7).

While Joshua won many notable victories among the Canaanites, he did not succeed in driving them all out or subjugating them, which we should bear in mind God commanded because of their evil ways. They worshipped false gods, indulged in sexual immorality, did terrible things like child sacrifice, and perpetrated other atrocities. We find at the start of the Book of Judges, the Israelites carrying on where Joshua left off; but that soon stopped. Not only were the Canaanite inhabitants left alone but the Israelites sought to reach some accord, including inter-marriage and adopting their wicked ways. Much of the Judges is about what happened as a consequence: it led to the Israelites being oppressed and subjugated by the inhabitants of the land, them crying to God for rescue, God raising up deliverers i.e. judges, followed by a period of peace; but the cycle continued with new judges and new oppressors, over and over again.

The Book of Judges discusses, at various lengths, what happened under the judges. For our purposes, we will cite three: Gideon, Jephthah and Samson; and that is as much because a lot is written about them and what they did. None of them can be classed as prophets but all of them were anointed by God to deliver His people, and their victories were emphatic because God was with them. In their particular ways their action might be regarded as prophetic. All were very flawed and would seem to be unlikely choices, with all having sad endings brought about by their own disobedience, which the recorded accounts of their judgeship do not gloss over. But all were mightily used by God and, under their leadership, the people experienced deliverance and a period of peace.

Gideon was ironically greeted by an angel as "a mighty man of valour" (when he was hiding from the enemy, no doubt in fear of being captured), and with some reluctance and a whittled down army defeated the Midianites. Jephthah was rejected by his brethren, who later turned to him to deliver them from the Ammonites, which he did. Samson was a Nazarite, whose strength was linked to his long hair, which he used to bring victory over the Philistines, who was a carnal man that in the end God used in an extraordinarily way to deliver Israel. And while God used all three men, they all fell in later life. This serves as a warning.

Besides Deborah, the only reference to prophets in the Book of Judges was a little prior to Gideon being called: "*And it came to pass, when the children of Israel cried unto the Lord because of the Midianites, That the Lord sent a prophet unto the children of Israel, which said unto them, Thus saith the Lord God of Israel, I brought you up from Egypt, and brought you forth out of the house of bondage; And I delivered you out of the hand of the Egyptians, and out of the hand of all that oppressed you, and drave them out from before you, and gave you their land; And I said unto you, I am the Lord your God; fear not the gods of the Amorites, in whose land ye dwell: but ye have not obeyed my voice."* (Judges 6:7-10.)

This prophet comes into the "unknown prophet" category, and is perhaps the first example we can cite (to be discussed further in Chapter 11) which teaches us about the paradigm later prophets operated, and God maintaining His keeping and concerns of His Covenant people. While for the purpose of this book, knowing about the lives of the prophets may be of particular interest, as far as the Bible is concerned their message was more important than the messenger.

While prophets seemed to pop up all the time under the kings, that was not so in this period between Moses' death and the appointing of the first King of Israel – Saul. We learn at the time God began to speak through Samuel the prophet: *"And the child Samuel ministered unto the Lord before Eli. And the word of the Lord was precious in those days; there was no open vision"* (1 Samuel 3:1).

Centuries later, after the death of Malachi, we experience a further period when there was no obvious prophetic voice, until John the Baptist. While one might surmise why this was the case, it should be borne in mind that God was always about keeping His Covenant with His people, and the issue we are faced with was that His people were unwilling to keep their part of the that Covenant. This can be readily seen as we survey the Book of Judges and the early chapters of Samuel.

Judges ends with the phrase, repeating an earlier observation, and pretty much encapsulates the worst of what people did: *"In those days there was no king in Israel: every man did that which was right in his own eyes."* (Judges 21:25.)

Ruth

With that depressing note, and before moving onto the Book of Samuel (one book in the Hebrew Bible; two in the Christian Bible), we should refer to the book wedged between Judges and Samuel – Ruth, which in the Hebrew Bible, and appropriately so, sees as part of the Book of Judges.

What God intended for His people can be seen in Ruth. Ruth was a Moabitess (often seen as enemies of Israel) woman who left everything to accompany the widowed mother of her deceased husband back to Israel. There she meets Boaz and marries him and becomes a direct ancestor to David and Jesus. What can be said about Ruth and Boaz is they are examples of how God wanted His people to be, including those who were not born Israelites, and of God's favour on such. It marks a refreshing contrast to a lot of the disturbing narrative we find in Judges.

Samuel

So what can we say about Samuel? Much of his coming into being and his early life was due to a praying mother, Hannah (discussed in Chapter 7). She was barren; she prayed for a child; God gave her Samuel; she gave Samuel back to God; God gave Hannah more sons. Samuel lived much of his life in and around the Temple under the mentorship of Eli the Priest. It was as a boy God spoke to Samuel, and it was words of judgement, which he reluctantly relayed to Eli, and which came to pass. From then on, we read: *"And Samuel grew, and the Lord was with him, and did let none of his words fall to the ground. And all Israel from Dan even to Beersheba knew that Samuel was established to be a prophet of the Lord. And the Lord appeared again in Shiloh: for the Lord revealed himself to Samuel in Shiloh by the word of the Lord."* (1Samuel 3: 19-21.)

Samuel rose to prominence while Israel was in conflict with their old enemy, the Philistines, with their fortunes being linked to whether their attitude to God was the right one. A time of peace followed a time of conflict, with Samuel judging wisely and the people following his godly counsel.

There came a time, as he grew old, when Israel demanded a king, not helped because Samuel's sons whom he elevated as judges were ungodly and a blight on Samuel's character. The author sees his nepotism and giving his sons authority when unmerited as a distinct flaw in Samuel's character and given his boyhood mentor, Eli, had done something similar, as ironic.

Despite Samuel trying to dissuade the people, God told him to accede to their request as it was all part of His will. This led to Samuel seeking out and anointing Saul as King, whom he sought to guide and encourage in the ways of the Lord. Saul began well but ended badly for, despite a promising start, he went against what God told him to do and reaped the consequences. The tragedy was that while he had all the natural qualities for a king and would have been the people's choice, Saul thought he knew better than God; even though for a time, with God's help, he was victorious in battle. When he was told to utterly destroy the Amalekites (1 Samuel 15), he failed to do so, and this triggered his downward spiral.

While Saul would not be regarded as a prophet, following him being anointed as

King we get a glimpse of what could have been when what Samuel said after he was anointed soon came to pass: *"And the Spirit of the Lord will come upon thee, and thou shalt prophesy with them, and shalt be turned into another man. And let it be, when these signs are come unto thee, that thou do as occasion serve thee; for God is with thee."* (1 Samuel 10: 6,7.)

After he had fallen from grace, and while he was pursuing his, rival, David, we find that *"the Spirit of God was upon him also, and he went on, and prophesied"*, 1 Samuel 19:23, teaching us that the gift of prophesy may be given by the Giver unconditionally, as He wills, to whoever He wills.

Because of Saul's disobedience, God chose another King, David, to replace him; and the man sent to anoint him was Samuel. A lot more could be said about David, described as a man after God's own heart (1 Samuel 13:14, Acts 13:22), including David as a prophet, but that will have to wait. We end this chapter by considering Samuel's farewell speech as an old man. While some of his speech seemed to be self-congratulatory over the way he had acted in the past, he gave sober warnings, much as Moses had done, on the consequences of straying from the Lord, and which we will see under later kings were to come to pass, as well as on a more positive note how great and wonderful were His intentions:

"Now therefore behold the king whom ye have chosen, and whom ye have desired! and, behold, the Lord hath set a king over you. If ye will fear the Lord, and serve him, and obey his voice, and not rebel against the commandment of the Lord, then shall both ye and also the king that reigneth over you continue following the Lord your God: But if ye will not obey the voice of the Lord, but rebel against the commandment of the Lord, then shall the hand of the Lord be against you, as it was against your fathers. Now therefore stand and see this great thing, which the Lord will do before your eyes ... For the Lord will not forsake his people for his great name's sake: because it hath pleased the Lord to make you his people. Moreover as for me, God forbid that I should sin against the Lord in ceasing to pray for you: but I will teach you the good and the right way: Only fear the Lord, and serve him in truth with all your heart: for consider how great things he hath done for you. But if ye shall still do wickedly, ye shall be consumed, both ye and your king." (1 Samuel 12:13-16, 22-25.)

What we can conclude is, Samuel was one who heard directly from God. While it might be argued he had weaknesses, e.g. his nepotism, he was mightily used by God to affect the transition from judges to kings, including anointing and mentoring the first two kings of Israel, and guiding the people aright. We might also want to give credit to his praying mother for what he was to become. Like all prophets, as one finished his work, new ones were raised to replace, and often there were marked differences in character and circumstances. But, as Charles Wesley, observed: *"God buries His workmen but carries on His work"*.

Chapter 9: David, Nathan and Gad

David

While the kings of the Bible are a fascinating lot, this book is about the prophets of the Bible (although even then, and even more importantly, it is about the God of the Bible), and in general kings are only discussed when they interacted with the prophets, which they often did. Following the demise of Saul, Israel's first king, David reigned as king in his place. While the prophet Samuel had a small, part to play, earlier in his life, in particular anointing David to be king to replace Saul, the prophets that played important parts in David's reign and doing so at critical points, were Nathan and Gad, whom we will get to. However, we make an exception to not discussing kings at length, when it comes to David, because:

1. David was arguably Israel's greatest king.

2. It was under David the land was secured and prospered, and was at peace.

3. A significant chunk of the Bible is devoted to the life of David.

4. While David sinned big time, he was as close as any to the heart of God.

5. He is referred to, positively, by a number of the later prophets, often linked to a hope that a descendant of David would be its future Messiah.

6. Unlike any other king, God made an everlasting covenant with David such that his descendants, notably the Messiah, would sit on the throne.

7. The little we know about Nathan and Gad from the Bible was tied in with David's story and was related to events at critical times in his reign.

8. We learn from the Gospels, Jesus was referred to as the Son of David.

9. The genealogy of Jesus listed in Matthew and Luke trace the line from David through several kings that we will encounter, to Jesus Himself.

10. While David is not usually regarded as a prophet, he did write Psalms (73 of them – half the Psalter), and some of these are messianic, i.e. prophetic.

Before discussing David further, we will mention two characters, Jehoiachin and his grandson Zerubbabel, and explain why they are significant. We read at the very end of the Book of Kings, concerning the last then living king of Judah, Jehoiachin, who had been taken captive and lived in Babylonian exile: *"And it came to pass in the seven and thirtieth year of the captivity of Jehoiachin king of Judah, in the twelfth month, on the seven and twentieth day of the month, that Eilmerodach king of Babylon in the year that he began to reign did lift up the head of Jehoiachin king of Judah out of prison; And he spake kindly to him, and set his throne above the throne of the kings that were with him in Babylon; And changed his prison garments: and he did eat bread continually before him all the days of his life. And his allowance was a continual allowance given him of the king, a daily rate for every day, all the days of his life."* (2 Kings 25:27-30.)

As for Zerubbabel, he returned to Jerusalem following the Exile, was involved in the building of the Temple and was governor of the City. He is mentioned in the Books of Chronicles, Ezra, Nehemiah, Haggai and Zechariah. Jehoiachin and Zerubbabel were descendants of David and mentioned in the New Testament genealogies concerning Jesus. We have jumped ahead five hundred years and make this diversion to reinforce the point that the line of David is hugely significant as far as the Bible narrative is concerned, and provides evidence that God's purposes matter, are not thwarted, and that He kept His promise to David.

There was a marked contrast between King Saul and King David. Saul was head and shoulders (literally) above his peers, outwardly looked the part and to begin with met the people's expectations. David, on the other hand, did not look the part. When Samuel came to Jesse to anoint one of his sons as kings, none of those paraded before him were God's choice. But there was one more son, the youngest, David, who was looking after the sheep and might have been overlooked, but for Samuel's insistence that he sees all the sons, including the one least likely. When David was brought before Samuel, he knew David was the man God chose, having been told by God that while man looks on outward appearances, God looks upon the heart. While he was anointed and was to have many adventures, it was not until many years later that David began to reign, after Saul's death.

Evidence that David was a man after God's own heart was borne out early on when he alone volunteered to fight Goliath, indignant he should be defying the armies of the living God, and trusting God to bring him victory, which He did. It was then David was thrown into the limelight and remained so until his death. *"So David slept with his fathers, and was buried in the city of David. And the days that David reigned over Israel were forty years: seven years reigned he in Hebron, and thirty and three years reigned he in Jerusalem."* (1Kings 2:10,11.) A NT commentary concerning David's life is poignant: *"For David, after he had served his own generation by the will of God, fell on sleep, and was laid unto his fathers, and saw corruption*" Acts 13:36. It is something we can all bear in mind when it comes to serving our own generation by the will of God.

It is nigh impossible to do justice to David's colourful career. After his victory, Saul appointed him as his personal harpist and David struck up a remarkable friendship with Saul's son, Jonathan. We learn *"the soul of Jonathan was knit to the soul of David, and Jonathan loved him as his own soul."* (1 Samuel 18:1). David was also enlisted in Saul's army and led Saul's troops, invariably to victory, with God's help. Saul's rejection by God took its toll and he became jealous of David and tried to kill him. David escapes and becomes an outlaw and also a mercenary, drawing a motley band of followers, including dwelling in the Cave of Adullam, a band of fellow outlaws and discontents, yet included in their number mighty warriors. David shows his mettle when on two occasions he could have killed Saul and saved himself but did not do so out of honour of Saul and fear of God. When Saul, along with Jonathan, dies in battle, and David learns this, he laments their loss: *"And David lamented with this lamentation over Saul and over Jonathan his son ..."* (2 Samuel 1:17). He takes over as king, wins more battles and establishes the kingdom, which was at its height during David's reign.

The one thing he wanted but was not allowed was to build a temple for the Lord. A critical point comes when he commits adultery with Bathsheba and kills her husband, Uriah. While he repents, the seeds of Israel's future demise had been sown. This can be seen in his sons. One rapes his sister; another murders the rapist and he then tries to humiliate and steal the throne from his father; and yet another, toward the end of David's life, tries to take the throne away from the appointed heir, his brother Solomon, by stealth and intrigue, when trying to effect a coup.

Before we turn to Nathan and Gad who, unlike David, were referred to as prophets (or seers - modern commentators see this as synonymous and it is not the purpose here to split hairs), we need to examine the biblical evidence that David prophesied, and this can be seen in the Psalms. Several Psalms, including those attributed to David, referred to the future Messiah and this interpretation is attested to by New Testament writers when making reference. What the Psalms reveal is someone whose heart is for God and, despite his many faults, which the biblical account does not gloss over, time and time again we find David seeking God's honour and glory. This is a key to understanding God's favour toward David, that remains so even in unfulfilled prophecy.

While we can refer to any number of David's psalms of praise, by way of example, we refer to three David Messianic psalms and their NT references.

Psalm 2 is about the Son and His victory over His enemies that oppose Him

Psalm 2:1-6 - Acts 4:25-26, Revelation 12:1-6

Psalm 2:7 - Matthew 3:17, Acts 13:33

Psalm 2:9 - Revelation 2:9

Psalm 22 may be seen as describing events relating to Jesus' death on the cross.

Psalms 22:1 - Matthew 27:46, Mark 15:34.

Psalms 22:7-8 - Matthew 27:39,43, Luke 23:35.

Psalms 22:18 - Matthew 27:35, Mark 15:24, Luke 23:34, John 19:23-24.

Psalms 22:22 - Hebrews 2:11-12.

Psalm 110 refers to the Melchizedek priesthood, which applied to Jesus:

Psalms 110:1 - Matt 22:44, Mark 12:36, Luke 20:42, Acts 2:34, Hebrews 1:13.

Psalms 110:4 – Hebrews 5:6, Hebrews 6:20, Hebrews 7:17,21.

Other examples of Psalms relating to prophecies of Jesus, referred to in the New Testament, include:

Psalm 8:6 – Ruler of all – Hebrews 2:8;

Psalm 16:10 – rises from death – Matthew 28:7;

Psalm 34:20 – bones unbroken – John 19:32-33, 36;

Psalm 35:19 – hated without cause – John 15:25;

Psalm 40:7-8 – delights in God's Word – Hebrews 10:7;

Psalm 41:9 – betrayed by friend – Luke 22:47;

Psalm 45:6 –the Eternal King – Hebrews 1:8;

Psalm 109:4 – prays for enemies – Luke 23:34.

Nathan

From the Bible account, we know little about Nathan the prophet other than he prophesied in David's reign and was associated with David's court; although there is extra-biblical material that concerns Nathan. What we learn about him is that he faithfully discharged his office. He heard from God and passed on the message to whom it was intended; namely, David, in the first two instances and the third, which we will get to, is more convoluted. He did so without fear or favour and showed extraordinary wisdom. Other than the three instances in which he plays a part, Nathan leaves the scene unobtrusively, without ostentation, as he entered it.

When we first read about Nathan we find: "*And it came to pass, when the king sat in his house, and the Lord had given him rest round about from all his enemies; That the king said unto Nathan the prophet, See now, I dwell in an house of cedar, but the ark of God dwelleth within curtains. And Nathan said to the king, Go, do all that is in thine heart; for the Lord is with thee.*" (2 Samuel 7: 1-3.) But that was not what God wanted: "*And it came to pass that night, that the word of the Lord came unto Nathan, saying ...*" (2 Samuel 7:4).

It is interesting how a prophet, even of Nathan's stature, could change his mind. While it was not God's intention for David to build the Temple (this task would be given to his son, Solomon), it was God's intention to "*stablish the throne of his* (David's) *kingdom for ever*" 2 Samuel 7:13. This Nathan conveyed to David. To David's credit, he accepted this as the word of the Lord, without any dissent and indeed gave glory to God.

The second time Nathan appears is soon after David had lusted after a married woman named Bathsheba. When she became pregnant with his child, he had her husband killed and married her to cover up his sin. However, this sin was not hidden from God. Thus, the Lord sent Nathan to David with a message. Nathan shows much wisdom in confronting David concerning his heinous sin. He does so indirectly, by telling David a story involving two men, a rich man and a poor man. The rich man had a large number of sheep, while the poor man only had one little lamb that he loved dearly and treated like his own child. When a traveller came to the rich man, instead of slaughtering one of his own sheep, the rich man took the poor man's lamb and prepared it for the traveller to eat.

David responded with anger. "*And David's anger was greatly kindled against the man; and he said to Nathan, As the Lord liveth, the man that hath done this thing shall surely die: And he shall restore the lamb fourfold, because he did this thing, and because he had no pity..*" (2 Samuel 12:5-6.) To which Nathan replied, "*Thou art the man!*" (2 Samuel 12:7). David had everything, yet took another man's wife. David repented of this wrongdoing (which he writes about: "*Against thee, thee only, have I sinned, and done this evil in thy sight: that thou mightest be justified when thou speakest, and be clear when thou judgest.*" Psalm 51:4.)

Nathan passes on God's message of forgiveness, even though the consequences of that sin were far reaching. Because of this sin, David's son with Bathsheba died. Nathan later brings another message to David after the birth of Bathsheba's second son, Solomon, telling him of God's love for the child (2 Samuel 12: 25).

The third time Nathan appears is in 1 Kings 1, in David's old age, when David's son Adonijah conspires to take the kingship. Nathan and Bathsheba confront David about the issue, and David declares that Solomon should be made king, as promised. Nathan teams up with, among others, Zadok the priest and some of David's mighty men. They are instrumental in putting down a coup and securing Solomon's kingship, after which Adonijah's cronies disperse.

One wonders what might have been if it were not for Nathan's prompt and wise action. The fourth son (third to live) of Bathsheba happened to be named Nathan. This Nathan is mentioned in Luke's genealogy as an ancestor of Jesus in Luke 3:31. One might imagine that this son was named after the faithful court prophet.

Gad

Gad the seer (or prophet) is first mentioned in 1 Samuel 22:5. He appears out of nowhere as a consultant to David while on the run from Saul. Significantly, Gad counsels David to leave Moab and return to Judah. Gad is not mentioned again until David took the throne as the king of Israel and Gad is named as his seer (2 Samuel 24:11). Unlike David's other counsellors, including Nathan, Gad represented the Lord's counsel and not merely a giver of good advice. He was a man of honour and faithfully spoke the Lord's words to David.

After David had sinned by numbering the troops, the Lord sent Gad to rebuke him and give three options of punishment (2 Samuel 24:11–14). Gad later went back to David to give him the Lord's command about making his sin right through offering a sacrifice (2 Samuel 24:18). Gad remained loyal to David throughout his reign. Gad must have been a young man when he first joined David's band, since he outlived David and wrote a history of his life (1 Chronicles 29:29).

Though rarely mentioned by name, Gad the seer must have played a crucial role in David's success as king. His initial advice, while David was on the run from Saul, not only kept David safe, but it allowed David to build a reputation as a mighty warrior, making him popular with the people (1 Chronicles 12:1–22). But the secret of David's success was not just that he had a heart for God but he was surrounded by wise people who understood God's Word and communicated God's message accurately, like Gad (and Nathan); and, moreover, he listened. Where David excelled, Gad's counsel was right behind him. When David failed, Gad's rebukes and advice quickly followed.

Gad worked in harmony with God's other influential prophet, Nathan (although there is no record of the two ever interacting), to keep David's heart and life pleasing to God and worthy of the throne. It was a formidable partnership: Gad was faithful to his calling and David had the benefit of godly insights needed to fulfil the role God gave him. How we could do with modern day Gads!

More on prophets in David's day

Before moving on from David to prophets associated with the kings that succeeded him, noting many prophets played crucial roles in the reigns of those kings, it is worth reflecting on two texts in the Book of Chronicles and something we do not read in the Bible concerning Nathan and Gad.

Firstly, we are told: "And *he set the Levites in the house of the Lord with cymbals, with psalteries, and with harps, according to the commandment of David, and of Gad the king's seer, and Nathan the prophet: for so was the commandment of the Lord by his prophets*" (2 Chronicles 29:25). The "he" in this case was another descendant of David, Hezekiah, some three hundred years later. Clearly, Nathan and Gad, had impacts more far-reaching than if we just read Samuel and Kings, written from a prophetic perspective, for Chronicles was written from a priestly perspective and emphasised the worship of YHWH, in His Temple.

While we are in Chronicles, which has quite different fixations than the Books of Samuel and Kings, we should reflect a little on David's contribution to the public worship of YHWH, the importance he gave to the Ark of the Covenant, and - even though God did not allow him to do this - his organising, to fine detail, the building of and activities taking place in the Temple. Besides what we read in Psalms, David was above all a worshipper of God, realising all he had was from God and no wonder he was a man after God's own heart. He was merely giving back to God what was rightfully His, a lesson we do well to remember.

We know this to be true because of what we read in Chronicles: "*All this, said David, the Lord made me understand in writing by his hand upon me, even all the works of this pattern. And David said to Solomon his son, Be strong and of good courage, and do it: fear not, nor be dismayed: for the Lord God, even my God, will be with thee; he will not fail thee, nor forsake thee, until thou hast finished all the work for the service of the house of the Lord.*" (1 Chronicles 28: 19-20.)

And regarding the theme of this Book, while it is true that the prophetic writers were preoccupied with how the people should live their lives, it is just as true that God is interested in right worship. Prophecy had many manifestations, yet what was important was God being worshipped.

The second example can almost be seen as an epitaph on the ministries of Nathan and Gad, and an encouragement to us to go and check out more: "*Now the acts of David the king, first and last, behold, they are written in the book of Samuel the seer, and in the book of Nathan the prophet, and in the book of Gad the seer*" (1 Chronicles 29:29). The point of this book is to focus on the Bible but, because context and background are all-important, we must not neglect other sources. The author's understanding is that both books are available to be studied and, while not part of the canon of scripture, provide a fascinating insight into the life of Nathan and Gad, and of David, especially prophetic ones relating to the Messiah.

To complete this section, we note: "*Now the rest of the acts of Solomon, first and last, are they not written in the book of Nathan the prophet, and in the prophecy of Ahijah the Shilonite, and in the visions of Iddo the seer against Jeroboam the son of Nebat?*" (2 Chronicles 9:29), making the point that the prophets provided a service to posterity of telling us what really went on, particularly in the reigns of the kings, and making us aware of what was important in God's eyes.

We are blessed that the Prophets of the Bible were the antithesis to what in modern parlance may be referred to as spin doctors or futurologists. They said whatever it was that needed saying, of how it really was because it was how God saw it, and how things will turn out, because God said it will be so.

Chapter 10: Elijah and Elisha

In the preceding chapters, we considered several prophets; and that would be still true in some cases if we were to take the traditional approach of associating individuals with that role only when their main job was that of a prophet, as being directed by the Lord to speak on behalf of God, notably when concerning the future, who heard and passed on directly messages they received from Him, and what they said would happen, did happen. Yet there is a temptation when thinking about Bible prophets to overlook these and begin with Elijah and Elisha, followed by those that are popularly labelled as the four major and twelve minor prophets.

There is no question though that Elijah and Elisha fitted the bill perfectly when it comes to identifying those who are the prophets of the Bible. They were the quintessential prophets of the Bible. A lot has been written and preached about their ministries, which included prophesying, doing often amazing miracles and having direct contact with the rulers of their day. While we can pick up a lot about their lives, the detail given is still limited. Concerning Elijah and Elisha, there are many lessons, including generic ones, we can learn, and spiritual applications.

Elijah

Elijah appears on the scene without any ado or context provided, other than the spiritually low state of the Northern kingdom and its ungodliness. *"And Elijah the Tishbite, who was of the inhabitants of Gilead, said unto Ahab, As the Lord God of Israel liveth, before whom I stand, there shall not be dew nor rain these years, but according to my word. And the word of the Lord came unto him, saying, Get thee hence, and turn thee eastward, and hide thyself by the brook Cherith, that is before Jordan. And it shall be, that thou shalt drink of the brook; and I have commanded the ravens to feed thee there. So he went and did according unto the word of the Lord: for he went and dwelt by the brook Cherith, that is before Jordan. And the ravens brought him bread and flesh in the morning, and bread and flesh in the evening; and he drank of the brook."* (1 Kings 17:1-6.)

Even from this opening, we learn a lot about Elijah, even though the only thing we are told about his background is that he is a Tishbite; and, as for his calling to the ministry and early life, we know very little. Clearly, he had the ear of the king, Ahab, but we learn elsewhere he was a weak king as well as a wicked one, and was married to someone more wicked than he, Jezebel, who in effect ran things.

We might surmise that the drought Elijah said would happen (and it did) was part of God's judgment. We learn that Elijah was obedient to and trusted in God when it came to confronting the king, which could have been life-threatening, and then following God's instruction where to hide and trusting God to take care of his temporal needs. He gives the impression of someone who is adept at roughing it.

It should be noted that Elijah ministered to the breakaway Northern kingdom. It was sixty years prior to when Ahab came to power that Israel had split into the ten tribes of the North under Jeroboam, and the two tribes (Judah and Benjamin) of the South under Rehoboam. While, as far as Elijah and Elisha goes, our focus is on events to do with the Northern Kingdom, known as Israel, as opposed to the Southern Kingdom, known as Judah, there was some interaction, even though the two kingdoms operated independently, sometimes cooperating; sometimes in conflict. Both, especially Israel, had been turning away from God, notably by practising idolatry; and yet, at least at the time Elijah came on the scene, they were experiencing a measure of prosperity and had been able to keep enemies at a measure of bay. While Ahab and his successors, Ahaziah and Joram, were wicked, the Judah kings, Asa and Jehoshaphat, were comparatively good.

A final point concerns the large number of little-known prophets, especially in the North. Some intersperse with the Elijah story and were his contemporaries. There is little clue of the prophets personally interacting, yet their ministries complemented and were significant. These will be considered in Chapter 11.

Back to the Elijah story, we read how the Cherith brook dried up, and the Lord told him: *"Arise, get thee to Zarephath, which belongeth to Zidon, and dwell there: behold, I have commanded a widow woman there to sustain thee. So he arose and went to Zarephath. And when he came to the gate of the city, behold, the widow woman was there gathering of sticks: and he called to her, and said, Fetch me, I pray thee, a little water in a vessel, that I may drink. And as she was going to fetch it, he called to her, and said, Bring me, I pray thee, a morsel of bread in thine hand."* (1 Kings 17:9-11.)

It happened exactly as God said. It was there he performed two more miracles. The woman was low in spirits and she, with her son, was expecting to die from starvation; and yet the food she had never run out. As for her son, he later died but was brought back to life through the intervention of Elijah, after which she believed in YHWH. Like so much of the Elijah (and Elisha) narratives, lessons can be drawn, but we will resist the temptation to over-elaborate and turn to Elijah going back to the king: "*And it came to pass after many days, that the word of the Lord came to Elijah in the third year, saying, Go, shew thyself unto Ahab; and I will send rain upon the earth. And Elijah went to shew himself unto Ahab. And there was a sore famine in Samaria.*" (1 Kings 18:1,2.)

1 Kings 18 recounts how Elijah met with Obadiah, a trusted servant of King Ahab but one who feared God and had hid one hundred prophets whom Queen Jezebel wanted to kill and, at significant personal risk, from being found out. He was able to set up a meeting between Elijah and the king, and what follows is a remarkable account of how Elijah suggests a contest between himself and the prophets of Baal on the top of Mount Carmel. The proposition was that the God who sends down fire to consume the sacrifice is the true God. The Baal and Asherah prophets had first chance to intreat their gods; and, despite their frantic efforts, failed to do so.

Elijah challenges the people: "*How long will you waver between two opinions? If the Lord is God, follow him; but if Baal is God, follow him…*" (18:21.) Eventually, "*he repaired the altar of the Lord, which had been torn down*" (18:30), before drenching the sacrifice with water so there would be no doubt that what followed would be a miracle. The result was spectacular: "*Then the fire of the Lord fell and burned up the sacrifice, the wood, the stones and the soil, and also licked up the water in the trench. When all the people saw this, they fell prostrate and cried, 'The Lord - he is God! The Lord - he is God!'*" (18:38, 39.)

The net outcome of the contest was that the onlookers believed and put to death the false prophets. After a short tense waiting period, the rain came, according to God's timetable and as Elijah had said it would. This may be seen as one of the highlights of Elijah's career, indeed of any of the prophets. After seeing God work, we might expect Elijah would follow it up by leading a revival. Except Jezebel had other ideas, and Elijah responded to her threat to kill him by running away and showing all the signs of burn out and spiritual depression. If nothing else, it should give us ordinary believers hope. "*…The effectual fervent prayer of a righteous man availeth much. Elias was a man subject to like passions as we are, and he prayed earnestly that it might not rain: and it rained not on the earth by the space of three years and six months. And he prayed again, and the heaven gave rain, and the earth brought forth her fruit.*" (James 5:16-18.)

1 Kings 19 describes Elijah running away, looked after by the angel, and his exchange with God at the holy mountain: "*And, behold, the Lord passed by, and a great and strong wind rent the mountains, and brake in pieces the rocks before the*

Lord; but the Lord was not in the wind: and after the wind an earthquake; but the Lord was not in the earthquake: And after the earthquake a fire; but the Lord was not in the fire: and after the fire a still small voice." (19:11,12.)

From being burned out, feeling he was all alone, wanting to die, and now getting off his chest his complaint, he is given a new commission by the Lord; and while he does not get all the answers, he is granted further insight into His purposes: *"And the Lord said unto him, Go, return on thy way to the wilderness of Damascus: and when thou comest, anoint Hazael to be king over Syria: And Jehu the son of Nimshi shalt thou anoint to be king over Israel: and Elisha the son of Shaphat of Abelmeholah shalt thou anoint to be prophet in thy room. And it shall come to pass, that him that escapeth the sword of Hazael shall Jehu slay: and him that escapeth from the sword of Jehu shall Elisha slay. Yet I have left me seven thousand in Israel, all the knees which have not bowed unto Baal, and every mouth which hath not kissed him."* (19:15-18.)

As for anointing the two kings, this was done by Elijah's successor, Elisha, whom he was to mentor. The fact that God appoints unlikely characters as kings (Hazael of Syria and Jehu of Israel) tells us something about how God chooses, and ought to be an item for praise, as is *"the king's heart is in the hand of the Lord"* Proverbs 21:1. The fact that God uses Elijah to anoint and then to train up his successor, tells us that the work of God does continue, even when a what seemed an irreplaceable legend like Elijah departs from the scene, and He uses unlikely instruments and quite different characters to accomplish His purposes.

Before we go onto Elisha, there are at least two further Elijah stories, involving Naboth and Ahaziah, worth mentioning.

The Naboth story begins: *"And it came to pass after these things, that Naboth the Jezreelite had a vineyard, which was in Jezreel, hard by the palace of Ahab king of Samaria. And Ahab spake unto Naboth, saying, Give me thy vineyard, that I may have it for a garden of herbs, because it is near unto my house: and I will give thee for it a better vineyard than it; or, if it seem good to thee, I will give thee the worth of it in money. And Naboth said to Ahab, The Lord forbid it me, that I should give the inheritance of my fathers unto thee."* (1 Kings 21:1-3.)

This upset Ahab, but Jezebel found a devious way to take the vineyard by force. Naboth and his family fell victims to a trap and were executed based on a false charge. As a result, Ahab was able to take possession of the vineyard. Elijah was told by God what had happened and confronted Ahab, telling him of the inevitability of God's judgment. But there was a twist because Ahab repented, in a measure, and because Ahab repented God showed mercy, although judgment was later to happen with Ahab's family; and all this was revealed to Elijah.

The Ahaziah story begins: *"Then Moab rebelled against Israel after the death of Ahab. And Ahaziah fell down through a lattice in his upper chamber that was in Samaria, and was sick: and he sent messengers, and said unto them, Go, enquire of Baalzebub the god of Ekron whether I shall recover of this disease. But the angel of the Lord said to Elijah the Tishbite, Arise, go up to meet the messengers of the king of Samaria, and say unto them, Is it not because there is not a God in Israel, that ye go to enquire of Baalzebub the god of Ekron? Now therefore thus saith the Lord, thou shalt not come down from that bed on which thou art gone up, but shalt surely die. And Elijah departed."* (2 Kings 1:1-4.)

The king sends out three companies of soldiers to arrest Elijah, and for the first two times fire is sent to consume them at Elijah's word. The third time, the captain, fearful of what might happen to him, asks for mercy and Elijah accompanies him back to the king. Elijah relays the message he gave the first time and the king dies. Like so many of the stories associated with Elijah and Elisha, there is hidden depth of meaning and, among other things we learn here, it is that God is not to be messed with, and neither were his prophets.

It is worth reflecting how esteemed Elijah was, including in the New Testament. Right at the end of the Old Testament we read: *"Behold, I will send you Elijah the prophet before the coming of the great and dreadful day of the Lord: And he shall turn the heart of the fathers to the children, and the heart of the children to their fathers, lest I come and smite the earth with a curse"* (Malachi 4:5-6).

We now turn to the New, specifically Matthew's gospel, where Elias equates to Elijah. The forerunner to Jesus, John the Baptist, was a prophet in the Elijah mould. *"For all the prophets and the law prophesied until John. And if ye will receive it, this is Elias, which was for to come."* (11:13-14.) When Jesus asked who do people say He was, the answer came back: *"And they said, some say that thou art John the Baptist: some, Elias; and others, Jeremias, or one of the prophets"* (16:14). Elijah, with Moses, appeared at Jesus' Transfiguration:

"And, behold, there appeared unto them Moses and Elias talking with him" (17:3). As far as Jesus was concerned: *"But I say unto you, That Elias is come already, and*

they knew him not, but have done unto him whatsoever they listed. Likewise shall also the Son of man suffer of them" (17:12). As Jesus was calling out to His Father as he was dying on the cross, we find that: *"Some of them that stood there, when they heard that, said, This man calleth for Elias"* (27:47).

Which brings us to Elijah's final act as he is whisked away in spectacular fashion. For his final journey, he is accompanied by his prodigy, Elisha, whom he invites to make a final request. Elisha's request is an audacious one but not inappropriate given the circumstances. It was for a double portion of Elijah's spirit, which he is informed will only happen if he sees Elijah taken; which is what happens, as Elijah is taken away (presumably) to heaven in a chariot of fire.

Elisha takes Elijah's cloak, depicting that the succession had been passed to him, and he does his first miracle, to part the waters just as Elijah had done a little earlier, answering the all-important question: *"Where now is the Lord, the God of Elijah?"* 2 Kings 2:14. Other miracles were soon to follow, starting with the healing of bitter waters and barren land, showing God to be the one who heals.

Elisha

Early on, we read of a group of youths coming to mock Elisha because of his bald head, Elisha cursing them in the name of the Lord and them being torn apart by bears. We mention this incident here precisely because it is one that some will have difficulty with. For just as King Ahaziah found he could not mess with Elijah, God's anointed, the people were soon to realise this also applied to Elisha. As for his anointing, this was evident - as we find out from reading on - and also necessary for Elisha's ministry.

"... and Elijah went up by a whirlwind into heaven. And Elisha saw it, and he cried, My father, my father, the chariot of Israel, and the horsemen thereof. And he saw him no more: and he took hold of his own clothes, and rent them in two pieces. He took up also the mantle of Elijah that fell from him, and went back, and stood by the bank of Jordan; And he took the mantle of Elijah that fell from him, and smote the waters, and said, Where is the Lord God of Elijah? and when he also had smitten the waters, they parted hither and thither: and Elisha went over. And when the sons of the prophets which were to view at Jericho saw him, they said, The spirit of Elijah doth rest on Elisha. And they came to meet him, and bowed themselves to the ground before him." (2 Kings 2:11-15.)

While Elijah was a hard act to follow, the work of God had to continue, even though this farmer from a well-to-do family may have been quite different to the one who was once described as *"an hairy man, and girt with a girdle of leather about his loins."* (2 Kings 1:8.) The importance of passing the cloak and mentoring is soon seen. As for having a double portion of Elisha's spirit, who can say it was not so? Someone who has counted the number of Elisha's miracles found the total when totted up was twice as many as Elijah's.

It is nigh impossible to do full justice to Elisha's prolific, varied and impactful ministry, but we will consider the early chapters of 2 Kings, where Elisha features, along with other happenings that were related or not to the ministry of Elisha.

Chapter 3: This is an unusual account when Joram, king of Israel, teams up with Jehoshaphat, king of Judah and the king of Edom, to bring Moab to heel for not paying Israel protection money. It was an awkward situation. Elisha's advice was sought by Joram, at the request of good king Jehoshaphat. While he showed contempt for Joram, he respected Jehoshaphat. He did not have a ready answer and only when the harpist played he got the word of the Lord (a further example of the link between music and prophecy). The outcome was that the triple alliance got a resounding victory, by God's hand and exposed the evil of Edom.

Chapter 4: This contains four fascinating stories which, like so many in the Elisha narrative, provide fertile ground for expository preachers. The first is about an impoverished widow. Elisha tells her to gather as many receptacles as she could get hold of and pour into them the little oil she had. Only when there were no more pots to be had did the oil run out, but at least now she could sell the oil, pay off her debts and support her family. The second involves a wealthy lady that thoughtfully made available a room in her house for Elijah to stay in. The one thing she wanted was a son and Elisha prayed and she got her son, who later died but was brought back to life by Elisha's prayer. The third involves death in the pot when unwittingly the meal being prepared contained something poisonous: *"But he said, then bring meal. And he cast it into the pot; and he said, pour out for the people, that they may eat. And there was no harm in the pot."* (4:41.) The fourth might be seen as the OT equivalent of the feeding of the five thousand.

Chapter 5: This tells one of the well recounted stories of the Bible told to children, and involves Naaman, the Syrian general and his being cured from his leprosy at the word of Elisha. If nothing else, it revealed to this pagan man something of the power of YHWH. Elisha accepted no reward when it was offered, as he wanted to give God all the glory. His servant, Gehazi, had other ideas, and saw a chance for enrichment. As a result of his duplicitous efforts that Elisha clearly saw because God revealed it, that leprosy came upon him.

Chapter 6: We are reminded here of such a thing as schools of prophets, and it would seem Elisha was their principal. The strange tale involved constructing a new building to accommodate the students and a borrowed axe falling into the water, but at Elisha's word was made to float and thereby could be recovered.

Then comes a story of the King of Syria, now at war with Israel, sending his men to capture Elisha. He had got wind that Elisha knew of his plans to attack Israel and, by warning the King of Israel, they (Israel) were able to fend off the attacks. Not only were Elisha's prophetic insights quite something (we could do with someone like that today!) but when the army detachment came to surround Elisha's house with the view to taking him, while that was all his servant could see, Elisha could also see a heavenly army and at his word the Syrians' eyes were blinded. Then came the rather bizarre spectacle of them being tricked and led off by Elisha into the city of Samaria, making them easy targets; but instead, under Elisha's command, they were given food and let go, after which the raids stopped.

The rest of the chapter is devoted to an account of a severe famine in Samaria as a result of a Syrian siege, with things getting desperate for the inhabitants, and the king of Israel venting his anger toward Elisha and wanting to kill him.

Chapter 7: Here we see the resolution to the siege story begun in the previous chapter. The siege was lifted as Elisha said it would, and the city spared; while in the panic when people from the city sought to take spoils from the Syrian camp, now vacated because of a rumour, the messenger who had been sent to take Elisha was trampled underfoot, just as Elisha predicted. Strange story, and make of it what you will. God is not mocked. He judges and He has mercy; and while the king wanted to kill Elisha the messenger, it was the messenger that knew what was happening, why it was happening and what would happen next.

Chapter 8: Here we see Elisha showing kindness to the woman who had earlier shown kindness to him, by warning of a famine to come; and when she returned, she intreated the king to restore her property to her. We read of his encounter with Hazael, the one Elijah had been told by God many years earlier to anoint as king. Again, a strange meeting as Elisha tells him that the king, whose health he was sent to enquire about of the prophet, would die and he would replace him; and, moreover, breaks down weeping, telling Hazael how he would inflict cruelty on the Israelites. Hazael goes back, kills the king, and becomes king in his place. The rest of the chapter is about Judah and does not involve Elisha.

Chapter 9: Interesting, but Elisha is not mentioned other than giving a young prophet the job of anointing Jehu (as Elijah had been told). Jehu begins the job of "cleaning the house" as per God's command, and it was the end of Jezebel.

Chapter 10: Interesting, but Elisha is not mentioned. However, we are given details of how Jehu was God's instrument in undoing Ahab's legacy, although the tragedy was that despite being God's anointed, he created his own awful legacy, which reading on we find God pouring out judgment over.

Chapter 11: Interesting, but Elisha is not mentioned.

Chapter 12: Interesting, but Elisha is not mentioned.

Chapter 13: King Jehoahaz took over from Jehu. "*And he did that which was evil in the sight of the Lord, and followed the sins of Jeroboam the son of Nebat, which made Israel to sin; he departed not there from. And the anger of the Lord was kindled against Israel, and he delivered them into the hand of Hazael king of Syria, and into the hand of Benhadad the son of Hazael, all their days.*" (2, 3.)

We were reminded in 2 Kings 8 that Hazael was to be anointed king even though he would oppress the Israelites, but then only as far as God allowed and with the purpose of getting His people to return to Him. This clearly had an effect because "*Jehoahaz besought the Lord, and the Lord hearkened unto him: for he saw the oppression of Israel, because the king of Syria oppressed them*" (2 Kings 13:4).

And later in the chapter we come to the last recorded act of Elisha, which concerned Jehoahaz son, Jehoash, who came to visit and pay his respects to Elisha as he lay sick and soon to die. The king shared his concerns over national security and, as was his custom, Elisha told him to do something strange.

"*And Elisha said unto him, Take bow and arrows. And he took unto him bow and arrows. And he said to the king of Israel, Put thine hand upon the bow. And he put his hand upon it: and Elisha put his hands upon the king's hands. And he said, Open the window eastward. And he opened it. Then Elisha said, Shoot. And he shot. And he said, the arrow of the Lord's deliverance, and the arrow of deliverance from*

Syria: for thou shalt smite the Syrians in Aphek, till thou have consumed them. And he said, Take the arrows. And he took them. And he said unto the king of Israel, Smite upon the ground. And he smote thrice, and stayed. And the man of God was wroth with him, and said, Thou shouldest have smitten five or six times; then hadst thou smitten Syria till thou hadst consumed it: whereas now thou shalt smite Syria but thrice. And Elisha died, and they buried him..." (13:15-20.)

It is interesting to note Elisha's prophecy changed, triggered by the king's lack lustre response. Therein lies a lesson, we see repeated later, and which might help us better understand the ways of God for our own day. God can be negotiated with and, while he is not like fickle man when it comes to changing minds, He can be persuaded to act differently according to how we are to respond.

While he did not have a spectacular exit like Elijah, the aftermath was no less impressive. We read "*And it came to pass, as they were burying a man, that, behold, they spied a band of men; and they cast the man into the sepulchre of Elisha: and when the man was let down, and touched the bones of Elisha, he revived, and stood up on his feet*" (13:21). And life went on, including oppression by Hazael but with limited respite, according to Elisha's final prophecy. It is worth recalling that it was Hazael that God had told Elijah to anoint, back in 1 Kings 19:17, and as strange as it may seem, given the oppressing, he was God's choice.

Applying lessons

The principles underlying the ministries of Elijah and Elisha can be universally applied. In days when details of Old Testament characters were taught with a view to finding out lessons we can learn, Elijah and Elisha might well have featured high on the list. Before going to the next chapter, talking about the prophets we have missed so far, and then concerning the four major and twelve minor prophets, of which the Bible record has much to say, let us pause and reflect on the lessons we have learned thus far, specifically on Elijah and Elisha.

What is all too clear is as remarkable as these two were, they were ordinary men (besides Elijah's foibles, we should recall that Elisha too, like many of the prophets, was also a reluctant prophet). They were contrasting characters, evident to the fact God uses willing vessels irrespective of conforming to a particular type. One is struck by the powerful miracles performed by each and the pin point accuracy of their prophecies. Yet Elijah and Elisha were merely the Lord's messengers whom He had powerfully anointed and equipped to speak truth to those in power and to guide and encourage the people in His ways (something, considering our own times, we might well see the benefit of), and they were faithful in carrying out the job God gave them to do, without fear or favour.

But the work of the Lord continues and new instruments for doing His will are raised up to do the work (including you and me), a work that continues to this day.

Chapter 11: Unnamed, unknown and less known prophets

In this chapter, we go through the Bible with a fine-tooth comb to find *all* of those that conform to the loose criteria we identified in Chapter 1 when defining what makes a prophet, who are *not* covered in the other chapters. One thing this exercise reveals is how all-pervading the prophetic ministry was.

By way of a checklist, but not one we have to agree with since it is not part of the Canon of the Word of God, the Talmud identifies forty-eight Old Testament prophets: Abraham, Isaac, Jacob, Moses, Aaron, Joshua, Phineas, Elkanah*, Eli*, Samuel, Gad, Nathan, David, Solomon, Iddo, Micaiah, Obadiah, Ahijah, Jehu, Azariah, Jahaziel, Eliezer, Hosea, Amos, Micah, Amoz*, Elijah, Elisha, Jonah, Isaiah, Joel, Nahum, Habakkuk, Zephaniah, Urijah, Jeremiah, Ezekiel, Shemaiah, Baruch, Neriah*, Seraiah*, Mehseiah*, Haggai, Zechariah, Malachi, Mordecai, Oded, Hanani. Without wanting to take issue with the Talmud, all, except for the ones marked with an asterisk (*), are referred to in this book as having a prophetic ministry of some sort.

There are others not named in the Talmud that we will argue in this book were prophets, including schools of prophets, such as operated in the days of Elijah and Elisha, or odd visitations to groups not necessarily seen as prophets. The Talmud names seven prophetesses: Sarah, Miriam, Deborah, Hannah, Abigail, Huldah, Esther, who are covered in Chapter 6.

Then there were those who had a perhaps unlikely prophetic ministry, even though not typically regarded as prophets, which we will consider at the end of the chapter. In this chapter, we will consider those Old Testament "prophets" that are not covered in the other chapters of this book, in the order (broadly) they appear in the Christian Bible, noting the Talmud lists the prophets in the order given in the Hebrew Bible. It should be added there were also false prophets, as covered in Chapter 7. The ideal intention is, by the end of this book, as far as the Old Testament goes certainly, to cover all the prophets and some that prophesied, although the final list could be disputed – not such a problem, as the intention is for our understanding of the ministry of the Bible prophets to be enhanced.

The New Testament is a challenge as few prophets can be identified, yet the gift of prophecy was widespread in the Church and the office of "Prophet" was one of five that were identified. As far as our book is concerned, the focus is on the message, the ministry, the man and the context, although to trump all that there is the Lord

Himself, and it is Him who should be our main focus.

The prophets listed in this chapter are not well known or well covered. What matters, as far as the Bible is concerned, was their message. While we may know very little about them, and often they entered some scene or other without fuss, did their significant bit and exited, never to be heard of again, the outstanding common factor was that they heard directly from God and faithfully did what God had told them to do. Moreover, we see in these accounts how precisely the words of prophecy were fulfilled and the seriousness of obedience to God.

As for the stories of these prophets, some are full of content and we know a lot about (at least what they said and why), like Micaiah; but with some just a few words are recorded, yet these should be seen as significant. It is likely there were prophets not identified or named, other than by statements like: *"Yet the Lord testified against Israel, and against Judah, by all the prophets, and by all the seers, saying, Turn ye from your evil ways, and keep my commandments and my statutes, according to all the law which I commanded your fathers, and which I sent to you by my servants the prophets"* (2 Kings 17:13).

Unnamed prophet (1)
Judges 6:8

"That the Lord sent a prophet unto the children of Israel, which said unto them, Thus saith the Lord God of Israel, I brought you up from Egypt, and brought you forth out of the house of bondage."

It is noteworthy that a number of the prophets referred to in this chapter are not given a name. The reason is simple: as far as the author in the biblical narrative relating their words and actions were concerned, what was important was just that, and their names were omitted. Our first unnamed prophet appeared a little prior to Gideon, one of the judges that delivered Israel from bondage, and was discussed in Chapter 8. He typified how God would send prophets at the right time, often when the hearers of their message were in danger or suffering in some way, to warn them of the errors of their ways or what they should do.

Unnamed prophet (2)
1 Samuel 2:27-29

"And there came a man of God unto Eli, and said unto him, Thus saith the Lord, Did

I plainly appear unto the house of thy father, when they were in Egypt in Pharaoh's house? And did I choose him out of all the tribes of Israel to be my priest, to offer upon mine altar, to burn incense, to wear an ephod before me? and did I give unto the house of thy father all the offerings made by fire of the children of Israel? Wherefore kick ye at my sacrifice and at mine offering, which I have commanded in my habitation; and honourest thy sons above me, to make yourselves fat with the chiefest of all the offerings of Israel my people?"

Going back to Chapter 8, it would be easy to think that Samuel was the only prophet around at the time. But before the boy Samuel heard God speak to him, including concerning Eli and his house, Eli had already been warned but did not respond. When Samuel later reinforced that message, it came as no surprise to Eli.

Ahijah
1 Kings 11:29

"*And it came to pass at that time when Jeroboam went out of Jerusalem, that the prophet Ahijah the Shilonite found him in the way; and he had clad himself with a new garment; and they two were alone in the field...*"

1 Kings 14:2

"*And Jeroboam said to his wife, Arise, I pray thee, and disguise thyself, that thou be not known to be the wife of Jeroboam; and get thee to Shiloh: behold, there is Ahijah the prophet, which told me that I should be king over this people.*"

1 Kings 14:18

"*And they buried him; and all Israel mourned for him, according to the word of the Lord, which he spake by the hand of his servant Ahijah the prophet.*"

2 Chronicles 9:29

"*Now the rest of the acts of Solomon, first and last, are they not written in the book of Nathan the prophet, and in the prophecy of Ahijah the Shilonite, and in the visions of Iddo the seer against Jeroboam the son of Nebat?*"

Ahijah appears twice on the scene to give words of prophecy. The first was before Jeroboam became king, when Ahijah told him he would take ten of the tribes. The second was years later, after what could have been a promising reign which had turned bad because of Jeroboam's idolatry. The message Ahijah gave that was fulfilled was the kingdom would be taken from him and that his son would die.

Shemaiah
1 Kings 12:22-24

"But the word of God came unto Shemaiah the man of God, saying, speak unto Rehoboam, the son of Solomon, king of Judah, and unto all the house of Judah and Benjamin, and to the remnant of the people, saying, thus saith the Lord, Ye shall not go up, nor fight against your brethren the children of Israel: return every man to his house; for this thing is from me. They hearkened therefore to the word of the Lord, and returned to depart, according to the word of the Lord."

2 Chronicles 12:5

"Then came Shemaiah the prophet to Rehoboam, and to the princes of Judah, that were gathered together to Jerusalem because of Shishak, and said unto them, Thus saith the Lord, Ye have forsaken me, and therefore have I also left you in the hand of Shishak."

When Jeroboam broke away from Rehoboam, who prior to that was king over all twelve tribes, it was understandable that Rehoboam would want to prevent this, and if need be at the cost of a bloody civil war. But he needed to be reminded that this breakaway was part of God's will and that his going to war was not. Shemaiah, who we know little else about other than the elaboration we read about in Chronicles, was sent by God merely to convey this message.

Unnamed prophet (3)
1 Kings 13:1-3

"And, behold, there came a man of God out of Judah by the word of the Lord unto Bethel: and Jeroboam stood by the altar to burn incense. And he cried against the altar in the word of the Lord, and said, O altar, altar, thus saith the Lord; Behold, a child shall be born unto the house of David, Josiah by name; and upon thee shall he offer the priests of the high places that burn incense upon thee, and men's bones shall be burnt upon thee. And he gave a sign the same day, saying, This is the sign which the Lord hath spoken; Behold, the altar shall be rent, and the ashes that are upon it shall be poured out."

The words of this unknown prophet came to pass, even those regarding Josiah (who he actually named) centuries later. God's hand was on the man even when the king tried to strike him and his hand withered. But there was a tragic end when this prophet was convinced by another, old prophet, to go with him for refreshment, when God had told him to return to Judah. He was tragically attacked and killed by a lion, which was God's punishment for his disobedience, much to the sorrow of the old prophet who buried him in his tomb. A strange story but with a twist when, under Josiah, the tomb in which he was buried was identified; and unlike in the cleaning-up exercise when bones of false prophets were burned, these were left alone. It is an amazing example how prophecies could be fulfilled centuries later and while this unknown prophet met an untimely end due to his foolishness, he would later be honoured. One is reminded God does not forget.

Hanani
2 Chronicles 16:7

"And at that time Hanani the seer came to Asa king of Judah, and said unto him, Because thou hast relied on the king of Syria, and not relied on the Lord thy God, therefore is the host of the king of Syria escaped out of thine hand."

The tragedy was King Asa did what many kings, even good kings, did before and after, in entering into an unwholesome alliance with an ungodly power. What was more tragic was that he had previously relied on the Lord to deliver Judah when oppressed by an enemy. Part of God's judgment was that from henceforth he would have wars. Sadly, rather than accept the rebuke, he imprisoned Hanani and began to oppress the people. In later life Asa succumbed to an illness and sought help in physicians but not, as he should have done, from the Lord.

Jehu
1 Kings 16:1-4

"Then the word of the Lord came to Jehu the son of Hanani against Baasha, saying, Forasmuch as I exalted thee out of the dust, and made thee prince over my people Israel; and thou hast walked in the way of Jeroboam, and hast made my people Israel to sin, to provoke me to anger with their sins; Behold, I will take away the posterity of Baasha, and the posterity of his house; and will make thy house like the house of Jeroboam the son of Nebat. Him that dieth of Baasha in the city shall the dogs eat; and him that dieth of his in the fields shall the fowls of the air eat."

2 Chronicles 19:1-2

"And Jehoshaphat the king of Judah returned to his house in peace to Jerusalem. And Jehu the son of Hanani the seer went out to meet him, and said to king Jehoshaphat, Shouldest thou help the ungodly, and love them that hate the Lord? therefore is wrath upon thee from before the Lord."

This hard-hitting message to King Baasha could have been all that we knew about Jehu the prophet, except later he has to rebuke good King Jehoshaphat for his unholy alliance with Ahab. The significance was that everything he prophesied came to pass, whether for the king of Israel or the king of Judah. Also significant is that Baasha was God's choice as king., Consider what might have been! And, as for Jehoshaphat, while God recognised the good that he had done, there was a price to be paid. Sadly, the record is that both kings' legacies were marred.

Unnamed prophet (4)
1 Kings 20:13, 22

"And, behold, there came a prophet unto Ahab king of Israel, saying, Thus saith the Lord, Hast thou seen all this great multitude? behold, I will deliver it into thine hand this day; and thou shalt know that I am the Lord... And the prophet came to the king of Israel, and said unto him, Go, strengthen thyself, and mark, and see what thou doest: for at the return of the year the king of Syria will come up against thee."

1 Kings 20:35, 38, 42

"And a certain man of the sons of the prophets said unto his neighbour in the word of the Lord, Smite me, I pray thee. And the man refused to smite him... So the prophet departed, and waited for the king by the way, and disguised himself with ashes upon his face... And he said unto him, Thus saith the Lord, Because thou hast let go out of thy hand a man whom I appointed to utter destruction, therefore thy life shall go for his life, and thy people for his people."

It is possible that there are two prophets mentioned in this chapter, the first to tell king Ahab that he would gain victory over this Syrian oppressor. The second rebuked Ahab, in this strange way, for his leniency to the Syrian king.

Micaiah
1 Kings 22:6-8

"Then the king of Israel gathered the prophets together, about four hundred men, and said unto them, Shall I go against Ramoth-gilead to battle, or shall I forbear? And they said, Go up; for the Lord shall deliver it into the hand of the king. And Jehoshaphat said, is there not here a prophet of the Lord besides, that we might enquire of him? And the king of Israel said unto Jehoshaphat, there is yet one man, Micaiah the son of Imlah, by whom we may enquire of the Lord: but I hate him; for he doth not prophesy good concerning me, but evil. And Jehoshaphat said, let not the king say so."

The scenario was that Ahab, the bad king of Israel, in alliance with Jehoshaphat, the good king of Judah, wanted to go to war against Syria but wanted divine affirmation that this was the right thing to do. Four hundred (false) prophets confirmed this to be the case. But there was one prophet, Micaiah, that went against the consensus and bravely warned the two kings of the disastrous consequences if they were to go to war. For his pains, Micaiah was struck and put in prison, but what happened after was what he said would happen. Sadly, the scenario of world leaders surrounding themselves with "yes" men is ever the case. Thankfully, good King Jehoshaphat asked the right question and Micaiah was ready to put aside popularity and personal safety to give the right answer.

Unnamed prophet (5)
2 Kings 9:1-3

"And Elisha the prophet called one of the children of the prophets, and said unto him, Gird up thy loins, and take this box of oil in thine hand, and go to Ramoth-gilead: And when thou comest thither, look out there Jehu the son of Jehoshaphat the son of Nimshi, and go in, and make him arise up from among his brethren, and carry him to an inner chamber; Then take the box of oil, and pour it on his head, and say, Thus saith the Lord, I have anointed thee king over Israel. Then open the door, and flee, and tarry not."

There is nothing remarkable it might seem about this young man doing what God originally told Elijah to do. He simply did what Elisha told him and Jehu became king. Yet we note his sheer courage. After anointing Jehu, he fled as he had been commanded. It was a great honour for this fledgling to anoint the new king and was no small task. It was effectively to initiate a coup against the House of Ahab.

Sons of Asaph
1 Chronicles 25:1

"Moreover David and the captains of the host separated to the service of the sons of Asaph, and of Heman, and of Jeduthun, who should prophesy with harps, with psalteries, and with cymbals: and the number of the workmen according to their service was..."

What is remarkable in this unusual text, which is to do with commissioning those for the service of worshipping the Lord, is the link between prophecy and music; something we have already seen in the ministries of Miriam and Elisha. In the verses that followed, there would seem to have been several musical prophets.

Iddo
2 Chronicles 9:29

"Now the rest of the acts of Solomon, first and last, are they not written in the book of Nathan the prophet, and in the prophecy of Ahijah the Shilonite, and in the visions of Iddo the seer against Jeroboam the son of Nebat?"

2 Chronicles 12:15

"Now the acts of Rehoboam, first and last, are they not written in the book of Shemaiah the prophet, and of Iddo the seer concerning genealogies? And there were wars between Rehoboam and Jeroboam continually."

The only thing we know about Iddo from the Bible account is that he was a seer (another name for a prophet); he had visions and he recorded genealogies.

Azariah
2 Chronicles 15:1

"And the Spirit of God came upon Azariah the son of Oded:"

Following the Spirit of God coming upon him, Azariah goes to meet King Asa of Judah to exhort him to carry out a work of reform. In response to Azariah's encouragement, Asa carried out a number of reforms, including the destruction of idols, and repairs to the altar of Yahweh in the Jerusalem Temple complex. A period of peace follows the carrying out of these reforms.

Eliezer
2 Chronicles 20:37

"Then Eliezer the son of Dodavah of Mareshah prophesied against Jehoshaphat, saying, Because thou hast joined thyself with Ahaziah, the Lord hath broken thy works. And the ships were broken, that they were not able to go to Tarshish."

Jehoshaphat was a good king, but here he had acted unwisely by making an alliance with the wicked king of Israel. Eliezer merely tells Jehoshaphat of God's displeasure and the consequences of his actions, which came to pass. It is ironic that another prophet (Jehu) had also passed on a similar rebuke to Jehoshaphat for making another unholy alliance with Ahaziah's predecessor as king of Israel (Ahab). Sadly, we learn that people do not learn and yet God continues to warn.

Unnamed prophet (6)
2 Chronicles 25:15-16

"Wherefore the anger of the Lord was kindled against Amaziah, and he sent unto him a prophet, which said unto him, why hast thou sought after the gods of the people, which could not deliver their own people out of thine hand? And it came to pass, as he talked with him, that the king said unto him, Art thou made of the king's counsel? forbear; why shouldest thou be smitten? Then the prophet forbare, and said, I know that God hath determined to destroy thee, because thou hast done this, and hast not hearkened unto my counsel."

Amaziah began as a righteous king but later turned to idols. The unnamed prophet was merely taking the king to task as directed by the Lord, but was told in no uncertain terms to shut up or else. This would have been a good chance for the king to repent rather than, as did happen, incur God's judgement.

Oded
2 Chronicles 28:9

"But a prophet of the Lord was there, whose name was Oded: and he went out before the host that came to Samaria, and said unto them, Behold, because the Lord God of your fathers was wroth with Judah, he hath delivered them into your hand, and ye have slain them in a rage that reacheth up unto heaven."

This unusual message from the Lord came at a time when Israel had won a victory in a war against Judah, but were told to have mercy on their captives.

Mordecai
Esther 2:5-7

"Now in Shushan the palace there was a certain Jew, whose name was Mordecai, the son of Jair, the son of Shimei, the son of Kish, a Benjamite; who had been carried away from Jerusalem with the captivity which had been carried away with Jeconiah king of Judah, whom Nebuchadnezzar the king of Babylon had carried away. And he brought up Hadassah, that is, Esther, his uncle's daughter: for she had neither father nor mother, and the maid was fair and beautiful; whom Mordecai, when her father and mother were dead, took for his own daughter."

In Chapter 7, we made a case for Esther being a prophetess. What Esther achieved was remarkable; and it would not be overstating the case that her actions saved the Jewish people, scattered as they were throughout the Persian empire, from complete annihilation. But it is unlikely that any of this would have been possible without the quick-wittedness and wise counsel of her uncle Mordecai, who understood the dangers and remedies.

From nearly losing his life, through his faithfulness and fortitude and wise actions, and God's overruling (although God is never mentioned), we find in the end he was exalted to high position: *"All the acts of his power and of his might, and the declaration of the greatness of Mordecai, whereunto the king advanced him, are they not written in the book of the chronicles of the kings of Media and Persia? For Mordecai the Jew was next unto king Ahasuerus, and great among the Jews, and accepted of the multitude of his brethren, seeking the wealth of his people, and speaking peace to all his seed."* (Esther 10:2-3.)

Urijah
Jeremiah 26:20-21, 23

"And there was also a man that prophesied in the name of the Lord, Urijah the son of Shemaiah of Kirjathjearim, who prophesied against this city and against this land according to all the words of Jeremiah. And when Jehoiakim the king, with all his mighty men, and all the princes, heard his words, the king sought to put him to death: but when Urijah heard it, he was afraid, and fled, and went into Egypt... And they fetched forth Urijah out of Egypt, and brought him unto Jehoiakim the king; who slew him with the sword, and cast his dead body into the graves of the common people."

Urijah was a contemporary of Jeremiah who reiterated the words of Jeremiah regarding God's judgment on the city. This displeased the king, just as Jeremiah's message had, but for Urijah it was a death sentence. We know nothing about Urijah other than his prophesy and his ending. While the outcome for the king and the city was disastrous, they had at least been warned. It begs the question when we see wrongdoing, how we respond and if we are prepared for the consequences of speaking truth to those in power, which may be at the cost of our very lives.

Baruch
Jeremiah 45:1-2

"The word that Jeremiah the prophet spake unto Baruch the son of Neriah, when he had written these words in a book at the mouth of Jeremiah, in the fourth year of Jehoiakim the son of Josiah king of Judah, saying, Thus saith the Lord, the God of Israel, unto thee, O Baruch..."

Baruch is mentioned several times in the Book of Jeremiah, and was in effect his right-hand man, messenger, scribe and personal assistant. While there is no evidence of him being a prophet in his own right, there is little doubt Jeremiah would not have been able to do what he did without the help of his faithful assistant. Baruch's role was not to seek the limelight but rather to do what was needed, with due diligence, without ostentation. How Jeremiah would have appreciated his support. How much we need backroom boys like Baruch today!

Prophets who are not recognised as prophets

Having gone through with a fine-tooth comb those who might qualify as being a prophet (or seer), in a commonly held understanding, we turn to examples of those who through words or actions said or did things that arguably may be seen as prophetic. While the Talmud identifies Solomon as a prophet, the same cannot be said for the others in the list below, which includes two pagan kings. The five names given here are by no means an exhaustive list, for the Bible provides many examples of deeds done and words said by those not regarded as prophets, that were arguably prophetic, to be received by those with receptive hearts. What happened may have significance for millennia after and be seen as prophetic because, while not necessarily predicting future events, these were able to reveal something of God's purposes to those whose lives they touched.

Job

Job is definitely one of the Bible good guys. Ezekiel names him as one of the three most righteous men to have lived – the others being Noah and Daniel. The patience of Job is legendary, and while his story does not fully answer the big question that has baffled great minds down the ages – why do the righteous suffer, especially considering God is just, etc.? – we can at least see in his story the bigger picture and an approach that works. If one were to quote a text that would endorse Job's prophetic credentials, especially as there is little in the scriptures prior to Job to endorse such a view, it is this: *"For I know that my redeemer liveth, and that he shall stand at the latter day upon the earth"* (Job 19:25).

Perhaps one of the most poignant of Job's utterances comes at the end of the book, after the Lord reveals himself to Job: *"Then Job answered the Lord, and said, I know that thou canst do every thing, and that no thought can be withholden from thee. Who is he that hideth counsel without knowledge? therefore have I uttered that I understood not; things too wonderful for me, which I knew not. Hear, I beseech thee, and I will speak: I will demand of thee, and declare thou unto me. I have heard of thee by the hearing of the ear: but now mine eye seeth thee. Wherefore I abhor myself, and repent in dust and ashes."* (Job 42:1-6.)

Solomon

Solomon started off as one of the Bible good guys; but, among other things, his foreign wives later helped lead him astray and sow the seeds for Israel's demise. When he began, he asked God at God's invitation that he would get wisdom and understanding to govern the people aright. Being pleased with this, God gave Solomon just that, and in addition peace and prosperity. Solomon is an example of someone who began well and was guided by God in his rule, but ended badly because he turned away from God. Maybe at the end of his he saw the errors of his ways, when he reflected in Ecclesiastes that so much in life is vanity and *"Let us hear the conclusion of the whole matter: Fear God, and keep his commandments: for this is the whole duty of man. For God shall bring every work into judgment, with every secret thing, whether it be good, or whether it be evil."* (12:13,14) but some of that legacy, we can now look back on, was damaging.

Evidence of Solomon's wisdom can be seen in the three Books of the Bible it is believed that he wrote: Proverbs, Ecclesiastes and Song of Solomon. Proverbs 8 is about wisdom and may be seen as a veiled reference to Christ, and therefore prophetic. While pundits down the ages have argued as to the interpretation of Solomon's Song of Songs, one which the author broadly supports and has written concerning, is that it depicts the sort of relationship that can be enjoyed between Christ and His Church, and is to be sought after. It could be argued that the Song is more than just about sexual ethics; it is also prophetic insofar as it looks forward to the time when the Church is finally married to Christ.

Nehemiah

There is nothing in what Nehemiah said that would mark him out as a prophet, and he does not even get mentioned in the New Testament; although from his prayers he showed deep insights into the prophetic and God's will. As we now rapidly approach the end of the Old Testament, it is with mixed emotions. Israel was far from where it expected to be in God's purposes, along with the promise of its Messiah, and that remains true two thousand, five hundred years later.

Yet his efforts as recorded in the Book of Nehemiah, when it comes to building the wall, restoring the true worship of YHWH, undertaking much needed social reforms, withstanding opposition, and his prayers (chapters 1 and 9) were remarkable concerning his understanding of the ways of God. While his efforts might be deemed moderately successful, his oft prayed prayer, "*Remember me, O my God, concerning this*" (13:14, etc.), is strangely poignant, considering what was to come, which like any OT prophetic character, he had only a glimpse.

Nebuchadnezzar

In his day, Nebuchadnezzar might be regarded as the most powerful man on earth, and in whose hands lay the fate of the Jewish people. He could not be regarded as particularly benevolent, although he did treat those Jews who had been exiled, like Daniel and his three friends: Shadrach, Meshach and Abednego, well and he recognised Daniel as a true prophet when he interpreted his dream. But he was also cruel and proud, as evidenced by his building a statute of himself that people had to worship or else face death, as happened with the three friends.

Yet, as he was to find out, God humbles the proud and exalts the humble. When he was restored, he could say: "*Now I Nebuchadnezzar praise and extol and honour the King of heaven, all whose works are truth, and his ways judgment: and those that walk in pride he is able to abase*" (Daniel 4:37). As for going from being a mighty king to a madman, and then once again restored, this was all God's doing, and his recognition of this would have had a profound effect. For those who heard those words, without knowing the Hebrew scriptures, it would have come across as prophetic, and may have helped turn the course of history.

Cyrus

One of the recurring wonders one finds studying the scriptures is seeing how God can use the most unlikely rulers (kings) to accomplish His purposes. Nowhere is this more evident than with the ruler of the Persian empire, Cyrus, who had the lives and future of his Jewish subjects in his hands. The very last verse of the Hebrew Bible says: *"Thus saith Cyrus king of Persia, All the kingdoms of the earth hath the Lord God of heaven given me; and he hath charged me to build him an house in Jerusalem, which is in Judah. Who is there among you of all his people? The Lord his God be with him, and let him go up."* (2 Chronicles 36:23.)

As for significance, it is that despite exile there was a future (Messianic) hope for Israel. This is the same Cyrus Isaiah prophesied of, two hundred years before the event: *"Thus saith the Lord to his anointed, to Cyrus, whose right hand I have holden, to subdue nations before him; and I will loose the loins of kings, to open before him the two leaved gates; and the gates shall not be shut"* (Isaiah 45:1). Cyrus played an important part in the story of Israel, along with its preservation and restoration, and whether or not he understood all the implications of what he had decreed and facilitated, he was used by God, just as was the case of other Persian kings: Darius the Mede, Darius 1 and Artaxerxes, as referred to in the books of Daniel, Ezra, Esther and Nehemiah. It should serve to encourage that God appointed kings, often not likely candidates in human terms, to bring about His purposes, which in this case concerned His specially chosen people, Israel.

Chapter 12: The major prophets (Isaiah to Daniel)

Overview

We come to the final set of recognised prophets in the Old Testament. Arguably, as far as many are concerned (but not this author), besides Elijah and Elisha (and perhaps Moses and Samuel), most mentioned thus far did not write down what they prophesied, these were the most significant of Bible prophets and, possibly with the exception of Daniel, are indisputably prophets since that was their main job that nigh everyone recognised. These comprise four major prophets (Isaiah, Jeremiah, Ezekiel, Daniel) and twelve minor prophets (Hosea, Joel, Amos, Obadiah, Jonah, Micah, Nahum, Habakkuk, Zephaniah, Haggai, Zechariah, Malachi). Key events during the period they wrote include the captivity of Israel by the Assyrians (around 722 BC) and Judah by the Babylonians (around 608 BC). Between them they wrote before, during and after the Exiles. In the case of most, they looked forward to a, yet to be realised, Messianic Kingdom.

Without exception, our sixteen prophets prophesied what the Lord told them to prophesy. If Amos was right (and he has to be) that *"the Lord God will do nothing, but he revealeth his secret unto his servants the prophets"* (Amos 3:7), then it was a serious business and what the prophets prophesied was important. Not that this was always recognised at the time, and often their message was rejected and the prophets made to suffer. Isaiah was told by God at the start that people would not hear him; and, while he had some intermediate success, his ending, if the Jewish historian Josephus was right, meant he got sawn in half at the command of wicked King Mannaseh. Jeremiah was not allowed to marry, in order to illustrate how God now viewed His relationship with Israel, and was once thrown into a slurry pit and left to die; Ezekiel had to perform all sorts of humiliating antics to put his message across; and Daniel was thrown into a lion's den – and that was just the major prophets! While able to listen in directly to the Lord, the job of being a prophet (as we have already seen) was not an enviable one. It is not a job that truly God-fearing types would volunteer for and instead need to be asked by the boss. While we may want to elevate a prophet, they simply acted as God's mouthpiece.

The use of "major" and "minor" is perhaps unfortunate, because all of these prophets made major contributions. Unlike Elijah and Elisha, these prophets are sometimes referred to as the writing prophets, because they wrote down what they prophesied. They are classified thus because the majors wrote a lot more than the minors, although there was a lot of repetition and variations on a theme.

As far as this book is concerned, this chapter deals with the major prophets and the next chapter deals with the minor prophets. We will take each prophet in the order they appear in the Christian Bible, which is not necessarily chronological order, although it was for the majors. A common approach for covering each of the sixteen aforementioned prophets will be adopted here, bearing in mind their messages were invariably deep and sublime. What we are about to do will hardly do justice to and barely scratch the surface concerning their message.

The message of each prophet ranged from prophecy already fulfilled in their day or after, e.g. concerning national and sometimes international events and the first coming of the Messiah (and they were – often remarkably), as well as yet to be fulfilled. A recurring theme was judgment and hope; and while the readership was often Israel or Judah, often other nations were addressed, and two to three thousand years on we who look back can take their message as important. The judgment was because of immorality, idolatry, injustice etc.; the hope invariably pointed to a nation restored, living in peace and prosperity under the Messiah.

While the focus was on Israel, there was invariably the sense that the Gentiles were to be included, harking back to the promise given to Abraham: "And *in thy seed shall all the nations of the earth be blessed...*", Genesis 22:18. While the prophets often could see events that Christians classify as pertaining to the first and second comings of the Messiah, the two events would have often have seemed one; and the notion of the Church, but a shadowy one.

Since some prophecies made were fulfilled often many years after (and often demonstrably), this is one reason for some raising doubts over things like date and authorship. It is not the intention to cover these arguments in this book; suffice to say, the view taken here is that each book was written by the named author and without the benefit of hindsight, because it was the word of the Lord. Not always apparent is the fact that the prophets wrote both in prose and poetry, appealing to both mind and heart, and invariably entreating listeners to respond.

They were often required to act out their message; their lives too were meant to reveal God. Readers are encouraged to look elsewhere for more detail concerning the many different prophesies that can be found, starting with the resources referred to in the Acknowledgements, and of course the Bible, in order to dig deeper into what those prophets wrote. In order to cover (hopefully) many of the keys points when considering each prophet in turn (and help keep the author on-track), the following general headings will be used in each case:

The prophet and his prophesy – an introduction to the prophet's life (where this is known – and often it is not much); and concerning their message.

Background and context – developing the argument laid out in Chapter 2, that in order to understand the book we need to know the background and context in which the prophet operated and how it relates to the rest of the Bible.

A synopsis of the book – (far from definitive statements) setting out in broad terms the main headings under which the book can be read and understood.

The message of the prophet – (the biggest challenge maybe) exploring what the prophet did prophesy and considering its significance and fulfilment. While missing out a lot of the detail, we will return to some prophecies in Chapter 15.

Without further ado, let us turn to Isaiah, followed by Jeremiah, Ezekiel, Daniel:

Isaiah

Isaiah and his prophesy

The Book of Isaiah is introduced: *"The vision of Isaiah the son of Amoz, which he saw concerning Judah and Jerusalem in the days of Uzziah, Jotham, Ahaz, and Hezekiah, kings of Judah"* (Isaiah 1:1). Uzziah was a good king who faltered toward the end, when Isaiah received his calling. *"In the year that king Uzziah died I saw also the Lord sitting upon a throne, high and lifted up, and his train filled the temple... Also I heard the voice of the Lord, saying, Whom shall I send, and who will go for us? Then said I, here am I; send me. And he said, Go, and tell this people, hear ye indeed, but understand not; and see ye indeed, but perceive not"* Isaiah 6:1,8-9. His vision was of the holiness of YHWH. Having realised "W*oe is me! for I am undone*" (v 5), it undoubtedly defined his ministry. His was a willing response to what he had seen and heard, but also it came with a warning that despite his best efforts, the people would not accept his message.

As far as we can make out, Isaiah came from the upper echelons of society and mingled with them in power, notably the kings. He began operating under Jotham (good king), continued under Ahaz (bad king) and reached his height of influence under Hezekiah (good king). He died during the reign of Manasseh (especially bad king who turned to someone approaching good at the end). A Jewish tradition was that under Manasseh he was forbidden to preach and was later sawn in two (Hebrews 11:37). As far as we can make out, he prophesied for over sixty years.

When scholars divide the book into two (some wrongly regard it as two books) – Judgment (1-39); Comfort (40-66) – this suggests what were two of the major themes of Isaiah. Isaiah's name means (appropriate to his key message) "Yahweh is salvation". We know Isaiah had a wife, referred to as *"the prophetess"* (Isaiah 8:3). They had three sons, naming the eldest Shear-jashub, meaning *"A remnant shall return"* (Isaiah 7:3), the next Immanuel, meaning *"God with us"* (Isaiah 7:14), and the youngest, Maher-Shalal-Hash-Baz, meaning, *"Spoil quickly, plunder speedily"* (Isaiah 8:3).

Background and context

Isaiah ministered (supposedly) 760 – 673 BC. He was based at Jerusalem and prophesied mainly to the southern kingdom of Judah. He did prophesy to the northern kingdom, Israel, too, but they were taken into captivity by the Assyrians in 722 BC. He also prophesied to surrounding nations, especially given their relationship to Israel and Judah. At the start of his prophesying, the Assyrians were the dominant power in the region, and while along with Syria and Egypt that power was to wane, they were Judah's main threat. Isaiah, just as did the other prophets, was all too conscious of the political dynamics of the surrounding nations, and the intrigues and alliances that took place. Chapters 36 to 39 tell the story of how Assyria sought to take captive Judah, but failed in spectacular fashion, thanks to YHWH's intervention and the prayer of a praying king (Hezekiah), encouraged by Isaiah. Following Assyria's demise, there was the rise and fall of Babylon, and later Persia, all of which Isaiah predicted. Hezekiah lived to witness the destruction of a 186,000 Assyrian army by the angel of the Lord (what just one angel can do), but his foolishness in welcoming emissaries from the new rising Babylonian empire set the scene for the later captivity of Judah.

While the Babylon captivity was a hundred years after Isaiah prophesied, he not only foretold it would happen but he looked forward to Israel's return from Exile, and the Messianic kingdom where there will be great blessing not just for Israel but to the Gentile nations. Isaiah also prophesied in amazing detail concerning the Messiah. Isaiah 53's "Suffering Servant" is a wonderful example that we will consider in more depth in Chapter 15.

Passages from the Book of Isaiah were cited many times in the New Testament, including by Jesus. Many such texts are memorable and are widely quoted. The author recalls as a youth a powerful sermon preached on the text: *"Come now, and let us reason together, saith the Lord: though your sins be as scarlet, they shall be as white as snow; though they be red like crimson, they shall be as wool*" (Isaiah 1:18). As this was being written, in an unrelated context, a friend shared: "*Thou wilt keep him in perfect peace, whose mind is stayed on thee: because he trusteth in thee*" (Isaiah 26:3). Shortly after, in another context, another friend shared: "*Fear thou not; for I am with thee: be not dismayed; for I am thy God: I will strengthen thee; yea, I will help thee; yea, I will uphold thee with the right hand of my righteousness*" (Isaiah 41:10).

Another feature of the Book of Isaiah worth mentioning is the many different references to God and God's character, such as the one used throughout the book: "the Holy One of Israel" (twenty-eight times). Some have referred to Isaiah as the fifth Gospel because its message touches on many, if not all, of the key gospel themes (if you want examples as to how, then you only need to listen to Handel's Messiah, which draws heavily upon Isaiah). Isaiah's contemporary prophet in Judah was Micah, and in Israel it was Amos and Hosea. Further background to his life and times can be found in the Books of Kings and Chronicles.

A synopsis of Isaiah

1. Messages of rebuke and promise (chs. 1–6).

2. Prophecies from Aramean and Israel threat against Judah (chs. 7–12).

3. Judgment against the nations (chs. 13–23).

4. Judgment and promise (the Lord's Kingdom) (chs. 24–27).

5. Six woes: five on unfaithful in Israel and one on Assyria (chs. 28–33).

6. More prophecies of judgment and promise (chs. 34–35).

7. Historical transition from Assyrian threat to Babylonian Exile (chs. 36–39).

8. The deliverance and restoration of Israel (chs. 40–48).

9. The Servant's ministry and Israel's restoration (chs. 49–57).

10. Everlasting deliverance and everlasting judgment (chs. 58–66).

The message of Isaiah

We can see right from the start of the book the two major themes of rebuke and judgement and of restoration and hope.

Rebuke: "*Hear, O heavens, and give ear, O earth: for the Lord hath spoken, I have nourished and brought up children, and they have rebelled against me. The ox knoweth his owner, and the ass his master's crib: but Israel doth not know, my people doth not consider. Ah sinful nation, a people laden with iniquity, a seed of evildoers, children that are corrupters: they have forsaken the Lord, they have provoked the Holy One of Israel unto anger, they are gone away backward.*" (Isaiah 1:2-4.)

Restoration: "*And it shall come to pass in the last days, that the mountain of the Lord's house shall be established in the top of the mountains, and shall be exalted above the hills; and all nations shall flow unto it. And many people shall go and say, Come ye, and let us go up to the mountain of the Lord, to the house of the God of Jacob; and he will teach us of his ways, and we will walk in his paths: for out of Zion shall go forth the law, and the word of the Lord from Jerusalem. And he shall judge among the nations, and shall rebuke many people: and they shall beat their swords into plowshares, and their spears into pruninghooks: nation shall not lift up sword against nation, neither shall they learn war any more. O house of Jacob, come ye, and let us walk in the light of the Lord.*" (Isaiah 2:2-5.)

As we read through Isaiah, and the fifteen prophets to follow, it becomes clear there is a lot of repetition and if not repetition, common themes. Often contrasting themes appear next to each other, such as here with God's complaint against His Covenanted people whom He was effectively wedded to, as well as His love and promises of future restoration – not just following the return from exile but in a future when Israel's Messiah reigns and, while sometimes veiled, the notion that the other nations were to benefit (after all, it was always God's intention that Israel should be a blessing to the nations) was also a theme that is repeated. These contrasting themes are taken up by the prophets to follow, and if it seems there is a good deal of repetition, it is that God was trying to get through to His people and wanting to reinforce what had been said before. Going back to Deuteronomy 27 and 28, they had a choice between blessings and curses. The tragedy of Israel was that too often they made the wrong choice, and they experienced cursing.

One of the focuses we have in these early chapters especially was that the old

Jerusalem, ripe for judgment, destruction and Exile, would one day give way to a new Jerusalem where blessings flow to the nations under the Messiah that will come from David's line. Here we are introduced to the Righteous Branch, "*in that day shall the branch of the Lord be beautiful and glorious*" (Isaiah 4:2), which is picked up again by Jeremiah 23:6, 33:15 and Zechariah 3:8, 6:12 as equating to the Messiah. It is worth noting that in the first half of Isaiah, while the emphasis is on judgment, we have references to future glory. Besides chapter 2, chapters 11-12 and 32 also speak of coming glory.

Not to be lost sight of, because this idea is developed in later chapters, and is the nature of the coming king: "*For unto us a child is born, unto us a son is given: and the government shall be upon his shoulder: and his name shall be called Wonderful, Counsellor, The mighty God, The everlasting Father, The Prince of Peace. Of the increase of his government and peace there shall be no end, upon the throne of David, and upon his kingdom, to order it, and to establish it with judgment and with justice from henceforth even for ever. The zeal of the Lord of hosts will perform this.*" (Isaiah 9:6,7). Then there is a thought of what is to come: "*And an highway shall be there, and a way, and it shall be called The way of holiness; the unclean shall not pass over it; but it shall be for those: the wayfaring men, though fools, shall not err therein. No lion shall be there, nor any ravenous beast shall go up thereon, it shall not be found there; but the redeemed shall walk there: And the ransomed of the Lord shall return, and come to Zion with songs and everlasting joy upon their heads: they shall obtain joy and gladness, and sorrow and sighing shall flee away.*" (Isaiah 35:8-10.)

Sadly, as we see from the opening chapters of Isaiah, the notion of Israel being a means for God to bless the nations was a distant proposition. It seemed that Judah had committed every sin imaginable, ranging from abandoning their God and worshipping idols, to sexual immorality and dealing injustice with the poor. One aspect not mentioned thus far was how many of the women were occupied with gaining luxuries: "*Rise up, ye women that are at ease; hear my voice, ye careless daughters; give ear unto my speech.*" (Isaiah 32:9.) The result would be devastation and eventually Exile, as many other prophets picked up on.

The notion of God allowing calamities to get the people's attention also applies. We also see in Isaiah reference to the marriage Covenant YHWH has with Israel and God's desire to re-establish that relationship in the way it had been intended. Making alliances with foreign powers was another common theme, already discussed in Chapter 11 concerning a number of prophets, and later this was developed under the ministries of other prophets, such as Jeremiah. God abhorred it because it was to do with compromise and not trusting Him. While lip service was given to the worshipping of YHWH, often that was all it was.

While the focus was on Israel, and especially Judah, Isaiah was mindful of the nations that impacted on them, especially Assyria and Babylon who were to take, respectively, Israel and Judah into Exile. But these were to be judged too along with other nations. While it was true, they were often the instruments of God's judgment, they also often overstepped the mark in their dealings with Israel and Judah, along with other wickedness that God found repugnant.

Some respite for Judah could be seen in the historical interlude in chapters 36-39 when, under Hezekiah, who intreated the Lord, Judah was delivered from the Assyrians who earlier conquered Israel. Later the king regressed when proudly he entertained a delegation from Babylon, with their "get well" card. He was warned they would later conquer Judah and take its treasures. Before we move to the second half of Isaiah, as Isaiah appears to be transported from present to future, we might also reflect on how these first half of his prophecies were fulfilled.

Isaiah now switches tack in chapters 40-66 with an emphasis on comfort and hope. In the second half, Isaiah looked forward to when the people would return from Exile, a glorious hope, the coming of the Messiah, and, beyond that, a new heaven and earth. This section begins: *"Comfort ye, comfort ye my people, saith your God. Speak ye comfortably to Jerusalem, and cry unto her, that her warfare is accomplished, that her iniquity is pardoned: for she hath received of the Lord's hand double for all her sins. The voice of him that crieth in the wilderness, Prepare ye the way of the Lord, make straight in the desert a highway for our God. Every valley shall be exalted, and every mountain and hill shall be made low: and the crooked shall be made straight, and the rough places plain: And the glory of the Lord shall be revealed, and all flesh shall see it together: for the mouth of the Lord hath spoken it."* (Isaiah 40:1-5.)

The section ends on a sober note, how things end up and God's promises to Israel finally fulfilled: *"For as the new heavens and the new earth, which I will make, shall remain before me, saith the Lord, so shall your seed and your name remain. And it shall come to pass, that from one new moon to another, and from one sabbath to another, shall all flesh come to worship before me, saith the Lord. And they shall go forth, and look upon the carcases of the men that have transgressed against me: for their worm shall not die, neither shall their fire be quenched; and they shall be an abhorring unto all flesh."* (Isaiah 66:22-24.)

It is in this second half of the book we are introduced to "The Servant", who can be equated to Israel, Israel's Messiah, and even King Cyrus. The first reference is: *"Behold my servant, whom I uphold; mine elect, in whom my soul delighteth; I have put my spirit upon him: he shall bring forth judgment to the Gentiles. He shall not cry, nor lift up, nor cause his voice to be heard in the street. A bruised reed shall he not break, and the smoking flax shall he not quench: he shall bring forth judgment unto truth. He shall not fail nor be discouraged, till he have set judgment in the earth: and the isles shall wait for his law."* (Isaiah 42:1-4.)

Two other Servant references, often cited by Christian preachers and New Testament writers as referring to Jesus, are: *"The Lord God hath given me the tongue of the learned, that I should know how to speak a word in season to him that is weary: he wakeneth morning by morning, he wakeneth mine ear to hear as the learned. The Lord God hath opened mine ear, and I was not rebellious, neither turned away back. I gave my back to the smiters, and my cheeks to them that plucked off the hair: I hid not my face from shame and spitting."* (Isaiah 50:4-6)

And *"Behold, my servant shall deal prudently, he shall be exalted and extolled, and be very high. As many were astonied at thee; his visage was so marred more than any man, and his form more than the sons of men: So shall he sprinkle many nations; the kings shall shut their mouths at him: for that which had not been told them shall they see; and that which they had not heard shall they consider."* (Isaiah 52: 13-15; plus Isaiah 53.)

One of the wonderments of Isaiah's ministry was how he could look forward to different points in time ranging from what was happening in his day to the final end state. In between that is what Christians see (and non-believing Jews do not), the first and second comings of the Messiah. As we have already pointed out, Isaiah would likely have seen the two events as one. Given that much of the first half of Isaiah focuses on the King to reign (second coming), we have to ask how this fits in with the Servant who dies to atone for the sin of the people (Isaiah 53) – how can it be? And also, pertinently, the need to be prepared and be rid of wrong attitudes (still a theme of Part 2), a message that John the Baptist, who fulfils some of Isaiah 40, gives to the people. A proper understanding of Isaiah needs to take into account all these things, for that is how God sees things, and to consider with prayerful concern: *"But we preach Christ crucified, unto the Jews a stumblingblock, and unto the Greeks foolishness..."* (1 Corinthians 1:23).

Let us consider the glorious hope: "*For, behold, I create new heavens and a new earth: and the former shall not be remembered, nor come into mind. But be ye glad and rejoice for ever in that which I create: for, behold, I create Jerusalem a rejoicing, and her people a joy. And I will rejoice in Jerusalem, and joy in my people: and the voice of weeping shall be no more heard in her, nor the voice of crying.*" (Isaiah 65: 17-19.) While there still is exhortation to live in accordance to the will of God, it is in the context of hope of what is to be: "*Arise, shine; for thy light is come, and the glory of the Lord is risen upon thee. For, behold, the darkness shall cover the earth, and gross darkness the people: but the Lord shall arise upon thee, and his glory shall be seen upon thee. And the Gentiles shall come to thy light, and kings to the brightness of thy rising.*" (Isaiah 60:1-3.)

With great confidence that can apply so much for the present day: "*So shall they fear the name of the Lord from the west, and his glory from the rising of the sun. When the enemy shall come in like a flood, the Spirit of the Lord shall lift up a standard against him. And the Redeemer shall come to Zion, and unto them that turn from transgression in Jacob, saith the Lord. As for me, this is my covenant with them, saith the Lord; My spirit that is upon thee, and my words which I have put in thy mouth, shall not depart out of thy mouth, nor out of the mouth of thy seed, nor out of the mouth of thy seed's seed, saith the Lord, from henceforth and for ever.*" (Isaiah 59:19-21.) But let us sign off:

Firstly – return to the Lord: "*Ho, every one that thirsteth, come ye to the waters, and he that hath no money; come ye, buy, and eat; yea, come, buy wine and milk without money and without price... Seek ye the Lord while he may be found, call ye upon him while he is near: Let the wicked forsake his way, and the unrighteous man his thoughts: and let him return unto the Lord, and he will have mercy upon him; and to our God, for he will abundantly pardon. For my thoughts are not your thoughts, neither are your ways my ways, saith the Lord. For as the heavens are higher than the earth, so are my ways higher than your ways, and my thoughts than your thoughts.*" (Isaiah 55:1, 6-9.)

Secondly – that hope is for (believing) Jew and Gentile: "*Thus saith the Lord, Keep ye judgment, and do justice: for my salvation is near to come, and my righteousness to be revealed. Blessed is the man that doeth this, and the son of man that layeth hold on it; that keepeth the sabbath from polluting it, and keepeth his hand from doing any evil. Neither let the son of the stranger, that hath joined himself to the Lord, speak, saying, The Lord hath utterly separated me from his people: neither let the eunuch say, Behold, I am a dry tree. For thus saith the Lord unto the eunuchs* *that keep my sabbaths, and choose the things that please me, and take hold of my covenant..."* (Isaiah 56: 1-4.)

Thirdly – that hope is embodied in the person of Jesus, who when He spoke at the synagogue in Nazareth, at the commencement of His ministry, He quoted up to *"to proclaim the acceptable year of the Lord"* in the passage that follows, much to the fury of those who heard Him. At the end when He announced: "T*his day is this scripture fulfilled in your ears*" (Luke 4:21). He was mindful the words from Isaiah that followed were yet to be fulfilled: *"The Spirit of the Lord God is upon me; because the Lord hath anointed me to preach good tidings unto the meek; he hath sent me to bind up the brokenhearted, to proclaim liberty to the captives, and the opening of the prison to them that are bound; To proclaim the acceptable year of the Lord, and the day of vengeance of our God; to comfort all that mourn; To appoint unto them that mourn in Zion, to give unto them beauty for ashes, the oil of joy for mourning, the garment of praise for the spirit of heaviness; that they might be called trees of righteousness, the planting of the Lord, that he might be glorified."* (Isaiah 61:1-3.)

Jeremiah

Jeremiah and his prophesy

We learn a lot about Jeremiah the man from the opening verses of the Book of Jeremiah, that contains his words and, more importantly, his prophesies; as well as background to the momentous events happening around him: *"The words of Jeremiah the son of Hilkiah, of the priests that were in Anathoth in the land of Benjamin: To whom the word of the Lord came in the days of Josiah the son of Amon king of Judah, in the thirteenth year of his reign. It came also in the days of Jehoiakim the son of Josiah king of Judah, unto the end of the eleventh year of Zedekiah the son of Josiah king of Judah, unto the carrying away of Jerusalem captive in the fifth month. Then the word of the Lord came unto me, saying, Before I formed thee in the belly I knew thee; and before thou camest forth out of the womb I sanctified thee, and I ordained thee a prophet unto the nations. Then said I, Ah, Lord God! behold, I cannot speak: for I am a child. But the Lord said unto me, Say not, I am a child: for thou shalt go to all that I shall send thee, and whatsoever I command thee thou shalt speak. Be not afraid of their faces: for I am with thee to deliver thee, saith the Lord. Then the Lord put forth his hand, and touched my mouth. And the Lord said unto me, Behold, I have put my words in thy mouth. See, I have this day set thee over the nations and over the kingdoms, to root out, and to pull down, and to destroy, and to throw down, to build, and to plant"* Jeremiah 1:1-10.

We might infer from this opening that Jeremiah was ordained a prophet before he was even born and did not even have any choice in the matter. Doing the job of the prophet was not going to be an easy one but God would be with him and protect him. His message was a consequential one. He was young (likely he was a teenager when he was called) and seemed to have been of a timid nature. He came from a priestly family; noting priests had a quite different undertaking to that of prophet. He lived in an especially tumultuous period of Judah history, beginning under good king Josiah (born in the same year), through four evil kings, although Jehoahaz and Jehoiachin, who each only reigned three months, were barely mentioned, and ending with Zedekiah and Babylonian captivity.

He began his ministry in 626 BC and ended not long after 586 BC. His name means "The Lord throws". It appears, after Jerusalem fell, despite being given protection by the Babylonian captors, he was kidnapped and taken to Egypt, where he died. He was based in Jerusalem and prophesied mainly to Judah although he did make significant prophesies regarding other nations too. His message, like Isaiah, was one of judgment but also hope, with a particular emphasis on the need to repent, and specifically on an individual basis. He saw the futility of outward religion and trusting in the Temple. He was told by God he could not marry, and that was partly to do with him not only speaking the part but also acting it, just like when he was told to bury some worn underwear and dig it up some time later, to smash a clay pot and to walk around with a yoke.

He was representing the aggrieved husband, God, whose spouse, Israel and Judah, had forsaken Him for other gods. Many of the sins that troubled Isaiah did so Jeremiah also, and major sections were Jeremiah pouring his heart out (it often appeared he was merged with God in this respect) because of the sins of the people, with their lack of contrition as part of the slippery slope to ruin. Which is where all this would end: in this there was no doubt; it would be destruction and no-one would help them. They would reach the point of no return.

We look in wonder at Jeremiah's faithfulness to God during his long ministry, passing a message of doom; interspersed, it is true, with a future message of hope and, with few exceptions, both message and messenger were rejected. Jeremiah was a man of faith, whose faith was tested. This is seen by his remonstrating with God while wicked people seemed to be let off. While he knew there was going to be a day of reckoning, he saw beyond that; and nowhere was this more evident than when he brought a field (Jeremiah 32:8), defying logic yet trusting God.

Background and context

With respect to the timelines and maps shown in Chapter 2, there was significant movement in the power structure of the region during Jeremiah's time. Israel no longer features in Jeremiah's prophesyings, other than in a distant future when the kingdom would be restored under its Messiah. Israel had already been taken into Assyrian captivity in 722 BC, one hundred years before Jeremiah began. But Assyria, along with the other significant power block at that time, Egypt, was on the decline. Tragically, it was at Megiddo in 608 BC that King Josiah fought a battle he need not have fought, which he lost along with his life. It was to stop the Egyptians linking up with the Assyrians to fight the emerging Babylonian power. While Egypt called the shots for a time, e.g. establishing Jehoiakim on the throne, the Babylonians were in the ascendancy in the control stakes. The destruction of Jerusalem in 586 BC, following a long siege, was preceded by them taking effective control of the land and two earlier Exiles: in 605 BC that took Daniel the Prophet, and 597 BC that took Ezekiel the Prophet (both we will return to). Ironically, part of Judah's plan to withstand Babylon was to make foreign alliances, one of which was Egypt, and all of which were ill-fated.

There was no question that Jeremiah's message was an unpopular one, and with very few exceptions he was opposed on every side, especially by members of the establishment, including those who claimed to be prophets. His life was threatened on several occasions. He was put in stocks, in prison and under house arrest. There were attempts on his life, including by people from his own community; and when he was cast into a cistern, where he would have died but for the timely rescue by Ebed-melech (a black official, whose black life it turned out, noting a present day-concern, really did matter). Ebed-melech was one of Jeremiah's few friends, another being his faithful assistant and scribe, Baruch, who likely compiled the final book of Jeremiah, which seems to dart backwards and forwards in the timeline and is often repetitious.

Jeremiah was a political prophet, all too aware of what was going on around him. It is worth noting when some say today preachers should be above politics. That maybe so, but they need to be politically aware and like Jeremiah give godly responses. He who warned the kings when they sought alliances with ungodly nations and not God, who advised them that they would do better to submit to the rule of Babylon than resist. This might have been avoided if his message of repentance had been accepted but it was not, and there came a point of no return.

Jeremiah is rightly seen as the weeping prophet, all too aware of the consequences of disobedience, especially if we take Lamentations as written by him. It should be noted that a lot of his writing was beautiful poetry, expressing God's heart.

Jeremiah's contemporary prophets, later in life, in Babylon were Ezekiel and Daniel, with Ezekiel especially viewing the same events Jeremiah commented on, albeit from different places. Jeremiah's ministry was immediately preceded by Zephaniah; Habakkuk was a contemporary. More background to Jeremiah's life and times can be found in the Books of Kings and Chronicles. 2 Kings ends, as does Jeremiah, with Jehoiachin, who had been taken captive to Babylon in 597 BC, being given special favour by the King of Babylon. Chronicles, written much later, could reflect on the return from Exile under Cyrus of Persia who conquered Babylon (just as Jeremiah predicted). The governor, upon the return from exile, was Zerubbabel, around 538 BC, laying the foundation of the rebuilt Temple. The significance in the two endings is that amidst the tumult there was hope; and that the royal line of David had been preserved (through Jehoiachin and Zerubbabel), and the promised Messianic kingdom would be restored.

There are, as we might expect, many parallels between the Book of Jeremiah and Isaiah; and, as we will see, that of other prophets also. Both are long books, and while Jeremiah has fifty-two chapters compared with Isaiah's sixty-six, Jeremiah has more words than any other book in the Bible (forty-two thousand). Both contain many memorable, quotable passages (some included in this account); and the only reason Isaiah is more so is that there is less doom and gloom, even though a careful reading of Jeremiah reveals messages of glorious hope and comfort. For example, "*The Lord hath appeared of old unto me, saying, Yea, I have loved thee with an everlasting love: therefore with lovingkindness have I drawn thee*" (Jeremiah 31:3), has encouraged many down the ages. "*Call unto me, and I will answer thee, and show thee great and mighty things, which thou knowest not*" (Jeremiah 33:3) is a text that has challenged this author; and, "*Blessed is the man that trusteth in the Lord, and whose hope the Lord is. For he shall be as a tree planted by the waters, and that spreadeth out her roots by the river, and shall not see when heat cometh, but her leaf shall be green; and shall not be careful in the year of drought, neither shall cease from yielding fruit. The heart is deceitful above all things, and desperately wicked: who can know it?*" (Jeremiah 17:7-9.) This has served as a check and balance for this author.

Like Isaiah, Jeremiah is quoted several times by New Testament writers. Matthew 2:17 and 27:9 point out specific Jeremiah prophesies fulfilled in Jesus' day. Jesus was Himself likened to Jeremiah when the question was asked who He was (Matthew 16:14).

Just as when reading Isaiah, we need to brace ourselves over the idea of God's disappointment when His people sin, similar lists of sins, consequences of this falling away, the unmet call to return and future hope following restoration; all themes that are repeated many times when reading Jeremiah. With Jeremiah it becomes that more intense because of the awful judgment that takes place toward the end of his ministry, and the loneliness and personal attacks he experienced throughout his ministry; yet he stuck to his task, even though he would remonstrate with God because of his enemies. He was right there at the centre of where suffering took place and teaches us that faithfulness to God mattered, even when much that took place seemed unjust. There is an irony, as God looks back, when there was a beautiful relationship as of a husband and wife who are truly in love; and yet realistically, nine hundred years on from the making of that Covenant on Mount Sinai, it was a topsy-turvy relationship, and it was Jeremiah's sad lot to witness the wickedness that took place around him, followed by Exile.

The end for Jerusalem (all else had fallen) is graphically described in chapters 39 and 52; and this after an eighteen-month siege, also referred to in the Book of Ezekiel. It represented the tragic demise of King Zedekiah (and his family), who tried to escape when it became clear the city could no longer be held. The other king of note, Jehoiakim, who was especially wicked, was earlier taken by the Babylonians after trying to break free from Babylonian rule by aligning with Egypt. Both kings were taken captive to Babylon in chains, and no-one was there to mourn their departure from the scene. Both dealt appallingly with Jeremiah and yet were given every opportunity to change their ways. The tragedy was their hardness of heart and what could have been.

While we are on the subject of kings, mention should be made of Jehoiachin, son of Jehoiakim, also an evil king, who after a three-month reign was also taken captive to Babylon, with Zedekiah taking his place. The hopeful note at the end (Jeremiah 52) was a reversal in his fortunes as captive, laying the hope that the line to the future Messiah would be restored.

The book at the very end of the Old Testament (Chronicles) ends on a hopeful note as discussed earlier, with the edict of Cyrus; just as did the book of Kings with the restoration of Jehoiachin, but not without first recognising the crucial ministry of Jeremiah (and others), who did what God told them to do by speaking from God's heart and mind, leaving the rest to God. Like Daniel (9:2), the chronicler recognised the significance of the seventy-year Exile:

"And the Lord God of their fathers sent to them by his messengers, rising up betimes, and sending; because he had compassion on his people, and on his dwelling place: But they mocked the messengers of God, and despised his words, and misused his prophets, until the wrath of the Lord arose against his people, till there was no remedy. Therefore he brought upon them the king of the Chaldees, who slew their young men with the sword in the house of their sanctuary, and had no compassion upon young man or maiden, old man, or him that stooped for age: he gave them all into his hand. And all the vessels of the house of God, great and small, and the treasures of the house of the Lord, and the treasures of the king, and of his princes; all these he brought to Babylon. And they burnt the house of God, and brake down the wall of Jerusalem, and burnt all the palaces thereof with fire, and destroyed all the goodly vessels thereof. And them that had escaped from the sword carried he away to Babylon; where they were servants to him and his sons until the reign of the kingdom of Persia: To fulfil the word of the Lord by the mouth of Jeremiah, until the land had enjoyed her sabbaths: for as long as she lay desolate she kept sabbath, to fulfil threescore and ten years. Now in the first year of Cyrus king of Persia, that the word of the Lord spoken by the mouth of Jeremiah might be accomplished, the Lord stirred up the spirit of Cyrus king of Persia, that he made a proclamation throughout all his kingdom, and put it also in writing, saying, Thus saith Cyrus king of Persia, All the kingdoms of the earth hath the Lord God of heaven given me; and he hath charged me to build him an house in Jerusalem, which is in Judah. Who is there among you of all his people? The Lord his God be with him, and let him go up." (2 Chronicles 36:15-23.)

A synopsis of Jeremiah

1. Call of the prophet (ch. 1).

2. Warnings and exhortations to Judah (chs. 2–11).

3. Complaints, conversations and conflicts of Jeremiah (chs. 12-20).

4. Bad kings, the Righteous Branch, false prophets and Exile (chs. 21-29).

5. Promises of future restoration (chs. 30-33).

6. Words to Kings Zedekiah and Jehoiakim (chs. 34-35).

7. Sufferings and persecutions of the prophet (chs. 36–38).

8. The fall of Jerusalem and its aftermath (chs. 39–45).

9. Judgment against the nations (chs. 46–51).

10. Historical appendix (ch. 52).

The message of Jeremiah

When it came to God's complaints concerning His people, the list of specifics was at least as long as Isaiah and not too dissimilar: idolatry, sexual immorality, child sacrifice, greed, lying, injustice, seeking help from Israel's enemies, forsaking the Covenant they had with God, worshipping God hypocritically; and it goes on and on and is repeated several times, without response other than attacking the messenger. For Jeremiah, the repetition and rejection was a painful experience that he felt acutely and had to commit to God who was His avenger, but who would judge righteously. In one summation we read: *"For my people have committed two evils; they have forsaken me the fountain of living waters, and hewed them out cisterns, broken cisterns, that can hold no water"* (Jeremiah 2:13). They had a choice between blessing and cursing, and chose the latter.

While studying much of Jeremiah's prophesying and experiences makes sad and sober reading, both because of the pain Jeremiah and the Lord felt as a consequence of the sin of the people and what he had to go through – which hurt him greatly and much more than merely physically – there is much in what is stated that is to do with hope for the future: *"Therefore, behold, the days come, saith the Lord, that it shall no more be said, The Lord liveth, that brought up the children of Israel out of the land of Egypt; But, The Lord liveth, that brought up the children of Israel from the land of the north, and from all the lands whither he had driven them: and I will bring them again into their land that I gave unto their fathers"* (Jeremiah 16:14-15).

He also picks up on the Righteous Branch theme, mentioned by Isaiah, relating to the future Messiah: *"And I will gather the remnant of my flock out of all countries whither I have driven them, and will bring them again to their folds; and they shall be fruitful and increase. And I will set up shepherds over them which shall feed them: and they shall fear no more, nor be dismayed, neither shall they be lacking, saith the Lord. Behold, the days come, saith the Lord, that I will raise unto David a righteous Branch, and a King shall reign and prosper, and shall execute judgment and justice in the earth. In his days Judah shall be saved, and Israel shall dwell safely: and this is his name whereby he shall be called, The Lord Our Righteousness."* (Jeremiah 23:3-6.)

His message was a practical one, revealing repeatedly a tender-hearted attitude, and a concern because of false prophets who would mislead them; for example to those who had already been sent into Exile: *"Thus saith the Lord of hosts, the God of Israel, unto all that are carried away captives, whom I have caused to be carried away from Jerusalem unto Babylon; Build ye houses, and dwell in them; and plant gardens, and eat the fruit of them; Take ye wives, and beget sons and daughters; and take wives for your sons, and give your daughters to husbands, that they may bear sons and daughters; that ye may be increased there, and not diminished. And seek the peace of the city whither I have caused you to be carried away captives, and pray unto the Lord for it: for in the peace thereof shall ye have peace. For thus saith the Lord of hosts, the God of Israel; Let not your prophets and your diviners, that be in the midst of you, deceive you, neither hearken to your dreams which ye cause to be dreamed. For they prophesy falsely unto you in my name: I have not sent them, saith the Lord."* (Jeremiah 29:4-9.)

As well as giving warnings, he could also encourage. Rather than merely a prophet of doom, his was one of hope: *"For thus saith the Lord, That after seventy years be accomplished at Babylon I will visit you, and perform my good word toward you, in causing you to return to this place. For I know the thoughts that I think toward you, saith the Lord, thoughts of peace, and not of evil, to give you an expected end. Then shall ye call upon me, and ye shall go and pray unto me, and I will hearken unto you. And ye shall seek me, and find me, when ye shall search for me with all your heart."* (Jeremiah 29:10-13.)

About the coming Messiah were his insights into the New Covenant that would be ushered in, referred to and elaborated on in Hebrews 8 and 10. *"Behold, the days come, saith the Lord, that I will make a new covenant with the house of Israel, and with the house of Judah: Not according to the covenant that I made with their fathers in the day that I took them by the hand to bring them out of the land of Egypt; which my covenant they brake, although I was an husband unto them, saith the Lord: But this shall be the covenant that I will make with the house of Israel; After those days, saith the Lord, I will put my law in their inward parts, and write it in their hearts; and will be their God, and they shall be my people. And they shall teach no more every man his neighbour, and every man his brother, saying, Know the Lord: for they shall all know me, from the least of them unto the greatest of them, saith the Lord: for I will forgive their iniquity, and I will remember their sin no more."* (Jeremiah 31:31-34.)

Before we leave the Book of Jeremiah, it is worth noting that chapters 46 to 51 concern nations other than Israel and Judah: Egypt, Philistia, Moab, Ammon, Damascus, Kedar, Hazor, Elam and Babylon, where most attention is devoted including, pertinent to this book, it being later overrun by the Medes. We learn among other things, just as we would expect from a true prophet, that the prophecies of Jeremiah were precisely fulfilled. God is interested in these other nations, especially when they relate to His Covenant people; and when they deal harshly with Israel, we find repeatedly that God sides with and will deliver Israel. God is concerned over the wickedness of these nations, especially the sin of pride. In some of the prophecies, and despite coming judgment, there is room for hope.

All the prophets had it hard; none more so than Jeremiah. His was definitely not a message of peace, hope and love; more judgment, woe and the need to repent, with some peace, hope and love thrown in. In our day, tolerance, diversity and inclusion are often the watchwords, so Christian preachers ought to take note. It would be easy to accuse Jeremiah of self-pity as he called out this or that pillar of the community, who seemed to prosper as they pummelled the poor prophet. But Jeremiah stuck to his guns when there seemed little respite from the flak that came his way. The consolation was, he was doing God's will and his reward would follow. Meantime, he had to accept that God had everything under control.

Lamentations

We cannot say for sure who wrote Lamentations. Many believe it was Jeremiah. While it might serve us if we were to go along with this thought, especially as there are pointers such as the themes covered and language employed; and, while lamenting was something many of the prophets did, it was something especially associated with Jeremiah, who we know wrote a lament about King Josiah after he died (2 Chronicles 35:25); but we must be careful not to read into the Bible what might conveniently reinforce our opinions. If the poetic language of Jeremiah was sublime, that of Lamentations (the entire book was poetry) was more so, and it cleverly used acrostics based on successive letters of the Hebrew alphabet to introduce each of the sentences of the first four of the five chapters:

- Chapter 1: Jerusalem's misery and desolation.

- Chapter 2: The Lord's anger against his people.

- Chapter 3: Judah's complaint and a basis for consolation.

- Chapter 4: Contrast between Zion's past and present.

- Chapter 5: Judah's appeal for God's forgiveness.

The devastating effects of the fall of Jerusalem are described in graphic and alarming detail. It begins and ends in sombre fashion: *"How doth the city sit solitary, that was full of people! how is she become as a widow! she that was great among the nations, and princess among the provinces, how is she become tributary! She weepeth sore in the night, and her tears are on her cheeks: among all her lovers she hath none to comfort her: all her friends have dealt treacherously with her, they are become her enemies... Turn thou us unto thee, O Lord, and we shall be turned; renew our days as of old. But thou hast utterly rejected us; thou art very wroth against us."* (1:1-2, 5:21-22.)

The penultimate verse (5:21) gives room for hope, along with this delightful reason for hope expressed right in the middle of the lament: *"This I recall to my mind, therefore have I hope. It is of the Lord's mercies that we are not consumed, because his compassions fail not. They are new every morning: great is thy faithfulness."* (3:21-23.)

Ezekiel

Ezekiel and his prophesy

As we reflected when we considered Jeremiah, the Exile to Babylon took place in three stages. The first was in 605 BC when Daniel was taken; the second was in 597 BC when Ezekiel was taken away to Babylon, aged 25, along with King Jehoiachin; and the third that gathered most of all who were still left, who were of any societal stature, in 586 BC, when Jerusalem fell. Ezekiel began his ministry aged thirty, the time he would have begun as a priest if there were a Temple. We do not know much about his life. We know he was married and that he lived in relative peace, in a place (interestingly) called Tel Aviv. He was a knowledgeable man and was respected by his community, who seemed to regularly consult him.

He was meticulous in his writings, and like another priest turned prophet after him (Zechariah), he dated his work. There was a symmetry when describing such things as the glory leaving the Temple and coming back at some future date, and when describing events surrounding the Temple in Jerusalem in chapters 8 to 11, and the new Temple in chapters 40 to 48. He would precisely date significant events, and while the prophecies concerning the nations were undated, unlike other prophets such as Jeremiah, these were laid out in date order.

It was from a vision of the glory of God, Ezekiel received his call to prophesy to his people and to be a watchman, warning the people of coming judgment. That vision, and the sense of God's holiness and of the glory of God, were to be hallmarks of his ministry; as was his continuous repetition (and hope) that the people, and later the nations, would know who the Lord truly is. Ezekiel was often referred to as a *"son of man"* (a term later applied to Jesus).

A lot of his prophesying was done through bizarre acting: building a model depicting the siege of and eventual fall of Jerusalem, cutting his hair with a sword and making three piles to depict aspects of God's judgment, laying on one side for 390 days and on the other for forty days, semi-naked, eating starvation rations cooked over a fire fuelled by cow (changed from human) dung to illustrate yet further divine truth. Another piece of acting was digging under a wall during the night, which like his other acting would be seen as bizarre, except that is what King Zedekiah would do (Jeremiah 39) in order to escape the city of Jerusalem when overrun by the Babylonians.

The saddest acting was when he was told his wife was going to die and he was not to mourn, since Ezekiel's wife's death prefigured the destruction of the Temple, *"the delight of your eyes"*. It should be noted Ezekiel often told stories (parables) to make important points, and there were times when he was literally tongue-tied, such that he was unable to prophesy in words. His prophesying was over twenty-two years, in three periods (soon after he received his call, around the time Jerusalem fell, and some time after that). From what we can work out, he died a natural death; his tomb is a place of pilgrimage to this day.

Ezekiel's commission was clear; and, as with Isaiah and Jeremiah, it was not going to be an easy one and there would be opposition and resistance to his message (although not physically as with Jeremiah): *"And he said unto me, Son of man, I send thee to the children of Israel, to a rebellious nation that hath rebelled against me: they and their fathers have transgressed against me, even unto this very day.*

For they are impudent children and stiffhearted. I do send thee unto them; and thou shalt say unto them, Thus saith the Lord God. And they, whether they will hear, or whether they will forbear, (for they are a rebellious house,) yet shall know that there hath been a prophet among them. And thou, son of man, be not afraid of them, neither be afraid of their words, though briers and thorns be with thee, and thou dost dwell among scorpions: be not afraid of their words, nor be dismayed at their looks, though they be a rebellious house. And thou shalt speak my words unto them, whether they will hear, or whether they will forbear: for they are most rebellious." (Ezekiel 2:3-7.)

These points are further amplified, but with it the assurance he would be God's spokesman, and would be toughened up for the task and withstand opposition: "*For thou art not sent to a people of a strange speech and of an hard language, but to the house of Israel; Not to many people of a strange speech and of an hard language, whose words thou canst not understand. Surely, had I sent thee to them, they would have hearkened unto thee. But the house of Israel will not hearken unto thee; for they will not hearken unto me: for all the house of Israel are impudent and hardhearted. Behold, I have made thy face strong against their faces, and thy forehead strong against their foreheads. As an adamant harder than flint have I made thy forehead: fear them not, neither be dismayed at their looks, though they be a rebellious house.*" (Ezekiel 3:5-9.)

An important aspect of Ezekiel's ministry was that of a watchman, whose job was to warn and thereby discharge his duties: "*Son of man, I have made thee a watchman unto the house of Israel: therefore hear the word at my mouth, and give them warning from me. When I say unto the wicked, Thou shalt surely die; and thou givest him not warning, nor speakest to warn the wicked from his wicked way, to save his life; the same wicked man shall die in his iniquity; but his blood will I require at thine hand. Yet if thou warn the wicked, and he turn not from his wickedness, nor from his wicked way, he shall die in his iniquity; but thou hast delivered thy soul.*" (Ezekiel 3:17-19.) This call to watch and warn would be further made in Chapter 33; it was going to be a solemn duty and he would be accountable to God. It was then up to those who heard his message to respond as God requires or face the consequences of disobedience; regardless of what others did, or whether or not they had lived as God required prior to that.

Background and context

The political, historical and geographical context for the Book of Ezekiel was the same as that for Jeremiah, although Jeremiah by the time Ezekiel came on the scene was now middle-aged. While reading Jeremiah and other prophets, we might conclude the Babylonians were cruel oppressors, yet it seems that just like Daniel, Ezekiel and the other captives were not treated too badly by their captors. While Jeremiah prophesied from where the important events were taking place (up to its destruction), i.e. Jerusalem, Ezekiel prophesied seven hundred miles away, in Babylon, but often about the same events and noting similar complaints.

Strangely, the two did not acknowledge each other, in spite of their messages being complementary, although Ezekiel did recognise Daniel (three times) who, along with Noah and Job, were in his view the three most righteous men who had lived, and even they could not change God's mind when it came to judging Israel. It is interesting that Israel was mentioned rather than Judah, when the ten Northern tribes had been judged over a hundred years earlier and were not on the scene. As with Isaiah and Jeremiah, Ezekiel was much aware of the nations around Judah and how these impacted on God's chosen people. Like other prophets, he prophesied accurately and was complementary to them on what would happen.

While Judah was all that was left of the kingdoms of Israel and Judah, after Israel's Assyrian captivity, Ezekiel would use "Israel" rather than "Judah" when referring to the people of God, and could see a day when the restored kingdom would include both: "*Say unto them, Thus saith the Lord God; Behold, I will take the stick of Joseph, which is in the hand of Ephraim, and the tribes of Israel his fellows, and will put them with him, even with the stick of Judah, and make them one stick, and they shall be one in mine hand*" (Ezekiel 37:19).

A lot of Ezekiel, unlike Jeremiah for example, was written in prose rather than poetry, although there was no doubt he felt God's pain. Like Jeremiah, he might be seen as a "doom and gloom" prophet, although also like Jeremiah, even when things were at their direst, his message recognised a benevolent God. When he received news of the fall of Jerusalem in chapter 33, his main message turned from judgment to come, because all he had foretold had happened, to future hope.

While Isaiah and Jeremiah contain many memorable verses, it may be argued the same cannot be said concerning Ezekiel, although this is a debatable point - as the author would testify when harking back to his youth: "*And I sought for a man among them, that should make up the hedge, and stand in the gap before me for the land, that I should not destroy it: but I found none*" (Ezekiel 22:30). The same might be said of what might be seen as text worthy of any gospel presentation:

"Have I any pleasure at all that the wicked should die? saith the Lord God: and not that he should return from his ways, and live?" (Ezekiel 18:23). Then, when looking far into the future of the New Jerusalem: "*…the name of the city from that day shall be, The Lord is there*" (Ezekiel 48:35).

Yet, when it comes to content, much of Ezekiel is a closed book for many. While there are certain passages - e.g. concerning the dry bones, the good and bad shepherds, and the amazing vision which kicked things off - that people may be aware of, much of its content they are not. That is a shame, as Ezekiel provides an important message that merits being reflected on today, and important prophecies that relate to end-time events. For example, messages that they (be it Israel or the nations) would know that He, YHWH, is indeed the Lord, and that of individual responsibility and the consequences for one's own actions. While not too many quotable passages, the four visions of Ezekiel were phenomenal.

A Vision of The Glory of the Lord – and Ezekiel's Call (chapters 1 – 3)

Words can barely encapsulate the vision Ezekiel saw. The central image comprised wheels within wheels, four creatures with four faces, lots of eyes, flames of fire, and a crystalline canopy upon which was a throne. On it was seated a glorious being and all were moving in unison in one or other direction.

A Vision of Idolatry in the Temple – the Lord's Departure (chapters 8 – 11)

Central to why God was judging Israel, was went on in the Temple back in Jerusalem by the leading figures at the time, specifically to do with idolatry. Ezekiel could see it all, including named persons dropping dead. During the vision he saw the glory of the Lord, long associated with the Temple, departing.

A Vision of a Valley of Bones – and Resurrection (chapter 37)

Ezekiel's message changed, once Jerusalem fell, into one of hope, around returning back to its land where Israel lives in peace and prosperity. The vision of dry bones is about bones coming together into human form with life breathed into them. What is shown is far more than anything we have seen up to now as it looks to the bringing together of Israel and Judah under one Good Shepherd,

A Vision of a New Temple, a New Land, and a New City (chapters 40 – 48)

This follows the great battle involving Gog and Magog, where Israel comes out on top. This final vision concerns a Temple to be built. While the focus was on the Temple, described here in great detail, description was also given of the City where it was and the restored kingdom of Israel, under the rule of the Messiah. The glory that departed in chapter 11 returns in chapter 43.

A synopsis of Ezekiel

Unlike with the other major prophets, we will tackle this section on the basis that Ezekiel had four 'Visions', thirteen 'Pictures' and eight 'Words':

1. A Vision of the Glory of the Lord - and Ezekiel's Call (chs. 1:1 - 3:15).

2. A Word about the people (ch. 3:16-27).

3. An Acted parable of siege (chs. 4 - 5).

4. A Word about idolatry (chs. 6 - 7).

5. A Vision of idolatry in the Temple - and God's departure chs. 8 - 11).

6. An Acted parable of Exile (ch. 12).

7. A Word to the 'prophets' (chs. 13 - 14).

8. The Illustration of the useless vine (ch. 15).

9. The Allegory of the adulterous wife (ch. 16).

10. The Parable of the eagles and the vine (ch. 17).

11. A Word to the people (ch. 18).

12. A Lament for the lion cubs and the vine (ch. 19).

13. A Word to the nation (chs. 20 – 22).

14. The Allegory of the two sisters (ch. 23).

15. The Parable of the cooking pot (ch. 24:1-14).

16. The Allegory of Ezekiel and his wife (ch. 24:15-27).

17. Words and laments for the nations (ch. 25 - 32).

18. The Allegory of Ezekiel the watchman (ch. 33).

19. A Word to the 'shepherds' (ch. 34:1-10).

20. The Allegory of God the Good Shepherd (ch. 34:11-31).

21. The Allegory of the land (ch. 35 - 36).

22. A Vision of a valley of bones - and resurrection (ch. 37:1-14).

23. The Acted parable of the sticks (ch. 37:15-27).

24. Seven Words against Gog (chs. 38 - 39).

25. A Vision of a new Temple, land, City (chs. 40 - 48).

The message of Ezekiel

The essence of Ezekiel's message of warning in chapters 1-11 was around the destruction of Jerusalem by the Babylonians, every bit as bad as described in the book of Lamentations. The twin complaint of idol worship and social injustice was similar to that given by Jeremiah. A lot of what he sought to convey was through acting, and what he could see through his vision of the Jerusalem Temple and the idol worship that took place, and where much of his message would be rejected by the people, as we have discussed earlier. Yet God does not abandon his people and it is, as it were, as if He goes into Exile with them.

At the end of his vision of idolatry in the Temple (Chapters 8-11), and just prior to seeing the significant departure of the glory from the Temple, Ezekiel can look in the future and see how Israel is scattered yet one day will be restored and be following God with a new heart – looking forward to the New Covenant:

"Therefore say, Thus saith the Lord God; Although I have cast them far off among

the heathen, and although I have scattered them among the countries, yet will I be to them as a little sanctuary in the countries where they shall come. Therefore say, Thus saith the Lord God; I will even gather you from the people, and assemble you out of the countries where ye have been scattered, and I will give you the land of Israel. And they shall come thither, and they shall take away all the detestable things thereof and all the abominations thereof from thence. And I will give them one heart, and I will put a new spirit within you; and I will take the stony heart out of their flesh, and will give them an heart of flesh: That they may walk in my statutes, and keep mine ordinances, and do them: and they shall be my people, and I will be their God." (Ezekiel 11:17-20.)

Before we come to the change in message, triggered by the Fall of Jerusalem, announced in chapter 33, there is the message of judgment, firstly against Israel in chapters 12-24 and then several of the surrounding nations in chapters 25-32. In pronouncing judgment against Israel, Ezekiel often resorted to allegory: a burnt useless stick (chapter 15), a rebellious wife (chapter 16), a dangerous lion that gets captured (chapter 19) and two promiscuous sisters (chapter 23), all representing Israel's foolish rebellion resulting in its justified punishment. They had reached the point of no return; and not even Daniel, Noah or Job could intercede on their behalf to prevent their Exile from happening.

In Chapters 25-32, Ezekiel turns his attention to some of the nations surrounding Israel: Ammon, Moab, Edom and Philistia. They rejoiced in Israel's downfall, showed contempt and took advantage of Israel's plight. Aside from their own internal wickedness, their attitude toward Israel made them ripe for judgment, all of which would take place as prophesied.

He also covers the two bigger powers in the region, Tyre and Egypt, both of which Judah had allied itself with. One of the notable features of these was their pride, viewing themselves as God, which God would bring down using the Babylonians.

Much contained in the later chapters (34 onwards) refers to a coming Messiah that is to reign over His people, specifically Israel, and relates to themes picked up by other prophets, e.g. Zechariah, and in Revelation. Ezekiel was typical of most prophets that saw glimpses of the last days, in that while he looked forward to a Messiah who reigns, he did not see someone coming twice (once to die two thousand years ago and once when He comes to Earth to establish His kingdom); neither did He foresee the Church. Ezekiel, like other prophets, used language and images that the people he was primarily addressing (in this case those exiled, only a remnant of whom would return) could understand, anticipating while not fully understanding the final outcome, to be bound up with the messianic kingdom.

Chapter 34 is about shepherds. Firstly, the bad shepherds that do not feed the flock and then the Good Shepherd – led by the Lord Himself, and His servant David (the Messiah), who will look after the flock.

Chapter 35 is about Edom and God's judgment on that nation that had so rejoiced in Israel's demise.

Chapter 36 depicts Israel restored to the land and living safely in it: "*For I will take you from among the heathen, and gather you out of all countries, and will bring you into your own land. Then will I sprinkle clean water upon you, and ye shall be clean: from all your filthiness, and from all your idols, will I cleanse you. A new heart also will I give you, and a new spirit will I put within you: and I will take away the stony heart out of your flesh, and I will give you an heart of flesh. And I will put my spirit within you, and cause you to walk in my statutes, and ye shall keep my judgments, and do them.*" (36:24-27.)

Chapter 37 is Ezekiel's vision of dry bones: "*Again he said unto me, Prophesy upon these bones, and say unto them, O ye dry bones, hear the word of the Lord. Thus saith the Lord God unto these bones; Behold, I will cause breath to enter into you, and ye shall live: And I will lay sinews upon you, and will bring up flesh upon you, and cover you with skin, and put breath in you, and ye shall live; and ye shall know that I am the Lord.*" (37:4-6.)

The prophesy comes to pass and great hope: "*Neither shall they defile themselves any more with their idols, nor with their detestable things, nor with any of their transgressions: but I will save them out of all their dwelling places, wherein they have sinned, and will cleanse them: so shall they be my people, and I will be their God. And David my servant shall be king over them; and they all shall have one shepherd: they shall also walk in my judgments, and observe my statutes, and do them. And they shall dwell in the land that I have given unto Jacob my servant, wherein your fathers have dwelt; and they shall dwell therein, even they, and their children, and their children's children for ever: and my servant David shall be their prince for ever. Moreover I will make a covenant of peace with them; it shall be an everlasting covenant with them: and I will place them, and multiply them, and will set my sanctuary in the midst of them for evermore. My tabernacle also shall be with them: yea, I will be their God, and they shall be my people. And the heathen shall know that I the Lord do sanctify Israel, when my sanctuary shall be in the midst of them for evermore."* (37:23-28.)

As we turn to the final chapters, that look into the far distant future, we note, firstly, Ezekiel's Gog and Magog account (Ezekiel 38,39). This is written in apocalyptic style, and is reminiscent of events in Revelation 16:16 and 20:8,9, although how these battles relate is for further study (see Chapter 15). Ezekiel 38 and 39 describe a final battle in which military forces from the far north make an all-out assault on the land of Israel. The names of these forces, Gog, Magog, Mechech and Tubal, along with many other nations (38:1-3), are obscure and undefined but represent evil. God defeats them completely before they engage in battle. Israel is resettled and the people are living peacefully and unprotected.

The section ends with great hope: *"When I have brought them again from the people, and gathered them out of their enemies' lands, and am sanctified in them in the sight of many nations; Then shall they know that I am the Lord their God, which caused them to be led into captivity among the heathen: but I have gathered them unto their own land, and have left none of them any more there. Neither will I hide my face any more from them: for I have poured out my spirit upon the house of Israel, saith the Lord God."* (Ezekiel 39:27-29.) Likewise, the final, in the far distant, prophecy (Ezekiel 40-48).

This section, which we might call "A Vision of a New Temple, a New Land, and a New City", appropriately rounds off Ezekiel's prophecy with a full-blown vision of what God's ultimate purposes might look like; with what amounts to a detailed picture of what that vision encompasses. We learn (40:1) that he has been twenty-five years in Exile when he wrote this and it has been thirteen years since the fall of Jerusalem, begging the question, perhaps, of what he was doing in the time since he last prophesied. The prophecy concerns a Temple yet to be built (and still has not been built; the Temple built on Israel's return from Exile was not it, and neither was that built by Herod and destroyed in AD 70).

While the focus was on the Temple, described here in meticulous detail, description was also given of the City where it was and the restored kingdom of Israel, under the rule of the Prince. The glory that departed in chapter 10 returns in chapter 43. One of the more remarkable descriptions was of a river of life flowing from the Temple to the Dead Sea, in chapter 47, giving life to the land. Fittingly and hopefully, "Yahweh Shammah", a Christian transliteration of the Hebrew "Yahweh is there", is the name at the end given to the City (48:35).

Daniel

Daniel and his prophecy

As we come to the last of the major prophets, we do so mindful there has been no let-up in the "wow" factor as wonderful truth is gleaned, sometimes for the first time. It has become increasingly clear, while the prophets were concerned with similar issues, each delivered the message God gave them from their own unique perspective, according to the situation prevailing at the time and the circumstances in which they were placed. We do not see the same message of Israel's judgment that we saw in Isaiah, Jeremiah and Ezekiel, other than delay in the setting up of the long-awaited Messianic kingdom, as God's chosen people were further refined, but we do read of a message of future hope that was meant to motivate faithfulness, as Daniel looked often way ahead into the future and spelled out in remarkable detail what was going to happen, some of which is still yet to happen.

We note in the Hebrew Bible, Daniel is not included with the other prophets but is rather included in "the Writings", illustrating that when it comes to who are the Prophets of the Bible, Daniel may be put in the category of one who prophesied rather that one who is a prophet, although we are mighty glad that he did.

As for that which has been fulfilled, it has been so precisely. It is one reason why taking a straightforward view that the Book of Daniel was completed by Daniel himself, soon after the Cyrus edict around 538 BC, toward the end of his life, is resisted by those who doubt that the future can be accurately predicted. Another stumbling-block is its reference to the miraculous. There are several miracles described in the Book of Daniel, which ought not to be dismissed. As has already been stated, this book takes the straightforward and, unless clearly not the case, literal interpretation of Daniel (recognising still significant gaps in the author's understanding, and differences among eminent scholars).

As fascinating as checking out historical and architectural verification is, and relevant in order to come to a view on the reliability of the text, it is not the intention to examine evidence in this book. It is worth noting Jesus had no doubt Daniel wrote the Book of Daniel, and he was a prophet: *"But when ye shall see the abomination of desolation, spoken of by Daniel the prophet"* (Mark 13:14).

Nevertheless, Daniel's prophecy was less to do with pronouncing oracles on the street and in the palaces so to speak, or messages of judgment or warning, as did many of the writing prophets, and was more to do with dreams and visions (his own and others), and their interpretation as was revealed to him by the Lord, along with a good deal of narrative concerning events happening at the time.

It makes Daniel an extraordinary book to come to grips with. Some parts are so easy to comprehend, such that when we teach it to children at Sunday School all who hear can readily understand what is happening and meant. But when it comes to the prophetic parts of Daniel, much of which is of an apocalyptic nature, matching and indeed complementing the Book of Revelation, as well as the writings of some of the other Hebrew prophets, that can and does present a challenge. Perhaps one of the stand out and endearing things about Daniel was his strength of character, seen over a long lifetime.

If there is a standout theme of the Book of Daniel, it is God's sovereignty and "*that the most high God ruled in the kingdom of men*" (Daniel 5:21). Daniel was the right person to convey that message. From the time, as a teenager, he was taken into captivity in Babylonian, throughout the seventy-year Exile period, until an old man and unlikely never to return to his country, he faithfully did so. He lived a godly life, serving God despite the obstacles and temptations. He was also endowed with extraordinary wisdom and ability, and was promoted to high positions in the governments of the Babylonian kings, Nebuchadnezzar and Belshazzar, and the Mede king Darius, who all recognised his abilities.

Background and context

We learn a lot about Daniel from the opening verses of the book, and while the Book of Daniel is about the message rather than the messenger, we find a lot more, particularly his prayer life and desire to serve God: "*In the third year of the reign of Jehoiakim king of Judah came Nebuchadnezzar king of Babylon unto Jerusalem, and besieged it. And the Lord gave Jehoiakim king of Judah into his hand, with part of the vessels of the house of God: which he carried into the land of Shinar to the house of his god; and he brought the vessels into the treasure house of his god. And the king spake unto Ashpenaz the master of his eunuchs, that he should bring certain of the children of Israel, and of the king's seed, and of the princes; Children in whom was no blemish, but well favoured, and skilful in all wisdom, and cunning in knowledge, and understanding science, and such as had ability in them to stand in the king's palace, and whom they might teach the learning and the tongue of the Chaldeans. And the king appointed them a daily provision of the king's meat, and of the wine which he drank: so nourishing them three years, that at the end thereof they might stand before the king. Now among these were of the children of Judah, Daniel, Hananiah, Mishael, and Azariah: Unto whom the prince of the eunuchs gave names: for he gave unto Daniel the name of Belteshazzar; and to Hananiah, of Shadrach; and to Mishael, of Meshach; and to Azariah, of Abednego. But Daniel purposed in his heart that he would not defile himself with the portion of the king's meat, nor with the wine which he drank: therefore he requested of the prince of the eunuchs that he might not defile himself.*" (Daniel 1:1-8.)

We see here further confirmation that Daniel was among the first exiles to Babylon and he likely was part of the privileged class. "Daniel" means, "God is my judge". His Babylonian name, Belteshazzar, means, "Keeper of the hidden treasures of Bel (a Babylonian god)". Having to adopt a new name and learning the wisdom of the Babylonians, some of it to do with their false worship, did not seem to phase Daniel and his three friends (who will henceforth be referred to as Shadrach, Meshach and Abednego – how the author was taught as a child), and they adapted to their new circumstances and excelled. But when it came to following the Law of YHWH, they would not compromise, and the rest of the chapter (and the book) is about YHWH honouring those who honoured him.

When it comes to background, Daniel was not just against the backdrop of Babylonian Exile but also the Medo-Persian empire that was to take over, and the prophecy of Jeremiah that the captivity would be for seventy years only. This happened, as will be detailed when we come to the post-Exile prophets – Haggai, Zechariah and Malachi; but by then Daniel was a very old man, who could only see this happening with the eyes of faith. A further backdrop was the kingdoms to follow: Greece, Rome and eventually that of Israel's Messiah.

There was much Daniel could not figure out but was assured by the angel he was beloved of God: "*And he said, Go thy way, Daniel: for the words are closed up and sealed till the time of the end*" (Daniel 12:9). It is worth reflecting, the rise and fall of kingdoms, where Christ will ultimately triumph by God's sovereign will, along with a spiritual dimension and battle, were major themes of Daniel's prophetic ministry, reminding us: "*For we wrestle not against flesh and blood, but against principalities, against powers, against the rulers of the darkness of this world, against spiritual wickedness in high places*" (Ephesians 6:12).

For the angel had also told him about the unseen conflict, indeed war, in the spiritual realm; and it was this, as brought out after he had been entreating the Lord in prayer on what was going to happen, that had caused him to become exhausted: "*And he *said unto me, O Daniel, a man greatly beloved, understand the words that I speak unto thee, and stand upright: for unto thee am I now sent. And when he had spoken this word unto me, I stood trembling. Then said he unto me, Fear not, Daniel: for from the first day that thou didst set thine heart to understand, and to chasten thyself before thy God, thy words were heard, and I am come for thy words. But the prince of the kingdom of Persia withstood me one and twenty days: but, lo, Michael, one of the chief princes, came to help me; and I remained there with the kings of Persia.*" (Daniel 10:11-13.)

The only other Old Testament reference to Daniel was by Ezekiel, discussed earlier, with Daniel perhaps being one of the three most righteous men to have ever lived up to then. While not named by the writer of Hebrews as one to be included in his hall of faith, he surely had Daniel in mind when he wrote: *"...of the prophets: Who through faith subdued kingdoms, wrought righteousness, obtained promises, stopped the mouths of lions..."* (Hebrew 11:32,33). Besides parallels to the Book of Revelation (although Daniel is not named), perhaps the most startling reference is that of Jesus' own end-times prophecy, *"When ye therefore shall see the abomination of desolation, spoken of by Daniel the prophet, stand in the holy place ..."* (Matthew 24:15), pointing out that a single prophecy (Daniel 11:31, 12:11) can be fulfilled at different levels, through Antiochus Epiphanes, the sacking of the Temple in AD 70, and the Antichrist.

A synopsis of Daniel

Here we offer two alternative breakdowns (each just as valid):

1. Daniel and his companions in Babylon, ch. 1.

2. Daniel and the dangerous dictator, chs. 2 – 4.

3. Daniel and the contemptuous king, ch. 5.

4. Daniel and the manipulated monarch   ch. 6.

5. Daniel's dream and his visions of the future chs. 7 – 12.

And:

1. Prologue: the setting (ch. 1; in Hebrew).

2. The destinies of the nations of the world (chs. 2–7; in Aramaic).

3. The destiny of the nation of Israel (chs. 8–12; in Hebrew).

At the time Daniel wrote, Hebrew was the language of the Jews; Aramaic was the *lingua franca* universally used. The choice of the language used in the Book of Daniel was likely due to who were the intended audience. It might be said that the Book of Daniel is like a game of two halves: the first half, 1-6, is mostly narrative, and the second, 7-12, mostly prophecy in the form of visions and dreams; with chapters 11 and 12 tying up many of the themes from the prophecies given. Noticeably, the first half is written in the third person (i.e. about Daniel and his world), and the second half is in the first person (i.e. about Daniel's prophecies).

The message of Daniel

Nebuchadnezzar saw an opportunity of training up these and other bright young men to exercise positions in his royal court (chapter 1). Daniel and his three friends were willing to do this, but not to compromise when it came to matters of faith, in particular on matters of diet. This act of faith set a precedence for Daniel's long life that followed, and he and his friends were not only healthier than those who compromised but they excelled in their studies and were promoted in the king's service. In Chapter 2 we read that Nebuchadnezzar had a dream which he could not remember, and decreed that if his wise men (which included the four friends) could not provide an interpretation, they would be put to death.

The dream was about kingdoms that were to follow after Babylon (golden head) – Persia (silver breast), Greece (brass belly), Rome (iron legs and feet of iron and clay), followed by the Messianic kingdom that will usurp all other kingdoms: "T*hou sawest till that a stone was cut out without hands, which smote the image upon his feet that were of iron and clay, and brake them to pieces*" (Daniel 2:34); something Daniel interpreted to the king's satisfaction, giving glory to God, and as a result the grateful king promoted Daniel to high office.

Chapter 3 is about the image of gold Nebuchadnezzar had built representing himself, demanding his subjects worship that image; and the blazing furnace Meshach, Shadrach and Abednego were cast into for refusing to do so; and how God miraculously delivered them from the furnace.

Chapter 4 might be seen in three sections: Nebuchadnezzar's dream of a tree,

Daniel interprets the dream and the dream is fulfilled. God had already used Nebuchadnezzar as his instrument of judgment, and had revealed himself both in the interpretation of his dream and the way God had delivered Meshach, Shadrach and Abednego; and yet the king remained proud despite a dream that he would be stripped of his power, something Daniel was able to interpret. A year later, the king was driven away from his palace and became crazy for seven years until he recognized that God was the true God whom he had to honour. And so he did and thus he was restored. As for Nebuchadnezzar, he could not have spoken a truer word: *"At the same time my reason returned unto me; and for the glory of my kingdom, mine honour and brightness returned unto me; and my counsellors and my lords sought unto me; and I was established in my kingdom, and excellent majesty was added unto me. Now I Nebuchadnezzar praise and extol and honour the King of heaven, all whose works are truth, and his ways judgment: and those that walk in pride he is able to abase."* (Daniel 4:36-37.)

Chapter 5 is about Nebuchadnezzar's successor, Belshazzar, who arrogantly made a feast for his subjects, and in doing so mocked the God of Israel. Here we witness the writing on the wall: *"And this is the writing that was written, Mene, Mene, Tekel, Upharsin. This is the interpretation of the thing: Mene; God hath numbered thy kingdom, and finished it. Tekel; Thou art weighed in the balances, and art found wanting. Peres; Thy kingdom is divided, and given to the Medes and Persians."* (Daniel 5: 25-28.)

This Daniel interpreted and, now an old man, was once again promoted to a high position. Like Nebuchadnezzar, Belshazzar's pride had been judged; and while Nebuchadnezzar repented and his throne was restored, in Belshazzar's case he did not and he was killed. That very night, the mighty Babylonian empire was overthrown by the Persians, and Darius the Mede became king in his stead. Darius, recognizing Daniel's qualities, retained him in his royal service and Daniel prospered. This made other high officials jealous, who tricked the king into making an edict that all were to worship King Darius, on pain of death. Naturally, Daniel refused to comply and he was thrown into the lion's den, but God delivered him, much to the king's relief.

Moving onto the second half of the book, our big challenge is understanding the dreams and visions given to Daniel. Chapters 7 and 12 are about end times and can be tied in with the Book of Revelation, while chapters 8 and 11 seem more to do with the future of the Medo-Persian empire and it being conquered by the Greeks, depicted by a ram and a goat in chapter 8, with many of the details remarkable in terms of historical correlation. Chapter 11 appears to be about what happens after Alexander the Great dies and the Greek empire is divided among his four generals; and both chapters remarkably detail events that have come and gone. One commentator has identified 135 specific prophecies fulfilled in chapter 11. It is worth noting too that chapter 11 may also be seen to have fulfilment in the reign of the Antichrist and an instance where two interpretations may apply.

The culmination of chapter 7 sees one, identified in the New Testament as the Antichrist, who is himself cast down; with the true king (the Messiah) taking over, with his saints: "And *he shall speak great words against the most High, and shall wear out the saints of the most High, and think to change times and laws: and they shall be given into his hand until a time and times and the dividing of time. But the judgment shall sit, and they shall take away his dominion, to consume and to destroy it unto the end. And the kingdom and dominion, and the greatness of the kingdom under the whole heaven, shall be given to the people of the saints of the most High, whose kingdom is an everlasting kingdom, and all dominions shall serve and obey him.*" (Daniel 7:25-27.) It is worth noting that both the Ancient of Days (7:9) and the Son of Man (7:13) are named by Daniel, along with much rich imagery; and we see a parallel with Revelation 1 and 4.

Regarding chapter 9, and to an extent 10 (in particular Daniel's remarkable prayer of chapter 9), this was two to three years after the end of the seventy-year Exile, after which the captives could return back to their land. Besides Jeremiah's prophecy, there is the prophecy about Cyrus in Isaiah 45. Daniel's prayer was one of contrition, and wanting to find out God's will and seeking God's honour. The answer was an extraordinary and unexpected one, which looked beyond merely returning from Exile but to the coming of the Messiah (in seventy weeks, including the missing one). Some commentators, relating sixty-nine weeks to a day being a year and 483 years to the coming of the King (Jesus), but this and the "missing" seventieth week is for further study (see Chapter 15).

Regarding chapter 10, linked to another Daniel prayer, we are reminded of a spiritual war in the heavenlies, with demonic powers seeking control of temporal powers. Daniel sees a vision of an amazing heavenly being, who comforts him: "*And he said unto me, O Daniel, a man greatly beloved, understand the words that I speak unto thee, and stand upright: for unto thee am I now sent. And when he had spoken this word unto me, I stood trembling. Then said he unto me, Fear not, Daniel: for from the first day that thou didst set thine heart to understand, and to chasten thyself before thy God, thy words were heard, and I am come for thy words*

... And said, O man greatly beloved, fear not: peace be unto thee, be strong, yea, be strong. And when he had spoken unto me, I was strengthened, and said, Let my lord speak; for thou hast strengthened me." (10:10-12,19)

Regarding chapter 11, it should be read as not just being fulfilled during the time of the Greeks but to be fulfilled in the time of the Antichrist. The final chapter, which is a continuation, makes sobering reading as it speaks how that time ends and resonates with what we see now. Yet there is hope; not least that the purposes of God will be fulfilled, and the reward for the righteous:

"And at that time shall Michael stand up, the great prince which standeth for the children of thy people: and there shall be a time of trouble, such as never was since there was a nation even to that same time: and at that time thy people shall be delivered, every one that shall be found written in the book. And many of them that sleep in the dust of the earth shall awake, some to everlasting life, and some to shame and everlasting contempt. And they that be wise shall shine as the brightness of the firmament; and they that turn many to righteousness as the stars for ever and ever. But thou, O Daniel, shut up the words, and seal the book, even to the time of the end: many shall run to and fro, and knowledge shall be increased." (Daniel 12:1-4.)

The warning is clear: "M*any shall be purified, and made white, and tried; but the wicked shall do wickedly: and none of the wicked shall understand; but the wise shall understand*" (Daniel 12:10); but so is the hope of the coming of the Messiah along with the saints (and that would include all His followers) to rule. As one person, reflecting on why was all this was revealed to Daniel, concluded, that besides being a warning to unbelievers and those who would try to usurp God's authority, it was to encourage God's people (then and now) to stand firm, do exploits, bring understanding, endure suffering, be refined, resist evil, find rest. As with the prophets generally, we are grateful Daniel stuck to his task.

As we close, we do so mindful that we have hardly scratched the surface concerning Daniel's prophecies; and, while we will revisit two of them in Chapter 15, the reader is encouraged to check these out themselves in a spirit of open humility, mindful of wide differences in interpretation among commentators. One thing that ought to be pondered is that these prophecies were history before it happened; and, as Daniel was able to witness first hand, the Sovereign God is in control of history. While some history was fulfilled before the first coming of Jesus, other parts spanned both comings, with some not actually taking place until after Jesus returns to planet earth. Daniel unlikely had more than basic insights into the period in between or the time elapsed. Each prophecy covers different periods. Some have both an initial and a final fulfilment, which is to be revealed. An example is the BC Antichrist, Antiochus Epiphanes; but there is one still to come that Daniel also referred to, the identity of which is yet to be revealed.

As can be the case with the prophets, the message and the messenger are closely linked, even though presenting the message was invariably done with due humility, honouring the message originator. Unlike with the other major prophets, we do not get the impression that Daniel's message was received negatively, and it was likely the exiled people needed hope and the despot rulers evidently welcomed some of his future insights. It is evident, where Daniel was concerned, that hearing from God was an emotionally draining experience, whenever God spoke to him in dreams and visions with vivid and alarming imagery, from which he could not detach. There is evidence of a meaningful prayer life and Daniel entreated God, we are told, three times a day, Daniel 6:10. Among his items of prayer, Daniel prayed on behalf of the people, pleading their plight.

The following is offered by way of summary of Daniel's life and ministry:

1. His whole life was marked by his faithfulness to God, and this was maintained from a young teenager until he was an old man.

2. He was diligent in all that he did, and God blessed him and made him a blessing to others.

3. While he submitted to ungodly authorities, it was always God first, even if it meant he had to die for adopting godly principles.

4. His extraordinary qualities as a result of God's blessing were recognized by those who did not recognize the God of Israel, including ungodly rulers, with whom he cooperated, working for the common good.

5. He was recognized and honoured by at least three kings: Nebuchadnezzar, Belshazzar and Darius, and that had a significant impact in the unravelling of God's plan for Israel, including influencing all of the kings in unexpected ways and impacting the divine plan.

6. He had glimpses of a still-to-happen future: "*And in the days of these kings*

shall the God of heaven set up a kingdom, which shall never be destroyed: and the kingdom shall not be left to other people, but it shall break in pieces and consume all these kingdoms, and it shall stand for ever" (Daniel 2:44).

7. He prayed amazing prayers, especially the one on behalf of his people and confessing their sins, which ends: "*O Lord, hear; O Lord, forgive; O Lord, hearken and do; defer not, for thine own sake, O my God: for thy city and thy people are called by thy name*" (Daniel 9:19).

8. He had a glimpse into the spiritual warfare that profoundly was going on in the background, and did so prophetically: "*But the prince of the kingdom of Persia withstood me one and twenty days*" (Daniel 10:13).

9. Just as he looked forward to the reign of the Christ and His everlasting kingdom that will usurp all before it, he saw the evil reign of the yet to be revealed Antichrist, and Antichrist-type figures before him, realizing: "*…yet he shall come to his end, and none shall help him*" (Daniel 11:45).

10. He understood a time of trouble for God's people, some of it still to be fulfilled: "*…there shall be a time of trouble, such as never was since there was a nation even to that same time: and at that time thy people shall be delivered, every one that shall be found written in the book*" (Daniel 12:1).

11. He understood and humbly accepted the limits of his own knowledge and understanding, and was patient: "*And he said, go thy way, Daniel: for the words are closed up and sealed till the time of the end*" (Daniel 12:9).

12. He could personally look forward to a wonderful end beyond the grave: "*But go thou thy way till the end be: for thou shalt rest, and stand in thy lot at the end of the days*" (Daniel 12:13).

Chapter 13: The minor prophets (Hosea to Malachi)

Overview

Having discussed the four major prophets (Isaiah, Jeremiah, Ezekiel, Daniel), we turn to the twelve minor prophets (Hosea, Joel, Amos, Obadiah, Jonah, Micah, Nahum, Habakkuk, Zephaniah, Haggai, Zechariah, Malachi), and thus complete our trawl through the Old Testament, with the view to picking up every prophet (and others who spoke or acted prophetically) we find along the way. We will cover here each minor prophet in the order they appear in the Christian Bible and adopt the same structure as with the major prophets, to keep us on track.

1. The prophet and his prophecy.

2. Background and context.

3. A synopsis of the book.

4. The message of the prophet.

THE MINOR PROPHETS (Update)

Prophet	Date (B.C.) Approx	Name Meaning	Prophesies To/About	King at Time (assumption)
Obadiah	845-750	'Servant of the Lord'	Israel/Edom	Jehoram (Ju) Joram (Is)
Joel	835-796	'Yahweh is God'	Judah	Joash (Ju) Jehu/Jehoahaz(Is)
Jonah	793-753	'Dove'	Nineveh	Jeroboam 11 (Is) Amaziah/(Ju)
Hosea	753-715	'Salvation'	Israel	Jotham/Ahaz (Ju) Jeroboam/Pekah/Hoshea (Is)
Amos	760-755	'Burden-bearer'	Israel/Judah	Jotham/Uzziah (Ju) Jeroboam/Pekah (Is)
Micah	770-710	'Who is like unto the Lord'	Israel/Judah	Jotham/Ahaz/Hezekiah(Ju) Zechariah – Hoshea (Is)
Nahum	655	'Consolation'	Nineveh	Manasseh (Ju) *
Zephaniah	625	'Yahweh hides'	Judah/Assyria. And Nations	Josiah (Ju)
Habakkuk	610	'Clings to'	Judah/Nations	Josiah/Jehoahaz/Jehoiakim
Haggai	520	'My Feast'	Judah	N/A
Zechariah	520	'Yahweh has remembered'	Judah	N/A
Malachi	460 - 420	'My Messenger'	Judah	N/A

Like most charts, the one above is a mixed blessing. Here the minor prophets are set in chronological order, although in some cases, specifically Obadiah and Joel, the dates are disputed by scholars. The author does not have a view other than, if it is over a hundred years later, as some argue, it does not much affect our understanding of the message, which - as we continually point out - is the most important aspect of our study. For the rest, we can be confident the dates are fairly accurate because of historical clues in the text; and with prophets like Zechariah, he dated his prophecy by both year and month. Other aspects – meaning of the prophet's name, intended audience and the king at the time – all help us to further understand the all-important context discussed in Chapter 2.

Many of the basic observations we made with the major prophets apply also to the minor prophets, but there is enough in each that is unique and merits study, which by ignoring we will miss out considerably on the important contributions made by these prophets. While most prophets dispensed variations on the theme of judgment and repentance, restoration and hope, each did so according to the circumstances prevailing at the time, the prophet's specific calling and their particular perspective and gifting. While what each major prophet prophesied was major, the same is true for the minor prophets; they just happened to write less. Like the major prophets, the minor prophets also experienced rejection. They were a mixed bag, from different strata of society, with a number from more humble backgrounds and called to minister in rural areas. They were called to different audiences, faithfully passing on the message God had given them. The common factor all major and minor prophets had was that they were used by God.

722 BC and 586 BC are two key dates to bear in mind; the first being when the Northern Kingdom (Israel) was taken into Assyrian captivity and the second when the Southern Kingdom (Judah) was taken into Babylonian captivity. Those two significant events overshadowed much of the prophesying of the minor prophets. 931 BC and 800 BC are two other dates worth keeping in mind: the first is when the kingdom was divided following the death of King Solomon; and the second approximates the death of the prophet Elisha. Elijah and Elisha were the two main prophets following the division of the kingdoms, and prophesied to Israel; and all the minor prophets followed them. While the major prophets operated in Judah, nearing the time of the Judean Exile, and then Babylon after the Exile, the minor prophets operated from before that time, and in both Israel (while around) and Judah, and following the return from Exile, ending with Malachi.

In the Jewish Bible, the twelve minor prophets featured in a single book, *The Book of the Twelve*, where the prophecies of the twelve minor prophets can be read as a single unit, notwithstanding the uniqueness of each. The twelve "books" in that book might be considered in three groups: (1) the books that came from the period of Assyrian power (Hosea, Joel, Amos, Obadiah, Jonah, Micah); (2) those written about the time of the decline of Assyria (Nahum, Habakkuk, Zephaniah); and (3) those dating after the Exile (Haggai, Zechariah, Malachi). Irrespective of how we might be inclined to view the minor prophets, what we can learn from their lives and ministries are every bit as important as what we found when we covered the major prophets; and so we begin with the first ...

Hosea

The prophet and his prophecy

His tragic marriage was the principal medium through which Hosea spoke God's message to God's people. We know nothing about Hosea except that he lived at the time of Isaiah prophesying complementary messages into different situations, and his serially unfaithful wife. His marriage reflected the heartache God was having with His beloved people. As with other contemporaries, Amos and Micah, he faithfully discharged his office: these were ordinary people who were often speaking to ordinary people. Hosea spoke for forty years during the last decades of the Northern Kingdom of Israel – in the reigns of Jeroboam II in Israel, and Uzziah, Jotham, Ahaz and Hezekiah in Judah (Hosea 1:1).

The prophecy of Hosea represented the last chance for Israel to avoid the disaster that would surely befall her if she did not repent of her sin. His complaint was that there was a lack of knowledge (*"yada"*) of YHWH in the land. The overriding theme of Hosea's message was God's love (*"chesed"*), which has no exact English translation and is more to do with covenant faithfulness, steadfast love and lovingkindness - which is how God feels regarding often faithless Israel. As with certain other prophets, God used marriage to make a point (Ezekiel was not allowed to mourn his wife's death, and Jeremiah was not allowed to marry). Hosea was told to marry a prostitute, love her and take her back, despite her committing adultery. As if his words were not powerful enough, this symbolic act was a powerful illustration of his key message.

Besides being married, Hosea had three children: a son called Jezreel, a daughter Lo-Ruhamah and another son Lo-Ammi; and it was not certain all were his. All the names are described in the text as having symbolic meaning, reflecting the relationship between God and Israel. Jezreel is named after the valley of that name. Lo-Ruhamah is named to denote the ruined condition of the Kingdom of Israel and

Lo-Ammi is named in token of God's rejection of His people. Just as God is ever seeking to restore His wife (Israel), Hosea is told to buy Gomer back, who because of her prostitution had been sold into some form of slavery, and he did so for fifteen shekels and a quantity of barley.

Background and context

Hosea preached to Israel, as did Amos; whose ministries may have overlapped, although Amos began some ten years earlier and prophesied for a much shorter period. Some of their message was also to Judah, and in Amos's case, surrounding nations too. Much of the background and context for the two prophets are the same, and since Hosea is first according to the order of the Christian Bible, we will describe some of the common features here and not repeat unnecessarily when we get to Amos. We will see by the time we have studied the two prophets, while they addressed similar grievances as far as God was concerned, their approach was different. Hosea appeared tender and Amos seemed tough; Hosea emphasised God's love; Amos, God's justice (although both did both). The net outcome was that both messages were rejected, and the fall of Israel in 722 BC, followed by Assyrian captivity, might have been avoided, but was not.

Both prophets began during the reign of King Jeroboam II (786 – 746 BC), although it is quite likely that Hosea was still prophesying come the Captivity, in which short time Israel got through six more kings. Both kingdoms of Israel and Judah were enjoying great prosperity during Jeroboam II's reign and had reached new political and military heights (cf. 2 Kings 14:23-15:7; 2 Chronicles 26). Israel at the time was politically secure and spiritually smug. About forty years earlier, at the end of his ministry, Elisha had prophesied the resurgence of Israel's power (2 Kings 13:17–19), and more recently Jonah had prophesied her restoration to a semblance of prosperity, not known since the days of Solomon (2 Kings 14:25).

The nation felt sure, therefore, that she was in God's good graces. But prosperity increased Israel's religious and moral corruption. God's past punishments for unfaithfulness were forgotten, yet His patience was at an end. Idolatry, pride, false prophets, bad and foolish leaders, unwise foreign alliances, child sacrifice, sham religion, intolerance of righteousness, trust in riches, social injustice, judicial corruption, breakdown in law and order, haves and have nots, were all features of national life, although different prophets emphasised different things; yet without the hoped-for response but with inevitable consequence for their sin. In keeping with revealing God's heart, Hosea's message was mainly poetry.

A synopsis of the book

1. Superscription (1:1).

2. The unfaithful wife and the faithful husband (1:2-3:5).

    - The children as signs (1:2-2:1).

    - The unfaithful wife (2:2-23).

        o The Lord's judgment of Israel (2:2-13).

        o The Lord's restoration of Israel (2:14-23).

    - The faithful husband (ch. 3).

3. The unfaithful nation and the faithful God (chs. 4-14).

    - Israel's unfaithfulness (4:1-6:3).

        o The general charge (4:1–3).

        o The cause declared and the results described (4:4-19).

        o A special message to the people and leaders (ch. 5).

        o The people's sorrowful plea (6:1-3).

    - Israel's punishment (6:4-10:15).

        o The case stated (6:4-7:16).

        o The judgment pronounced (chs. 8-9).

        o Summary and appeal (ch. 10).

    - The Lord's faithful love (chs. 11-14).

        o The Lord's fatherly love (11:1-11).

        o Israel's punishment for unfaithfulness (11:12-13:16).

        o Israel's restoration after repentance (ch. 14).

The message of the prophet

As far as God was concerned, according to Hosea, those whom He was betrothed to (priests, prophets, princes, profiteers, people) had committed the heinous sin of rejecting Him, worshipping false gods, making unholy alliances with God's enemies and doing evil: infidelity, independence, intrigue, idolatry, ignorance, immorality and ingratitude. So much of the book of Hosea is about God pleading with His people with warnings of judgment if they did not repent, yet His yearning that they return to Him and find healing, blessing and restoration. They were beloved of Him; and, while they were faithless, God remained faithful, and yet could not overlook their sin, using prophets like Hosea as His mouthpieces. As for the prophet and the prostitute, it was clear that Hosea's relationship with his wife was a metaphor as to how it was then between YHWH and Israel.

Our attention is drawn to Hosea's marriage to Gomer and the obvious parallels with God's marriage to Israel, in the first three chapters, culminating with him rescuing her from slavery. Hosea looks to the future: *"And I said unto her, Thou shalt abide for me many days; thou shalt not play the harlot, and thou shalt not be for another man: so will I also be for thee. For the children of Israel shall abide many days without a king, and without a prince, and without a sacrifice, and without an image, and without an ephod, and without teraphim: Afterward shall the children of Israel return, and seek the Lord their God, and David their king; and shall fear the Lord and his goodness in the latter days."* (3:3-5.)

He then turns to the crux of his message – God's complaint and the consequences and inevitable outcome if the people of God do not repent from their wicked ways: *"Hear the word of the Lord, ye children of Israel: for the Lord hath a controversy with the inhabitants of the land, because there is no truth, nor mercy, nor knowledge of God in the land. By swearing, and lying, and killing, and stealing, and committing adultery, they break out, and blood toucheth blood. Therefore shall the land mourn ..."* (4:1-3.)

Chapters 6 - 7 sees God lamenting over the fact that His people are unrestrained and unrepentant in their sin: *"Come, and let us return unto the Lord: for he hath torn, and he will heal us; he hath smitten, and he will bind us up. After two days will he revive us: in the third day he will raise us up, and we shall live in his sight. Then shall we know, if we follow on to know the Lord: his going forth is prepared as the morning; and he shall come unto us as the rain, as the latter and former rain unto the earth. O Ephraim, what shall I do unto thee? O Judah, what shall I do unto thee? for your goodness is as a morning cloud, and as the early dew it goeth away."* (6:1-4.) There are muggings and murders in the countryside (6:9), deceit and burglary in the town (7:1), drunkenness and sexual immorality everywhere (7:4-6). It's sapping their strength as if they're growing old before their time (7.8-9). *"Ephraim also is like a silly dove without heart: they call to Egypt, they go to Assyria"* (7:11). *"And they have not cried unto me with their heart ... They return, but not to the most High..."* (7:14, 16).

Chapters 8 - 10 make it clear there is no hope for Israel on the trajectory they are on. The name of God is on their lips (8:2), but because of their continuing idolatry and rejection of God's call to repentance, their end is in sight (10:15). They worshipped idols (8.1-6). *"They have sown the wind, and they shall reap the whirlwind..."* (8:7). They run backwards and forwards between Assyria and Egypt instead of turning to God for help (8:9,10), but this to no avail (8:14). The day of reckoning is nigh, *unless* they change their ways: *"Sow to yourselves in righteousness, reap in mercy; break up your fallow ground: for it is time to seek the LORD, till he come and rain righteousness upon you. Ye have plowed wickedness, ye have reaped iniquity; ye have eaten the fruit of lies: because thou didst trust in thy way, in the multitude of thy mighty men."* (10:12-13.)

Chapters 11-13 continue in similar vein: God pleading for Israel to return and reminding them of past foolishness. In the last chapter (14), Israel is called to repentance, with God promising healing and fruitfulness. *"O Israel, return unto the LORD thy God; for thou hast fallen by thine iniquity. Take with you words, and turn to the LORD: say unto him, Take away all iniquity, and receive us graciously: so will we render the calves of our lips. Asshur shall not save us; we will not ride upon horses: neither will we say any more to the work of our hands, Ye are our gods: for in thee the fatherless findeth mercy. I will heal their backsliding, I will love them freely: for mine anger is turned away from him. I will be as the dew unto Israel: he shall grow as the lily, and cast forth his roots as Lebanon."* (14:1-5.) The book ends with the people being called to wise up and to no longer rebel: *"Who is wise, and he shall understand these things? prudent, and he shall know them? for the ways of the LORD are right, and the just shall walk in them: but the transgressors shall fall therein"* (14:9).

Joel

The prophet and his prophecy

We know little about Joel the man, or the devastating plague of locusts spoken of at the start of his message. This, for Joel, was a clarion call for Zion to turn to the Lord. As far as this plague went, this was a current event and yet Joel looks far into the future, linking the Day of the Lord to the time recorded in the New Testament that is to do with the coming of the Holy Spirit and spanning to the end time battle that precedes the ushering in of the restored Kingdom of Israel and a time of peace and vindication for the people of God.

Background and context

The book contains no references to datable historical events. Many interpreters date it somewhere between the late seventh and early fifth centuries BC. In any case, its message is not significantly affected by its dating. The Book of Joel has linguistic parallels to that used by other prophets, and addresses some of their themes, especially around different aspects associated with the Day of the Lord.

A synopsis of the book

1. Title (1:1).

2. Judah experiences a foretaste of the Day of the Lord (1:2-2:17).

    - A call to mourning and prayer (1:2-14).

    - The announcement of the Day of the Lord (1:15-2:11).

    - A call to repentance and prayer (2:12-17).

3. Judah Is assured of salvation in the Day of the Lord (2:18-3:21).

    - The Lord's restoration of Judah (2:18-27).

    - The Lord's renewal of His people (2:28-32).

    - The coming of the Day of the Lord (ch. 3).

        o The nations judged (3:1-16).

        o God's people blessed (3:17-21).

The message of the prophet

Joel sees the massive locust plague and severe drought devastating Judah as a harbinger of the *"great and dreadful day of the Lord"* (2:31). Confronted with this crisis, he calls on everyone to take stock on what is happening and repent and pray: old and young (1:2–3), drunkards (1:5), farmers (1:11) and priests (1:13). *"And rend your heart, and not your garments, and turn unto the Lord your God: for he is gracious and merciful, slow to anger, and of great kindness, and repenteth him of the evil"* (2:13). While the locusts were likely for real, he describes them as the Lord's army and sees in their coming a reminder that the Day of the Lord is near. He describes it as one of punishment of unfaithful Israel as well as the nations. Restoration and blessing will come only after judgment and repentance: *"And I will restore to you the years that the locust hath eaten ... And ye shall know that I am in the midst of Israel, and that I am the Lord your God, and none else: and my people shall never be ashamed."* (2:25, 27.)

The verses that follow are referred to by Peter at the Day of Pentecost (Acts 2:17-21), ushering in the Day of the Lord; and yet two thousand years on we are still to see the complete fulfilment: *"And it shall come to pass afterward, that I will pour out my spirit upon all flesh; and your sons and your daughters shall prophesy, your old men shall dream dreams, your young men shall see visions: "And also upon the servants and upon the handmaids in those days will I pour out my spirit. And I will shew wonders in the heavens and in the earth, blood, and fire, and pillars of smoke. The sun shall be turned into darkness, and the moon into blood, before the great and terrible day of the Lord come. And it shall come to pass, that whosoever shall call on the name of the Lord shall be delivered: for in mount Zion and in Jerusalem shall be deliverance, as the Lord hath said, and in the remnant whom the Lord shall call."* (2: 28-32.)

Then we come to end-time battles, referred to in Ezekiel, Daniel, Zephaniah, Zechariah, Revelation (discussed in Chapter 15): *"I will also gather all nations, and will bring them down into the valley of Jehoshaphat, and will plead with them there for my people and for my heritage Israel, whom they have scattered among the nations, and parted my land ... Proclaim ye this among the Gentiles; Prepare war, wake up the mighty men, let all the men of war draw near; let them come up: Beat your plowshares into swords and your pruninghooks into spears: let the weak say, I am strong ... Multitudes, multitudes in the valley of decision: for the day of the Lord is near in the valley of decision ... "* (3:2, 9-10, 14.)

After which God Himself secures the final victory; there is a time of blessing for Israel: "*The Lord also shall roar out of Zion, and utter his voice from Jerusalem; and the heavens and the earth shall shake: but the Lord will be the hope of his people, and the strength of the children of Israel. So shall ye know that I am the Lord your God dwelling in Zion, my holy mountain: then shall Jerusalem be holy, and there shall no strangers pass through her any more. And it shall come to pass in that day, that the mountains shall drop down new wine, and the hills shall flow with milk, and all the rivers of Judah shall flow with waters, and a fountain shall come forth out of the house of the Lord, and shall water the valley of Shittim ... But Judah shall dwell for ever, and Jerusalem from generation to generation. For I will cleanse their blood that I have not cleansed: for the Lord dwelleth in Zion.*" (16-18, 20-21.)

Amos

The prophet and his prophecy

Amos (whose name means "burden") was from Tekoa (1:1), a small town in Judah about six miles south of Bethlehem and eleven miles from Jerusalem. He was not a man of the court like Isaiah, nor was he a member of a priestly family like Jeremiah and Ezekiel. He earned his living from the flock and the sycamore-fig grove (1:1; 7:14–15), and was of humble means. Whether he owned the flocks and groves or only worked as a hired hand is not known. His skill with words, and the strikingly broad range of his general knowledge of history and the world, preclude his being an ignorant peasant. Though his home was in Judah, he was sent to announce God's judgment on the Northern Kingdom (Israel).

He ministered for the most part at Bethel (7:10-13), Israel's main religious sanctuary where the upper echelons of the Northern Kingdom, including the priests that opposed him, worshipped. The book brings prophecies together in a carefully organised form intended to be read as a unit. It offers few, if any, clues as to the chronological order of his spoken messages – he may have repeated them on many occasions to reach everyone who came to worship. The book is ultimately addressed to all Israel (hence the references to Judah and Jerusalem).

While Amos is best known as God's mouthpiece, doing the job God had given him, it was evident he had a relationship with God, such that he could even change God's mind: "*Thus hath the Lord God shewed unto me; and, behold, he formed grasshoppers in the beginning of the shooting up of the latter growth; and, lo, it was the latter growth after the king's mowings. And it came to pass, that when they had made an end of eating the grass of the land, then I said, O Lord God, forgive, I beseech thee: by whom shall Jacob arise? for he is small. The Lord repented for this: It shall not be, saith the Lord. Thus hath the Lord God shewed unto me: and, behold, the Lord God called to contend by fire, and it devoured the great deep, and did eat up a part. Then said I, O Lord God, cease, I beseech thee: by whom shall Jacob arise? for he is small. The Lord repented for this: This also shall not be, saith the Lord God."* (7:1-6.)

Background and context

From the outset we are introduced to *"the words of Amos, who was among the herdmen of Tekoa, which he saw concerning Israel in the days of Uzziah king of Judah, and in the days of Jeroboam the son of Joash king of Israel, two years before the earthquake"* (1:1). Amos prophesied during the reigns of Uzziah over Judah (792–740 BC) and Jeroboam II over Israel (793–753). The main part of his ministry was probably carried out 760–750 BC. The background and context to Amos's ministry was as described above (see under his contemporary, Hosea).

A synopsis of the book

1. Superscription (1:1).

2. Introduction to Amos's message (1:2).

3. Oracles against the nations, including Judah and Israel (1:3-2:16).

    - Judgment on Aram (1:3-5).

    - Judgment on Philistia (1:6-8).

    - Judgment on Phoenicia (1:9-10).

    - Judgment on Edom (1:11-12).

    - Judgment on Ammon (1:13-15).

    - Judgment on Moab (2:1-3).

    - Judgment on Judah (2:4-5).

    - Judgment on Israel (2:6-16).

        - Ruthless oppression of the poor (2:6-7a).

- Unbridled profanation of religion (2:7b-8).
- Contrasted position of the Israelites (2:9-12).
- The oppressive system will perish (2:13-16).

4. Oracles against Israel (3:1-5:17).
   - Judgment on the chosen people (ch. 3).
     - God's punishment announced (3:1-2).
     - The announcement vindicated (3:3-8).
     - The punishment vindicated (3:9-15).
   - Judgment on an unrepentant people (ch. 4).
     - Judgment on the socialites (4:1-3).
     - Perversion of religious life (4:4-5).
     - Past calamities brought no repentance (4:6-11).
     - No hope for a hardened people (4:12-13).
   - Judgment on an unjust people (5:1-17).
     - The death dirge (5:1-3).
     - Exhortation to life (5:4-6).
     - Indictment of injustices (5:7-13).
     - Exhortation to life (5:14-15).
     - Prosperity will turn to grief (5:16-17).

5. Announcements of Exile (5:18-6:14).
   - A message of woe against Israel's perverted religion (5:18-27).
   - A message of woe against Israel's complacent pride (6:1-7).
   - A sworn judgment on the proud and unjust nation (6:8-14).

6. Visions of divine retribution (7:1-9:10).
   - Judgment relented (7:1-6).

- A swarm of locusts (7:1-3).
- A consuming fire (7:4-6).
- Judgment unrelented (7:7-9:10).
    - The plumb line (7:7-17).
    - The basket of ripe fruit (ch. 8).
    - The Lord by the altar (9:1-10).
7. Restored Israel's blessed future (9:11-15).
    - Revival of the House of David (9:11-12).
    - Restoration of Israel to an Edenic Promised Land (9:13-15).

The message of the prophet

In his prophesying, primarily to Israel and to a lesser extent Judah, it was what God told him to do – for they were particular objects of God's interest – which was to get His special people to turn back to Him – if need be using natural disasters to shake them up; and, later (from 722 BC), more drastically, letting them be taken into captivity by a hostile, foreign power (Assyria). While obedience to YHWH and practising justice and righteousness, especially to the poor and weak, may these days be seen as two separate messages, as far as Amos was concerned the two were closely linked. If they truly loved God, they would love their neighbour too. He also prophesied against the nations surrounding Israel (Damascus, Philistia, Tyre, Edom, Ammon and Moab – see map in Chapter 2), which between them did many wicked acts and God would punish them. There was much repetition in Amos's utterances, but the sense of indignation over the wickedness he observed was all too evident. His images, like a basket of over-ripe fruit that the people were compared to, and a plumb line that could be used to expose crookedness, in the main fell on deaf ears.

Amos is not the only prophet to speak out against social injustice or the exploitation of the poor, but he was one of the more prominent to do so; and it is not surprising that Christians on the Left like to quote from Amos about justice and righteousness. Amos's message was more directed at individuals rather than institutions, who were expected to obey God's commands. The government was under a king who, along with most of the kings of Israel and Judah, was a bad king, and was also an object of rebuke. Not only that, but the judges were corrupt and could be bribed by the rich and powerful. As for the priests, who were the custodians of the law and meant to be the conscience of the nation, they should have been teaching the way of God but were unfaithful to what should have been their calling. Their main fixation was to maintain the *status quo* and threaten, which they did, and shut up Amos, which they could not.

As with many prophets, they wanted to kill him if they could. The situation in Amos's time, while different to that of today, had similarities; like the rich doing well at the expense of or ignoring those who are poor or with a just grievance. We might well reflect that Amos's plea to practice justice and righteousness and return to God is just as relevant for us at this time as it was to 750 BC Israel. We might also reflect that Amos was fully engaged and even changed God's mind.

One simple breakdown of Amos message is:

1. Indictments x 8 (chapters 1-2).

2. Oracles x 3 (chapter 3-6).

3. Visions x 5 (chapters 7-9).

We close with the following (memorable) individual verses (to be read in context), that the author has found helpful when it comes to meditation.

3:2 *"You only have I known of all the families of the earth: therefore I will punish you for all your iniquities."* Israel remains God's special people and it seems, as such, He will deal harshly with them in order to bring them back to Himself.

3:7 *"Surely the Lord God will do nothing, but he revealeth his secret unto his servants the prophets."* In the Old Testament, certainly, God consistently told His people what He was about to do, using the prophets as His mouthpieces; even though they were often rejected and the messages were often repeated.

3:14 *"That in the day that I shall visit the transgressions of Israel upon him I will also visit the altars of Bethel: and the horns of the altar shall be cut off, and fall to the ground."* The horns of the altar were signs of strength (it was what escaped fugitives held onto when fleeing justice), but the people could no longer trust in this as the horns would be removed.

4:1 *"Hear this word, ye kine of Bashan, that are in the mountain of Samaria, which oppress the poor, which crush the needy, which say to their masters, Bring, and let us drink."* This so graphically illustrates people (in this case the women) who were preoccupied with their own comforts and were happy to continue to do so even if it meant exploiting the weak and vulnerable.

5:14-15 *"Seek good, and not evil, that ye may live: and so the Lord, the God of hosts, shall be with you, as ye have spoken. Hate the evil, and love the good, and establish judgment in the gate: it may be that the Lord God of hosts will be gracious unto the remnant of Joseph."* The need for justice was especially pertinent at the time of Amos and remains so as we see deep injustices in our society; including the rehabilitation of offenders through reconciliation with victims and the community at large.

5:24 *"But let judgment run down as waters, and righteousness as a mighty stream."* This is probably the key verse in Amos and is what Martin Luther King quoted in his "I have a dream" speech – but it needed repentance first.

6:1 *"Woe to them that are at ease in Zion, and trust in the mountain of Samaria, which are named chief of the nations, to whom the house of Israel came!"* The people – at least, the "haves" of that society – thought they were set and secure, given it was a time of peace and prosperity (at least for them); but how wrong they were, and so are we if we were to think on those lines.

7:1-3 *"Thus hath the Lord God shewed unto me; and, behold, he formed grasshoppers in the beginning of the shooting up of the latter growth; and, lo, it was the latter growth after the king's mowings. And it came to pass, that when they had made an end of eating the grass of the land, then I said, O Lord God, forgive, I beseech thee: by whom shall Jacob arise? for he is small. The Lord repented for this: It shall not be, saith the Lord.* Swarms of locusts then and now can be devastating. Just as remarkable is how prayer can bring about God's mercy.

7:7-8 *"Thus he shewed me: and, behold, the Lord stood upon a wall made by a plumbline, with a plumbline in his hand. And the Lord said unto me, Amos, what seest thou? And I said, A plumbline. Then said the Lord, Behold, I will set a plumbline in the midst of my people Israel: I will not again pass by them any more:"* A plumb line is used to helped ensure straightness building a wall or whatever construct; God wants His people to be straight in all their dealings.

7:10 *"Then Amaziah the priest of Bethel sent to Jeroboam king of Israel, saying, Amos hath conspired against thee in the midst of the house of Israel: the land is not able to bear all his words."* Here is an example of how standing for God comes at a price. Like most prophets, it amounted to being persecuted by the establishment; in this case, the priest.

8:1-2 *"Thus hath the Lord God shewed unto me: and behold a basket of summer fruit. And he said, Amos, what seest thou? And I said, A basket of summer fruit. Then said the Lord unto me, The end is come upon my people of Israel; I will not again pass by them any more."* A basket of over-ripe fruit, is what the people were likened to, as with so much of Amos prophesying, was a poignant and devastating picture of how God saw His people, who were now over-ripe for judgment.

9:11,15 *"Thus hath the Lord God shewed unto me: and behold a basket of summer fruit. And he said, Amos, what seest thou? And I said, A basket of summer fruit. Then said the Lord unto me, The end is come upon my people of Israel; I will not again pass by them any more ... And I will plant them upon their land, and they shall no more be pulled up out of their land which I have given them, saith the Lord thy God."* After his message of God's displeasure and imminent judgment, Amos looks forward to a time of restoration and the bringing in of the Gentiles, a theme that is picked up in Acts 15 and is further discussed in Chapter 15.

Obadiah

The prophet and his prophecy

The author's name is Obadiah, which means "servant (or worshipper) of the Lord". It was a common name; his father's name and the place of his birth is not given. The Book of Obadiah is the shortest in the Old Testament and contains a message of judgment against the land of Edom, which lay immediately south of the Dead Sea. It was hostile mountainous terrain, making it ideal for defending against enemies. Its inhabitants were descendants of Esau, the twin brother of Jacob whom God had renamed Israel. They were cousins to the Israelites, but they had a long history of animosity towards them – from refusing to let them pass through their territory as they approached the Promised Land to taking land from them as Judah was conquered and exiled by the Babylonians. Just as the two books preceding Obadiah, Joel and Amos, take a global, future approach, so Obadiah considers Edom's pride as an example of the human condition, and Edom's downfall pointing to the coming of God's Kingdom over all nations.

Background and context

The date and place of composition are disputed. Dating the prophecy is mainly a matter of relating *"In the day that thou stoodest on the other side, in the day that the strangers carried away captive his forces, and foreigners entered into his gates, and cast lots upon Jerusalem, even thou wast as one of them"* and their indifferent, hostile response (11-14) to one of two specific events in Israel's history: the invasion of Jerusalem by Philistines and Arabs during the reign of Jehoram (853-841 BC), or the Babylonian attacks on Jerusalem (605-586). Like Joel, with credible backgrounds separated by centuries, it does not matter which is correct as far as understanding of the prophecy goes. What mattered is a long history of antagonism between Israel and Edom, going back to Jacob and Esau:

1. Genesis 25:22-25 – the birth of Jacob and Esau.

2. Genesis 33:4 – two brothers reconciled, despite a tetchy relationship.

3. Numbers 20:14-21 – Edom will not let Israel pass on their journey.

4. Deuteronomy 2:4,5 – instructions for when passing through Edom.

5. Joshua 24:4 – Edom, God's gift to Esau.

6. 1Samuel 22:18 – Deog the Edomite - an enemy.

7. Jeremiah 49:10 – God's punishment of Edom is foretold.

8. Ezekiel 35:2-4 – Prophesy against Mount Seir.

9. Amos 1:11 – Edom pursues his brother.

10. Malachi 1:2-4 – Edom is thrown down.

11. No reference – The family of Herod were Edomites.

A synopsis of the book

1. Title and introduction (1).

2. Judgment on Edom (2-14).

    - Edom's destruction announced (2-7).

        o The humbling of her pride (2-4).

        o The completeness of her destruction (5-7).

    - Edom's destruction reaffirmed (8-14).

        o Her shame and destruction (8-10).

        o Her crimes against Israel (11-14).

3. The Day of the Lord (15-21).

4. Judgment on the nations but deliverance for Israel (15-18).

5. The Lord's Kingdom established (19-21).

The message of the prophet

Obadiah's short, far-seeing message is that Edom, proud over her security, confident in her alliances, had gloated over Israel's devastation by foreign powers. Edom's participation in that disaster, not just as an indifferent onlooker but cheering on, assisting in and benefiting from attacks on Israel, will bring on God's wrath. She will be utterly destroyed; it will be a devastating demise, and Mount Zion and Israel delivered, with God's Kingdom ultimately triumphing. Since Edom is related to Israel, their hostility is all the more reprehensible. Edom is fully responsible for her failure to assist Israel and her open aggression. Edom, snug in its mountain strongholds, will be dislodged and sacked.

- Their pride is their downfall; they will be pushed from their land (1-7).

- Their treatment of the Israelites will lead to them being cut down (8-14).

- As they have done, it will be done to them when Mount Zion is delivered and the Lord redistributes the lands of the nations (15-21).

While Obadiah's prophecy is specifically directed towards Edom, it might also be taken as a warning for any nation opposed to Israel; and, in keeping with other prophets, it looks forward to the Day of the Lord scenario and Israel's future blessing: *"For the day of the Lord is near upon all the heathen: as thou hast done, it shall be done unto thee: thy reward shall return upon thine own head ... But upon mount Zion shall be deliverance, and there shall be holiness; and the house of Jacob shall possess their possessions ... And saviours shall come up on mount Zion to judge the mount of Esau; and the kingdom shall be the Lord's. Israel will prosper because God is with her"* (1:15,17,21).

Jonah

The prophet and his prophecy

Jonah is best known as the reluctant prophet that was swallowed by a big fish, spewed out and eventually carried out the mission God gave him. While most of his ministry, of which we have a record, was not to Israel and Judah, in the divine scheme of things it was significant. The book is named after its principal character, whose name means "dove". Although the book does not identify its author, tradition has ascribed it to the prophet himself, Jonah son of Amittai (1:1), from Gath-Hepher (2 Kings 14:25) in Zebulun (Joshua 19:10,13). Besides the fish story, there are many miracles recounted in the Book of Jonah; but as we have argued throughout this book, if God is God then that is not an issue.

Background and context

There are two references to Jonah outside the Book of Jonah. The first is 2 Kings 14:25-26, shortly after bad king Jeroboam II came to power (782 BC). It was not long after that, but before 722 BC, when Israel was taken into captivity by the very people Jonah was commissioned to prophesy against, that Jonah was called to prophesy to the king – not a word of rebuke as might be expected, but rather that God would bless Israel by restoring to them some of the land that had earlier been taken from them. As we will see, this side of God's character is important in understanding the events that followed. It is notable that in the half-century during which the prophet Jonah ministered (800-750 BC), this significant event affected the Northern Kingdom of Israel: King Jeroboam II (793-753) restored her traditional borders, ending a century of sporadic seesaw conflict between Israel and Damascus. This contributed to a period of relative peace and prosperity (and complacency) for Israel prior to its rapid demise, providing part of the backdrop for Hosea and Amos's ministry. Assyria was a threat and could be a strange ally and this no doubt influenced Jonah when called to prophesy.

The other reference is Matthew 12:39-41, when Jesus was asked for a sign, and the one He gave was of Jonah who spent three days and nights in the belly of the fish. Of significance is the fact that this was not just a powerful illustration of Jesus' death and resurrection, but Jonah was the only prophet Jesus cited in this manner and was from the same place as Jesus, Nazareth. Also significant was that those coming from Nazareth and the Galilee area were often looked down on by those from Judea with their more purist outlook to religion; they were less affected by the passing international trade, and yet it was here that Jesus had His greatest ministry successes. While Jonah's ministry overlapped with his Northern Kingdom contemporaries, Hosea and Amos, none referred to any of the others.

A synopsis of the book

1. Jonah flees his mission (chs. 1-2).

    - Jonah's commission and flight (1:1-3).
    - The endangered sailors' cry to their gods (1:4-6).
    - Jonah's disobedience exposed (1:7-10).
    - Jonah's punishment and deliverance (1:11-2:1; 2:10).
    - His prayer of thanksgiving (2:2-9).

2. Jonah reluctantly fulfils his mission (chs. 3 - 4).

    - Jonah's renewed commission and obedience (3:1-4).
    - The endangered Ninevites' repentant appeal to the Lord (3:5-9).
    - The Ninevites' repentance acknowledged (3:10-4:4).
    - Jonah's deliverance and rebuke (4:5-11).

The message of the prophet

Chapter 1 is the chapter people are generally more aware of, it recounts how Jonah was told by God to preach to the people of Nineveh, seven hundred and fifty miles from where he was based, about forthcoming judgment. Instead he tries to escape (foolishly, given that God is omnipresent) and gets on a ship bound for Tarshish, two thousand miles away in the opposite direction. Then came the storm and the response by the pagan sailors this was to do with divine judgment, the need to pray, drawing of lots to find the culprit, Jonah who was the culprit offering to be thrown overboard, the sailors reluctantly agreeing, Jonah being swallowed by the huge fish, and the storm calming - which greatly impressed the sailors.

Chapter 2 contains Jonah's remarkable prayer of contrition, at the time he was thrown into the sea – and, for all we know, his actual death - before being brought back to life. If there was a time to get one's attention, then this was it, as Jonah cried to God, reflected on his helpless state and dedicated himself to doing God's commands. *"In my distress I called to the Lord, and he answered me. From deep in the realm of the dead I called for help, and you listened to my cry ... Those who cling to worthless idols turn away from God's love for them. But I, with shouts of grateful praise, will sacrifice to you. What I have vowed I will make good. I will say, 'Salvation comes from the Lord.'"* (Jonah 2:2,8-9.)

Chapter 3 shows Jonah being recommissioned, having been vomited by the fish. He goes to Nineveh as commanded and delivers what is likely the most effective sermon ever delivered, and one that was contained in a mere five words. Without giving whys and wherefores or elaborating, he tells the Ninevites their city will be destroyed in forty days, and led by the king who commanded all its citizens, as well as its animals, that the people fast as an act of penitence. The people did repent and God's judgment was averted, at least for the time being.

Chapter 4 sees Jonah throwing a tantrum; he objected to God showing mercy on these wicked people and angry. *"And he prayed unto the Lord, and said, I pray thee, O Lord, was not this my saying, when I was yet in my country? Therefore I fled before unto Tarshish: for I knew that thou art a gracious God, and merciful, slow to anger, and of great kindness, and repentest thee of the evil. Therefore now, O Lord, take, I beseech thee, my life from me; for it is better for me to die than to live."* (4:2-3.) God's reply was – do you have the right to be angry?

We next see Jonah sitting at an outside-the-city vantage point to check out what was to happen, thinking maybe repentance might be short-lived and God might revert to Plan A. By miraculous design, God causes a plant to grow up to give Jonah shade; and just as quickly He sent a worm to kill it, followed by the scorching wind to make Jonah even more uncomfortable; whereupon Jonah embarks on yet another sulk, and wishes again that he were dead. God in response reminds Jonah of His sovereignty and His mercy, to do what He willed and to show compassion on Nineveh's one hundred and twenty thousand residents who could not tell their right hand from their left, and also many animals.

As we reflect on lessons that can be drawn, the one that stands out is how God showed mercy on a people renowned for being wicked, who from Jonah's perspective deserved all that had been threatened upon them. But it is not all one way, and a hundred years later a near neighbour of Jonah, Nahum, also pronounced God's judgment over Nineveh, and this time the people of Nineveh had not repented and God's judgment was carried through as the Assyrian Empire fell. We may well be intrigued at the gracious manner in which God handled His rebellious spokesperson, who, as far as we can make out, screwed up several times during the story, and yet God persisted with him as His prophet.

If we were in Jonah's shoes, we might have done what Jonah did; after all, if any deserved judgment rather than mercy it was the people of Nineveh. Yet, as we can see, Jonah was full of hate and anger, and flawed theology. While the Old Testament is a Jewish book, it also shows God is interested in those outside of the Covenant, and nowhere better seen than with Jonah. Besides His great mercy, God knows what He is doing and He has the right to do what He will; our response should be simply to trust and obey. Flawed as Jonah was compared with other, almost-too-good-to-be-true prophets, he still had a heart for God; and despite his hypocrisy and rebellion, God saw something of merit in Jonah (fear of God) and the people of Nineveh (penitence); important things, not to be missed.

Micah

The prophet and his prophecy

Little is known about the prophet Micah beyond what can be learned from the book itself and from Jeremiah 26:18 (discussed later). Micah was from the town of Moresheth (1:1), probably Moresheth Gath (1:14) in southern Judah. He prophesied concerning Israel and Judah. We do not know about his family but, unlike Isaiah with court connections, he was likely from a humbler background; and while there was much in his message that was similar, as with Amos there was a particular sensitivity on social justice issues, which he had witnessed first-hand, especially as they affected the towns and villages of his homeland. Micah means "who is like the Lord?", which was also reflected in his message.

Background and context

Micah prophesied some time between 750 and 686 BC, during the reigns of Jotham, Ahaz and Hezekiah, kings of Judah (1:1). He was a contemporary of Isaiah, Amos and Hosea. Micah predicted the fall of Samaria (1:6), which took place in 722–721. His early ministry was toward the end of the reigns of Jotham and during the reign of Ahaz (732–716) (a particularly bad king). Micah's message reflects social conditions prior to the religious reforms under Hezekiah (715–686). Micah's ministry most likely fell within the period 735–700.

The background of the book is the same as that found in the earlier portions of Isaiah, though Micah does not exhibit the same knowledge of Jerusalem's political life as Isaiah does, living his life as he did in a Judean village. What we wrote earlier concerning context, under Hosea, applies also to Micah. Relevant Biblical texts covering this period are 2 Kings 15:32-20:21; 2 Chronicles 27-32. Israel was in an apostate condition. Micah predicted the fall of her capital, Samaria (1:5–7), and also foretold the inevitable desolation of Judah (1:9–16).

A synopsis of the book

1. Title (1:1).
2. First cycle: judgment and restoration of Israel and Judah (1:2-2:13).

    - Judgment on Israel and Judah (1:2-2:11).
        - The predicted destruction (1:2-7).
        - Lamentation over the destruction (1:8-16).
        - Woe to oppressive land-grabbers (2:1-5).
        - Condemnation of wealthy wicked and false prophets (2:6-11).
    - Restoration of a remnant (2:12-13).

3. Second cycle: indictment of Judah's leaders, but future hope (chs. 3-5).

    - Indictment of Judah's leaders (ch. 3).
        - Guilty civil leaders (3:1–4).
        - False prophets of peace and Micah's response (3:5-8).

- - Corrupt leaders and Zion's fall (3:9-12).
  - Future hope for God's people (chs. 4-5).
    - The coming Kingdom (4:1-5).
    - Restoration of a remnant and Zion (4:6-8).
    - From distress to deliverance (4:9-10).
    - From siege to victory (4:11-13).
    - From helpless ruler to ideal King (5:1-4).
    - The ideal King delivers His people (5:5-6).
    - The remnant among the nations (5:7-9).
    - Obliteration of military might and pagan worship (5:10-15).
4. Third cycle: God's charges, ultimate triumph (chs. 6-7).
   - God's charges against His people (6:1-7:7).
     - A divine Covenant lawsuit (6:1-8).
     - Further charges and the sentence (6:9-16).
     - A lament over a decadent society (7:1-7).
   - The ultimate triumph of God's Kingdom (7:8-20).
     - An expression of trust (7:8-10).
     - A promise of restoration (7:11-13).
     - A prayer, the Lord's answer, and the response (7:14-17).
     - A hymn of praise to God (7:18-20).

The message of the prophet

Micah's message alternates between oracles of doom and oracles of hope, God's "sternness" and His "kindness". The theme is divine judgment and deliverance. Micah also stresses that God hates idolatry, injustice, rebellion and empty ritualism (see 3:8), but delights in pardoning the penitent (see 7:18–19). Finally, the prophet declares that Zion will have greater glory in the future than ever before (e.g. 4:1–2).

The Davidic Kingdom, though it will seem to come to an end, will reach greater heights through the coming Messianic Deliverer (see 5:1–4), whose first and second comings are anticipated, yet not distinguished.

Chapter 1 - while making it clear the vision Micah shared concerned Samaria and Jerusalem (representing Israel and Judah) and coming judgment, that message is for the whole world (1.2). The incurable wound of God's people will result in the deaths of Israel and Judah, and will lead the people into Exile (1.8-16).

Chapter 2 makes clear God's complaint and the outcome: "*Woe to them that devise iniquity, and work evil upon their beds! when the morning is light, they practise it, because it is in the power of their hand. And they covet fields, and take them by violence; and houses, and take them away: so they oppress a man and his house, even a man and his heritage. Therefore thus saith the Lord; Behold, against this family do I devise an evil, from which ye shall not remove your necks; neither shall ye go haughtily: for this time is evil ... Even of late my people is risen up as an enemy: ye pull off the robe with the garment from them that pass by securely as men averse from war. The women of my people have ye cast out from their pleasant houses; from their children have ye taken away my glory for ever*" (2:1-3, 8-9.) Micah criticises the false prophets who could be bought (2:7, 11). Yet there is hope for a future remnant: "*I will surely assemble, O Jacob, all of thee; I will surely gather the remnant of Israel... and their king shall pass before them, and the Lord on the head of them.*" (2:12,13.)

Chapter 3 addresses God's complaint against the leaders: "*Who hate the good, and love the evil; who pluck off their skin from off them, and their flesh from off their bones*" (3:2); and the result: "*Then shall they cry unto the Lord, but he will not hear them: he will even hide his face from them at that time, as they have behaved themselves ill in their doings*" (3:4). As for God's judgment on the leaders who behave wickedly and claim they are on God's side and are safe: "*The heads thereof judge for reward, and the priests thereof teach for hire, and the prophets thereof divine for money: yet will they lean upon the Lord, and say, Is not the Lord among us? none evil can come upon us*" (3:11).

Chapter 4 begins with the same future, glorious yet-to-be-fulfilled expectation of Isaiah 2:1-5: "*But in the last days it shall come to pass, that the mountain of the house of the Lord shall be established in the top of the mountains, and it shall be exalted above the hills; and people shall flow unto it*" (4:1).

Chapter 5 looks forward to the first coming of the Messiah, just as Micah (4:1-5) and Isaiah (2) looked forward to His Second Coming: *"But thou, Bethlehem Ephratah, though thou be little among the thousands of Judah, yet out of thee shall he come forth unto me that is to be ruler in Israel; whose goings forth have been from of old, from everlasting. Therefore will he give them up, until the time that she which travaileth hath brought forth: then the remnant of his brethren shall return unto the children of Israel. And he shall stand and feed in the strength of the Lord, in the majesty of the name of the Lord his God; and they shall abide: for now shall he be great unto the ends of the earth"* (3:2-4), and while part of this was fulfilled (as we are reminded each Christmas), some of this prophecy has yet to be fulfilled. While Micah sees the soon invasion of the Assyrians, they will not ultimately win. A remnant will survive and triumph, and there will be a purified people of God! (5.5-15). *"I will execute vengeance in anger and fury upon the heathen, such as they have not heard"* (5:15).

Chapter 6 sees God bringing charges against His people. He asks how He has wronged them that they should treat Him like this, and recounts His history of caring for them (6.1-5), with Micah spelling out what God requires: *"He hath shewed thee, O man, what is good; and what doth the Lord require of thee, but to do justly, and to love mercy, and to walk humbly with thy God?"* (6:8). The chapter ends with, again, Israel's guilt and punishment made clear: dishonesty, violence and deceit will lead to their ruin and to public scorn (6.9-16).

Chapter 7 is Micah's tragic lament for the appalling state of his society (7.1-7), *"The good man is perished out of the earth: and there is none upright among men: they all lie in wait for blood; they hunt every man his brother with a net"* (7:2). Yet there is also hope: *"Therefore I will look unto the LORD; I will wait for the God of my salvation: my God will hear me. Rejoice not against me, O mine enemy: when I fall, I shall arise; when I sit in darkness, the LORD shall be a light unto me"* (7:7,8). And Micah ends on a high: *"Who is a God like unto thee, that pardoneth iniquity, and passeth by the transgression of the remnant of his heritage? he retaineth not his anger for ever, because he delighteth in mercy. He will turn again, he will have compassion upon us; he will subdue our iniquities; and thou wilt cast all their sins into the depths of the sea. Thou wilt perform the truth to Jacob, and the mercy to Abraham, which thou hast sworn unto our fathers from the days of old."* (7:18-20.) Not only is this reminiscent of the gospel message but it offers hope to the Jewish people and of God's promise.

One of the less obvious Micah texts referred to in the New Testament was when

Jesus quoted: *"For the son dishonoureth the father, the daughter riseth up against her mother, the daughter in law against her mother in law; a man's enemies are the men of his own house"* (7.6); and He did so in order to prepare His disciples for some of the struggles they would face (Matthew 10.35-36 and Mark 13.12). The one place outside the Book of Micah when Micah was quoted in the Old Testament was: *"Micah the Morasthite prophesied in the days of Hezekiah king of Judah, and spake to all the people of Judah, saying, Thus saith the Lord of hosts; Zion shall be plowed like a field, and Jerusalem shall become heaps, and the mountain of the house as the high places of a forest. Did Hezekiah king of Judah and all Judah put him at all to death? did he not fear the Lord, and besought the Lord, and the Lord repented him of the evil which he had pronounced against them?"* (Jeremiah 26:18,19.) Not only do we read of an example of a king heeding a prophet's warning, but this was used by Jeremiah's supporters when dissuading some who talked of putting him to death for his warnings.

Nahum

The prophet and his prophecy

The book contains the "vision of Nahum" (1:1), whose name means "comfort". The fall of Nineveh, which represented Assyria, was Nahum's theme, although the warnings given would apply to all nations that oppress in a similar way and would bring comfort to Judah. Little is known about Nahum except his home town (Elkosh). Like Jonah, one hundred and twenty years before him, Nahum preached to Nineveh in their city, a message of judgment. Unlike with Jonah, they had reached the point of no return. The Tomb of Nahum remains to this day in the town of Alqosh, fifty kilometres north of Mosul, near the site of the city of Nineveh that fell as Nahum predicted, and excavated the early twentieth century.

Background and context

In 3:8-10 the author speaks of the fall of Thebes, which happened in 663 BC, as already past. While in the first chapter Nahum appears to be speaking generally, in the second and third chapters, specifically, Nahum prophesied Nineveh's fall, which was fulfilled in 612 BC. Nahum therefore uttered this oracle between 663 and 612 BC, perhaps near the end of this period since he represents the fall of Nineveh as imminent (2:1; 3:14,19). This would place him during the reign of Josiah and make him a contemporary of Zephaniah, who also did prophesy concerning the destruction of Nineveh, and the young Jeremiah.

Assyria arose as one of the world's first great empires. Assyria had already destroyed Samaria (722–721 BC), resulting in the captivity of the Northern Kingdom of Israel, and posed a present threat to Judah. The Assyrians were brutally cruel, their kings often being depicted as gloating over the gruesome punishments inflicted on conquered peoples. They conducted their wars with shocking ferocity, uprooted whole populations as state policy and deported them to other parts of their empire. The leaders of conquered cities were tortured and killed. No wonder the dread of Assyria fell on her neighbours.

About 700 BC, King Sennacherib made Nineveh the capital of the Assyrian Empire. Soon after, during the reign of King Hezekiah, he attempted without success to conquer Judah and besieging Jerusalem. Nineveh remained Assyria's capital until it was destroyed in 612. Jonah had announced its destruction earlier (Jonah 3:4), but the people repented and the destruction was temporarily averted (see Jonah 3:10). Not long afterwards, Nineveh reverted to its extreme wickedness, cruelty and pride. The brutality reached its peak under Ashurbanipal (669–627), the last great ruler of the Assyrian Empire. After his death, Assyria's power waned until 612, when Nineveh was overthrown by Babylon. Nahum could see what was to happen to this proud and "impregnable" city and not long after it happened just as he saw it, down to the red uniforms of those who sacked it.

Some words are addressed to Judah (1:12–13,15), but most are addressed to Nineveh (1:11,14; 2:1,13; 3:5–17,19) or its king (3:18). The book, however, seemed to be intended particularly for Israelite readers living in Judah. The book is written largely in poetry form, and in the first chapter uses the technique of starting each line with the next letter of the Hebrew alphabet. The contents are primarily made up of judgment oracles, with appropriate descriptions and vocabulary, expressing intense moods, sights and sounds. There is frequent use of metaphors and similes, vivid word pictures, repetition and many short, often staccato, phrases (e.g., 3:1–3). Rhetorical questions punctuate the flow of thought, which has a marked stress on moral indignation toward injustice.

A synopsis of the book

1. Title (1:1).

2. Nineveh's Judge (1:2-15).

    - The Lord's kindness and sternness (1:2-8).

- Nineveh's overthrow and Judah's joy (1:9-15).

3. Nineveh's judgment (ch. 2).

    - Nineveh besieged (2:1-10).

    - Nineveh's desolation contrasted with her former glory (2:11-13).

4. Nineveh's total destruction (ch. 3).

    - Nineveh's sins (3:1-4).

    - Nineveh's doom (3:5-19).

The message of the prophet

Chapter 1 presents a complete "A - Z" of God's indignation and vengeance against a nation that had fallen from the repentant attitude of Jonah's time to the militaristic cruelty and economic corruption at the time of Nahum. Nahum's oracle paints a terrifying picture of an awesome God dealing with His enemies. *"The Lord is slow to anger, and great in power, and will not at all acquit the wicked"* (1:3). He is jealous, avenging, full of wrath, destructive like a whirlwind, like a terrible drought, like an earthquake and like a fire.

This chapter can also be seen in more generic terms, for it is about how God will deal decisively with wicked nations down the ages, of which Nineveh is but an example. While serving as a warning to violent nations, it also provides hope to God's faithful remnant: *"The Lord is good, a strong hold in the day of trouble; and he knoweth them that trust in him"* (1:7). There is good reason for Judah to rejoice: *"Behold upon the mountains the feet of him that bringeth good tidings, that publisheth peace! O Judah, keep thy solemn feasts, perform thy vows: for the wicked shall no more pass through thee; he is utterly cut off"* (1:15).

Chapter 2 presents a picture of God laying siege to Nineveh, pillaging it and finally overthrowing it. Nahum describes in graphic detail how God is as a terrible army, shining red and flashing in the sunlight, advancing on the town, darting from street to street and coming hard up against the city walls. The people of Nineveh cannot resist because the Lord is set to free His people from this oppressor. Resistance is futile and the city collapses (2:1-6). The detail, including the red uniforms and the way Nineveh's defences were breached, is precisely what happened. What the Assyrians did to God's people will happen to them. Terrified, they'll be plundered, pillaged, stripped of all their assets and carried away into Exile! (2:7-10). The war picture ends by likening the Assyrian capital to a pride of lions, once so proud, predatory and well-fed, but now they had disappeared (2:11-13). Notably, their conquerors were the Babylonians whom God subsequently used to punish the Southern Kingdom of Judah.

Chapter 3 completes Nahum's prophecy by giving God's reasons for His anger and judgment on the Assyrians. It opens with a curse: *"Woe to the bloody city! it is all full of lies and robbery; the prey departeth not"* (3:1). They were ripe for judgment because of two major sins in particular. The first was the brutality and inhumanity of their conquering armies (3.1-4). They did not just conquer, they destroyed and enslaved. God declares He is their enemy because of this, and He will punish and humiliate them as an adulterous prostitute. *"And I will cast abominable filth upon thee, and make thee vile, and will set thee as a gazingstock. And it shall come to pass, that all they that look upon thee shall flee from thee, and say, Nineveh is laid waste: who will bemoan her? whence shall I seek comforters for thee?"* (3:6,7.)

Secondly, He charges them with unscrupulous, asset-stripping business practice. Just like corrupt businessmen, when God strikes them, their guards and officials will disappear like a thief in the night (3:12-17). The end has come for the cruel Assyrian Empire, and the whole world will applaud: *"Thy shepherds slumber, O king of Assyria: thy nobles shall dwell in the dust: thy people is scattered upon the mountains, and no man gathereth them. There is no healing of thy bruise; thy wound is grievous: all that hear the bruit of thee shall clap the hands over thee: for upon whom hath not thy wickedness passed continually?"* (3:18,19.)

Notably, the ruins of the city lay buried and undiscovered until the nineteenth century. We might reflect God is in control of history and He will always have the last word. History shows that the "Woe" Nahum pronounced did come to pass.

Habakkuk

The prophet and his prophecy

Little is known about Habakkuk (whose name means "clinger"), except that he was a contemporary of Jeremiah and ministered some twenty years after Zephaniah (whose book comes after). He was a man of vigorous faith rooted deeply in the religious traditions of Israel. He was bold enough to remonstrate with the Almighty over the sort of issues that have occupied humankind since the time of Job – "Why does such-and-such occur? – it just isn't right!" and with the Lord, rather than rebuking his audacity, explaining His actions in a way that was able to put Habakkuk's mind at rest.

Background and context

The prediction of the coming Babylonian invasion (1:6) indicates Habakkuk lived in Judah toward the end of Josiah's reign (640–609 BC) or the beginning of Jehoiakim's (609–598). The prophecy is generally dated a little before or after the battle of Carchemish (605), when Egyptian forces, which had earlier gone to the aid of the last Assyrian king, were routed by the Babylonians under Nabopolassar and Nebuchadnezzar, and were pursued as far as the Egyptian border (Jeremiah 46). Habakkuk, like Jeremiah, probably lived to see the initial fulfilment of his prophecy, with Jerusalem attacked by the Babylonians in 597. He wrote clearly and with great feeling, using poetic language, and unlike Zephaniah he came up with many memorable phrases (2:2,4,14,20; 3:2,17-19).

A synopsis of the book

1. Habakkuk's first complaint: Why does the evil go unpunished? (1:2-4.)

2. God's answer: The Babylonians will punish Judah (1:5-11).

3. Habakkuk's second complaint: How can a just God use wicked Babylon to punish a people more righteous than themselves? (1:12-2:1.)

4. God's answer: Babylon will be punished; faith will be rewarded (2:2-20).

5. Habakkuk's prayer: After asking for manifestations of God's wrath and mercy (as seen in the past), he confesses trust and joy in God (ch. 3).

The message of the prophet

Among the prophetic writings, Habakkuk is somewhat unique in that it includes no oracle addressed to Israel. It contains, rather, a dialogue between the prophet and God. In the first two chapters, Habakkuk argues with God over His ways that appear to him unfathomable, if not unjust. Having received replies, he responds with a beautiful confession of faith (Chapter 3). This account of wrestling with God is, however, not just a fragment from a private journal that has somehow entered the public domain; it was composed for Israel. No doubt it represented the voice of the godly in Judah, struggling to comprehend the ways of God. God's answers therefore spoke to all who shared Habakkuk's troubled doubts. And Habakkuk's confession became a public expression.

Habakkuk was perplexed that wickedness, strife and oppression were rampant in Judah but God seemingly did nothing. When told that the Lord was preparing to do something about it through the "ruthless" Babylonians (1:6), his perplexity only intensified: How could God, *"too pure to look on evil"* (1:13), appoint such a nation *"to execute judgment"* (1:12) on a nation that is *"more righteous than themselves"* (1:13)? God makes it clear that eventually the corrupt destroyer will itself be destroyed. In the end, Habakkuk learns to rest in God's sovereign appointments and await his working in a spirit of worship. He learns to wait patiently in faith (2:3-4) for God's Kingdom to be expressed universally (2:14).

Chapter 1 begins with an anguished cry to God: *"O Lord, how long shall I cry, and thou wilt not hear!"* (1:2). There is violence, injustice, conflict and lawlessness in Judah, just as Jeremiah and contemporary prophets observed. Why does God not do something (1.1-4)? Incredibly, God's response is that He is going to raise up an idolatrous and pagan nation to use as an instrument of punishment on His own people! Babylonia was a superpower feared throughout that part of the world, and God was going to use them to punish sin (1.5-11)! But still this does not satisfy Habakkuk. In Chapter 1.12 - 2.1 he continues to complain. He still cannot understand how God can tolerate such high levels of evil - even using the wickedness in other nations as part of His purpose. How can God use wrong to punish wrong? How can God use the Babylonians, who worship their own prowess and abilities like a fisherman might worship the nets and hooks he has made for himself? Can God really tolerate the Babylonians as they cruelly "catch" and conquer more and more nations - and even His own people?

Chapter 2 - Habakkuk concludes his complaining with some reticence *"I will stand upon my watch, and set me upon the tower, and will watch to see what he will say unto me, and what I shall answer when I am reproved"* (2:1). God's answer is that He is fully aware of the evil in the empire He proposes to use, and He uses them at this particular time as part of His longer-term plans. He tells Habakkuk to write down what He is going to tell him, because His purpose will be worked out - but in His time (2.2-3). In responding, God makes it clear how His people should act, which is picked up three times in the New Testament: Romans 1:17, Galatians 3:11, Hebrews 10:38: *"Behold, his soul which is lifted up is not upright in him: but the just shall live by his faith"* (2:4).

The Lord knows Babylon is arrogant, drunken and greedy for conquest, but the time will come when they too will face a day of reckoning. In a series of five "woes" God outlines their crimes and prophesies their punishment: piling up stolen goods, becoming wealthy by extortion, wholesale destruction of people and property, building an arrogant kingdom by unjust gain, building cities by bloodshed, drawing other nations into sin and immorality to exploit them, worship of idols and man-made things. God sees all this. In due course all will rebound on the Babylonian Empire: *"Woe to them…"* But with these "woes" are declarations of the victory and sovereignty of God:*"For the earth shall be filled with the knowledge of the glory of the Lord, as the waters cover the sea ... But the Lord is in his holy temple: let all the earth keep silence before him."* (2:14,20.)

Chapter 3 - this encounter with God was deep and life-changing for Habakkuk. His mood turns to one of understanding and trust, even though the outward situation has not changed. He begins by declaring that he heard about God's great deeds of the past, and appeals to Him to *"Revive Thy work ... in wrath remember mercy"* (3:2). Then he calls upon God to come in power and judgment as He did to the people of Israel at Mount Sinai. He pictures the Lord coming like the sunrise, like a gathering storm, like a plague and like an earthquake. And he asks, Why does He come in this way? It is not because He is angry with His creation, but rather He is coming as a mighty Warrior-God to destroy the leaders of the wicked and *"even for salvation with thine anointed"* (3:13). The truth of who God is and what He will do overwhelms the prophet: *"When I heard, my belly trembled; my lips quivered at the voice: rottenness entered into my bones, and I trembled in myself, that I might rest in the day of trouble: when he cometh up unto the people, he will invade them with his troops"* (3:16).

The book ends on a wonderfully optimistic note: *"Although the fig tree shall not blossom, neither shall fruit be in the vines; the labour of the olive shall fail, and the fields shall yield no meat; the flock shall be cut off from the fold, and there shall be no herd in the stalls: Yet I will rejoice in the Lord, I will joy in the God of my salvation. The Lord God is my strength, and he will make my feet like hinds' feet, and he will make me to walk upon mine high places. To the chief singer on my stringed instruments."* (3:17-19.)

As those looking on two thousand, six hundred years later, with consternation at the evil of our own times and what appears to be an unsatisfactory response, we should take heart: God is control. While Israel's evil is a given, unlike other prophets this was not Habakkuk's focus. Rather, it was him taking his concerns to God in prayer and finding rest in God's answer. Habakkuk shows how, come what may, the righteous can (must) live by faith.

Zephaniah

The prophet and his prophecy

We know little about Zephaniah ("Yahweh hides"), who is not referred to by name anywhere else in the Bible, other than in the opening verse of the book: *"The word of the Lord which came unto Zephaniah the son of Cushi, the son of Gedaliah, the son of Amariah, the son of Hizkiah, in the days of Josiah the son of Amon, king of Judah"* (1:1). What we might deduce is that he was a descendant of good King Hezekiah, and of royal blood, and he came on the scene after the rapid downward spiral in the moral and religious life of Judah, and may have been just the spur the next good king (Josiah) needed for his short-lived reforms. Like so many of the prophets, his message was one of judgment (Yahweh is *not* to be messed with) and the future (how far, he knew not, Messianic) hope.

Background and context

Zephaniah may have begun his prophesying around 621 BC, around the time Josiah began his reforms. We know that Josiah, who was king 640-609 BC, came to the throne aged eight, and before he took the deliberate decision to go along the righteousness way, with an all too sad limited impact, while still a minor who might have continued in the evil ways of his predecessors. Who knows to what extent Zephaniah was instrumental in that decision, but there was no ambiguity or mincing of his words when following the introduction, he declares: *"I will utterly consume all things from off the land, saith the Lord"* (1:2.) While the main audience of the prophecy was Judah, there was a message too for the nations surrounding Judah on all its sides, all of which were to face judgment under (not named by Zephaniah) God's instrument, Babylon.

As for hope, while that realisation was for a future time, including some of it in a still to be manifest future, there was still the prospect, even then, that if the people turned to the Lord, He would relent concerning future judgment, for that was an important part of God's character. Tragically, what might have been a God leaning trajectory, following Josiah's reforms, was not to be.

After, four more kings, who between them did not reign long and were in effect puppets to foreign masters, exile to Babylon was the fate in store for Judah, and would be a theme that Habakkuk would pick up some twenty years later, as well as Jeremiah who picked up the pieces that was the result of Judah not heeding Zephaniah's warnings. Besides, following similar judgment and then hope themes of other prophets, some of these, with God judging His people and then the surrounding nations, before seeing in a Kingdom where His rule and blessing dominates, are picked up in the Book of Revelation.

A synopsis of the book

1. Introduction (1:1–3).
   - Title: The prophet identified (1:1).
   - Prologue: Double announcement of total judgment (1:2-3).
2. The Day of the Lord coming on Judah and the nations (1:4-18).
   - Judgment on the idolaters in Judah (1:4-9).
   - Wailing throughout Jerusalem (1:10-13).
   - The inescapable Day of the Lord's Wrath (1:14-18).
3. God's judgment on the nations (2:1-3:8).
   - Call to Judah to repent (2:1-3).
   - Judgment on Philistia (2:4-7).
   - Judgment on Moab and Ammon (2:8-11).
   - Judgment on Cush (2:12).
   - Judgment on Assyria (2:13-15).
   - Judgment on Jerusalem (3:1-5).
   - Jerusalem's refusal to repent (3:6-8).
4. Redemption of the remnant (3:9-20).
   - Nations purified, remnant restored, Jerusalem purged (3:9-13).
   - Rejoicing in the city (3:14-17).
   - The nation restored (3:18-20).

The message of the prophet

Chapter 1.1 - 2.3 gives dire warnings of punishment and destruction for Judah. The prophet begins with an all-embracing prophecy of destruction, possibly for the whole of mankind (1:2-3), but focuses on the people of God. "*I will also stretch out mine hand upon Judah, and upon all the inhabitants of Jerusalem; and I will cut off the remnant of Baal from this place, and the name of the Chemarims with the priests*" (1:4). God says He will punish them for their worship of other "gods", "*that are turned back from the Lord; and those that have not sought the Lord, nor enquired for him*" (1:6). God's complaint and punishment is described in graphic detail, His righteous cause and devastating effect.

"*And it shall come to pass at that time, that I will search Jerusalem with candles, and punish the men that are settled on their lees: that say in their heart, The Lord will not do good, neither will he do evil. Therefore their goods shall become a booty, and their houses a desolation: they shall also build houses, but not inhabit them; and they shall plant vineyards, but not drink the wine thereof. The great day of the Lord is near, it is near, and hasteth greatly, even the voice of the day of the Lord: the mighty man shall cry there bitterly*" (1:12-14.) In the light of this terrible prospect, God calls upon His people to turn back to Him before it is too late, for there is still hope: "*Seek ye the Lord, all ye meek of the earth, which have wrought his judgment; seek righteousness, seek meekness: it may be ye shall be hid in the day of the Lord's anger*" (2:3).

Chapter 2:4-15 turns our attention to other nations near to Judah, in fact to all four points of the compass; for, having invoked God's simmering anger, it was about to boil over. They will also be judged by the same instrument of the Lord, i.e. Babylon, a rising power, whom He used to bring about Judah's downfall:

- West – Philistia (2:4-7).
- East – Moab, Ammon (2:8-11) – pride; and oppressed God's people.
- South – Egypt, Ethiopia (2:12).
- North – Assyria (2:13-15) – full of pride (reminiscent of Nahum).

Chapter 3 - Zephaniah returns to God's own people. He starts with the coming judgment and accuses them of rebellion and resistance; he uses the strongest of warnings of the direst of judgements: "*Woe to her that is filthy and polluted, to the* *oppressing city! She obeyed not the voice; she received not correction; she trusted not in the Lord; she drew not near to her God. Her princes within her are roaring lions; her judges are evening wolves; they gnaw not the bones till the morrow. Her prophets are light and treacherous persons: her priests have polluted the sanctuary, they have done violence to the law. The just Lord is in the midst thereof; he will not do iniquity: every morning doth he bring his judgment to light, he faileth not; but the unjust knoweth no shame"* (3:1-5).

They had exhausted God's patience, and judgment was coming to Judah and the nations; through not named, Babylon in a matter of a few years, but looking far into the future, all the nations will face the wrath of God. *"Therefore wait ye upon me, saith the Lord, until the day that I rise up to the prey: for my determination is to gather the nations, that I may assemble the kingdoms, to pour upon them mine indignation, even all my fierce anger: for all the earth shall be devoured with the fire of my jealousy."* (3:8.) This theme, considered elsewhere by the prophets, for example Joel 3:1-2, and is discussed later, in Chapter 15, when we consider the final great battle before Jesus returns.

But there is hope and there is a remnant: *"For then will I turn to the people a pure language, that they may all call upon the name of the Lord, to serve him with one consent ... I will also leave in the midst of thee an afflicted and poor people, and they shall trust in the name of the Lord."* (3:9,12.) Zephaniah ends with a song of encouragement and joy for the future – punishment is taken away, hope is restored, and enemies are brought to justice. God promises that He will bring His scattered people back to their land, and they will be honoured by the nations of the world instead of being their victims (3:9-20). *"The Lord thy God in the midst of thee is mighty; he will save, he will rejoice over thee with joy; he will rest in his love, he will joy over thee with singing ... At that time will I bring you again, even in the time that I gather you: for I will make you a name and a praise among all people of the earth, when I turn back your captivity before your eyes, saith the Lord"* (3:17,20). Having started the chapter with a curse (justice), it ends with a blessing (mercy), for Israel and those from all the nations that trust in the Lord. Our job is to make known His message!

Haggai

The prophet and his prophecy

Haggai (meaning "festive") was a prophet who, along with Zechariah, encouraged the returned exiles to rebuild the Temple: *"In the second year of Darius the king, in the sixth month, in the first day of the month, came the word of the Lord by Haggai the prophet unto Zerubbabel the son of Shealtiel, governor of Judah, and to Joshua the son of Josedech, the high priest, saying, Thus speaketh the Lord of hosts, saying, This people say, The time is not come, the time that the Lord's house should be built"* (1:1-2).

Haggai is referred to in the Book of Ezra, along with Zechariah the prophet who overlapped him at the end of his ministry, and two key figures, also referred to by Ezra: Zerubbabel (the governor – a direct descendant of David and ancestor of Jesus) and Joshua (the High Priest): *"Then the prophets, Haggai the prophet, and Zechariah the son of Iddo, prophesied unto the Jews that were in Judah and Jerusalem in the name of the God of Israel, even unto them. Then rose up Zerubbabel the son of Shealtiel, and Jeshua the son of Jozadak, and began to build the house of God which is at Jerusalem: and with them were the prophets of God helping them"* Ezra 5:1-2.

We know little about Haggai, the man, although some have argued he may have witnessed the destruction of Solomon's Temple and therefore was an old man.

Background and context

In 538 BC, the conqueror of Babylon, Cyrus King of Persia, issued a decree allowing the Jews to return to Jerusalem and rebuild the Temple (see Ezra 1:2–4; 6:3–5). Led by Zerubbabel, about fifty thousand Jews returned and began work on the Temple. About two years later (536), they completed the foundation amid great rejoicing (Ezra 3:8–11). Their success aroused the Samaritans and other neighbours, who feared the political and religious implications of a rebuilt Temple in a thriving Jewish state. They opposed the project vigorously and managed to halt work until 520, after Darius the Great became king of Persia in 522, who encouraged the building to continue. Notably, the two Persian kings between Cyrus and Darius were ambivalent regarding the project and, just as significantly, did not provide financial support, unlike Cyrus. However, the Jews were more to blame due to their inactivity, and Haggai tried to arouse them from their apathy.

Unlike most pre-Exile prophets, he was successful in that task, with the four messages he gave, which were recorded, happening over a period of four months: August 29th, October 17th and December 18th (twice). In 516 the Temple was finished and dedicated (Ezra 6:15–18). This was seventy years after the First Temple had been destroyed, just as Jeremiah had prophesied. Haggai uses a number of questions to highlight key issues (see 1:4,9; 2:3,19). He also makes effective use of repetition: *"Give careful thought"* occurs in 1:5,7; 2:15,18, and *"I am with you"* in 1:13; 2:4. *"I will shake the heavens and the earth"* is found in 2:6,21. The major sections of the book are marked off by the date on which the word of the Lord came. Several times the prophet appears to reflect on other passages of Scripture (compare 1:6 with Deuteronomy 28:38–39 and 2:17 with Deuteronomy 28:22). The threefold use of *"Be strong"* in 2:4 echoes the encouragement given in Joshua 1:6–7,9,18. The writing was all in prose.

A synopsis of the book

1. First message: the call to rebuild the Temple (1:1-11).
    - The people's lame excuse (1:1-4).
    - The poverty of the people (1:5-6).
    - The reason God has cursed them (1:7-11).
2. The response of Zerubbabel and the people (1:12-15).
    - The leaders and remnant obey (1:12).
    - The Lord strengthens the workers (1:13-15).
3. Second message: the Temple to be filled with glory (2:1-9).
    - The people encouraged (2:1-5).
    - The promise of glory and peace (2:6-9).
4. Third message: a defiled people purified and blessed (2:10-19).
    - The rapid spread of sin (2:10-14).
    - Poor harvests because of disobedience (2:15-17).
    - Blessing to come as the Temple is rebuilt (2:18-19).
5. Fourth message: the promise to Zerubbabel (2:20-23).
    - The judgment of the nations (2:20-22).
    - The significance of Zerubbabel (2:23).

The message of the prophet

In **Chapter 1**, we note his message, on behalf of God, to the governor and High Priest, which was: "Rebuild my Temple!" When the people had returned to the land, after starting on the task set, they took little interest in completing it. They had built themselves fine houses but hadn't got around to what should have been their priority: rebuilding the Temple, which had been destroyed when the city fell in 587 BC. The Lord points out accordingly that they had not prospered since they returned, despite His promise of blessing. Food, clothes, drink and wages had not met their needs. God had withheld rain and allowed drought because of their slowness to honour Him by building the Temple (1:1-11). *"Ye have sown much, and bring in little; ye eat, but ye have not enough; ye drink, but ye are not filled with drink; ye clothe you, but there is none warm; and he that earneth wages earneth wages to put it into a bag with holes. Thus saith the Lord of hosts; Consider your ways. Go up to the mountain, and bring wood, and build the house; and I will take pleasure in it, and I will be glorified, saith the Lord."* (1:6-8.)

Led by Zerubbabel, and encouraged by Haggai, the response from the people was swift and positive: *"Then Zerubbabel the son of Shealtiel, and Joshua the son of Josedech, the high priest, with all the remnant of the people, obeyed the voice of the Lord their God, and the words of Haggai the prophet, as the Lord their God had sent him, and the people did fear before the Lord. Then spake Haggai the Lord's messenger in the Lord's message unto the people, saying, I am with you, saith the Lord. And the Lord stirred up the spirit of Zerubbabel the son of Shealtiel, governor of Judah, and the spirit of Joshua the son of Josedech, the high priest, and the spirit of all the remnant of the people; and they came and did work in the house of the Lord of hosts, their God, In the four and twentieth day of the sixth month, in the second year of Darius the king."* (1:12-15.)

In **Chapter 2:1-9**, four weeks after the building work had commenced, Haggai brings a word of encouragement when it seems initial zeal was flagging. There were those who could still remember the glory of the former Temple. And the present building site could not have looked very promising! But the Lord saw things differently and that was all that mattered, as well as looking forward to beyond the immediate aftermath of the Temple rebuilt: *"Yet now be strong, O Zerubbabel, saith the Lord; and be strong, O Joshua, son of Josedech, the high priest; and be strong, all ye people of the land, saith the Lord, and work: for I am with you, saith the Lord of hosts ... And I will shake all nations, and the desire of all nations shall come: and I will fill this house with glory, saith the Lord of hosts. The silver is mine, and the gold is mine, saith the Lord of hosts. The glory of this latter house shall be greater than of the former, saith the Lord of hosts: and in this place will I give peace ...* (2:4-9).

In **Chapter 2:10-23,** Haggai begins his word with an illustration from the Law, to drive home the message of the need for purity and putting away that which defiles and hinders God's blessing. It appears the people did respond, and we read in the word that follows (3:20-23) of a glorious future for God's people: *"Speak to Zerubbabel, governor of Judah, saying, I will shake the heavens and the earth; And I will overthrow the throne of kingdoms, and I will destroy the strength of the kingdoms of the heathen; and I will overthrow the chariots, and those that ride in them; and the horses and their riders shall come down, every one by the sword of his brother. In that day, saith the Lord of hosts, will I take thee, O Zerubbabel, my servant, the son of Shealtiel, saith the Lord, and will make thee as a signet: for I have chosen thee, saith the Lord of hosts"* (3:21-23).

Zechariah

The prophet and his prophecy

Like Haggai, Zechariah's prophetic ministry took place in the post-Exilic period; and, like him, his focus (in his early ministry, at least) was on the building of the Temple. He first prophesied in November 520 BC (Haggai last prophesied in December 520 BC), and likely prophesied for at least a further twenty years. As in Jeremiah (1:1) and Ezekiel (1:3), Zechariah was not only a prophet (1:1) but also a member of a priestly family. He was born in Babylonia and was among those who returned to Judah in 538/537 BC, under the leadership of Zerubbabel and Joshua. At a later time, when Joiakim was High Priest, Zechariah may have succeeded Iddo (1:1,7) as head of that priestly family (Nehemiah 12:10–16).

Zechariah ("Yahweh remembers") was a common OT name. A good deal of what he wrote was referred to elsewhere in several books of the Bible. The book is remarkable in its use of rich imagery, insights into the spiritual (angelic) realm and its apocalyptic nature. In the second half (chapters 9-14) it refers to events in detail relating to the first and second coming of the Messiah. As an aside, for this author the insights it has provided in piecing together the big prophetic picture have been extraordinary, and its neglect in Bible study is regrettable, which is one reason why extra space is given here to Zechariah's prophecies.

Background and context

The background for Zechariah was much the same as described under Haggai and in the "Exile" section of Chapter 3. Regarding the end time events part, this was significant and not only was it consistent with that given by many of the writing prophets discussed earlier in this book, but was referred to as being fulfilled in the life of Jesus (e.g. thirty pieces of silver; riding into Jerusalem on a donkey) but will be fulfilled when it comes to the great final battle and the coming in glory of Jesus (the second time) as detailed in the later chapters of Revelation and of Israel's conversion, referred to by Paul in Romans 11:26: *"and so all Israel shall be saved"*. If there is an overarching message to the book, it is that, however long it takes, or strange it may appear, God is in control of history.

A synopsis of the book

1. Introduction (1:1-6).
    - The date and the author's name (1:1).
    - A call to repentance (1:2-6).
2. A series of eight visions in one night (1:7-6:8).
    - The horseman among the myrtle trees (1:7–17).
    - The four horns and the four craftsmen (1:18–21).
    - A man with a measuring line (ch. 2).
    - Clean garments for the High Priest (ch. 3).
    - The gold lampstand and the two olive trees (ch. 4).
    - The flying scroll (5:1-4).
    - The woman in a basket (5:5-11).
    - The four chariots (6:1-8).
3. The symbolic crowning of Joshua the High Priest (6:9-15).
4. The problem of fasting and the promise of the future (chs. 7-8).
    - The question by the delegation from Bethel (7:1-3).
    - The rebuke by the Lord (7:4-7).
    - The command to repent (7:8-14).
    - The restoration of Israel to God's favour (8:1-17).
    - Kingdom joy and Jewish favour (8:18-23).

5. First prophetic oracle: Messiah comes and is rejected (chs. 9-11).

    - The coming of the Messianic King (chs. 9-10).

        o Destruction of surrounding nations; Zion's preservation (9:1-8).

        o The coming of Zion's King (9:9-10).

        o The deliverance and blessing of Zion's people (9:11-10:1).

        o The leaders warned and the people encouraged (10:2-4).

        o Israel's victory and restoration (10:5-12).

    - The rejection of the Messianic Shepherd-King (ch. 11).

        o The prologue (11:1-3).

        o The rejection of the Good Shepherd (11:4-14).

        o The rise and fall of the worthless shepherd (11:15-17).

6. Second prophetic oracle: Messiah's coming and reception (chs. 12-14).

    - The deliverance and conversion of Israel (chs. 12-13).

        o The siege of Jerusalem (12:1-3).

        o The divine deliverance (12:4-9).

        o Israel completely delivered from sin (12:10-13:9).

    - The Messiah's coming and His Kingdom (ch. 14).

        o The siege of Jerusalem (14:1-2).

        o The Messiah's return and its effects (14:3-8).

        o The establishment of the Messianic Kingdom (14:9-11).

        o The punishment of Israel's enemies (14:12-15).

        o The universal worship of the holy King (14:16-21).

The message of the prophet

Chapter 1:1-6 introduces the word of the Lord that came to Zechariah. Like Haggai, he urges the people to take commitment to the Lord more seriously. Their forefathers had been warned by earlier prophets. They had not listened, and were deservedly punished by Exile. His message was unequivocal; this was their opportunity to take note and be blessed: *"Turn ye unto me, saith the Lord of hosts, and I will turn unto you, saith the Lord of hosts"* (1:3).

Two months later, **Chapter 1:7-6:15**, Zechariah had a series of visions (full of strange imagery and remarkable symmetry: visions 1 and 8, 2 and 7, 3 and 6, 4 and 5 all having a correlation) during the night, speaking of God's burning desire to see Jerusalem, the city of Zion, rebuilt and restored for the fulfilment of His future purposes:

The first vision (1:7-17) is of God surveying the whole earth by four horsemen during the seventy years when God's people were in Exile, noting the world was at peace (thanks to King Cyrus). The angel (not having predictive powers) appeals to God on the nation's behalf. The Lord, with displeasure, notes the oppressing nations at ease and declares that He will bless Jerusalem – *"the Lord shall yet comfort Zion, and shall yet choose Jerusalem"* (1:17) – but all in His time.

The second vision (1:18-21), involving blacksmiths and horns, is God sending His agents (likely Persia) to overthrow nations who had scattered His people.

The third vision (2:1-13) is of a man measuring Jerusalem and God telling him that great numbers will live there in the future because He is going to bring so many people home. The Lord also says that He will come and live among them, giving us a first glimpse of God's promises for the far future in which those who are not Israel will join with Israel in worshipping the Lord and knowing His protection (for which man-made walls are not required): *"For I, saith the Lord, will be unto her a wall of fire round about, and will be the glory in the midst of her ... And many nations shall be joined to the Lord in that day, and shall be my people: and I will dwell in the midst of thee, and thou shalt know that the Lord of hosts hath sent me unto thee. And the Lord shall inherit Judah his portion in the holy land, and shall choose Jerusalem again. Be silent, O all flesh, before the Lord: for he is raised up out of his holy habitation."* (2:5, 11-13.)

The fourth vision (3:1-10) is of Joshua the High Priest having filthy clothes removed and fresh clothes put on. This is a poignant picture of how Satan (often in the shadows and never far away, as far as the OT narrative goes) is apt and keen, accusing God's people, especially their leaders. The Lord has a wonderful response (worth us all now to bear in mind) and a glorious future prediction, involving the future Messiah and the wiping away of sin: *"And the Lord said unto Satan, The Lord rebuke thee, O Satan; even the Lord that hath chosen Jerusalem rebuke thee: is not this a brand plucked out of the fire? ... Thus saith the Lord of hosts; If thou wilt walk in my ways, and if thou wilt keep my charge, then thou shalt also judge my house, and shalt also keep my courts, and I will give thee places to walk among these that stand by. Hear now, O Joshua the high priest, thou, and thy fellows that sit before thee: for they are men wondered at: for, behold, I will bring forth my servant the Branch. For behold the stone that I have laid before Joshua; upon one stone shall be seven eyes: behold, I will engrave the graving thereof, saith the Lord of hosts, and I will remove the iniquity of that land in one day. In that day, saith the Lord of hosts, shall ye call every man his neighbour under the vine and under the fig tree."* (3:2, 7-10.)

The fifth vision (4:1-14) is reminiscent of Haggai 2:20-23 where Zerubbabel the governor of Judea is given greater authority. It also presents us with the picture of the golden lampstand (that stood in the Holy Place of the Temple) replenished with oil (symbolic of the Holy Spirit) in never-ending supply through two (not identified by name, but likely Zerubbabel and Joshua, *anointed ones*, whom God had called to their tasks). The message is one full of hope and encouragement, and a reminder of how God's work done in His way will assuredly be carried out: *"Who art thou, O great mountain? before Zerubbabel thou shalt become a plain: and he shall bring forth the headstone thereof with shoutings, crying, Grace, grace unto it. Moreover the word of the Lord came unto me, saying, The hands of Zerubbabel have laid the foundation of this house; his hands shall also finish it; and thou shalt know that the Lord of hosts hath sent me unto you. For who hath despised the day of small things? for they shall rejoice, and shall see the plummet in the hand of Zerubbabel with those seven; they are the eyes of the Lord, which run to and fro through the whole earth."* (4:7-10.)

The sixth vision (5:1-4) is of a flying scroll whose purpose is to curse all unrighteousness amongst God's people, for stealing and lying cannot be.

The seventh vision (5:5-11) is of a woman in a basket, representing the wickedness of God's people. She is exported to Babylon in place of God's people who have been re-imported from Babylon into their land. Yet there is a salutary note, as part of God's sovereign plan permits evil to establish itself elsewhere: *"Then said I to the angel that talked with me, Whither do these bear the ephah? And he said unto me, To build it an house in the land of Shinar: and it shall be established, and set there upon her own base."* (5:10-11.)

And the eighth vision (6:1-8) recalls the first: four chariots riding out from the presence of God to do His will. All the history of Israel and the surrounding nations has been God's work. And now His Spirit is at rest, even in the land of the north (Babylonia). It implies His work must surely be complete.

The visions are rounded off with a word from God about crowning Joshua the High Priest as King - a picture of the future Messiah, fulfilled ultimately in Jesus, our great High Priest, who sits on the throne of David for ever (6:9-15). *"Thus speaketh the Lord of hosts, saying, Behold the man whose name is The Branch; and he shall grow up out of his place, and he shall build the temple of the Lord: Even he shall build the temple of the Lord; and he shall bear the glory, and shall sit and rule upon his throne; and he shall be a priest upon his throne: and the counsel of peace shall be between them both ... And they that are far off shall come and build in the temple of the Lord, and ye shall know that the Lord of hosts hath sent me unto you. And this shall come to pass, if ye will diligently obey the voice of the Lord your God."* (6:12-13,15.)

In **Chapters 7 and 8**, two years after these night visions, God gave Zechariah prophetic words for a delegation who came from the worship centre at Bethel. They had come to ask if they should continue observing fasts in the fifth and seventh months, which were memorials of the destruction of the Temple in 586 BC and the murder of the governor Gedaliah a little later. God's answer was: "Yes" and "No". Yes – do not forget the disaster and punishment came seventy years ago, because the message God's people refused to hear then must be obeyed by the present generation. Do not forget the lesson the Lord is teaching (7:1-14). No – forget the destruction of the Temple and the murder of the governor. The Lord is going to restore and bless Jerusalem and His people, such that all memory of the past will be blotted out. God is going to bless the remnant of His people and they will be able to grow old in peace again. If there is a moral for now, fasting and feasting both have a place, but as unto the Lord.

The question of whether to fast or feast was therefore not an unreasonable one, but better if it could be turned around. It could read: will you become the people ready to participate in God's Kingdom? Two thousand, five hundred years on, we still await the full answer, which will gloriously come to pass with Israel restored; and we read again, along with those not of Israel joining them: *"Thus saith the Lord of hosts; The fast of the fourth month, and the fast of the fifth, and the fast of the seventh, and the fast of the tenth, shall be to the house of Judah joy and gladness, and cheerful feasts; therefore love the truth and peace. Thus saith the Lord of hosts; It shall yet come to pass, that there shall come people, and the inhabitants of many cities: And the inhabitants of one city shall go to another, saying, Let us go speedily to pray before the Lord, and to seek the Lord of hosts: I will go also. Yea, many people and strong nations shall come to seek the Lord of hosts in Jerusalem, and to pray before the Lord. Thus saith the Lord of hosts; In those days it shall come to pass, that ten men shall take hold out of all languages of the nations, even shall take hold of the skirt of him that is a Jew, saying, We will go with you: for we have heard that God is with you."* (8:19-23.)

Chapters 9 - 14 are not always easy to understand; they pick up on events in the far future and speak concerning God's final intervention in history. While still concerned with Israel's future, it is more concerned with Israel's Messiah. It can be viewed in two parts: national (Israel) restoration (chapters 9-11) and international (furthest future) repercussion (chapters 12-14). There appears to be a certain amount of darting backwards and forwards. Like the other OT prophets, Zechariah had but a bare inkling of elapsed time. While the modern reader may want sequential presentation of events (some having happened with Jesus' first coming; others yet to happen with his second coming), as far as this presentation goes, besides that which is further discussed in (our) Chapter 15, we will take each section as it comes, concentrating on the main highlights. We are reminded that *"God, who at sundry times and in divers manners spake in time past unto the fathers by the prophets, Hath in these last days spoken unto us by his Son"*, Hebrews 1:1-2, and Revelation when the pieces come together.

National restoration (9-11)

- Vanquished enemies (9:1-8), speaks of Israel's enemies being vanquished. Jerusalem is God's eternal city and will be there, come what may (until the New Jerusalem in Revelation 21); and the day will come when the enemies will be no more and some will even join with Israel.

- Peaceful king (9:9-10), speaks of a King who has dominion from *sea even to sea* (9:10). The words, *"Rejoice greatly, O daughter of Zion; shout, O daughter of Jerusalem: behold, thy King cometh unto thee: he is just, and having salvation; lowly, and riding upon an ass, and upon a colt the foal of an ass*" (9:9), were fulfilled when Jesus entered Jerusalem on a donkey, a few days before being put to death; although those who acclaimed "Hosanna!" wrongly assumed that He was coming to liberate them, and then turned against Him when He did not (for His time had not then come).

- Mighty God (9:11-10:7), speaks of He who fights on Israel's behalf, like the good shepherd. "*And the Lord their God shall save them in that day as the flock of his people: for they shall be as the stones of a crown, lifted up as an ensign upon his land*" (9:16). He will rid Israel of bad shepherds, destroy her enemies: "*And I will strengthen the house of Judah, and I will save the house of Joseph, and I will bring them again to place them; for I have mercy upon them: and they shall be as though I had not cast them off: for I am the Lord their God, and will hear them*" (10:6).

- Gathered people (10:8-12), speaks of those who were dispersed among the nations coming home: "*And I will sow them among the people: and they shall remember me in far countries; and they shall live with their children, and turn again. I will bring them again also out of the land of Egypt, and gather them out of Assyria; and I will bring them into the land of Gilead and Lebanon; and place shall not be found for them.*" (10:9-10.)

- Deforested neighbours (11:1-3), speaks, somewhat surprisingly, of the trees of some of Israel's neighbours being removed.

- Worthless shepherds (11:4-17) contains a parable about three shepherds that had been sacked for not doing their jobs and then throwing back their wages. This also looks to a time when God raises up worthless shepherds who, rather than look after the sheep, do the very opposite. There is also a NT fulfilment with Judas Iscariot: "*And I said unto them, If ye think good, give me my price; and if not, forbear. So they weighed for my price thirty pieces of silver. And the Lord said unto me, Cast it unto the potter: a goodly price that I was prised at of them. And I took the thirty pieces of silver, and cast them to the potter in the house of the Lord.*" (11:12-13.)

International Repercussion (12-14)

- Invading army (12:1-9), shows that while Jerusalem is the main focus, and up to the end of the book when becoming the centre of world government, some things need to happen first. It begins with a siege against Jerusalem (and Judah), with the nations gathered against it. We are introduced to a concept considered in both OT and NT – "the Day of the Lord". We now come to the culmination of world events prior to the Messianic reign. As for the outcome of this attack: *"And it shall come to pass in that day, that I will seek to destroy all the nations that come against Jerusalem"* (12:9).

- Grieving inhabitants (12:10-14), is where we reach the glorious climax of the Day of the Lord, before going back and once again fore tracking: *"And I will pour upon the house of David, and upon the inhabitants of Jerusalem, the spirit of grace and of supplications: and they shall look upon me whom they have pierced, and they shall mourn for him, as one mourneth for his only son, and shall be in bitterness for him, as one that is in bitterness for his firstborn. In that day shall there be a great mourning in Jerusalem, as the mourning of Hadadrimmon in the valley of Megiddon."* (12:10-11.) The glory is He whom Israel had hitherto rejected, the Lamb of Calvary; He is the one who now comes to rescue them. *"Behold, he cometh with clouds; and every eye shall see him, and they also which pierced him: and all kindreds of the earth shall wail because of him"* (Revelation 1:7).

- Banished prophets (13:1-6), are those who have been a scourge to the people, but the land will be banished of the now shamed false prophets.

- Reduced population (13:7-9), reflects that the population had been reduced to a third (some may speculate: Holocaust or Antichrist?).

- Plagued attackers (14:1-8), is where we return to Israel under attack (with parallels to Ezekiel 38-39 and Joel 3), with the Lord gathering the nations for battle and defending Israel, with the armies turning on each other, and with Jesus returning to the Mount of Olives as He said he would (Acts 1:11): *"Behold, the day of the Lord cometh, and thy spoil shall be divided in the midst of thee. For I will gather all nations against Jerusalem to battle; and the city shall be taken, and the houses rifled, and the women ravished; and half of the city shall go forth into captivity, and the residue of the people shall not be cut off from the city. Then shall the Lord go forth, and fight against those nations, as when he fought in the day of battle. And his feet shall stand in that day upon the mount of Olives, which is before Jerusalem on the east, and the mount of Olives shall cleave in the midst thereof toward the east and toward the west, and there shall be a very great valley; and half of the mountain shall remove toward the north, and half of it toward the south."* (14:1-4.) And with living waters going out from Jerusalem (4:8); and *"the Lord shall be king over all the earth: in that day shall there be one Lord"* (4:9). There will be geographic changes with the City elevated and the people living in safety.

- Universal worship (14:16-21) follows. The Lord establishes Jerusalem. It becomes the place from where He rules and all nations recognise and submit to His authority, including the celebration of the Feast of Tabernacles. Significantly, this feast celebrates the final ingathering of the harvest. It is the most important one for Jews, and is one where they are again married to the Law and when they expect their Messiah to come, just as the Church celebrates the Marriage Supper of the Lamb (Revelation 19:7): *"And it shall come to pass, that every one that is left of all the nations which came against Jerusalem shall even go up from year to year to worship the King, the Lord of hosts, and to keep the feast of tabernacles. And it shall be, that whoso will not come up of all the families of the earth unto Jerusalem to worship the King, the Lord of hosts, even upon them shall be no rain. ... Yea, every pot in Jerusalem and in Judah shall be holiness unto the Lord of hosts: and all they that sacrifice shall come and take of them, and seethe therein: and in that day there shall be no more the Canaanite in the house of the Lord of hosts."* (14:16-17, 21.)

Malachi

The prophet and his prophecy

The book is ascribed to Malachi, whose name means "my messenger", of which we know little. A high percentage of the narrative is the actual word of the Lord; and, given it is His last, at least explicit, word for four hundred years, it is one we need to note carefully. While a hard-hitting one, which is nothing new of course, there is a sense of sadness as God tells the people to get their act together; and, as it were, slips away until they do – or, at least, until the coming of Jesus. Remarkably, the words of the prophecy resonate today and might be encapsulated in the phrase "take God seriously". Malachi is the last Old Testament prophet, although the date when he wrote we cannot be certain of. As far as canonical writings go, there are no more prophets until John the Baptist. Israel continued to be ruled, with varying degrees of benevolence (from sympathetic to exactly the opposite) by occupying powers (and that remained the case until 1948 when the Jewish State of Israel was formed), with moral leadership shifted toward priests. It should be added the return of Jews to live in Israel in significant numbers is a relatively recent phenomenon, with most still living outside of Israel.

Background and context

Spurred on by the prophetic activity of Haggai and Zechariah, the returned exiles, under the leadership of their governor Zerubbabel, finished the Temple in 516 BC. In 458 BC the community was strengthened by the coming of the priest Ezra, and several thousand more Jews. Artaxerxes, King of Persia, encouraged Ezra to reconstitute the Temple worship (Ezra 7:17) and to make sure the law of Moses was being obeyed (Ezra 7:25–26). Fourteen years later (444), the same Persian king permitted his cupbearer Nehemiah to return to Jerusalem and rebuild its walls (Nehemiah 6:15). As newly appointed governor, Nehemiah also spearheaded reforms to help the poor (5:2–13), and he convinced the people to shun mixed marriages (10:30), to keep the Sabbath (10:31) and to bring their tithes and offerings faithfully (10:37–39). In 433 BC, Nehemiah returned to the service of the Persian king, and during his absence the Jews fell into sin once more.

Nehemiah later came back to Jerusalem to discover the tithes were ignored, the Sabbath was broken, the people had intermarried with foreigners, and the priests had become corrupt (13:7–31). One hundred years after the first return, as Malachi preached to people, things had got worse, despite mini revivals under Ezra and Nehemiah; and the people were despondent and depressed. Several past sins are cited after repeating them in Malachi's time (Malachi 1:6–14; 2:14–16; 3:8–11). Malachi's prophecy (1:1) is written in lofty prose. The text features a series of questions asked by God and the people. Frequently, the Lord's statements are followed by sarcastic questions, introduced by "(But) you ask" (1:2,6–7; 2:14,17; 3:7–8,13; cf. 1:13). In each case the Lord's response is given. Repetition is a key element in the book. The name "Lord Almighty" occurs twenty times.

A synopsis of the book

1. Title (1:1).

2. Introduction: God's faithful Covenant love for Israel affirmed (1:2-5).

3. Israel's unfaithfulness rebuked (1:6-2:16).

    - The unfaithfulness of the priests (1:6-2:9).

        o They dishonor God in their sacrifices (1:6-14).

        o They do not faithfully teach the law (2:1-9).

    - The unfaithfulness of the people (2:10-16).

4. The Lord's coming announced (2:17-4:6).

- The Lord will purify the priests and judge the people (2:17-3:5).
- Call to repentance in view of the Lord's coming (3:6–18).
    o An exhortation to faithful giving (3:6-12).
    o An exhortation to faithful service (3:13-18).
- The Day of the Lord announced (ch. 4).

The message of the prophet

Introduction (1:1)

"The burden of the word of the Lord to Israel by Malachi" (1:1). While "burden" may not be the best translation, it was something this messenger carried.

Jacob loved, Esau hated (1:2-5)

We have already set the scene of a people that were disconsolate. God is saying He loves them and their response is, "How come?", given their situation. God's response is to remind them of the ongoing story of Jacob and Esau, and how He has ever since, and demonstratively so, favoured Jacob over his brother, Esau,

Blemished sacrifices (1:6–14)

We come to one of the crunch issues in God's complaint: the people giving to God what is second best, and thinking they can get away with something that, in any normal father-son relationship, or between the people and the governor, would be seen as wholly unacceptable. This occurred in the matter of sacrifice: rather than offering the best animals, they offered the worst. As for God, we are reminded: *"For from the rising of the sun even unto the going down of the same my name shall be great among the Gentiles"* (1:11); and, *"I am a great King, saith the Lord of hosts, and my name is dreadful among the heathen"* (1:14).

Admonition for the priests (2:1–9)

Attention turns to the priests, who were leading the people. They were meant to teach them what is right, arbitrating in matters of justice, but had fallen from the high standard set when the priesthood, notably the Levites, were established under Moses: "*The law of truth was in his mouth, and iniquity was not found in his lips: he walked with me in peace and equity, and did turn many away from iniquity. For the priest's lips should keep knowledge, and they should seek the law at his mouth: for he is the messenger of the Lord of hosts. But ye are departed out of the way; ye have caused many to stumble at the law; ye have corrupted the covenant of Levi, saith the Lord of hosts.*" (2:6-8.) There would be dire consequences as a result of them falling short of the standards and expectations that God had set.

Judah unfaithful (2:10–16)

God makes a further complaint against the people, despite outward religious observance, and in two specific areas. Firstly, they had intermarried with those who were outside the faith (something we are reminded was an issue in the Book of Ezra): "*...for Judah hath profaned the holiness of the Lord which he loved, and hath married the daughter of a strange god*" (2:11). Secondly, there was unfaithfulness in marriage: "*...the Lord hath been witness between thee and the wife of thy youth, against whom thou hast dealt treacherously: yet is she thy companion, and the wife of thy covenant. And did not he make one? Yet had he the residue of the spirit. And wherefore one? That he might seek a godly seed. Therefore take heed to your spirit, and let none deal treacherously against the wife of his youth.*" (2:14-15.) It is a salutary thought that believers marrying unbelievers, and Christians divorcing and re-marrying, are significant issues among Christians today, and that Malachi's message on these matters is relevant.

The Day of Judgment (2:17 – 3:5)

One complaint calling right wrong and wrong right, thinking that with God it does not matter: "*Ye have wearied the Lord with your words. Yet ye say, Wherein have we wearied him? When ye say, Every one that doeth evil is good in the sight of the Lord, and he delighteth in them; or, Where is the God of judgment?*" (2:17.) As with most writing prophets, Malachi considers future events, developing thoughts on the Day of the Lord. He talks of one preparing the way (John the Baptist) "*Behold, I will send my messenger, and he shall prepare the way before me*" (3:1a); and the Lord Himself (in the person of Jesus): "*...and the Lord, whom ye seek, shall suddenly come to his temple, even the messenger of the covenant, whom ye delight in: behold, he shall come, saith the Lord of hosts*" (3:1b).

There will be a time of refinement: "*But who may abide the day of his coming? and who shall stand when he appeareth? for he is like a refiner's fire, and like fullers' soap: And he shall sit as a refiner and purifier of silver: and he shall purify the sons of Levi, and purge them as gold and silver, that they may offer unto the Lord an offering in righteousness."* (3:2,3.) This is followed by evil purged and of blessing: *"Then shall the offering of Judah and Jerusalem be pleasant unto the Lord, as in the days of old, and as in former years. And I will come near to you to judgment; and I will be a swift witness against the sorcerers, and against the adulterers, and against false swearers, and against those that oppress the hireling in his wages, the widow, and the fatherless, and that turn aside the stranger from his right, and fear not me, saith the Lord of hosts."* (3:4,5.)

Robbing God (3:6–18)

The Lord reminds His people that He does not change, for if He did they would have been consumed. This has implications for now, given so much else does change. He invited them to return to Him. Their response, yet again, is "Why?" and "How?". God is clear: they are robbing Him and they need to give Him what is His due; for until they do, they will remain under a curse, and if they give Him what is His due there will be a great blessing (yet another poignant lesson for today): *"Will a man rob God? Yet ye have robbed me. But ye say, Wherein have we robbed thee? In tithes and offerings. Ye are cursed with a curse: for ye have robbed me, even this whole nation. Bring ye all the tithes into the storehouse, that there may be meat in mine house, and prove me now herewith, saith the Lord of hosts, if I will not open you the windows of heaven, and pour you out a blessing, that there shall not be room enough to receive it"* (3:8-10).

The issue of tithes and offerings is one we might pick up on. While it was true the people lost out by withholding that which was God's due, the author is of the view that under the New Covenant we are not obliged to tithe, and yet our whole life should be characterised by good stewardship in our giving to God, including in financial matters. As for the people being addressed here, if they do these things, God will protect them from their enemies, and the surrounding nations will recognise that they are indeed blessed of God. Such is the twisted minds of some, though, that they still think people are better off doing wicked than doing right.

This section ends on a heart-warming note, concerning those who fear God, and what God will do for them: *"Then they that feared the Lord spake often one to another: and the Lord hearkened, and heard it, and a book of remembrance was written before him for them that feared the Lord, and that thought upon his name.*

And they shall be mine, saith the Lord of hosts, in that day when I make up my jewels; and I will spare them, as a man spareth his own son that serveth him. Then shall ye return, and discern between the righteous and the wicked, between him that serveth God and him that serveth him not." (3:16-18.) Again, a practical application for now, for those who fear the Lord (and there is nothing to say that under the New Covenant fear does not matter) should be encouraging one another in the things of God, and this is something in which He delights.

The Day of the Lord (4:1–6)

So we end looking forward to the Day of the Lord; although, as we now know, two thousand, four hundred years on it has still to happen; yet Christians see part fulfilment in the first coming of Jesus, which again was declared by His forerunner, John the Baptist (again, talked of in this section). It will be a time when wickedness will be judged and righteousness vindicated: *"For, behold, the day cometh, that shall burn as an oven; and all the proud, yea, and all that do wickedly, shall be stubble: and the day that cometh shall burn them up, saith the Lord of hosts, that it shall leave them neither root nor branch. But unto you that fear my name shall the Sun of righteousness arise with healing in his wings; and ye shall go forth, and grow up as calves of the stall. And ye shall tread down the wicked; for they shall be ashes under the soles of your feet in the day that I shall do this, saith the Lord of hosts."* (4:1-3.) Again, we see a lovely picture of them who fear the Lord along with the thought of calves skipping freely. As for the here and now, the God who had not changed still required His people to keep the Law.

Back to John the Baptist, who is referred to as Elijah, we note: *"Behold, I will send you Elijah the prophet before the coming of the great and dreadful day of the Lord: And he shall turn the heart of the fathers to the children, and the heart of the children to their fathers, lest I come and smite the earth with a curse"* (4:5-6). This is referred to when the angel speaks to Zacharias, four hundred years later, concerning the birth of his son, John: *"And many of the children of Israel shall he turn to the Lord their God. And he shall go before him in the spirit and power of Elias, to turn the hearts of the fathers to the children, and the disobedient to the wisdom of the just; to make ready a people prepared for the Lord"* Luke 1:16,17. John was an Elijah-type figure when it came to lifestyle, and he did what Malachi and the angel said before Jesus embarked on His ministry, that is yet to be fully fulfilled. It is a sobering thought, though, that the very last verse is a threat of a curse, should the hearts of the people not be changed. For while the last word of the Old Testament has been spoken, the story is far from ended!

Chapter 14: Prophets of the New Testament

Transitioning from the Old to the New

The challenge we face for this chapter is, where do we begin? After all, the God of the New Testament is the same as the God of the Old and He has not changed. But when it comes to stuff about prophets and prophecy, other than the fascinating subject of Old Testament prophecy fulfilment, with two notable (prophet) exceptions (and a third covered elsewhere), it seems there is little to be said. Big questions loom, like, what is New Testament (where we are at now) prophecy and how does this differ from the Old? Other than John the Baptist and John the Apostle (by virtue of his Book of Revelation), who are the New Testament prophets, what were their ministries and how did this differ from the OT?

Even if we come up with a shortlist (and when it comes to names it is short), unlike the sixteen Old Testament "writing" prophets, and the umpteen non-writing prophets, there is not much that we can write about the messenger or the message; other than concerning the two Johns; and, of course, Jesus, who is much more than a prophet, and whom we have considered back in Chapter 3. Some of these more contentious questions, where even a basic Internet search will reveal there are many differing views, will be touched on in the final chapter of this book; but, as for this chapter, the intention is, as has been the case throughout the earlier chapters, to concentrate on Bible exegesis, rather than venture a personal opinion.

We ended our journey through the Old Testament, checking out the prophets, with the prophet Malachi; and that was over four hundred years before the next prophet of significance appeared – John the Baptist. That is not to say there were not those who prophesied in the interim, especially if we adopt the looser definition used in this book. We also have an example of a New Testament prophet, before John the Baptist even got going: *"And there was one Anna, a prophetess"* (Luke 2:36).

Between the two Johns (Baptist in preparing the way for Jesus, and Apostle when he writes the Book of Revelation) one senses that many had prophetic words, although few were named who did. Putting aside apostles who wrote the Letters section of the New Testament, like Peter and Paul, who also prophesied along the way, the standout prophet we can name in the New Testament, who actually predicted the future, was Agabus (Acts 11:28, 21:10). Two that many miss are the "Two Witnesses" (to come) in Revelation 11:1-14, whose identities Bible scholars disagree on, which we will consider in Chapter 15. An example of Peter practically prophesying was in Acts, concerning the demise of Sapphira (Acts 5:9) and the conversion of the Roman centurion, Cornelius (Acts 10). As for Paul, while like Peter he is seen as an apostle rather than as a prophet, when we read his letters we are reminded by the "thus saith the Lord" like authority in the way he writes, and may be seen as the NT version of the office of prophet in the OT.

Examples of the office of prophet include, "And *in these days came prophets from Jerusalem unto Antioch"*, Acts 11:27; "Now *there were in the church that was at Antioch certain prophets and teachers"*, Acts 13:1; and "And *Judas and Silas, being prophets also themselves, exhorted the brethren with many words..."*, Acts 15:32. It was evident that when believers received the gift of the Holy Spirit they often prophesied (as well as spoke in tongues) at the same time.

One memorable example relating to the gift of prophecy concerned the daughters of Philip, for we are told: "And *the same man had four daughters, virgins, which did prophesy"* (Acts 21:9).

Throughout the New Testament, it was evident that great respect was given to the Old Testament prophets, who were often held up as examples to follow: "T*ake, my brethren, the prophets, who have spoken in the name of the Lord, for an example of suffering affliction, and of patience"* (James 5:10). When teaching and preaching, many specific examples were cited of Old Testament prophecies being fulfilled, typically when relating these to the events around Jesus.

When considering prophets of the New Testament, many commentators often make the distinction between the office of a prophet, confined to the few, and the gift of prophecy, concerning which all Christian believers have the potential of exercising. Regarding offices in the church, five have been identified: *"And he gave some, apostles; and some, prophets; and some, evangelists; and some, pastors and teachers"* (Ephesians 4:11). As for gifts, nine have been identified: *"But the manifestation of the Spirit is given to every man to profit withal. For to one is given by the Spirit the word of wisdom; to another the word of knowledge by the same Spirit; To another faith by the same Spirit; to another the gifts of healing by the same Spirit; To another the working of miracles; to another prophecy; to another discerning of spirits; to another divers kinds of tongues; to another the interpretation of tongues..."* (1 Corinthians 12:7-10.)

The office of prophet is foundational to the Church: *"And are built upon the foundation of the apostles and prophets, Jesus Christ himself being the chief corner stone*" (Ephesians 2:20). The gift of prophecy is to help build up the Body (a depiction of the Church), which true believers are part of and have specific roles to play. Moreover, we (all of us) are told, *"Follow after charity, and desire spiritual gifts, but rather that ye may prophesy"*, and also to *"covet to prophesy"* (1 Corinthians 14:1,39); and one of the startling results of the gift being exercised, as has been testified to down the ages, is: "*...there come in one that believeth not, or one unlearned, he is convinced of all, he is judged of all: And thus are the secrets of his heart made manifest; and so falling down on his face he will worship God, and report that God is in you of a truth*" (1 Corinthians 14:24,25).

Some of the questions raised, as a result of these brief reflections, include: how does the office of the prophet and gift of prophecy in the New Testament compare with that of the Old? - and, looking at our own time, can we expect *bona fide* prophets today and the gift (and, indeed, any or all of the nine gifts identified earlier) to be exercised today? We will attempt to address these questions, noting Bible expositors differ widely in their answers; but not fully, and, as far as it is possible, non-controversially. The author has a non-definitive view and this he will elaborate in the Chapter sixteen, when he attempts to relate lessons learned.

Going back to the Old Testament, it has been argued throughout this book that there were both those who held the office of prophet and those who exercised the gift of prophecy from time to time. The former encompassed the latter but not *vice versa*. If one were to name a quintessential prophet, few would dispute Elijah. If one were to name someone who prophesied without being a prophet, King Saul would qualify; and he did so more than once, and might have done so more if he did not turn away from the Lord. When one compares the Old and New Testaments, one might have a field day identifying differences. After all, those who are New Testament believers are saved by grace due to what Jesus accomplished when He died on the cross and rose again, whom they follow. Old Testament believers were required to obey the Covenant God made with Moses. The New Covenant, while foretold in the Old Testament, was only revealed in the New, and intrinsic within that was the writing of the Law on our hearts.

Yet there was one significant difference between the Old and New Testaments, explaining why in the New, unlike in the Old, the gift of prophecy should be desired and expected by believers. Rather than being given to a few who are privileged, it is something for all. That is the Holy Spirit that Jesus promised: *"Nevertheless I tell you the truth; It is expedient for you that I go away: for if I go not away, the Comforter will not come unto you; but if I depart, I will send him unto you...*

Howbeit when he, the Spirit of truth, is come, he will guide you into all truth: for he shall not speak of himself; but whatsoever he shall hear, that shall he speak: and he will shew you things to come." (John 16:7,13.)

The promised Holy Spirit was poured out spectacularly on the Day of Pentecost: *"And when the day of Pentecost was fully come, they were all with one accord in one place. And suddenly there came a sound from heaven as of a rushing mighty wind, and it filled all the house where they were sitting. And there appeared unto them cloven tongues like as of fire, and it sat upon each of them. And they were all filled with the Holy Ghost, and began to speak with other tongues, as the Spirit gave them utterance... But this is that which was spoken by the prophet Joel; And it shall come to pass in the last days, saith God, I will pour out of my Spirit upon all flesh: and your sons and your daughters shall prophesy, and your young men shall see visions, and your old men shall dream dreams: And on my servants and on my handmaidens I will pour out in those days of my Spirit; and they shall prophesy..."* (Acts 2:1-4, 16-18.)

When it comes to the message of the prophet, it cannot be dogmatically stated that the Old Testament was almost entirely about judgment (and rebuke), and some hope (and comfort), with a strong element of future prediction; while the New Testament was almost entirely about encouraging believers in the church and convincing unbelievers of their need to repent and have faith, with a lesser emphasis on future prediction; when the latter was present it was more to do with ministry in the church and what God is saying to and through the church, and less to do with the deliberations of rulers and nations. And yet it does seem like that!

As for prophets and prophecy no longer applying today, other than what is set out in Scripture, the Canon of which is now, unlike then, complete: while this may be the view of some, cessation of gifts like prophecy, with obvious supernatural connotations, may well tie in with unbelief in a God that speaks in that way today, it is not something (in the author's understanding) that has scriptural warrant; even though the gift of prophecy has been widely abused and, as we will later reflect, there have been many false prophets, just as Jesus warned.

Dealing with false prophets (as well as teachers) was something the Early Church faced, and this has been the experience of the church ever since, until the time when Jesus comes again. As for what constitutes true prophecy and why it is needed today, this is a subject we will return to in the Chapter 16. As for specific prophecies, such as in Matthew 24 and some parts of the Book of Revelation, we will revisit this in Chapter 15. But to complete this chapter, we will return to the two Johns, whom we identified earlier as having something substantially prophetic to say, and we start with John the Baptist.

John the Baptist

If we were to be asked who was the greatest prophet, we might be hard-pressed to come up with an answer, for our studies thus far reveal a number of prophets we can rate as outstanding, which is why Jesus' testimony is so relevant, noting that John the Baptist was the only prophet He fully did acclaim: *"But what went ye out for to see? A man clothed in soft raiment? behold, they that wear soft clothing are in kings' houses. But what went ye out for to see? A prophet? yea, I say unto you, and more than a prophet. For this is he, of whom it is written, Behold, I send my messenger before thy face, which shall prepare thy way before thee. Verily I say unto you, Among them that are born of women there hath not risen a greater than John the Baptist: notwithstanding he that is least in the kingdom of heaven is greater than he. And from the days of John the Baptist until now the kingdom of heaven suffereth violence, and the violent take it by force. For all the prophets and the law prophesied until John."* (Matthew 11:8-13.)

John's ministry was indeed a remarkable one. It was he who prepared the way for Israel's Messiah. He declared in John 1:23, *"I am the voice of one crying in the wilderness, Make straight the way of the Lord, as said the prophet Esaias."* Not only is John foretold in Isaiah 40:3, *"The voice of him that crieth in the wilderness, Prepare ye the way of the Lord, make straight in the desert a highway for our God"*, but Jesus affirms this to be the case when he refers to Malachi 3:1, *"Behold, I will send my messenger, and he shall prepare the way before me: and the Lord, whom ye seek, shall suddenly come to his temple, even the messenger of the covenant, whom ye delight in: behold, he shall come..."*

His ministry began before he was born and was filled with the Holy Spirit from that point onward, evidenced when pregnant Mary came to visit Elisabeth, John's mother, then six months into her pregnancy: *"And it came to pass, that, when Elisabeth heard the salutation of Mary, the babe leaped in her womb; and Elisabeth was filled with the Holy Ghost"* (Luke 1:41). Just as Mary's pregnancy was extraordinary, so was that of Elisabeth: *"They* (Elisabeth and Zacharias) *were both righteous before God, walking in all the commandments and ordinances of the Lord blameless. And they had no child, because that Elisabeth was barren, and they both were now well stricken in years"* (Luke 1:6-7).

Zacharias received a visitation from an angel, while carrying out his priestly duties *"But the angel said unto him, Fear not, Zacharias: for thy prayer is heard; and thy wife Elisabeth shall bear thee a son, and thou shalt call his name John. And thou shalt have joy and gladness; and many shall rejoice at his birth. For he shall be great in the sight of the Lord, and shall drink neither wine nor strong drink; and he shall be filled with the Holy Ghost, even from his mother's womb. And many of the children of Israel shall he turn to the Lord their God"* Luke 1:13-16. We know nothing of John's life before he appears on the scene, a little prior to when Jesus began His ministry, but might reflect that God's choice of his parents was not incidental, and had a bearing on his character and ministry. Having God-fearing parents in Zacharias and Elisabeth no doubt impacted what John did.

John's ministry was to prepare the way for Jesus, Israel's Messiah. Soon after Jesus began his ministry, John, typical of his character, withdrew away from the limelight. So significant was that ministry that *all* four Gospels provided a record: *"In those days came John the Baptist, preaching in the wilderness of Judaea, And saying, Repent ye: for the kingdom of heaven is at hand"* (Matthew 3:1-2). *"As it is written in the prophets, Behold, I send my messenger before thy face, which shall prepare thy way before thee. The voice of one crying in the wilderness, Prepare ye the way of the Lord, make his paths straight. John did baptize in the wilderness, and preach the baptism of repentance for the remission of sins."* (Mark 1:2-4.) *"…the word of God came unto John the son of Zacharias in the wilderness. And he came into all the country about Jordan, preaching the baptism of repentance for the remission of sins."* (Luke 3:2-3.) *"There was a man sent from God, whose name was John. The same came for a witness, to bear witness of the Light, that all men through him might believe. He was not that Light, but was sent to bear witness of that Light."* (John 1:6-8.)

Going back to the account of John's ministry in Matthew 3, we learn:

1. Like Elijah, with whom John is often compared, his was a rough and ready, no-frills existence: "… *John had his raiment of camel's hair, and a leathern girdle about his loins; and his meat was locusts and wild honey*" (4).

2. His ministry attracted a sizable crowd who listened to him, even though his was a hard-hitting message of repentance: *"Then went out to him Jerusalem, and all Judaea, and all the region round about Jordan, And were baptized of him in Jordan, confessing their sins"* (5,6).

3. He did not mince his words, for example when speaking to members of the religious establishment he was forthright: *"O generation of vipers, who hath warned you to flee from the wrath to come? Bring forth therefore fruits meet for repentance..."* (7,8).

4. Always, he would be pointing people to Jesus, their rightful King: *"I indeed baptize you with water unto repentance. but he that cometh after me is mightier than I, whose shoes I am not worthy to bear: he shall baptize you with the Holy Ghost, and with fire"* (11).

5. He baptized Jesus at Jesus' request, even though reluctant to do so because of his unworthiness. He saw the Holy Spirit descending on Jesus in the form of a dove, and heard *"a voice from heaven, saying, This is my beloved Son, in whom I am well pleased"* (17).

His message was remarkably practical and down to earth, understanding what repentance meant in practical terms: *"Then came also publicans to be baptized, and said unto him, Master, what shall we do? And he said unto them, Exact no more than that which is appointed you. And the soldiers likewise demanded of him, saying, And what shall we do? And he said unto them, Do violence to no man, neither accuse any falsely; and be content with your wages."* (Luke 3:12-14.) While John was looking forward to the Kingdom to come, with Jesus as the King, he also understood something profound that most missed: *"Behold the Lamb of God, which taketh away the sin of the world. This is he of whom I said, After me cometh a man which is preferred before me: for he was before me. And I knew him not: but that he should be made manifest to Israel..."* (John 1:29-31.)

Other than a discussion that was had on why John's disciples fasted and Jesus' did not, we next read of John when he is put in prison, from where he sent two disciples to ask Jesus the key question: *"Art thou he that should come, or do we look for another?"* (Matthew 11:3), which Jesus answered; and then went on to commend John, as we considered earlier.

It is worth reflecting that John was human with weaknesses like the rest of us. After all, he more than any should have known that Jesus was the real deal; but then, as we consider Old Testament prophecy, the expectation would have been for a king exercising full authority, and that might have included overturning wicked King Herod, who had put him in prison in the first place.

As for the reason for John being put in prison: "*For Herod had laid hold on John, and bound him, and put him in prison for Herodias' sake, his brother Philip's wife. For John said unto him, It is not lawful for thee to have her.*" (Matthew 14:3,4.) The tragic outcome is one many are aware of: through now humiliated but still scheming with evil intent, Herodias, John lost his head.

John may be the last of the prophets in the traditionally understood sense. We could take many lessons from John, not so dissimilar to when we considered the Old Testament prophets. For John, the message was all important; and, in his case, it was to prepare the way of the Lord (Jesus the Messiah). His message was uncompromising and fearless; it was to call people, and especially the leaders, to repentance. Gaining popularity and acceptance was furthest from his thoughts, and his austere and lonely life was void of many of the comforts most take for granted (modern-day prophets take note!) and he paid a hefty price. Few dispute that John was one of the good guys; but one wonders, if he were around today, how he might have gone down with "saints" and sinners alike – perhaps he would be rejected by the saints but welcomed by sinners because of his message of hope?

John the Divine (Apostle)

"*The Revelation of Jesus Christ, which God gave unto him, to shew unto his servants things which must shortly come to pass; and he sent and signified it by his angel unto his servant John: Who bare record of the word of God, and of the testimony of Jesus Christ, and of all things that he saw. Blessed is he that readeth, and they that hear the words of this prophecy, and keep those things which are written therein: for the time is at hand. John to the seven churches which are in Asia: Grace be unto you, and peace, from him which is, and which was, and which is to come; and from the seven Spirits which are before his throne; And from Jesus Christ, who is the faithful witness, and the first begotten of the dead, and the prince of the kings of the earth. Unto him that loved us, and washed us from our sins in his own blood, And hath made us kings and priests unto God and his Father; to him be glory and dominion for ever and ever. Amen. Behold, he cometh with clouds; and every eye shall see him, and they also which pierced him: and all kindreds of the earth shall wail because of him. Even so, Amen. I am Alpha and Omega, the beginning and the ending, saith the Lord, which is, and which was, and which is to come, the Almighty. I John, who also am your brother, and companion in tribulation, and in the kingdom and patience of Jesus Christ, was in the isle that is called Patmos, for the word of God, and for the testimony of Jesus Christ.*" (Revelation 1:1-9.)

Revelation is often seen as a mystery book, given its rich imagery that lends itself to various interpretations, and begging the question whether and when to interpret literally or figuratively. It has been ignored or downplayed by some, including by the Reformers, Luther and Calvin, but some are so obsessed with it that they do so at the expense of other parts of the Bible, as they try to relate it to world events and speculate concerning what the book says about the future, and the meaning of unfulfilled prophecy. We see, even now, church leaders taking both extremes. Trying to unravel the message of the book, including by the saintly and learned, is a challenge, which may be one reason some avoid it; but it should be borne in mind that Revelation was written to ordinary, often of humble means, hard-pressed Christians, members of one of the seven named churches in Asia Minor: Ephesus, Smyrna, Pergamon, Thyatira, Sardis, Philadelphia, Laodicea.

For five out of the seven churches, there were words of rebuke as they failed to do what God required of them; along with a call to repent, and the promise of blessing for those who are faithful amidst persecution. It is interesting to note that the variety of complaints range from allowing false teaching to lack of life. They were living in a time of, and had experienced first-hand, persecution and there was the prospect of more to come, albeit for a season, so the letter would have been especially meaningful, and comforting, with exhortations such as: "*...they overcame him by the blood of the Lamb and by the word of their testimony, and they did not love their lives to the death*", Revelation 12:11; "H*ere is the patience of the saints: here are they that keep the commandments of God, and the faith of Jesus*", Revelation 14:12; and "*the testimony of Jesus is the spirit of prophecy*", Revelation 19:10. Sadly, long ago, the lampstand for all these churches have been removed, the very warning Jesus had given them if there was a lack of repentance.

Unlike the letters of Peter, John and Paul, which form a major part of the New Testament, this was from Jesus Himself. It is the one book of the New Testament that attaches a blessing for readers and a warning to those who add to the words of the book. While much of the message is apocalyptic in nature, with fearful predictions of what is going to happen, there is the assurance that Jesus wins emphatically in the end and that He is coming soon. Regarding the author, while most accept it as the Apostle John, we cannot be certain; but, as with most prophecy, the message is more important than the messenger. What is evident is that the author was well known to and respected by the letter's recipients.

It is also important to point out Revelation (especially the last four chapters), like Genesis (especially the first eleven chapters), are essential books of the Bible, even though often dismissed by scoffers. Genesis tells us how it (life, the universe and everything) came into being; Revelation tells us how it all will end. Given where we are now, the growing tide of evil despite hopes for a better world, persecution of believers we are seeing all around us, and expected in the West that hitherto has got off relatively lightly, Revelation's message and the attached blessing to them who read it is important; as are related themes like the need to be prepared, of patient endurance and perseverance, and Jesus wins in the end.

Following the specific messages to the seven churches (Chapters 2-3), we get a glorious glimpse of heaven. In Chapter 4, the Lord God Almighty is on His Throne and is worshipped. In Chapter 5, the Lamb is on His Throne and is worshipped: *"And they sung a new song, saying, Thou art worthy to take the book, and to open the seals thereof: for thou wast slain, and hast redeemed us to God by thy blood out of every kindred, and tongue, and people, and nation; And hast made us unto our God kings and priests: and we shall reign on the earth"* (Revelation 5:9,10). The book is full of sevens: seven seals, seven trumpets and seven bowls. From Chapter 6 on, we read of events which a plain rendering is yet to happen, which includes divine judgment, hardening of people's hearts, the persecution of believers, the mystery of Babylon, the rule of the Antichrist, and an increase in the ongoing conflict between good and evil, light and darkness.

Consideration of the order of events from Revelation 6 onward (e.g., are they the order to be expected if read in sequence?), and to what extent the events can be taken as literal / futuristic or non-literal / historic is one that lends itself to many arguments among Bible students. One concerns the "rapture" and who are the saints who are attacked by the evil forces that are around, identified in Chapters 6 to 18, whether the Church or Israel or both? There is no shortage of examples throughout Christian history of well-intentioned attempts at relating the chapters of Revelation to actual events, many we can reflect on now as being dubious.

Yet the neglect of the one book in the New Testament where a blessing is attached to them who read it, is also regrettable. While the author has a view, which will be touched on in future chapters, in line with the approach taken by this book, the intention is to open up an important subject that merits further and careful study.

Chapter 19 is about the coming to the earth of the King of kings, and Lord of lords, in glory; and not this time as a babe born in a manger, who ended up dying on a cross. This is what the Hebrew prophets had looked forward to: He of the line of David, and who was to rule with a rod of iron. We see here, as throughout Revelation, allusion and reference to Old Testament prophecy. Then comes the Marriage Supper of the Lamb, when Jesus marries His Bride, the Church. Then comes the one-thousand-year reign. Satan is bound, but afterwards let loose for a short time to cause havoc; but in the end: "And *the devil that deceived them was cast into the lake of fire and brimstone, where the beast and the false prophet are, and shall be tormented day and night for ever and ever*" (Revelation 20:10).

Then comes the Day of Judgment. There is no escape: "*And I saw a great white throne, and him that sat on it, from whose face the earth and the heaven fled away; and there was found no place for them. And I saw the dead, small and great, stand before God; and the books were opened: and another book was opened, which is the book of life: and the dead were judged out of those things which were written in the books, according to their works... And whosoever was not found written in the book of life was cast into the lake of fire.*" (Revelation 20:11-12,15.)

It is a sobering thought, given the eternal consequences, worth emphasising: Is your name written in the book of life? Chapters 21 and 22 look forward to the final and glorious end and builds on the theme: "*And I saw a new heaven and a new earth: for the first heaven and the first earth were passed away; and there was no more sea. And I John saw the holy city, new Jerusalem, coming down from God out of heaven, prepared as a bride adorned for her husband. And I heard a great voice out of heaven saying, Behold, the tabernacle of God is with men, and he will dwell with them, and they shall be his people, and God himself shall be with them, and be their God.*" (Revelation 21:1-3.)

We close with the closing verses of the whole Bible, which contain a wonderful invitation and a sober warning. It also reminds us that Jesus is coming soon and we should be living in that expectation and be ready: "*And the Spirit and the bride say, Come. And let him that heareth say, Come. And let him that is athirst come. And whosoever will, let him take the water of life freely. For I testify unto every man that heareth the words of the prophecy of this book, If any man shall add unto these things, God shall add unto him the plagues that are written in this book: And if any man shall take away from the words of the book of this prophecy, God shall take away his part out of the book of life, and out of the holy city, and from the things which are written in this book. He which testifieth these things saith, Surely I come quickly. Amen. Even so, come, Lord Jesus. The grace of our Lord Jesus Christ be with you all. Amen.*" (Revelation 22:17-21.)

As for today

One final thought is, while this chapter on New Testament prophecy is dominated by the prophetic ministries of the two Johns, that would be an unfair reflection of the importance placed on the office of prophet and the gift of prophecy in New Testament times; and begs the question concerning the Church that is operating today, as part of the still being enacted "Acts 29", and what is the significance for God's people today? The author will later venture a view, but it is far from complete, and this is a question those reading this may wish to further reflect on.

Some may feel disappointed, comparing our coverage of NT prophets with that of the OT, as lightweight in comparison. Like any author, there will be strengths and weaknesses. As we consider in the next two chapters, we are still thinking NT and the prophetic, even for those Christians who do not believe in genuine prophets today, yet it is mighty significant, especially given the rapid unravelling of alarming and perplexing events we now see. Some (including the author) yearn for the prophetic voice to help us unravel what is truly going on around us and how best to respond. There is much to alarm and church leaders do *not* sing from the same hymn sheet. We may be tempted to look in strange places for answers.

Neither wanting to acquiesce to official lines, nor going after unproven conspiracy theories, it might help if we recall the counsel of an OT prophet on how to respond to what is going on now – "*Do not call conspiracy all that this people calls conspiracy, and do not fear what they fear, nor be in dread. But the Lord of hosts, him you shall honor as holy. Let him be your fear, and let him be your dread*" (Isaiah 8:12,13 ESV) – as well as Jesus' words, "*Let not your hearts be troubled*" (John 14:1), and "*…lo, I am with you always*" (Matthew 28:20.) Many have maintained while the Lord guides in different ways, especially the Bible, this does not include new revelation of the "thus saith the Lord" variety.

In trying to figure out the position pertaining to prophets, between when the canon of the New Testament was completed and today, we find the history of the Church is a mixed one that ranged from glory to ignominy, unity to schism, true to false doctrine, acceptance to rejection, gospel fervour to lukewarmness and everything in-between. Within that 1900-year span, while many would not have recognised the office of "prophet" or the gift of prophecy, many were faithful to the Lord and kept the torch burning, often at great cost, when it came to persecution from both outside of and inside the professing church. It sometimes included people laying down their lives, for the gospel message they faithfully handed down from one generation to the next, until the present day. While it is not our place to judge who are genuine Christians and who are not, the true Church is ever a faithful remnant of those who truly believe and faithfully follow the Lord whatever anyone says.

These lived and spoke the word of the Lord despite opposition, acting in the best traditions of the prophets, including proving the words of Jesus when called to suffer or speak because of the gospel: "*But when they deliver you up, take no thought how or what ye shall speak: for it shall be given you in that same hour what ye shall speak. For it is not ye that speak, but the Spirit of your Father which speaketh in you*" Matthew 10:19,20. No doubt many also did what was urged in scripture: "*If any man speak, let him speak as the oracles of God*" 1 Peter 4:11, and those who were hearing them knew all too well that God was speaking to them. Heaven only knows who among our spiritual forefathers were prophets or spoke prophetically, but we who are alive today owe many, many whose names we will never know this side of eternity, a huge debt of gratitude.

The Church's One Foundation is a Christian hymn written in the 1860s by Samuel John Stone, which captures some of the salient sentiments:

The church's one foundation is Jesus Christ her Lord;
She is his new creation by water and the Word.
From heaven he came and sought her to be his holy bride;
with his own blood he bought her, and for her life he died.

Elect from every nation, yet one o'er all the earth;
Her charter of salvation, one Lord, one faith, one birth;
One holy name she blesses, partakes one holy food,
and to one hope she presses, with every grace endued.

Though with a scornful wonder we see her sore oppressed,
by schisms rent asunder, by heresies distressed,
yet saints their watch are keeping; Their cry goes up, "How long?"
and soon the night of weeping shall be the morn of song.

Mid toil and tribulation, and tumult of her war,
she waits the consummation of peace forevermore;
Till, with the vision glorious, her longing eyes are blest,
and the great church victorious shall be the church at rest.

Yet she on earth hath union with God the Three in One,
and mystic sweet communion with those whose rest is won.
O happy ones and holy! Lord, give us grace that we
like them, the meek and lowly, on high may dwell with thee.

Chapter 15: Digging deeper into prophecy

Making the case

If we were to thoroughly cover every prophecy we can find in the Bible, in this book, and even if we were then to restrict this to those we deem to be especially significant, this would still end up as a very long book and it would take an inordinately long time to complete. If nothing else, this book is intended to encourage ordinary readers to study for themselves the Bible, in particular the prophets and what they prophesied, and provide a framework in which to do so.

It should be noted, though, that while many prophecies have not been covered in detail in this book, many have at least been touched on. By way of compromise, we have identified twenty Bible specific prophecies or groups of prophecies in this chapter, which the author reckons to be significant, challenging and controversial with some (and there are more we might select); and in many cases these attract plausible alternative interpretations.

Usually some of the content of a particular prophecy is also contained within another prophecy, or when there is mention of the prophecy being fulfilled in some other scripture. The challenge for us is making the connections and joining the dots, mindful there will be those who know more than we do and may disagree. With all this in mind, and resisting the temptation of going down too many rabbit holes, the author has restricted himself to writing more or less a page on each of the twenty identified, trying to make sense of each and drawing out as much pertinent detail as the space restriction allows.

An important matter regarding Bible prophecy is the question of what we are to make of and how to approach it. We live in a day when knowledge of the Bible, even among Christians, is as poor as it ever has been, despite many helpful resources that are readily (*e.g.* via the Internet) and freely available. This is, of course, lamentable; and knowledge of prophetic scriptures is even weaker (and those who do "know" are often, with some justification, bracketed with the "crazies"), despite predictive prophecy being more than one quarter of the Bible, with an important bearing on much of the rest of it. Even among saintly scholars and Christian leaders keen not to upset the apple cart, certain prophecies come in the "don't go there" category; and those that do, often get it wrong.

As far as the author, with no reputation to protect or audience to appease, is concerned, he is concerned that we live in a time when ordinary folk are dissuaded from searching the Scriptures for themselves and may be patronised or worse if they do. What is suggested is, check out prophecy, even no-go ones, humbly, holding our hands up when we cannot make firm conclusions, and to *"be diligent to present yourself approved to God, a worker who does not need to be ashamed, rightly dividing the word of truth"* (2 Timothy 2:15). If this book encourages people to study the Bible for themselves, with open minds, that is a great result and, speaking from long experience, we all need to be encouraged.

But what about the part played by Bible prophecy, especially what is yet to be fulfilled? A common approach is to consider prophecies relating to Christmas and Easter but not the Second Coming and Last Days, although often we see churches give emphasis to one or the other. For liberals, the focus may be to make the world a better place, and prophecy outside what has a direct bearing may be discounted.

For non-liberals, unless prophecy has clear interpretation, it may be shelved as an inconvenient distraction, although some - like the Plymouth Brethren and USA Fundamentalists – are often into things pertaining to the Second Coming of Jesus. Some may react – for example, old men like the author who know their Bible, have had their day and can safely pontificate from their armchairs! Some may build a whole theology and worldview around a narrow, controversial interpretation of selected prophecies, when the aim should be both to truly search out the matter and couple it with a yearning for truth and balance.

A point that the author would like to make is that there is a lot concerning which he has still to come to a firm view, and this is why controversial subjects prominently feature in the examples selected. Sometimes, we are not meant to know the precise interpretation other than what we need to know to operate as God's servant for this present time. Sometimes, our interpretation will depend on our taking a view on certain matters. Some place particular store on certain things happening in the world, such as the rise and influence of Islam. Christians disagree on subjects like the Millennium, the Rapture and Israel, and this has a bearing. Sometimes, we may have a view on interpretation that may differ from others who are holy, knowledgeable and wise, but need to graciously agree to disagree. In following the history of prophetic interpretation, it is clear many have not got it right. But at all times we should adopt the approach of the Bereans who *"searched the scriptures daily, whether those things were so"* (Acts 17:11).

All the prophecies chosen in some way relate to the Messiah and / or the Last Days.

They have been chosen because they have been deemed problematic by some / many; and, without overly sticking his neck out regarding their interpretation, or over pressing the links to other related prophecies when not fully sure, what is written is to not only encourage readers to search the Scriptures (and by that we mean closely examine the text and compare scripture with scripture, before going to learned commentaries), but also to make the point that we can do so and still maintain a balanced, biblical stance.

Those prophecies that fall into this category are usually regarded as unfulfilled, noting that some try to get round this "conundrum" by saying we should not expect them to be fulfilled, or if they are to be, they cannot be taken literally (especially when it comes to Israel – that has been noted elsewhere, that some view promised to Israel as either been retracted or Israel has been replaced by the Church). It is suggested that the approach adopted in considering examples below could be adapted for any Bible study, and providing it is not an unhelpful distraction, can be a fruitful area for study.

One undertaking not covered thus far is proving Bible prophecy is true, despite much hard evidence of their fulfilment. If we were to enquire along these lines, proof of fulfilled prophecy is a powerful argument for Bible authenticity. Two thousand, five hundred prophecies appear in the pages of the Bible, about two thousand of which already have been fulfilled to the letter. In most examples referred to in the rest of this chapter, the prophecies have yet to be fully fulfilled, and to do so requires the coming of the Messiah (for a second time), but arguably if all the Bible prophets are genuine, as we here claim, we ought to expect all these to come to pass in due course. And so far, that is exactly what has happened!

One more caveat besides expecting prophecy that has not yet been fulfilled to be fulfilled, even if we do not know when, is that it will be done so literally, unless that is obviously not the case, including a glorious future for Israel living in its restored Messianic kingdom reigned over by the Messiah. This subject has long divided Bible scholars. While not wanting to assign labels or disrespect those with different views, the author's view (just from these studies) is that many scriptures point to Israel (the people) gathered to the land promised to Abraham and living in peace and prosperity; and it has not been replaced by the Church. As for the actuality / timing of the Rapture, the author is in the "not made up his mind" camp. Another area of dispute that should be recognised concerns the sequence and details of end-time events just prior to and following the Second Coming.

Before introducing the twenty "one pagers", let us return to the question: why study prophecy and, in particular, unfulfilled prophecy? The author has already given several reasons, not least it is a significant part of the Bible; if God thought it important enough to put it there, then who are we to argue? He has also noted that, at least from his experience, the study of the prophets is a particular interest of but a minority of Christians, notably old men like him who have had their day, and in their day were trailblazers and go-getters. Whether one is a "conservative" with a fixation on personal holiness, doctrinal purity, getting people "saved", or a "liberal" with a fixation on social justice, equality and diversity, helping the poor (all, incidentally, having their place) – even though there seems more than enough to get one's teeth into without being over-bothered trying to understand prophecy – we are beholden to declare the whole counsel of God.

While it may be an over-simplification, after the first century AD (when the New Testament Canon closed), until about two hundred years ago, in-depth studies of unfulfilled prophecy seemed few, or had been spiritualised; and, when it was, the leading pundits at the time seemed rather beholden to what was going on around them, leading one now to think with the benefit of hindsight that their pontifications were rather ambitious, if not foolish. Nevertheless, as part of his research, the author has latched on the thoughts of scholars of a by-gone era and have found many to be remarkably insightful. The world has changed enormously in that period and, in that light, pundits might well say that what we are seeing now is further evidence that the prophets were right and the end really is nigh. But what if the world carries on as it is for another two hundred years, without the Messiah coming back to earth? How should that influence our take on life?

As far as this author is concerned, having, or so he had thought, come to the end of his writing, and while waiting on certain happenings before sending the manuscript off to them who would print the book, it was the opportunity to explore more nooks and crannies and go down more rabbit holes, when it comes to digging deep into the prophetic scriptures. Besides reading and re-reading the relevant sections of the Bible and referring to the learned books that might have a bearing, there was a temptation to listen to what the experts said, typically on YouTube. In fairness, this was a fruitful exercise, and if nothing else he was introduced to new and valid ideas he did not consider before.

One example was "Daniel's seventy weeks" – one of the twenty examples selected for this chapter. It was interesting how different experts had different takes on what to make out concerning these weeks, and especially the last (missing) week. But rather than being confused, it was a time to come to a view, including that for some scriptures he had to do what Daniel did: *"But thou, O Daniel, shut up the words, and seal the book, even to the time of the end: many shall run to and fro, and knowledge shall be increased"* (Daniel 12:4).

It is important to be cautious and thorough and not to be negligent in our studies. There are still big areas still not covered satisfactorily by this author in this book; for example, concerning the prophecies of Daniel and Revelation, about which readers are encouraged to undertake their own studies. But always we come back to the need for maintaining balance and not to be carried away and obsessed with the spectacular; for example, when it comes to Apocalyptic prophecy, which is, undeniably, a significant part of all prophecy. There is, after all, a lot of more mundane things also we need to attend to, and a world to win for Christ, and that too is important. The God we serve is awesome and what he rates important, such as every day kindness and doing the ordinary things of life to the best of our ability, is not what man rates. While the pieces of the jigsaw are coming together, it would seem at a far greater rate than students of prophecy, two hundred years ago, could ever have imagined, we still do not know for sure a lot of the detail.

But we worship a glorious God, and that is a central theme of the message of the prophets. He only has to give the word and things will change (just as we have been seeing since the author embarked on this project) in remarkable, unforeseen ways; and, for that, we look on what is happening in awesome wonder. To illustrate his final point before we end it, the author searched out an example text from Ezekiel and came up with: *"Then shall they know that I am the Lord their God..."* (Ezekiel 39:28). As in the other forty-odd *"then shall they know"* references in Ezekiel, the point behind studying prophecy, both prediction and fulfilment, is with a view that people shall know the Lord for who He truly is.

There you have it – but just one more thought: What we have covered already, and are about to cover, are grave subjects and very real, because God is very real; because He means and does what He says, as numerous prophecies bear out. We can look around us in despair, thinking "Why do we matter?" and "How can we make a difference?", yet mindful that these scriptures can encourage us and guide us on our way. The world is clearly not going the way it ought, *i.e.* as per God's purposes, and we may feel inconsequential, frustrated and powerless. But the point is, we do matter because God says we do, and we need to hang in there, for we can make a difference; and, however forlorn things may seem, God is in control of history, and by His grace we can be part of His grand purposes. Bible prophecy both assures us God's Word will come to pass and of His perfection.

About Daniel, at the centre of some of these more challenging texts, we note: "*And I heard, but I understood not: then said I, O my Lord, what shall be the end of these things? And he said, Go thy way, Daniel: for the words are closed up and sealed till the time of the end. Many shall be purified, and made white, and tried; but the wicked shall do wickedly: and none of the wicked shall understand; but the wise shall understand ... But go thou thy way till the end be: for thou shalt rest, and stand in thy lot at the end of the days.*" (Daniel 12:8-10,13.)

Here then are the twenty topics we have selected that demonstrate these and many other points made and offer a short introduction for further study. It comes with a caveat that others might have different interpretations on these challenging texts, but we need to search the Scriptures, realising we do not have all the answers.

1. Bruising the Serpent's head (Genesis 3:14,15).
2. Enoch and the Lord's coming with His saints (Jude verses 14,15).
3. The Lord, my Lord and Melchizedek the Priest (Psalm 110).
4. The Suffering Servant (Isaiah 52:13-53:12).
5. The time of Jacob's trouble (Jeremiah 30:7).
6. The New Covenant (Jeremiah 31:31-34 etc.).
7. The battle of Gog and Magog (Ezekiel 38,39).
8. The new (third) Temple (Ezekiel 40-48).
9. Daniel and the Antichrist (Daniel 7).
10. Daniel's seventy weeks (Daniel 9:24-27).
11. The restoration of Israel (and the Gentile inclusion) (Amos 9:10-15).
12. The destruction of the Temple and signs of the End Times (Matthew 24).
13. The Abomination of Desolation (2 Thessalonians 2:3-4).
14. The Two Witnesses (Revelation 11:1-14).
15. The woman and the dragon (Revelation 12:1-3).

16. The Mark of the Beast (Revelation 13:15-18).

17. The Mystery of Babylon (Revelation 17:1-9).

18. The Battle of Armegeddon and the Lord's return (Revelation 19 etc.).

19. The Millennium (the thousand-year reign of Christ) (Revelation 20:1-6).

20. The new heaven and the new earth (Revelation 21,22).

But before we get going, take note … unsurprisingly, when it comes to "difficult" and "controversial", the Book of Revelation provides rich pickings, which has most recently been evidenced by the author when he has checked out the "experts" and found sharp differences in their varied understanding; although there have also been amidst this many valid perspectives shared, which the author, in seeking circumspection and balance, has tried to take into account – all points readers should take note of. We include in our selection of topics to be covered, seven "Revelation titles", including two that are specifically about hugely different women. We could have easily added a further six, but these are well covered under Daniel (twice), Ezekiel (twice), Matthew and 2 Thessalonians. Tantalizingly, given his trying to "keep it to a page" remit, many questions remain begged.

The beauty of studying the Bible is when different parts of it talk about the same subject, albeit approaching from different angles, and the challenge for the serious Bible student is how to piece them all together. Also, we can always gain fresh insights and learn new things, even from those with who we disagree.

While we are talking about Revelation, a confession has to be made. It was never the author's intention to major on the Apocalyptic, partly because he found, especially in his youth, this to be a distraction. He hopes there is enough in what precedes to demonstrate this has been achieved; but while this may challenge those who get embarrassed about those who do, if we are sincere in our quest to understand the prophets of the Bible, all aspects of prophecy need to be covered, ranging from what some might class as social justice type issues and therefore fair game, to the more spectacular, often latched onto by the "crazies".

Bruising the Serpent's head (Genesis 3:14,15)

We begin with the first prophecy given in the Bible: "*And the Lord God said unto the serpent, Because thou hast done this, thou art cursed above all cattle, and above every beast of the field; upon thy belly shalt thou go, and dust shalt thou eat all the days of thy life: And I will put enmity between thee and the woman, and between thy seed and her seed; it shall bruise thy head, and thou shalt bruise his heel.*" (Genesis 1:14,15.) The matter of bruising the serpent (Satan) is picked up again, at the end of Paul's letter to the Romans: "*And the God of peace shall bruise Satan under your feet shortly.*" (Romans 16:20.)

While we cannot say for sure who passed on these words that God spoke to Satan, for posterity, we note from the account given in Genesis that just prior and just after doing so, God spoke to Eve, and after that to Adam. This prophecy is significant because underlying it is one of the great themes of the Bible: the battle between good and evil, light and darkness, God and Satan. Satan is often given limited free reign to do his mischief, beginning with enticing Adam and Eve to eat the forbidden fruit, resulting in their expulsion from the garden and accounting for when sin first came into the world. It reaches a crescendo in the Book of Revelation, when he wages war against those who follow God and even seems to prevail; yet it ends with him being cast into the Lake of Fire (Revelation 20).

This issue of sin and salvation, the Fall and redemption, is again another great Bible theme. When Jesus (the seed of Eve) died on the Cross, Satan had truly bruised His heel, as he has been doing so ever since, throughout the history of humankind, and is a part explanation for the suffering in the world. But Jesus did not remain in the grave; He rose from the dead in triumph. It appeared Satan had won, but God had other ideas, and going back four thousand years before that, we find God telling Satan that his head shall be bruised by Eve's seed. The Bible, including the prophets, tells us how this was happened:

1 Low in the grave he lay, Jesus my Savior,
waiting the coming day, Jesus my Lord!

Refrain:
Up from the grave he arose;
with a mighty triumph o'er his foes;
he arose a victor from the dark domain,
and he lives forever, with his saints to reign.
He arose! He arose! Hallelujah! Christ arose!

2 Vainly they watch his bed, Jesus my Savior,
vainly they seal the dead, Jesus my Lord! [Refrain]

3 *Death cannot keep its prey, Jesus my Savior;*
he tore the bars away, Jesus my Lord! [Refrain]

Robert Lowry (1874)

Enoch and the Lord's coming with His saints (Jude verses 14,15)

We might not give Enoch, about which whose only statement in the Old Testament is, "*And Enoch lived sixty and five years, and begat Methuselah: And Enoch walked with God after he begat Methuselah three hundred years, and begat sons and daughters: And all the days of Enoch were three hundred sixty and five years: And Enoch walked with God: and he was not; for God took him*" (Genesis 5:21-24), a second thought, if he were not mentioned as belonging to the Hebrews 11 Hall of Faith or cited in the penultimate book in the Bible (Jude): "*And Enoch also, the seventh from Adam, prophesied of these, saying, Behold, the Lord cometh with ten thousands of his saints, To execute judgment upon all, and to convince all that are ungodly among them of all their ungodly deeds which they have ungodly committed, and of all their hard speeches which ungodly sinners have spoken against him*" (Jude verses 14,15).

Jude was written as a warning and an exhortation to his readers to "*earnestly contend for the faith which was once delivered unto the saints*" (v3), in the light of false teachers who had crept into the church to lead it astray. In doing so, he quotes from the Book of Enoch. Whilst not considered part of the Canon, it held much sway in the early Church. The Book of Enoch is an ancient Hebrew apocalyptic religious text, ascribed by tradition to Enoch, the great-grandfather of Noah (this is significant because his son Methuselah's name means, "When he is dead it (being the *Flood*) shall be sent", which is what happened). The Book of Enoch contains unique material on the origins of demons and giants, why some angels fell from heaven, an explanation of why the Great Flood was morally necessary, and prophetic exposition of the thousand-year reign of the Messiah.

This prophecy is the first indisputably recorded in the Bible and yet is looking forward to End Times, reminding us of texts like Revelation 19:14 that present similar teachings. It is a thought, and is parked here for future consideration, that while Enoch was the seventh from Adam via Seth (the son who replaced Abel whom Cain murdered), that Lamech was the seventh from Adam via Cain; and while Enoch was godly, the Genesis 4 record reveals that Lamech was not, and is an early indication of the ongoing conflict between the children of light and those of darkness. As for the Book of Enoch's fixation with demons and giants, it is worth bearing in mind, prior to the flood in Genesis 6, *"the sons of God saw the daughters of men that they were fair; and they took them wives of all which they chose... There were giants in the earth in those days ..."* (Genesis 6:2,4.)

In relating this unusual, yet pertinent to make Jude's case, prophecy of Enoch, we should ever be mindful of the spiritual warfare that is taking place around us and be encouraged to maintain hope, notably God's long-term purposes that are detailed in many more obvious places in the Bible, and shall surely come to pass.

The Lord, my Lord and Melchizedek the Priest (Psalm 110)

Psalm 110 is the most quoted Psalm in the New Testament. It contains the epitome of the gospel: the Coronation of Christ as King-Priest. Contained here are core doctrinal principles: 1) Godhead/Trinity (v.1); 2) suffering as Priest (v.4); 3) resurrection (v.7); 4) completed work (5-6); 5) Ascension (1, sit at my right hand); 6) Church (v.3); 7) final judgment (1b); 8) eternal life (v.4, "for ever").

When He was being asked various trick questions by the Pharisees, Jesus turned the table on them by asking his own question: *"While the Pharisees were gathered together, Jesus asked them, Saying, What think ye of Christ? whose son is he? They say unto him, The son of David. He saith unto them, How then doth David in spirit call him Lord, saying, The Lord said unto my Lord, Sit thou on my right hand, till I make thine enemies thy footstool? If David then call him Lord, how is he his son? And no man was able to answer him a word, neither durst any man from that day forth ask him any more questions."* (Matthew 22:41-46.)

Reference to this Psalm formed an important part of the gospel presentation by the Early Church, such as quoted on the Day of Pentecost: *"Therefore being by the right hand of God exalted, and having received of the Father the promise of the Holy Ghost, he hath shed forth this, which ye now see and hear. For David is not ascended into the heavens: but he saith himself, The Lord said unto my Lord, Sit thou on my right hand, Until I make thy foes thy footstool."* (Acts 2:33-35.)

This aspect of the Messiah, with support of willing followers: *"...rule thou in the midst of thine enemies. Thy people shall be willing in the day of thy power"* (110:2,3), and how He subdues His enemies, and is refreshed on the way – *"The Lord at thy right hand shall strike through kings in the day of his wrath. He shall judge among the heathen, he shall fill the places with the dead bodies; he shall wound the heads over many countries. He shall drink of the brook in the way: therefore shall he lift up the head*" (110:5-7) – speaks of Christ's ultimate victory.

But the verse forming the backbone of the argument that Christ's (Melchizedek) priesthood is better than the Law's (Aaronic) priesthood, and is our way back to a holy God, is: "*The Lord hath sworn, and will not repent, Thou art a priest for ever after the order of Melchizedek*" (110:4) This is often referred to in Hebrews: "*As he saith also in another place, Thou art a priest for ever after the order of Melchisedec ... Called of God an high priest after the order of Melchisedec.*" (5:6,10.) "*Which hope we have as an anchor of the soul, both sure and stedfast, and which entereth into that within the veil; Whither the forerunner is for us entered, even Jesus, made an high priest for ever after the order of Melchisedec*" (6:19,20). "*For this Melchisedec, king of Salem, priest of the most high God, who met Abraham returning from the slaughter of the kings, and blessed him...*" (7:1).

The Suffering Servant (Isaiah 52:13-53:12)

The most referred to OT passage in the NT is one of the Servant Songs, this one to do with the Suffering Servant. As far as Bible-believing Christians go, there is a fair amount of unanimity as to how this prophecy related to the events around Jesus, as were recorded in the NT and other historical texts. The problem liberals raise is, "How could Isaiah have known?" – although the text was included, e.g. in the Dead Sea scrolls, long before Christ came. More significant is what referred to a Messiah that had to suffer, as this is not an interpretation many Jews accept.

In terms of how what was prophesied related to Jesus, we can make reference to each verse, all with a NT fulfilment, in the life and especially the death of Jesus. (It is suggested that a useful study will be to check each point for NT fulfilment.)

1. His visage was so marred more than any man (52:14).

2. So shall he sprinkle many nations (52:15).

3. The kings shall shut their mouths at him (52:15).

4. There is no beauty that we should desire him (53:2).

5. He is despised and rejected of men (53:3).

6. A man of sorrows, and acquainted with grief (53:3).

7. We hid as it were our faces from him (53:3).

8. He was despised, and we esteemed him not (53:3).

9. He hath borne our griefs, and carried our sorrows (53:4).

10. Yet we did esteem him stricken, smitten of God, and afflicted (53:4).

11. He was wounded for our transgressions, bruised for our iniquities (53:5).

12. With his stripes we are healed (53:5).

13. The Lord hath laid on him the iniquity of us all (53:6).

14. He was oppressed, and he was afflicted (53:7).

15. He opened not his mouth (53:7).

16. He is brought as a lamb to the slaughter (53:7).

17. As a sheep before her shearers is dumb, so he openeth not his mouth (53:7).

18. For he was cut off out of the land of the living (53:8).

19. For the transgression of my people was he stricken (53:8).

20. He made his grave with the wicked (53:9).

21. and with the rich in his death (53:9).

22. Yet it pleased the Lord to bruise him (53:10).

23. Thou shalt make his soul an offering for sin (53:10).

24. The pleasure of the Lord shall prosper in his hand (53:10).

25. He shall see of the travail of his soul, and shall be satisfied (53:11).

26. By his knowledge shall my righteous servant justify many (53:11).

27. He shall bear their iniquities (53:11).

28. He bare the sin of many, and made intercession for the transgressors (53:12).

The time of Jacob's trouble (Jeremiah 30:7 etc.)

The author recalls a meeting several years ago, when in a conversation with a lovely Jewish lady, he expressed a view, based on his then understanding of Scripture, which was a lot less than it is now, that Israel's troubles are *not* all behind them. Her response was, "*Don't you think Israel has had more than its fair share of trouble and what it now wants and expects is peace?*"

The truth is, a correct reading of Scripture would show that Jacob has always had troubles and this was predicted going back to Moses, yet always with a message of hope: "*When thou art in tribulation, and all these things are come upon thee, even in the latter days, if thou turn to the Lord thy God, and shalt be obedient unto his voice; (For the Lord thy God is a merciful God;) he will not forsake thee, neither destroy thee, nor forget the covenant of thy fathers which he sware unto them.*" (Deuteronomy 4:30,31.) It was not enough for the chosen people of God to possess the land and live in peace thereafter. Ever since and until the present day, Jacob has been troubled and, according to Jeremiah, will be so again.

One rendering of, "*Alas! for that day is great, so that none is like it: it is even* **the time of Jacob's trouble***, but he shall be saved out of it*" (Jeremiah 30:7, emphasis added), is that their being taken into Babylonian exile was what Jeremiah had in mind. But other scriptures, like Daniel 12:1, Zechariah 12-14, Matthew 24, 1 Thessalonians 5:3, point to a time of trouble after the return from exile and pertaining to the End Times, suggesting otherwise. It may be argued that "Jacob's trouble" refers to the difficulties the Jewish people will face during the seven-year Tribulation period, detailed in Revelation. During this time, the Temple will be rebuilt, later to be desecrated. The Antichrist will break the covenant he makes with Israel, eager to find peace, and set himself up as ruler, expect to be worshipped and force people to receive his mark. In addition, many calamities will occur, with Jews fleeing Jerusalem to the mountains.

But many scriptures also speak of a glorious ending to follow, for example: "*In that day shall the branch of the Lord be beautiful and glorious, and the fruit of the earth shall be excellent and comely for them that are escaped of Israel,*" (Isaiah 4:2). If we continue with Jeremiah, we find: "*For it shall come to pass in that day, saith the Lord of hosts, that I will break his yoke from off thy neck, and will burst thy bonds, and strangers shall no more serve themselves of him: But they shall serve the Lord their God, and David their king, whom I will raise up unto them.*" (30:8,9.) What we must not lose sight of is God's greater purpose for Israel. While the natural mind would be antipathetic to the notion of God choosing the Jews and then allowing them to experience centuries of troubles from then until the time Jesus comes again, His purposes are ever glorious. to do with His Covenant. As is discussed elsewhere, it will culminate in the Messianic Kingdom.

The New Covenant (Jeremiah 31:31-34 etc.)

We are talking here of: "*Behold, the days come, saith the Lord, that I will make a new covenant with the house of Israel, and with the house of Judah: Not according to the covenant that I made with their fathers in the day that I took them by the hand to bring them out of the land of Egypt; which my covenant they brake, although I was an husband unto them, saith the Lord: But this shall be the covenant that I will make with the house of Israel; After those days, saith the Lord, I will put my law in their inward parts, and write it in their hearts; and will be their God, and they shall be my people. And they shall teach no more every man his neighbour, and every man his brother, saying, Know the Lord: for they shall all know me, from the least of them unto the greatest of them, saith the Lord: for I will forgive their iniquity, and I will remember their sin no more.*" (Jeremiah 31:31-34.) This theme is repeated in Ezekiel 36:26-27, is what Moses had seen as coming, in Deuteronomy 28 and 29, and is elaborated upon in Hebrews 8 and 9.

The Bible is full of covenants God made, for example with Adam, Noah, Abraham, Moses and David; all of which are good, and not necessarily replaced by later covenants. But the Covenant mentioned here in Jeremiah is significant, for at least two good reasons. Up to Chapter 31, a lot of what Jeremiah had prophesied was dire and depressing, and would culminate in a matter of a few years with Judah being taken into Exile; but now there is more than a glimmer of hope: "*At the same time, saith the Lord, will I be the God of all the families of Israel, and they shall be my people. Thus saith the Lord, The people which were left of the sword found grace in the wilderness; even Israel, when I went to cause him to rest. The Lord hath appeared of old unto me, saying, Yea, I have loved thee with an everlasting love: therefore with lovingkindness have I drawn thee ... They shall come with weeping, and with supplications will I lead them: I will cause them to walk by the rivers of waters in a straight way, wherein they shall not stumble: for I am a father to Israel, and Ephraim is my firstborn.* (31:1-3,9.)

Jeremiah looked forward to Israel restored into their land and to God; and he likely had but a basic knowledge of the New Covenant as applied to Gentile believers. The NT points out the limitations of the Mosaic Covenant, which was powerless to deal with sin as it did not address the issue of the heart. Not only did Jesus tell a leading Jew of His time that he needed to be born again (John 3:3), but just prior to His death Jesus celebrated the Passover with His disciples: *"And as they were eating, Jesus took bread, and blessed it, and brake it, and gave it to the disciples, and said, Take, eat; this is my body. And he took the cup, and gave thanks, and gave it to them, saying, Drink ye all of it; For this is my blood of the new testament, which is shed for many for the remission of sins."* (Matthew 26:26-28.)

The battle of Gog and Magog (Ezekiel 38, 39)

Having identified this as one of the "twenty", the author felt to drop it, thinking it could be referred to when we come to "the Battle of Armageddon"; but then, when it became apparent that unlike several other OT last battle prophecies, this may be a different event and, moreover, in the light of the subtly and confusingly changing Middle East picture, this is especially relevant and therefore merited inclusion. It could even be the next big event, and one that could precede the Great Tribulation, when the Antichrist has his wicked way. However, here is an example of where different scholars have different views, including it being yet another view of the Battle of Armageddon; although some think this is when Gog and Magog appear at the end of the millennium (Revelation 20:8).

The prophesy begins: *"Son of man, set thy face against Gog, the land of Magog, the chief prince of Meshech and Tubal, and prophesy against him, And say, Thus saith the Lord God; Behold, I am against thee, O Gog, the chief prince of Meshech and Tubal: And I will turn thee back, and put hooks into thy jaws ... in the latter years thou shalt come into the land that is brought back from the sword, and is gathered out of many people, against the mountains of Israel"* (38:2-4,8). Several nations are part of this unholy alliance, led by Russia, supported by Iran, Turkey, and countries in North Africa and Islamic Asia, but from the "hooks" statement we know God has their measure. Israel is at peace and the target is the mountains or the West Bank aka Judea-Samaria. *"Thus saith the Lord God; It shall also come to pass, that at the same time shall things come into thy mind, and thou shalt think an evil thought: And thou shalt say, I will go up to the land of unwalled villages; I will go to them that are at rest, that dwell safely, all of them dwelling without walls, and having neither bars nor gates"* (38:10-11).

While this is a large army, they suffer an emphatic defeat, followed by a seven-year clear-up operation, because of God's intervention using "natural" events, and with the attacking armies turning on each other: *"And it shall come to pass at the same time when Gog shall come against the land of Israel, saith the Lord God, that my fury shall come up in my face"* (38:18). But God's perspective is the one that matters: *"Thus will I magnify myself, and sanctify myself; and I will be known in the eyes of many nations, and they shall know that I am the Lord"* (38:23); and the people, Israel, and her enemies, will know it was God who had won the victory and this will be a trigger for some turning to God.

Given the state of the world, and specifically Middle East events today, the Palestinian question, Russian aspirations for regional control and influence, antipathy towards Israel by nations like Turkey and Iran, we can see how all this fits in a way that would not have been the case not so long ago. But we must also avoid precipitous conclusions. The question may well be begged: where are the superpowers, like the USA and China? As for Britain (which some have argued is Tarshish), consider: *"Sheba, and Dedan, and the merchants of Tarshish, with all the young lions thereof, shall say unto thee, Art thou come to take a spoil?"* (38:13), but realise the victory is the Lord's alone!

The new (third) Temple (Ezekiel 40-48)

This is one part of Scripture where Ezekiel's vision of the Temple lends itself, unsurprisingly, to varied interpretations, and is presented here as another instance where the author has not come to a definitive view on something he considers as important. Even if we maintain the literal approach to interpretation, given such a Temple has yet to be built, and much of what is described has not happened and cannot be, at least before the return of the Messiah, even though there is a temple in Revelation, still to be built, the question is begged, why is a Temple needed and why is a sacrificial system needed, given Jesus has dwelt (tabernacled) among us and is the ultimate sacrifice, which means no more sacrifices are required?

It should be borne in mind Temple worship played a pivotal part in Jewish life, starting with the building of the Tabernacle in the wilderness; and when it came to instituting various aspects of worship and religious life under Moses, building the Temple under Solomon, and the Second Temple after the return from Exile. Herod's rebuilt Second Temple was destroyed in 70 AD, and from then until the present day there has been no Temple, and animal sacrifice plays no part in the Jewish religion; although that would appear to change in the Tribulation period. The Temple was seen as God's dwelling place, where His glory was manifested.

Some of the highlights concerning the Temple, as well as the City and the Land:

1. The precise detail given of the Temple construction.

2. Similarities with Solomon's Temple but significant differences too.

3. Everyone had and knew their place in the well-ordered life of the Temple.

4. The sense of order and purpose; divine peace and blessing.

5. The sense of righteousness and justice.

6. The priests of Zadok, the Levites and the Prince.

7. The glory of God that left the Temple in chapters 10 and 11, returns in 43.

8. The river that flows from the Temple in chapter 47 that gives life to all.

9. The unusual apportionment of the Land.

10. *"The name of the city from that day shall be, The Lord is there"* (48:35).

The author is inclined to the view that Ezekiel's Temple vision is *not* to be taken entirely literally, given it cannot take place until Jesus returns, and then the Temple system is no longer needed. However, reading the detailed description, the exiled Jews, who looked forward to the restored kingdom with its Temple, could well understand how things might be under its Messiah. As for when this will happen, it could be in the Millennium, and if it were not for the fact the Temple is not mentioned, it could happen in the New Jerusalem (described in Revelation 21 and 22) where much of the imagery presented in Ezekiel's vision was picked up by John in his vision of the New Jerusalem. But in the final analysis, hands are held up high, as we declare we must wait and find out!

Daniel and the Antichrist (Daniel 7)

The Antichrist is prophesied by the Bible to oppose Christ and substitute himself in Christ's place just prior to the Second Coming, in a period sometimes referred to as the Great Tribulation. Besides identifying the "Antichrist spirit" the Bible identifies many Antichrist-type figures, going back to Genesis with Lamech and Nimrod; and notably Antiochus Epiphanes, spoken about, but not by name, in Daniel 11. Besides Jesus' teaching in Matthew 24, John writes of the Antichrist in 1 John 2:18-27, as does Paul in 2 Thessalonians, as someone yet to come.

The Antichrist features prominently in Revelation, with the opening of the First Seal: *"And I saw, and behold a white horse: and he that sat on him had a bow; and a crown was given unto him: and he went forth conquering, and to conquer"* (6:2). In chapter 13, we read a fuller description starting with his arrival: *"And I stood upon the sand of the sea, and saw a beast rise up out of the sea, having seven heads and ten horns, and upon his horns ten crowns, and upon his heads the name of blasphemy. And the beast which I saw was like unto a leopard, and his feet were as the feet of a bear, and his mouth as the mouth of a lion: and the dragon gave him his power, and his seat, and great authority."* (13:1-2.) It describes how he deceives and subjugates the world and opposes the saints.

He comes to the end following the Battle of Armageddon, and meets his downfall with the coming of Christ in Chapter 19. This is borne out in Daniel 11, which appears to be an example of prophecy having more than one fulfilment, when *"he shall plant the tabernacles of his palace between the seas in the glorious holy mountain; yet he shall come to his end, and none shall help him"* (11:45).

We are first introduced to the Antichrist in Daniel 7: *"After this I saw in the night visions, and behold a fourth beast, dreadful and terrible, and strong exceedingly; and it had great iron teeth: it devoured and brake in pieces, and stamped the residue with the feet of it: and it was diverse from all the beasts that were before it; and it had ten horns. I considered the horns, and, behold, there came up among them another little horn, before whom there were three of the first horns plucked up by the roots: and, behold, in this horn were eyes like the eyes of man, and a mouth speaking great things ... Then I would know the truth of the fourth beast, which was diverse from all the others, exceeding dreadful, whose teeth were of iron, and his nails of brass; which devoured, brake in pieces, and stamped the residue with his feet; And of the ten horns that were in his head, and of the other which came up, and before whom three fell; even of that horn that had eyes, and a mouth that spake very great things, whose look was more stout than his fellows. I beheld, and the same horn made war with the saints, and prevailed against them..."* (7:7-8, 19-21.) Yet it is only for a season. Daniel 7 is more concerned with the Ancient of Days and the Son of Man: *"...judgment was given to the saints of the most High; and the time came that the saints possessed the kingdom"* (7:22).

Daniel's seventy weeks (Daniel 9:24-27)

"Seventy weeks are determined upon thy people and upon thy holy city, to finish the transgression, and to make an end of sins, and to make reconciliation for iniquity, and to bring in everlasting righteousness, and to seal up the vision and prophecy, and to anoint the most Holy. Know therefore and understand, that from the going

forth of the commandment to restore and to build Jerusalem unto the Messiah the Prince shall be seven weeks, and threescore and two weeks: the street shall be built again, and the wall, even in troublous times. And after threescore and two weeks shall Messiah be cut off, but not for himself: and the people of the prince that shall come shall destroy the city and the sanctuary; and the end thereof shall be with a flood, and unto the end of the war desolations are determined. And he shall confirm the covenant with many for one week: and in the midst of the week he shall cause the sacrifice and the oblation to cease, and for the overspreading of abominations he shall make it desolate, even until the consummation, and that determined shall be poured upon the desolate."

These verses appear at the end of Daniel 9, which starts off with Daniel's prayer. The prayer is important, because it follows Daniel's earlier vision, recounted in Daniel 7, concerning the Messianic Kingdom, his realization that the seventy years mentioned in Jeremiah's prophecy had now elapsed, and the need to intreat the Lord. The prayer starts: *"In the first year of his reign I Daniel understood by books the number of the years, whereof the word of the Lord came to Jeremiah the prophet, that he would accomplish seventy years in the desolations of Jerusalem. And I set my face unto the Lord God, to seek by prayer and supplications, with fasting, and sackcloth, and ashes..."* (9:2,3). The prayer ends: *"O my God, incline thine ear, and hear; open thine eyes, and behold our desolations, and the city which is called by thy name: for we do not present our supplications before thee for our righteousnesses, but for thy great mercies. O Lord, hear; O Lord, forgive; O Lord, hearken and do; defer not, for thine own sake, O my God: for thy city and thy people are called by thy name"* (9:18:19). Gabriel's response (9:20-27) was a direct response to Daniel's amazing prayer.

All relevant: 7+62+1=70. One week often equates one year in Bible terms. The Hebrew *"shabua"* is translated as "week"; *shabua*: a period of seven (days, years) (Strong). Years 0 BC and 0 AD do not exist. We take one year, based on the solar calendar, to be 365 or 366 days; the Hebrew take, based on the lunar calendar, is, one year is 360 days. There were a number of decrees – *"the commandment to restore and to build Jerusalem"* – that fit the bill. Several worthy commentators have done the maths and have come up with the sixty-ninth week falling during the life of Jesus, which ends with the *"Messiah be cut off, but not for himself"*. The point here is besides agreeing broadly, there are disagreements on specifics, for example: Daniel's seventieth week, yet we have a timetable for Jesus return.

Since we have come to the end of our allocated space, the author suggests:

1. One week or seven days is taken as seven years, as far as Daniel 9 goes.

2. The command to restore Jerusalem was by Artaxerxes, 444/445 BC.

3. Jerusalem was rebuilt in 408 BC (seven weeks).

4. Add a further 62 weeks and we come to when Jesus died (33 AD).

5. While scholars argue over where the seventieth week fits in, this looks as if it applies to the Tribulation period described in Revelation 6-19.

6. As for discussion on the "Covenant" and "Abomination", read on.

7. Gabriel's unexpected answer to Daniel's prayer has had and will have a remarkable fulfilment, and these points deserve further study.

The restoration of Israel (and the Gentile inclusion) (Amos 9:10-15)

The subject of Israel's bright, future hope is covered by many of the Hebrew prophets, and this is what Amos writes after concluding his prophecy of future judgment for Israel: "*All the sinners of my people shall die by the sword, which say, The evil shall not overtake nor prevent us*" (9:10). But looking to the future, he sees a glorious future: "*In that day will I raise up the tabernacle of David that is fallen, and close up the breaches thereof; and I will raise up his ruins, and I will build it as in the days of old: That they may possess the remnant of Edom, and of all the heathen, which are called by my name, saith the Lord that doeth this. Behold, the days come, saith the Lord, that the plowman shall overtake the reaper, and the treader of grapes him that soweth seed; and the mountains shall drop sweet wine, and all the hills shall melt. And I will bring again the captivity of my people of Israel, and they shall build the waste cities, and inhabit them; and they shall plant vineyards, and drink the wine thereof; they shall also make gardens, and eat the fruit of them. And I will plant them upon their land, and they shall no more be pulled up out of their land which I have given them, saith the Lord thy God.*" (9:11-15.)

We might be tempted to conclude that while this is very nice, other Hebrew prophets made the same point, maybe better; except this was a key text when the Early Church met for its first and only recorded Council (of Jerusalem), when it had to come to terms with the problematic question of how they were to include Gentiles who did not first convert to Judaism and follow the Law of Moses. But it was James whose argument carried the day: "*Simeon hath declared how God at the first did visit the Gentiles, to take out of them a people for his name. And to this agree the words of the prophets; as it is written, After this I will return, and will build again the tabernacle of David, which is fallen down; and I will build again the ruins thereof, and I will set it up: That the residue of men might seek after the Lord, and all the Gentiles, upon whom my name is called, saith the Lord, who doeth all these things. Known unto God are all his works from the beginning of the world. Wherefore my sentence is, that we trouble not them, which from among the Gentiles are turned to God..."* (Acts 15:14-19.)

The restoration of Israel (which their long-awaited Messiah was expected to bring about) was no doubt an Early (mostly Jewish) Church preoccupation, as was the vexed question of whether you need to be a Jew before becoming a Christian, something we see in the early chapters of Acts and Galatians that was hotly debated. It was not so much Gentiles replacing Jews as the beneficiaries of God's promises, but rather they were to be included in those very promises, being among them *"which are called by my name"* that Amos writes about.

The destruction of the Temple and signs of the End Times (Matthew 24)

The chapter starts with the Temple and a pertinent question: *"And Jesus went out, and departed from the temple: and his disciples came to him for to shew him the buildings of the temple. And Jesus said unto them, See ye not all these things? verily I say unto you, There shall not be left here one stone upon another, that shall not be thrown down. And as he sat upon the mount of Olives, the disciples came unto him privately, saying, Tell us, when shall these things be? and what shall be the sign of thy coming, and of the end of the world?"* (24:1-3.) Jesus comes up with several signs and observations leading to His Second Coming, beginning with something that was to take place less than forty years later – the utter destruction of the Temple (in AD 70) - and something still to happen two thousand years on, His coming in the clouds; along with warnings and advice.

1. The Abomination of Desolation, spoken of by Daniel the prophet (24:15) is one prophecy that one might argue was fulfilled in 166 BC, would be fulfilled in 70 AD and again in the time of Great Tribulation under the Antichrist, ending with Great Tribulation, not seen since the beginning of the world. It is also the event that will trigger a time of great (The Great Tribulation).

2. There will be false Christs, false prophets and widespread deception. These shall shew great signs and wonders and may *"deceive the very elect"* (24:24).

3. There will be wars and rumours of wars and all sorts of "natural" disasters.

4. There will be hatred toward and persecution of those who are His followers.

5. Many will be offended, and shall betray and hate one another.

6. Iniquity shall abound, the love of many shall wax cold.

7. The gospel of the kingdom shall be preached in all the world.

8. *"And then shall appear the sign of the Son of man in heaven: and then shall all the tribes of the earth mourn, and they shall see the Son of man coming in the clouds of heaven with power and great glory. And he shall send his angels with a great sound of a trumpet, and they shall gather together his elect from the four winds, from one end of heaven to the other ... But of that day and hour knoweth no man ... but my Father only."* (24:30-31, 36).

9. It will be like the days of Noah, when the floods came destroying the earth, and: *"Then shall two be in the field; the one shall be taken"* (24:40).

10. *"Watch therefore: for ye know not what hour your Lord doth come ... Therefore be ye also ready: for in such an hour as ye think not the Son of man cometh ... Blessed is that servant, whom his lord when he cometh shall find so doing ... But and if that evil servant shall say in his heart, My lord delayeth his coming ... The lord of that servant shall come in a day when he looketh not for him, and in an hour that he is not aware of. And shall cut him asunder, and appoint him his portion with the hypocrites: there shall be weeping and gnashing of teeth."* (24:42, 44, 46, 48, 50-51).

The Abomination of Desolation (2 Thessalonians 2:3-4)

"Let no man deceive you by any means: for that day shall not come, except there come a falling away first, and that man of sin be revealed, the son of perdition; Who opposeth and exalteth himself above all that is called God, or that is worshipped; so that he as God sitteth in the temple of God, shewing himself that he is God." (2 Thessalonians 2:3-4.)

"'Abomination of desolation' is a phrase from the Book of Daniel describing the pagan sacrifices with which the 2nd century BCE Greek king Antiochus IV replaced the twice-daily offering in the Jewish temple, or alternatively the altar on which such offerings were made" (Wikipedia). This is the view of several commenters

concerning the Daniel references mentioned: 9:27, 11:31, 12:11. It can also apply to Jesus' Matthew 24 prophecy, discussed in the previous section, concerning the ransacking of the Temple that took place in AD 70. However, there is an alternative view it marks the start of the final 42 months of the Tribulation.

Given the significance Jesus attached to Daniel's prophecy and the Abomination of Desolation as marking the beginnings of great tribulation, which as a key (possible the key) event in the seven year period preceding the Second Coming, it is well to remind consider pertinent points: "*And arms shall stand on his part, and they shall pollute the sanctuary of strength, and shall take away the daily sacrifice, and they shall place the abomination that maketh desolate. And such as do wickedly against the covenant shall he corrupt by flatteries: but the people that do know their God shall be strong, and do exploits. And they that understand among the people shall instruct many: yet they shall fall by the sword, and by flame, by captivity, and by spoil, many days. Now when they shall fall, they shall be holpen with a little help: but many shall cleave to them with flatteries.*" (Daniel 11:31-34.) While this will be a terrible time for the people of God who stand true to the faith, as the Antichrist reigns and blasphemes, Daniel also reminds us how it will end: "*And he shall plant the tabernacles of his palace between the seas in the glorious holy mountain; yet he shall come to his end, and none shall help him ... And at that time shall Michael stand up, the great prince which standeth for the children of thy people: and there shall be a time of trouble, such as never was since there was a nation even to that same time: and at that time thy people shall be delivered, every one that shall be found written in the book*". (11:45, 12:1.)

Besides the Daniel reference, there is: "*And there was given unto him a mouth speaking great things and blasphemies; and power was given unto him to continue forty and two months. And he opened his mouth in blasphemy against God, to blaspheme his name, and his tabernacle, and them that dwell in heaven.*" (Revelation 13:5-6.) Antiochus IV is but a foreshadow of the real Antichrist, who, according to the author's understanding, breaks the covenant he made with Israel, halfway (42 months) into the seven-year Tribulation period.

It would be quite valid to use the Daniel or Revelation texts as the centrepiece of our consideration of the Abomination of Desolation, but since we have already cited both books more than once in this chapter, it would be useful to consider from a new perspective, here relating to the writings of the Apostle Paul. While part of his gifting was as a prophet, much of what Paul argues is as an interpreter of prophecy, in particular Daniel. In verses cited above, he is responding to a concern:

"T*hat ye be not soon shaken in mind, or be troubled, neither by spirit, nor by word, nor by letter as from us, as that the day of Christ is at hand*" (2:2).

We are not about speculating on events around the Second Coming, but it is worth summarising some of the context and events around this important happening:

1. There will be a falling away first.

2. The man of sin, i.e. the Antichrist, will be revealed.

3. He will oppose and exalt himself above God.

4. He sits as God in the temple (to be built) – the abomination of desolation.

The Two Witnesses (Revelation 11:1-14)

"*The two witnesses are two of God's prophets who are seen in a vision by John of Patmos, who appear during the Second woe recorded in Revelation 11:1-14. They have been variously identified by theologians as two individuals, as two groups of people, or as two concepts*" (Wikipedia).

"*And I will give power unto my two witnesses, and they shall prophesy a thousand two hundred and threescore days, clothed in sackcloth. These are the two olive trees, and the two candlesticks standing before the God of the earth. And if any man will hurt them, fire proceedeth out of their mouth, and devoureth their enemies: and if any man will hurt them, he must in this manner be killed.*" (Revelation 11:3-5.)

The identity of the two witnesses is one keenly debated among prophecy students. This includes Enoch and Elijah, and Moses and Elijah. There are also those who suggest two groups. All of which appear credible and the author is undecided. What he does believe, though, is that the Two Witnesses operate during the first half of the Tribulation period, to the point when the Antichrist "ups the anti" by double-crossing the Jews, and going after and killing Jews and followers of Jesus, following the manifestation of the Abomination of Desolation.

It is at this halfway point that we read: "*And when they shall have finished their testimony, the beast that ascendeth out of the bottomless pit shall make war against them, and shall overcome them, and kill them. And their dead bodies shall lie in the street of the great city, which spiritually is called Sodom and Egypt, where also our*

Lord was crucified." (11:7,8.) It appears Antichrist has finally got his way, with his followers glad in the "fact", but God has the final say: *"And after three days and an half the spirit of life from God entered into them, and they stood upon their feet; and great fear fell upon them which saw them. And they heard a great voice from heaven saying unto them, Come up hither. And they ascended up to heaven in a cloud; and their enemies beheld them."* (11:11,12).

It is important, though, to understand something of the scenario in which the Two Witnesses came to operate. The Antichrist had come to power and was calling the shots. He did so as the bright hope to fix the troubles the world had got itself in, and was widely acclaimed as the great deliverer. Besides the 144,000 Jewish evangelists that opposed the Antichrist, described in Revelation 7, there were the two witnesses; who, rather than toe the line with the Antichrist's "peace and security" and, "Follow me, for I can sort things out", message, delivered old fashioned gospel-type preaching, telling the people they needed to repent or else face God's wrath. The battle between the two opposing factions is a central theme of the Book of Revelation, but when we read to the end, we see who wins. Putting aside the question of whether or not true Christians are around during this period (discussed in chapter 17), the key challenge for us all is deciding who to follow.

The woman and the dragon (Revelation 12:1-3)

"And there appeared a great wonder in heaven; a woman clothed with the sun, and the moon under her feet, and upon her head a crown of twelve stars: And she being with child cried, travailing in birth, and pained to be delivered. And there appeared another wonder in heaven; and behold a great red dragon, having seven heads and ten horns, and seven crowns upon his heads." (12:1-3.)

We come to the first of our two women (here the goodie, later the baddie), and along with it a dragon who opposes her. There is much symbolism in this chapter, and inevitably different "worthies" having different views. The dragon is Satan and is identified as such (chapter 17 also relates). Interpreters have different views on who the woman is; for example, the Church; Mary; and Israel, with the sun, moon and stars reminding us of Joseph's dream (Genesis 37). The male child would appear to be Jesus (for example *"who was to rule all nations with a rod of iron"* (12:5)), although other ideas include the Church or even the "144,000".

Notable in this chapter is the part played by the followers of Christ: *"And I heard a loud voice saying in heaven, Now is come salvation, and strength, and the kingdom of our God, and the power of his Christ: for the accuser of our brethren is cast down, which accused them before our God day and night. And they overcame him by the blood of the Lamb, and by the word of their testimony; and they loved not their lives unto the death."* (12:10,11.) And since Michael has been mentioned, it is worth relating what John saw with what Daniel saw: *"And at that time shall Michael stand up, the great prince which standeth for the children of thy people: and there shall be a time of trouble, such as never was since there was a nation even to that same time: and at that time thy people shall be delivered, every one that shall be found written in the book."* (Daniel 12:1.)

What we have in this chapter is a chiasmus: a rhetorical or literary figure in which words, grammatical constructions, or concepts are repeated in reverse order.

1. The dragon pursues the woman and her child (12:1-5).

2. The woman is nourished 1,260 days (12:6).

3. Michael overcomes the dragon (12:7,8).

4. The dragon is cast out of heaven (12:9,10)

5. The saints overcome the dragon (12:11-12)

6. The woman is nourished times, times and half a time (12:13-16).

7. The dragon pursues the woman's other children (12:17).

Interestingly, the centrepiece of this chiasmus is the dragon being cast out of heaven; and given the events surrounding this in Revelation, this is one of the key ones and has a bearing on much of the carnage that follows. One explanation is that the first half relates to a war fought in heaven culminating with the dragon being cast out; and the second half on earth, with the saints prevailing in the end. The war in heaven goes back to the time Satan rebelled, and his antagonism toward the Christ relates to the first prophecy in the Bible (discussed earlier). While the chapter ends on a somber note, *"And the dragon was wroth with the woman, and went to make war with the remnant of her seed, which keep the commandments of God, and have the testimony of Jesus Christ"* (12:17), when we read on, we will see that it is not the dragon (Satan) who wins that war but Christ.

The Mark of the Beast (Revelation 13:15-18)

"And he had power to give life unto the image of the beast, that the image of the beast should both speak, and cause that as many as would not worship the image of the beast should be killed. And he causeth all, both small and great, rich and poor, free and bond, to receive a mark in their right hand, or in their foreheads: And that no man might buy or sell, save he that had the mark, or the name of the beast, or the number of his name. Here is wisdom. Let him that hath understanding count the number of the beast: for it is the number of a man; and his number is Six hundred threescore and six." (Revelation 15:16-18.)

Even for those who do not know their Bibles, they will likely have heard of the "Mark of the Beast", and the number "666" printed on one's person that is needed in order to buy and sell. We live in the day that not only does the technology exists for this type of operation, by way of electronic implants or even ingredients in vaccines, but that technology is being used, occasionally imposed and sometimes welcomed – it does not need much imagination to see beyond any obvious benefits that comes with technology, the darker side. But none of this is the Mark of the Beast, which is about open, conscious worship of the Antichrist. The call for Christ followers is to endure and have faith in Him. While we may have valid opinions on how to respond to what some see now as the Mark, the "what" is *not* it. When the time comes, we will know "what" is and "what" is not the Mark.

According to the Bible narrative, the imposition of the Mark comes in the second half (last forty-two weeks) of the Tribulation period, brought in following the setting up of the Abomination of Desolation by the Antichrist (discussed earlier) where the unholy trinity of Satan, the False Prophet and the Antichrist are given free reign and are able to impose their evil will on the world population, often with their acquiescence, and in particular on the Jewish people and those who follow Jesus, which they will do ruthlessly. The Mark is something that is only given to those who worship the Antichrist. From what we can read in the chapters before and after in Revelation, it will be a terrible time for true believers, who are encouraged to stand firm and in doing so will receive a martyr's crown.

"And there was given unto him a mouth speaking great things and blasphemies; and power was given unto him to continue forty and two months. And he opened his mouth in blasphemy against God, to blaspheme his name, and his tabernacle, and them that dwell in heaven. And it was given unto him to make war with the saints, and to overcome them: and power was given him over all kindreds, and tongues, and nations.

And all that dwell upon the earth shall worship him, whose names are not written in the book of life of the Lamb slain from the foundation of the world." (13:5-8.)

The Mystery of Babylon (Revelation 17:1-9)

Two chapters (17 and 18) are devoted to our second woman, the Mystery of Babylon, referred to also as the "Great Whore", who is introduced: *"And there came one of the seven angels which had the seven vials, and talked with me, saying unto me, Come hither; I will shew unto thee the judgment of the great whore that sitteth upon many waters: With whom the kings of the earth have committed fornication, and the inhabitants of the earth have been made drunk with the wine of her fornication. So he carried me away in the spirit into the wilderness: and I saw a woman sit upon a scarlet coloured beast, full of names of blasphemy, having seven heads and ten horns. And the woman was arrayed in purple and scarlet colour, and decked with gold and precious stones and pearls, having a golden cup in her hand full of abominations and filthiness of her fornication. And upon her forehead was a name written, Mystery, Babylon The Great, The Mother Of Harlots And Abominations Of The Earth. And I saw the woman drunken with the blood of the saints, and with the blood of the martyrs of Jesus: and when I saw her, I wondered with great admiration."* (Revelation 17:1-6.)

The identity of the Mystery is a keenly debated one among prophecy students. It includes Rome (and the Roman Catholic Church); major economic centres, such as New York; Jerusalem in its impenitent state; and, more recently (and with some credibility, given what we have been seeing in recent years), something to do with the Muslim world - for example: a rebuilt Babylon or a new mega-city now being built in Saudi Arabia. We cannot say for sure concerning the identity and events, but it cannot be ignored, for it plays an important part in the Tribulation period.

The image depicts the woman riding on the Beast (the Antichrist) with whom she has a strong relationship. She represents a major commercial and religious centre. She holds extraordinary power and influence on the world stage (*"which reigneth over the kings of the earth"*, 17:18); and it is easy to imagine, in his quest for world domination and adulation, why the Beast would want to team up with her; although at some point, and the trigger is unclear, he turns against her. She is responsible, along with the Antichrist, for the persecution of "the saints".

Her demise is sudden and emphatic, and with it comes a warning for believers: *"Babylon the great is fallen, is fallen, and is become the habitation of devils, and the hold of every foul spirit, and a cage of every unclean and hateful bird. For all nations have drunk of the wine of the wrath of her fornication, and the kings of the earth have committed fornication with her, and the merchants of the earth are waxed rich through the abundance of her delicacies. And I heard another voice from heaven, saying, Come out of her, my people, that ye be not partakers of her sins, and that ye receive not of her plagues. For her sins have reached unto heaven, and God hath remembered her iniquities."* (18:2-5.)

So many points can be elaborated – such as Babylon representing a long line of pseudo-spiritual, socio-economic entities, opposed to the true God and His people, yet wielding power and influence, going back to Nimrod and the Tower of Babel and Babylon itself, about which Isaiah 47:8,11 and Jeremiah 50 relate, and notably some of the imagery on display then is also in John's vision.

The Battle of Armageddon and the Lord's return (Revelation 19 etc.)

"For they are the spirits of devils, working miracles, which go forth unto the kings of the earth and of the whole world, to gather them to the battle of that great day of God Almighty. Behold, I come as a thief. Blessed is he that watcheth, and keepeth his garments, lest he walk naked, and they see his shame. And he gathered them together into a place called in the Hebrew tongue Armageddon." (Revelation 16:14-16.)

"And I saw heaven opened, and behold a white horse; and he that sat upon him was called Faithful and True, and in righteousness he doth judge and make war. His eyes were as a flame of fire, and on his head were many crowns; and he had a name written, that no man knew, but he himself. And he was clothed with a vesture dipped in blood: and his name is called The Word of God. And the armies which were in heaven followed him upon white horses, clothed in fine linen, white and clean." (19:11-14.)

Other pertinent references relating the last great battle on Earth, known as the Battle of Armageddon, which is ended in spectacular manner when Christ returns to the earth, when He defeats the armies from many nations that have come up to do battle, specifically against Israel, are: Isaiah 34:1-6, Isaiah 63:1-6, Daniel 9 and 11, Joel 3, Zephaniah 3:8, Zechariah 14. The nature of the battle (or battles) is not entirely clear; and while the Revelation reference suggests it takes place on the plains of Megiddo, the crossroads of the world, where many of battles in the past had taken place, if we take these references to relate to the same event, then it could also be in locations a hundred miles radius of Jerusalem: Valley of Jehoshaphat (Joel), Bozrah (Isaiah) and Jerusalem itself (Zechariah).

From the Revelation account, it is in the context of the destruction of the great mystery (Babylon); the rise and rule of the Antichrist; the enmity between the "saints" and those who follow the Antichrist and the False Prophet; and divine judgments upon the earth starting with the seven seals and leading to the seven trumpets and seven bowls. While the period involved is seven years (and the worst in the final three and a half years when the Antichrist turns against Israel, with which he had made a covenant), it is one of suffering for the saints and also for Israel, many of whom had yet to accept Yeshua their Messiah, but in the light of His intervening will do so at the end, Zechariah 12:10, with weeping and joy.

The Millennium (the thousand-year reign of Christ) (Revelation 20:1-6)

There is a verse in Isaiah (and also in Micah) that has been cherry-picked (because it misses out the key ingredient – the Messiah – who is needed to make it happen) by the United Nations, in coming up with some form of mission statement, which to quote fully reads: *"And he shall judge among the nations, and shall rebuke many people: and they shall beat their swords into plowshares, and their spears into pruninghooks: nation shall not lift up sword against nation, neither shall they learn war any more"* (Isaiah 2:4). Isaiah begins his book with a rebuke, and yet he looks forward to a reign of peace, that is referred to as the Millennium.

And not just Isaiah: the other major prophets (Isaiah, Jeremiah, Ezekiel, Daniel) and twelve minor prophets (Hosea, Joel, Amos, Obadiah, Jonah, Micah, Nahum, Habakkuk, Zephaniah, Haggai, Zechariah, Malachi) too. Most of them looked forward to the Day of the Lord, the coming of Israel's Messiah; and Israel's fortunes restored, and far, far better, in a time referred to here as the Millennium. For most of them recognized, lived through or lived after the result of YHWH's judgment - exiled by the Assyrians (Israel) and by the Babylonians (Judah). While a measure of restoration occurred following the return from Exile by decree of Persian King Cyrus, what was experienced was a shadow of that prophesied.

In Revelation, the Millennium text falls between Christ's Second Coming and Judgment Day: *"And I saw thrones, and they sat upon them, and judgment was given unto them: and I saw the souls of them that were beheaded for the witness of Jesus, and for the word of God, and which had not worshipped the beast, neither his image, neither had received his mark upon their foreheads, or in their hands; and they lived and reigned with Christ a thousand years. But the rest of the dead lived not again until the thousand years were finished. This is the first resurrection. Blessed and holy is he that hath part in the first resurrection: on such the second death hath no power, but they shall be priests of God and of Christ, and shall reign with him a thousand years"* (20:4-6).

Christian pundits over the centuries come into different schools of thought: A-, Post- and Pre- (and even Pan - i.e. it will all pan out in the end) millennialist; and within each group there are significant variations, for example Pre-millennialists who do not believe in the "Secret Rapture". A-millennialists do not believe in a literal Millennium. Post-millennialists believe we may be in it. Pre-millennialists (including the author) believe the above text, and the many related in the Old Testament, should be taken literally. Christ reigns and those who had been killed for witnessing to Jesus will reign with Him. The restored Kingdom (of David) has finally arrived! It will be a time of peace and prosperity. The world, with Satan and the bad guys removed, and Christ ruling, will function as God intended.

The new heaven and the new earth (Revelation 21,22)

As we have noted, Christians are in general agreement about the actuality of the Second Coming but attach varying importance and applications according to their particular understanding. The same goes for the eternal state: while in agreement that there is life after death, there is considerable variance on what this life actually is. Some, maybe many, will view our eternal destiny as being either Heaven – a place of continuous spiritual bliss somewhere in Outer Space – or Hell, which is just the opposite, although many these days dispute such a place exists.

When the Millennium ends, the devil is released from captivity and allowed one more opportunity to reek havoc on the earth, including another Gog and Magog battle, before God intervenes and the devil is consigned to the Lake of Fire, a place of eternal torment. Then comes the final great judgment when all: *"…were judged every man according to their works… And whosoever was not found written in the book of life was cast into the lake of fire"* (20:13,15). We are then told: *"And I saw a new heaven and a new earth: for the first heaven and the first earth were passed away; and there was no more sea. And I John saw the holy city, new Jerusalem, coming down from God out of heaven, prepared as a bride adorned for her husband. And I heard a great voice out of heaven saying, Behold, the tabernacle of God is with men, and he will dwell with them, and they shall be his people, and God himself shall be with them, and be their God."* (21:1-3).

Since we only have a page, all the author can add is that it is glorious, for the whole of creation is redeemed, the universe and everything in it is made new and, for once, what seems too good to be true is better than true. Read chapters 21 and 22 and see for yourself. It was what Abraham looked forward to four thousand years ago when leaving home comforts to take up the mission God gave him: *"For he looked for a city which hath foundations, whose builder and maker is God"* (Hebrews 11:10). It is something Peter could see when writing: *"But the day of the Lord will come as a thief in the night; in the which the heavens shall pass away with a great noise, and the elements shall melt with fervent heat, the earth also and the works that are therein shall be burned up"* (2 Peter 3:10).

The Bible ends by presenting a stark choice that we all have to make, the gospel invitation to come to Jesus, and the heart-felt cry of His followers for Him to come: *"He that is unjust, let him be unjust still: and he which is filthy, let him be filthy still: and he that is righteous, let him be righteous still: and he that is holy, let him be holy still ... And the Spirit and the bride say, Come. And let him that heareth say, Come. And let him that is athirst come. And whosoever will, let him take the water of life freely ... Even so, come, Lord Jesus."* (22: 11,17,20.)

Chapter 16: Learning from the prophets

Personal reflections

Throughout the preceding fifteen chapters, it was the deliberate intention of the author to avoid use of first person, singular pronouns, such as "I", "me", "my" and "mine". The reason is simple – this book is not about the author, any more than the prophecies of the prophets of old were about the prophets. While his interests, perspectives, preoccupations, and prejudices even, cannot be ignored, and that is true for probably every author, he wanted it to reflect his straightforward journey through the Bible, often forensically, picking up on anything to do with prophets and prophecy that seem relevant for the now, and so much is (in his view). But more important than that, given the Bible is His Book, he wanted this book to be more about God, with His prophets as mere messengers.

From now on, I will throw off the restraint of having to find ways of avoiding use of the first person singular because I want to be up front when it comes to offering a personal view and sharing personal examples of how the prophetic impacts my life and changed my view of the world, how God is working in it, wants to work in it and will work in it, and the part we can all play, doing what the title of this chapter suggests, learning from the prophets. There is no doubt, researching for this book has been a far bigger undertaking than I ever envisaged and inevitably there are areas remaining that could, and some might argue should, be developed further; but there comes a time to call it a day and I use this chapter and those that follow as opportunities to tie up some loose ends and draw lessons. (I was given an unexpected second chance to develop certain points in the second edition.)

As those, especially if familiar with my blogs, will know, I often offer views of what is going on in the world that challenge the official line and it is often at odds with Christian leaders, including those from my own theological stable. But readers who have got this far will realise, if they thought that I was going to come out with controversial statements, they may come away disappointed. I especially wanted to adhere to sound principles of exegesis, checking what I write against Bible text and sound Bible scholars. If there have been controversial statements, this will include the view that the prophets of the Bible were the real deal, *i.e.* they prophesied what God told them and, unless clearly not the case, prophecies should be taken literally. There is a special place still for Israel; there is a lot of prophecy still to be fulfilled, including a literal millennium and some of the discussion in the previous chapter, interpreting "difficult" prophecy. Less controversially, I believe, even more than when I began, is we can learn much from the prophets; and, while open as to how this might look, we can do with a prophetic voice today.

When I began this project at the beginning of 2020, it was with the thought that this could be my most significant contribution to the advancement of the Kingdom of God to date, and part of my doing what those similarly situated from previous generations have done, which is to pass on the baton to the next generation, in the knowledge that God alone will decide when baton-passing ends because Christ is back reigning on earth. I do not write because I am better than anyone else, and can look back on times in life when it seemed I had blown my chances, spiritually speaking, and had squandered opportunities. I am merely a *"brand plucked out of the fire"* (Zechariah 3:2), an *"unprofitable servant"*, Luke 17:10, and if there is any good, "by *the grace of God I am what I am*", 1 Corinthians 15:10. I should add that while I know the Bible well, and better than most, and can hold my own in many theological debates, to my shame, I still do not know it well enough.

But I do believe certain things need saying that are not being said. It is with a degree of frustration, not only are our secular leaders and movers and shakers doing bad or mad things, but the leaders of that part of the "Church" that non-Christians are aware of, and many actual Christians look to for leadership, are not being a voice of correction. What is lacking, as I saw / see it, was / is a prophetic voice. I make no claim to being a prophet – it is not something I would anyway volunteer for, now that I am aware of the deprivations *pukka* prophets have had to suffer. I feel called to be a watchman on the wall though, whose job is to warn without fear or favour. Little did I realise the events that would take place, even though it should come as no surprise with a proper understanding of the prophetic Scriptures. One of the good things, for me at least, of the Covid-19 lockdown is that it has been an opportune time to write a book; and, given the nature of events taking place and a renewed interest in the prophetic, also a good time.

To explain why I am thinking on the lines I am, I would like to go back to the beginning, or at least early on in my Christian life. It was while I was in my school Sixth Form, in 1969. I had become a Christian aged fifteen and, while carrying lots of excess baggage, had a desire to follow the Lord. One of my school mates was Paul Tait, who was the son of the pastor of Providence Chapel, Southend. One of my mentors was Paul Bullivant, who was a member of Coleman Street Chapel who became one of the leaders of the Charismatic movement in Southend, in the early 70's. Providence (Strict Baptist) is the church I am a member of today, and Coleman Street (Plymouth Brethren) is the church I was a member of for forty years.

Pertinently, neither church could be regarded at any time as "Charismatic" leaning, and little did I imagine I would end up at Providence, that might be best described as a church in the Reformed tradition and one that eschews controversy.

The event was, Martyn Lloyd-Jones was in town and was speaking at Providence Chapel. The Doctor, as he is still fondly referred to in hushed tones, was arguably the greatest preacher, at least in the opinion of those in my own theological-leaning stable, of his day, and this was an opportunity not to be missed; and neither did I, and was encouraged to attend by the two Pauls. I imagine that, like many who are reading this now, we have heard many sermons, most of which we cannot recall. But I do recall this one, or at least the text and the impression it left with me at the time. The passage expounded was 1 Corinthians 14:1-25, which begins: *"Follow after charity, and desire spiritual gifts, but rather that ye may prophesy"* (v1). The impression that remains was what might happen if the Apostle Paul's words were to come to pass: *"But if all prophesy, and there come in one that believeth not, or one unlearned, he is convinced of all, he is judged of all: And thus are the secrets of his heart made manifest; and so falling down on his face he will worship God, and report that God is in you of a truth"* (24,25).

Since that time, Coleman Street Chapel closed (around six years ago) due to declining numbers, and Providence Chapel might have followed a similar path but in recent years has enjoyed an expansion in numbers and activities. I cannot speak for the Doctor as to what were his thoughts on prophecy, but I imagine what he had in mind was that the preaching we should yearn for would be so powerful, and the Holy Spirit be so present, that knowingly or otherwise what the preacher preached would go right to the hearts of his hearers such that it produces the effect stated in our text. After all, there have been many named examples of people giving a "word" that, unbeknown to them at the time, touched on some intimate detail of some listener's life that they could not have possibly known about. One powerful preacher around that time was named Dick Saunders and he often did just that. Several who heard him recall him speaking words that precisely matched their situation. He could not have known, and he was not even Charismatic! I wonder, considering Providence today, if the Doctor's words were prophetic?

If I can move on a couple of years with my own testimony, and how it impacts on my writing as I do, it concerns how God has been dealing with me, and, pertinently, prophetically speaking. My own background, as I explained at the beginning of this book, is that after becoming a Christian from a non-Christian family, but who were not unfavourably disposed, those who taught me were very into sound doctrine and often had antipathy toward those they considered unsound, which happened to be most other churches. What I began to see, though, was that their light was not matched by their life. I, like many at the time, was attracted to the Charismatic movement that gave more prominence to the prophetic because I wanted reality and life to match the light. My experience was mixed and, while my main association with Christian groups thereafter have been with those of the non-Charismatic variety, including some who were outright cessationist, I have little doubt that while needing to avoid excess and imbalance, the spiritual gifts, including that of prophecy, have a place in today's church.

The tricky questions of who are the prophets today, what is their remit, etc. are not ones I wish to duck, but in the interests of maintaining the non-partisan, non-controversial etc., as I can, approach, I began with, I do not name many names. As for my own Christian testimony, on the one hand there has been a desire to serve the Lord, honour His word etc, yet on the other, there has been a holding back, a sense of failure and rejection (one reason why prophets fascinate me). Even during this present period, while spending a lot more time studying the Bible, things have come to light that the Lord has had to deal with me concerning.

One thing brought to mind was a time when, as a young Christian, I came across, possibly for the first time, a true prophet. His name was Alex Buchanan. He prophesied something concerning me at a very low ebb in my life, and what he said was specific for that time, as well as this time now, which has been one of the reasons I have continued to follow the path I am now on. While many in my church do not hold with modern-day prophets, and many early mentors were cessationists, my belief is that while there are many charlatans, there are real prophets too. I have observed enough to think the gift of prophecy is being exercised for good, more than occasionally. I recall the words of Moses, *"would God that all the Lord's people were prophets, and that the Lord would put his spirit upon them"*, (Numbers 11:29,) and would add my own "Amen".

From our study of New Testament prophets, we ought to expect there to be prophets today, and maybe many more than what we are seeing because God's promise to pour out His Holy Spirit on all flesh has not been revoked, but when it comes to those who are touted as such, there is considerable variance among Christian leaders as to whether or not they fall into the true or the false prophet / teacher category, often linked to where they stand spiritually. After all, there are enough warnings given in the Bible that we are to expect false prophets as well as a falling away in matters of faith. Such is my sheltered existence, I rarely rub shoulders with those claimed to be prophets, true or false. The Lord moves in mysterious ways, though, and reveals to us only what is necessary.

I believe we should take seriously the words: "*Quench not the Spirit. Despise not prophesyings. Prove all things; hold fast that which is good.*" (1 Thessalonians 5:19-21.) Moreover, given "*that in the last days perilous times shall come*", 2 Timothy 3:1, this is a time to encourage one another rather than doing the opposite, while at the same time, "*earnestly contend for the faith*" (Jude v 3).

Before considering the lessons we can learn from the prophets of the Bible and modern-day applications and implications, I would again reiterate, I am not a prophet and I cannot claim to have had visions and dreams; and, while I seek to be accountable, I do not have a wide circle putting me on any pedestal – often the opposite is the case. My best claim to having any credibility is that what I write is based on a prayerful consideration of the Word of God (the Bible), which I have been studying regularly since I was a child, testing what I write against the words of others, especially of good spiritual standing (some who afford me opportunity to teach and preach), and the ancient creeds of the Church – mindful of a tendency which most of us have to gravitate to those who happen to share our views – and what I believe the Lord has laid on my heart. Perhaps more controversially, as part of my watchman remit, I do check out what is going on in the world and have a certain disdain for mainstream news because of its untruthfulness, and this begs the question of where we look to find truth, other than, of course, the Bible?

I invite those reading to check out what I have written thus far against the Bible, putting aside what does not agree. I make no attempt to predict the future; and my focus in this book, at least, is on what the prophets of the Bible have said and written. But as a watchman of what is going on in the world around me, I take into account what is happening when we come to applying the lessons we have learned. What I write here, and even more openly in my other writings, is as a result of "*test and weigh*", "*watch and pray*"; mindful a watchman's job is to warn and not seek popularity. If I have a role model, it is the children of Issachar, "*which were men that had understanding of the times, to know what Israel ought to do*", 1 Chronicles 12:32. I counsel that more important than having a right view on the prophetic is to have a right relationship with God and His people. While breathing in and breathing out is essential for human life, so is both studying the Word (breathe in) and praying to the Lord (breathe out) essential for spiritual life.

I now come to my most controversial argument (possibly) in this whole book (putting aside chapter twenty-one that came only with the second edition – lol). I intimated earlier that some church leaders neglect and reject prophecy, and some, notably "prosperity preachers", claim a prophetic anointing; claiming things that might put them in a similar false prophet category, as we have discovered was the case in the time of Isaiah, Jeremiah and Ezekiel. Those who are the true prophets may then be rejected. I suspect, also, the climate in many churches will anyway discourage prophesying. The question is, what is the Lord saying, and if we don't know, how can we find out; and what should we be pursuing and what should we let lie as previous generations of spiritual giants have done? After all, our job includes praying without ceasing, loving God and our neighbour, playing our part in the Body of Christ (a challenge sometimes when churches do not encourage us to do so), being salt and light, being His witnesses to the uttermost ends of the earth. In that alone, there is enough to keep us occupied without having to try and respond to the obstacles that face us, so it might seem, on a daily basis.

Part of my own spiritual journey is the many and varied experiences I have had that have helped me to deal with the present. Something, I have become more aware of is the polarization among Christians, which if Jesus' words are to be taken seriously (e.g. John 17) should not be so. Instead, there should be unity. I see two "poles" emerging; please excuse the simplicity and alliteration. Group 1, I call loony, luvvie, lefties and Group 2, I call rabid, reactionary, righties. I have gone full circle, twice. When a teen, I was moving toward Group 1. After I got converted, given the sort of Christians I associated with, I moved toward Group 2. When, twenty years ago, I found interest in community activism, I reverted back to Group 1. Five or so years ago, when I became more a watchman, I reverted back to Group 2. Brexit, Islam, race, LBGT, climate change, immigration, globalism, popularism, socialism, certain leaders have become contentious issues, and I am of a view many have got it wrong, with negative consequences. I have managed to upset "friends", including Christian ministers, from both groups.

We need to disagree agreeably and recognise God is above human ideology. He has the big picture. His righteous agenda is what we are called to follow. I watch what is going on around me with disquiet. A lot of what I witness is *not* righteous: those who report, lie; those who lead, lead badly. We may look to others for information and hope as a result, who may be vilified or dismissed as conspiracy theorists (a pejorative term, even when proved factual). There is a propensity for us to gravitate toward narratives that match our opinions. I too have been as guilty!

We need to seek truth and learn wisdom when it comes to when to speak, avoid the extremes of unproven alternative narratives and untrue official ones, yet question everything we are told and look to God. While we may not know a lot of what is happening about us, and who are the good, mad and bad guys, we do know from the Bible that there is a conspiracy, led by Satan, to deceive and enslave humanity. If there is an example to take from the prophets, it is that they had a firm grasp of what was going on around them and were beholden to the truth; and their zeal for God and love for humanity was such that they would not be shut up.

New Testament prophets operated in a different paradigm to that of the Old, and often in the context of the Church – especially the local manifestation. As for Old Testament prophets, it was more often than not a precarious undertaking and a lonely one, where deprivations might be expected as a price to pay. They were merely God's messengers, and while blessing those who heard and heeded, they challenged and rebuked those doing wrong, inviting hostility. While all God's people are expected to live holy lives, this was especially important concerning prophets; and straying from the straight path could have dire consequences. Yet their job was vital as they communicated God's thoughts, and, as important, His feelings, to hearers, who gave them a glimpse into the unseen spiritual world. Without their contribution, those living then and now would be all the poorer.

While I have tried to cover almost all of the prophets of the Bible, I apologise for anything significant I missed. If I have an excuse, while there is a lot I could develop further, it is necessary to draw things to a close, else I would never finish. While my coverage of the prophets of the New Testament and modern-day prophets is lighter than some might wish, I nevertheless yearn for true prophets. I believe now, as much as ever, we need the prophetic anointing, not just to make sense of the world but to help guide the church in its mission.

As for what is going to transpire in the next few years, I will not be drawn. I am reminded that many of the Old Testament prophets spoke of both judgment (if no repentance) and hope (according to God's gracious purposes). Often the voices people listened to were prophets in the peace when there was no peace camp. Whether in the days ahead there will be ruin based on the current trajectory of the culture, with its prevailing godlessness, turning from the Lord etc., allowing for the rule of the Antichrist, or whether to expect revival and a reprieve, I leave that with God, praying for His blessing: "M*ercy-drops round us are falling, but for the showers we plead.*" My job is to be faithful to Him and leave the rest to Him.

I would like to finish with a final word of wisdom: my hope is for readers to check out themselves the prophets and to love more deeply the one prophets prophesied on behalf of ... THE END ... or at least the end of the beginning – but new thoughts keep swirling around in my head! But before I do close, I would like to share a light-bulb moment (actually, there have been several, but this one is particularly pertinent); and then some final personal thoughts and a prayer!

It came when I was researching Hosea, although it could just have easily been the case with other prophets like his contemporaries, Amos and Micah, who saw similar. This was the scenario, and it got me thinking about similarities in my own country, Great Britain, and the USA, a country I am following on the basis that what happens there will have a significant impact on the rest of the world. Idolatry (tick✓), pride (tick), false prophets and false teachers (tick), bad and foolish leaders (tick), unwise foreign alliances (tick), child sacrifice (tick – we abort babies), sham religion (tick), intolerance of righteousness (tick), trust in riches (tick), social injustice (tick), judicial corruption (tick), breakdown in law and order (tick), haves and have-nots (tick). Soon after Hosea prophesied, judgment came to Israel, having ignored his warning, in the form of Assyrian captivity.

But there is a difference: in Israel's case, religion and the nation were intrinsically linked because of the Covenant relationship it had with God. Yet, it might be argued, both Britain and America have enjoyed a measure of God's blessing because it has in the past, at least to an extent, followed God's laws and there were godly people, but blessing will be withheld as it goes further away from those laws. While there is a case for a Jonah-type proclamation to get the people to repent, the message should be directed firstly to the Church. After all, "For *the time is come that judgment must begin at the house of God: and if it first begin at us, what shall the end be of them that obey not the gospel of God?*" (1 Peter 4:17).

Before considering the Church and the place of the prophetic, I want to make my final point. When I began the project (to write this book) back at the start of the year (2020), I had little inkling concerning the momentous events that would transpire, and we are not out of the woods yet. I wrote my Preface, setting out my store, at the start, not realising how big an undertaking the project would be and what was about to happen in the world. As I write, we are coming out of an unprecedented (in my lifetime) period of (near six months) lockdown due to Covid-19 and we are still a long way from getting back to normal (whatever that is; and, besides, many are talking about a new "normal"). There is a lot else that can be said but this is not the place. There is no doubt that what has happened has had a devastating effect on life and also impacts the prophetic. From a personal perspective, it has been a great opportunity to write with minimal disturbance and, given what is happening, the subject matter appears as relevant as ever.

Some see the taking away of long taken-for-granted freedoms, the economic uncertainty and instances of breakdown in law and order to be the very signs the Bible has warned us of (*e.g.* Matthew 24) to usher in the period described in Revelation 6 - 18, referred to as the Great Tribulation, when the Antichrist holds sway for a season, prior to Jesus coming again, described in Revelation 19, to set up His Kingdom. I am not going to pontificate on what will happen next (I do not know and God has not told me); and while I will continue my watchman role, and will listen to those with prophetic words, I take the view while we want to hope for the best (nations will be all the stronger following these calamities and adopt kingdom principles), but prepare for things to get a whole lot worse. Sadly, I observe both strengthening of people's faith and the hardening of hearts.

But going back to the Church and prophecy, people can take different views. I have seen a lot of good when it comes to "loving thy neighbour", as well as bad when we do not do what God requires of us. There is a need for a prophetic voice, given that church leaders (bishops, etc.) who are reported on seem to come out with pious platitudes responding to an agenda set out by the ungodly, whereas whenever calamity struck in Bible times, the question that needed asking was, "What is God saying?" We need a prophetic voice today. Christ will build His Church as He promised, and souls will be saved, even if it has to, as seems likely, go through turbulent and testing times (already many experience persecution).

If there is a word to end with, it is that we need to be faithful to the Lord and have faith in Him. I encourage readers (and myself) to:

- Read and reflect (read the Bible; reflect on its varied applications to life).

- Suffer and serve (suffer for and serve the Lord – in His Church, this world).

- Test and weigh (test prophecy and weigh anything we hear from any news).

- Watch and pray (watch what is going on; pray to the Lord God Almighty).

- Trust and obey (trust Him who we follow; obey the Lord Jesus Christ).

More afterthoughts

I have a habit, and I am (hopefully) not unique in this, that whenever I return to something I have written, I find new things I want to add. This chapter, which I originally completed before perhaps the biggest challenge of this project, writing about the Minor Prophets in Chapter 13, is a case in hand. I realised I had not addressed, at least to more than a basic level, the lessons that we can learn from studying of the prophets. We did address this, albeit implicitly, at the time we discussed each prophet, and it is hoped readers can draw their own conclusions.

As we have already observed, the prophets could be likened to messenger boys passing on instructions from the chief to his underlings, where their identity, character and circumstances were very much of secondary importance. While it was not quite like that, when we consider the prophets of the Bible, as the message and the messenger were often strongly bound, it is the message that is of primary importance; and, depending on what one's perspective is, different lessons can be drawn, all perfectly valid. While I had, or I thought I had, a pretty sound understanding of what those lessons were before I started the project, some new things, particularly concerning God and His ways, did jump out of the pages as I continued with my studies, which highlights I share, in the Minor Prophets' case:

1. Hosea – God continuously entreats His Covenant yet faithless people.

2. Joel – God will assuredly and decisively act on the Day of the Lord.

3. Amos – God can be persuaded to change His mind.

4. Obadiah – God comes down hard on those who do wrong to His people.

5. Jonah – God uses unlikely and flawed instruments to do His work.

6. Micah – God hates immorality, idolatry *and* social injustice.

7. Nahum – God gives more chances, yet there comes a point when no more.

8. Habakkuk – God can be argued with, but He always win the argument.

9. Zephaniah – God who judges His people also restores them.

10. Haggai – God requires us to carry on with the job he has given us to do.

11. Zechariah – God is in control of history, and it ties up perfectly in the end.

12. Malachi – God requires genuine worship and rejects what is second best.

If there is an overriding lesson from our more in-depth exploration of the prophecies of the Bible, it is that there are always more lessons to be learned. I feel blessed as a result of one or other Bible teacher sharing his (or occasionally her) thoughts on this or that prophet. Often, when I go to another expositor on the same prophet, different thoughts are presented, often just as valid and, usually, not contradictory. There is no doubt that even now I can revisit what I wrote and find more, sometimes profound, thoughts that I may have missed or not given due prominence to. I started my book with an apology, recognising this would likely be the case, and I end with the same apology. I realise that I have not been even-handed in the amount of coverage given. For example, I devote four pages to Hosea and yet eight pages to Zechariah, both important and both comprising fourteen chapters (although I only give eight to Isaiah, with its sixty-six chapters).

My excuse, and maybe it is a poor one, is that in Zechariah I learned stuff I was barely aware off beforehand and I was blown away, and I just had to carry on; and in doing so, I fell into the trap old men of my ilk have often fallen into; and being more obsessed, compared with many sound, more traditional scholar types, with the more apocalyptic and the end-time predictions (noting mine is a minority view, insofar that these will come to pass, as many prophecies previously have done, with actual – not replaced – Israel being a centrepiece). I have also been inclined to adopt different approaches to presentation, ranging from section by section analysis of what is written about or by a particular prophet, to one of taking the approach and sometimes words of one or other commentator who, in my opinion, "gets it". Even so, in all these cases there were lessons to learn and I have done my best to draw those lessons or write enough for readers to do so.

And it is also back to the point made near the start: the prophets of the Bible were a varied and eclectic bunch and while many prophesied concerning common themes, around warning, reminding, judgment, future hope, etc., they were all so very different, both in character and their circumstances, and in the message they presented. The fact that their message was not just relevant for the day they lived in but also today, and the fact that in the experience of so many churches and individual believers that message has been neglected and ignored has served as a spur to my persisting with the project rather than taking it easy.

To recap what I wrote in the Preface, I began writing this book in January 2020, with a good deal of it based on thoughts I previously had; not realising, as this book is ready to go to print in September 2020, all the momentous and strangely pertinent happenings to take place in the interim. I fully anticipate more to come but dare not predict what; because I believe, to quote one historical figure, "*You ain't seen nothing yet*" – and even if we cannot quite identify what that is, it will likely be very soon and will relate to the content of this book. Consequently, I am keen to not delay. I am torn between seeing a near future with the people waking up, the bad guys exposed, revival, and one with a continued downward spiral of evil and mass deception, leading to the Great Tribulation. While it is a bit flippant to say, "*Hope for the best and prepare for the worst*", whatever scenario does unfold, we need ourselves to be right with God and to be instruments He can use.

Given what became so evident when reflecting on the message of the Hebrew prophets, I believe God is displeased with His Church, just as He was with Israel. Refining it has to happen, and will have a bearing on what the God who controls history does next. There is also the matter of the growing persecution of Christians around the world. I suspect there will be a major shaking in the churches, more than we might think. God is tired of the counterfeit and desires hearts that are inclined to Him. Trust in Him, learn from the prophets and recall Jesus' words: "*Peace I leave with you, my peace I give unto you: not as the world giveth, give I unto you. Let not your heart be troubled, neither let it be afraid.*" (John 14:27.)

Going back to lessons learned, I can imagine those who have read thus far will have learned or at least been reminded of many lessons and no doubt they are not all the same and, moreover, will not be the sum total of lessons that could be learned. Speaking personally and mindful of where I am in this brief sojourn called life, these lessons provide a refreshing antidote to the despair, frustration, feeling of hopelessness I am prone to feel, observing and feeling as I do. Above all, these men and women who prophesied, ordinary and faithful as they were, stuck to their task through thick and thin. They found God, while He was not to be messed with, was ever faithful and true to His Word. However dire things looked, however fierce the opposition, however apathetic and antipathetic those around them were, God was always right and there will come a day when his righteousness will prevail in men's affairs and the righteous shall be vindicated.

While there is much to be learned from our study of the prophets, it is the ways of the God of the prophets, who has everything under control, whose purposes are glorious, and is the one we need to serve, and it is Him and His lessons matters most. And on this note of hope, *here endeth the lesson*! Thanks for listening!

Prayer of praise and thanksgiving

you are the Lord God Almighty who is sovereign over all

your mercies, your grace, mercy and lovingkindness endure forever

your glory that will one day cover the whole earth

you are holy and all your ways are truth, justice and righteousness

you are all knowing, all powerful, all present, all wise

you have ever been raising up your prophets to speak your word

you have chosen the foolish things of this world to confound the wise

you have said you will do nothing without revealing your plans to your prophets

the testimony of Jesus is the spirit of prophecy

the promise that in Abraham's seed shall all the nations of the earth be blessed

even when your prophets were rejected, their words speak and bless us now

the words of the prophets that have all come to pass and will come to pass

the prophets and other persons of faith, whose example down the ages inspire us

you ever sought a bride, be it Israel or the Church, to have a relationship with

you are ever faithful to your promises and keep the covenant you have made

the Word became flesh and dwelt among us, full of grace and truth

he who rides prosperously because of truth and meekness and righteousness

my beloved who is white and ruddy, the chiefest among ten thousand

your only begotten Son, Jesus, who died, was raised and is coming again

your Spirit that was on Jesus, anointing him to preach good tidings to the meek

you forgive and forget our sins and save us for eternity, because of your grace

you have told us how you want us to live and have given us the power to do so

they overcame by the blood of the Lamb, who loved not their lives unto death

those redeemed by Jesus' blood out of every kindred, tongue, people and nation

your promise that in the Last Days you will pour out your Spirit on all flesh

amazing grace, how sweet the sound, that saved a wretch like me

Prayer of intercession and supplication

your name to be exalted in all the earth and we your people to revere your name

your kingdom to be extended throughout the whole world

your church, especially those members who are suffering, and for revival

we will be found faithful in our time of trial and not yield to temptation

faith to believe great things from a great God that manifests in our works

a greater sense of the riches of your grace and the wonders of your love

we know the power of your Holy Spirit, including the spirit of prophecy

you will vindicate your people who continually cry out to you

a new generation that will diligently study your Word, taught by you

a true understanding of your Word and as doers and not just hearers

us oldies, to pass on a worthwhile legacy to those we leave behind

the peace of Jerusalem and for all Israel to be saved

there will be raised up a prophetic voice in this generation

church leaders and those you raise up to faithfully shepherd the flock

you will send labourers into your harvest that is ripe for harvest

people to be saved and delivered from evil, especially our family members

the troubled parts of the world, for peace, for men to bow to the Prince of peace

those who have been displaced from their homes and who are refugees

world leaders and all those who are in authority; for wise government

those in caring professions and who keep us safe; for grace to do their work

our children and young people, that you will keep them from the Evil One

healing of those who have been hurt and wounded and who suffer calamity

truth to be honoured and vindicated and for falsehood to be exposed

justice to roll on like a river, righteousness like a never-failing stream

unity among your people, especially when there is disunity

Lord have mercy; Christ have mercy; Maranatha

Chapter 17: Tying up loose ends

Why a new ending when the lesson is endeth?

Early on in this project, I came to a view that I ought to produce sixteen chapters, albeit unequal in length, to cover all the ground (and there is a lot of it) needing to be covered (to at least an acceptable and satisfactory level); and yet there remains more that could be said, some of which should be said. The reason I have written as I have, is that my approach to writing has veered toward exegesis and avoiding letting rip with my views on certain subjects. Having reached the end of my book, or so I had thought, and all set for a thorough proof reading, and then the challenging task (at least for this little-known author) of getting it published and distributed, I found that a number of big topics were still swirling around in my mind, pertinent to my subject, which I will use a single word in each case to identify, and which I will follow up in this chapter, by way of elaboration:

1. Bible.
2. Truth.
3. Church.
4. Israel.
5. Rapture.
6. Community.
7. Spirit.
8. Apologetics.
9. Blood.
10. Gospel.

While there are many topics I think important, which views I am happy to share with any who are interested, concerning each one of the ten I have identified here (and I daresay if I were to cogitate, more could be added to the list), these I would argue are pertinent to the main theme of this book, which is to do with helping toward better understanding the prophets of the Bible and relating this to the times we live in. Besides which, this may be my last chance to write a book before I go the way of all humankind. At least, here is my chance to set the record straight, etc., for these are subjects that not only have a bearing upon our study of the prophets but provide some of the impetus for doing this study. I have set a limit of two pages to cover each topic, even though much more could be usefully said.

While readers might not always agree with me, if they take time to read and reflect, they may find these thoughts helpful. Our goal, and I hope here readers will agree, should be to get to know God better, appreciate Him more and become better equipped and more effective in His service, because in the final analysis it is doing that and glorifying the Lord that truly matters.

Bible

While nearing my allocated three score and ten years is no guarantee that I have the needed wisdom to pass onto the next generation, there is nevertheless a lot I would like to say that I think will be of benefit, on a wide range of topics, among which is, "Read your Bible." I have been privileged that from an early age I have been exposed to those who knew and loved the Bible. I remember as a seven or eight-year-old being taught in Sunday School the chorus: *"The best book to read is the Bible. The best book to read is the Bible. If you read it every day, it will help you on your way. The best book to read is the Bible"*. Later, in my teens, I became associated with the Plymouth Brethren. The PBs were far from perfect but one thing they helped instill into me was a love of the Bible and a desire to understand what it had to say (which is a lot). While I have often failed to apply what I know, ever since that time it seemed to me a matter of great importance to know what the Bible really says and then apply it to how I live my life.

Fifty years on, it is still the best book because it is God's book; I still read it every day and it still helps me on my way. While many acknowledge I know the Bible well, I lament I do not know it well enough. Even so, every day when I do study the Bible, even those sections I know very well, I discover new things. It is why if I were to imagine that I am in a room of young people and exhorting them on things they should attend to, near the top of that list is, "Diligently study the Bible, but always with humility." I confess, I prefer to use the KJV, although if I were starting again it might well be the ESV. The reasons for preferring the KJV are, I love the language, I am familiar with that translation, I remember specific verses in the KJV, it is still a good translation despite its archaic language, and deep down I believe the manuscripts used by the KJV translators may be more accurate than the ones used for most modern versions.

What matters more is actually reading the Bible, and this is a far more important matter than arguing the relative merits of different translations. We need to do so carefully, meditate prayerfully, comparing wisely scripture with scripture and apply practically what we learn. Often it is worth reading it in more than one translation as this often gives fresh insights into the meaning; and, bear in mind, some are better at conveying God's thoughts and some God's feelings. While some sections may seem more relevant than others (I generally suggest start with the Gospels), all sixty-six books, Genesis to Revelation, warrant study to get full understanding. Even in the most unlikely sections, there is gold to be found.

"It is the story of how God was seeking a bride for his son. Each book is different from every other book. I am trying to give you the keys for you to unlock the key itself." That is how the late David Pawson introduced his "Unlocking the Bible" talks (often referred to in preparing this book). At the beginning of his book, *A Pathway into the Bible* (also referred to while preparing this book), Stuart Kimber quotes William Tyndale: *"I marvel greatly, dearly beloved in Christ, that any man would ever contend or speak against having the scripture available in every language, for every man"*. Tyndale played an important part in seeing this desire realized, and it is worth pausing to think that he considered it important enough to do so, such that in the end it was to the cost of his life.

I have found ***www.biblegateway.com*** and ***www.biblestudytools.com*** provide some great online resources: reading the Bible in any number of versions, and listening to it being read. The truth is, when it comes to resources (online and those in traditional book form) to help us in our study of the Bible, we are spoiled for choice. I have named some used in my "prophets" studies in the "Acknowledgements" section of this book, and there is so much more, including excellent aids to help us in regular Bible study. We are without excuse. The Bible is to be read, with open hearts and minds and with an enquiring spirit. It is all a matter of discipline and application.

Undoubtedly, we live in a time when people are largely ignorant of the contents of the Bible, and sadly we note the consequences. It is evident that the teachings of the Bible have often been distorted, including by church leaders who we would like to think should know better, yet sadly do not. It sometimes seems "ignorance is a virtue" and worldly wisdom are promoted. Those with knowledge often disagree on interpretation and application. While knowledge of the Bible is no guarantee against embracing false teaching or living in a way that is at odds with how the God of the Bible would have us live, too often ignorance of the Bible is a factor for people *not* living in the way God would have us live.

I am not going to insist on those reading this what is the right interpretation, and I recognize even the best of scholars and saints differ at times; and sometimes the challenge is differentiating between what is essential or important and what is not, but I am going to encourage you to diligently search the Scriptures for yourself. Many metaphors can be used to describe the Word of God that are given in the Bible: gold, hammer, fire, light, sword, etc., and the very images these conjure up should enthuse us to want to study. The most important reason is, it will lead us to the knowledge needed for having an all-important personal relationship with the God of the Bible and knowing the way which we ought to be going.

If you want a goal, why not read the Bible through at least once every year, and when possible commit sections of it to memory, maybe a verse each day? The Bible is the only set of books I can say is divinely inspired; and, while there will be parts we will struggle with, it covers the whole plethora of human experience from how humankind began to how it will end; the meaning of life; a guide to living in a turbulent world; and the source of true wisdom and precious promises.

Truth

"*What is truth?*" was the question that Pontius Pilate asked Jesus; although it was doubtful he was that anxious to find the answer, for shortly after he condemned this innocent man to death and released a notorious murderer in His stead, in order to placate the crowd. I get the impression that many try to claim the moral high ground when saying they are beholden to truth, and it seems to me this includes outright liars who try to get one over the genuine seekers after the truth. Putting aside the notion of relative truth (what is true for you may not be for me, etc.), or alternative truths, for a moment, all of us fall short, even if we are not like Pilate and allow expediency to override nobler goals. We are subject to our prejudices and axioms, and even if we try to see other viewpoints, and find out the relevant facts, we often fall short. There is a tendency to confuse opinion with truth; and, given opinions differ, it follows they cannot all be true. There is also a tendency to be selective on material, ignoring that which does not support our case.

Jesus claimed He is the Truth; it was said of Him, He was full of Truth; He spoke about the truth setting us free. Of all people, Christians should be those who place truth very high on their list of priorities, if only because that is what the Bible tells us to do. Before I go on about something that is bugging me, and one of the key triggers behind writing this book – which was trying to figure out what was going on in the world so that I can work out how best to respond, and be one that leads people toward truth and away from error – I should make some personal statements. Truth has been a principal driving force behind my community activism and Christian service. It is not an academic exercise, because dealing with the real world, and the messy situations I am confronted with all the time, means I do not always have the luxury to pontificate over philosophical niceties.

I do not set myself up as a paragon of virtue, and admit sometimes to being a hypocrite. After all, if we are serious about truth, it should affect all our relationships, especially our family and those close to us, and govern how we live. Truth can be found in many places, besides the Bible. I am intrigued by the sign inscribed over the Cavendish Laboratories, Cambridge: "*The works of the Lord are great, sought out of all them that have pleasure therein*" (Psalm 111:2), suggesting scientific endeavour is one way of discovering truth; one might add many other fields of human endeavour. The last point is, truth needs to be coupled with things like grace, love and humility (as it was with Jesus) and a realization that there is a lot we do not know and lots we cannot be sure of.

If asked who my sources of inspiration are in the Bible, I would be spoiled for choice; but if pressed, I might say Jeremiah, and add the sons of Issachar, of whom it was written "*were men who understood the times, with knowledge of what Israel should do*" (1Chronicles 12:32). It seems quite obvious that people like that are rarities, yet if one takes Jesus' words, "Watch and pray", seriously then this is something we need to do. Such is the state of the Church, it is hard to identify modern-day sons of Issachar, as too often leaders do not address the issues of the times as they ought; they have their own agendas that too often are not God's, and, rather than taking a lead, follow the ways of the world. Jesus' warning in these last days, that the very elect will be deceived, should be taken seriously.

Over fifty years, I have seen a shift on things that bother Christians. Back in the day, whether or not to take the Bible literally, free will or predestination, the gifts of the Spirit, believers or infant baptism, creation or evolution, pre-, post- or a-millennialism, social activism or evangelism, Bible versions, women in ministry, church government, which church to join - were all issues keenly debated among

Christians, and to a lesser extent still are. Besides a drift from some sort of consensus, there is a new list, items I do not recall being discussed much back in the day. Brexit, Islam, Race, LBGT issues, climate change, immigration, globalism, popularism, socialism, and most recently things to do with Covid-19, have all become contentious issues, including among Christians. If I can be more specific: something like is Donald Trump good for the world? is one such issue for the present time. Should we take a view and what should that view be?

And there is another of the elephants in the room: how much store do we give to conspiracy theories, for the answer to that may determine one's approach? Another change, at least for me (but I know there are many others) is that fifty years ago we trusted mainstream media, especially the quality press and even more so the BBC; we trusted the government, even when not our choice, to a significant extent; and, in general, we trusted academia and authority figures. That is no longer the case. The temptation is to look elsewhere; conspiracy theories is one such place. I am not going to be drawn much further into this, other than to say, I do believe that evil forces conspire and many have a spiritual dimension.

I am inclined to question everything and counsel people to do the same, and resist cultural dumb down. I am still learning when to speak and when to keep silent, and being careful not to get sidetracked from things that matter. For this, wisdom is needed. We are privileged, unlike our forefathers, of being allowed (at least in the UK – but for how much longer, as restrictions get imposed?) of saying what we believe to be true. While there is lots we don't know, we have access to a lot more information. As for conspiracy theories, these may be false or unproven, and yet over time some have been proven true and often more credible than the official narrative. My own watchword, besides "watch and pray" (and "trust and obey"), is to "test and weigh". My parting word on the matter is: *"Buy the truth, and sell it not; also wisdom, and instruction, and understanding"* (Proverbs 23:23).

Church

When I refer to the Church (as opposed to churches), I usually do not have in mind buildings or clubs, but rather those who follow the Lord Jesus Christ with sincere hearts. Sadly, many "churchy" people are not real Christians and do not belong to the Church. The prayer Jesus prayed just before He was arrested and put to death: *"I pray for them ... That they all may be one; as thou, Father, art in me, and I in thee, that they also may be one in us: that the world may believe that thou hast sent me"* (John 17:9, 21) – has yet to be fully realised. My hope is to see entirely different people become as one. I have seen glimpses, but the actuality is – now it is not so, but will be awesome with breakthroughs that will follow when it is.

While there is a future role for Israel, the Church is God's chosen instrument to bless the world, despite Hebrew prophets seeing such as but a shadow. Sometime in the future (Revelation 19 relates) there will be the marriage between Christ and the Church, followed by the full manifestation of the Kingdom of God. To serve humanity is ever important, as is to do so with likeminded people. My hope that the Church take a lead in this as well as going about its business of mission and discipling, has at best been part realised. My heart is for the Church to fulfil her God-given potential and role to live as salt and light in the world. This should be intrinsically linked with spreading the Christian message throughout the whole world and making disciples who wholeheartedly follow the Lord Jesus Christ.

Throughout my Christian life, I have heard well-meaning Christians exhort other Christians to join a local church. Usually, they had in mind one or other Christian fellowship, without which one becomes like a coal removed from a blazing fire. Having reflected on which church is best, I know none are perfect and, if I found one that is, I should leave it. It is a place for sinners to be saved and grow in grace, not put on "holy" airs. I see good and bad in most fellowships; and, sadly, signs of apostasy becoming all too evident. The notion of a remnant meeting in people's homes is a real one. I have seen many Christians give up on "church", sometimes because of backsliding but also because they are disappointed at the corruption and lukewarm attitudes they see in church.

My advice is, go or rather associate with those where God is honoured and where there is life, where you are welcome and can contribute (including encouraging others), but don't expect too much (no-one is perfect), although you will want to find a spiritual home. Let your approach to others be a winsome one, with denominational labels being of secondary importance. For many, the church they end up in is as a result of accident or circumstance, or where they can best contribute or feel comfortable or are drawn closer to God. Sadly, there are those who were once active in "church" but are no longer. Reasons may be many, including backsliding, but also disillusionment and discouragement.

While I have a sense of trepidation as to what might happen in the near future, given some of the unsavoury happenings going on in all sorts of situations, and in the light of pressure on and persecution of Christian people the world over, I am confident too that it will turn out glorious in the end, and that God's perfect plan will be enacted, even if it means going through torrid times. Right now, I sense opposition toward Christians, especially the more earnest types, and that should cause us to turn even more so to God in trust and dependence. For those in the UK, while we might not be physically attacked, there can be insidious pressure to conform to anti-Christian ideology and pay the price if we don't.

Two aspects about the church that need to be emphasised are first the Great Commission: "*And Jesus came and spake unto them, saying, All power is given unto me in heaven and in earth. Go ye therefore, and teach all nations, baptizing them in the name of the Father, and of the Son, and of the Holy Ghost: Teaching them to observe all things whatsoever I have commanded you: and, lo, I am with you always, even unto the end of the world. Amen.*" (Matthew 28:18-20.) The second is the universality of the church that is above denomination, ethnic, national etc. considerations. Given the persecution that is taking place in many countries of the world, this fact alone should be a spur to solidarity and action.

While I can look at the church in my own country with a tinge of sadness, e.g. dwindling congregations, compromise and lack of spiritual life and effectiveness in mission (although I see change afoot), we see the reverse in some countries, especially the less well off, where churches are experiencing real growth. My sadness is that my own country has rejected God and is paying the price in terms of calamities that have befallen us, including natural disasters, inept leaders, lack of cohesion and direction. When trying to apply the message of the Hebrew prophets, it should be with the thought "*judgment begins in the house of God*". In the words of Charles Wesley's hymn: "*Oh, that in me the sacred fire might now begin to glow, burn up the dross of base desire ... and sanctify the whole!*"

To individual Christians, I would say, you are a member of the Church if you are a follower of Christ. This includes being a unique and essential part of His Body, which is joined to other body parts. You are part of the Bride of Christ which has been betrothed to the Bridegroom, who is Christ. You are also part of a great Building that is inhabited by the Spirit of God and founded on Christ the cornerstone. I would add that in order to follow these ideas through, you need to try and relate to other Christians, typically through one or other local church, but not to exclude the other groupings. There is always room for individuals with a good heart, who don't just adopt the *status quo;* but we are most effectively employed when we relate to other Christians. I would urge church leaders to encourage such folk (including weak and wavering); accept your congregation is not the local church, but rather part of it, and the Lord works in mysterious ways.

I am reminded of the old adage: *"unity in necessary things; liberty in doubtful things; charity in all things"*. Jesus' word to His followers is to *"love one another"* (John 13:24). For me, the necessary things start with recognizing the person of Christ (perfect humanity and divinity combined), the need to preach faith and repentance and the historical truth that, *"Christ died for our sins according to the scriptures; and that he was buried, and that he rose again the third day according to the scriptures"*, (1Corinthians 15:3,4). We who follow Jesus should be loving God and our neighbour, and also *"earnestly contend for the faith which was once delivered unto the saints"* (Jude v3). Much can be said about Church – just don't give up on it! Like Israel of old, the Church (not the organisation) is God's chosen instrument to bring about His grand purposes in the world. *"*T*his is a great mystery: but I speak concerning Christ and the church"* (Ephesians 5:32).

Israel

A good deal of this book is about ancient Israel and an Israel in a time that is yet to come. The Bible closes with Israel under Roman occupation, the last big event being the destruction of the Temple in AD 70. Following this was occupation by the Byzantines, Arabs, Crusaders, Mamluks, Ottomans and the British. It was not until 1948 that the modern state of Israel was formed, which was a fulfilment of the Balfour Declaration in 1917; and, for the first time since the Babylonian Exile, the Jewish people had autonomous control over some of the land that had been promised to Abraham. Since 1948, there have been several wars (all of which Israel have won) and conflicts over the land; and, while Israel has managed to maintain sovereignty over the land given to it and even gain new territory, there are many formidable powers at work that would seek to bring about its demise.

The Palestinian question and allowing them self-government over some of that land remains a huge one that has occupied many a great and well-meaning mind. One area of contention is the conflict between Israelis and Palestinians; another is Israel's security. Despite many a peace plan having been hatched and attempted, a fully satisfactory solution for all parties has not been managed. The return of the Jews in any great number to Israel is a modern occurrence, although many still remain scattered around the world. Few Jews believe in Jesus as their Messiah. The history of the Jewish people since the Exile has seen them, in the main, seeking to live peacefully with their hosts, and often prospering, while maintaining their distinctiveness. History has also seen many atrocities being perpetrated toward the Jews. Anti-Semitism has always been an issue and still is.

Much more could be said about modern Israel, which is never far from the news. As interesting as that subject is, we do not want to stray too far from the subject of this book or enter into avoidable controversy, given among sound Christians there are big differences in opinions. It is quite likely only a minority believe there remains a special purpose for Israel in God's plans. Even without the benefit of biblical hindsight, it is quite clear that Israel continues to play an important and pivotal role on the world stage, including in numerous complex conflicts in the Middle East. One senses, with the benefit of hindsight, there will be much more. The following are, in my opinion, some of the more important points to consider:

1. Israel and the Church are distinct, although one can be a Jew and belong to the Church. The Church has not replaced Israel. Faith and obedience, and the principles of saving grace, govern them all.

2. While a special Covenant (like a marriage) has been made with both Israel and the Church, the merging and culmination of which is in the future.

3. The promise made to Abraham, that through his descendant Jacob (Israel) would arise a great nation, has not been revoked.

4. It was always God's intention, through Israel, for the world to be blessed.

5. The preservation of the nation of Israel and re-emergence of its homeland might be regarded as miraculous but also is Israel's divine destiny.

6. There are many biblical prophecies yet to be fulfilled relating to Israel, both regarding the land and its people.

7. There is a small number of Jews who have accepted Yeshua as their Messiah. There will be a future turning to Him by a large section of them.

8. There will be days of great blessing for Jews, preceded by more suffering.

9. God holds nations accountable for their mistreatment of Jews, of which there have been many instances. He will bless those who bless Israel.

10. The fact that one third (six million) of the Jewish people were exterminated during the Nazi era (1933-1945) must never be forgotten.

11. Some of Israel's woes are as a result of its disobedience and rebellion, and this may also be a means used by God to bring Israel to repentance.

12. Looking at history, while some Christians have acted sympathetically toward Jews, others have not, and this must be a cause of deep regret.

13. There will be a Millennial age under the rule of Israel's Messiah, which will be its golden age. The babe of Bethlehem will reign as King in Jerusalem.

14. Proclaiming the gospel to the Jew (first) and then the Gentiles, is a matter of primary importance, and we should not ignore the need to do so.

15. While the Church should seek ways to effectively proclaim the gospel of repentance and of the grace of God toward the Jews, it should at the same time be offering friendship and providing support wherever it can.

16. We should uphold the need for social justice toward the Arab. Sadly, due to complexities, politics, prejudices, antagonism, it remains a challenge.

17. While some Christians are as much a Zionist as the most ardent among those who are Jewish, many see no place for the Jews in God's plans today.

18. As far as the Scriptures are concerned, peace and prosperity and other blessings in the land are linked to national repentance.

19. Some Christians see Israel as doing no wrong and others see them as doing no right. The truth (as it often is) lies somewhere in-between.

20. The development of Israel to become an advanced technological state with incredibly talented people, from humble beginnings, is truly amazing.

21. With few exceptions, Israel's closest neighbours are not particularly well disposed and sometimes hostile to the existence of the State of Israel.

22. The "Palestinian question" has long occupied great and noble minds, but is an important one that ought not to be ignored or dealt with prejudicially.

23. The Jewish people retain a special place in God's heart and purposes.

24. *"And so all Israel shall be saved ... There shall come out of Sion the Deliverer, and shall turn away ungodliness from Jacob: For this is my covenant unto them, when I shall take away their sins"* Romans 11:26,27

Rapture

According to Wikipedia: *"the rapture is an eschatological concept of a minority of Christians, particularly within branches of American evangelicalism, consisting of an end-time event when all Christian believers who are alive, along with resurrected believers, will rise "in the clouds, to meet the Lord in the air""* 1 Thessalonians 4:17 ... *Differing viewpoints exist about the exact timing of the rapture and whether Christ's return will occur in one event or two. Pretribulationism distinguishes the rapture from the second coming of Jesus Christ to earth. This view holds that the rapture will precede the seven-year Tribulation, which will culminate in Christ's second coming and be followed by a thousand-year Messianic Kingdom. Adherents of this perspective are referred to as premillennial dispensationalists"* and goes onto say *"Dispensationalism is a religious interpretive system and metanarrative for the Bible. It considers biblical history as divided by God into dispensations, defined periods or ages to which God has allotted distinctive administrative principles"*.

While Wikipedia is hardly an authoritative source for theological definitions, I do not wish to disagree with the above statements but would want to elaborate. As far as orthodox Christian belief goes, Christ is coming again; which, noting the focus of this book, was what the Hebrew prophets looked forward to. When Jesus ascended into heaven, we read: *"And while they looked stedfastly toward heaven as he went up, behold, two men stood by them in white apparel; Which also said, Ye men of Galilee, why stand ye gazing up into heaven? this same Jesus, which is taken up from you into heaven, shall so come in like manner as ye have seen him go into heaven"* (Acts 1:10,11). The Nicene Creed reminds us: *"He ascended into heaven and is seated at the right hand of the Father. He will come again in glory to judge the living and the dead, and his kingdom will have no end."* While Bible-believing Christians will agree on the Second Coming, as Wikipedia reminds us, only a minority believe in the Rapture that is to take place before the Lord comes, typically before the Tribulation period, which is discussed in Revelation 6-18, begins, but some argue it is at any time before Christ returns in Revelation 19.

During the course of my writing this book, I have tried not to get sidetracked by going down paths that are controversial and unprofitable. Besides which, it is a huge subject and I am merely able to give headlines. I am conscious there will be those reading this book who will regard themselves as "Pre-tribulation Rapture, Dispensational, Pre-millennialists" and those who are not. The only part of that label I fully subscribe to is "Pre-millennialist", for reasons discussed in this book. A plain understanding of end-time prophecy leads me to that conclusion. I believe those telling believers they need not concern themselves with the great trouble to be in error. We need to be prepared for anything, to remain faithful whatever that is, and leave the rest to God. I am also of the view that Israel has not been replaced by the Church, and regret that except probably for the first three centuries this has not been the dominant view throughout two thousand years of church history.

While I am a mild Dispensationalist (I am not going down that rabbit hole to explain what that amounts to), I understand, when it comes to the Jewish enigma (a people chosen by God, yet presently rejecting their Messiah, Jesus) why, with the Rapture, and the focus of attention turned once again on the Jews (with the Christians having left the scene), the question is begged, how things will change, and Dispensationalism may help provide answers. The Jews will come into their own and turn to their Messiah. It becomes a question for Bible students to marry the teachings of the Hebrew prophets with that of Revelation. But as I have said all along, other than opening up these scriptures and now recognizing the different positions of the Church and Israel, more study is required on how it ends up, and it may well be more needs to happen in the world before it becomes very clear.

We read, at the end of the Tribulation: *"And I will pour upon the house of David, and upon the inhabitants of Jerusalem, the spirit of grace and of supplications: and they shall look upon me whom they have pierced, and they shall mourn for him, as one mourneth for his only son, and shall be in bitterness for him, as one that is in bitterness for his firstborn ... And his feet shall stand in that day upon the mount of Olives, which is before Jerusalem on the east, and the mount of Olives shall cleave in the midst thereof toward the east and toward the west, and there shall be a very great valley; and half of the mountain shall remove toward the north, and half of it toward the south"* Zechariah 12:10, 14:4. That is a truly marvelous thing and should cause us to wonder and worship God.

As a young Christian, in a Brethren assembly, it would be true to say that the majority view was: "pre-tribulation rapture, dispensational, pre-millennialist", but because I have done what I encourage readers to do and taken on the Berean mindset and check everything out, I refuse to accept any position unless I can be convinced by the Scriptures. Moreover, I find the thought that Christians escape any tribulation, when Jesus tells us to expect it, goes counter to what He taught, what many of my brethren experience and our calling to bless our communities – the need to get involved, yet are taken from Earth when we are needed most?

Regarding when Jesus is coming again, even though Jesus told us nearly two thousand years ago, "*Surely I come quickly*" (Revelation 22:20), I am happy to accept that it can be any time (just as Jesus said would be the case, Matthew 24:36), and leave the unravelling to God. The main thing for us is that we are ready for His return. Whether His return comes in two stages (secret Rapture and openly in glory), I will not debate here other than declare my view that Christians will do through at least part of the Tribulation. What I do know, and in the light of the various yet to be fulfilled prophecies picked up in the course of our studies, is when Jesus does come, all will become clear. The future is a glorious one for the Church and believing Israel but a fearful one for those who reject Him.

Community

If I had not set a one-word limit to these headings, I might have come up with "social justice", which in the day this is written is a huge subject and is one that has contributed to churches both keeping on the rails and going off the rails. But "community" is OK too, given that twenty years ago I changed my job spec. to "community activist", which my first Google hit tells me is "*a member of a community who is voluntarily working with others from that community to achieve common aims (Delivering Change). Someone who takes individual action or action with others in a community, in a planned way*". Actually, I tried to make a living out of it, although not financially lucrative even though satisfying from the perspective of making a difference; but these days, as a retired person, it is nearly all voluntary. My story, going from being a secondary school teacher, to computer consultant, to "gospel preaching, community activist, watchman on the wall" is told in my book ***Outside the Camp***, now overdue for an update.

One of the lessons drawn from studying the prophets was finding that not only were they concerned with pure worship but also with social justice. It is a salutary lesson for Christians, both on the right and on the left (if I dare use those terms), that God is concerned with all these aspects of life, and not to claim the spiritual high ground when righteously indignant concerning our brethren who see things differently, as often happens; as this author can testify, with the "scars" to prove it. There is a certain irony in laying claim to the title "Community Activist", given that my church background, in most of the fifty-four years I have been a Christian, is Plymouth Brethren, which renowned church historian David Bebbington once described as an "Adventist Sect", and might I add with some justification.

A story indelibly fixed on my mind concerns Frank Newman, brother of recently sainted John Newman. He was with the PB in its early years and had a lot to do with its leading light, John Nelson Darby, who did more than many to popularize Dispensationalism and the Pre-tribulation Rapture. Newman once commented to the effect that if one were to follow Darby's teaching there was not much point committing the next thirty years to becoming the next LaPlace (great French mathematician), if the Lord is going to return in the next twenty-nine. Not getting involved in activities to improve the wider (outside the church) community has often been a feature of PBism. However, that is a bit of a caricature, as Brethren have often excelled at being good neighbours and been responsible for setting up such worthy community enterprises as orphanages, hospitals and schools.

But it does go to show that Christians across the ecclesiological spectrum do take widely different views on involvement in community activity and, putting aside factors like spiritual fervour, may have something to do with whether one is Post-millennialist, and beholden to improve society prior to Christ's coming, or a Pre-millennialist that might see such attempts as futile and rather focus on living pure Christian lives, doing good when obvious and urging those who do not believe to flee from the wrath to come. It is simplistic, but it was the prospect of making a difference and finding out what is really meant by *loving thy neighbour*, in the light of societal inequalities and the prospect of meeting real need, that required taking a wider view; combining doing what we can and challenging social injustice, along with the spiritual that recognizes the big issue is sin and being saved from it, that was the spur going down the route I did, with varying success.

I wrote in Chapter 16, "*Brexit, Trump, Islam, race, LBGT, climate change, immigration, globalism, popularism, socialism, have become contentious issues*" in my experience have led to deep divisions among Christians, when one would like to suggest that these should come into the "agreeing to disagree" bracket. It is true that we can, and many do, operate in our own bubble, when trying to do good outside the strict confines of one's local church activity; but, as I tried to point out, while there is much to be said about addressing real needs, going about it, especially when helping the many rather than the few, is not without pitfalls; and sometimes it touches on these subjects, pits us against those who are hostile to the Christian gospel and forces us to come to a view as to where the truth lies, as well as ask when to sacrifice "Christian" principles to become more inclusive.

These are among many issues I have not dealt with here, as these do not fit into the remit of this book, although I hope to revisit when I update **Outside the Camp**. I suspect there will be some (perhaps many) interested in doing social justice, who question whether taking an interest in prophets of the Bible is an unhelpful distraction. They might rather learn how best to get involved in their communities (outside the church). There is no simple answer here, and I can only share my own experience and urge things like making wise choices. As for what cause one picks up, it will be an individual one depending on various factors. I would also add, don't expect the world to get better, but still get involved.

If there is one myth that studying the prophets should have dispelled, it is that while the Bible looks forward to a "God in control" Millennium and New Heaven and New Earth, He is not disinterested in the present earth or lets us off the hook when it comes to doing our part here and now. Besides, using this unusual time to write this book and, mindful of personal limitations and circumstances, my main community activism interest is connected with helping the homeless; and more often than not with those of all beliefs and none, mindful there are many other aspects of our society where we can make a difference. In fact, the needs are limitless, and, as well as the need for wisdom, there is a need for balance. It is not a matter of one thing or another. I can't help feeling as the prophets looked on what was going wrong in the community, the question was being begged concerning doing something about it. How I went about it, and now that I know more, I will discuss. The fact "community" is listed as one of ten subjects covered in this chapter is indicative of why I consider these things matter.

Spirit

The mainstream Christian view is, there is only one God but three persons in the Godhead (Father, Son and Holy Spirit). Much of this book is about God the Father and some about God the Son. It is because this is the way Christians view the Messiah, whose coming was keenly anticipated by most prophets. Not much has been said about God the Holy Spirit, other than by implication or in passing, but it was He (the Holy Spirit is a person) who inspired prophets to prophesy. Another area touched upon is the spiritual world (as opposed to the natural). In our trawl through the prophets, we find the world of the unseen played important parts in the experiences of Enoch, Daniel and Zechariah, to name but three. "Spirit" is a further loose end meriting "tying up" and, again, another huge subject.

I suspect that part of our propensity toward imbalance is deciding wrongly where the balance lies between the natural and the spiritual. While, as Christians, we reject the notion that the only real world is the natural, we may, having recognised we are spiritual beings, be in danger of ignoring the importance of the natural. When I embarked on this project, which was mainly about the Old Testament, I decided to view the prophetic scriptures through a Hebrew lens. I was mindful of the observation, possibly simplistic, of some who had been on this journey, that the church over two thousand years has been predominantly influenced by Greek thought that had a tendency to despise the natural, whereas it should have been more influenced by Hebrew thought that recognised the importance of the natural; and one simple example in this book is how I have adopted such an approach in contentious areas of biblical interpretation, where I inclined toward the natural.

But if we ignore the spiritual dimension, we miss out. Regarding the three prophet examples given above, Enoch predicted the coming of the Lord with His saints in the light of a mighty hiatus involving spiritual beings; Daniel found out following his intense praying and patient waiting, the big factor was a battle going on behind the scenes involving the angels; and as for Zechariah, when he considered Joshua's wretched mental state, it was a lot to do with Satan acting behind the scenes. The New Testament is clear *"for we wrestle not against flesh and blood, but against principalities, against powers, against the rulers of the darkness of this world, against spiritual wickedness in high places."* (Ephesians 6:12.)

Many things, often perplexing, that happen in the natural are because of what is happening in the spiritual, often unbeknown to us. One phrase I used to hear a lot in my youth is, one can be too heavenly minded to be earthly good. The aim ought to be so heavenly minded (because thereby we see things so much clearer) that we can do earthly good by following the way of wisdom. One explanation concerning the reasons for many schisms and heresies in two thousand years of church history is that often it is due to not getting the right balance between recognising, appreciating and apportioning the natural and spiritual worlds.

When we go back to the start of the Bible, we read, *"In the beginning God created the heaven and the earth"* (Genesis 1:1), *"the Spirit of God moved"* (1:2), and, *"Let us make man in our image"* (1:26); we see the Holy Spirit there at the outset. Concerning the Holy Spirit, besides inspiring the prophets, we find He is active throughout the Old Testament in many different ways. In the New, Jesus told His disciples, "*I will pray the Father, and he shall give you another Comforter, that he may abide with you for ever*" (John 14:16), which Christians usually take as having been fulfilled fifty days after Jesus' resurrection, when the Holy Spirit descended on the disciples on the Day of Pentecost, as detailed in Acts 2.

As a young Christian, the issue Baptism in the Holy Spirit was a contentious one (although many other controversial issues have since taken its place), and like many I was caught in the middle, without knowing enough to come to a fully thought-out view. It forced Christians into one of two camps: "haves" and "have nots". The "haves" might have seen themselves as spiritually superior and the "have nots" might have gone into self-justification mode to explain they were good Christians despite having not been "zonked" as on the Day of Pentecost, and likely more balanced. This is, admittedly, somewhat of a caricature, but to this day I fail to align with either camp. I refuse to take the Cessationist position that such visitations of the Holy Spirit do not occur today and that gifts, including prophecy, are no longer available today, any more than I take a view that Christians that have not had a Pentecostal-type experience, typically accompanied by speaking in tongues, have *not* been baptised in the Holy Spirit.

There is no question that the Holy Spirit plays an important part in the New Covenant (discussed in Chapter 15), and is needed to enable us to live fruitful and effective lives in the Lord's service; as well as meriting a series of Bible studies. Being filled with the Holy Spirit (which happened at the baptism of Jesus) was essential when it came to power and authority in Jesus' ministry. We are commanded to be filled and to go on being filled with the Holy Spirit (Ephesians 5:18), not to quench the Holy Spirit (1 Thessalonians 5:19), and not to grieve Him (Ephesians 4:30). It is the Holy Spirit who will lead us into all truth (John 16:13); and since, as we discussed earlier, truth should be the mantra under which we engage in the world, having the Holy Spirit is vitally important.

Our focus, besides the prophets of the Bible, is on prophecy, identified as one of the gifts of the Spirit as listed in 1 Corinthians 12:7-11. We are told: "*Follow after charity, and desire spiritual gifts, but rather that ye may prophesy*" (14:1), and prophesying is mentioned to reinforce a point. But let us end: "*For to be carnally minded is death; but to be spiritually minded is life and peace. Because the carnal mind is enmity against God: for it is not subject to the law of God, neither indeed can be. So then they that are in the flesh cannot please God.*" (Romans 8:6-8.)

Apologetics

Peter wrote: "*Knowing this first, that no prophecy of the scripture is of any private interpretation. For the prophecy came not in old time by the will of man: but holy men of God spake as they were moved by the Holy Ghost*" (2 Peter 1:20,21). He also wrote: "*But sanctify the Lord God in your hearts: and be ready always to give an answer to every man that asketh you a reason of the hope that is in you with meekness and fear*" (1 Peter 3:15). Christian Apologetics is that discipline that seeks to defend the "truths", encapsulated in the Christian faith, against objections. It can take many forms. The apologetic type we are concerned with here is that to do with prophecy and how prophecy can have precise and literal fulfilment, years, sometimes millennia, after the prophecies were originally made.

In order not to become sidetracked from the main purpose behind writing this book, I have avoided thus far going down the Christian apologetics route, even when tempted to do so, mindful of discussion made in learned commentaries concerning those prophets that uttered prophecies that often were fulfilled long after they were supposed to have written them, as to whether this was possible, *unless* God had inspired them. Questions of authorship and date aside, strong arguments can be made that the record shows what the prophet prophesied at the time, sometimes centuries before a predicted event happening; not added later. The question is begged, if the prophecies were genuine, now go and prove it!

In a Web article, "***Fulfilled Prophecy: Evidence for the Reliability of the Bible by Hugh Ross - August 22, 2003***", the argument is made: "*Unique among all books ever written, the Bible accurately foretells specific events-in detail-many years, sometimes centuries, before they occur. Approximately 2,500 prophecies appear in the pages of the Bible, about 2,000 of which already have been fulfilled to the letter—no errors. The remaining 500 or so reach into the future and may be seen unfolding as days go by.*"

We are spoiled for choice, but I would cite the following examples Ross made:

1. The prophet Daniel proclaimed that Israel's long-awaited Messiah would begin his public ministry 483 years after the issuing of a decree to restore and rebuild Jerusalem (Daniel 9:25-26). He further predicted that the Messiah would be "cut off", which is what happened when Jesus died.

2. In approximately 700 BC, Micah named the tiny village of Bethlehem as the birthplace of Israel's Messiah (Micah 5:2).

3. Zechariah declared that the Messiah would be betrayed for thirty pieces of silver, according to Jewish law, and this money would be used to buy a burial ground for Jerusalem's poor foreigners (Zechariah 11:12-13).

4. Some four hundred years before crucifixion was invented, David and Zechariah described the Messiah's death in words that perfectly depict that mode of execution. Further, they said that the body would be pierced and that none of the bones would be broken, contrary to customary procedure in cases of crucifixion (Psalm 22 and 34:20; Zechariah 12:10).

5. Isaiah foretold that a conqueror named Cyrus would destroy seemingly impregnable Babylon and subdue Egypt along with most of the rest of the known world. Cyrus would decide to let the Jewish exiles in his territory go free without any payment of ransom (Isaiah 44:28; 45:1; and 45:13). Isaiah made this prophecy 150 years before Cyrus was born.

6. Mighty Babylon, 196 miles square, was enclosed not only by a moat, but also by a double wall 330 feet high, each part 90 feet thick. It was said by unanimous popular opinion to be indestructible, yet two Bible prophets declared its doom (which happened when the city of Babylon was sacked, just as the prophets said, by the Persian invaders). These prophets further claimed that the ruins would be avoided by travelers, that the city would never again be inhabited, and that its stones would not even be moved for use as building material (Isaiah 13:17-22 and Jeremiah 51:26, 43).

7. An unnamed prophet said a future king of Judah, named Josiah, would take the bones of all the occultic priests (priests of the "high places") of King Jeroboam and burn them on Jeroboam's altar (1 Kings 13:2 and 2 Kings 23:15-18). This event occurred three hundred years after it was foretold.

Ross gives a further six solid examples of prophesies being precisely fulfilled, centuries after the prophesies were made; and, if we were to continue our search of the Internet, several other significant examples could be added to the list. I would refer back to the comment I made in Chapter 12 regarding Daniel 11: "[It] *is about what happens after Alexander the Great dies and the Greek empire is divided among his four generals, and both chapters remarkably details events that have come and gone. One commentator has identified 135 specific prophecies fulfilled in Daniel 11.*" Another "favourite" is the prophecy made by Ezekiel (Chapter 26), specifically, and other prophets, concerning Tyre. Tyre was considered impregnable, priding itself that it could not be conquered, just as were Nineveh (discussed under Nahum) and Edom (discussed under Obadiah). Yet years after the prophecies were made, those cities fell (to Alexander the Great in Tyre's case), and prophecies were fulfilled with remarkable precision.

We could go on; and I have not even got onto the numerous Old Testament types, such as the Lamb, *e.g.* in Exodus 12, being a type of Christ, and as prophesied in Isaiah 53 (another example of prophecy being precisely fulfilled). While the subject of prophecy Apologetics can be usefully further explored, there is enough here to more than suggest that the Bible record is more than merely credible.

Blood

Sacrificing animals to atone for sin was an important feature throughout the Bible. We see animal sacrifices being made by Abel, Noah and Abraham; and there are many more places in the OT where animal sacrifices were carried out. A poignant example in the life of Abraham was being told by God to sacrifice his son; and, just before doing the act, God stopped him and made available a ram instead, pointing to the time when God was not only prepared to sacrifice His Son but did.

Sacrificing a lamb and applying the blood on their doors was an essential part of the Passover ritual that meant the firstborn in the houses of those who did so was spared: *"And the blood shall be to you for a token upon the houses where ye are: and when I see the blood, I will pass over you"* (Exodus 12:13). Sacrifice became a central feature of Tabernacle (and Temple) worship. Applying the blood of sacrificed bulls and goats was an essential part of what took place on the Day of Atonement, whereby the people's sins could be atoned for, along with the different sacrifices that could be made; although not all involved animal sacrifice.

Making animal sacrifices was a central aspect of OT Law, whereby sinful man could be reconciled with a holy God. But it was David who understood what God really wanted: *"The sacrifices of God are a broken spirit: a broken and a contrite heart, O God, thou wilt not despise"* (Psalm 51:17). The words of Samuel are also pertinent: *"Hath the Lord as great delight in burnt offerings and sacrifices, as in obeying the voice of the Lord? Behold, to obey is better than sacrifice, and to hearken than the fat of rams."* (1 Samuel 15:22.) And so are the words of Hosea: *"For I desired mercy, and not sacrifice; and the knowledge of God more than burnt offerings"* (Hosea 6:6). And yet blood sacrifices were incredibly important.

We are told in the Old Testament: "*For the life of the flesh is in the blood, and I have given it to you upon the altar to make atonement for your souls; for it is the blood that makes atonement for the soul*" (Leviticus 17:11). We are reminded in the New: "*And almost all things are by the law purged with blood; and without shedding of blood is no remission*" (Hebrews 9:22). The central purpose of Jesus' ministry is encapsulated in His own words: "*For even the Son of man came not to be ministered unto, but to minister, and to give his life a ransom for many*" Mark 10:45. In predicting His own death, Jesus was merely confirming what was spoken concerning Him by the prophet Isaiah: "*He was oppressed, and he was afflicted, yet he opened not his mouth: he is brought as a lamb to the slaughter, and as a sheep before her shearers is dumb, so he openeth not his mouth ... Yet it pleased the Lord to bruise him; he hath put him to grief: when thou shalt make his soul an offering for sin, he shall see his seed, he shall prolong his days, and the pleasure of the Lord shall prosper in his hand.*" (Isaiah 53:7,10.)

While "blood", specifically, shedding the blood of innocent animals, might seem out of place in a book about prophets (if was about priests, whose job included offerings sacrificing animals, we might better understand); yet the big picture, which each prophet had only part of, could only be seen if we take into account the significance of blood and of atoning sacrifices. Going back to the Passover feast, it was when celebrating this with his disciples that Jesus could say, "*For this is my blood of the new testament, which is shed for many for the remission of sins*", (Matthew 26:28); and telling His disciples in future to remember Him in this way, knowing for Him the next step would be betrayal and ending up being crucified, where He really did shed His blood for the remission of sins.

The writer to the Hebrews speaks of the significance of what took place when Jesus died on the Cross, and how this achieved far more than what took place in the OT Law: "*Neither by the blood of goats and calves, but by his own blood he entered in once into the holy place, having obtained eternal redemption for us. For if the blood of bulls and of goats, and the ashes of an heifer sprinkling the unclean, sanctifieth to the purifying of the flesh: How much more shall the blood of Christ, who through the eternal Spirit offered himself without spot to God, purge your conscience from dead works to serve the living God? And for this cause he is the mediator of the new testament, that by means of death, for the redemption of the transgressions that were under the first testament, they which are called might receive the promise of eternal inheritance.*" (Hebrews 9:12-15.)

Before turning to our next section, about the Gospel, with its central tenet being

Christ dying on a Cross and shedding His blood for our sin, it is worth considering what the last of our "Prophets of the Bible" (John in Revelation) said about blood, applying firstly to Christ washing us from our sins in His own blood; secondly, how the Lamb that had been slain, now on the Throne, redeemed us by His blood and is worthy; thirdly, how those coming out of the Great Tribulation had washed their robes in His blood; and fourthly, overcoming by the blood of the Lamb.

1. *"And from Jesus Christ, who is the faithful witness, and the first begotten of the dead, and the prince of the kings of the earth. Unto him that loved us, and washed us from our sins in his own blood."* (1:5.)

2. *"And they sung a new song, saying, Thou art worthy to take the book, and to open the seals thereof: for thou wast slain, and hast redeemed us to God by thy blood out of every kindred, and tongue, and people, and nation"* (5:9).

3. *"These are they which came out of great tribulation, and have washed their robes, and made them white in the blood of the Lamb"* (7:14).

4. *"And they overcame him by the blood of the Lamb, and by the word of their testimony; and they loved not their lives unto the death"* (12:11).

Gospel

"It's news I'm most proud to proclaim, this extraordinary Message of God's powerful plan to rescue everyone who trusts him, starting with Jews and then right on to everyone else! God's way of putting people right shows up in the acts of faith, confirming what Scripture has said all along: 'The person in right standing before God by trusting him really lives.'" (Romans 1:16, *The Message*).

One secular definition is: "*The word gospel comes from the Old English god meaning 'good' and spel meaning 'news, a story.' In Christianity, the term 'good news' refers to the story of Jesus Christ's birth, death, and resurrection.*" Proclaiming the gospel (whether by word or deeds) is a most important activity. Jesus commanded His disciples: *"Go ye therefore, and teach all nations, baptizing them in the name of the Father, and of the Son, and of the Holy Ghost: Teaching them to observe all things whatsoever I have commanded you: and, lo, I am with you always, even unto the end of the world"* (Matthew 28:19-20).

Paul writing to the Romans argues whether a Jew, supposedly following the Law, or a Gentile, guided by conscience, we all fall short of God's standard, are subject to God's condemnation and unable to save ourselves: *"For all have sinned, and come short of the glory of God"* (3:23). But here comes the good news: *"For when we were yet without strength, in due time Christ died for the ungodly. For scarcely for a righteous man will one die: yet peradventure for a good man some would even dare to die. But God commendeth his love toward us, in that, while we were yet sinners, Christ died for us."* (5:6-8). And: *"For the wages of sin is death; but the gift of God is eternal life through Jesus Christ our Lord"* (6:23).

As far as the Hebrew prophets go, many looked forward to Israel's Deliverer and had insights into His character and ministry. When the risen Christ walked along the Emmaus Road, talking with two disconsolate "wannabe" followers of their hoped-for Messiah, confounded at the way His life had ended, He remonstrated with them: *"Then he said unto them, O fools, and slow of heart to believe all that the prophets have spoken: Ought not Christ to have suffered these things, and to enter into his glory? And beginning at Moses and all the prophets, he expounded unto them in all the scriptures the things concerning himself."* (Luke 24:25-27.) Even though the prophets' understanding were incomplete, we could do as Jesus did and preach the gospel from what the prophets said, something Philip did when explaining Isaiah 53 to the Ethiopian eunuch and leading him to Christ (Acts 8).

Some have said that the gospel is like our ABC: A – Admit you are a sinner; B – Believe in Christ to save you; and C – Confess Christ before others. The plain fact is, some of the simplest of folk get and welcome this message, and some of the most sophisticated fail to get and welcome it. I am not alone in recollecting the first Bible verse I learned by heart as a child: *"For God so loved the world, that he gave his only begotten Son, that whosoever believeth in him should not perish, but have everlasting life"*; and, yes, the gospel message is simple and sublime, but once it is embraced it has profound consequences for the rest of our lives.

Like the Hebrew prophets, we would be remiss if we just focused on God's love and mercy, and neglected His righteousness and holiness. We who follow Jesus are told to *"put on the new man, which after God is created in righteousness and true holiness"* (Ephesians 4:24). Jesus made it clear: *"If any man will come after me, let him deny himself, and take up his cross daily, and follow me"* (Luke 9.23). After Paul eruditely sets out the gospel message in Romans 1-8, in 9-16, after discussing the conundrum of unbelieving Jews to whom that message was initially directed, he turned to our response: *"I beseech you therefore, brethren, by the mercies of God, that ye present your bodies a living sacrifice, holy, acceptable unto God, which is your reasonable service. And be not conformed to this world: but be ye transformed by the renewing of your mind, that ye may prove what is that good, and acceptable, and perfect, will of God."* (12:1-2.)

As one of my Sunday School choruses so sublimely put it: *"Oh, the love that drew salvation's plan! Oh, the grace that brought it down to man! Oh, the mighty gulf that God did span At Calvary! Mercy there was great, and grace was free; Pardon there was multiplied to me; There my burdened soul found liberty, At Calvary".* That gulf could not be spanned by human endeavor or way known to man, but only through what Jesus accomplished at the Cross and rising from the dead – the very heart of the gospel message. As Paul told the church at Corinth: *"For I delivered unto you first of all that which I also received, how that Christ died for our sins according to the scriptures; And that he was buried, and that he rose again the third day according to the scriptures"* (1 Corinthians 15:3,4).

The prophets were strongest when looking forward to Christ's Second Coming, not so much the Man of Calvary sent to atone for our sins, but as the one who would reign as King. *"My heart is inditing a good matter: I speak of the things which I have made touching the king: my tongue is the pen of a ready writer. Thou art fairer than the children of men: grace is poured into thy lips: therefore God hath blessed thee for ever. Gird thy sword upon thy thigh, O most mighty, with thy glory and thy majesty. And in thy majesty ride prosperously because of truth and meekness and righteousness; and thy right hand shall teach thee terrible things."* (Psalm 45:1-4.) Paul wrote: *"But made himself of no reputation, and took upon him the form of a servant, and was made in the likeness of men: And being found in fashion as a man, he humbled himself, and became obedient unto death, even the death of the cross. Wherefore God also hath highly exalted him, and given him a name which is above every name: That at the name of Jesus every knee should bow, of things in heaven, and things in earth, and things under the earth; And that every tongue should confess that Jesus Christ is Lord, to the glory of God the Father."* (Philippians 2:7-11.) It is our privilege, not just to open up the prophetic scriptures, but to tell people of the one whom the prophets foretold.

"Neither is there salvation in any other: for there is none other name under heaven given among men, whereby we must be saved." (Acts 4:12.)

"For when we were yet without strength, in due time Christ died for the ungodly. For scarcely for a righteous man will one die: yet peradventure for a good man some would even dare to die. But God commendeth his love toward us, in that,

while we were yet sinners, Christ died for us." (Romans 5:6-8.)

"But we preach Christ crucified, unto the Jews a stumblingblock, and unto the Greeks foolishness; But unto them which are called, both Jews and Greeks, Christ the power of God, and the wisdom of God." (1Corinthians 1:23,24.)

Chapter 18: More loose ends

In the previous chapter, I identified ten topics encapsulated by a single word to do with an important Bible theme that somehow related to the subject of the Prophets of the Bible and which the prophets, if they were around today, may well be able to offer a valuable perspective. I recognized then that this was not the end of the matter but, since I was keen to get on with publishing the book, I left it there. Now I am able to produce a second edition. As it happens, I have come across ten further topics, also important and relevant, that I would like for us to consider. I have decided to reflect on these in this chapter, adopting a similar approach as before, and restricting our thoughts to two or three pages:

1. Covenant.
2. Fear.
3. Holiness.
4. Idolatry.
5. Trinity.
6. Suffering.
7. Eternity.
8. Prayer.
9. Faith.
10. Grace.

Covenant

One of the major concerns of the Hebrew prophets, as they prophesied to Israel, was that of keeping the Covenant, notably the one God made with them through Moses, when giving the Law on Mount Sinai, during their wilderness journey, and reminding them of the blessings and curses that would surely follow as a result of keeping or not keeping the Law, something that inevitably came to pass, even though God often showed mercy. The fact that God makes covenants and expects these to be kept is a vital consideration when it comes to trying to understand his dealings with humankind and in our understanding of the Bible.

The Christian Bible comprises Old and New Testaments (Testament is another word for Covenant), even though there are a number of covenants discussed in the Old Testament. The subject of "covenant" can be a contentious one but it is also very important. God has always been making covenants with His creation, the nation of Israel, the Church or individuals. A covenant is more than just a contract between two parties, since a contract suggests two equal parties. It is an agreement whereby God, who is not obligated to or dependent on anyone, who can be 100% guaranteed to keep His part of any agreement arrived at even if that is not reciprocated (unlike when a contract is broken), makes promises and often but not always expecting certain responses. As Israel found out and as the prophets often reminded them, their failure to keep God's covenant has consequences. An example of a covenant that can be found in everyday life is that of marriage, the keeping of which imposes an obligation on both parties.

While the New Covenant, such as symbolized when Jesus celebrated the Passover feast with His disciples (*likewise also the cup after supper, saying, this cup is the new testament in my blood, which is shed for you* – Luke 22:20), is the one that particularly interests Christian Gentile believers because of its obvious application to do with salvation, and it supersedes that of the Mosaic covenant in terms of personal obligations, most of the other covenants, which are discussed below (seven have been identified by this author), still apply.

The Edenic Covenant (Genesis 1:28-30, 2:15-17)

The Bible begins with an account of God's creation, the pinnacle of which was man, with who He wanted a relationship. He put Adam in a garden and told him to look after it and the rest of His creation. Adam effectively had free sway but the one thing he was forbidden from doing was to eat of a certain tree. Adam disobeyed and he was expelled from that garden and a curse followed. The mandate to look after planet Earth and its resources and inhabitants remains.

The Adamic Covenant (Genesis 3:14-19)

Following Adam's Fall, while there was a curse, there was also a promise that in Adam's descendants (Jesus) there will come a victory over the serpent (Satan) and along with it comes redemption and restoration for humankind.

The Noahic Covenant (Genesis 8:20-9:17)

Much of the story of humankind following Adam was one of rebellion toward God. Making man *grieved him at His heart* (6:6) and as a result He sent a Great flood that destroyed all living creatures on the planet, except for Noah's family and the animals to continue God's creation. After the flood, He makes a covenant with Noah, representing humanity that was to follow, and gave a rainbow as a sign: "*While the earth remaineth, seedtime and harvest, and cold and heat, and summer and winter, and day and night shall not cease*" (8:22).

The Abrahamic Covenant (Genesis 12:1-3)

Following the Flood, humanity continued its downward trajectory and this was seen in God's destruction of the Tower of Babel. Then He calls Abraham, a faithful man, and promised him the land known as Israel and promised that his descendants would be a great nation, who God will bless and they would bless other nations. The sign of that covenant was the practice of male circumcision.

The Mosaic Covenant

So the nation that followed, which was also called Israel, grew in numbers but found itself eventually enslaved in Egypt. God appointed Moses to lead them out of Egypt to take possession of the land He promised Abraham. During their Wilderness journeyings, God established His covenant with Israel and promised He would bless them, providing they obeyed the Law that God gave to them.

The Davidic Covenant (2 Samuel 7:4-17)

David, a man after God's own heart, was Israel's most important king. God promised that come what may (and what did come eventually was a divided kingdom and exile for both the Northern and Southern kingdoms) there would always be one of His descendants to sit on the throne of Israel.

The New Covenant (Hebrews 8:7-13)

As the chosen people of God were to go into exile, God promised they will return to the land He gave them and give them a new heart and make with them a new covenant. While this was promised specifically to Jews, Gentiles would also benefit and that was because the Messiah, Jesus, came from heaven to earth to die and atone for our sins and thus bring in the New Covenant.

Fear

"The fear of the Lord is the beginning of wisdom: and the knowledge of the holy is understanding" Proverbs 9:10.

We begin this section on fear with a verse (one of many) that points to the benefits that result when the Lord is feared. I do so mindful many Christians, including pillars of the church, downplay the role of fear in a believer's life and rather they focus on love and grace that supposedly replaces and is superior to fear. But having gone through the 500 Bible references to "fear" and trying to understand its meaning in the original Hebrew and Greek, I believe it is a wrong view, often promoted to ingratiate church spokespeople to the very people who need to fear God and, as a result, dumbs down the gospel message that should be presented, done in order not to upset saved and unregenerate sinners alike.

I begin with a rather basic explanation, using an extraction from Strong's concordance concerning one of the Hebrew and one of the Greek words that the KJV and others have translated as "fear", which I understand tries to convey anything ranging from respect and reverence to terror and dread:

Hebrew: *yârê', yaw-ray'; a primitive root; to fear; morally to revere; causatively to frighten:—affright, be (make) afraid, dread(-ful), (put in) fear(-ful, -fully, -ing), (be had in) reverence(-end), see, terrible (act, -ness, thing).*

Greek: *εὐλάβεια eulábeia, yoo-lab'-i-ah; properly, caution, i.e. (religiously) reverence (piety); by implication, dread (concretely):—fear(-ed).*

This lack of the fear is part of the reason why the church finds itself in an inept and powerless condition and, notwithstanding the many Bible exhortations not to fear or to be precise not to fear the wrong things, and the importance of grace and love in the Christian experience, there is a need to rediscover the fear of the Lord as the following text illustrates. We are told to fear a holy, praise a wonder working God: *"Who is like unto thee, O Lord, among the gods? who is like thee, glorious in holiness, fearful in praises, doing wonders?"* Exodus 15:11.

God's desire is that His specially chosen people fear Him and in so doing thereby derive benefit: *"O that there were such an heart in them, that they would fear me, and keep all my commandments always, that it might be well with them, and with their children for ever!"* Deuteronomy 5:29.

A key characteristic attributed to one of the most righteous men to have ever lived was his fear of God: *"There was a man in the land of Uz, whose name was Job; and that man was perfect and upright, and one that feared God, and eschewed evil"* Job 1:1.

A clear statement how to serve the Lord with fear, and with it comes joy, is: *"Serve the Lord with fear, and rejoice with trembling"* Psalm 2:11.

Rather than having negative connotations, we discover: *"The fear of the Lord is clean, enduring for ever: the judgments of the Lord are true and righteous altogether"* Psalm 19:9.

There is something precious to be got from fearing God: *"The secret of the Lord is with them that fear him; and he will shew them his covenant"* Psalm 25:14.

Naturally, there is much to fear but not if the Lord is the strength of our lives: *"The Lord is my light and my salvation; whom shall I fear? the Lord is the strength of my life; of whom shall I be afraid?"* Psalm 27:1.

What blessings come from being released from our natural fears and replacing these with the fear of God: *"I sought the Lord, and he heard me, and delivered me from all my fears. They looked unto him, and were lightened: and their faces were not ashamed. This poor man cried, and the Lord heard him, and saved him out of all his troubles. The angel of the Lord encampeth round about them that fear him, and delivereth them. O taste and see that the Lord is good: blessed is the man that trusteth in him. O fear the Lord, ye his saints: for there is no want to them that fear him. The young lions do lack, and suffer hunger: but they that seek the Lord shall not want any good thing. Come, ye children, hearken unto me: I will teach you the fear of the Lord"* Psalm 33:4-11.

In an invitation to worship God, fear comes into it: *"O worship the Lord in the beauty of holiness: fear before him, all the earth"* Psalm 69:9.

Blessings results from fearing God: *"Blessed is every one that feareth the Lord; that walketh in his ways"* Psalm 128:1.

The importance and rich rewards comes from fearing God: *"My son, if thou wilt receive my words, and hide my commandments with thee; So that thou incline thine ear unto wisdom, and apply thine heart to understanding; Yea, if thou criest after knowledge, and liftest up thy voice for understanding; If thou seekest her as silver, and searchest for her as for hid treasures; Then shalt thou understand the fear of the Lord, and find the knowledge of God*" Proverbs 2:1-5.

Fear brings confidence, refuge and life: "*In the fear of the Lord is strong confidence: and his children shall have a place of refuge. The fear of the Lord is a fountain of life, to depart from the snares of death*" Proverbs 14:26,27.

True treasure comes with the fear of God: "*Better is little with the fear of the Lord than great treasure and trouble therewith*" Proverbs 15:16.

A salutary warning is given us for when we are tempted to envy those who do not fear God: "*Let not thine heart envy sinners: but be thou in the fear of the Lord all the day long*" Proverbs 23:17.

Fear can be misplaced and when it is stumbles us: "*The fear of man bringeth a snare: but whoso putteth his trust in the Lord shall be safe*" Proverbs 29:25.

One way to summing up the whole duty of man is: "*Let us hear the conclusion of the whole matter: Fear God, and keep his commandments: for this is the whole duty of man*" Ecclesiastes 12:13.

The fear of God is a key attribute of the coming Messiah: "*And there shall come forth a rod out of the stem of Jesse, and a Branch shall grow out of his roots: And the spirit of the Lord shall rest upon him, the spirit of wisdom and understanding, the spirit of counsel and might, the spirit of knowledge and of the fear of the Lord; And shall make him of quick understanding in the fear of the Lord: and he shall not judge after the sight of his eyes, neither reprove after the hearing of his ears*" Isaiah 11:1-3.

Wisdom and knowledge and the stability that results are brought about when there is the fear of God, which is treasure indeed: "*And wisdom and knowledge shall be the stability of thy times, and strength of salvation: the fear of the Lord is his treasure*" Isaiah 33:6.

The fear of the Lord is something that unites His people and withstands the enemy: "*So shall they fear the name of the Lord from the west, and his glory from the rising of the sun. When the enemy shall come in like a flood, the Spirit of the Lord shall lift up a standard against him*" Isaiah 59:19.

One of God's irrefutable promises is so the beneficiaries may fear Him: "*And I will give them one heart, and one way, that they may fear me for ever, for the good of them, and of their children after them"* Jeremiah 32:39.

Those of us who fear the Lord should be encouraging each other: *"Then they that feared the Lord spake often one to another: and the Lord hearkened, and heard it, and a book of remembrance was written before him for them that feared the Lord, and that thought upon his name"* Malachi 3:16.

Another precious promise to those who fear God is: *"But unto you that fear my name shall the Sun of righteousness arise with healing in his wings; and ye shall go forth, and grow up as calves of the stall"* Malachi 4:2.

Fearing God was an important characteristic of the early church: *"Then had the churches rest throughout all Judaea and Galilee and Samaria, and were edified; and walking in the fear of the Lord, and in the comfort of the Holy Ghost, were multiplied"* Acts 9:31.

Fear should be a factor in living our faith: *"Wherefore, my beloved, as ye have always obeyed, not as in my presence only, but now much more in my absence, work out your own salvation with fear and trembling"* Philippians 2:12.

Fear was not just an Old Testament matter: *"And so terrible was the sight, that Moses said, I exceedingly fear and quake"* Hebrews 12:21.

We should conduct ourselves in godly fear: *"Wherefore we receiving a kingdom which cannot be moved, let us have grace, whereby we may serve God acceptably with reverence and godly fear"* Hebrews 12:28.

Holiness to which we are called and fear of the Lord are irrevocably linked: *"But as he which hath called you is holy, so be ye holy in all manner of conversation; Because it is written, Be ye holy; for I am holy. And if ye call on the Father, who without respect of persons judgeth according to every man's work, pass the time of your sojourning here in fear"* 1Peter 1:15-17.

One good motto for life includes in it the entreaty to fear God: *"Honour all men. Love the brotherhood. Fear God. Honour the king"* 1 Peter 2:17.

Fear is a good thing when we consider how holy and worthy of worship God is: *"Who shall not fear thee, O Lord, and glorify thy name? for thou only art holy: for all nations shall come and worship before thee; for thy judgments are made manifest*" Revelation 15:4.

Fear is called for when Jesus comes again to judge: "*And a voice came out of the throne, saying, Praise our God, all ye his servants, and ye that fear him, both small and great*" Revelation 19:5.

In today's culture, fear is often seen in negative terms, even if many succumb to it, one way or the other. Although sometimes there is a place, e.g. warning us of danger, but too often people fear the wrong things. As we have seen in the aforementioned texts, fear if properly directed is an excellent thing with many benefits, especially if it is the fear of the Lord. We round off our meditation with a text that reminds us how fear can play both a negative and positive part in our lives. I write at a time when a second lockdown has just been announced to combat the Coronavirus. Different people have different reactions to this.

Some see conspiracy theories being played out in society, just as did Israel in our text below, when the threat of invasion was all too real. Some who follow the rules religiously will tut tut at those who succumb to such theories. Yet criticism might apply to those who fear what happens if correct precautions are not taken but at huge cost, where the fear of death has been a factor in getting the populace to do what they are told and lose their freedoms in the bargain. Neither are correct responses, but to fear God, and that includes dread, is!

As we will see later, fear relates to grace. John Newton understood this when he wrote: "*Twas grace that taught my heart to fear, and grace my fears relieved. How precious did that grace appear the hour I first believed.*" As for fearing God rather than conspiracies: "*For the Lord spoke thus to me with his strong hand upon me, and warned me not to walk in the way of this people, saying: Do not call conspiracy all that this people calls conspiracy, and do not fear what they fear, nor be in dread. But the Lord of hosts, him you shall honor as holy. Let him be your fear, and let him be your dread*" Isaiah 8:11-13.

Holiness

One of the major recurring themes of the Bible that the Hebrew prophets continually referred to was the holiness of God, and along with that was God's demand that His people be holy: "*And ye shall be unto me a kingdom of priests, and a holy nation. These are the words which thou shalt speak unto the children of Israel*" Exodus

19:6 and *"Speak unto all the congregation of the children of Israel, and say unto them, Ye shall be holy: for I the Lord your God am holy"* Leviticus 19:2. A major reason for God's displeasure with His people and for their demise was they were not living as holy people. An important principle and purpose in God's dealings with his people is to make them holy.

For modern minds, the notion of holiness can often be looked on with suspicion because of negative connotations, such as an emphasis on the inconsequential things some concentrate on doing and ignoring consequential things some refrain from doing, and foreboding because holy people often come across as judgmental "holier than thou" and are not particularly nice people. There is also the claim such folk are joyless and legalistic, too heavenly minded to be any earthly good. In God's eyes, holiness, at least in the biblically held sense, is a very good thing. To be holy is something that is worth pursuing. The same command given to the Israelites applies to the Church: *"Follow peace with all men, and holiness, without which no man shall see the Lord"* Hebrews 12:14.

There is a wide discrepancy among churches when it comes to how holiness is taught. For some, it is a matter of lots of dos and don'ts, often ignoring what it means to truly love thy neighbor, and has negative implications or it is taught at the expense of other important Bible doctrines. For others, it is something that is ignored because it is seen to be divisive, intolerant and judgmental and not to put off the assorted group of sinners who might take umbrage. Then there are some whose focus is on getting people saved such that what comes after and the call to live a holy life and encouragement to do so is too easily overlooked. Some will take a view that holiness will follow automatically once saved and talk of it is thus downplayed. Yet it is truth and balance that is needed.

While not perfect correlations or synonyms to the word holiness as used in the Bible, the following are near matches: set-apartness, separateness, devotedness, godliness, righteousness, piety, virtue, consecration, sacredness, sinlessness, sanctification. Yet none do full justice to this important aspect of God's character and one we are called to emulate, as part of our own act of devotion and worship. It does involve ritual cleanliness and manifests itself, especially in Jewish religion, in the way God was worshiped and the things people did or did not do, but more importantly it is a matter of the heart: *"Who shall ascend into the hill of the Lord? or who shall stand in his holy place? He that hath clean hands, and a pure heart; who hath not lifted up his soul unto vanity, nor sworn deceitfully. He shall receive the blessing from the Lord, and righteousness from the God of his salvation"* (Psalm 24:3-5).

In preparing for this section on holiness, besides checking out OT prophets and NT writers e.g. Paul, Peter, John, I checked out what great men of God in the past, whose insights I particularly respect, said about holiness: Jonathan Edwards, John Owen, John Wesley, C.H.Spurgeon and J.C.Ryle (a personal favourite) as well as people who have lived during my lifetime: A.W.Tozer, Derek Prince, David Wilkerson, David Pawson and J.I.Packer. In all these cases, I was blown away, not so much because of the gravity of what they shared but because what they shared was so important and that I had a long way to go.

As I look around me and ponder on Gods dealing with humankind, past and present, the more I see a significant factor when it came to outcomes was God's holiness. True God deals with us in judgment and mercy, but also to vindicate His holy name and make us a holy people. As we look with consternation at world events and try to make sense out of it all, it is worth bringing to that mix the notion that God, as ever, is seeking a holy people.

Before rounding off by quoting a few of the many significant verses of the Bible that contain the word "holy" or "holiness", bearing in mind there are many more texts where those words are not mentioned that are equally relevant, I would like to offer the following thoughts:

Ten holiness thoughts:

1. An important theme of the prophets is the Salvation of God. For those of us who believe, we have been saved (justification); we are being saved (sanctification) and we shall be saved (glorification). Intrinsic in all three is the need to depart from sin and to pursue holiness.

2. It is a grave truth: heaven is a holy place and if you are not interested in being holy on earth it is unlikely you will be able to experience the joys of heaven or the presence of a holy God.

3. Anyone serious about God will want to be holy because they want to please and honour Him in all things. It is not just for those we call saints but it is something for all true children of God.

4. Those who are truly saintly are invariably those most concerned about overcoming their sinfulness.

5. Becoming holy is not something that occurs overnight. We come to God as sinners and while there should be a desire and expectation to overcome sin, it remains a lifelong exercise.

6. A holy person is as much concerned with doing the right thing (e.g. in our dealings with others, such as the poor and suffering) as things that might cause us to drift away from God (and is why cultivating good habits and not doing things that might lead us into temptation is important).

7. A holy person is more concerned about being holy rather than being happy, with the praise of God rather than the praise of men and doing the right thing rather than being successful. Yet often (as I have observed) true happiness happens when there is holiness.

8. While a holy person may possess an aura of the presence of God and a sense of "the other", often those who are truly holy are among the most empathetic, wholesome, and productive examples of humanity.

9. A holy person grieves for the sin that is all too apparent in those around him / her (as well as his / her own) and desires and wants to help such people to be saved and that means them becoming holy.

10. A holy person, above everything else, seeks to please God. Holiness is his / her mantra, and reason for living. Often it is the most unlikely people who are the most holy, although it is the Lord alone can pass judgement.

Ten "holiness" texts:

1. Exodus 15:11: *"Who is like unto thee, O Lord, among the gods? who is like thee, glorious in holiness, fearful in praises, doing wonders?"*

2. Exodus 28:36: *"And thou shalt make a plate of pure gold, and grave upon it, like the engravings of a signet, Holiness to the Lord."*

3. Psalm 29:2: *"Give unto the Lord the glory due unto his name; worship the Lord in the beauty of holiness."*

4. Isaiah 35:8: *"And an highway shall be there, and a way, and it shall be called The way of holiness; the unclean shall not pass over it; but it shall be for those: the wayfaring men, though fools, shall not err therein."*

5. Obadiah 1:17: "*But upon mount Zion shall be deliverance, and there shall be holiness; and the house of Jacob shall possess their possessions.*"

6. 2 Corinthians 7:1: "*Having therefore these promises, dearly beloved, let us cleanse ourselves from all filthiness of the flesh and spirit, perfecting holiness in the fear of God.*"

7. Ephesians 4:24: "*And that ye put on the new man, which after God is created in righteousness and true holiness*".

8. 1 Thessalonians 3:13: "*To the end he may stablish your hearts unblameable in holiness before God, even our Father, at the coming of our Lord Jesus Christ with all his saints.*"

9. Hebrews 12:10: "*For they verily for a few days chastened us after their own pleasure; but he for our profit, that we might be partakers of his holiness.*"

10. Hebrews 12:14: "*Follow peace with all men, and holiness, without which no man shall see the Lord:*"

Ten "holy" texts:

1. Exodus 19:6: "*And ye shall be unto me a kingdom of priests, and an holy nation. These are the words which thou shalt speak unto the children of Israel.*"

2. 1 Samuel 2:2: "*There is none holy as the Lord: for there is none beside thee: neither is there any rock like our God.*"

3. Psalm 15:1: "*Lord, who shall abide in thy tabernacle? who shall dwell in thy holy hill?*"

4. Psalm 103:1: "*Bless the Lord, O my soul: and all that is within me, bless his holy name.*"

5. Isaiah 6:3: "*And one cried unto another, and said, Holy, holy, holy, is the Lord of hosts: the whole earth is full of his glory.*"

6. Habakkuk 2:20: *"But the Lord is in his holy temple: let all the earth keep silence before him."*

7. Romans 12:1: *"I beseech you therefore, brethren, by the mercies of God, that ye present your bodies a living sacrifice, holy, acceptable unto God, which is your reasonable service."*

8. Ephesians 5:27: *"That he might present it to himself a glorious church, not having spot, or wrinkle, or any such thing; but that it should be holy and without blemish."*

9. 1 Peter 2:5,9: *"Ye also, as lively stones, are built up a spiritual house, an holy priesthood, to offer up spiritual sacrifices, acceptable to God by Jesus Christ ... But ye are a chosen generation, a royal priesthood, an holy nation, a peculiar people; that ye should shew forth the praises of him who hath called you out of darkness into his marvellous light."*

10. Revelation 22:11: *"He that is unjust, let him be unjust still: and he which is filthy, let him be filthy still: and he that is righteous, let him be righteous still: and he that is holy, let him be holy still."*

Idolatry

Closely connected to the call to holiness is that of turning from idolatry, which when doing a dictionary search to find meaning we find that an idol is *"an image or representation of a god used as an object of worship"* or *"a person or thing that is greatly admired, loved, or revered"*.

The notion of bowing down to an inanimate object representing something animate is not one that most modern minds particularly identify with. Yet they might also concur with the scornful ridicule of the prophet: *"They that make a graven image are all of them vanity; and their delectable things shall not profit; and they are their own witnesses; they see not, nor know; that they may be ashamed ... He burneth part thereof in the fire; with part thereof he eateth flesh; he roasteth roast, and is satisfied: yea, he warmeth himself, and saith, Aha, I am warm, I have seen the fire: And the residue thereof he maketh a god, even his graven image: he falleth down unto it, and worshippeth it, and prayeth unto it, and saith, Deliver me; for thou art my god"* Isaiah 44:9, 16-17.

But idolatry goes far beyond the obvious that Isaiah had observed. Besides making the observation that idolatry was widely practiced in the times of the Hebrew prophets and that practice as much as anything did cause Yahweh to punish his special people: Israel, it is evident that it is something that everyone of us could slip into, knowingly or unknowingly, because all too often its roots may be found in replacing God with self on the throne of our hearts. The first two of the Ten Commandments that most Christians, except for keeping the Sabbath, see as binding, tell us *"You shall have no other gods before me"* and *"You shall not make yourself a carved image, or any likeness of anything ..."*, which both encapsulate the notion of avoiding idolatry as being very important.

While most examples of idol worship can be found in the OT, it is clear in the NT God is angry with and judges ANY who practice idolatry, and this becomes a central plank in Paul's argument as to why humankind stands condemned before an idol hating God: *"For the wrath of God is revealed from heaven against all ungodliness and unrighteousness of men, who hold the truth in unrighteousness ... And changed the glory of the uncorruptible God into an image made like to corruptible man, and to birds, and fourfooted beasts, and creeping things. Wherefore God also gave them up to uncleanness through the lusts of their own hearts, to dishonour their own bodies between themselves: Who changed the truth of God into a lie, and worshipped and served the creature more than the Creator, who is blessed for ever"* Romans 1:8, 23-25.

In terms of avoiding (fleeing, killing maybe better words) idolatry, the NT writers are unequivocal in their exhortations, knowing full well from the OT what were the consequences when that did not happen. Notwithstanding, this is now the age of grace, there is a danger people can fall into practicing idolatry, even if momentarily or not all that deeply or even when the idol is something that is basically good. For example: *"Wherefore, my dearly beloved, flee from idolatry"* 1 Corinthians 10:14, *"For this ye know, that no whoremonger, nor unclean person, nor covetous man, who is an idolater, hath any inheritance in the kingdom of Christ and of God"* Ephesians 5:5, *"Mortify therefore your members which are upon the earth; fornication, uncleanness, inordinate affection, evil concupiscence, and covetousness, which is idolatry"* Colossians 3:5, *"Little children, keep yourselves from idols"* 1 John 5:21 and *"The fearful, and unbelieving, and the abominable, and murderers, and whoremongers, and sorcerers, and idolaters, and all liars, shall have their part in the lake which burneth with fire and brimstone: which is the second death"* Revelation 21:8.

As one might expect, if one were to check out some of the many sermons and meditations on the subject of idolatry, we would find many examples of idolatry given, including what is good, but somehow it usurps the place of God who tells us to have no other god before him. Success, prosperity, power, status, fame, ambition, prestige, family, things, hobbies, sports, science, knowledge, sex, persons come to mind. All may have their place, but if these come before the worship of the Almighty, it can quickly turn into idolatry as well as things we know we should not be doing – and as for images – in this modern age where self and sophistication is prized in the culture, these may seem not to feature.

When we turn back to the Old Testament, idolatry was something that seriously concerned the prophets, although it was evident idolatry was widespread outside the confines of Israel among its close neighbors. The building of and bowing to the Golden Calf while Moses was up in the mountain receiving the Law is an early example of what led to severe judgement on the idolaters. God was very clear *"Ye shall make you no idols nor graven image, neither rear you up a standing image, neither shall ye set up any image of stone in your land, to bow down unto it: for I am the Lord your God"* Leviticus 26:1, and yet repeatedly in their history, at least until after the Exile, we find the Israelites doing the very thing that God forbade and in doing so found to be reaping the consequences.

As for the Hebrew prophets and how God viewed idolatry, the following are some examples of how vehemently it was opposed: *"Their land also is full of idols; they worship the work of their own hands, that which their own fingers have made"* Isaiah 2:8, *"A drought is upon her waters; and they shall be dried up: for it is the land of graven images, and they are mad upon their idols"* Jeremiah 50:38, *"Son of man, these men have set up their idols in their heart, and put the stumblingblock of their iniquity before their face: should I be enquired of at all by them?"* Ezekiel 14:3, *"What profiteth the graven image that the maker thereof hath graven it; the molten image, and a teacher of lies, that the maker of his work trusteth therein, to make dumb idols?"* Habakkuk 2:18, and *"For the idols have spoken vanity, and the diviners have seen a lie, and have told false dreams; they comfort in vain: therefore they went their way as a flock, they were troubled, because there was no shepherd"* Zechariah 10:2.

In the Old Testament especially, many of these false gods / idols are named but two that keep cropping up and which I will focus were: Baal and Molech. *"And they built the high places of Baal, which are in the valley of the son of Hinnom, to cause their sons and their daughters to pass through the fire unto Molech; which I commanded them not, neither came it into my mind, that they should do this abomination, to cause Judah to sin*" Jeremiah 32:35. Baal crops up many times and notably in that great contest between Elijah and the prophets of Baal when the true God, Yahweh passed judgement over the false and when Elijah asked the Israelites why that were wavering between two opinions: whether to serve Yahweh or Baal? Molech crops up, as in this verse, with the sacrifice of children. Today people need to decide which god / God they are to serve. Much of the abortion industry and child sex trafficking is a sacrifice to Molech. Much of the hatred we are seeing directed toward Christians who oppose cultural norms such as with sexual identity and orientation, is linked to Baal worship.

Trinity

"*The Christian doctrine of the Trinity holds that God is one God, but three coeternal and consubstantial persons, each corresponding to its own hypostasis: the Father, the Son, and the Holy Spirit, as one God in three Divine Persons. The three persons are distinct, yet are one "substance, essence or nature"* Wikipedia

"*I believe in one God, the Father almighty, maker of heaven and earth, of all things visible and invisible. I believe in one Lord Jesus Christ, the Only Begotten Son of God, born of the Father before all ages. God from God, Light from Light, true God from true God, begotten, not made, consubstantial with the Father; through him all things were made ...*" Nicene Creed (AD 325)

"*... we worship one God in Trinity, and Trinity in Unity; Neither confounding the Persons: nor dividing the Substance. For there is one Person of the Father, another of the Son: and another of the Holy Ghost. But the Godhead of the Father, of the Son, and of the Holy Ghost, is all one: the Glory equal, the Majesty co-eternal. Such as the Father is, such is the Son: and such is the Holy Ghost. The Father uncreate, the Son uncreate: and the Holy Ghost uncreate. The Father incomprehensible, the Son incomprehensible: and the Holy Ghost incomprehensible. The Father eternal, the Son eternal: and the Holy Ghost eternal. And yet they are not three eternals: but one eternal. As also there are not three incomprehensibles, nor three uncreated: but one uncreated, and one incomprehensible ...*" Athanasian Creed (AD 500)

The Christian doctrine of the Trinity has proved to be controversial ever since the Christian religion began 2000 years ago and in order to combat heretical teaching the two (of the three) main creeds adopted by Catholic, Orthodox, Anglican and major Protestant denominations, quoted above, were produced. There have been huge disputes concerning the person hood of Father, Son and Holy Spirit, down the ages, which continue, and this has often given rise to huge disruption and schism. As far as mainstream Christianity goes, belief in the doctrine of the Trinity is an essential tenet of faith, even more so perhaps than that of Justification by Faith. Yet the word "Trinity" does not appear in the Bible and arguably it is not something that is formulated so strongly as it is in the two creeds quoted above. But as far as this writer is concerned, the doctrine of the Trinity is not only essential but is a key to understanding the prophets.

Our main focus has been on God the Father, followed by God the Son and God the Holy Spirit (dealt with in an earlier section because, even if only implied, the Holy Spirit played an important part in our story of the Prophets of the Bible). As far as Judaism is concerned there is only one God: *"Hear, O Israel: The Lord our God is one Lord"* Deuteronomy 6:4. This message is continually reinforced by the prophets even though, without exception, the nations surrounding Israel worshiped other gods, sometimes many, and often Israel turned to such gods. While the Christian doctrine of the Trinity may be an anathema as far as much of Judaism is concerned, Christianity is monotheistic.

The expectation of the coming Messiah, which Christians see as having been fulfilled in David's descendant, Jesus, who is also coming again to reign as king, was as we have discussed a major preoccupation of the prophets, harking back to God's promise to Abraham: *"in thy seed shall all the nations of the earth be blessed"* Genesis 22:18, but whose expected coming intensified during and following the Exile. The Messiah was seen both in human terms *e.g. "He is despised and rejected of men; a man of sorrows, and acquainted with grief: and we hid as it were our faces from him; he was despised, and we esteemed him not. Surely he hath borne our griefs, and carried our sorrows: yet we did esteem him stricken, smitten of God, and afflicted"* Isaiah 53:3-4 as well as bordering on the divine: *"I saw in the night visions, and, behold, one like the Son of man came with the clouds of heaven, and came to the Ancient of days, and they brought him near before him. And there was given him dominion, and glory, and a kingdom, that all people, nations, and languages, should serve him: his dominion is an everlasting dominion, which shall not pass away, and his kingdom that which shall not be destroyed"* Daniel 7:13,14, but it is unlikely the prophets quite saw their Messiah as divine, as their belief was in the one God.

The point here is not to make a case for the Trinity in the way some Christian apologists have done so in the past. While some have pointed to verses in the Old Testament that might suggest the Trinity, *e.g.* as part of the creation story when we read "*And God said, Let us make man in our image, after our likeness: and let them have dominion over the fish of the sea, and over the fowl of the air, and over the cattle, and over all the earth, and over every creeping thing that creepeth upon the earth. So God created man in his own image, in the image of God created he him; male and female created he them*" Genesis 1:26,27, when the word for God used, **Elohim**, suggests plurality, it may be rather stretching the point to affirm the Hebrew prophets embraced the Trinitarian view.

We need to consider the New Testament to find stronger evidence to support the Trinitarian position, and several verses can be cited. Perhaps one of the most compelling, and is often used, is in the prologue to John's gospel: "*In the beginning was the Word, and the Word was with God, and the Word was God. The same was in the beginning with God. All things were made by him; and without him was not any thing made that was made ... And the Word was made flesh, and dwelt among us, (and we beheld his glory, the glory as of the only begotten of the Father,) full of grace and truth*" John 1:1-3,14. It is often said that the synoptic gospels (Matthew, Mark, Luke) focus on Jesus humanity, whereas John's gospel focuses on Jesus divinity, and gives several examples, with the blending of the two natures being one of the great wonders of the faith.

That wonderful unity can be seen in the giving of the Holy Spirit: "*But when the Comforter is come, whom I will send unto you from the Father, even the Spirit of truth, which proceedeth from the Father, he shall testify of me*" John 15:26. It is notable in the closing commission given to His disciples, mention is made of all persons of the Trinity. Jesus said: "*Go ye therefore, and teach all nations, baptizing them in the name of the Father, and of the Son, and of the Holy Ghost: Teaching them to observe all things whatsoever I have commanded you: and, lo, I am with you always, even unto the end of the world*" Matthew 28:19,20.

The doctrine of the Trinity is a hard one to swallow because of the impossibility of such in human terms and is one, especially those who are new to faith, some may find it difficult to come to grips with. But if we are to give Son and Holy Spirit the honour due to them and hold a balanced understanding of the unique parts played by Father, Son and Holy Spirit in the workings of the universe, not least in the salvation of humankind, how each has a specific role yet ones that are beautifully complementary, an acceptance of this triune God is essential.

Suffering

The subject of suffering has occupied greater and lesser minds from the beginning of time, and where libraries are needed to contain all what has been thought, said and written. Like many, I have been confronted by those who have either lost their faith or have made radical adjustments because of what they have seen and witnessed and in the light of the Bible has to say about suffering and related topics. It is also something I have personally had to deal with, *e.g.* when carrying a chip on my shoulder for perceived injustices that I have personally experienced or wanting to get back at those who do bad to those I care for.

It is therefore appropriate to say something, while admitting I do not have many of the answers, to help set the record straight, noting that in the best part of a year researching this book, the subject of suffering in various guises has cropped up several times, even if only in passing. The background in which I operated with severe restrictions due to Covid-19 shows many have suffered. Suffering was introduced into the world following the Fall, when Adam and Eve disobeyed God. The result was they were expelled from their idyllic garden and this has been the experience of humanity ever since. The one thing the Bible does not do and that is to unravel in full the mysteries behind suffering.

There is a side of God which Christians, especially those of a more liberal persuasion, present: loving, kind, patient, merciful, gracious etc., all of which is true of course. But there is another side: holy, righteous, judgmental, vengeful, jealous etc. and that too is true. For the sake of balance, we need to recognise both sides. A few years back, I read Richard Dawkin's "***The God Delusion***". I was struck when Dawkins laid into those who believed in and followed God (even though he put God into the same category as fairies at the bottom of the garden) and made the point – how could they, given the evidence of God's cruelty that can be traced back to the Bible itself? After all, did he not command Joshua and Saul to wipe out whole cities – men, women and children? If it happened today, Joshua and Saul might be hauled before an international court on charges of genocide and few "right thinking" people would object. I should add, if Dawkins were to come to me, I could give many more examples. While I may question his context, I can't dispute his examples. There is a lot in the Bible, especially Old Testament, narrative, when God does not make sense.

The proposition that has bothered many down the ages is while it may not be unreasonable to expect bad people to suffer, i.e. get their just desserts for their bad deeds, there are countless examples of good people who suffer (as well as the bad people who don't). We can all think of examples of when that is the case and I will resist giving examples, but we can all think of examples in our own lives, or those we care about, when life has dealt them a poor hand. It is tempting, like Job's comforters, to question why this seemingly very righteous man should suffer as badly as he did, and that maybe he was not quite as good as he appeared to be. But we know from reading the book with that title they got it wrong and there was an eternal dimension involving God and Satan that no-one saw, not even Job. It was Job who said: *"for I know that my redeemer liveth, and that he shall stand at the latter day upon the earth: And though after my skin worms destroy this body, yet in my flesh shall I see God"* Job 19:25-26 and as for being confident in God, he declared: *"though he slay me, yet will I trust in him: but I will maintain mine own ways before him"* Job 13:15.

If we were to read through the whole Bible, looking for examples of suffering, we would soon be inundated with many examples. Sometimes people suffered because of their own wrong actions and there are lessons that can be derived. Sometimes people suffered because of the wrong actions of others and cannot be blamed. Both are universal experiences. Sometimes people suffered because they did the right thing. This book has furnished numerous examples of the prophets suffering, often as a result of being attacked by those who did not like their message. While we read about the prophets' pain and sometimes bemusement, we also find they trusted God. For New Testament Christians, suffering was a common place experience. Perhaps the most profound of the prophetic books of the Bible was Revelation and its profoundness was not so much because of the number of prophetic statement but because it was addressed to those who had experienced and would experience persecution.

When it comes to suffering, however much we might try to arrange things (assuming we can – and many do not have that luxury because of the circumstances in which they live) suffering is still nigh unavoidable, for such are the vagaries of life and the best we can do is hope for the best and prepare for the worst (although often that is impossible because often we cannot predict what that "worst" is going to be). Persecution is a form of suffering that particularly impacts people of faith. It may be something that can be avoided by renouncing the faith. Going back to Revelation, the readers were encouraged to stand fast and look forward to an eternal reward for doing so. *"And I heard a loud voice saying in heaven, Now is come salvation, and strength, and the kingdom of our God, and the power of his Christ: for the accuser of our brethren is cast down, which accused them before our God day and night.*

And they overcame him by the blood of the Lamb, and by the word of their testimony; and they loved not their lives unto the death" Revelation 12:10,11. Looking around the world about me at this time, as I write, I am astounded by the amount of persecution happening all over the world and the way things are heading, soon in my own country. The watchword is we must prepare to suffer.

I daresay it is easy to come up with pious platitudes in the light of suffering, especially if it is other people's, and it is something that we should avoid. Rather we need to seek to encourage, pray for and give comfort and whatever limited practical help we can to those who do suffer, especially our brothers and sisters, some we do not know, who are suffering for Christ. We are reminded that it is our Lord "*who comforteth us in all our tribulation, that we may be able to comfort them which are in any trouble, by the comfort wherewith we ourselves are comforted of God*" 2Corinthians 1:4.

We should see suffering in positive terms and character building: "*we glory in tribulations also: knowing that tribulation worketh patience; And patience, experience; and experience, hope: And hope maketh not ashamed; because the love of God is shed abroad in our hearts by the Holy Ghost which is given unto us*" Romans 5:3-5. Then there is the Day of Judgement and the Eternal State (covered in the next section) when true justice is served ("*shall not the Judge of all the earth do right*" Genesis 18:25) and mysteries around suffering are resolved. Finally, we should remember the amazing truth that God suffered on our behalf. Jesus the Son died on the Cross and was rejected by His Father, and all that was necessary in order that He could atone for our sins.

Eternity

The subject of eternity is one that most of us, I have no doubt, have given a good deal of thought to. As the "Preacher" noted, God has set eternity in the hears of me (Ecclesiastes 3:11). One of my earliest childhood memories was a sense of fear when I contemplated eternity – realising it has no beginning and no end. Along with this was the notion that God is eternal and, as for me, I was a mere infinitesimal speck in the timeline between no beginning and no end. The 1662 Book of Common Prayer captures some of these sentiments: "*Man that is born of a woman hath but a short time to live, and is full of misery. He cometh up, and is cut down, like a flower; he fleeth as it were a shadow, and never continueth in one stay*". It was some years later that I gained the assurance this insignificant nobody could and would spend eternity with an infinite God, not on the basis of any intrinsic merit etc. but because I had been saved by His grace.

These days I attend (at least before Covid lockdown) funerals on a regular basis. They tend to fall into two categories, depending on the deceased's beliefs and those of his/her family, firstly: those that reflect on the delights that the one who is mourned is now experiencing or one day experience in God's presence, often irrespective of the deceased religious beliefs or practices, and secondly: those that ignores such considerations, but with perhaps the rather whimsical hope that something of that persons life's energy and qualities will continue with future generations. Whichever our position is, if we are to take the Bible seriously, the question of how one spends eternity remains an important one.

In my studies of the Hebrew prophets, it appeared that eternity was not a major preoccupation. Rather, their major concern was the future of Israel, with only a passing interest in the destiny of other nations and that the people of YHWH be obedient to Him and leave a worthy legacy for their families and Israel. But a careful examination of the Law, *e.g.* Deuteronomy 31:16, the Writings, *e.g.* Psalm 16 10, Psalm 17:15, Psalm 49:14-15, Psalms 71:18, Proverbs 14:32, Daniel 7:18, Daniel 12:1, 13 and Job 12-13-14, as well as the prophets, *e.g.* Isaiah 25:8-9, 26:19, Ezekiel 37:12-14, Hosea 13:14, will dismiss the notion that the Old Testament was ***not*** concerned with eternity. Even what appears to be a euphemism often used when talking about someone's death *"he slept with his fathers"* implied that death is not the end and there is something after death.

Perhaps one of the more sobering utterances from the mouth of the prophets, because it alludes to what we might equate to notions of heaven and hell, comes at the end of Isaiah: *"For as the new heavens and the new earth, which I will make, shall remain before me, saith the Lord, so shall your seed and your name remain. And it shall come to pass, that from one new moon to another, and from one sabbath to another, shall all flesh come to worship before me, saith the Lord. And they shall go forth, and look upon the carcases of the men that have transgressed against me: for their worm shall not die, neither shall their fire be quenched; and they shall be an abhorring unto all flesh"* Isaiah 66:22-24.

What heaven and hell are like, who goes there and on what basis, the actual timelines between Old and New Covenants, the significance of the Day of Judgement, the New Heaven and New Earth, our ultimate destinies and where the royal we fits into all this, are yet further huge questions that this chapter has been raising, because they are important and while hardly scratching the surface it opens up these subjects, encouraging further study, mindful that considerable false teaching abounds. As far as the New Testament is concerned, toward the outset we are presented with two major and influential camps within Judaism: the liberal, rationalists, the Sadducees, who did not believe in the resurrection of the dead, and the sanctimonious, hypocrites, the Pharisees, who did. Jesus own theological position was clear when he declared "*I am the resurrection, and the life: he that believeth in me, though he were dead, yet shall he live*" John 11:25. One of the best known and loved texts in the whole Bible makes it clear: "*For God so loved the world, that he gave his only begotten Son, that whosoever believeth in him should not perish, but have everlasting life*" John 3:16.

Paul teaches what the pre-requisite for eternal life is: "*For all have sinned, and come short of the glory of God; Being justified freely by his grace through the redemption that is in Christ Jesus: Whom God hath set forth to be a propitiation through faith in his blood, to declare his righteousness for the remission of sins that are past, through the forbearance of God; To declare, I say, at this time his righteousness: that he might be just, and the justifier of him which believeth in Jesus. Where is boasting then? It is excluded. By what law? of works? Nay: but by the law of faith*" Romans 3:23-27. Paul develops this theme: "*What shall we say then that Abraham our father, as pertaining to the flesh, hath found? For if Abraham were justified by works, he hath whereof to glory; but not before God. For what saith the scripture? Abraham believed God, and it was counted unto him for righteousness. Now to him that worketh is the reward not reckoned of grace, but of debt. But to him that worketh not, but believeth on him that justifieth the ungodly, his faith is counted for righteousness. Even as David also describeth the blessedness of the man, unto whom God imputeth righteousness without works, Saying, Blessed are they whose iniquities are forgiven, and whose sins are covered. Blessed is the man to whom the Lord will not impute sin. Cometh this blessedness then upon the circumcision only, or upon the uncircumcision also? for we say that faith was reckoned to Abraham for righteousness*" Romans 4:1-9.

Even Gentiles who know nothing of the Law or the Gospel are not excluded: "*For there is no respect of persons with God. For as many as have sinned without law shall also perish without law: and as many as have sinned in the law shall be judged by the law; (For not the hearers of the law are just before God, but the doers of the law shall be justified. For when the Gentiles, which have not the law, do by nature the things contained in the law, these, having not the law, are a law unto themselves: Which shew the work of the law written in their hearts, their conscience also bearing witness, and their thoughts the mean while accusing or else excusing one another;) In the day when God shall judge the secrets of men by Jesus Christ according to my gospel*" Romans 2:11-16. While the above provides great hope and reassurance to the Christian believer, it is well to be reminded that *"faith without works is dead"* James 2:20 and it is *"he who endures to the end shall be saved"* Matthew 24:13.

The matter of Hell is a problematic one and I doubt few if any find the notion of eternal punishment for unbelievers a palatable one humanly speaking and most could name those close to them who we cannot, hand on heart say, died as believers, and therefore they stand condemned. If we avoid the sentimentality that often surrounds loved ones who die, we cannot say with assurance we will be reunited with those who died as unbelievers. Harking back to the previous section on suffering, for some the idea of Hell is the most difficult example of suffering to stomach. But it was Jesus who called Hell (however we wish to describe it) a place *"where their worm dieth not, and the fire is not quenched"* Mark 9:48 and *"where there shall be weeping and gnashing of teeth"* Luke 13:28. One of the most sobering verses in the whole Bible because of its grave warning is what happens following the Day of Judgement: *"whosoever was not found written in the book of life was cast into the lake of fire"* Revelation 20:15.

Our eternal destiny should be a cause of great concern for self and others, including, however hard it is to fathom, what a person's eternal destiny is, yet God will always do what is right and we leave it with Him, as I and many have done, contemplating the death of a loved one. For our part, we are responsible both for making the right decision and not resting there but living a holy life, and for telling others how they stand before God and what they must do to be saved. Like the apostles, we must proclaim: *"neither is there salvation in any other: for there is none other name under heaven given among men, whereby we must be saved. Neither is there salvation in any other: for there is none other name under heaven given among men, whereby we must be saved"* Acts 4:12. *"It is appointed unto men once to die, but after this the judgment"* Hebrews 9:27. The question of where "after this" is of paramount importance. The idea of spending eternity with one's Saviour, is one that should bring great comfort.

Since this book is about the prophets of the Bible, it is appropriate to give one of them the last word: *"For since the beginning of the world men have not heard, nor perceived by the ear, neither hath the eye seen, O God, beside thee, what he hath prepared for him that waiteth for him"* Isaiah 64:4, which Paul quotes, while explaining something of the wisdom of God and the true wonder and mystery of the gospel message (1Corinthians 2:1-9).

Prayer

I do not feel particularly well qualified to write on the subject of prayer, but since I am a Christian who prays, knows well most of the passages in the Bible that concern prayer, have been a participant in countless prayer meetings, many of which I have led, and have many times seen God answer prayer, I believe I have something to bring to the party. Just like "Bible", discussed earlier, prayer is something even the humblest among us can participate in with great effect.

As an old dodderer who society might consign to sit on the sidelines and with no demand to contribute to the economy, I can do so knowing I must do my bit as a Watchman on the Wall, encourager of saints and sinners alike and as a Bible student and teacher, and share what the Lord has laid on my heart. I have long known this of course but my effectiveness is linked to my prayer life and I have no excuse for not praying, whether it is an individual (in secret as Jesus told us) or part of a collective. The days of national emergency, such as during World War 2 when the King called the UK to pray, seem to have gone and yet we face an emergency now. While I don't want to use this as an opportunity to bash church or government, I regret such calls don't happen and my reading of the Bible is God allows calamities to wake His people up. An earlier topic was holiness, and it there is a connection, God (YHWH) wants both a holy people and a praying people and the one leads to the other. While we may stand in awe at saints in bygone days who prayed daily for hours on end, it remains true: *"the devil trembles when he sees the weakest saint upon his knees"*.

Before I give my list of areas to pray into, I offer some "qualifying" thoughts by way of a precursor:

1. It is quite clear that the prophets of the Bible were men and women of prayer and that prayer and prophecy were linked. Often they had to wait a long time (or never) before seeing answers to their prayers or fulfillment of their prophecies, but they persisted and were patient, and so should we.

2. I often precede studies like this with a Bible search, in this case on the word "pray", and feed this into my online Bible application (BibleGateway) and use as a basis to meditate. There are passages of the Bible, particularly the Psalms, that we do well to meditate on. I commend this practice. Besides studying the Bible, I have read many helpful books on prayer, which I commend, but confess the revolution and transformation that should follow is very much work in progress.

3. There have also been many "heroes of the faith" to supplement those mentioned in the Bible, who took God at his word, and prayed, and as a result of their praying often saw wonderful, unexpected, unusual, miraculous, powerful answers to prayer. Like Elijah they were those of likes passions as we are. Reading their biographies can be inspirational.

4. Prayer is no substitute for obedience to God, living a holy life, taking action and having a contrite heart and a penitent spirit. The practice of confession as a prelude to prayer is one I would also commend. *"If I regard iniquity in my heart, the Lord will not hear me"* Psalm 66:18.

5. Prayer must lead to action. The likes of Wilberforce and Bonhoeffer prayed and it led to needful political action. The likes of George Carey and Hudson Taylor prayed and it led to fruitful missionary endeavour, as in the unchristianised lands of India and China. The likes of Mueller and Booth prayed and it led to much needed social action being undertaken, like caring for widows and orphans. The likes of Bonnke and Prince prayed and it led to Pentecostal revival. The likes of numerous church planters down the ages prayed and it led to new churches being opened. The likes of many martyrs prayed, right up to this present time, and it while it led to their deaths it brought new life to the wider church. So often, the likes of you and me have prayed and it did lead to wonderful breakthroughs in what might often be seen as small things.

6. We must be careful not to pre-empt God – who while He will answer our prayers, it may not be in the way we hope of expect. We must be reliant on the Holy Spirit to help us to pray.

7. We are beholden to pray and the subjects for our prayers are countless, but we must begin somewhere. It doesn't require fancy words or well thought out schemes. God knows it all.

8. Prayer, including supplication and intercession, should accompany worship, including praise and thanksgiving. In fact, worship God for who He is and praise for what He has done should be central to our prayer time. It also means we have to forgive those who have wronged us. It also involves spiritual warfare and is an weapon in this important undertaking.

9. While our prayers are often general e.g. bless Aunt Soandso, we need to learn to go from the general to the specific and be like Jacob, not to let God go until he has blessed us.

10. Prayer involves spiritual warfare and those who take prayer seriously, as opposed to a token exercise, are spiritual warriors. There is much that is happening behind the scenes, typically in the spiritual realm, we cannot see because we do not have the big picture, but the Lord and his heavenly army does and delights when his earthly army engages in such warfare.

11. As members of the Body (the Church), which is universal and includes people from every walk of life and who we may not like or agree with, we need to pray for them, and especially for the suffering church.

12. Prayer, like so much in life is a discipline and it can happen at any time and in any place and take any form (including use of set prayers). It can be done privately and individually and publicly and corporately. It may accompany fasting. It needs to be done regularly and freely. Prayer is a sincere response of the heart to our loving heavenly Father who can and does give us far more than we can ever ask or imagine.

As for items of prayer, I offer here what is a halfway house between the general and the specific. I also have a view of world events as does the reader and will do my best not to force my view.

1. There is so much going on in the world and the picture changes by the day and we don't know half. As I write, the matter of the US Presidential election is a contentious one that has huge implications, not just for the USA but for the world at large. Pray that truth and justice will prevail. Pray that America like Britain return to what was good in its godly heritage.

2. 2020 has been the year of the Corona virus which has affected us all. For some the effects are devastating. As I write, we do not know how it will all end or what nefarious schemes are afoot. There is much confusion, even within the church. We pray God's will be done.

3. As far as my country, the UK, goes, Brexit has overshadowed so much among its concerns. It is shortly due to completely leave the EU, and there remains uncertainty as to whether it is with a deal or no deal. Pray for a righteous transition and for the UK's future outside of the EU.

4. It has become increasingly evident that the Church (true followers of Christ) is not united and false teaching and unspiritual leaders holds sway.

Yet Christ loves the Church and seeks a bride, pure and holy. Pray He will stir up His people and raise up leaders, like King David, after His own heart. Pray for revival in the church and be ready for it start with us.

5. Many of our brothers and sisters in many countries across the world suffer severe persecution who we should pray for. Every day, the likes of the Barnabas Fund give examples of persecution for us to pray about.

6. There are many mission agencies, including those known to and supported by us individually, who do sterling work, but under great pressure and all sorts of constraints, including financial ones. We pray, as overwhelming as these needs are, recognising *"the fields are white for harvest"* John 4:35 and that *"the Lord of the harvest to send out laborers into His harvest"* (Matthew 9:37), and for those who are doing the work.

7. We may have little confidence in the leaders of this world but we must pray for kings and all those in authority, that we may live peaceful and quiet lives in all godliness and holiness.

8. There is much to concern us in our own community, family, friends, neighbours etc. It is likely that included in their number are those who are unsaved. We must pray for them.

9. In our own circle and fellowships there is the elderly, young, perplexed, lonely, disaffected, sick etc. There may be outreaches to these and the wider community to pray concerning.

10. Israel remains God's special people and is at the heart of so much happening in the world: *"Pray for the peace of Jerusalem"* Psalm 122:6.

11. The call to love our neighbour, from the top of the societal ladder to the bottom, those who are key workers and those who aren't, those who like and support us and the very opposite, the decision makers and influencers and those who aren't; whatever age, gender, sexual orientation, race, religion, disability etc. There is enormous scope for prayer.

12. Pray for the worldwide furtherance of the gospel and the extension of God's kingdom, for true disciples of the Lord Jesus who disciple others.

Faith

When I did my customary Bible search on a word or idea I want to discuss, I found there to be 56 references in the Old Testament to the text "faith" and 280 in the New Testament. Most of the OT references were the words "faithful" and "faithfulness", something that is intrinsically related to faith and is confirmed when doing a Strong's Concordance check – someone with faith will be faithful, just as God is. Then there was the concept of faith, encapsulated in words like "trust", "confidence", "reliance", bringing me to the view if I were to check out all such references, I would soon get lost down the many rabbit holes.

What has become very clear is that faith is an essential element in our study of the Prophets of the Bible and without it we might well conclude the prophets were deluded or worse and we would be wasting our time and energy in pursuing such studies if God was not for real. The crux question concerning God is not does religion keep one civilized and happy or, as Karl Marx put it, act as *"the opium of the people"*, but is it true and if so which variant, given that if A contradicts B then either A or B or both are false? In an earlier loose end, on "Apologetics", I argued given the weight of Bible prophecy that has been fulfilled, this is powerful reason why I know the God I have faith in, as revealed in the Bible, is for real. Another is the resurrection of Jesus. I concur with Paul (as a "fundamentalist" – do I have a choice?) *"And if Christ be not risen, then is our preaching vain, and your faith is also vain"* 1 Corinthians 15:17.

Which brings me to "what is faith" and specifically faith in the God of the Bible? One basically sound online Bible dictionary defined faith thus: *"belief, trust, and loyalty to a person or thing. Christians find their security and hope in God as revealed in Jesus Christ, and say "amen" to that unique relationship to God in the Holy Spirit through love and obedience as expressed in lives of discipleship and service"* and in elaborating on the subject: *"Faith is in general the persuasion of the mind that a certain statement is true. Its primary idea is trust. A thing is true, and therefore worthy of trust. It admits of many degrees up to full assurance of faith, in accordance with the evidence on which it rests"*.

One of the great faith chapters in the Bible is Hebrews 11, which gives several examples of characters in the Bible who had faith and it was this that governed the way they lived. The writer of the Hebrews begins with Abel: *"by faith Abel offered unto God a more excellent sacrifice than Cain"* (11:4) and ends considering the efficacy, trials and rewards of faith: *"Who through faith subdued kingdoms, wrought righteousness, obtained promises, stopped the mouths of lions. Quenched the violence of fire, escaped the edge of the sword, out of weakness were made strong, waxed valiant in fight, turned to flight the armies of the aliens. Women received their dead raised to life again: and others were tortured, not accepting deliverance; that they might obtain a better resurrection: And others had trial of cruel mockings and scourgings, yea, moreover of bonds and imprisonment: They were stoned, they were sawn asunder, were tempted, were slain with the sword: they wandered about in sheepskins and goatskins; being destitute, afflicted, tormented; (Of whom the world was not worthy:) they wandered in deserts, and in mountains, and in dens and caves of the earth. And these all, having obtained a good report through faith, received not the promise: God having provided some better thing for us, that they without us should not be made perfect"* (11:33-40).

As for why faith matters and what faith actually is, the Hebrews writer helpfully points out: *"Through faith we understand that the worlds were framed by the word of God, so that things which are seen were not made of things which do appear... Now faith is the substance of things hoped for, the evidence of things not seen... But without faith it is impossible to please him: for he that cometh to God must believe that he is, and that he is a rewarder of them that diligently seek him"* (11:1,3,6). The one verse that links OT and NT and is quoted by Paul when discussing the essence of the gospel, and is the doctrine more than any central to the Reformation, "Justification by Faith", is: *"the just shall live by his faith"* Habakkuk 2:4. This is his central plank as he expounds the gospel in Romans, chapters 1-11. *"For I am not ashamed of the gospel of Christ: for it is the power of God unto salvation to every one that believeth; to the Jew first, and also to the Greek. For therein is the righteousness of God revealed from faith to faith: as it is written, the just shall live by faith"* Romans 1:16,17.

It would be rather simplistic to say that when it comes to having a relationship with God, while the OT was more about obeying the Law and the NT was more to do with having faith, having faith and doing as God tells us go hand in hand. My own Christian background encouraged me to hang onto the notion that, when I had my conversion experience aged 15, that settled the matter of my eternal salvation. I was presented with texts like *"Believe in the Lord Jesus, and you will be saved"* (Acts 16:31) to support that assertion. The question *"once saved, always saved!?"* is one that has divided Bible teachers, including those I respect, like R.T.Kendal and David Pawson. They have both written books with that very title. Kendal concludes in answer to that statement – yes and Pawson no. While I am more inclined to the Kendal position, I continue to urge folk to read the Bible, which teaches salvation is ongoing and of the need to be faithful. Faith manifests itself in actions and Jesus own solemn teaching is *"but he that shall endure unto the end, the same shall be saved"* Matthew 24:13.

The subject of law and grace, faith and works, how it impacts on our prayer life and life's decisions and whether or not one can lose one's salvation are lofty ones and beyond the scope of a book, which is primarily about the prophets. One might reflect on the use of the word "faith" by Jesus and His followers. On several occasions Jesus healed those who had faith. Jesus said: *"If ye have faith as a grain of mustard seed, ye shall say unto this mountain, Remove hence to yonder place; and it shall remove; and nothing shall be impossible unto you"* Matthew 17:20 and the history of the church is full of examples of those who had faith, even as small as a grain of mustard seed, who accomplished great things for the Kingdom and whose exploits we should emulate, just as urged by the writer to the Hebrews when considering the OT saints. The implications are enormous as we examine the world around us and its many conundrums.

When it comes to faith, one OT man of faith and a prophet, was Abraham, who was cited by Paul when tackling some of the great questions of his day (which still hold): *"Even as Abraham believed God, and it was accounted to him for righteousness. Know ye therefore that they which are of faith, the same are the children of Abraham. And the scripture, foreseeing that God would justify the heathen through faith, preached before the gospel unto Abraham, saying, in thee shall all nations be blessed. So then they which be of faith are blessed with faithful Abraham. For as many as are of the works of the law are under the curse: for it is written, cursed is every one that continueth not in all things which are written in the book of the law to do them. But that no man is justified by the law in the sight of God, it is evident: for, the just shall live by faith. And the law is not of faith: but, the man that doeth them shall live in them. Christ hath redeemed us from the curse of the law, being made a curse for us: for it is written, cursed is every one that hangeth on a tree: That the blessing of Abraham might come on the Gentiles through Jesus Christ; that we might receive the promise of the Spirit through faith"* Galatians 3:6-14. If nothing else, these verses demonstrate the importance of faith and it is this that saves us (and not our good works) and it is this that should govern how we live.

It is difficult to know how to wrap up discussion on a subject when there is so much more that could be usefully said. My own watchword and one that is strongly linked to my own church background is the call: *"Beloved, when I gave all diligence to write unto you of the common salvation, it was needful for me to write unto you, and exhort you that ye should earnestly contend for the faith which was once delivered unto the saints*" Jude 1:3. If there is anything I can usefully do, notwithstanding physical and circumstantial limitations, it is to be an exemplar of the faith I claim and be an encourager to others to have faith and hang in there come what may: "*Here is the patience of the saints: here are they that keep the commandments of God, and the faith of Jesus*" Revelation 14:12. Which brings us to the faithful one we follow and one who as one by-product of faith we expect to return to Earth in glory: "*And I saw heaven opened, and behold a white horse; and he that sat upon him was called Faithful and True, and in righteousness he doth judge and make war*" Revelation 19:11.

When it comes to examples of persons of faith and given it is relevant to this book, we need go no further than the Hebrew prophets even though other than the Habakkuk reference given above the word "faith" is not to be found in the narrative. Yet faith and faithfulness oozes throughout their lives and ministries. While we stand in awe at the startling revelations the prophets received, it still required faith to be those who not just heard from God but who at any cost were prepared to pass on the message to those God directed them toward and live accordingly. This also brings us to faithfulness. The prophets were faithful just as the one in whose name they prophesied is faithful. Faith may seem a scary thing for we ordinary folk but, without it, however tiny the "it" is, we can never please God or doing anything significant for God. As for faithfulness, however ordinary we are, we can and should be faithful and it is that, as was pointed out to this once rather naïve, zealous young Christian, what truly matters.

Grace

There are a number of attributes of YHWH God that ought to thrill us and on which Christians of different theological leanings broadly agree: love, mercy, goodness, faithfulness, compassion to name but five. Many of these attributes, it may be argued, can be found in other religions, as applying to their gods. Many have been touched on in this book because they were of interest to the prophets. But I want to add one more, and this some may argue is a precious truth that is unique to Judaism and Christianity. It is the word grace.

While the word translated as grace or gracious is used 124 times in the New Testament, it is far just a Christian concept because Christians are interested in grace and Jews law (John 1:17), for it is used 69 times in the Old Testament, including by several of the Hebrew prophets. Many have tried to explain and define "grace" but for this consideration I will define grace to be *love, mercy and favour given to us by God because God simply desires us to have it and not because of anything we have done or are to earn it; it is an attribute of God that is especially manifested in the salvation of sinners*. As far as giving examples of grace, I will cite four examples from the Bible, followed by twelve random verses, along with a brief explanation why I believe these to be relevant.

When Moses was communing with God on Mount Sinai, when giving the Law, and at the same time the Israelites misbehaved down below, Moses made an audacious request, which God granted, and in so doing Moses saw something, maybe just a glimpse, of the grace of God as well as His glory: *"And he said, I beseech thee, shew me thy glory. And he said, I will make all my goodness pass before thee, and I will proclaim the name of the Lord before thee; and will be gracious to whom I will be gracious, and will shew mercy on whom I will shew mercy. And he said, thou canst not see my face: for there shall no man see me, and live. And the Lord said, behold, there is a place by me, and thou shalt stand upon a rock: And it shall come to pass, while my glory passeth by, that I will put thee in a clift of the rock, and will cover thee with my hand while I pass by: And I will take away mine hand, and thou shalt see my back parts: but my face shall not be seen"* Exodus 33: 18-33.

One blessing a Jew may bestow on another and is found in the Bible and is how we may wish to bless those we care about is: *"The Lord bless thee, and keep thee: The Lord make his face shine upon thee, and be gracious unto thee: The Lord lift up his countenance upon thee, and give thee peace"* Numbers 6: 24-26.

The prologue to John's gospel is about the Word who was in the beginning, who became flesh, but also about Law and Grace and the Word, full of Grace and Truth: *"In the beginning was the Word, and the Word was with God, and the Word was God. The same was in the beginning with God. All things were made by him; and without him was not any thing made that was made. In him was life; and the life was the light of men ... And the Word was made flesh, and dwelt among us, (and we beheld his glory, the glory as of the only begotten of the Father,) full of grace and truth. John bare witness of him, and cried, saying, This was he of whom I spake, He that cometh after me is preferred before me: for he was before me. And of his fulness have all we received, and grace for grace. For the law was given by Moses, but grace and truth came by Jesus Christ"* John 1: 1-4, 14-17.

Grace is an essential component of the Gospel, and is a point Paul strongly argued in his letter to the Romans: *"Therefore being justified by faith, we have peace with*

God through our Lord Jesus Christ: By whom also we have access by faith into this grace wherein we stand, and rejoice in hope of the glory of God ... Nevertheless death reigned from Adam to Moses, even over them that had not sinned after the similitude of Adam's transgression, who is the figure of him that was to come. But not as the offence, so also is the free gift. For if through the offence of one many be dead, much more the grace of God, and the gift by grace, which is by one man, Jesus Christ, hath abounded unto many. And not as it was by one that sinned, so is the gift: for the judgment was by one to condemnation, but the free gift is of many offences unto justification. For if by one man's offence death reigned by one; much more they which receive abundance of grace and of the gift of righteousness shall reign in life by one, Jesus Christ.) ... Moreover the law entered, that the offence might abound. But where sin abounded, grace did much more abound: That as sin hath reigned unto death, even so might grace reign through righteousness unto eternal life by Jesus Christ our Lord" Romans 5: 1, 2, 14-17, 20, 21.

The following are Bible verses to do with grace along with a simple application:

1. An example of one who possessed something that truly mattered: "*But Noah found grace in the eyes of the Lord*" Genesis 6:8.
2. Grace must not be an excuse for sin: "*What shall we say then? Shall we continue in sin, that grace may abound? By no means! We are those who have died to sin; how can we live in it any longer?*" Romans 6:1,2.
3. The grace of God can make us what God wants: "*But by the grace of God I am what I am: and his grace which was bestowed upon me was not in vain; but I laboured more abundantly than they all: yet not I, but the grace of God which was with me*" 1Corinthians 15:10.
4. What better example of grace is that which Jesus accomplished when dying for us sinners: "*For ye know the grace of our Lord Jesus Christ, that, though he was rich, yet for your sakes he became poor, that ye through his poverty might be rich*" 2 Corinthians 8:9.
5. God's grace is all sufficient to cope with the challenges of life: "*My grace is sufficient for thee: for my strength is made perfect in weakness. Most gladly therefore will I rather glory in my infirmities, that the power of Christ may rest upon me*" 2 Corinthians 12:9.
6. Many feel that a "fitting" way to end a church service is to say the grace: "*May the grace of the Lord Jesus Christ, and the love of God, and the fellowship of the Holy Spirit be with you all*" 2Corinthians 13:14.
7. It is grace that saves us: "*In whom we have redemption through his blood, the forgiveness of sins, according to the riches of his grace ... Even when*

we were dead in sins, hath quickened us together with Christ, (by grace ye are saved;)" Ephesians 1:7, 2:5.
8. God's gracious, eternal intention is clear: *"That in the ages to come he might shew the exceeding riches of his grace in his kindness toward us through Christ Jesus. For by grace are ye saved through faith; and that not of yourselves: it is the gift of God"* Ephesians 2:7,8.
9. Grace should define how we live: *"Let the word of Christ dwell in you richly in all wisdom; teaching and admonishing one another in psalms and hymns and spiritual songs, singing with grace in your hearts to the Lord"* Colossians 3:16.
10. Grace is there for all those who seek it: *"Let us therefore come boldly unto the throne of grace, that we may obtain mercy, and find grace to help in time of need"* Hebrews 4:16.
11. We are called to grow in grace: *"But grow in grace, and in the knowledge of our Lord and Saviour Jesus Christ. To him be glory both now and for ever. Amen"* 2 Peter 3:18.
12. A fitting way to end the Bible is as it invokes the idea of grace: *"The grace of our Lord Jesus Christ be with you all. Amen"* Revelation 22:21.

Dietrich Bonhoeffer was asked in 1943 how it was possible for the Church to sit back and let Hitler seize absolute power. His firm answer: *"It was the teaching of cheap grace ... Cheap grace is the preaching of forgiveness without requiring repentance, baptism without church discipline, communion without confession, absolution without personal confession. Cheap grace is grace without discipleship, grace without the cross, grace without Jesus Christ."* We live in a time and culture when all too often the church not only teaches cheap grace but praises it. Such attitudes, we all need to repent of.

A fitting end to this section is words of the much-loved hymn by John Newton: *"Amazing grace, how sweet the sound that saved a wretch like me. I once was lost, but now I am found, was blind, but now I see ... Through many dangers, toils and snares I have already come, 'Tis grace has brought me safe thus far and grace will lead me home"*. Newton also said: *"I am not the man I ought to be, I am not the man I wish to be, and I am not the man I hope to be, but by the grace of God, I am not the man I used to be"*. Many share these sentiments.

Despite my many flaws, I am a trophy of God's grace. I believe my life experience thus far, including some that has been painful, is evidence of God's gracious workings. Rather than living a life with a chip on one's shoulder, we do better to thank God for the experiences we have had and see these as ways that God can use us. I therefore commend God's grace to the wavering, anxious, perplexed, discouraged and disbelieving. It is what enables us to live as disciples of Jesus in an often hostile world, and it is what will lead us home.

Chapter 19: My twelve favourite Bible characters

Introduction

If I were to enquire as to your twelve favourite Bible characters by virtue of their legacy of notably blessing you personally, what would your answer be?

I would be surprised if your answer is the same as mine and would not be surprised if none on your list appear on mine. I suspect a major reason for this is none of our journeys, temperaments, interests, outlooks, axioms, *etc.*, are the same, often far from it, yet these are the very factors that influence our choices. As far as my choices go, which I am about to identify, along with reasons why they are my choices, three are widely recognised as prophets, although in one case it was not his main job; and the rest have, as I have argued before, acted prophetically. None were perfect and some had a notably darker side.

While there are many other worthy characters that deserve to be included, these are the ones I would cite as being my twelve favourite Bible characters if one were to press me. I have deliberately excluded Jesus of Nazareth from my list because He is more than human, for if He were to be included, since He is my Lord and Saviour, perfect in every way, He would be far at the top of the list. I should add, whatever way we look at it, we are spoiled for choice. If I think about it, there are many more "favourite Bible characters", starting with most of the prophets. One more thought is, as fascinating all these characters were and as praiseworthy were their endearing qualities, even more significant is the way God dealt with and used ordinary people, and if we are willing, He can do the same with us too.

Jephthah

This guy was an outsider. He was kicked out of his family home (his mother was a prostitute) and he was rejected by his community. If anyone had a reason for having a chip on his shoulder, it was him. While on the outside, he attracted around him a band of dodgy characters who, from what we can figure out, operated as a bunch of mercenaries. Yet this was just what was needed as Israel fell yet again under the cosh by enemies in their midst, frustrated they could do little to protect themselves, and as often happens in times of crisis they look to any who can help. They then called on a bemused Jephthah to help free them from their oppressors. He did so successfully by the power of the Holy Spirit (*i.e.* God used him) and was appointed their leader. His weak theology, coupled with doing the wrong thing, is evidenced by his willingness to sacrifice his daughter because of a foolish vow he had made to God, and afterward playing a key part in a short, bloody civil war, even though arguably he was on the right side. While his credentials for favourite may be questionable, Jephthah shows us how God can use willing outsiders, who are flawed, for His glory. And it isn't just me that recognise his faith; he is after all mentioned in the Hebrews 11 Hall of Faith, along with other dubious characters: Gideon, Barak, Samson.

Job

As we have already reflected, the book of Job begs the question, although not answered to our entire satisfaction, that has been asked from time immemorial: why do the innocent and righteous suffer? It is likely set in the time of the Patriarchs and Job's story is recounted in cultures other than that of Israel. In a nutshell, Job was a man who had everything, was materially well off, well respected and life as far as he was concerned was hunky-dory. Moreover, he honoured God, and importantly God recognised him as righteous. Unbeknown to Job, there was a confab going on in heaven involving God and Satan. Satan told God that Job only honoured Him because God had blessed Job. As if to test this proposition, God allowed Satan to take everything away from Job that he had, except his life and, after he did, Job still worshipped God. We then trawl though many chapters of dialogue between Job and his three comforters, plus toward the end with a young fellow, Elihu, who wanted to chip in with his own two penneth. In short, Job's friends suggested Job was not quite as good as he was made out to be and this was the reason why he suffered; and, as for Job, he tried hard to figure out, far from satisfactorily, "why me?" In the end, God intervenes, but without entirely answering Job's concerns, while telling him that he did not know what he was talking about and as God He could do whatever He wanted. He then restored to Job all that he had lost, and did so with interest. Faced as we are with perplexing conundrums, including the unfairness of life, and a God who does not always / often intervene in the way we want, it is well to reflect on Job's patience and his trust in God while undergoing suffering.

Abraham

Abraham is a fascinating character, starting with him being the founding father of the Jewish race who, whether modern humanity recognise it or not, still have a central part to play in the unravelling of God's great purposes. Just as amazing was how God plucked Abraham out of what might be seen as obscurity, telling him to leave his country, family, and father's home for a land God will show him. Abraham literally stepped into the unknown, because of his faith in God's promise. Abraham did what he was told and never stopped believing God would do what He said, including Abraham being the father of a great nation special to God. While there were signs of his faith floundering, because the promise was delayed, including him not possessing any of the Promised Land other than a plot for a family tomb, and a long delay to the arrival of his son and heir, Isaac, he continued to honour God and God blessed him. One example of Abraham's faith was his willingness to sacrifice his own son because that was what God had instructed him to do. A further example concerned his interceding on behalf of Sodom and Gomorrah which God said he would destroy, but was prepared not to do so if according to Abraham's request enough righteous people were found. God refers centuries later to Abraham, his friend; what better accolade?

Jacob

The first thing I notice about Jacob was how unlikeable he was. Comparing Jacob with his older brother, by a minute, Esau, we see Jacob as sneaky and a mummy's boy and Esau as not sneaky and more a man's man. Yet God, who always knows what is best, chose Jacob to take and pass down the all-important birthright. Two key events stood out in Jacob's life: the first was at Bethel when he dreamed a dream of angels ascending and descending stairs between earth and heaven, when God promised His protection and reaffirmed the promise He gave to his grandfather Abraham; the second was at Peniel, twenty years later, having acquired two wives, several children and lots of animals. He had been outconned and chastened by his dealings with Uncle Laban and was not looking forward to again facing the brother he wronged, Esau, who he had cheated and may still be carrying a grudge, as he returned home. It was at Peniel, Jacob had his all-night wrestling match with the Angel, who he would not let go until the Lord (represented by the Angel) had blessed him, which blessing he received along with a limp he carried for the rest of his life. Peniel was where Jacob experienced true brokenness. While after, flaws in character could still be seen, there was wisdom, an aura of serenity and evidence of God's blessing. If God can do that with Jacob the Supplanter, He can do that with us. God's dealings with Jacob of humbling over a lifetime, breaking before finally using him, sets an example for us to follow. It helps us to counter feelings of self-pity as whatever our good intentions are and however any blows we received, God can use all these.

Elijah

Elijah pops up out of nowhere and without further ado predicts a drought that will only end when he says so. Such audacity raised the anger of wicked king Ahab and even more wicked queen Jezebel and Elijah goes into hiding and in full dependence on God, until such time God instructs him to confront the king. Israel was then widely practising Baal worship, encouraged by Ahab, and Elijah challenges the prophets of Baal to a contest to reveal who was the true God. YHWH God won by sending fire from heaven to consume the water-soaked animal sacrifice and the onlookers were awestruck and killed the priests of Baal and was soon followed by rain. This angered Jezebel who vowed to kill Elijah and Elijah fled for his life and in a fit of depression. Three things at least warm me to Elijah. Firstly, he said it as it was without mincing his words or trying to please others, out of obedience to God. Secondly, it was clear from the various descriptions he was a rough and ready sort and did anything but live it up in comfort. Thirdly, he was human, for he might have stood his ground given what happened on Mount Carmel but instead he ran scared and his depression was such he wanted just to roll over and die. But God in His grace uses flawed instruments like Elijah and there was work God still had for him before being whisked away in a chariot of fire. It included anointing two kings and his successor, Elisha, who he mentored. One remarkable story was exposing Ahab who, along with Jezebel, had been complicit in the murder of a righteous man, Naboth. The wonder of the Elijah narrative is as much to do with how God can use willing vessels. Before moving on to our next character, it is good to reflect there is a NT Elijah in the form of John Baptist, who lived rough, told people straight what God thought of them, who also had his moments of doubt.

Obadiah

The Bible is full of people who had small walk-on roles, never to be heard of again – and if one does not know one's Bible, may not even be recognised – and yet played significant, even heroic roles. We first come across Obadiah (not to be confused with the minor prophet) as one who was in charge of the palace of King Ahab. Obadiah feared the Lord and was very devout, yet this did not stop him doing his job doing the bidding of his wicked master, at least as far as his conscience allowed. No doubt he did perform his job admirably, and it was while about the king's business that he bumped into the prophet Elijah. During the period while Elijah had been away, wicked Queen Jezebel was busily rounding up the true prophets of the Lord and killing them, while Obadiah was doing his best to secretly protect them by hiding them in caves and ensuring their temporal needs were being met. Understandably, Obadiah was fearful meeting the great man, as being seen to be colluding with the king's enemy might well cost him his life. But he did what Elijah asked and set up a meeting between Ahab and Elijah, and we hear no more about him after that. Obadiah was one of those people I admire that just gets on with life, making the best out of whatever was thrown at him, using the unique opportunity afforded him by doing something amazingly significant (in his case by hiding the prophet), being clearly the right person to do this important job, and thus he honoured God.

Jeremiah

Jeremiah will forever be known as the doom and gloom prophet, and for good reason. He started young and was not too confident, but God called him, said He would tell him what to say and that he needed to toughen up. He had to do some daft things from a human perspective. He did so at God's bequest and suffered terribly at the hands of them he managed to upset, all because he spoke God's truth and did so with pinpoint accuracy. While he was a contemporary of good King Josiah, the four southern kingdom kings that followed, prior to Judah being taken into exile, were bad, and so were the people. God had had enough; they had reached the point of no return despite many warnings and they were ripe for judgment. The people somehow expected that everything would turn out alright, a message that most of the other prophets proclaimed and which was one the people wanted to hear. But Jeremiah stuck to his guns, despite knowing that doing so would harm him. His message was Judah had reached the point of no return and God's judgment was they would go into Babylonian exile for 70 years and the best they could do is accept the inevitable and make peace, which also made Jeremiah seem like a traitor. Notwithstanding, he spoke words of comfort too – judgment would be followed by mercy, and ruin by revival. If there is an example that I would want to follow, it is that of Jeremiah who spoke needed truth to power and did what God required of him. It also serves as an example that it is never too young to start being used by God. Today, his message strangely resonates in the light of events we see unravelling around us.

Daniel

If you want a best example of a goody two-shoes character in the Bible, then Daniel is your man. We first find out about him when as a teenager he was taken into exile, right at the beginning and, seventy years later, at the end of the exile, he was still around. For that entire period, he was faithful to God, obeying the Law down to a tee, even when it meant being thrown into the lion's den. But he also won favour with three pagan kings by the way he conducted himself, impressed by his wisdom and ability as a civil servant, as well as how spot-on were his dreams and visions; although he also attracted enemies who were jealous of him. Some of Daniel's prophecies are still to be fulfilled and some are remarkably significant today. Given the accuracy of his prophecies that were fulfilled, down to the fine detail, we can ponder on those words with confident expectancy. He lived a disciplined life, exemplified by his prayer life (three times daily) and his eating habits. He loved God and His people. The fervour, passion and serious intent in his prayers were amazing. The old Sunday School chorus, *"Dare to be a Daniel, dare to stand alone! dare to have a purpose firm! dare to make it known"*, pretty much summarises what Daniel was about and throws down the gauntlet: whether we are young or old, we too can dare to be a Daniel, who stayed the course, in good times and bad. What is there not to like?

Stephen

Stephen will forever be known as the first Christian martyr. He died not long after the Church began on the Day of Pentecost, following Jesus' death and resurrection. He first comes to our attention when it became clear in those early days that the practical needs of the Church, specifically in taking care of the poor, including widows, needed to be attended to by persons other than the Apostles, to ensure their needs were properly met. Therefore, they appointed seven deacons, one of which was Stephen. We are told Stephen was a man full of faith and the Holy Spirit; he brimmed with God's grace and energy. Besides no doubt effectively carrying out this important practical job, Stephen was keen to win people to Christ and was diligent in doing so, and to such an extent that detractors could not refute his arguments. This upset some of the Jewish religious folk, who felt threatened by the new sect. They had him before the High Council on a trumped-up charge. Whence Stephen gave an amazing defence of the Christian faith, but it only went to anger his accusers. In the end, Stephen was stoned to death, and died ever gracious and forgiving his killers. While many reading this will not have to face what Stephen faced, we live in a day when Christians are being persecuted in many countries throughout the world, because of their Christian faith. Should that time ever come to us, we can take inspiration from Stephen, a faithful follower of Jesus, even until death.

Barnabas

Barnabas will be remembered as one who looked out for others, especially those needing support and encouragement, whom the Apostles looked to, to sort out tricky situations like how to respond when Gentiles were becoming Christians. He was the man who mentored Paul after his Damascus Road experience, when other believers would not touch him with a barge pole, and who would later accompany Paul on his missionary journeys, willing to play second fiddle until they parted company on a matter of principle. He is depicted as a good man, full of the Holy Spirit, and an encourager. My own background tends to put Paul on such a pedestal that to criticize him might be considered sacrilegious, and yet Barnabas stood up to him when he considered Paul to be in the wrong. Barnabas represents an example of how Christian discipleship should be carried out. We first learn of him as one who was dedicated to the cause when he sold land so that the proceeds could be used for gospel ministry. We later see him encourage new believers who had nothing worldly wise to repay him and then stick his neck out to support the one forever known as the great apostle, Paul. Given it is an obvious need today, what stands out for me, was how he went out of his way and at personal cost, to encourage others, especially in the ways of God.

Ruth

Ruth was an amazing woman. Before I found my own "Ruth", she would have been the sort of girl I would have liked to marry, and her husband (Boaz) the sort of man I wanted to be. If it were not for the fact Ruth married two (not at the same time) Israelites who were to be important links in the Messianic line, and whose story is told in the Bible, we would never have known about her. She was a Moabitess and, generally in the Bible, anything to do with Moab was seen negatively. She is introduced as one of the daughters-in-law to Naomi, who, while living in Moab, her husband and two sons died. She decided to return home and told her two daughters-in-law to remain where they were. But Ruth insisted she return with her, despite bleak prospects. Her "*Where you go, I go; and where you live, I'll live. Your people are my people, your God is my God; where you die, I'll die, and that's where I'll be buried, so help me God – not even death itself is going to come between us*" speech is beautiful. In one of those remarkable "God instances" that the Bible is good at recounting, she met Boaz, an honourable, righteous man, who happened to be Ruth's kinsman-redeemer. They fall in love, marry and have a son who happened to be in direct line to Jesus. Ruth's virtue was there for all to see, and it was at a premium, given the story took place in the time of the Judges. Just as Boaz showed the sort of character men should emulate, Ruth did much the same for women.

Mary Magdalene

The jury has been out for two thousand years as to what sort of woman Mary Magdalene was. While it is often thought she was an immoral woman and a prostitute, maybe the same person who anointed Jesus with precious ointment and washed His feet with her hair, we cannot be sure. What we do know is that Jesus cast from her seven demons, suggesting up to then she was a troubled woman with perhaps a dark past. She became one of his followers, along with other women who took care of some of the practical needs of Jesus' disciples. She features particularly at the end as she witnesses first hand Jesus dying on the cross. Then, on that third day, she is first to arrive at the tomb to anoint the body, and to her surprise and great joy she discovered that Jesus is *alive*. Her Jesus encounter was thrilling: *"She, thinking that he was the gardener, said, "Sir, if you took him, tell me where you put him so I can care for him." Jesus said, "Mary." Turning to face him, she said in Hebrew, "Rabboni!" meaning "Teacher!"* She was first to witness His resurrection (and this was a woman!) It was she who told Jesus' disciples of this wonderful news. Mary was a faithful follower of Jesus with a caring, serving heart who, despite whatever her earlier life had been, Jesus was pleased to reveal Himself to before anyone else.

Conclusion

Having completed "my twelve", I can easily come up with a second (and even a third) list, e.g., Moses, Caleb, Boaz, Hannah, David, Isaiah, Hosea, Hezekiah, Nehemiah, John the Baptist, Paul, Priscilla (and I do so in the chapter that follows this). When two friends shared what their lists were, I found them to be a lot different to mine, but it only goes to show how spoiled for choice we are. It is worth being reminded while most of the folk chosen the Bible commends, none were given a free pass when they did the wrong thing or showed flaws in character or limitations, which makes it all the more amazing God uses fallible humans to accomplish His purposes. Many memorable Bible characters did much in the Lord's service. Just as He used them, He can do so with us too!

Chapter 20: Twelve more favourite Bible characters

Moses

I count myself blessed for having been sent along to Sunday School as a child. One of the characters that kept cropping up in our lessons was Moses. Stories of him being put in a basket and hidden in the bulrushes away from the clutches of the wicked Pharaoh, meeting with God at the burning bush and him leading the Children of Israel out of Egypt bondage, crossing the Red Sea and wandering in the wilderness are three of many that come to mind. In my teens, I remember reading a commentator make the point Moses spent forty years thinking he was a somebody, forty years learning he was a nobody and forty years experiencing how God could use a nobody, and the thought impacted me.

Given how much is written about Moses, much of which is positive, that he is the major figure in four of the books of the Bible and referred to in many more, with no shortage of evidence of Moses' qualities, the fact is that he was not allowed to enter the Promised Land despite being the one person more than anyone else, other than the Almighty, who had made it possible. It only goes to show his human failures were significant enough for God not to allow it. It was the high price he had to pay for his disobedience when he struck the rock.

After Moses had his God encounter, aged 80, while looking after his father-in-law's sheep, putting aside his striking the rock, he was obedient in all what God told him to do, keeping faith and being faithful, even when the natural odds for the desired outcome and the going was getting tough with God delaying doing what He promised. While he could only get a glimpse of God's backside, given he could not stand in the midst of His glory, he did in effect speak to God face to face and God confided in Moses in a way God has rarely otherwise done with others. Moses showed his compassion and intimacy with God when he was able to successfully intercede on behalf of Israel after God said He would cut them off because of their unbelief, and even managed to change God's mind, because of the Golden Calf incident, one of many when Israel rebelled against God.

Perhaps the one thing that stands out among his many other qualities was Moses meekness: *"Now Moses was a very humble man, more humble than anyone else on the face of the earth"* Numbers 12:3. While this quality is often not one that is highly rated according to many human standards, it is important when it comes to God deciding to use us, and one now in my dotage I rate highly.

Caleb

Not long after entering into the wilderness, Caleb was one of the twelve spies sent by Moses into Canaan (one from each of the twelve tribes). Their task, over a period of 40 days, was to explore the land God had promised to Israel, and to make an assessment of the geographical features of the land, the strength and numbers of the population, the agricultural potential (including bringing back samples of the produce), the actual performance of the land, and settlement patterns (including where there were strongholds).

Moses asked them to be courageous and to bring back reports. All the spies came back and testified that this was indeed a land flowing with milk and honey, but ten of them advised against trying to possess it because of the giants who lived there would prevent them. Caleb (aged 40) along with Joshua gave contrary counsel and said Israel could and should enter the land because God was with them. Tragically, Israel was persuaded by the argument of the ten that it would be fool hardy to try to possess the land, and it was not until 45 years later Caleb, who kept the faith throughout and along with Joshua were the only people allowed in to possess the land, under Joshua's leadership.

In laying claim to his inheritance, Caleb reminded Joshua of the promise God gave Moses many years prior: *"Surely there shall not one of these men of this evil generation see that good land, which I swore to give unto your fathers. Save Caleb the son of Jephunneh; he shall see it, and to him will I give the land that he hath trodden upon, and to his children, because he hath wholly followed the Lord"* Deuteronomy 1:35 - 36.

Moreover, it was the land where those very giants that so frightened off the people were concentrated that he asked for: *"Now therefore give me this mountain, whereof the Lord spake in that day; for thou heardest in that day how the Anakims were there, and that the cities were great and fenced: if so be the Lord will be with me, then I shall be able to drive them out, as the Lord said. And Joshua blessed him, and gave unto Caleb the son of Jephunneh Hebron for an inheritance"* Joshua 14:12 -13.

What I find attractive about Caleb is he kept his strong faith over all these years, not allowing age or fear to get in the way of claiming his inheritance, holding onto the promise he had received, maintaining his commitment to the Lord and, unlike many, was whole hearted when it came to following the Lord.

Boaz

Boaz was an amazing guy that was lucky enough to marry one of the loveliest ladies in the Bible – Ruth. The entire story, told in the book of Ruth, comes as a refreshing interlude. It took place in a tumultuous time in Israel's history that often was not sweetness and light – that is recounted in the Book of Judges.

I love Boaz because he was an honourable and God-fearing man, who lived in a time when honour and the fear of God were at a premium. He was, from what we can make out, a prosperous land owner, who happened to care for the poor. If anyone wants an example of why capitalism is better than communism, Boaz is it. The fact there was not too many of his ilk around is a reason why it may not be. The Law, under which Israel was meant to operate, made few demands on individual entrepreneurs, but made ample provision where the haves had to take care of the have nots, and when that happened society thrived. Boaz discharged all his obligation, e.g. relating to gleaning – and more.

It happened (brilliant Bible euphemism for a God instance) that at that time impoverished Ruth gleaned in Boaz's field and he ensured she was more than taken care of. I particularly like his first entrance on the scene when he greeted his workers with "the Lord bless you" (now wouldn't that be nice if it happened today). The wonderful happenstance bit concerns Boaz as Ruth's kinsman redeemer. Being a close relative of Ruth's late husband, he had the right to marry her according to Jewish Law. Except he was not first in line to marry the widow Ruth. Someone else had first refusal, so to speak.

Which brings me to another great aspect of Boaz's character and why honour comes to mind. He did everything by the book (something this ducker and diver especially notes), treating Ruth, after she dropped the bombshell in what had been a beautiful set-up, and everyone involved with great respect. In the end he married the lovely Ruth and their son, Obed, was a direct ancestor of Jesus. There is no better example in the Bible of how to conduct oneself than Boaz.

Hannah

There are two amazing things about Hannah that makes her one of my favourite Bible characters. Firstly, she was a barren woman who desperately wanted a child, not helped as she was taunted by her (loving, God fearing) husband's other wife, and so she prayed to the Lord ... *"she vowed a vow, and said," O Lord of hosts, if thou wilt indeed look on the affliction of thine handmaid, and remember me, and not forget thine handmaid, but wilt give unto thine handmaid a man child, then I will give him unto the Lord all the days of his life, and there shall no razor come upon his head"* 1Samuel 1:11.

God answered Hannah's prayer. The result was Samuel, who eventually became one of the great prophets, her fulfilling her vow and God giving her five more children. When she handed Samuel over into the custody of Eli the priest, she prayed a remarkable prayer that revealed such a tender heart, a love for the poor and lowly, and a simple trust in the Lord that is reminiscent to that of Mary, in her Magnificat, that was likely inspired by Hannah's prayer.

"... My heart rejoiceth in the Lord, mine horn is exalted in the Lord: my mouth is enlarged over mine enemies; because I rejoice in thy salvation. There is none holy as the Lord: for there is none beside thee: neither is there any rock like our God ... The Lord killeth, and maketh alive: he bringeth down to the grave, and bringeth up. The Lord maketh poor, and maketh rich: he bringeth low, and lifteth up. He raiseth up the poor out of the dust, and lifteth up the beggar from the dunghill, to set them among princes, and to make them inherit the throne of glory: for the pillars of the earth are the Lord's, and he hath set the world upon them ..." (1Samuel 2:1, 2:6-8).

The second amazing thing about Hannah's story is it reminds us that there have been many great men of God down the ages who were indebted to a praying mother. While we cannot make our children into what we would like them to be, we can still pray for them that God will have His way in their lives.

David

David is an interesting character. There are things about him I dislike and that goes beyond his murder of Uriah the Hittite to cover up his adulterous affair with Uriah's wife, Bathsheba. While David lived in a violent age, he could also be violent toward those who crossed him. He couldn't have been much of a father. Two of his sons tried to steal the throne from him. David's ego led to him doing a not-needed census which attracted divine judgment. YET how many among the good and the great in the Bible could be called a man after God's own heart besides David? It was David's heart, something the Bible rates as very important, that draws him to our attention in the first place.

David was the youngest among eight brothers, a mere shepherd boy, who was almost overlooked when the prophet Samuel called by to anoint the next king Israel, knowing only it was to be a son of David's father, Jesse. In checking out sons one to seven, God had to tell Samuel that, while man looks at the outward appearance, God looks at the heart. Given that David was the one who fitted the bill and was God's choice, it was he who Samuel anointed.

Soon all could see that special quality which God saw. The armies of Israel were set against those of the Philistines. Their champion, Goliath, challenged Israel's champion to single handed combat, with the winner taking the spoils. David alone responded to the call. Goliath had defied the armies of the living God and all that mattered to David was to fight in God's name.

There is much about his story that is of interest, including how he established the kingdom, going from his father's house, to be part of the Royal Court, an outlaw on the run and then ruling as king, and that from his lineage the future Messiah would come. The importance he attached to the Ark of the Covenant and to the building of the Temple are especially noteworthy. Incredible but true, half of the 150 Psalms were likely written by David and these have blessed many besides myself in the 3000 years that since have passed. His significance throughout the Bible after his death is huge, including his association with the Messiah, who when he came first time was referred to as "the Son of David".

Back to the business of the heart, David could and did stray from the Lord, but was willing to be corrected and quick to repent. Besides establishing Israel to be the most secure it has ever been, because his heart was for God, incorporating doing His will and a desire for God to be honoured and glorified, the messianic promise, and his amazing Psalms that continue to bless lovers of God today, all that and more are reasons for his greatness and making him a favourite.

Isaiah

When I look at Isaiah, I do not see an outstandingly charismatic in personality character but rather a modest, faithful servant of the Lord. Isaiah effectively wrote what my early mentors referred to as the fifth gospel, touching on all aspects of the gospel story. He combined magnificently aspects such as judgement and mercy, holiness and love, righteousness and hope. His wonderfully memorable quotes, taken together, exceed that of any other book of the Bible in terms of number, profoundness and sublimity.

Isaiah is known as the court prophet and was of royal descent and was able to regularly rub shoulders with the high and mighty. Yet in having that access it did not corrupt him. Over a period of more than forty years he faithfully prophesied without fear or favour, under five different kings, ranging from the very good to the very bad. It is believed that under the fifth, wicked Manasseh, he was told not to prophesy and was so hated that he suffered a martyr's death. But Isaiah first comes to our attention under, what started off as good and ended up as a bad king, Uzziah, for: "*In the year that king Uzziah died I saw also the Lord sitting upon a throne, high and lifted up, and his train filled the temple ... And one cried unto another, and said, Holy, holy, holy, is the Lord of hosts: the whole earth is full of his glory*" Isaiah 6:1,3.

It was Isaiah's vision of this thrice holy God that defined his ministry from then on. Thereafter, he repeatedly referred to God as "*the Holy One of Israel*". Following that vision, there was the call of God, which the now humbled and purged of sin Isaiah responded to. However, it came with the salutary warning that people were not going to heed his words: "*Also I heard the voice of the Lord, saying, "Whom shall I send, and who will go for us?" Then said I," Here am I; send me." And he said, "Go, and tell this people, Hear ye indeed, but understand not; and see ye indeed, but perceive not. Make the heart of this people fat, and make their ears heavy, and shut their eyes; lest they see with their eyes, and hear with their ears, and understand with their heart, and convert, and be healed*" Isaiah 6:8-10.

How blessed, we who live now are, that Isaiah was able to prophesy such tremendous stuff. Much of which has been fulfilled down to the letter, *e.g.* concerning the first coming of the Messiah, and will be, e.g. the second coming of the Messiah, but that he faithfully and consistently responded to God's call.

Hosea

When we think of Hosea, we might well want to compare him with another outstanding prophet, his near contemporary, Amos (whose concern for social justice, for example, could also qualify him as a favourite). Both prophesied to the Northern Kingdom, Israel, and were the last to do so before Israel was taken into captivity by the Assyrians.

What they each saw was quite similar – a nation where many (but not all) were doing well, often were smug and self-satisfied but, as was manifest in many different ways, had turned from God and broken their covenant with Him. It was only a matter of time, unless they repented, for God to judge. While, as would be expected, Amos and Hosea messages had much in common, their approaches were far different. One commentator has associated the notions of affection, wooing, tender and mercy with Hosea and justice, accusation, warning and toughness with Amos. The truth for any gospel preacher today is that both emphases are needed.

Hosea introduces and develops the importance of what is encapsulated in the Hebrew as *"Chesed"*. This is used to depict kindness or love between people, of the devotional piety of people and faithfulness towards God and love or mercy of God towards humanity. It is seen in the marital motif of troth and betroth. The thrilling thing to note in Hosea's story is how the message and the man interacted, for God often used the life experiences of individual prophets in their respective ministries. Hosea married a prostitute but, despite her unfaithfulness, went out of his way and at personal cost to woo her back into the marital home. What Hosea was doing with Gomer, his wife, is what God has been doing all along with his faithless people, Israel. From his own painful experience, he gained insight into how God felt.

"Sow to yourselves in righteousness, reap in mercy; break up your fallow ground: for it is time to seek the Lord, till he come and rain righteousness upon you" Hosea 10:12 and *"I will heal their backsliding, I will love them freely: for mine anger is turned away from him"* Hosea 14:4. These passages have ever been God's desire for His people.

I am encouraged God uses our painful experiences as we serve Him and while my experience was nothing like Hosea's, it somehow particularly resonates.

Hezekiah

As to my reasons for making Hezekiah a favourite, we need go no further than how he is introduced in the Book of Kings.

"Twenty and five years old was he when he began to reign; and he reigned twenty and nine years in Jerusalem. His mother's name also was Abi, the daughter of Zachariah. And he did that which was right in the sight of the Lord, according to all that David his father did. He removed the high places, and brake the images, and cut down the groves, and brake in pieces the brazen serpent that Moses had made: for unto those days the children of Israel did burn incense to it: and he called it Nehushtan. He trusted in the Lord God of Israel; so that after him was none like him among all the kings of Judah, nor any that were before him. For he clave to the

Lord, and departed not from following him, but kept his commandments, which the Lord commanded Moses. And the Lord was with him; and he prospered whithersoever he went forth: and he rebelled against the king of Assyria, and served him not" 2 Kings 18:2-7.

As for context and what makes Hezekiah so remarkable is that his father Ahaz was a bad king, the people had largely turned away from God and he had his work cut out in order to turn things around. While good and bad can be seen as relative terms, following the divided kingdom, all 19 kings of Israel may be deemed as bad and 12 of the 20 kings of Judah. Hezekiah went that step further as far as good is concerned by removing the High Places. However, even though we read he stopped serving the king of Assyria, he paid a hefty price to be left alone, having to pay him tribute, as well as, later in life, when his flaws could be seen and facing an early death at the hands of God for not putting his house in order, he was granted a reprieve due to his repentance.

Hezekiah's finest hour perhaps, that showed his admirable character, was when the Assyrians invaded. They were threatening to completely subjugate Judah, just as they had done not so many years earlier with Israel. Humanly speaking, there was little to be done to stop them. What follows is one of many amazing prayers we find in the Bible, as Hezekiah laid the threatening letter from the Assyrians, which advised surrender, before the Lord.

"*Incline thine ear, O Lord, and hear; open thine eyes, O Lord, and see: and hear all the words of Sennacherib, which hath sent to reproach the living God. Of a truth, Lord, the kings of Assyria have laid waste all the nations, and their countries, and have cast their gods into the fire: for they were no gods, but the work of men's hands, wood and stone: therefore they have destroyed them. Now therefore, O Lord our God, save us from his hand, that all the kingdoms of the earth may know that thou art the Lord, even thou only*" Isaiah 37:16-20.

As for the answer to prayer, it was truly miraculous and shows what just one angel can do: "*Then the angel of the Lord went forth, and smote in the camp of the Assyrians a hundred and fourscore and five thousand: and when they arose early in the morning, behold, they were all dead corpses*" Isaiah 37:36.

Nehemiah

Like most of our chosen favourites, if we wanted to know what made them tick, we should get to know the context in which they operated. This is particularly so in the case of Nehemiah. Readers are referred to earlier chapters of this book and the books of Nehemiah and of his close contemporary (another amazing fellow) Ezra. Nehemiah appears on the scene nearly one hundred years after the first exiles returned to Judah and things weren't looking good. The glorious return that had been anticipated, culminating with the arrival on the scene of Israel's Messiah, had not materialised and wouldn't do so for another 400 years. Most of those who were exiled never returned.

Nehemiah's job was an interesting one. He was the cupbearer to King Artaxerxes, there in Babylon, watching the fortunes of the returnees with concerned interest from afar. While his job meant that if, when tasting the king's food and drink, it was found to be poisoned, he would be the first to know. It was a responsible position and one in which he could and did gain the king's confidence, a thing he could exploit to bring about the purposes of God.

As for news about those exiles, it was concerning: "*Hanani, one of my brethren, came, he and certain men of Judah; and I asked them concerning the Jews that had escaped, which were left of the captivity, and concerning Jerusalem. And they said unto me, The remnant that are left of the captivity there in the province are in great affliction and reproach: the wall of Jerusalem also is broken down, and the gates thereof are burned with fire*" Nehemiah 1:2-3.

Where Nehemiah's greatness stood out was in his response that began, like so much of what he later did, with prayer: "*And it came to pass, when I heard these words, that I sat down and wept, and mourned certain days, and fasted, and prayed before the God of heaven, And said, I beseech thee, O Lord God of heaven, the great and terrible God, that keepeth covenant and mercy for them that love him and observe his commandments: Let thine ear now be attentive, and thine eyes open, that thou mayest hear the prayer of thy servant, which I pray before thee now, day and night, for the children of Israel thy servants, and confess the sins of the children of Israel, which we have sinned against thee: both I and my father's house have sinned ...*" Nehemiah 4:3-7. This was followed by Nehemiah claiming God's promise and asking God's favour regards what he could do about remedying the situation.

The rest of the Book of Nehemiah revolves round narrative of his practical response, including supervising building the wall and encouraging and organising the people, often taking the side of the underdog and joining with them. At the same time, he took to task, without fear or favour, those who had acted wrongly, despite all sorts of barriers, both from within and without, always prayerfully entreating God, often with pithy, down to earth prayers. One can't help but admire his tenacity and long for Nehemiah types in our own day!

John the Baptist

John the Baptist is the New Testament version of Elijah and the reasons that drew me to Elijah, drew me to John as well. While Elijah suddenly appears on the scene to prophesy a period of drought, John was in action before he was even born (an important fact in today's pro-life deliberations), when he leaped in his mother's womb when she came face to face with Mary, who was herself carrying Jesus.

Then before Jesus starts His ministry, being himself baptized by John, we find him as *"The voice of him that crieth in the wilderness, Prepare ye the way of the Lord, make straight in the desert a highway for our God"* Isaiah 40:3. Like Elijah, he was fully sold out when it came to doing the job God had given him to do and it including living out what has come across as an austere, no frills existence: *"John had his raiment of camel's hair, and a leathern girdle about his loins; and his meat was locusts and wild honey"* Matthew 3:4.

It appears he was effective as many showed their repentance by being baptized. His message was simple, fearless, direct and effectual: *"Repent ye: for the kingdom of heaven is at hand"* Matthew 3:2. However, it gained him some powerful enemies, such as the religious establishment, who he referred to as a generation of vipers and King Herod, who he rebuked for taking his brother's wife. This led to John's arrest, a period of self-doubt and finally losing his head. But always he was pointing people to the Christ: *"Behold, the Lamb of God, who takes away the sin of the world!"* John 1:29 and away from himself: *"He must increase, but I must decrease"* John 3:30.

There is no greater commendation than that given by Jesus: *"Verily I say unto you, among them that are born of women there hath not risen a greater than John the Baptist: notwithstanding he that is least in the kingdom of heaven is greater than he. And from the days of John the Baptist until now the kingdom of heaven suffereth violence, and the violent take it by force"* Matthew 11:11-12.

While the vital task of preaching the gospel nowadays requires wisdom and sometimes tact and discretion, we could do with more John the Baptists who say what needs saying, without fear or favour or concern at upsetting those sinners who need to repent. While one may question use of his methods in today's snowflake culture, his message remains pertinent. We all have good reason to be grateful for John, who prepared the way for Jesus.

Paul

I was reticent including Paul in my favourites list as I felt sure, if I were around in his day, we might not have got on and I might have reacted against his self-assuredness. To put it in another way – his perspective was the only one that truly mattered. The parting of ways between him and Barnabas suggests it may not just be me! Yet it is also easy to see why Paul should be included, if for no other reason than, if you are on my theological wavelength, your understanding of the glorious gospel likely owes more to the writings of the Apostle Paul than to anyone else, and in that regard we are kindred spirits.

Having set out his store: "*For I am not ashamed of the gospel of Christ: for it is the power of God unto salvation to every one that believeth; to the Jew first, and also to the Greek*" Romans 1:16, Paul meticulously provides the most powerful argument as to why the gospel needs to be proclaimed, received and lived out that I have ever come across. "*For all have sinned, and come short of the glory of God; Being justified freely by his grace through the redemption that is in Christ Jesus*" Romans 3:23,24 is but one of many memorable Paul statements.

Paul's writings virtually dominate the New Testament. 13 of its 27 books were written by him and in one other (Acts) is the major player. And there are so many more strings to Paul bow, beginning with his conversion experience. No one is born a Christian and to become one you need to be converted. Paul's conversion experience was as dramatic as it comes, encountering the risen Christ on his way to Damascus to arrest the very Christians he was persecuting. From that point onward he was wholehearted in discharging the commission Jesus had given him, by way of his various missionary journeys, culminating in his imprisonment in Rome and likely execution. The variety of approaches and methods Paul used is text book stuff when it comes to carrying out the Great Commission, showing how "*he that winneth souls is wise*" Proverbs 11:30.

"*For to me to live is Christ, and to die is gain*" Philippians 1:21 and "*I press toward the mark for the prize of the high calling of God in Christ Jesus*" Philippians 3:14. These are two of many memorable, profound Pauline quotes. Paul will be forever remembered as the great apostle, serving the Church that Christ himself had founded and His cause, yet was Christ's humble servant, who could say: *"by the grace of God I am what I am"* 1 Corinthians 15:10. Christians down the ages owe Paul a huge debt.

Priscilla

So we come to the last of my favourites, notwithstanding there is still room for many more. Priscilla is part of a formidable husband and wife team: Aquila and Priscilla. Every time her name is mentioned: Acts 18:2, Acts 18:18, Acts 18:26, Romans 16:3, 1 Corinthians 16:19 and 2 Timothy 4:19, so is Aquila's. Despite this I have selected Priscilla rather than her other half.

We live in a day when we see many attempts to redress millennia of gender imbalance, even re-writing history, but the fact remains that the Bible, like most ancient books, says a lot more about men than it does women. Without wanting to patronise, Priscilla's role, in what might be seen as a minor character part, was a significant one, not just because of the part they she along with her husband played in the lives of two significant men, Paul and Apollos. What I found as outstanding is the couple showed what is so often is sadly not seen, that is, how husbands and wives can play a powerful complementary role in the cause of the Kingdom and much else besides. Aquila was a blessed man.

We first come across them when they had been expelled from Rome and set up in their business as tent makers in Corinth, at a time when the Apostle Paul was about to come to town. They were kindred spirits in sharing the same trade and the same faith, and Paul lodged with the couple for over a year before they all moved onto Ephesus. It was at Ephesus that they met an earnest, eloquent preacher, Apollos, who was deficient in certain important aspects of doctrine. The way the couple took Apollos under their wing and explained the faith more fully to him is a great example of how "it" should be done.

As for the rest of their story, we are left to read between the lines. Their impact on the early church was likely considerable, evidenced when Paul warmly commends the couple as his co-workers in three of his letters. As for hospitality, this is further seen with them hosting a house church. As for business, which they were likely proficient in, this was a vehicle they were able to use to share the gospel. As for how couples ought to work together, there is no better example in all of the Bible than Aquila and Priscilla.

While in failing to live up to the demands of being "head of the house" men often have a lot to answer for. If the household happens to be a dysfunctional one, there is a lot to commend the supportive role of women like Priscilla, reminiscent of the wife of noble character described in Proverbs 31:10-31.

Chapter 21: 2020, 2021 and the prophetic

An extraordinary undertaking

Writing this chapter has been a challenging undertaking, unlike with that taken in the chapters preceding this. There I offered "a view" when it seemed appropriate to do so, and tried to concentrate on adopting principles of sound exegesis, and to an extent emulate the approach of past Bible teachers I admired: the likes of people like John Stott, Jim Packer and David Pawson, to name but three, and before that: C.H.Spurgeon, J.C.Ryle and the great Puritan writers. In this chapter, I go down rabbit holes these great men may not have ventured, or, if they had, they might have seen what was down there and turned back early. I did check out some of those who I describe as "political prophets" though, along with secular types dismissed by many as conspiracy theorists, many of which may not be rated much by those who approve my list of exegetical greats. I found, I often had to go out on a limb, not finding encouragement where I might have expected it, yet sometimes finding it in surprising quarters. I say so with a degree of trepidation, since history is full of people adopting such an approach and going off the proverbial rails. I therefore add my customary "test and weigh" rider. I am talking about what is happening in the world right now and what might happen in the near future, a topic many Prophets of the Bible were familiar and occupied with. I also write by way of a journal. Between December 2020 and February 2021, as I sought to do what I encourage my readers to do – besides "test and weigh", to "watch and pray", I found myself deeply exercised by what was going on in the world and trying to reconcile what was happening with my own hopes and what some of these political prophets said, and was humbled in the process, realising how little I knew and that God's ways are greater than I could ever imagine.

2020

Writing this final chapter of my book as a momentous year (2020 – it would not be hyperbole to say it could be the most momentous of my entire life thus far) draws to an end, but I wish to raise what I consider to be an important subject to add to the many already covered – relating the present to the prophetic. I do so with a health warning. In other "Chapters" of the book I have tried to follow my exegetical heroes of the past, but here I divert somewhat and shoot from the hip as it were, sharing what some might see as my own controversial views – yet some of these pertain to what divides Christians today and are thus relevant because it is God's intention to present His Son with a radiant, pure and unified bride and for His people to respond appropriately and not how I, or anyone else, thinks.

Ever since the beginning of the year (2020), things were happening in the world to draw our attention, ranging from bush fires in Australia to plagues of locusts in Africa and, from a British perspective, the UK formally announcing it would be leaving the EU (deal or no deal), thus honouring the 2016 EU Referendum outcome. But in my view, there are two stories that stand out and both have yet to fully play out. The first involves USA President Donald Trump. The year began with his, as it turned out, unsuccessful impeachment trial; the year ended, following the USA Presidential election, with his opponent Joe Biden claiming victory and Trump alleging there was massive fraud and disputing the result.

The world awaits final confirmation as to who will be inaugurated as the next President on January 20th 2021. The second involves the Coronavirus crisis. It would not be overstating it to say this has had a dramatic effect on the whole world in terms of economic fall-out, poor mental health, social isolation and loss of freedoms and, in the midst of it, riots and protests over racial injustice. Many with anguish ask how much longer; some ask what is God saying in this? As with the Presidential election, we cannot tell what twists and turns are ahead of us and how this will play out. A third one, we could add, concerns how the long running (getting on for five years) Brexit saga will play out. In a strange way this and other "unrelated" ongoing events are more related than it seems.

As many who have read so far will know, much of 2020 has been taken up with my writing this book. It focuses on Bible exegesis and, at least in the main chapters, avoids extensively commenting on events such as highlighted in the previous paragraph or on modern-day prophets. Whilst tempting to do so given what is taking place, I have resisted, other than what I write in the rest of this section. This is partly out of respect to those interested in my insights on Bible prophecy but not my political opinions. If people want to know what I think about Trump, Coronavirus and Brexit, I refer them to articles on my blog, which I have been regularly updating over these past seven years.

My Christian upbringing, while in the main dismissive of modern-day prophets, often tried to relate events unravelling about them with the prophetic scriptures, particularly concerning the End Times. Again, I will resist the temptation, other than re-iterate my view expressed earlier that we are seeing many examples to indicate the end is near and unfulfilled prophecy fulfilled does just that. I cannot help wonder what the prophets of old would have made out of current events if they were standing in our shoes today – maybe, like one mentor of old, I could ask them that very question when I eventually get to meet them in heaven!

On the subject of modern-day prophecy, I confess I am going outside of the original remit I set myself when I began this project. After all, the title of the book is "Prophets of the Bible" and not "Prophets Today". Moreover, given my own background, there will be some interested in the subject of the title and not prophets today, especially if they are "cessationist" in their theology. So, when I refer to prophecy today, please bear with me. I believe the pronouncements of "prophets" who are around today should be considered, maybe not quite as intensely but at least seriously, as we have attempted to do with our Prophets of the Bible studies. Although others may see things differently, I have suggested today's "prophets" could be categorised into three groups:

1. False prophets (I discuss what makes a prophet false in Chapter 6);

2. Charismatic prophets who tend to operate in churches that attach importance to the present exercising of the gifts of the Spirit, including prophecy – albeit in most cases, when words of prophecy are given, these usually relate specifically to the ministry of their own church and the lives of individuals and what God intends for them;

3. Political prophets, who are perhaps a subset of the second group (including those who prophesied a second term for Trump as President), believing God speaks into the affairs of men and the world, although, in my experience, often not accepted by some in the second group.

I best speak for myself here, for while there are some who mostly agree, some do not. While there are a few friends on my page in terms of understanding what is happening in the world, many are not, including some who are close to me. One leader friend has stated that we are a people of praise, not politics, and we should focus on being upright Christians. There are also no shortage of Christian leaders bashing Christians in their flock who subscribe to a different narrative about world events than that which is presented by official sources and mainstream media, including subscribing to suspect and frowned upon "conspiracy theories".

Those so bashed react to being patronised, especially when some of those leaders are themselves following suspect agendas, *e.g.* Black Lives Matter or climate change activism, which may be seen as a diversion from the gospel. More conservative types might accept what we are seeing, even though they may be disapproving, as something God has allowed and to leave it there, and as we have seen this results in disruption in the ranks including those who agree on gospel truth. The result is often schism. Sadly, my observation, too often, is that there is spiritual one upmanship and a lack of both truth and charity on either side.

The term "conspiracy theory" has pejorative undertones and, if not based on proven fact, should be avoided or, at least some of them, tested. But what is the truth, given those we expect / hope to tell it, *e.g.* our politicians, the media, lie? Maybe 9/11, the JFK assassination, US Presidential election outcomes and the story behind Covid-19 were not according to the official narrative, as many now realise, and people are waking up. As for "Q", even if the religious consensus thinks it/they are bogus, maybe there are over 100,000 sealed indictments waiting to be served on bad guys who think they can buck the system because they own it, and maybe there are millions of children who are being trafficked by Satanic paedophiles and a global financial cabal overseen by robber barons with corrupt politicians and other elites who are firmly in their pockets, who are assisted by an evil Deep State, who see themselves to be above the law because they control it.

I have observed enough to at least ask questions. There is a lot more to what is going on in the world than what we see or are told and God who so loved the world is interested. I have come to a view, which deviates from my early Christian upbringing, that, given the stakes are high, it would be wrong if we adopt a head-in-the-sand mentality that would consign many of our fellow humans to have to face evil unchecked when we might be able to help. And what if we let things ride until we are 101% sure and even then we might ignore it? Then it will be too late.

Sadly, for some, living under oppressive regimes, the ability to resist bad government is limited and is why passages like Romans 13, that are to do with submitting to authority, are so relevant. For many, particularly Christians living under authoritarian regimes, simply to practice what their conscience tells them is right extracts a high price. It is unbiblical and anti-God to merely stand by and observe when injustice is perpetuated as it means we break the second Great Commandment, which is to love our neighbour. I should add, for the record, I am neither Conservative nor Labour, neither Republican nor Democrat. I believe it folly to put our hope in man or human institutions more than we do God, although I will support those of whatever political colour who work toward achieving justice. Rather, I am a nobody, a brand plucked from the fire, that has responded to the call of being a Watchman on the Wall, who watches and prays.

In my recent ***Red-pilling others, especially Christians*** blog, I asked, perhaps somewhat provocatively, the following questions:

1. Is Trump better for the USA and the world than Biden?
2. Was there an attempt to steal the recent USA election?
3. Is China the major threat when it comes to world powers?
4. Is Islam the major threat when it comes to religious ideology?
5. Are abortion and child sex trafficking the top social justice issues?
6. Is climate change something that is wrongly hyped up?
7. Is there a concerted effort to destroy marriage, family and religion?
8. Should we be concerned about imposition of Covid-19 vaccines?
9. Should the UK leave the EU with no deal, should it come to it?
10. Is "global reset" about empowering elites and enslaving others?
11. Is globalism / socialism worse than nationalism / conservatism?
12. Should we be concerned with 5G and merging man and machine?
13. Is the demon of political correctness trying to suppress truth?
14. Are Gates, Soros, and many politicians (all sides) villains?
15. Should we be more concerned with groups like BLM, Antifa?
16. Is much of mainstream media about peddling fake news?
17. Is big tech, like Facebook, trying to censor questioning voices?
18. Is the recent interest in racial justice an unhelpful distraction?
19. Is the professing Church largely led by hireling shepherds?
20. Should Christians be particularly concerned with the above?

I confess that my answer is *YES* to all these questions but I recognise that some of my brothers and sisters in Christ, including some reading this book, may answer *NO* and may raise important questions themselves, and there we may disagree. Some questions may have been dealt with by the time people read this and new questions arisen. I am conscious that some who share many of my theological views may answer *NO* to question 20, feeling it rather unseemly for Christians to adopt a position on the other questions. Moreover, since following the Lord Jesus Christ, promoting His Kingdom and making Christian disciples should be what unites us, holding different views on these questions should **not** be a cause for division, when in reality and regrettably in my experience it *is*. I may be wrong but, if my experience is anything to go by, the consensus once seen in the evangelical camp has now been replaced by acrimonious polarisation.

The seeming absence of a prophetic voice among church leaders is cause for lament. I have upset some by saying much of "the flock" are being led by hireling shepherds but even if that is overstating the case, poor leadership and confusion in the ranks is the disturbing reality of where the church is at. If there is a positive side to the wokeness I see, it is that I do detect a greater awareness of *the other* and resolve to find ways to do good to others, especially the less well-off. If there is a positive side to the sense of unease I see in the Body of Christ, it is seeing God work in the lives of believers who desire a greater intimacy with Him.

While I have a view as to what is right and a desire for truth (and in fairness, so do many of my detractors), the reason I make this point is that I note sadly there are entrenched opinions among Christians in different camps, which lead to intolerance and division. Often a concern for biblical holiness fails to include that for social justice. Often an acceptance of the status quo disallows for, and even opposes, those who question the official narrative. While it will not resolve what is clearly an impasse, whatever camp one may feel inclined toward, it is worth bearing in mind Paul's exhortation: "*And now abideth faith, hope, love, these three; but **the greatest of these is love***" 1 Corinthians 13:13.

There is much we do not know, which is why we have to be careful concerning *conspiracy theories,* some / many of which should be deliberately discounted or at least kept in abeyance until more facts emerge. The exponential increase in knowledge in more recent years has meant that we know much more than our forefathers did about what is truly going on, especially what is, humanly speaking, behind evil deeds. It truly has been made worse because there would seem to be a dearth of honest journalism and those journalists who are honest are not allowed to ply their craft by those who own and control said media.

I have often quoted Paul's exhortation that "*supplications, prayers, intercessions, and giving of thanks, be made for all men; for kings, and for all that are in authority"*, and the reason given is so *"that we may lead a quiet and peaceable life in all godliness and honesty"*, 1 Timothy 2:1-2; and notwithstanding our assessment that such people often fall in the bad guy camp, our priority has to be living godly lives and leave the rest to God. Another of my often referred to texts is *"for we wrestle not against flesh and blood, but against principalities, against powers, against the rulers of the darkness of this world, against spiritual wickedness in high places"* Ephesians 6:12, and that too must be borne in mind when faced with and confronting the growing tide of evil.

Again, speaking for myself, this has been a challenging personally. I hark back to my youth when a spiritual mentor pronounced God was into the business of shaking at that time, especially the Church. It seems to me, now at this time, this is particularly so as we see the professing Church fall short, led by leaders who have got it wrong. Yet the true Church arises – albeit a remnant and it has ever been thus. It has been a time to get my own house in order and rise to the challenge of practicing biblical holiness, and is something that is ongoing. It has been a time when I experienced deep depression and frustration, and was tempted to lose hope for my nation, observing a lukewarm, woke, inept church acquiescing to its enslavement and allowing the bad guys free reign to call the shots.

There is much going on to disturb us, although I still see many examples of human kindness, especially in helping the homeless, my own sphere of activity. Top of the list of disturbing matters, and the list above shows there are many, is the way Covid-19 is being handled, with more lockdowns and restrictions and every indication the forthcoming vaccine is likely to be mandatory if we are to have some semblance of freedom. As for me, my time on earth is running out as I approach my three score and ten years. Whilst I have a measure of health and *compos mentis,* it is declining. Nevertheless, I find by God's grace there is still work for this unprofitable servant to do, including writing my book, raising alarm bells, passing on the baton, showing kindness and doing good, often in small things. And there is a world to save from a Christless eternity, God's righteous kingdom to promote and sheep to be rescued from the wolves, and a part to play in bringing the glorious gospel of the Lord Jesus Christ to a runaway world with all its pitfalls and with the devil seeking whom he may devour.

Regarding modern day prophets, I confess there are some I listen to, but always with the "Test and Weigh" caveat, which I believe is biblical. Some are endorsed by charismatic churches, who believe, rightly, that God still guides His people, including through the office of prophet and the gift of prophecy. Others are false prophets, just as Jesus predicted there would be, notably those who promote prosperity teaching. While noting what I earlier titled as my group two charismatic prophets, I will not discuss much further here as it is not my subject *per se*. I do though believe we will see more of the genuinely prophetic. Some I have found oppose the views I offer above and oppose my third group, the political prophets. This I will consider, as it is within my subject of reflecting on the today's world, with the caveat that discussing individuals is too big an exercise for this reflection.

The modern-day prophets differ in what they cover. Often, it's a lot more than the future of Trump – more like the future of the world and insights into what is going on, and no doubt not all are genuine. While I am far from hanging on their every word, having considered many of their characters and theology, as well as prophecies, some of which have come to pass remarkably, I incline to the view amidst the bogus many are genuine. I have no doubt God will have the last word.

Among other things, some have boldly predicted Trump will get a second term as President. But their detractors, often with an ear to mainstream media, may have already joined with those crowning Biden as King, pointing out if their prophecies do not come to pass, it would show them up to be false, and with an added bonus that it might help shut up those "annoying Christian conspiracy theorists". I should also add: I am finding Bible prophecy, e.g. as found in the Book of Revelation, and modern-day events, increasingly aligning.

I should counsel, while we must not dismiss prophecy that is God given, we must test prophecy and not be hasty to accept a "prophet" because he happens to share our view of the world. *"Do not listen to the words of the prophets who prophesy to you, filling you with vain hopes. They speak visions of their own minds, not from the mouth of the Lord"* Jeremiah 23:16, remains true. One thing Jeremiah and company had in common was to shake people out of their complacency.

Regarding the prophetic, while my background is non-Conformist, Evangelical, non-Charismatic, I am broad in my theology. Twenty years ago, I wrote a paper entitled **Who are the Brethren?** and concluded: *"At the risk of being dismissed as a spiritual schizophrenic by my readers or a heretic by my (Plymouth) brothers, I am inclined toward a vision of the church that is Catholic in spirituality, Liberal in social activism, Reformed in doctrine, Charismatic in experience, Evangelical in zeal, Puritan in living, Methodist in organisation and Brethren in ecclesiology, but above all passionate for Jesus. Finally, although an enthusiastic researcher of Brethren history who is keen to "get it right", I am much more concerned that men* *and women, and boys and girls, walk the way, trust the truth and live the life of the Lord Jesus Christ (John 14v6); and may He be exalted, by whatever instrument He chooses, Brethren or otherwise. And may all God's people receive a touch from heaven so that they may touch earth in His glorious cause. O Lord grant us grace to lose what is dear, so we may gain Him who is dearest, and may Thy Kingdom come!"* Twenty years on, those same sentiments still apply.

I began writing this section three weeks before the end of 2020 and now we are at the end. There is much going on. It is impossible to predict what twists and turns there will be, and what new happenings will occur, much unforeseen. *"The Fat Lady has not yet sung"* may well apply to many of these situations, notably the final outcome of the USA Presidential election, and again without wanting to overstate my case, this matters as two quite different futures beckon for the world depending on what that outcome is. I have a view, and as for expounding what that is, it will have to be for another time and for another place.

Minor in the scheme of things, but significant even so, given we are talking about prophecy, is where this will place these modern-day political prophets in one's esteem? As for me, I hope they will be vindicated but only if they have truly prophesied. But my focus must be on God and His honour and glory, recognising He does things His way and in His timeframe. I will continue to watch and pray and do what little I can for humanity, including fighting for truth, justice and righteousness. Always bear in mind, God's priorities are often not those of man. It is one reason why things happen which we find uncomfortable. Associated with this is the importance of the (real) Church in God's plan.

A reoccurring theme, throughout the Old Testament especially, is how God's mercy and God's judgement interact. Revival or ruin; mercy or judgment; and blessings or curses? Such was the way forward often facing ancient Israel, as we discussed, and we face it today. One friend who shares many of my theological and political perspectives believes, regarding the US Presidency, that if Biden wins God will be exercising judgement and if Trump then mercy. I think it is not quite as straightforward as that and right now we do not know which. It should also be noted that some sound Christians believe Trump to be very bad. I am of a view that many have been over influenced by lying mainstream media.

Because we are fallen, fallible beings, however holy and switched on to what is going on around us we are, we are not going to get everything right, including the way we respond to, for example, the twenty questions asked above. It would be remiss of me *not* to spend time arising out of my watching and praying, to share what I know, hoping I may wake up some but, even more importantly, point them to the Lord I love – for example, by writing this book which is more about the Lord of the prophets than the prophets themselves and always with the rider we test and weigh everything. I do so partly because we have been betrayed, not just by our secular but our spiritual leaders too, from whom we might expect better, the elites of this world who are merely looking out for their own interests rather than those of the rest of humanity, and mainstream media who fail to tell the truth. Sadly, most have us have fallen short by not searching out a matter and coming to wrong conclusions. These are partly reasons why many Christians are asleep.

My early spiritual mentors told me we should be seeking a kingdom not of this world (and an over preoccupation with world events has inherent dangers). That is true, and as I have both observed and experienced personally, it can be an unhelpful distraction, compared with bringing people into God's Kingdom and authentic Christian living. My reading of the prophets of the Bible is they were well aware of what was going on around them. In speaking about what they saw with their eyes and heard with their ears, they would not be shut up, and literally it cost some of their lives, for they wanted to see a righteous outcome.

I should say, in the interest of balance, something we all are in danger of not having: our eyes must be firmly fixed on the Lord God of Israel, and our priorities should include at the top of our list, pursuing holiness, along with carrying out the Great Commission, serving the Church, advancing God's Kingdom, being a humble, faithful believer and loving our neighbour. Be patient; it is worth remembering God is not in a hurry, is always on time and does things His way.

2021

I begin to write this second section on the very last day of this most momentous of years, with a lot of water going under the bridge since I began writing the chapter, and do so with some trepidation. I am humbled that some things, like the US Presidential election, have not worked out as I hoped and predicted and yet I also see the hand of God – in fact in an unexpected way more so than if things had worked out the way I hoped. Just as I do not claim to be a prophet, I do not claim to be God's answer to secular pundits when it comes to what will take place in 2021. But I will venture an opinion on how I see things going forward, based on my study of the Bible, what the "prophets" are saying and happenings I see.

Referring to some of the "loose ends" when it comes to events playing out at the end of 2020, the most obvious one is the Brexit agreement. While opinions are divided as to whether it is good or not, the general consensus, including among the most ardent of Brexiteers, is it is and now begs the question what next? As for the Coronavirus, the agony continues with, as far as the UK is concerned (and in several countries it us worse), further lockdowns happening, despite hopes we are over the worse, as well as issues arising out of the roll-out of a vaccine against the virus, a vaccine most of us are expected to and could even be forced to take, but which many are seeing as the key to our resuming some form of normality.

No doubt, many of "hot" issues in pre-Covid days that have been temporarily put to bed, *e.g.* climate change, will likely again come to the fore. There will, no doubt, be surprises in store, including the possibility of further, often natural, calamities, despite many hoping 2021 will be better than 2020. My hope is it will be a time for people to turn to God and the church regains its nerve in proclaiming such a message. While I cannot say some of our present calamities, such as a pandemic that just goes on and on, is God's judgment, the response the prophet Joel gave to calamities in his day is applicable: "*Therefore also now, saith the Lord, turn ye even to me with all your heart, and with fasting, and with weeping, and with mourning: And rend your heart, and not your garments, and turn unto the Lord your God: for he is gracious and merciful, slow to anger, and of great kindness, and repenteth him of the evil*" Joel 2:12,13. Part of the reason for writing is to encourage this to happen and the Church to repent of unbelief.

For me, the most important question that I was hoping would be answered, both from a worldly and a spiritual perspective, concerns the outcome of the US Presidential election. For most that outcome is all but settled, even though some hope for a turnaround with legislatures and judiciary seeing "the light". I see this with my human eyes as a pivotal event for so much happening in the world. I had hoped by now what is right would have been made abundantly clear to all, but it has not. The issue is not so much did "my man" win – in a democracy we know that does not always / often happen and we accept the fact. It is far graver than that – did the other man win fairly and has he the right to be called the winner? As for the twenty questions posed earlier, I have little doubt what outcome is better, and it is more to do with what I believe will be better for the world as well as America than which person I prefer, yet what God allows is what matters.

A very important and confounding factor concerns election integrity. Since I wrote last, I am convinced more than ever that industrial scale fraud has taken place and

Trump won legally, despite almost everything pointing to Biden soon to be declared as President. Not just that, I sense behind many events we see unfolding before our very eyes, there are wicked people pulling the strings; and any thought of such people being allowed to be let of the hook is abhorrent. Issues range from child trafficking and killing babies in the womb to election fraud on an industrial scale, the elevation of corrupt politicians, a nefarious Deep State, manipulation of the world financial system, the controlling of free speech and the Chinese Communist Party trying to take over the world by subterfuge. Some dismiss all such thinking as conspiracy theory, but I believe such is the case.

Six weeks on, I have delayed sending my second edition to the printers because I wanted to be bang up-to-date. Already I see some earlier projections to be wrong – certainly disqualifying me from secular punditry. The presidential outcome is pertinent to how I wanted to wrap things up, not least because of prophets who confidently predicted a Trump second term, not because they slavishly endorsed Trump necessarily but because they had sought to listen to God and be faithful.

Given we now know it is Biden and not Trump who has been crowned as the 46th US president, many have been calling out these political prophets, especially as weeks following on from his inauguration most have come to terms with the situation. I confess things are different to what I had expected and, while it has led to some self-doubt and heaviness of spirit, it has turned me more to God. I think if there is a lesson even the most ardent of "Trump second termers because the prophets said so" should take away, is we should not trust in human imaginations but God alone, and to learn the lessons of the ancient gnostic heresy.

But then the Lord who alone has the big picture, intending grander purposes than what we imagine, ever moving in mysterious ways, including how he speaks through prophets today. We also know that in the cases of Jonah with Nineveh, Elisha with Jehoash, Nathan with David and Isaiah with Hezekiah, things do sometimes turn out differently to what prophets first said. As for me, I continue to weigh up world events as any watchman should, looking to God for a righteous outcome, including Trump becoming president as these prophets foretold. Noah is one of many prophets that looked foolish until events proved them correct.

As for the political prophets, some remind me of the children of Issachar, of whom it was said: "*And of the children of Issachar, which were men that had understanding of the times, to know what Israel ought to do*" 1 Chronicles 12:32. This unexpected insertion in the chronicles of Israel is because what they did mattered. Given few do respond in the way God would rather they would in secular life, and even more disappointingly, in religious life too, we could do with such understanding children today. *"The fear of the Lord is the beginning of wisdom: and the knowledge of the holy is understanding"* Proverbs 9:10. While Israel was unique among the nations at that time as being one who was supposed to be under God, it is our hope that righteous government should prevail and at the very least the people of God (the real church), instead of being taken in by all sorts of assorted nonsense, should know what they ought to do.

Not my thought originally, but one I am inclined to agree with – we (the people of God expecting a miracle) may be facing the modern equivalent to a "Moses Red Sea moment" or the fire coming from heaven to consume Elijah's sacrifice on Mount Carmel. For only God can overturn the works of the powers of darkness that is gripping the world right now, of which the stolen US Presidential election is merely the tip of an iceberg. In doing so we must never discount the part played by the prophetic and the prophets when it comes to bringing about the desired, longed for righteous outcome: *"And by a prophet the Lord brought Israel out of Egypt, and by a prophet was he preserved"* Hosea 12:13.

While the Great Tribulation precedes the millennial kingdom when righteousness will truly reign on the earth, the prayers of God's people for justice will surely not go unheard when it comes to the here and now. As for reconciling thoughts around a time of great revival with that of Great Tribulation, other than referring to what I believe the Bible teaches in earlier chapters of this book, I must leave it to Him.

I have little doubt, while there will be much more to come out in the open these next few days and months. Some will shock us concerning what has been done in darkness. Many of these much-maligned political prophets will be vindicated, albeit chastened. More importantly, we must live by faith and God must get all the glory. The picture when people get to read this will be a lot different to how we see it as I write now. If God did call many of these "Trump will serve a second term" prophets (as I believe He had), then just as He has always done, He will stand by His true prophets. As for the how's etc., He will do it His way. The same is true, incidentally, concerning Trump, for if he is indeed God's anointed one to drain the swamp etc., he will be back and there is nothing anyone can do to prevent it. If I am wrong as some well-respected Christians suggest, I will apologise.

I also sense there is a lot more to be manifest in the genuinely prophetic as well as in the fulfilment of unfulfilled prophecy, as we look forward to our Lord's coming.

After all, the full pouring out of the Holy Spirit, including the gift of prophecy, foretold in Joel 2 and partly fulfilled in Acts 2, is yet to be seen in a way Joel's prophecy had suggested. But we need to be people of discernment, including applying the lessons of the Bible when it comes to evaluating prophecy that we want to be true *e.g.*: *"A wonderful and horrible thing is committed in the land; The prophets prophesy falsely, and the priests bear rule by their means; and my people love to have it so: and what will ye do in the end thereof?"* Jeremiah 5:30,31. As for His people, our job on earth is to faithfully serve Him. As ever, we must be *"wise as serpents, and harmless as doves"* Matthew 10:16.

Finally, and having read many well-known Christian leaders writing concerning political prophets, often doing so negatively, I continue to ponder. A new President is looking set to continue and with him a radical agenda, often aligning with the "wrong" answers to the twenty questions raised earlier, despite hopes by some sharing my views of a different outcome. Going by recent experience, events will continue to unfold rapidly and not what as we might expect, such that when people do get to read this, things will likely look a lot different. If there is a point to be made, we should not be putting our trust in political or religious leaders, including the prophets. Rather, our hope must be in the Lord, who raises up and puts down kings, as we have seen in our study of prophets of the Bible. But we can take comfort: *"The king's heart is in the hand of the Lord, as the rivers of water: he turneth it whithersoever he will"* Proverbs 21:10. And as Nebuchadnezzar and Belshazzar found out, their pride can be judged very quickly.

And we can still pray with the prophet: *"O Lord, I have heard thy speech, and was afraid: O Lord, revive thy work in the midst of the years, in the midst of the years make known; in wrath remember mercy"* Habakkuk 3:2. While my studies have taught me that God honours the true prophets, even if they have a hard time, his timing and the way prophecy is fulfilled is up to Him. Our part is to be God's faithful people, including being fervent in intercessory prayer.

As well as His love for the world, for people to be saved, and for the poor and suffering, His purposes for His Church and Israel, notwithstanding their assorted trials and tribulations, are glorious and, to such an extent, this has a significant bearing on some of the conundrums we have raised, without there being full and satisfactory resolution. We need more humility to recognise our own prejudices, ignorance, and fallibility. The Lord alone knows all and has the full big picture. I have had to personally repent concerning my attitude to those who see things differently, especially real Christians who I have strongly disagreed with.

I hope soon there will be a revival on a monumental scale, as many political prophets have been predicting, rather than a new normal following the dumping of Trump and a vaccine for the Coronavirus, and with it a new dark age to be overseen by a nefarious New World Order, leading to the rule of the Antichrist. Either way, there is a world to win for Christ and, if we are His, this must be our priority. I also sense that God's priority is the Church that he has been shaking, as evidenced by the calamities, confusion and division we are now seeing. This has taken its toll, including earnest Christians with a heavy spirit. God wishes to purify, embolden and unite the Church, which comprise those who are truly His, and is why things are as they are, including the heavens appearing at times to be like brass. Our part is to keep faith, hope and love, to draw closer to God, and to be humble and available to do all his bidding, whatever that is, whatever the circumstances, allowing for our all-wise, loving heavenly Father to do the rest.

Some reading this may well add their loud Amens, and others may be of a view I have ended a book with a chapter they would rather I omitted as, what otherwise might have been a book showing promise concerning biblical exegesis on an important subject, seems to detract from what they were led to believe from the title as to what was to follow. I do not apologise for doing this, because although Bible prophecy can be taken as something to do with times past or time future, it is also related to time present. We, who are the people of God, should not be afraid of trying to connect the proverbial dots, in order to gain understanding of the times we live in and, like the children of Issachar, knowing how best to respond. We also should long for the prophetic, something that in the main does not happen. But we do so mindful of those in the past who were more learned and holy than us, who got it totally or partially wrong and other learned and holy people of God, living today, who see things a whole lot differently to the way we see things.

In drawing to a close, we will give the final words to two who we have identified as being Prophets of the Bible. The first reminds us of how to approach life and God, whether you agree with my opinions of not. The second, in the light of all the above, is the Psalmist's perspective on what we are now seeing.

"For thus saith the high and lofty One that inhabiteth eternity, whose name is Holy; I dwell in the high and holy place, with him also that is of a contrite and humble spirit, to revive the spirit of the humble, and to revive the heart of the contrite ones." (Isaiah 57:15.)

Psalm 2

1 Why do the heathen rage, and the people imagine a vain thing?

2 The kings of the earth set themselves, and the rulers take counsel together, against the LORD, and against his anointed, saying,

3 Let us break their bands asunder, and cast away their cords from us.

4 He that sitteth in the heavens shall laugh: the LORD shall have them in derision.

5 Then shall he speak unto them in his wrath, and vex them in his sore displeasure.

6 Yet have I set my king upon my holy hill of Zion.

7 I will declare the decree: the LORD hath said unto me, Thou art my Son; this day have I begotten thee.

8 Ask of me, and I shall give thee the heathen for thine inheritance, and the uttermost parts of the earth for thy possession.

9 Thou shalt break them with a rod of iron; thou shalt dash them in pieces like a potter's vessel.

10 Be wise now therefore, O ye kings: be instructed, ye judges of the earth.

11 Serve the LORD with fear, and rejoice with trembling.

12 Kiss the Son, lest he be angry, and ye perish from the way, when his wrath is kindled but a little. Blessed are all they that put their trust in him.

Prophets' Poem

"God, who at sundry times and in divers manners spake in time past unto the fathers by the prophets, Hath in these last days spoken unto us by his Son, whom he hath appointed heir of all things, by whom also he made the worlds; Who being the brightness of his glory, and the express image of his person, and upholding all things by the word of his power, when he had by himself purged our sins, sat down on the right hand of the Majesty on high..." (Hebrews 1:1-3)

Lord, You have always been speaking to the fathers

And You have always been using Your prophets as Your spokespersons

From the day You said "Let there be light" and from eternity past

To the day You bid us "Come" and to eternity future

You spoke with our first father in that idyllic garden, so beautiful, so tranquil

A relationship, so wonderful, so perfect

And he decided to forsake Your way and follow a way You did not intend

As did his descendants from henceforth and unto now

But You have ever been wooing them back to You

And have been using Your prophets to speak Your words

Like Enoch, whom You walked with, and was not because You took him

Like Noah, who preached righteousness to a wicked people

Year after year; then the rain came and the flood; only eight escaped in the Ark

And You called Abraham and promised to make of his descendants a great nation

That would be wedded to You and to the covenant You would make with them

To be a blessing to all other nations; to convey something of Your glory

Abraham, Isaac and Jacob and then for four hundred years, waiting in Egypt

And it seemed You were silent, but You were merely biding Your time

You raised up Moses to lead Your people out of Egypt

And they wandered forty years in the wilderness

They continued to rebel and You continued to woo them

And You raised up Joshua to lead them into the land You promised

And they possessed the land and still they rebelled

And when they cried to You, You raised up judges, over three hundred years

Prophets like Deborah and Samuel, who led Your people

And other prophets, Nathan, Gad and many whose names we don't have

And You gave Your people a king, because that is what they wanted

Saul who blew it, and then the man who was after Your own heart, David

And still they were guided by Your prophets

Then there was Solomon, who began so well and ended so badly

And the Kingdom divided

And still You continued to speak to the people through Your prophets

Some whose names we will never know; most whose stories we cannot tell

The likes of Elijah and Elisha, mighty and anointed men of faith and faithfulness

Marvellous workers of miracles and yet men with like passions as us

Prophets who knew exactly what was going on and what needed to be done

And the people still rebelled and You still continued to woo them

Sometimes the people listened but more often they did not

You kept warning them; You sent calamities; You raised up oppressors

Idolatry, injustice and immorality; robbing the poor and killing the innocent

These were Your complaints, and You who are holy cannot stand evil

But You did not give up on Your people; You honoured those who honoured You

You raised up more prophets to say what concerned You, to say what You will do

In all shapes, sizes, backgrounds, temperaments, circumstances and dispositions

Yet faithfully passing onto the people the words You had given them

We thank You for the prophets; it couldn't have been easy for them

Ignored, attacked, deprived, rejected, despised, hated, vilified and killed

But they were faithful and did what You told them to do; this You will not forget

They did not have the big picture and, while we see things they didn't, nor do we

We wept for them as they endured hardship; we sensed some of Your own anguish

In the end, You allowed Your people to go into exile

And still You did not give up on "the fathers"

You brought Israel back to the land You promised them

And beyond that, there was the promise of the Messiah from David's line

A prospect of a glorious kingdom; a time of peace and prosperity

And yet, ardour abated, passions waned and the people forgot their God

And another four hundred years, when things seemed to have gone quiet

And then the Messiah did come, in the person of Your Son

It was the same one whom Your prophets had foretold and anticipated

Our Lord and Saviour, Jesus Christ, the glorious One

He came unto his own, and His own received him not

But as many as received Him, to them gave He power to become the sons of God

Thank You for Your gift of Jesus; thank You for Your gift of sonship

Thank You that He died for our sins and You raised Him from the dead

Thank You that He is coming again to set up His glorious Kingdom

Wherefore God also hath highly exalted Him

And given Him a name which is above every name

That at the name of Jesus every knee should bow

And that every tongue should confess

That Jesus Christ is Lord, to the glory of God the Father

We thank You for Israel, who You have not forgotten

Whose day of salvation is yet to come

We Gentiles who believe thank You for saving our souls

Questions

Based on the previous chapters, here are some questions you may wish to consider, either individually or in group discussion. It is far from a complete list and there are no precise right or wrong answers, but it may help your thinking.

Chapter 1:

1. Why might you *not* want to take on the job of the prophet?

2. What should the main attributes and qualifications be of a prophet?

Chapter 2:

1. Why is studying the Bible in context so important?

2. Besides the Bible itself, what resources do you find helpful in studying?

Chapter 3:

1. What were the strengths and what were the weaknesses in having prophets, priests and kings operating in tandem?

2. How did Jesus so perfectly combine all three of these offices?

Chapter 4:

1. Why is an understanding of Genesis important when it comes to our overall understanding of the Bible?

2. Genesis is not well known for its prophets; is that view justified?

Chapter 5:

1. Why is Moses often considered to be one of the greatest of all prophets?

2. In what ways were Israel's experiences in the wilderness significant when it comes to our study of the prophets?

Chapter 6:

1. What is the hall-marks of a false prophet?

2. Are there false prophets today and, if so, what makes them false?

Chapter 7:

1. The role of women in ministry has been a contentious one – how might our consideration of female prophets have a bearing on our understanding?

2. We have identified seven female OT prophets – is this justified?

Chapter 8:

1. How significant were the ministries of Jephthah, Gideon and Samson?

2. In what ways did Joshua and Samuel exercise a prophetic ministry?

Chapter 9:

1. David is not known as a prophet; in what ways did he act prophetically?

2. In what ways were David well supported by the prophets Nathan and Gad?

Chapter 10:

1. Why are Elijah and Elisha regarded as typical prophets?

2. What comparisons might you draw between Elijah and Elisha?

Chapter 11:

1. How would you define "prophet" and "prophecy"?

2. Our list of "not well-known prophets" is a long one. Is this justified?

Chapter 12:

1. How might Daniel be seen as different when it comes to the office of prophet, compared to that of Isaiah, Jeremiah and Ezekiel?

2. What is the justification for studying apocalyptic prophecy?

Chapter 13:

1. How might you compare "minor" prophets with "major" prophets?

2. When it comes to social justice and issues for today, what applications might we find from our study of the minor prophets?

Chapter 14:

1. Our study of New Testament prophets is lightweight compared with that devoted to the Old Testament. Have we missed something significant?

2. Is the gift of prophecy and the office of prophet for today?

Chapter 15:

1. This chapter tackles several "controversial" topics. Do you agree or disagree with the conclusions given in this chapter and can you add more?

2. Why can a study of the prophets be a profitable exercise?

Chapter 16:

1. What main lessons have you learnt studying the prophets of the Bible?

2. What changes do you intend to make as a result of doing these studies?

Chapter 17:

1. We have selected ten broadly related topics linked to our study of the prophets. Do you agree they are relevant to our study of the prophets?

2. Of the ten topics, how would you rate them in order of importance?

Chapter 18:

1. Concerning the ten further topics we have selected, is there is anything significant worth adding that we may have missed?

2. Are there other topics worth considering for our studies?

Chapter 19:

1. What are your twelve favourite Bible characters and why?

2. Is there anything else significant, concerning our choice of characters in this and the next chapter, that we may have missed?

Chapter 20:

1. The overwhelming majority of favourite characters chosen have been men. Why do you think this is and is this justified?

2. What other considerations would you want to make when it comes to you choosing your own favourite characters?

Chapter 21:

1. What importance should be attached to prophecy in the life of the church?

2. In terms of priority, what message should be brought to the church concerning the days we live in and the part the church should be playing?

"Lord, how long?" – a phoenix from the ashes – a Covid prayer

The world of COVID-19 through one man's lens – a personal perspective and cry to the Lord by John Barber – a prayer inspired by the prophet Habakkuk 03/04/20

Pious platituders
Armchair activists
Obedient oppressors
Omniscient observers
Conspiracy complainers
Irresponsible ignorers
Who ignore calls to
Do as you're told
To self-isolate
Stay at home
Stay safe
And by the way
Wash your hands
Put on a face mask
Keep your distance
Keep out of the way
Don't pass anything on
Especially if not needed
Especially if old or infirm
But let those who can – do
Our wonderful NHS workers
Menial workers matter now
Essential service providers
Matters of life and death
Free and not free
Heavy handed
Sudden and cruel
Concerned and willing
Knowledge and ignorance
Disempowered and uninformed
Proportionate and disproportionate
Official and alternative narratives
Communicate and miscommunicate
Information and misinformation

Responsible and irresponsible
Unexpected and unavoided
Reaction and over-reaction
National and international
Freedom and slavery
Hoax and truth
What is going on
Fools and villains
And the good guys
Deciding who is who
More collateral damage
Re-discover what matters
Shut it all down – unless
We need it to survive
Open spaces open
Unless at home
Social lockdown
Social distancing
Can't visit relatives
Economic meltdown
Economy via the ether
Small business going under
Taken over by the big guns
Internet is now a utility
Cyber police reigns in
Smart apps rescue us
Shop for essentials
Queues and gaps
The blame game
Fear and anger
People are scared
People in the dark
People are confused
People are deceived
People are manipulated
Knowing what we should do
Wisdom before the event
Wisdom during the event
Wisdom after the event

Experts divided on
What is going on
What is needed
False religion
Fake news
But who
Cyber Censor
Only the truth
Truth covered up
Anything to save us
Wanting to know the truth
It is that which will set us free
Many questions and few answers
Helplessness and hopefulness
Encouraged and discouraged
Unexpected opportunities
Noble and crass
Help the helpless
Everyone matters
Trump the villain
Trump the hero
Boris in charge
Boris in bed
Gates the hero
Gates the villain
Heads in the sand
WHO can't be serious
Regards Chinese virus
CCP the good guys
CCP the bad guys
Obedience to God
Or the government
Trust the government
Distrust the government
Media manipulation
Concerned citizens
Frustrated citizens
Deceived citizens
Social distancing

Social isolation
Social media
Clean air
Sabbath rest
Heroes and heroism
Kindness and empathy
Tolerance and patience
Trying to help
Doing our bit
Helping others
When and as best we can
Taking each day as it comes
Thankful for each new day
Homeless with no home
Gaps and do gooders
Simple things matter
What is important
What is not
Positivity
Catch up
Tidy the house
Affairs in order
Take up a hobby
Talk to loved ones
Help a neighbor
Phone a friend
Draw a picture
Solve a puzzle
Write a book
Read and reflect
Cultivate garden
Time to fret fritter
Time to seek the Lord
While He may be found
Watch and pray and do
For all the whole world
Counting your blessings
Bless those who suffer
Happened o so quickly

Alarms from China but will blow away
From Italy to Iran onto everywhere
From living life normally
And in no time at all
Complete lockdown
Church to conform
Citizens to comply
Heavy handed
Lock or unlock
It could get worse
It could get better
Abnormal
Post normal
What is normal
Accept what you are told
Question what you are told
How long – who knows
Lord - You know
Pandemic
Happenstance
Ginormous hoax
God's judgment
Government knows
Government ignorant
Government inept
Conspiracy theory
Conspiracy fact
Evidence
Models
5G
JFK
9/11
1984
Pizzagate
Darkness exposed
Abortion genocide
Vaccine heals
Vaccine kills
Killing the saints

Satan's throne
Deep State
Brave new world
Control by hidden hand
People dependent on drugs
People merged with machines
Know outcome; know journey
Big brother is watching you
New World Order saves us
False prophet; world religion
One world government
The elite, your masters
Global re-alignment
Coerce and control
Conform or else
Little people
Pushed aside
Bow to tyranny
Virus to destroy
Vaccinate to restore
Movements tracked
And more control
Freedom denied
Cashless society
Mark of the Beast
Deceive the Elect
False flags to dupe
Climate change hoax
Usher in the bad guys
World under a cosh
Untold distress
Lord have mercy
Christ have mercy
God wants our attention
Wake up you good people
New World Order pushed back
Good guys are winning
End times harvest
Bad guys exposed

For a period
Time to reap
Startling revelations
Righteousness and justice
Scales falling from our eyes
Perspectives valid and not
And after the darkness
Before the darkness
And then the light
When He reigns
A door of hope
A time of grace
Phoenix from Ashes
Back to normal
A new normal
How long Lord
Lord have mercy
Christ have mercy
Honour of Thy name
Judgment and mercy
Return now to the Lord
Remember the Covenant
Call on the Lord to save us
O man, He is your only hope
Church shut (unless Rodney)
Churches react
Churches comply
Christians awoke
Christians awake
Real church arises
Body bride building
Its finest hour looms
That they may be one
That the world will know
Saviour of mankind
Lord of lords
King of kings
Kingdom authority
Worship His majesty

Power flows from His Throne
To Him be glory, honour and praise
Making a way when no other way
Unprecedented opportunity
Passover and Pentecost
Awesome is our God
It's about Him; not us
It is time to seek the Lord
God works in mysterious ways
His wonders to perform
He is on His Throne
He never left it
He has our number
And He can't be shut down
His is the ONLY agenda
That truly matters
And will prevail
He comes soon
Great God
Great Command
Great Commission
As for me, I will trust in the Lord

Psalm 91

1 He that dwelleth in the secret place of the most High shall abide under the shadow of the Almighty.

2 I will say of the Lord, He is my refuge and my fortress: my God; in him will I trust.

3 Surely he shall deliver thee from the snare of the fowler, and from the noisome pestilence.

4 He shall cover thee with his feathers, and under his wings shalt thou trust: his truth shall be thy shield and buckler.

5 Thou shalt not be afraid for the terror by night; nor for the arrow that flieth by day;

6 Nor for the pestilence that walketh in darkness; nor for the destruction that wasteth at noonday.

7 A thousand shall fall at thy side, and ten thousand at thy right hand; but it shall not come nigh thee.

8 Only with thine eyes shalt thou behold and see the reward of the wicked.

9 Because thou hast made the Lord, which is my refuge, even the most High, thy habitation;

10 There shall no evil befall thee, neither shall any plague come nigh thy dwelling.

11 For he shall give his angels charge over thee, to keep thee in all thy ways.

12 They shall bear thee up in their hands, lest thou dash thy foot against a stone.

13 Thou shalt tread upon the lion and adder: the young lion and the dragon shalt thou trample under feet.

14 Because he hath set his love upon me, therefore will I deliver him: I will set him on high, because he hath known my name.

15 He shall call upon me, and I will answer him: I will be with him in trouble; I will deliver him, and honour him.

16 With long life will I satisfy him, and shew him my salvation.

Psalm 69 – a meditation for times of trouble

Contained within the Psalm is a treasure trove. Many years ago, I came across and was fascinated by a collection of seven books entitled: ***The Treasury of David***, which has been described as "*C. H. Spurgeon's enduring classic, The Treasury of David has long been regarded as the most comprehensive pastoral and inspirational study of the Psalms ever written*". This, along with another great Bible commentator, Matthew Henry, has been referred to in the thoughts that follow concerning this wonderful and relevant Psalm 69 (one of many).

Recently in our church prayer meeting, when the prayer focus was Christians round the world facing persecution, my wife shared this psalm, and it got me thinking. As far as prophets of the Bible goes, there are several reasons why this psalm is relevant. As far as my wife goes, this was a much-loved psalm in her native country, India, often read by Christians who had to suffer because of their faith. As for me, the words, "*I restored that which I took not away*", resonated, as it was often included in an "extempore" prayer by one brother in a time past, typically as part of a Brethren breaking-of-bread meeting. Moreover, as I came to further meditate on Psalm 69, I realised the term "treasury" is not just apt but there is always new treasure to discover for them who seek it.

Persecution of Christians in all sorts of insidious ways, across many lands, is on a sharp increase as we see the spirit of the Antichrist often manifesting itself in plain sight and often wanting to suppress the people of God. This ranges from outright physical attack to subtle infringements on religious freedom. We should be left in no doubt there will be no let-up as the war between darkness and light intensifies. Not that I want to keep harking back to the book of Revelation, but I am reminded that it and other prophetic writings are there to encourage us for such a time as this. This is where the Psalms (including this one) come in. David, who we understand wrote along these lines on many occasions, knew evildoers were all around him with evil intent and seemed to be operating with impunity. It is why he would call upon the name of the Lord to plead his case, and while it did not mean the bad guys would be crushed by the Almighty right away, he knew He had their measure and would act justly; and as for David, the more he prayed the more confident he became in God.

I reflected in my earlier studies that the prophets of the Bible often had a hard time. They were often not listened to and were beaten up in all sorts of ways when they tried to faithfully declare the word God had given them. Moreover, they were not perfect (unlike in the case of Jesus the Messiah): *"O God, thou knowest my foolishness; and my sins are not hid from thee"* (69:5). Not only did they suffer for doing the right thing, their oppressors were able to do further damage by doing the wrong thing. Like many psalms, it begins on a low, dire note: *"Save me, O God; for the waters are come in unto my soul. I sink in deep mire, where there is no standing: I am come into deep waters, where the floods overflow me. I am weary of my crying: my throat is dried: mine eyes fail while I wait for my God. They that hate me without a cause are more than the hairs of mine head: they that would destroy me, being mine enemies wrongfully, are mighty: then I restored that which I took not away"* (69:1-4).

It ends on a high and triumphant note, rejoicing in the salvation of the Lord: *"But I am poor and sorrowful: let thy salvation, O God, set me up on high. I will praise the name of God with a song, and will magnify him with thanksgiving. This also shall please the Lord better than an ox or bullock that hath horns and hoofs. The humble shall see this, and be glad: and your heart shall live that seek God. For the Lord heareth the poor, and despiseth not his prisoners. Let the heaven and earth praise him, the seas, and every thing that moveth therein. For God will save Zion, and will build the cities of Judah: that they may dwell there, and have it in possession. The seed also of his servants shall inherit it: and they that love his name shall dwell therein"* (69:29-36).

Between the start and the end, the psalmist pours out his heart before God, pleading his cause. There is a sense that he wants his oppressors to suffer because of their unkind actions, begging the question that this attitude contravenes Jesus' words to His disciples to bless and pray for those who persecute them. On two separate occasions the "bashing one's detractor" verses are picked up by New Testament actors. *"Let their table become a snare before them: and that which should have been for their welfare, let it become a trap. Let their eyes be darkened, that they see not; and make their loins continually to shake"* (69:22,23) – is quoted by Paul when he was considering Israel's unbelief (Romans 11:9,10). *"Let their habitation be desolate; and let none dwell in their tents"* (69:25) – is quoted by Peter, justifying the call to appoint a new disciple to replace Judas (Acts 1:20).

The prophetic element of this Psalm is even more poignant when we consider the Messianic aspect, and a further example of a "not a prophet" (David) speaking prophetically, for some of the points made are not too dissimilar in vein to that in Psalm 22, which begins *"My God, my God, why hast thou forsaken me?"*, and where there are remarkable parallels, which we refer to when reflecting on the sufferings of Jesus, particularly when it came to His death on the cross. When we think of the Psalms pointing to the Passion of the Christ and the account of that Passion in the Gospels, the following verses all resonate and find NT fulfilment:

1. *"Because for thy sake I have borne reproach; shame hath covered my face"* (69:7).

2. *"For the zeal of thine house hath eaten me up; and the reproaches of them that reproached thee are fallen upon me"* (69:9).

3. *"I made sackcloth also my garment; and I became a proverb to them"* (69:11).

4. *"Reproach hath broken my heart; and I am full of heaviness: and I looked for some to take pity, but there was none; and for comforters, but I found none"* (69:20).

5. *"They gave me also gall for my meat; and in my thirst they gave me vinegar to drink"* (69:21).

Like many of the Psalms, it should lead us to praise and prayer, thanking God:

1. For the prophets who faithfully did His bidding despite the cost.

2. He vindicates those who trust in Him.

3. He hears and answers prayer.

4. He keeps faith with us, despite our sins.

5. Jesus did all what is laid out here, for me!

The Brethren

Why the Brethren

"The Brethren Assembly movement emerged around 1826-27 (although it was not seen as such until a few years later), when a few met together in a private house (later, as numbers grew, it was in a hired hall) in Dublin, not to start a new sect, but for the purpose of Christian fellowship, to study the Bible and (later) to share in the Lord's Supper. They felt that their spiritual aspirations and concerns for God's work to prosper could not be addressed in the churches they came from, and had a spiritual hunger that needed to be satisfied. Not being under any particular leader, all were at liberty to contribute and did so, for among other things theirs was a reaction against clericalism or minister domination and a movement for spiritually empowering the people. (The extempore nature of Christian gatherings was an important Brethren principle, in order to allow for God's leading. But the need or desire for organisation and order was never far away. Putting into practice this principle gave rise to some of the tensions and conflicts that later followed.)"

It might seem strange the above quote, from my **Who are the Brethren?** paper that I wrote over twenty years ago (downloadable from my website) should appear in a book about prophets of the Bible. The reason is to do with legacy and heritage, which are two driving forces behind this book; and also, to clear up potential misunderstanding, given I mention I have been a member of the Plymouth Brethren for much of my Christian life, even though these days I join with the Strict Baptists. I should say, I am not particularly hung up about denominations and see good and not so good in all of them, including the PBs and the SBs.

While neither a Liberal nor a Catholic, I work with Liberal pastors on matters like homelessness, asylum seeking and mental health, and mentor, advise and volunteer for a Catholic organization that is helping the poor and marginalized in my community. In my pessimism, I see the future, not in any denomination, or group, including the PB – whose heyday has likely passed and, as far as the UK goes, has mostly died or reinvented itself, often ignoring their roots – but rather a faithful remnant meeting in homes or wherever, who love and follow the Lord.

But back to legacy and heritage: the older I get, the more importance I attach to these two things. Part of the legacy I wish to leave, to them who come after me, is this book. As for heritage, the reason why some twenty odd years ago I produced this paper and wrote a thesis titled: ***The hearts and minds of J.N.Darby and***

E.B.Pusey, and a book about the Brethren assembly I have been involved with for much of my life, ***Coleman Street's Children*** (all available on my website) was that my associations with the Plymouth Brethren have formed an important part of my own heritage (at least the "Christian" part of it), and I was keen to find out more, *warts and all*. A further reason, and pertinent to the subject in hand, was that heritage was a significant driving force behind writing this book and might go some way to explain why I have written as I have; and while I completely get why we must "move on", a good deal of credit must go to the PBs.

About the Brethren

I should explain more about this often misunderstood and maligned group, the Plymouth Brethren, and its history. There were many factors behind the origins of the PBs, what they stood for etc., but to know more, read my paper or a book like ***Gathering to His Name*** by Tim Grass. One early development was a centre where people met based in Plymouth (thus the name) where many PB principles were on display. A further development was the split (around 1845), based more, in my view, on personality than principle. This resulted in two distinct groupings: Exclusive and Open Brethren – with splits of the splits that were to follow.

None too salubrious, one might say, but all part of that heritage. One of the key persons in the split was J.N.Darby, whose thoughts on prophetic interpretation are touched on later. It should be added, for the sake of balance, that while Darby was arguably the most influential figure in PBism, not just because of his eschatology but as much due to his ecclesiology (including his view, I was once inclined toward, of a church that was in ruins), other key influences, and much wider than just PBs, were George Muller (founder of a faith mission to orphans) and A.N.Groves (overseas, cross cultural missions). They form some of the rich tapestry that has influenced this author's thoughts and in selection of material.

Going back to the quote, the PBs were not minister (priest, pastor etc.) led and were anti-clericalism, although ironically this did lead to dominant personalities as bad as any Pope, and also led to suspicion by other denominations (which was often mutual), while attracting many who defected from them, looking for a purer form of Christian experience. The PBs put a good deal of store on all parts of the body ministry and the doctrine of the "Priesthood of All Believers". It is this, along with the PB commitment that all its members were potential missionaries, mandated to preach the gospel to the whole world, called to forsake worldliness, love Scripture, beholden to this rather than the traditions of men, meticulously searching out of nooks and crannies other denominations hardly touched, spurred on by its fascination with unfulfilled prophecy and Christ's Second Coming, that have been factors behind this author undertaking this project in the way he has.

These days, my association with the Brethren is a lot less, although I do preach in Brethren assemblies, especially in the country that is my second home, India. I am often touched by those folks who sincerely and sacrificially serve the Lord. While I am keen to reach all and sundry with an interest in Bible prophets, especially if coupled with wanting to follow the Lord, I am mindful of the debt of gratitude I owe past members of the Plymouth Brethren (including their Bible scholarship) many who held responsible "secular" jobs – most recently it was Sir Robert Anderson's thoughts on Daniel's seventy weeks. No doubt their insights, preoccupations and perspectives (along with ubiquitous faults and foibles) have been significant factors behind my selection of material and approach to writing.

One piece of feedback from those who read the first edition of this book was that by discussing the Brethren movement as I have done, and doing so early on, in a book about prophets, it might put off some potential readers who are not particularly interested in the Brethren (it is one reason why this section has now been moved to near the end of the book). My response is, I wanted to be upfront on matters to do with heritage and legacy, and the Brethren story has a significant bearing. One example that springs to mind and has a bearing on why I wrote this book in the first place, notwithstanding debatable theological implications, is not just the disdain leading lights had concerning clericalism and the "priestly class" but their emphasis on the teaching of the "priesthood of all believers".

They did this to encourage their men especially to be skilled as preachers of the Gospel. I recall not long after my conversion as a fifteen-year-old being invited to preach in open air meetings or not long after assisting a seasoned preacher in some gospel service. I imagine a good number of my readers will share some of that heritage, even though things are a lot different these days and many Brethren assemblies have closed, yet may identify with what I have written. I realise the history of the Church contains numerous examples of movements that began in response to a specific need at the time, yet often over time lost their way, as well as not grasping everything that mattered in the first place. Like many, groups ditch some of their distinctiveness in later years. The Brethren are no exception.

The Pilgrim Church

In a book entitled *The Pilgrim Church* by E.H.Broadbent, who was himself a Brethren missionary, the author gives many examples of movements of radical dissent throughout two millennia of Church history, who were often despised, attacked and rejected by mainstream Christianity at the time and were often in a small minority. Yet often they emphasized much neglected and overlooked truth and brought with them new life. The Brethren were cited as one such example, and in a strange way my own Brethren background played a part when it came to selection of material. Besides taking an interest in Bible prophecy, especially that to be fulfilled, some of what the Brethren did and said was arguably prophetic.

Rightly or wrongly, they gladly accepted being looked upon unsympathetically by many in mainstream denominations, even seeing it as a badge of honour, as they deemed faithfulness to the Lord as more important than being approved by men, even Christians. I have little doubt the Brethren, since their inception, have made valuable contribution to the life of the Church, even if they did not get everything right, whose faults these days are there for all to see and are no longer the force they once were, with leading lights in recent decades abandoning ship.

My ecclesiology is nowadays rather eclectic and it is not my intention to promote Brethrenism or any other "ism" (the truth is no church grouping has ever got it 100% right). Finding a church to join can be a tetchy subject, evidenced by the number of "prodigals" who have all but given up, but is beyond the scope of this book. As discussed in Chapter 17, fellowship between and unity among believers is a matter of great importance. But we are entering into a paradigm when people seeking to be faithful to the Lord will once again (or maybe it has ever been the case) find themselves reviled or side-lined, not just by a world that rejects the ways of the Lord, but by elements in the professing church. They may well have come to a view they are unable to associate with egregious errors they see in much of contemporary Christianity, and as a result become part of a despised "remnant", but it is also important such a remnant operates as the Body of Christ ought.

While "*endeavouring to keep the unity of the Spirit in the bond of peace*" (Ephesians 4:3) among fellow believers is something that cannot be dismissed, and neither can the importance of "*encouraging one another and building one another up*" (1 Thessalonians 5:11) – "another" being all true believers, and neither can "*love one another; as I have loved you*" (John 13:34), joining the ranks of this despised and rejected remnant may well become an inevitability for some.

The Unprofitable Servant

J.N.Darby and E.B.Pusey

One of my passions is history, especially church history and doubly especially the movers and shakers who down the ages have impacted the church and the wider world, finding out what made them tick and how they made a difference.

(Left) J.N.Darby; (Right) E.B.Pusey (both 1800 - 1882)

There are many fascinating characters I would like to have checked out, but two characters I did research, and I produced a paper about them (available on my website), were J.N.Darby and E.B.Pusey, who both lived 1800 to 1882, whose impact on the church, then and now, has been monumental. Both started off Anglican. Darby left to join the Plymouth Brethren and Pusey was considered by many to be more Catholic than Anglican. In later life, they were ecclesiologically poles apart in terms of low and high church (although arguably, the two had a much higher view of the church than most), and eschatologically concerning end time events, such as the millennium. They were both flawed (theologically and personally), enigmatic and even eccentric in their characters, and yet they had a lot in common, such as their personal piety; they were Bible scholars of the highest calibre and wrote prolifically (writings still available); they served and were empathetic toward the poor (notwithstanding the fact they both came from privileged backgrounds) and they were staunch and effective defenders of the faith in an age when past certainties were increasingly coming under attack.

Since our book is about prophets, it should be noted that few historians would regard either of these two men as prophets, even though it can be argued they were acting prophetically with respect to what they saw happening around them, in a way that is not often seen in our present day. Darby helped to establish and lead the Plymouth Brethren movement, partly in response to what he saw as a church that was in ruins. Pusey helped to establish and lead the Tractarian (Oxford) movement, partly in response to the latitudinarian tendencies he saw in the Church of England. What is of special interest to this author is that both men saw themselves (with some justification) as unprofitable servants and both men would return to Jesus parable of "The Unprofitable Servant" in their preaching.

The Parable applied

It is worth re-acquainting ourselves with the Parable, which is about a servant (Greek: *doulos* – slave) who having worked hard for his master was not thanked but rather he was expected to do more, and even then, as unprofitable servants, expect no token of appreciation. Such is the example we should be following:

"*But which of you, having a servant plowing or feeding cattle, will say unto him by and by, when he is come from the field, Go and sit down to meat? And will not rather say unto him, Make ready wherewith I may sup, and gird thyself, and serve me, till I have eaten and drunken; and afterward thou shalt eat and drink? Doth he thank that servant because he did the things that were commanded him? I trow not. So likewise ye, when ye shall have done all those things which are commanded you, say, We are unprofitable servants: we have done that which was our duty to do*" Luke 17:7-10

Much can be said about how we, who are God's people, should view serving others as being something of high priority and, as we consider Prophets of the Bible, is something to keep in mind. We can do no better than follow the example of Jesus, who is the Servant King, just as Graham Kendrick's song reminds us:

"*From heaven you came helpless babe*
Entered our world, your glory veiled
Not to be served but to serve
And give Your life that we might live
This is our God, The Servant King
He calls us now to follow Him
To bring our lives as a daily offering
Of worship to The Servant King"

Jesus (the Servant King) is the one who came from the highest place (in the form of God) to the lowest place, in order to die on the cross because of our sin, and has once again been established in the highest place and will one day return to earth as judge and king. It is such a mindset that ought to determine our conduct:

"Let this mind be in you, which was also in Christ Jesus: Who, being in the form of God, thought it not robbery to be equal with God: But made himself of no reputation, and took upon him the form of a servant, and was made in the likeness of men: And being found in fashion as a man, he humbled himself, and became obedient unto death, even the death of the cross. Wherefore God also hath highly exalted him, and given him a name which is above every name: That at the name of Jesus every knee should bow, of things in heaven, and things in earth, and things under the earth; And that every tongue should confess that Jesus Christ is Lord, to the glory of God the Father. Wherefore, my beloved, as ye have always obeyed, not as in my presence only, but now much more in my absence, work out your own salvation with fear and trembling" Philippians 2:5-12.

Another twelve favourite Bible characters

I have already devoted two chapters to a consideration of twenty-four of my favourite Bible characters and why they are "favourites", chosen not because there are no just as worthy other candidates to consider, but somehow what they did particularly resonated with my own experience. I am using this opportunity to write about twelve more (and, even then, I can see that I am still far from done, if I were to get back to reflecting on what the Bible says concerning those I didn't include) and with that I repeat the challenge (dear reader) for you to come up with your own list. I confine my comments on each character to single sentences.

Bible Characters

Enoch *"walked with God: and he was no more; for God took him"* is as much as we know of him from the OT record, but in the NT we find a quote from his amazing book that revealed so much what went on behind the scenes (i.e. in the heavenly realm); but more importantly, in a time when people were already beginning to turn away from God, he kept the faith and he remained faithful.

Noah *"found grace in the eyes of the Lord"* at a time when *"God saw that the wickedness of man was great in the earth, and that every imagination of the thoughts of his heart was only evil continually"*; for he was one of the three most righteous men to have ever lived according to Ezekiel, and his faith and obedience to God, over a period of several decades, while he built the Ark, to escape a Flood that looked unlikely, and urged people to repent, that will ever endear him to us.

Joshua *"fought the battle of Jericho ... and the walls came tumbling down"* hardly does justice to the monumental part he played leading Israel into the Promised Land, which included capturing this key city; for it was Joshua who, along with Caleb, spied out the land forty years earlier and alone brought back favourable reports, was mentored by Moses all that time and faithfully led Israel so they could take possession of the land and enjoy a measure of peace.

Samuel as a young boy heard the voice of God, responding with *"speak; for thy servant heareth"*, which words were to mark how he was to carry out his long ministry as a judge and prophet from that time on, as he led Israel until King Saul followed by King David (both kings he was to anoint) took over, providing timely counsel and the word of the Lord at crucial times when it was most needed.

Mephibosheth was the crippled grandson of King Saul, who David took over from, and in wanting to show kindness to those left of Saul's house, particularly to his dear friend, Jonathan, he found Mephibosheth, who although wary given the history of conflict between the houses of Saul and David, greatly appreciated the grace that was given to him, for *"he did eat continually at the king's table"*, as in another sense so can we, for the invite includes *"such a dead dog as I am"*.

Amos was simply a shepherd on a mission for God, as one who had taken the prophetic task on a temporary basis, but for the short but intense time in which he bravely, and pulling no punches, prophesied a hard-hitting message of God's judgment to a people who were reluctant to respond, but ticked all the boxes when it came to why God wanted to rebuke them: idolatry, social injustice, immorality; as Israel faced almost its last chance to save itself before being taken into exile.

Josiah was eight years old when he began to reign as king in Judah (the last good one), for it was said *"he did that which was right in the sight of the Lord, and walked in all the way of David his father, and turned not aside to the right hand or to the left"*, repairing the Temple, re-introducing true worship of God and removing the false, bringing in much needed reform, yet sadly too little, too late.

Ezekiel faithfully prophesied, through visions, pictures and words from the Lord, a hard hitting but much needed message, where he had to partake in some strange actions, and at personal cost, to bring home the point to his audience, concerning the final destruction of Jerusalem, and when all that had come to pass was then able to bring a message of restoration and hope, looking far ahead into the future.

Esther was the beautiful queen who was married to the most powerful man in the world at the time, who from a God perspective, even though God was never mentioned, was raised up for *"such a time as this"*; for it was her brave (she could accept *"if I perish, I perish"*), timely and wise actions, along with those of her Uncle Mordecai, that was to save the Jewish people from complete annihilation.

Anna was an 85-year-old prophetess, who had been long widowed but spent much of her time in the Temple, fasting and praying, who had the joy of seeing the eight-day old Jesus and thanked God, speaking concerning Jesus *"to all them that looked for redemption in Jerusalem"*, for this was an amazing lady, who undertook this much needed ministry and who God was to openly reward.

Zacchaeus *"was a very little man and a very little man was he; he climbed up into a sycamore tree for the Saviour he wanted to see; and when Jesus passed that way he looked into the tree and said "now Zacchaeus, you come down, for I'm coming to your house for tea"* is how the old Sunday School chorus went; but he was also a very bad man who knew something was missing in his life and found his Saviour, restoring four-fold all that he had taken by crooked dealings.

Philip was one of the first batch of (seven) deacons to be appointed by the Early Church but, with persecution, he had to leave Jerusalem, but made effective use of the situation he found himself in, by preaching the Gospel and leading a revival that was accompanied by many amazing miracles; and yet when the angel told him to go and meet the Ethiopian eunuch on his long journey home, he was able to seize the opportunity and led this man, who was hungry for the truth, to Christ.

Of making many books

"And further, by these, my son, be admonished: of making many books there is no end; and much study is a weariness of the flesh. Let us hear the conclusion of the whole matter: Fear God, and keep his commandments: for this is the whole duty of man. For God shall bring every work into judgment, with every secret thing, whether it be good, or whether it be evil." (Ecclesiastes 12:12-14.)

I begin this section quoting salient wisdom from the Book of Ecclesiastes in order to help keep me in my place and establish my priorities, along with the advice I received a long time ago: *not* to exercise delusions of grandeur when it comes to expecting lots of people to want to hang onto my every word of wisdom. As folk who follow my writings may gather, I love to write (as well as read), and this has been so since my youth. As I enter my dotage and am expected to find interests to occupy my time, reading (especially the Bible), including generally taking an interest in what is going on in the world, and writing, have come top of that list.

Despite my best efforts, I am not a big-named author (and don't expect to be) and the best I can claim is some people, having read what I have written, have told me they found my writings helpful. Most of my writings (books, articles, leaflets) are no longer available in book form. A lot of what of what I wrote over many years is freely available in electronic form from my website: ***jrbpublications.com***. Go to the writing tab for my writings and my blog tab for my (at the time of writing) nearly 1800 blog articles, which I typically add to 3-4 times a week.

Past writings

The following refers to links to my non-blog writings:

Community activism

1. Outside the Camp
2. Onward and Upward
3. Theological Musings
4. Spirituality and Mental Health
5. The Gay Conundrum

Education

1. A Parent's Guide to the 11 Plus

Community research

1. Missing Communities
2. Faiths and Africa
3. Southend Mental Health Directory
4. Rough sleeper leaflet: where to go for help if homeless in Southend

Church history

1. Who are the Brethren?
2. The Hearts and Minds of J.N.Darby and E.B.Pusey
3. Coleman Street's Children

Solomon's Song of Songs

Solomon's Song of songs – Pure Intimacy is a devotional that is in print and it supersedes my earlier works:

1. Fired up
2. Love as strong as death
3. Conference paper

Blog e-books

Reflections from Outside the Camp introduces twelve e-collections covering many of my blogs, which cover a wide range of subjects that interest me:

Book 1: Homeless reflections

Book 2: Donald J. Trump

Book 3: Immigration and Islam

Book 4: Education, education, education

Book 5: Sexual identity and sexual orientation

Book 6: Christianity and community action

Book 7: Political perspectives

Book 8: Israel and the Middle East

Book 9: Biographies, obituaries and tributes

Book 10: Culture wars

Book 11: Community matters

Book 12: Personal interests

Future plans

The Bible encourages us to not get carried away concerning what we might do in the future. As for the wherewithal, circumstances and whether we are still around to implement our well-intended plans, we need to accept that it is all in the Lord's hands and the best we can do is make the most of the time we have left, which given my age and condition may not be that long. There are a lot of writing projects, and if circumstances were different and I was a lot younger, I might be interested and able to pursue, including under the headings given to some of my earlier writings above, particularly to do with one of my passions: church history and another: community activism, which realistically I do not expect to happen.

Regarding my ***Solomon's Song of songs,*** I intend supplementing this with daily meditations based on Solomon's two other books: Proverbs and Ecclesiastes and include in a book I propose to title: ***Song of songs, Proverbs and Ecclesiastes – mediations from Solomon's three Bible books***.

As for ***Outside the Camp***, which is my chance to tell my story of how I became a community activist and some of the lessons I learned on the way, that might help those I pass the baton to, I intend to update and incorporate some of the writings this spawned as well as reflect how, some years after I first wrote, I see what going outside the camp amounts to and some of the issues involved when we do.

I hope to make, the currently work in progress, ***Song of songs, Proverbs and Ecclesiastes*** and, the soon to be updated, ***Outside the Camp***, along with future published books, available through outlets like Ingram and Amazon, so anyone anywhere might be able to get hold of these books in paper form for themselves.

The big project, and one that will likely take up most of my time (DV) in 2021, is to write a new book, which I propose to title: ***Kings and Priests of the Bible***. It will be a sequel to, logical continuation of and is intended to complement this book: ***Prophets of the Bible***, doing for kings and priests, what I did for prophets. I say this with the caveat these bright ideas will only happen if I still have the enthusiasm, energy and *compos mentis* and of course if the Lord allows it.

I hope too to keep adding to the blogosphere, covering a wide range of subjects, based on my reflecting on the world around me, ranging sacred and secular, from minor to major, from the sublime to the ridiculous. As they say – watch this space!

Back to my, at this time of writing, two thirds completed project on the three books of Solomon. I leave readers with three sets of verses covering each of these books and encapsulating what are arguably the major themes to be found in each one. I do so by way of wetting one's appetite concerning things to come.

"*Set me as a seal upon thine heart, as a seal upon thine arm: for love is strong as death; jealousy is cruel as the grave: the coals thereof are coals of fire, which hath a most vehement flame. Many waters cannot quench love, neither can the floods drown it: if a man would give all the substance of his house for love, it would utterly be contemned.*"
Song of Solomon 8:6-17

"*Give instruction to a wise man, and he will be yet wiser: teach a just man, and he will increase in learning. The fear of the Lord is the beginning of wisdom: and the knowledge of the holy is understanding. For by me thy days shall be multiplied, and the years of thy life shall be increased. If thou be wise, thou shalt be wise for thyself: but if thou scornest, thou alone shalt bear it.*"
Proverbs 9:9-12

"*Vanity of vanities, saith the Preacher, vanity of vanities; all is vanity. What profit hath a man of all his labour which he taketh under the sun? ... Let us hear the conclusion of the whole matter: Fear God, and keep his commandments: for this is the whole duty of man. For God shall bring every work into judgment, with every secret thing, whether it be good, or whether it be evil.*"
Ecclesiastes 1:2-3; 12:13-14

Join all the glorious names

Join all the glorious names
Of wisdom, love, and pow'r,
That mortals ever knew,
That angels ever bore;
All are too mean to speak His worth,
Too mean to set my Savior forth.

Great Prophet of my God,
My tongue would bless Thy name;
By Thee the joyful news
Of our salvation came;
The joyful news of sins forgiv'n,
Of death annulled, and Thy life giv'n.

Jesus, my great High Priest,
Offered His blood, and died;
My guilty conscience seeks
No sacrifice beside:
His pow'rful blood did me redeem,
'Tis worthy of my heart's esteem.

I love my Shepherd's voice:
His watchful eye shall keep
My wand'ring soul among
The thousands of His sheep:
He feeds His flock, He calls their names,
His bosom bears the tender lambs.

My Savior and my Lord,
My Conqu'ror and my King,
Thy scepter and Thy sword,
Thy reigning grace I sing:
Thine is the pow'r; behold I sit
In willing bonds beneath Thy feet.

Isaac Watts (1674-1748)

While we are thinking of dear Isaac Watts, we will give him the very last word. Whatever our views on the prophets and their prophecies, I believe his priorities, when he wrote the following words, ought to be our own. I have little doubt that the Hebrew prophets of old, with limited knowledge concerning their expected Messiah, would echo these sentiments if they only knew what we know now:

> When I survey the wondrous cross
> On which the Prince of glory died,
> My richest gain I count but loss,
> And pour contempt on all my pride.
>
> Forbid it, Lord, that I should boast,
> Save in the death of Christ my God!
> All the vain things that charm me most,
> I sacrifice them to His blood.
>
> See from His head, His hands, His feet,
> Sorrow and love flow mingled down!
> Did e'er such love and sorrow meet,
> Or thorns compose so rich a crown?
>
> Were the whole realm of nature mine,
> That were a present far too small;
> Love so amazing, so divine,
> Demands my soul, my life, my all.

The Prophets and the Gospel

"And, behold, two of them went that same day to a village called Emmaus, which was from Jerusalem about threescore furlongs. And they talked together of all these things which had happened. And it came to pass, that, while they communed together and reasoned, Jesus himself drew near, and went with them. But their eyes were holden that they should not know him. And he said unto them, What manner of communications are these that ye have one to another, as ye walk, and are sad? And the one of them, whose name was Cleopas, answering said unto him, Art thou only a stranger in Jerusalem, and hast not known the things which are come to pass there in these days? And he said unto them, What things? And they said unto him, Concerning Jesus of Nazareth, which was a prophet mighty in deed and word before God and all the people: And how the chief priests and our rulers delivered him to be condemned to death, and have crucified him. But we trusted that it had been he which should have redeemed Israel: and beside all this, to day is the third day since these things were done. Yea, and certain women also of our company made us astonished, which were early at the sepulchre; And when they found not his body, they came, saying, that they had also seen a vision of angels, which said that he was alive. And certain of them which were with us went to the sepulchre, and found it even so as the women had said: but him they saw not. Then he said unto them, O fools, and slow of heart to believe all that the prophets have spoken: Ought not Christ to have suffered these things, and to enter into his glory? And beginning at Moses and all the prophets, he expounded unto them in all the scriptures the things concerning himself. And they drew nigh unto the village, whither they went: and he made as though he would have gone further. But they constrained him, saying, Abide with us: for it is toward evening, and the day is far spent. And he went in to tarry with them. And it came to pass, as he sat at meat with them, he took bread, and blessed it, and brake, and gave to them. And their eyes were opened, and they knew him; and he vanished out of their sight. And they said one to another, Did not our heart burn within us, while he talked with us by the way, and while he opened to us the scriptures?" (Luke 24:13-32.)

One of the lovely stories often revisited during the Easter season is the meeting of Jesus with two disciples along the Emmaus road, shortly after He rose from the dead. They had hoped Jesus would turn out to be their long-awaited Messiah, with his riding into Jerusalem on a donkey, and being hailed as the king the Hebrew prophets had prophesied would redeem Israel, the previous Sunday. But having had their hopes raised these were soon dashed when Jesus was executed as a common criminal the following Friday. They were disappointed and confused, but had heard reports of the empty tomb and Jesus risen from the dead.

Speaking personally, if I had a time machine, the one thing I would love to be able to do is eavesdrop on the conversation Jesus had with these two persons, so distraught and bemused, concerning what it was the prophets of old had said about his first coming. With reference to the preceding chapters, it is quite evident that a lot had been written concerning Jesus life, death and resurrection, often down to the minutest details, in the Hebrew scriptures, such as contained in Psalm 22 and Isaiah 53 or even Zechariah 9 about entering Jerusalem on a donkey, and there is even more about His second coming as King of kings and Lord of lords – what these two disciples had been hoping would happen in the person of Jesus.

Most of the Christian church celebrate special days, especially the Christmas and Easter seasons, sometimes preceded by Advent and Lent respectively, as times of sober reflection and preparation. Both these special seasons and the OT Feasts of Yahweh, that some Christians argue are even more worth recognising, point to important Gospel truths. The Incarnation (when God entered the world in human form), the Atonement (when God in the person of Jesus died on the cross as the sacrificial lamb to reconcile mankind with God) and the Resurrection (when Jesus rose from the dead) are three significantly glorious truths central to the Gospel message, as is that of Jesus coming again (we do not know when) to reign in glory – all of these truths having been wonderfully foretold by the Hebrew prophets. As for "unfulfilled" Bible prophecy, methinks surprises are soon in store for us.

The above is a reinforcement of the Gospel message discussed in Chapter 17, and I have shared these thoughts here by way of providing balance to earlier thoughts on the modern day "political" prophets and what to make of and how to respond to events unfolding in the world today, discussed in Chapter 21, and the section that is to follow. We live in a time when it is easy to become side-tracked, taken in by deception, lose hope, and become less than whole-hearted in our discipleship. Whatever importance we attach to and interpretation we may give to modern day events and the pronouncements of these modern prophets, we must not lose sight that as followers of Jesus, we are firstly mandated to preach the gospel – and "when necessary, use words" (according to St. Francis of Assisi). The truth Jesus is alive should give us hope, and remind us God wins in the end!

Chapter 22: A New Ending

Final thoughts on modern day prophecy

"Though the mills of God grind slowly, yet they grind exceeding small; Though with patience He stands waiting, with exactness grinds He all" Henry Wadsworth Longellow (1807-1882).

I wrote Chapter 21 by way of a reflective diary that ended in February 2021, with the intention of relating Bible prophecy, modern prophecy and today's events. It is now mid-April and, while I had hoped something dramatic would have happened by now with regard to the concerns and hopes I raised and, pertinent to the book, it would confirm (or even refute, if false) the credibility of some whom I chose to label as modern-day political prophets, I am still waiting, yet there is enough going on, largely unreported, to give me hope. Sometimes it feels like I am watching a pantomime, barely aware of the twists and turns ahead, but hoping the villains get their comeuppance and the good guys win. I sense too God is testing and refining His people for great things to come and that He is looking to make Christ's bride a pure and radiant one, as opposed to impure and defeated. I know too there is a spiritual war being fought in the heavenlies, and one where the repercussions are being felt down here on Earth, and yet one which the armies of God along with the Church will win. While the thoughts of Longfellow are not the Word of God, he made the important point that any sincere followers of the Lord should note. He does things His way, and in His time that is always on time.

It seems to me there are broadly three categories of Christians when it comes to formulating a response to what is happening in the world right now and, such is the "divide and rule" paradigm we are now living in, we often find members of each group antipathetic to the views of those who are not in their group. Firstly, there are those who seek to rise above and often ignore what is going on, emphasising rather the importance of preaching the gospel and being faithful. Secondly, there are those who seek to respond to world events but are content to be guided by what political and societal leaders and mainstream media say. Thirdly, there are those who also seek to respond but, since disregarding such leaders and media (to use the picture painted in the Book of Proverbs) as fools (mix of liars, villains and those who simply, naïvely have got it wrong), some of them are more likely to be informed by "conspiracy theorists" and/or political prophets. In my lifetime, I have belonged to all three groups and, while I would rather be part of the first one, I am finding myself increasingly drawn to the third, while at the same time seeking out truth and maintaining balance. There is also a danger of Christians losing hope and abandoning sound doctrine, and the ever-present danger of the Laodicean spirit of lukewarmness taking hold.

While what the future holds, once we come (supposedly) out of the Covid-19 crisis, may by uppermost in people's minds, I am inclined to the view that what we are faced with is a future dominated by either what has come to be labelled as the "Great Reset" or the alternative "Great Awakening" and, for those in the don't know camp, it is the question of which one is going to prevail that should be concerning us. In a strange way, the Corona virus is part of the big picture and it is a matter of connecting the dots. One is dominated by the "black hats" that wish to control (and coerce) the masses. The other is dominated by the "white hats", who among other things are pulling the lid off international child trafficking, the evils of the world financial systems, election fraud and attempts to enslave the masses by deception and even get them to acquiesce to their enslavement. The difficulty for many often is working out who is good and who is bad. The reality is if God is at the centre of it all, what we may see is merely a shade of grey.

In eschatological terms, I cannot discount that as well as the fact the Lord is coming back to planet earth soon, before then there will be a time of major disruption and wickedness as part of a three-and-a-half-year period referred to as the Great Tribulation, overseen by the Antichrist and, while I would love to be wrong, that is where the world seems to be heading at this time. Yet, many political prophets are prophesying a time of imminent great revival along with, at least for a season, the white hats orchestrating many world events, and that includes Donald J. Trump serving a second term as US President to help in, among other things, more draining of the swamp. Other "Christian" views range from a new Enlightenment to a great falling away, and not forgetting those who see the rising tide of evil but before the Great Tribulation the Church will be raptured.

As for me, I will endeavour, with God's help, to do what I wrote on my Facebook page: "*I am a gospel preaching, community activist, watchman on the wall*". The more I watch, the more convinced I am that: not only God will win in the end (and therefore, dear reader, I invite you to join God's winning side), but evil will be exposed to an extent unprecedented since the Great Flood, with God acting both in mercy and in judgment. "*And we know that we are of God, and the whole world lieth in wickedness*" 1 John 5:19. We need to be like faithful Daniel, who humbly and prayerfully intreated God concerning perplexing events that were happening around him and the future, barely aware of the battle raging in the spiritual realm

(Daniel 9,10). But we know: *"for the weapons of our warfare are not carnal, but mighty through God to the pulling down of strong holds"* 2 Corinthians 10:4.

I expect, when most people get to read this, the world will appear to be a quite different place to when this was written, much of which, as far as this author is concerned, will come in the unforeseen and unexpected categories. Just as I don't claim to be a prophet, neither am I a political pundit (my track record confirms); nor am I (and this is definitely a no-go area) a soothsayer or crystal ball gazer. I am not going to go down conspiracy theory rabbit holes, besides which, there are others who do so better than me; all I can say is – do your own research and don't trust the media. I am me, a "nobody"; church layman, a sinner saved by grace, a brand plucked from the fire, who wants to make a difference. I love the Lord and want to share what I know; to wake people up and to encourage others. And what better way than give the last word of this section to a prophet of the Bible: *"He hath shewed thee, O man, what is good; and what doth the Lord require of thee, but to do justly, and to love mercy, and to walk humbly with thy God?"* Micah 6:8.

Eight months on ...

"Moreover the Lord answered Job, and said, Shall he that contendeth with the Almighty instruct him? he that reproveth God, let him answer it. Then Job answered the Lord, and said, Behold, I am vile; what shall I answer thee? I will lay mine hand upon my mouth. Once have I spoken; but I will not answer: yea, twice; but I will proceed no further" Job 40:1-5.

All of the above, barring some minor tinkering for this final chapter, was written more than eight months ago and formed the second edition of this book. During that time, I have reflected on where the world is from a prophetic perspective and do see how little I know on what is going on etc., feeling perhaps a bit like dear Job when God finally caught up with him and put him in his place. While I have made my book freely available on my website as an electronic download and did get some hard copies printed to give out to folk who were interested, or to pass on as a gift to friends etc., I did not particularly promote what I wrote. For one reason, I lacked the confidence to do so and wanted to find the most opportune moment. Significantly, I did not make the book available to the wider world through Ingram, Amazon etc. and thus have no compunction to add these extra thoughts along with tinkers and claim this as the second edition – so please bear with me. After this, no more changes (this edition at least); it is *"publish and be damned"*.

I have resisted the temptation revise earlier content for, if I did, I might, for example, bring up to date the section titled "*On making many books*". As I write this, the number of *jrbpublications.com* blog entries stand at 1930 and I fully expect it to be over 2000 in the next few months. Some of the new entries are on subjects relating to the content of this book. As for writing projects, I am now resigned *not* to update "*Outside the Camp*", which tells my story. While to "*go forth to Him outside the camp, bearing His reproach*" etc., Hebrews 13:13, still defines my own approach as a gospel preaching, community activist, watchman on the wall, I feel I need to focus my energies elsewhere, as my time is short and, besides, I want my future writing efforts to be more about Him and less about me.

While I don't regret doing what I did, as it was well intentioned and often made a real difference, I do regret some of my naïvety in wanting to get along with and having my priorities defined by those who do not love God, a tendency I see all too often in the next generation of Christian community activists. Regarding my forthcoming book: "*Kings and Priests of the Bible*", it is as I had expected a big undertaking and is still work in progress, to be made available in 2022. But I did complete "*Song of Songs, Proverbs and Ecclesiastes*" (a set of daily meditations) since writing that section and, while not to do with prophets, the main themes of that book: "*Love is Strong as Death*" – Song of Songs, "*The Way of Wisdom*" – Proverbs and "*Life under the Sun*" – Ecclesiastes, all have prophetic implications.

I had a strong sense when I came to this final chapter of this book, which was meant to take a final hard, long, last look at the state of the world that is unravelling before our very eyes as opposed to in the shadows, and do so from a prophetic perspective by relating this to what the Bible prophets had to say and what our own response should be, noting that the world is changing rapidly and, by the time people would come to read my book, there would have been a lot more change to reflect upon. Paradoxically, while in eight months I have been made even more aware of nefarious goings on and the resistance to them, resulting in huge changes that when we look back at them in years to come will see as of major significance, yet the words of Longfellow have been proven true. My hope for justice in the light of the November 3rd 2020 US Election steal though has still not happened and neither has there been an appropriate resolution to the Covid-19 pan(scam)demic. Perhaps, one thing we can take comfort in, along with Longfellow's inspirational words, is we can have confidence in the Lord and His righteous plans for humanity: "*For I am the Lord, I change not*" Malachi 3:6.

The nice thing about getting extra bites of the proverbial cherry is the author is given the opportunity to add further profound thoughts that have arose since last writing. The first thing to say is I hope I have not been an unnecessary stumbling block to any. While I regret not always being gracious, I do not apologise for upsetting some folk, including respected Christian leaders, when I know they should be taken to task for not acting as shepherds ought with their flock, and from own experience gentle rebukes are how God frequently deals with us, and at the same time I don't wish to lead people astray at a time when many Christian brothers and sisters, as well as the world at large, are being led astray by the Evil One. Except for ***Chapter 21: 2020, 2021 and the prophetic***, and mindful some good Christian folk do not go along with all my views on eschatology, literal, pre-millennial etc., I make no apologies for my Conservative Evangelical, non-replacement of Israel views. I have tried in the previous chapters to be meticulous in keeping to what the Bible says, recognising there are depths not yet fully delved into, because I feel I don't know the Bible or the God of the Bible well enough.

As for Chapter 21, while I do not claim to be a prophet, I have no doubt, besides teaching the Bible, I am called to be a watchman on the wall, whose job was to warn the people of imminent threats etc. Chapter 21 and this final chapter is offered by way of sharing with readers what I am seeing, as it matters, along with the caveat, when checking out what I write, you "***test and weigh***" and hear from the Lord alone. In the eight months since I wrote what I did, I have noted with alarm the squashing of the prophetic voice, with real prophets under attack and those who are acclaimed as prophets more likely to be in the false prophet category, discussed in Chapter 6. Often those in church leadership are more likely to be providing support to the false narratives, *e.g.* over Covid-19 as pushed by government. What is needed is the authentic prophetic voice as prophesied in Joel 2 and Acts 2. If there is to be a Great Awakening of the spiritual sort, I hope and pray it includes true prophets of the Lord and the gift of prophecy in the Church.

At the beginning of this chapter, as well as in Chapter 21, I laid out two alternative views on how the world will turn out in the next few months and years. I felt it can either be the Great Reset led by the "black hats" or the Great Awakening led by the "white hats". A third view, of course, is it will be neither or a mix and a fourth one, perhaps, is it is not for us to know – it is in the Lord's hands. I write now with a certain trepidation, not wanting to mislead anyone. People get quite hung up over definitions and the best thing I can do for those wanting to know my own understanding is to suggest they read what I have written so far in this book or my recent blogs. As to which it is going to be, in the natural, I fear the former (because that is the way it is looking) but I hope for the latter, both from the point of view of more evidence since I wrote eight months ago of people waking up to assorted wicked, satanic inspired goings on and resisting the evil cabal (and if "Q" is for real, and it is not some New Age fantasy to wrongly raise hopes and we can "trust the plan" (whatever that is), as unlikely as it seems, the good guys may indeed be control). Then there are longed for spiritual revivals, some already happening, which in the past were often referred to as great awakenings. Not to forget, Satan is ever at work trying to deceive us all and oppose all that is of God.

While some of the modern "political" prophets seem sometimes to agree with the New Age, syncretic, Gnostic leaning conspiracy theorists types when it comes to a soon Great Awakening that includes overturning of the Babylon system spoken of in Revelation 17 and 18 and by some of the Hebrew prophets, they often appear to overlook the view my former spiritual mentors came to when considering end time prophecy – the world is getting steadily worse and, given the AntiChrist (Revelation 13) has not yet been revealed and neither has the Great Tribulation begun that goes with it, we have no basis to expect the evil cabal to receive their comeuppance before Christ returns to planet earth to, amongst other things, judge evil and usher in His righteous kingdom (Revelation 19). I could go on and elaborate but, as far as this book is concerned, I have said enough, other than make the point – Trust **His** plan, for it is the only one we can be entirely confident in!

Many years ago, as a youngish preacher, about to set out on a preaching tour in what was to become the country of my second home – India, I was offered two bits of sage advice, by wiser, older mentors, that I would like to pass on to those reading this book, especially if like me the reader is intent on preaching the gospel. Firstly, we must put aside personal hang ups about this or that issue or pet subject, but rather focus on encouraging listeners, something this book seeks to do for its readers. Secondly, we must not ignore the subject of suffering, even though all too often there is no pat answer for those who have suffered or are experiencing suffering. After all, the last book of the Bible, which is almost entirely all prophecy, Revelation, was written to prepare its readers for suffering. I would like to begin these final thoughts by considering something that goes hand in hand with encouragement – that of warning, specifically given our proneness to deception, reflect further on the subject of suffering, something no true follower of Jesus can avoid (see also Chapter 18) and consider the writing on the wall.

Before elaborating on these two bits of advice that I can now see are needed more than ever for such a time as this and coming up with a suitable new conclusion, let me reiterate that I fully stand by what I wrote, now over a year ago, that went out as the First Edition. I was, after all, trying to do what I have long tried to do – faithfully expound the scriptures as best I can, adopting certain principles that many great Bible scholars of the past have adhered to, even though maybe taking different views and, understandably, emphasising different things. Where I get more controversial is concerning how to apply prophecy to the current situation and what to make out of modern-day prophecy, given my own church background were not much into such things and many who are do not go along with my views, yet noting that even in the course of one year my views have developed, if not changed, and will do so again. It is unlikely, however, any one understands it all.

While "test and weigh" is something I urge people do whenever they receive new information, insights etc., I particularly urge they do so regarding what is going on right now, my take on events, the future etc., and especially when it comes to modern day "prophets", some of whom have sadly been found wanting. I continue to take as my role model the children of Issachar, of whom it is written *"were men that had understanding of the times, to know what Israel ought to do"* 1 Chronicles 12:32. Along with modern day Elishas, who knew what was spoken in the king's bedroom, we could do with the modern equivalent of Children of Issachar. As I turn my attention to the kings and priests of the Bible, it seems to me we have more than enough of their modern-day equivalents, although often not of the desired calibre, but when it comes to genuine prophets, there is a dearth, especially given the need and for balance sake the prophetic voice is desperately needed.

Deception

"And the great dragon was cast out, that old serpent, called the Devil, and Satan, which deceiveth the whole world: he was cast out into the earth, and his angels were cast out with him" Revelation 12:9.

When it comes to issues and concerns for fellow Christians, there may be many, not least that we all are found united (reference Jesus' High Priestly prayer of John 17) and living holy lives experiencing the power and blessing of the living God. More down to earth, perhaps, is the matter of deception.

"Beloved, when I gave all diligence to write unto you of the common salvation, it was needful for me to write unto you, and exhort you that ye should earnestly contend for the faith which was once delivered unto the saints" Jude 3.

"For God so loved the world, that he gave his only begotten Son, that whosoever believeth in him should not perish, but have everlasting life" John 3:16.

We all have a tendency to align with those who echo and support our opinions, often based on our own life experiences and axioms we live by. Perhaps, one sign of maturity is to live serenely with difference, accept that sometimes we are wrong, realise there is much we don't know and prioritise what matters (*"get wisdom, get understanding"* and *"wisdom is the principal thing; therefore get wisdom"* Proverbs 4:5,7). Often it is safer to align with groups as it suits us etc., for the result of not doing so is like what may happen walking in the middle of the road, with the danger of being knocked down by traffic coming in either direction. We may want to join with a particular theological stable, especially if we are looking to associate with sound doctrine, as long as we realise none are 100% correct. The trick is to avoid bigotry and to discern – knowing / doing what is right and humility, adopting the maxim we can trace back to St. Augustine: *"in essentials unity, in non-essentials liberty, in all things charity"* and the prayer of Reinhold Niebuhr: *"God, grant me the serenity to accept the things I cannot change, courage to change the things I can, and wisdom to know the difference"*.

As I wrote earlier, my own stable for a lot of my life has been the Plymouth Brethren, which some see as a cult and others as those who more than any follow the text in Jude 3 and believe the text in John 3. One good lesson I did learn from the PBs is in their eagerness to be right and custodians of the truth, they could be unnecessarily dismissive of some of those who saw things differently yet truly, and not always gracious. More than twenty years back, I wrote a paper titled: "**Who Are The Brethren**" (available on my website) and my concluding paragraph reads: "*At the risk of being dismissed as a spiritual schizophrenic by my readers or a heretic by my (Plymouth) brothers, I am inclined toward a vision of the church that is Catholic in spirituality, Liberal in social activism, Reformed in doctrine, Charismatic in experience, Evangelical in zeal, Puritan in living, Methodist in organisation and Brethren in ecclesiology, but above all passionate for Jesus. Finally, although an enthusiastic researcher of Brethren history who is keen to "get it right", I am much more concerned that men and women, and boys and girls, walk the way, trust the truth and live the life of the Lord Jesus Christ (John 14v6); and may He be exalted, by whatever instrument He chooses, Brethren or otherwise. And may all God's people receive a touch from heaven so that they may touch earth in His glorious cause. O Lord grant us grace to lose what is dear, so we may gain Him who is dearest, and may Thy Kingdom come*". I should add, I still cannot find a perfect role model when it comes to eschatology.

If you were to ask well known atheist, Richard Dawkins, the question we want to attempt to answer (*i.e.* are most Christians deceived?) he would probably say any who believe in the equivalent to fairies at the bottom of your garden are likely to be deceived. As for me, when I was aged 15, I accepted the Lord Jesus Christ as my Lord and Saviour, recognising He died on the cross to redeem me and save me from Hell and, while there have been many hiccups in the 55 years up to now, I have followed and still follow Him and seek after truth. I have a love for His Church and, in writing as I do, I try to warn and encourage the Church (*i.e.* believers in Him) as well as those who are not the Church, mindful of His High Priestly prayer of John 17, praying disciples in the future, including today, be One, as He is with His Father. It appears to be a long way from being answered in its entirety. My writings and blogs are evidence of my own concerns and perspectives even though it has come at a cost of upsetting several Christian ministers, including those from my own theological stable, and going through refining fire.

But what I want to get to is the subject of deception and all of us have it in us to be deceived, just as Jesus pointed out in His Mount Olivet discourse (Matthew 24) *e.g.* "*for there shall arise false Christs, and false prophets, and shall shew great signs and wonders; insomuch that, if it were possible, they shall deceive the very elect*" (24:24), and particularly as we come to "End Times". When it comes to the End, the culmination of the sequence of events to be expected is the return of Jesus, described in Revelation 19. The Apostle Paul elaborates on the theme of deception in the light of this, in 2 Thessalonians 2. I wish to focus on one example of deception as my ear has been bent in recent days by Christians of good standing *e.g.* quoting the Jude 3 text that is pivotal, citing concerns like "New Age", "Gnostic", "Syncretic", "Theosophy" and the occult, who have spoken particularly against those involved in a "Reawaken America" tour (meant to do just that) that is taking place in the USA as I write (www. timetofreeamerica.com), although to wake people up and enthuse them is one thing, leading them to a true knowledge of God, which faithful gospel preachers should be doing, is another.

Others have expressed concern I am going down these rabbit holes as many of those who do so often push New Age notions not in accordance with the teachings of the Bible, although (rightly) pointing out that the world right now is anything but what it ought to be, and all this can only be a distraction and not good for one's mental well-being. But we can't ignore what is going on in increasing plain sight and should ask what if anything we should be doing about it. If I can cite one Bible teacher, J.D.Farag, who is no friend from what I can make out of modern day political prophets yet who, other than some of his end time views, is deemed as sound by most, he gives reasons why he believes a lot of the end of the world stuff, talked about in the Book of Revelation, is coming to pass right now *e.g.* his belief that the bad guys are looking to control humanity because they have access to peoples' DNA is especially alarming, and anyone who has seen the latest James Bond movie, "No Time to Die", will know just what I mean.

Before I examine further the New Age deception, I would like to refer to another deception that is just as insidious and perhaps even more widespread. Since Satan, the father of lies, is the instigator of all deceptions there is some commonality. He is, after all, the quintessential past master, having tempted Eve to eat the forbidden fruit in the Garden of Eden. When I began my Christian journey 55 years ago, I was made aware of broadly three groups of Christians: Evangelicals, Liberals and Catholics, who joined forces when it suited them and kept their distance and outrightly opposed each other when it didn't. As for the cults, and non-Christian religions, they could be safely ignored as too far away from the truth to count.

My Plymouth Brethren mentors, while decidedly Evangelical in their beliefs, often distanced themselves from other Evangelicals, such as the Pentecostals, because of their views on the Holy Spirit, and many mainline denominations because of their ecclesiology and eschatology beliefs. The "Christian" landscape has changed much in the period following and my own journey has brought me in contact with many, who if they were around, my PB mentors would likely disapprove of. While I now value alternative perspectives on Christian living in accordance with Bible principles and have learned a lot from such folk, my gospel related beliefs, broadly outlined above, have firmly remained.

Few would disagree we live in interesting times and some will come up with more apt adjectives. Of course, at the same time, we know there is nothing new under the sun; Christians ever since New Testament days have been in contention with other Christians on what Christians should believe etc. But Solomon did not have to contend with issues like the US Presidential Election fraud and the Corona pandemic and would not have had to come to a view on climate change, LBGTQ inclusion and Critical Race Theory. What I have noted, sadly, is many ministers have fallen in line with the ideas of globalists calling for the Great Reset (it used to be referred to as the New World Order) and have allowed social justice issues to take priority over preaching the gospel and either dismiss or ignore evils such as child sex trafficking, mega financial theft, agendas to depopulate and enslave humanity and the attack on God taking place in our institutions and culture as well as evils such as abortion, these often go unchallenged. It seems to me that many ministers have lost their nerve when it comes to putting into action gospel certainties, preferring to be contemporary and relevant instead, and in doing so have become more awoke than awake. While there is a need for wisdom, as for the prophetic voice, as far as church is concerned, it appears to be dismissed.

Besides those falling for these deceptions, what also bothers me is those opposing some purporting to be Christian, claiming these endorse New Age etc. teaching, yet at the same time ignore the important matters they raise. Then there are those who seek to rise above what is going on and choose not to get involved. Cowardice is no excuse and, subtly, is yet another form of deception. When we consider Christians who are taken in by the false narrative promoted by government and endorsed by the media and the elite, when it comes to Covid-19 and how to approach the pan (scam) demic, together with those not taken in, yet are beholden to conspiracy theories, expecting a Great Awakening, along with all other groups discussed so far, the question is begged: who is not deceived? And that includes those Christians who can truly say they have not been taken in by any of the above deceptions yet have indulged in some sin or other, without having truly repented.

When I once wrote about "New Age", I considered both the accusation and what some accused of New Ageism were saying. After all, New Age when applied to spirituality etc. outside the God of the Bible, is a deception and, as we have discussed, all deception has at its root Satan. On reflection, I don't wish to go off on tangents by discussing the views of others that all too often get misrepresented by those who take issue, nor will I take sides without knowing the facts. I am in no doubt good people on any side can hold erroneous views and it is important to stand firm on the truth (I give my understanding of what that is, when it comes to the Gospel, in Chapter 17). What is particularly sad from where I stand is seeing people getting up on their spiritual high horses and seeing Satan's divide and rule strategy working. While valuing a lot of my early PB upbringing, I regret that all too often a lot more importance was attached to light at the expense of life.

While my own Bible understanding is things will get worse, I would love to see a temporary respite from the evil that I see in the world and deception that has befallen greater humanity, and I even expect a Great Awakening, at least of the spiritual kind (albeit with more deception, just as Jesus said would be the case) – but then I can only be fully assured of what is taught in the Bible. While the scene is being set for the coming of the AntiChrist and the Great Tribulation, he has not been revealed and it has not happened yet. As for timings, the Lord alone knows, and we need to be patient. My sadness is not so much such folk are deceived but that those who know the truth have set such a bad example. Therein lies a great opportunity for the people of God and to get their act together, beginning with taking seriously the John 17 prayer, and bringing people back to the true God.

The Lord ever works in mysterious ways, but always there is Satan to oppose and do all he can to prevent the glorious church Jesus prayed for, that is so authentic that people believe the truth. In the meantime, all Hell is let loose to prevent this. It seems to me there are all sorts of deceptions, some not mentioned here, for example Christians thinking too highly of themselves or not high enough – the result is the same, Satan gains a foothold, including hidden sin, which needs to be resisted and can if we put on the armour of God. For Christians awake to Satan's devices, these do well to meekly warn and encourage those who do succumb.

But this is what I believe ***does*** matter… We should not be putting our hope in man or what we think ought to be happening and neither should we be fearing what man says and does – the only one we should fear is the Lord God Almighty. We must be mindful of the human tendency to gravitate to what it wants to hear and finding ways to reinforce one's prejudices and resisting that which doesn't, and be careful that reflecting on what is going on around us, especially what we don't know for sure, does not replace things like prayer, Bible study and fellowship and hearing what God is saying. We should be alert to deception (for us and others). In her book "***War on the Saints***" (published 1915), Jessie Penn Lewis provides many examples of deception and traps even the sincerest Christians have fallen into, that applied then and apply today. We should humbly accept not only there is much we don't know but it is unlikely we will know this side of eternity.

I have decided to follow Jesus;
I have decided to follow Jesus;
I have decided to follow Jesus;
No turning back, no turning back.

Tho' none go with me, I still will follow,
Tho' none go with me, I still will follow,
Tho' none go with me, I still will follow;
No turning back, no turning back.

My cross I'll carry, till I see Jesus;
My cross I'll carry, till I see Jesus,
My cross I'll carry, till I see Jesus;

No turning back, No turning back.

The world behind me, the cross before me,
The world behind me, the cross before me;
The world behind me, the cross before me;
No turning back, no turning back.

We should trust the Lord and search the scriptures. We are called to serve Him (check out the section on ***the Unprofitable Servant***). There is much we don't know and much we cannot change, including egregious examples of evil that have been pointed out by some of those folk whose deception we take issue with (it seems to me Christians often outdo one another in calling out those they disagree with), but even if we are powerless, God is able to do more than we can ask or think. He has given each one of us unique opportunities (often making it clear if we have eyes to see etc.) to make a difference and play our part in His great purposes for human kind, and this should be our focus. Included in this is the need to take seriously the Great Commission. There is more that can be said and more to be checked out. I reaffirm the truth: "*For I am not ashamed of the gospel of Christ: for it is the power of God unto salvation to every one that believeth; to the Jew first, and also to the Greek*" Romans 1:16. I preceded this paragraph with a song that influenced me as a young Christian and I end with another song that was also popular in my youth and pray that these sentiments may bless you too.

O soul are you weary and troubled
No light in the darkness you see
There's light for a look at the Savior
And life more abundant and free

Chorus
Turn your eyes upon Jesus
Look full in his wonderful face
And the things of earth will grow strangely dim
In the light of his glory and grace

His word shall not fail you he promised
Believe him and all will be well
Then go to a world that is dying

His perfect salvation to tell

Suffering

"If we suffer, we shall also reign with him: if we deny him, he also will deny us" 2 Timothy 2:12.

I had an interesting recent experience visiting a soup kitchen I am involved with, which provides meals for the homeless and other disadvantaged persons. I got into a conversation with a couple, who had been homeless, who asked me how I spent my retirement. When I told them I write books, such as this one, we got into a discussion about faith in God and some of the things that stopped people having faith, such as the fact that innocent people suffer. I pointed out that God was not indifferent to human suffering. An example of this is Jesus (who is both God and man (the only man completely innocent)) who suffered, bled and died on a cross to save us from our sins. I hope it at least got my homeless friends thinking.

It also got me thinking again about a subject that has exercised humanity from time immemorial and has stumbled many – why do the innocent suffer? I could give examples of all sorts of suffering that has been experienced by human kind, several of which most readers will be aware of and none of us are immune from suffering, which seems a lottery, but I won't as that is not the point of my writing on the subject. Neither will I rate different types of suffering in order of severity – it is neither my field of expertise nor my right to do so. The wisest original thing I can say is the things people suffer, as much as anything, affect what they think, say, do etc. and it is well to make allowances when formulating a response. Even wiser, is to turn our attentions to the Bible, which includes many texts pointing out that suffering is something we should come to expect and, positively, it produces character in us and makes us more empathetic toward others suffering.

Before considering the Book of Job, let us recap on some home truths. Suffering is something all of us experience to a greater or lesser extent and it is not for any of us to pontificate on who has suffered more or many of the whys or wherefores or to offer pious platitudes to the sufferer. The best that can be said, and why what happened in Job's case, even though he did not realise it at the time, is so pertinent – is God is in control and has all the answers. The salutary observation is people respond to suffering in different ways. While anger or grief may be a laudable and understandable response, at least initially, when one becomes twisted or bitter it is counterproductive and it is easy to point to individuals so scarred by suffering. The best longer-term responses, in my judgment, are when people develop good character as a result of their painful experiences and even use these positively, such as in their empathetic dealings with others suffering in similar ways.

It is also worth bringing the Devil into the discussion (after all he paid a key role in Job's story). There is, for example, suffering brought on by trials and temptations, which may or may not be instigated by the Devil and where we are not, partly or wholly to blame in some way. It is why suffering ties in with the other main topic of this section, deception. We should see suffering for what it is and take a godly view rather than a know it all human one! Also, given our central theme is prophets of the Bible, having gone through almost all of them, we might make another salutary observation. They suffered in many different ways and such was their solemn mission and opposition by the ungodly, it was often more than most, but God is not mocked, He saw them through it all and because of it what they said and did blessed people then and continue to bless us now.

The obvious book of the Bible to turn to when considering the subject of suffering is that of Job, which provides a human angle that we can identify with today, even though it is reckoned Job was around at the time of Abraham (*i.e.* 2000 BC). More pertinently, it gives a perspective of what is going on, often missed when people discuss why suffering exists – that of God. We read how Job started off doing well by both human and divine standards and then his own world came crashing down before him, leaving him barely alive, with everything gone (including his ten children), a barely sympathetic wife and "friends" whose attempts to comfort him, were anything but, before God intervenes at the end, restoring two-fold what Job had lost. While Job's "happily ever after" ending is not one many sufferers can claim for themselves, there are still many lessons we can draw from his story.

According to Wikipedia: "*The Book of Job addresses the problem of theodicy, meaning why God permits evil in the world ... Job is a wealthy and God-fearing man with a comfortable life and a large family; God, having asked Satan for his opinion of Job's piety, decides to take away Job's wealth, family and material comforts, following Satan's accusation that if Job were rendered penniless and without his family, he would turn away from God.*" The bulk of the book of Job is taken up with Job and his three "comforters", and a fourth "friend" who comes in later on speaking his two penny-worth, pontificating over the problem of suffering (especially for people like Job that purport to be righteous), before God comes in at the end (chapter 38 onwards) and without necessarily giving them too many of the answers to their concerns, after putting Job and his friends straight, including telling all parties, including righteous Job, that they did not know what they were talking about (how could they – after all they did not witness what was going on behind the scenes between God and Satan) it merely reminds us we need to be in awe of Him, who in the end brings it all to a satisfactory conclusion. A further exposition of Job is outside the scope of this book but in ending we will cite two items of Job wisdom and follow this up from the Book of Revelation, which shows why the subject of suffering matters from a prophetic perspective, because that is what we should expect and prepare for, especially in these Last Days.

"Though he slay me, yet will I trust in him: but I will maintain mine own ways before him" Job 13:15.

"For I know that my redeemer liveth, and that he shall stand at the latter day upon the earth: And though after my skin worms destroy this body, yet in my flesh shall I see God" Job 18:25-26

"After this I beheld, and, lo, a great multitude, which no man could number, of all nations, and kindreds, and people, and tongues, stood before the throne, and before the Lamb, clothed with white robes, and palms in their hands; And cried with a loud voice, saying, Salvation to our God which sitteth upon the throne, and unto the Lamb. And all the angels stood round about the throne, and about the elders and the four beasts, and fell before the throne on their faces, and worshipped God, Saying, Amen: Blessing, and glory, and wisdom, and thanksgiving, and honour, and power, and might, be unto our God for ever and ever. Amen. And one of the elders answered, saying unto me, What are these which are arrayed in white robes? and whence came they? And I said unto him, Sir, thou knowest. And he said to me, These are they which came out of great tribulation, and have washed their robes, and made them white in the blood of the Lamb. Therefore are they before the throne of God, and serve him day and night in his temple: and he that sitteth on the throne shall dwell among them. They shall hunger no more, neither thirst any more; neither shall the sun light on them, nor any heat. For the Lamb which is in the midst of the throne shall feed them, and shall lead them unto living fountains of waters: and God shall wipe away all tears from their eyes" Revelation 7:9-17.

The Writing on the Wall

"And I heard another voice from heaven, saying, Come out of her, my people, that ye be not partakers of her sins, and that ye receive not of her plagues" Revelation 18:4.

Mene, mene, tekel, upharsin (ˈmiːni miːni tɛkəl juːˈfɑrsɪn) was the writing on the wall that followed Belshazzar's Feast, interpreted by Daniel, the Hebrew prophet, to mean that God had weighed Belshazzar and his kingdom, had found them wanting, and was about to swiftly destroy them, and it was done so by stealth, as the Persian army diverted a river to enable them to enter and conquer what was considered at the time the impregnable city of Babylon, and on that very night (read all about it in Daniel 5). This was also to mark a major turning point in Israel's history as their 70 years in exile was about to come to an end and they would be free to return home under the decree issued by the Persian King, Cyrus.

Like many, I tend to use the term *"writing on the wall"* pretty loosely, as I look at what is happening around me and try to figure out the significance of various signs that might suggest what is going to happen next, albeit with less confidence than what happened with Daniel, who rightly interpreted the writing that appeared on the wall out of nowhere, as King Belshazzar and his entourage were indulging at their feast in defiance of the God of Israel. Seeing the mysterious hand writing on the wall would have been terrifying to all who witnessed it. *Mene, mene, tekel, upharsin* literally means "numbered, numbered, weighed, divided", and that is what God decreed and what happened to Belshazzar and his kingdom.

As I write, looking at the latest developments in the Corona saga, I take the writing on the wall to mean further draconian measures in the offing for the people of the UK as a result, as is already happening in different places in the world, especially to those who go against the official line, and who can say what is going to happen next, and especially significant if as seems likely it is for the worse? No doubt, if I were to write this in a month's time, say, I could come up with a new example of what I think constitutes writing on the wall – an end to the US Election Steal saga maybe. Unlike Daniel, I am not a prophet and, while there are signs if we take the time and effort to check these out, these are nothing so dramatic as what took place with the writing on Belshazzar's wall on that fateful day.

Who can say for sure which direction the world is soon to take other than what the Bible teaches, noting plausible diverse views "out there"? When we think of the wickedness of government and institutions, for example, we are reminded of the words *"He that sitteth in the heavens shall laugh: the Lord shall have them in derision"* Psalm 2:4. His calling is that people *"Serve the Lord with fear, and rejoice with trembling"* Psalm 2:11. In another Psalm we are told: *"The Lord bringeth the counsel of the nations to nought; He maketh the thoughts of the peoples to be of no effect"* 33:10. As far as the writing on the wall goes for our times, we do well to remember that all actions have consequences and wrongdoers will one day be required to give an account of these to God, the righteous judge.

Two quite different directions the world may be about to take have already been discussed: "The Great Reset" and "The Great Awakening". It has given rise to heated debate and fall outs, including among those broadly in my own theological camp, who reject both notions. Few would have predicted the events seen since the "Great US Election Steal": further cover ups, more Covid-19 relating shenanigans (including jab related and coercion of citizens to comply to government overreach), miscellaneous world events of a disturbing nature that has exposed more of the evil and evil doers in the world and, importantly, as far as this book is concerned, all sorts of responses from among Christian folk, which from where I am watching and, as I have argued, are often not the right ones.

Will it lead to the Great Reset, talked about by many elements of an unholy trinity of politicians, media and societal leaders, and with it the eventual emergence of the Antichrist, discussed in Revelation 13, or will it lead to the Great Awakening that is predicted or at least hoped for by elements of yet another trinity, here comprising New Age conspiracy theorists, modern day political prophets and certain Christians, who I label as "the church of the deplorables" (the Remnant), which comprise one or both of a great spiritual revival and the fall of the Cabal, like that prophesied concerning the modern day Babylon equivalent, in Revelation 17 and 18? As for the notion of an evil cabal running the world and controlling its institutions etc., this is being increasingly realized by people waking up to the reality of this. Whether what is being proposed as an alternative, such as a "good" alternative to the New World Order, is questionable. But, as far as spiritual Babylon is concerned, the word to God's people remains: *"come out of her"*. Moreover, we are called to be faithful to our God, love our neighbour, especially our Christian brethren, announce His Kingdom to all and preach His Gospel.

It is worth pondering a little more on the "***Mystery of Babylon***", elaborating on thoughts I penned on the subject some eighteen months ago when I wrote Chapter 15 to address twenty of the more challenging and controversial unfulfilled or partially fulfilled prophecies of the Bible. As I re-read what I wrote then on this topic, while I still hold with what I wrote, I feel I did not do full justice to a subject that is so pertinent to these times, not least due to the Babylonian system we now see. It is quite evident, on this subject, there is a wide range of views and it is not my intention to try to articulate the right one. My spiritual forefathers often had a simpler view of the Great Whore seated on the Beast, of whom it is written *"upon* *her forehead was a name written, Mystery, Babylon The Great, The Mother Of Harlots And Abominations Of The Earth*" Revelation 17:5, this representing the Roman Catholic Church in cahoots with the AntiChrist led global social, economic, political system he oversees, at the height of her power during the time of the Great Tribulation. They did make one point worth reminding ourselves of – despite our knowing more, it will not stop what the Bible says will happen. Factors they would not have seen include new major centres of global power, *e.g.* China, the rise of Islam, notably under Saudi Arabia, increasing exposure of an evil cabal, involving elements of the Illuminati, certain "bloodline families", the Deep State, the World Economic Forum, the United Nations, to enslave the masses, the push for globalism, including global corporations etc., usurping the middle classes, the Corona "pandemic" and the power wielded by Big Pharma.

Deeper discussion on the subject of Babylon the Great is outside the scope of this last chapter but it is worth pointing out Revelation 17 and 18, coupled with Jeremiah 50 and 51 and other Bible texts, is a major and significant chunk of prophecy and one that is particularly pertinent to these modern times. It relates to earlier discussions in this chapter on the Great Reset and the Great Awakening, where some of those hoping for and expecting the latter should consider that while it may be desirable to see an end of the Babylonian system, the Bible suggests it will be around until the time just prior to Christ's return in Revelation 19 and any advocacy of an Age of Aquarius is inviting the very deception the Antichrist will exploit. But we can look forward to "*And the light of a candle shall shine no more at all in thee; and the voice of the bridegroom and of the bride shall be heard no more at all in thee: for thy merchants were the great men of the earth; for by thy sorceries were all nations deceived. And in her was found the blood of prophets, and of saints, and of all that were slain upon the earth*" Revelation 18:23,24. The definition given in Strong's Concordance for the Greek word the KJV translates as sorcery, ***pharmakeia***, is sorcery or witchcraft in the use or the administering of drugs and also sorcery and magical arts, often found in connection with idolatry and fostered by it, along with the deceptions and seductions of such idolatry.

Much as I shudder when, for example, I listen again to Prince Charles' speech at the recent COP26 conference, where among other things he alludes to someone about to sort out the world's problems (the Antichrist maybe), I see that is where we may be heading right now. While some mainly sound Christians dismiss notions of a Great Awakening, I can understand their rationale, especially since many pushing this promote error. Even so, an awakening to the truth was my hope ever since the US Election was stolen on November 3rd 2020 and long before that even, ever since I became a Christian in fact. While Conspiracy Theorists have often been proven right over time, many subscribe to New Age, syncretic, Gnostic notions, which are erroneous. As for the modern-day prophets, while there are many instances of prophecy fulfilled, some have been found wanting.

As for the deplorables, which to qualify means being sold out for God and His Word, and unconcerned if it means going against the flow (church and state), some of whom have the temerity to say things like Corona is a ginormous hoax orchestrated by the Black Hats who are using this with the intention of enslaving the masses to bring about their twisted notions of a New World Order and some take issue with Great Awakening ideas because of links to the occult. Those who recoil at the thought of a Great Reset often have the tendency of clutching at straws, looking for respite by way of the NWO plans being somehow nullified, despite evidence pointing to the Antichrist led, Great Tribulation looming large. As I discussed earlier, there is a real danger of replacing one form of deception with another. As for true Christian believers, the ideology we should subscribe to and promote is the Gospel of Salvation (as set out in Romans 1:16).

The more I watch and pray, the less certain which, if any, of Great Reset or Great Awakening it will be (or whether there will be a mixture since the world knows not yet Christ), although having no doubt there will be a righteous kingdom and God wins in the end. Even though a Great Awakening sounds attractive, anything not of God is of the Devil, and needs to be rejected. The Lord has everything figured out and is in complete control and is testing and refining His people, calling them to simply trust and obey. We are being tested, with more to come (to remind ourselves: one of the main reasons why the Book of Revelation was written was to prepare us for suffering but with a glorious hope that is to follow). One thing I do believe is many good Christians are about to find out they have been conned and need a comforting arm and many who we least expect are about to come into God's Kingdom and we need to be there to encourage them. And for the sake of balance, I share yet another Psalm to help guide out thoughts and give us peace, so come what may we should be still and know that He is God.

"God is our refuge and strength, a very present help in trouble. Therefore will not we fear, though the earth be removed, and though the mountains be carried into the midst of the sea; Though the waters thereof roar and be troubled, though the mountains shake with the swelling thereof. Selah. There is a river, the streams whereof shall make glad the city of God, the holy place of the tabernacles of the most High. God is in the midst of her; she shall not be moved: God shall help her,

and that right early. The heathen raged, the kingdoms were moved: he uttered his voice, the earth melted. The Lord of hosts is with us; the God of Jacob is our refuge. Selah. Come, behold the works of the Lord, what desolations he hath made in the earth. He maketh wars to cease unto the end of the earth; he breaketh the bow, and cutteth the spear in sunder; he burneth the chariot in the fire. Be still, and know that I am God: I will be exalted among the heathen, I will be exalted in the earth. The Lord of hosts is with us; the God of Jacob is our refuge. Selah" Psalm 46.

Conclusion

"And he said, Go thy way, Daniel: for the words are closed up and sealed till the time of the end. Many shall be purified, and made white, and tried; but the wicked shall do wickedly: and none of the wicked shall understand; but the wise shall understand." Daniel 12:9,10.

If you have read all the way from the beginning, then congratulations although, seriously, I hope despite being told hard truths and feeling the alarm that Daniel felt when he was told, you are encouraged and will consider and act on what you find in God's word (just as I speak this to myself). I pray we both *"along with the people that do know their God shall be strong, and do exploits"* Daniel 11:32.

We live in crazy days and while "unprecedented" seems a bit strong if a student of history, as there is nothing new under the sun, but that is how it looks to me. We have no right to criticise the students of prophecy from previous generations who did not get it spot on in their interpreting and attempts to understand the times they lived in. The same might be said by future generations about us, should the Lord tarry with His return, as they will see things we could never have seen or predicted, our being not party to knowledge that has been hidden from us.

While there is a lot we do know, should we be prepared to check things out (and it is why I write as I do), there is a lot we don't know, even if we spend all our time doing research, and moreover the Lord has chosen not to reveal all to us. The events we are witnessing right now are often disturbing and may be tempted to despair. But as for what He does require, along with what Micah tells us (6:8), is we be faithful, holy, kind, peaceful, patient and wise etc., until when He comes in the clouds and we meet Him or we die before and He takes us to be with Him.

I am sure, many authors, like me, offer up what they write, mindful there is more they could say and when they reflect may be conscious some things might have been better left unsaid. I am luckier than many because of the way I operate of having more than one bite of the cherry but knowing it is time to move on – kings and priests beckon. I close, wanting to give encouragement, by way of more related Bible texts which, better than what my words can achieve, encapsulate many of the themes covered in this section in particular and the book in general.

It has ever been my desire to help people to know the scriptures. This is one of the most worthwhile activities one can be engaged in, providing we are doers of the Word. I have deliberately alternated between OT and NT as the two testaments perfectly complement one another. We follow the risen Christ and while trials and tribulations, and we do not know what is round the corner, the end is a glorious one and we need to take to heart words of the Prophets of the Bible, especially the greatest prophet of them all, who is more than a prophet – the Lord Jesus Christ.

Before we turn to our twenty Bible texts that have blessed me (and I hope will bless you too), to do with the message of this book, given we are trying here to encourage one another "in the Lord", we might do well to recap certain home truths. The first one goes back to the very first chapter of the Bible – God created man, *i.e.* including me and you, in His own image, and that makes us special and unique. The second is that God has given us the freedom to choose between good and evil, truth and error, right and wrong etc., but in choosing Him and His ways (even though we may have been party to that all too human trait of "blowing it") we can live out His perfect plan for our lives (He is ever so patient), however dire or unfavourable our personal circumstances, disposition etc., appear to be.

As for the times we live in, it is not for me to say they are better or worse than what our forefathers experienced, especially if subject to plague, war, oppression, famine etc., which is just as well for know so little. What we can say, the world is *not* at peace and at the precipice of events taking place, taking us into unknown and quite likely less than comfortable territory (which is one reason why I release this new edition of my book at this time). Not only are things not what they ought to be, they are more often than not what they seem to be. Many are beginning to wake up to this reality and in doing so turn to the spiritual that is not necessarily the Holy Spirit. Our job is clear: to point people to the God that the true Prophets of the Bible served and to be part of that faithful remnant through which He acts. Finally, I want to thank Una Campbell for proof reading these latest changes.

Fear God and obey Him

"Let us hear the conclusion of the whole matter: Fear God, and keep his commandments: for this is the whole duty of man. For God shall bring every work into judgment, with every secret thing, whether it be good, or whether it be evil" Ecclesiastes 12:13,14.

Submission to authorities placed in context

"Love worketh no ill to his neighbour: therefore love is the fulfilling of the law. And that, knowing the time, that now it is high time to awake out of sleep: for now is our salvation nearer than when we believed. The night is far spent, the day is at hand: let us therefore cast off the works of darkness, and let us put on the armour of light. Let us walk honestly, as in the day; not in rioting and drunkenness, not in chambering and wantonness, not in strife and envying. But put ye on the Lord Jesus Christ, and make not provision for the flesh, to fulfil the lusts thereof" Romans 13:10-14.

My baptismal text; encouraging strength and courage

"Only be thou strong and very courageous, that thou mayest observe to do according to all the law, which Moses my servant commanded thee: turn not from it to the right hand or to the left, that thou mayest prosper withersoever thou goest. This book of the law shall not depart out of thy mouth; but thou shalt meditate therein day and night, that thou mayest observe to do according to all that is written therein: for then thou shalt make thy way prosperous, and then thou shalt have good success. Have not I commanded thee? Be strong and of a good courage; be not afraid, neither be thou dismayed: for the Lord thy God is with thee whithersoever thou goest" Joshua 1:7-9.

Our commission; His promise

"And Jesus came and spake unto them, saying, All power is given unto me in heaven and in earth. Go ye therefore, and teach all nations, baptizing them in the name of the Father, and of the Son, and of the Holy Ghost: Teaching them to observe all things whatsoever I have commanded you: and, lo, I am with you always, even unto the end of the world. Amen" Matthew 28:18-20.

More on how we should conduct ourselves

"*Sow to yourselves in righteousness, reap in mercy; break up your fallow ground: for it is time to seek the Lord, till he come and rain righteousness upon you*" Hosea 10:12.

Keep looking to the Lord, who has gone before us

"*Wherefore seeing we also are compassed about with so great a cloud of witnesses, let us lay aside every weight, and the sin which doth so easily beset us, and let us run with patience the race that is set before us, Looking unto Jesus the author and finisher of our faith; who for the joy that was set before him endured the cross, despising the shame, and is set down at the right hand of the throne of God. For consider him that endured such contradiction of sinners against himself, lest ye be wearied and faint in your minds*" Hebrews 12:1-3.

It may look bad now but we can still rejoice

"*Although the fig tree shall not blossom, neither shall fruit be in the vines; the labour of the olive shall fail, and the fields shall yield no meat; the flock shall be cut off from the fold, and there shall be no herd in the stalls: Yet I will rejoice in the Lord, I will joy in the God of my salvation. The Lord God is my strength, and he will make my feet like hinds' feet, and he will make me to walk upon mine high places. To the chief singer on my stringed instruments*" Habakkuk 3:17-18.

The law and the prophets placed in a nutshell

"*Jesus said unto him, Thou shalt love the Lord thy God with all thy heart, and with all thy soul, and with all thy mind. This is the first and great commandment. And the second is like unto it, Thou shalt love thy neighbour as thyself. On these two commandments hang all the law and the prophets*" Matthew 22:37-40

We can always hope in the Lord and that hope is never misplaced

"*And thou hast removed my soul far off from peace. I forgat prosperity. And I said, My strength and my hope is perished from the Lord: Remembering mine affliction and my misery, the wormwood and the gall. My soul hath them still in remembrance, and is humbled in me. This I recall to my mind, therefore have I hope. It is of the Lord's mercies that we are not consumed, because his compassions fail not. They are new every morning: great is thy faithfulness. The Lord is my portion, saith my soul; therefore will I hope in him. The Lord is good unto them that wait for him, to the soul that seeketh him. It is good that a man should both hope and quietly wait for the salvation of the Lord. It is good for a man that he bear the yoke in his youth"* Lamentations 3:17-27.

Jesus prays for us that we may be one and the world may know

"Neither pray I for these alone, but for them also which shall believe on me through their word; That they all may be one; as thou, Father, art in me, and I in thee, that they also may be one in us: that the world may believe that thou hast sent me. And the glory which thou gavest me I have given them; that they may be one, even as we are one: I in them, and thou in me, that they may be made perfect in one; and that the world may know that thou hast sent me, and hast loved them, as thou hast loved me. Father, I will that they also, whom thou hast given me, be with me where I am; that they may behold my glory, which thou hast given me: for thou lovedst me before the foundation of the world. O righteous Father, the world hath not known thee: but I have known thee, and these have known that thou hast sent me. And I have declared unto them thy name, and will declare it: that the love wherewith thou hast loved me may be in them, and I in them" John 17:20-26.

Conspiracy theories and the fear of the Lord

"For the Lord spoke thus to me with his strong hand upon me, and warned me not to walk in the way of this people, saying: Do not call conspiracy all that this people calls conspiracy, and do not fear what they fear, nor be in dread. But the Lord of hosts, him you shall honor as holy. Let him be your fear, and let him be your dread" Isaiah 8:11-13 (ESV).

Life in the Spirit and with it a glorious expectation

"Likewise the Spirit also helpeth our infirmities: for we know not what we should pray for as we ought: but the Spirit itself maketh intercession for us with groanings which cannot be uttered. And he that searcheth the hearts knoweth what is the mind of the Spirit, because he maketh intercession for the saints according to the will of God. And we know that all things work together for good to them that love God, to them who are the called according to his purpose. For whom he did foreknow, he also did predestinate to be conformed to the image of his Son, that he might be the firstborn among many brethren. Moreover whom he did predestinate, them he also

called: and whom he called, them he also justified: and whom he justified, them he also glorified. What shall we then say to these things? If God be for us, who can be against us? He that spared not his own Son, but delivered him up for us all, how shall he not with him also freely give us all things? Who shall lay any thing to the charge of God's elect? It is God that justifieth. Who is he that condemneth? It is Christ that died, yea rather, that is risen again, who is even at the right hand of God, who also maketh intercession for us. Who shall separate us from the love of Christ? shall tribulation, or distress, or persecution, or famine, or nakedness, or peril, or sword? As it is written, For thy sake we are killed all the day long; we are accounted as sheep for the slaughter. Nay, in all these things we are more than conquerors through him that loved us. For I am persuaded, that neither death, nor life, nor angels, nor principalities, nor powers, nor things present, nor things to come, Nor height, nor depth, nor any other creature, shall be able to separate us from the love of God, which is in Christ Jesus our Lord" Romans 8:26-39.

Seek the Lord who wants to be found

"Ho, every one that thirsteth, come ye to the waters, and he that hath no money; come ye, buy, and eat; yea, come, buy wine and milk without money and without price. Wherefore do ye spend money for that which is not bread? and your labour for that which satisfieth not? hearken diligently unto me, and eat ye that which is good, and let your soul delight itself in fatness. Incline your ear, and come unto me: hear, and your soul shall live; and I will make an everlasting covenant with you, even the sure mercies of David. Behold, I have given him for a witness to the people, a leader and commander to the people. Behold, thou shalt call a nation that thou knowest not, and nations that knew not thee shall run unto thee because of the Lord thy God, and for the Holy One of Israel; for he hath glorified thee. Seek ye the Lord while he may be found, call ye upon him while he is near: Let the wicked forsake his way, and the unrighteous man his thoughts: and let him return unto the Lord, and he will have mercy upon him; and to our God, for he will abundantly pardon. For my thoughts are not your thoughts, neither are your ways my ways, saith the Lord. For as the heavens are higher than the earth, so are my ways higher than your ways, and my thoughts than your thoughts" Isaiah 55:19.

From the lowest to the highest place; an example to follow

"Look not every man on his own things, but every man also on the things of others. Let this mind be in you, which was also in Christ Jesus: Who, being in the form of God, thought it not robbery to be equal with God: But made himself of no reputation,

and took upon him the form of a servant, and was made in the likeness of men: And being found in fashion as a man, he humbled himself, and became obedient unto death, even the death of the cross. Wherefore God also hath highly exalted him, and given him a name which is above every name: That at the name of Jesus every knee should bow, of things in heaven, and things in earth, and things under the earth; And that every tongue should confess that Jesus Christ is Lord, to the glory of God the Father" Philippians 2:4-11.

Thank God for the Psalms – our confidence is in God

"The Lord is my light and my salvation; whom shall I fear? the Lord is the strength of my life; of whom shall I be afraid? When the wicked, even mine enemies and my foes, came upon me to eat up my flesh, they stumbled and fell. Though an host should encamp against me, my heart shall not fear: though war should rise against me, in this will I be confident. One thing have I desired of the Lord, that will I seek after; that I may dwell in the house of the Lord all the days of my life, to behold the beauty of the Lord, and to enquire in his temple. For in the time of trouble he shall hide me in his pavilion: in the secret of his tabernacle shall he hide me; he shall set me up upon a rock. And now shall mine head be lifted up above mine enemies round about me: therefore will I offer in his tabernacle sacrifices of joy; I will sing, yea, I will sing praises unto the Lord. Hear, O Lord, when I cry with my voice: have mercy also upon me, and answer me. When thou saidst, Seek ye my face; my heart said unto thee, Thy face, Lord, will I seek. Hide not thy face far from me; put not thy servant away in anger: thou hast been my help; leave me not, neither forsake me, O God of my salvation. When my father and my mother forsake me, then the Lord will take me up. Teach me thy way, O Lord, and lead me in a plain path, because of mine enemies. Deliver me not over unto the will of mine enemies: for false witnesses are risen up against me, and such as breathe out cruelty. I had fainted, unless I had believed to see the goodness of the Lord in the land of the living. Wait on the Lord: be of good courage, and he shall strengthen thine heart: wait, I say, on the Lord." Psalm 27:1-14.

Putting on all of God's armour

"Finally, my brethren, be strong in the Lord, and in the power of his might. Put on the whole armour of God, that ye may be able to stand against the wiles of the devil. For we wrestle not against flesh and blood, but against principalities, against powers, against the rulers of the darkness of this world, against spiritual wickedness in high places. Wherefore take unto you the whole armour of God, that ye may be

able to withstand in the evil day, and having done all, to stand. Stand therefore, having your loins girt about with truth, and having on the breastplate of righteousness; And your feet shod with the preparation of the gospel of peace; Above all, taking the shield of faith, wherewith ye shall be able to quench all the fiery darts of the wicked. And take the helmet of salvation, and the sword of the Spirit, which is the word of God: Praying always with all prayer and supplication in the Spirit, and watching thereunto with all perseverance and supplication for all saints" Ephesians 6:10-18.

What a great God we serve

"Ah Lord God! behold, thou hast made the heaven and the earth by thy great power and stretched out arm, and there is nothing too hard for thee: Thou shewest lovingkindness unto thousands, and recompensest the iniquity of the fathers into the bosom of their children after them: the Great, the Mighty God, the Lord of hosts, is his name, Great in counsel, and mighty in work: for thine eyes are open upon all the ways of the sons of men: to give every one according to his ways, and according to the fruit of his doings" Jeremiah 32:17-19.

The cost and reward of discipleship

"Then said Jesus unto his disciples, If any man will come after me, let him deny himself, and take up his cross, and follow me. For whosoever will save his life shall lose it: and whosoever will lose his life for my sake shall find it. For what is a man profited, if he shall gain the whole world, and lose his own soul? or what shall a man give in exchange for his soul?" Matthew 16: 24-26.

Let us keep encouraging one another

"Then they that feared the Lord spake often one to another: and the Lord hearkened, and heard it, and a book of remembrance was written before him for them that feared the Lord, and that thought upon his name. And they shall be mine, saith the Lord of hosts, in that day when I make up my jewels; and I will spare them, as a man spareth his own son that serveth him. Then shall ye return, and discern between the righteous and the wicked, between him that serveth God and him that serveth him not" Malachi 3:16-18.

Our hope for where it could well end

"For I am now ready to be offered, and the time of my departure is at hand. I have fought a good fight, I have finished my course, I have kept the faith: Henceforth there is laid up for me a crown of righteousness, which the Lord, the righteous judge, shall give me at that day: and not to me only, but unto all them also that love his appearing" 2 Timothy 4:6-8.

www.ingramcontent.com/pod-product-compliance
Lightning Source LLC
Chambersburg PA
CBHW071850290426
44110CB00013B/1094